OXFORD READINGS IN SOCIO-LEGAL STUDIES

A Reader on The Law of the Business Enterprise

D0784815

OXFORD READINGS IN SOCIO-LEGAL STUDIES

Forthcoming titles in this series

Criminal Justice
Edited by Nicola Lacey

Family Law
Edited by John Eekelar and Mavis Maclean

Punishment
Edited by David Garland and Antony Duff

A READER ON

The Law of the Business Enterprise: Selected Essays

EDITED BY

Sally Wheeler

OXFORD UNIVERSITY PRESS
1994

Oxford University Press, Walton Street, Oxford ox2 6dp

Oxford New York Toronto
Delhi Bombay Calcutta Madras Karachi
Kuala Lumpur Singapore Hong Kong Tokyo
Nairobi Dar es Salaam Cape Town
Melbourne Auckland Madrid
and associated companies in
Berlin Ibadan

Oxford is a trade mark of Oxford University Press

Published in the United States
by Oxford University Press Inc., New York

© Oxford University Press 1994

British Library Cataloguing in Publication Data
Data available

Library of Congress Cataloging in Publication Data
Data available
ISBN 0-19-876346-8
ISBN 0-19-876347-6 (pbk.)

Set by Hope Services (Abingdon) Ltd.
Printed in Great Britain
on acid-free paper by
Bookcraft Ltd., Midsomer Norton, Avon

Contents

The Business Enterprise: A Socio-Legal Introduction

SALLY WHEELER

An overview of the corporate form

In capitalist economies the corporate structure is the principle organized form of economic association for business enterprise offered by the state. In the UK, statutes and the literature of legal scholarship refer to the corporate form as the 'company', in the USA the equivalent discourse refers to the 'corporation'. In this introductory essay the terms 'company' and 'corporation' are used interchangeably. The enterprises that we encounter on a day-to-day basis as employers, providers of food, utilities, and consumer goods are likely to have adopted the company form as the basis of their economic association. Within the legal model there are two variants of the company form; the public company and the private company.[1] The central difference between public and private companies concerns the acquisition of equity (or, as it can also be described, risk) capital. Public companies fit our popular perception of the company as a large impersonal organization in which a member of the public, another company or an institutional investor (e.g. a pension fund or an investment trust) can purchase a stake. A public company can, through judicious acquisitions of other companies,[2] and through capital generation of its own, create a group structure of holding and subsidiary companies which wields immense economic power. The possibility of vertical integration (e.g. the control of a whole sector of the economy from raw materials to retail outlets) and/or diversification into a number of different sectors

---

[1] Under Companies Act 1985 s. 1(3) a public company is a company which has a share capital and which is registered as a public company. Under CA 1985 s. 118 the minimum share capital for a public company is £50,000 of which, under s. 117(1)(4), a quarter must be paid up. A private company is defined by exclusion under the Companies Act 1985 as any company which is not a public company.

[2] The conduct and regulation of takeovers is governed by the City Code on Takeovers and Mergers and CA 1985 ss. 314–16 and 428–30F. Controls on competition aspects of mergers are dealt with at national level by Part IV of the Fair Trading Act 1973 and at EC level by Council Regulation (EEC) No. 4064/89.

creates endless possibilities and also, some would argue, responsibilities for the exercise of this power. Private companies cannot offer shares to the public.[3] This apart, under the prevailing legal model, both company types share certain basic characteristics: a separate legal personality distinct from its shareholders and management, perpetual succession, management functions presided over by a board of directors or single director, which is possible in the case of a private company,[4] a group of shareholders, and, in the overwhelming majority of cases, limited liability.

Power within the company is divided between the management, personified by the board of directors, and the capital providing investors, the shareholders. The existence of the company as a separate legal personality is evidenced not least by the line of cases examined by Stokes in her essay, in the context of the separation of the functions of ownership and management, which ascribe to the directors the role of agents of the company and not of the shareholders.[5] Article 70 of the Table A[6] of the Companies Act 1985 describes the legal relationship between investors and management thus: 'Subject to the provisions of the Act, the memorandum and the articles and to any directions given by special resolution, the business of the company shall be managed by the directors who may exercise all the powers of the company . . .'. As Article 70 makes clear, general management powers are exercised by the directors, with shareholders able to intervene either where statute demands a special resolution or where shareholders have reserved themselves the power to intervene by special resolution through the forum of the shareholders' meeting. The guiding principle for shareholders is majority rule as long as votes are cast 'bona fide in the best interests of the company'.[7] Control of directors by investors is achieved by allowing investors to appoint[8] and dismiss[9] directors and by provisions governing directors' service contracts.[10] Monitoring of the performance of directors by investors is possible through the medium of various sections of the Companies Act and the operation of common law rules. For example, statute requires the

---

[3] See CA 1985 s. 81.   [4] See CA 1985 s. 282.

[5] See *Automatic Self-Cleansing Filter Syndicate Co. Ltd.* v. *Cunningham* [1906] 2 Ch. 34, *Shaw* v. *Shaw* [1935] 2 KB 113, *Scott* v. *Scott* [1943] 1 All ER 582.

[6] Adoption of Table A in whole or part is not obligatory, although in the absence of any articles of association CA 1985 s. 8(2) would dictate Table A's inclusion as the company's articles.

[7] *Greenhalgh* v. *Arderne Cinemas Ltd.* [1951] Ch 286 *per* Evershed MR at 291.

[8] See CA 1985 s. 292.   [9] See CA 1985 s. 303.

[10] See CA 1985 ss. 318 and 319.

drawing up of a directors' report[11] and the disclosure of interests in contracts[12] and at common law there exists a general rule of no profit from office.[13] This common law rule is usually described as part of the directors' fiduciary duties and is accompanied by a duty of skill and care.[14] These duties are enforceable by the company. This means, in practice, by a shareholder who sues the wrongdoers on behalf of the company in a derivative action.[15] Disaffected shareholders can also sue the wrongdoers in either a personal action to enforce rights derived under the articles of the company and related statutory provisions[16] (put colloquially, the rules of membership) or a representative action to enforce the rules on behalf of other shareholders.

The legal model of the company does not orientate itself towards the economic function or purpose of the company. The legal model is in fact most appropriate to public limited companies where the company will have sufficient non-management investors for there to be a meaningful

[11] A directors' report must be appended to the annual accounts of a company. The precise form the report must take and the information required for it is contained in CA 1985 s. 234.

[12] CA 1985 s. 317 requires directors to disclose interests in contracts to the board of directors. See, however, the judgment of the House of Lords in *Guinness* v. *Saunders* [1990] 2 AC 663, which appears to decide that a company may contract out of the section in its articles.

[13] This is found in cases such as *Regal Hastings* v. *Gulliver* [1967] 2 AC 134 and *Industrial Development Consultants Ltd.* v. *Cooley* [1972] 2 All ER 162. Clearly the position is much more complicated than presented here and extends to issues such as what constitutes a corporate opportunity and who can ratify and what can be ratified. The textual comments here are intended only to indicate that in the legal model of the corporation limits are ascribed to the power of directors.

[14] See *Re City Equitable Fire Insurance* [1925] Ch 407.

[15] The so-called rule in *Foss* v. *Harbottle* (1843) 2 Hare 461. As was the case in n. 12 above, this presents a very simplified account. To launch a successful derivative action a shareholder has to bring himself within one of the exceptions to the rule. This in turn feeds back into the question of ratification and the definitions placed on concepts such as fraud and control. For a thorough discussion of these concepts in judicial eyes see *Prudential Assurance* v. *Newman* (no. 2) [1982] Ch 204, *Smith* v. *Croft (no. 3)* [1987] 3 All ER 909 and *Barrett* v. *Duckett* [1993] BCC 778. There is a view that breach of the duty of skill and care cannot be brought within the exceptions to the rule in *Foss* v. *Harbottle* and can only be enforced as a breach of CA 1985 s. 459 if the appropriate criteria for the operation of that section are present. See Finch, 'Company Directors: Who Cares about Skill and Care' (1992) 55 *MLR* 179, specifically on this point at p. 204.

[16] See CA 1985 s. 14 (CA 1948 s. 20 as was). There is an extensive literature on the debate about its precise effect on the relationship between the shareholders *inter se* and the shareholder and the company. See for example Wedderburn, 'Shareholder Rights and the Rule in Foss v Harbottle', [1957] *CLJ* 193; Goldberg, 'The Enforcement of Outsider Rights under Sec 20(1) of the CA 1948', (1972) 33 *MLR* 362; Gregory, 'The Section 20 Contract', (1981) 40 *MLR* 562; Goldberg, 'The Controversy on the Section 20 Contract Revisited', (1985), 48 *MLR* 121; and Drury, 'The Relative Nature of a Shareholder's Right to Enforce the Company Contract', [1986] *CLJ* 219.

distinction between the directors, on the one hand, and the shareholders in general meeting, on the other. For private companies, the legal model is relevant in an ever-diminishing scale dependant upon size. There has, in recent years, been some evidence of an acceptance of the differing purposes for which the legal model of the company may be used. To this end, accounting requirements for private companies which are defined for the purposes of the Companies Act, as 'small' or 'medium sized' are scaled down.[17] As private companies are not permitted to offer their shares to the public, there is, presumably, not thought to be the same need for transparency in their financial affairs. Perhaps in recognition of the more informal way that private companies, depending on the number of investors and their relationship with the management, can be run, the Companies Act also spares them some of the legal formalities of decision-making within the company.[18] However, these reforms are too piecemeal to have moved us away in any real sense from the legal model described above.[19]

The Essays in Perspective

Stokes refers at the beginning of her essay to a popular disaffection with company law as being 'technical . . . and dull', and to company lawyers as lacking an intellectual tradition which centres on the broader concerns of the business enterprise.[20] This is true to a certain extent if we take as our sole basis of enquiry the statutory and common law rules which surround the legal model of the company. Most discussion of company law on this micro-level is centred on narrowly confined legal debate or a description of the historical progression and development of rules within a legal context only.[21] This collection of essays seeks to broaden debate on company law and place in context the legal model presented by the

---

[17] See CA 1985 ss. 246–50. The Budget speech of Nov. 1993 indicated that proposals would be brought into force in April 1994 that would remove the requirement of audited accounts from companies with turnover below a certain financial threshold. Audit will be replaced by a compilation report from an accountant which will confirm that accounts have been drawn from the company's records and that the company has complied with relevant statutory requirements.

[18] See Companies Act 1985 s. 381A, which permits private companies to operate shareholder decision-making by written resolution in the absence of a meeting. Any resolution passed in this way is subject to scrutiny by the company's auditors.

[19] *A New Form of Incorporation for Small Firms: A Consultation Document* Cmnd. 8171 (1981).

[20] Stokes is not alone in this observation: see Manning, 'The Shareholder's Appraisal Remedy: An Essay For Frank Coker' (1962) 72 *Yale Law Journal* 233 at 245.

[21] A notable exception to this is the literature available on the development of company accounting practices. See for example Edwards, 'Companies, Corporations and Accounting Change 1855–1933: A Comparative Study', (1992) 23 *Accounting and Business Research* 59 and the references contained therein.

Companies Act and by the EC Directives and Regulations which are becoming increasingly important. A number of questions are posed (and in some cases answered) by all of these essays. At the centre of this enquiry are economic and sociological questions[22] about the power relationship within the company; how is and should control be divided between capital providers and managers? In turn this leads to questions grounded in political theory about how the company derives its power from the state and how the state deals with cross-border concentrations of corporate power in the shape of multinationals. This feeds into the question of state sovereignty and whether the large corporation is best controlled by the creation of supra-national legal models. The final section in this collection examines the use made of the private business enterprise by the state to achieve particular political goals. The two examples used here of privatization are similar in underlying philosophy, but start from very different points of departure. The first example examines the impact of the promotion of market economy values through the techniques of privatization and contracting-out in the UK which are used to stimulate competition, consumer choice, and accountability. The second example is that of the dismemberment of the old state-trading economies, in particular in Central and Eastern Europe, and the creation of fledgling market economies.

The purpose of this introduction is not to introduce the essays in this reader as such but to offer a series of brief pen portraits of the key issues raised by the phenomenon of the business enterprise, some of which are the subject of the selected essays.

As shown by the essays in the first section, many of the theoretical contributions to a broader conception of the company have come from the USA. It is often implicit within these approaches that limited liability for the corporation is a given construct. Indeed, in the USA, limited liability arrived rather earlier.[23] However, in the UK, the debate surrounding

---

[22] A general introduction to the type of analyses offered by the disciplines of economics and sociology can be found in Hirsch, Michaels, and Friedman, 'Clean Models v Dirty Hands: Why Economics is Different from Sociology', in Zukin and DiMaggio (eds.), *Structures of Capital: The Social Organisation of the Economy* (Cambridge, 1990). For a 'people' rather than a themes based approach see Martinelli and Smelser 'Economic Sociology: Historical Threads and Analytic Issues', in Martinelli and Smelser (eds.), *Economy and Society* (London, 1990).

[23] See *Spear* v. *Grant* (1819) 16 Mass 9, 12 and *Wood* v. *Dummer* 30 P Cas 435, 436 (CCD Me 1824) (no. 17, 944). A general discussion can be found in Livermore 'Unlimited Liability in Early American Corporations', 43 *J. of Pol. Econ.* (1935), 674 and Blumberg, *The Law of Corporate Groups: Tort, Contract and other Common Law Problems in the Substantive Law of Parent and Subsidiary Corporations* (Boston, 1987), ch. 1.

the merits of limited liability provoked many of the questions about corporate structure and power divisions within the corporation that have occupied later US theorists. Jurisprudential debate on the nature of the corporation at that time and for a while subsequently centred on the issue of separate personality.[24]

Rise of the Corporate Form

Although it is possible to trace the origins of the corporate form from the Middle Ages onwards,[25] debates about the desirability of the corporate form did not really begin in earnest until the eighteenth century. By 1844 the corporate form was generally available[26] and limited liability became so in 1856. By 1880, after a somewhat muted beginning, the use of the corporate form had increased rapidly.[27] In 1907 the division of companies into public and private occurred.[28]

As early as 1776, in *The Wealth of Nations*,[29] Adam Smith made the point, later to be enlarged upon by Berle and Means in their classic work of 1933,[30] that by allowing separation of management and stock ownership (and with it control) through proliferation of the corporate form, shareholders would lack the power to ensure efficiency of management. This is the classic position of the managerialist and the debate that has sprung from this observation is well surveyed by both Bratton and Stokes in their essays and is discussed later. For Smith the free availability of the corporate form was connected with monopoly and was considered by him to stand in the way of innovative competition. Incorporation with

[24] See Stein, 'Nineteenth Century English Company Law and Theories of Legal Personality', (1983) 12 *Quaderni Fiorentini* 502 and the references contained therein for a review of UK jurisprudential contributions and judicial debates.

[25] See Scott, *The Constitution and Finance of English, Scottish and Irish Joint Stock Companies to 1720* (Cambridge, 1909–12). Halho, 'Early Progenitors of the Company' (1982) *Juridical Review* 139; Formoy, *The Historical Foundations of Modern Company Law* (London, 1923).

[26] The Bubble Act of 1719–20, which had held back the development of the corporate form, was repealed in 1825. For an account of the South Sea Bubble and its aftermath see Carswell, *The South Sea Bubble* (rev. edn. London, 1993), Patterson and Reiffen, 'The Effect of the Bubble Act on the Market for Joint Stock Shares' (1990) 50 *J. of Econ. Hist.* 163, and Neal, *The Rise of Financial Capitalism* (Cambridge, 1990), 89–117.

[27] See Shannon 'The First Five Thousand Limited Companies and their Duration', (1932) 3 *Economy History* 396 and 'The Limited Companies of 1866–83' (1933) 4 *Economic History Review* 290 and Robb, *White-collar Crime in Modern England* (Cambridge, 1992), 24–30, for a discussion of what happened to the early joint stock companies.

[28] CA 1907 s. 37.

[29] Adam Smith, *The Wealth of Nations*, Book V (Everyman Library edn.); see also Williams, *The Emergence of the Theory of the Firm* (London, 1978), ch. 2 and the references contained therein.

[30] *The Modern Corporation and Private Property* (New York, 1933).

limited liability could only be justified if the capital required was so great that private venturers would not otherwise provide it and the industry was of the greatest public utility. Smith identified four industries as coming into this category; insurance, water supply, banking, and canal construction. Smith's connection between increased availability of the corporate form and monopoly is not surprising given that the companies of the pre-Bubble Act 1719 era enjoyed joint stock status through the grant of a royal charter and were synonymous with monopoly.[31]

Smith's identification of incorporation as being connected with public utility is a statement of the early eighteenth- and nineteenth-century view of incorporation of a company as a separate legal personality derived as a concession from the state; that incorporation occurs as the result of a privilege conferred by the state in return for the constituted company undertaking functions which benefit the public good as well as those within the matrix of ownership through investor stake. This idea of state concession gave the company form a public character which could then be used as the basis for state intervention into corporate affairs to monitor public benefit. Other theories which try to explain corporate power are examined later in this introductory chapter deny or downgrade this element of public benefit.

In statutes of 1844[32] and 1856[33] incorporation, on registration, with limited liability became generally available. Prior to this the association of incorporation with the exercise of state privilege was a historically justifiable fact. A Royal Charter was required for incorporation and the monopoly rights which so worried Smith usually followed it. In the early nineteenth century many of the Royal Charters granted concerned the creation of transport systems (railways and canals for example) and other service industries such as banking[34] which were essential to the development of the economy and clearly satisfied the criterion of public benefit while also using the corporate form to secure the considerable capital necessary for the viability of these schemes.

Once incorporation became generally available the corporate form could not be said to have any more of a public character than any other form or institution given legal recognition. Consequently the attraction

---

[31] See Ekelund and Tollison, 'Mercantilist Origins of the Corporation' (1980) *Bell Journal of Economics* 715; and Hahlo, 'Early Progenitors of the Modern Company', (1982) *Juridical Review* 139.

[32] Companies Registration and Regulation Act 1844.

[33] Limited Liability Act 1856.

[34] For a detailed breakdown of the Royal Charters granted in 1835–6, see Hunt, *The Development of the Business Corporation* (Cambridge, Mass., 1936).

of the concession theory as an explanation of the corporate form and its legal status has paled somewhat. It is true that incorporation and limited liability are still described in terms of privilege[35] in certain circumstances but that is primarily in relation to protecting the interests of creditors from abuses of these institutions. In that context description and intervention is no different from the role the courts and legislature play and have played in say the control of exclusion clauses in contract. Contract is an institution traditionally viewed very much as a system of private ordering with state intervention occurring as a restraining hand on the worst excesses of market forces, not as a system with a strong public character where state intervention is justified on the grounds of public benefit. If the state had for itself felt the authority to assume this role, there would have been less incentive to take certain assets and industries into public ownership following a policy of nationalization, particularly in the post-war years.[36] The last section of this introductory chapter looks at the decline of nationalization and the rise of privatization.

Both Bratton briefly and Stokes, at rather more length, deal with the concession theory of incorporation. Both place it with the fiction theory, so offering the two terms as interchangeable. The fiction theory of incorporation is traditionally formulated to describe the company as an artificial entity separate from its members[37] and can be viewed as distinct from the concession theory. The idea of state concession offers a platform for state involvement in corporate affairs that is missing in the fiction theory. The attraction is that it offered both a justification and a balancing weight, albeit one overtaken by circumstances, for corporate power, the fiction theory merely sets us off on our enquiries by supplying us with a platform that embodies the following statement: 'a corporation has none of the features which characterizes a living person, a mind which can have knowledge or intention or be negligent and has hands to carry out his intentions'.[38]

Limited Liability

A rich example of the diversity of views about the desirability of the corporate form generated by discussion of limited liability can be seen from

[35] See for example the judgment of Harman J. in *Re Crestjoy Products Ltd.* [1990] BCLC 677 at 681.

[36] For a historical charting of the rise of nationalization policies, see Foreman Peck, 'The Privatization of Industry in Historical Perspective', (1989) 16 *J of L & S* 129.

[37] See Maitland, 'The Corporation's Soul', in *Collected Papers*, iii (Cambridge, 1911), 210.

[38] Wells, *Corporations and Criminal Responsibility* (Oxford, 1993), 108, quoting in part from Lord Reid's speech in *Tesco* v. *Nattrass* [1971] 2 WLR 1166 at 1177.

Ker's report to the government in 1837[39] on the merits of adopting the limited partnership as an enterprise form.[40] The report came out against the idea but many of those who submitted evidence to Ker used the opportunity to offer a more general treatise. Thomas Tooke adopted the classic Victorian stance of individualism and saw the corporate form as a relaxation of individual responsibility which could only be justified in the public interest.[41] Limited liability would, according to Tooke, push capital into the hands of others who would not be as careful with it as they would with their own—the classic conundrum of corporate control. Took's one concession to limited liability and the expected growth in investment that would result was that it would create a more productive avenue for the use of savings.[42] Nassau Senior's evidence to Ker represents the complete antithesis to Took's.[43] Senior saw the increased availability of limited liability as a way of encouraging the use of capital as an investment in commerce and manufacture. He also saw this as stimulating competition rather than stifling it as Smith had done, because more people would be able to carry on business aided by capital injections from others. Without limited liability these investors would be fewer in number, thus generating a monopoly on capital and a restriction on its availability.[44] A view that does not appear to receive much discussion in the literature taking a historical perspective on limited liability is that the limited liability company emerged out of the 'merchant cartels' of the Middle Ages as a response to the need for a system for the transfer of property rights in these organizations. This approach rejects the idea that capital raising was the moving force behind limited liability.[45] It is

[39] BPP (1837) 530 XLIV 339.

[40] This was in use on the continent and known as the *société en commandite*, see Cornish and Clark, *Law and Society in England 1750–1950* (London, 1989), 252–4. The limited liability partnership was introduced by an Act of the same name in 1908. However, it never became popular as an enterprise form, see Ireland, 'The Rise of the Limited Liability Company', (1984) 12 *Int. J. of Soc. of Law* 239.

[41] Ibid. 431 paras. 5 and 6.

[42] This sentiment was broadly echoed by John Stuart Mill in evidence to a subsequent Select Committee on Investments for the Savings of the Middle and Working Classes, see BPP (1850) XIX qus 837 and 846. More of Mill's views will be advanced later in our discussion of Coase.   [43] BPP (1837) 530 XLIV 461.

[44] For a general discussion of the economic background of this period see Amsler, Bartlett, and Bolton, 'Thoughts of Some British Economists on Early Limited Liability and Corporate Legislation', *History of Political Economy* (1981), 774 and Shannon, 'The Coming of General Limited Liability' (1931) 2 *Economic History* 267. For a discussion of the development of a theory of the firm in relation to pricing and production decisions, see Williams *The Emergence of the Theory of the Firm* (London, 1978).

[45] See expressly Ekelund and Tollison *supra* n. 31 and more peripherally Demsetz, 'Toward a Theory of Property Rights', (1967) 57 *Am. Econ. Rev.* 347.

difficult to see why this property rights theory gives rise to a limited liability form and not just a corporate form giving greater rights of transferability of stake than partnership. Transferability of shares is, as outlined
above, an aim achieved by the form of public rather than private companies. A further weakness of the primacy of transferability theory is that by
1914 four-fifths of registered companies were private rather than public
companies.[46]

Current thinking on limited liability offers us a positive assessment of
its worth, generated in an American law and economics analysis. The
most comprehensive account comes from Easterbrook and Fischel.[47]
Their starting-point is the proposition of Manne[48]—and coincidently
Senior—that without limited liability those with capital to invest will
concentrate it in particular firms and monitor it closely rather than
indulging in a diversification of investment to offset the risk of business
failure. This will result in increased costs to firms of pursing capital as
they try to break the monopoly on it.

Easterbrook and Fischel identify five additional factors which support
limited liability. The first two factors are based on a reduction of monitoring costs; limited liability reduces both the need to monitor management, as investment diversification is possible and stakes in each
company will be lower and at less risk, and the need to monitor other
shareholders. Without limited liability the wealth of other shareholders
would be crucial to evaluating the potential risks of investment. An
assessment in these terms evades the issue as to whether there are effective systems for monitoring the activities of management even within the
limited area of need identified by Easterbrook and Fischel. One of the
arguments examined later in this introduction is the idea that the very
diversification of investment identified by Easterbrook and Fischel,
amongst others, prevents investors grouping together to form an effective monitoring unit to check the activities of management, hence the
formulation of alternative strategies of corporate governance.[49]

The third factor concerns the level of management efficiency which is

---

[46] Balfour Committee on Factors in Industrial and Commercial Efficiency (1927), as
quoted in Hannah, *The Rise of the Corporate Economy* (2nd edn., London, 1983), 24.

[47] Their classic article is 'Limited Liability and the Corporation', (1985) 52 *U. Chi. L. Rev.*
89; much of this material is also reproduced in Easterbrook and Fischel, *The Economic
Structure of Corporate Law* (Cambridge, Mass., 1991), ch. 2.

[48] Manne, 'Our Two Corporation Systems: Law and Economics' (1967) 53 *Virginia Law
Review* 259.

[49] Tricker provides a definition of corporate governance by drawing a distinction
between the running of the business (management) and seeing that it is run properly (corporate governance), Tricker, *Corporate Governance* (Vermont, 1984).

secured by limited liability; greater management efficiency results because disaffected shareholders can sell their shares and the lower risk offered by limited liability to investors encourages other investors to purchase these shares and to use their voting power to install new management personnel and structures. If investors have the voting power to achieve this when they buy into the enterprise, it is difficult to see why existing shareholders do not simply exercise this power without selling their shares. Factor 4 is built on this relationship between limited liability and the alienability of shares; a purchaser of shares in a limited liability concern is buying a stake in the enterprise which reflects that enterprise's asset base and is not a statement about the wealth of the shareholders. There is also one price for shares, and investors need not spend time and resources investigating the right price.[50] This part of the analysis really only works in relation to publicly quoted companies which can dispose of their shares to investors through the medium of the market and it also makes an assumption about the ability of the market to reflect 'a fair price'. For private companies, a decision to invest is likely to encompass exactly the sort of considerations which Easterbrook and Fischel assert are irrelevant in a limited liability forum—the wealth of other shareholders who are likely to be involved in management, the efficiency of management and the prospects for effective monitoring of both shareholders and management. The final factor concerns the type of investment decisions the management of enterprises with limited liability make. Easterbrook and Fischel argue that they can make the most efficient use of investors' capital by investing in high risk enterprises with the possibility of high return, without exposing individual investors to ruin. Without limited liability, they would have to reduce risk for investors by not investing in this way.

This final factor begs the question whether all limited liability does is to shift the risk of failure away from investment capital providers and onto creditors, with raised costs for the enterprise. Easterbrook and Fischel answer this in the negative for several reasons. Shareholders lose their capital stake first before creditors. Perhaps a clearer way of expressing this is to say that creditors rank above shareholders in the priority list in the event of the firm's insolvency. To this end, secured creditors may feel the need to consider only the value of their security and not the firm as a whole. Creditors do not need intra-group monitoring under either limited or unlimited liability as it does not assist their position. Creditors

---

[50] This gains support from Demsetz, *Ownership, Control and the Firm* (Oxford, 1988), 114.

may have superior knowledge about management activities—if we take the primary creditors to be institutional investors through the mechanism of debt, i.e. secured finance. They may have an industry-wide knowledge of markets and activities through other investments etc., which individual investors do not have, and will employ this knowledge because of the greater risk they take. Of course, these institutional investors may choose to buy shares on the market and not use the debt mechanisms available. In this instance they will be investors with superior knowledge and could as a result exercise influence over management decisions in a way in which individual investors never could, since the only recourse for them is the market for their shares. If institutional investors act in this way then, provided the problems of capital diversification and capital monopoly can be overcome, it would not matter whether an enterprise's liability was limited or unlimited.

Easterbrook and Fischel consider the desirability of leaving firms to insure against failure to protect their investors' capital rather than relying on limited liability. This is rejected as failing to provide an answer to the question of who insures the insurer and whether insurers would be effective monitors of management. There is also the question of the availability of insurance for small firms[51] and the cost of negotiating insurance cover on an individual firm-by-firm basis. For Easterbrook and Fischel, the rationale for limited liability and its enduring appeal lie in its partial risk-shifting function: equity investors carry more risk than debt investors who still carry substantial risks, but neither can lose more than their original stake.[52] Other groups such as trade creditors can protect their position by raising their prices or changing their conditions of sale.

This risk-shifting analysis then leads Easterbrook and Fischel to assert that the piercing of the corporate veil (i.e. the removal of corporate personality and its benefits from an undertaking) by the courts to enable creditors to attack the assets of shareholders is evidence of a judicially undertaken cost–benefit analysis; if limited liability has provided minimal gains from investment diversity and the firm has undertaken a socially unacceptable level of risk-raking, then the cost of limited liability has exceeded its benefits and creditors should be able to have recourse to shareholder assets. This may be capable of substantiation in the US

---

[51] See Halpern, Trebilcock, and Turnbull, 'An Economic Analysis of Limited Liability in Corporation Law', (1980) 30 *U. Toronto LJ* 117 where it is concluded that there would be problems of insurance availability for small firms.

[52] For a discussion of how the risk bearing differentials in a limited liability scenario affect a lower cost of capital see Ricketts, *The Economics of Business Enterprise: New Approaches to the Firm* (Brighton, 1987), 105.

where there is a greater readiness to pierce or lift the veil of incorporation than in the UK. In the UK this occurs only in certain limited circumstances and simply where the justice of the case may seem to require it.[53] Much more significant in this area are the statutory inroads that have been made into limited liability in the context of imposing personal liability on company directors. This is not strictly lifting the veil of incorporation to allow an attack by creditors on the assets of shareholders but it does have the effect of stepping outside the principle of limited liability and asking management to account for their running of the company in certain situations where limited liability would offer them protection. The best recent example is the creation of the concept of wrongful trading, for which the insolvency of the company concerned is a prerequisite.[54] A successful action for wrongful trading results in a company director being assessed as liable for a contribution to the assets of the insolvent company, thus swelling the amount available for creditors and shareholders based on debts acquired by the company after a date on which a reasonable director would have concluded that the only future for the company was insolvent liquidation.[55]

Berle and Means and the separation of ownership and control

Passing reference has been made to the work of Berle and Means.[56] This, together with the work of Coase which is examined later, has become the linchpin of twentieth-century thought on the corporate form. In 1932, Berle and Means presented a seminal work, based on the shareholding structure of the largest 200 companies in the USA, on the divorce between ownership of stock in public companies and the management of these concerns. Ownership was vested in a disparate number of shareholders who were then not in a position to effect any meaningful control over directors. The situation is described by Berle and Means in the following terms: 'we have reached a condition in which the individual

---

[53] The most thorough review in recent years of the circumstances in which the veil will be lifted by the courts can be found in *Adams* v. *Cape Industries PLC* [1990] Ch 433.

[54] See the Insolvency Act 1986 s. 214 and *Re Produce Marketing Consortium* [1989] 1 WLR 745. This was the first case on this section and provides an interesting insight into its operation.

[55] Other examples include fraudulent trading (Insolvency Act 1986, s. 213) and more peripherally the disqualification of directors from holding office in the future under the Company Directors Disqualification Act 1986, s. 6. Once again insolvency is a prerequisite as is a finding of unfitness by the courts.

[56] *The Modern Corporation and Private Property* described by Prentice, 'Aspects of Corporate Governance Debate', in Prentice and Holland (eds.), *Contemporary Issues in Corporate Governance* (Oxford, 1993) 11 as part of 'our intellectual luggage'.

interest of the shareholder is definitely made subservient to the will of a controlling group of managers even though the capital of the enterprise is made up out of the aggregated contributions of perhaps many thousands of individuals'.[57] For Berle and Means control within the company progressed through three stages; (1) the ability in legal terms to vote the majority of the shares was defined as majority control; (2) as diversification progressed, control was vested in those who did not have a majority of the shares but could effect control in other ways, perhaps because there was no other large enough group to oppose them, this they defined as minority control; (3) finally, if the minority group reduced in size through further diversification, then management control resulted. Control can be defined as the ability to determine the company's actions, long-term objectives and resource allocation to achieve those objectives. This requires control of the board of directors in terms of ability to appoint or ability to influence. The advantages of management control identified by its supporters are set below.

Dissenters from the Model

There are some dissenters, however, from the initial Berle and Means proposition that minority control has descended into management control. There are those who question the way in which Berle and Means interpreted their data[58] and there are those who assert that the pattern of ownership identified by Berle and Means does not, as a matter of empirical fact, give rise to the propositions they claim for it.[59] There is an overlap between these two groups: a central factor in rejecting the Berle and Means model is the definition applied to control and what is required for a group to have control of an enterprise. For Berle and Means, minority control required a shareholding of 20 per cent or less; others have put the figure as low as 5 per cent. It is also argued that a numerical figure cannot

[57] *Modern Corporation*, 277.

[58] See, however, Leech, 'Corporate Ownership and Control: A New Look at the Evidence of Berle and Means', (1987) 39 *Oxford Economic Papers* 534 and the references contained therein. Leech applies a probabilistic voting model to the data used by Berle and Means and suggests that in fact their designation of companies in their sample as management controlled should have been considerably lower. See also Burch, *The Managerial Revolution Assessed* (Lexington, Mass., 1972), who makes a similar point.

[59] In the UK this movement got off to a slow start; apart from the work of Florence, 'The Statistical Analysis of Joint Stock Company Control', (1947) part 1 and *Ownership, Control and Success of Large Companies* (London, 1961) significant contributions were not made until the late 1970s; see Scott, *Corporations, Classes and Capitalism* (London, 1985) and Francis, 'Families, Firms and Finance Capital: The Development of UK Industrial Firms with Particular Reference to their Ownership and Control' (1980) 4 *Sociology* 1.

be put on control and that it is something which has to be assessed in the light of the overall pattern of share ownership within that enterprise.[60] These dissenters posit an alternative model of the consequences of diversified ownership; what results is control effected through a coalition of interests. A coalition of interests will only be effective where the shareholders involved have sufficient in common and will always be inherently unstable, but nevertheless it does leave the way open for control to be effected by a 'constellation of interests';[61] shareholders who negotiate with each other and who together are too powerful for the board of directors to ignore. Scott, the principal proponent of this approach in the UK, parallels the rise of control through a constellation of interests with the rise of institutional investors.[62] The question for research that develops out of this approach is the effect of this dominance on corporate performance.[63]

Managerialist and Anti-managerialist

Notwithstanding the above discussion of the detractors from the Berle and Means proposition, for many scholars, particularly legal ones, the paradigm has, as Bratton points out in his essay, been widely accepted without challenge. For those who accept it as a given construct, there is then a division of view into managerialist who welcome the position of management as reflecting their superior business knowledge etc. and as giving management an opportunity, free from the constraints of ownership, to act with 'corporate conscience'. The obvious difficulty with this concept is its definition: what exactly is corporate conscience and who decides this? To assert that it is the will of the corporation itself is an unacceptable reification of an inanimate body albeit one which enjoys legal personality. To assert that these decisions are made by a group within the company simply begs the question about how the views of competing groups within the corporation are evaluated and given effect to.[64] Against this position can be juxtaposed the view of the anti-managerialists who see power as being wielded by management without

---

[60] See Zeitlin, 'Corporate Ownership and Control: The Large Corporation and the Capitalist Class', (1974) *Am. J. of Soc.* 5.

[61] Scott, *Corporations*, 49.

[62] Ibid. 79–83, where he reviews several studies which have analysed the number of shareholders and shareholdings in major companies from 1950 onwards.

[63] Zeitlin, 'Corporate Ownership'.

[64] For an interesting review of this position see Lipton and Rosenblum, 'A New System of Corporate Governance: The Quinquennial Election of Directors', (1991) 58 *Univ. of Chicago LR* 187.

authority. Berle posited the idea of the market for corporate control acting as a check on management power; shareholders could sell their
shares and control would be lost to a new management group installed
by the new shareholders.[65]

The Market for Corporate Control

The use of the market for corporate control is the subject of Bradley's
essay. The principal advantage claimed for this method of control is that
fear of take-over promotes management efficiency. The counterpoint to
this is that it is also claimed that it leads to short-termism—profit maximization by management to avoid the threat of take-over[66] from dissatisfied shareholders resulting in neglect of the medium- and long-term
development of the company.[67] Indeed it has been suggested that this
was a driving force behind the current debate on corporate governance
as much as the forces discussed below.[68] The market for control was
Berle's ultimate sanction. Implicit in the managerialists' arguments is the
idea that corporate managers will exercise their power with responsibility
and that there are mechanisms[69] within the corporate structure to ensure
that they do so, such as fiduciary duties[70] and rules on the conduct of
meetings.[71] It is important to articulate at this point the type of investors
we are concerned with when we consider the market for corporate con-

---

[65]   58 *Univ. of Chicago LR* 287.

[66]   For a fascinating account of the evolution and formulation of devices to defend against
hostile take-over bids see Powell, 'Professional Innovation: Corporate Lawyers and Private
Lawmaking', (1993) 18 *Law and Social Inquiry* 423.

[67]   There is a huge literature on the merits or otherwise of the market for corporate con-
trol; references to this literature is provided in Bradley's essay. See also Farrar (ed.),
Takeovers, Institutional Investors and the Modernisation of Corporate Law (Oxford, 1993);
Daniels, 'Stakeholders and Takeovers: Can Contractarianism be Compassionate', (1993) 43
Univ. of Toronto LJ 315.

[68]   See Davies, 'Institutional Investors: A UK View', [1991] 57 *Brooklyn Law Rev.* 129. See
also *Creative Tensions*, National Association of Pension Funds (London, 1990). This is an
extremely informative overview of the positions taken by industry and institutional
investors respectively.

[69]   Lipton and Rosenblum 'Corporate Governance', 189 reject the idea of control mechanisms over management within corporate governance as a strategy that emphasizes the
confrontational aspects of corporate governance and which, as a result, harms what should
be 'the ultimate goal of corporate governance . . . the creation of a healthy economy
through the development of business operations that operate for the longterm and compete
successfully in the world economy'.

[70]   These include statutory obligations like the duty to disclose an interest in contracts
discussed above and rules drawn from equitable restrictions on the conduct of trustees such
as the duty not to make a profit from office. For a general discussion on this see ch. 21 of
Gower, *Principles of Modern Company Law* (London, 1992).

[71]   CA 1985 ss. 366–83.

trol and other devices that can conceivably be used to censure the activities of management. These are institutional investors. We have already seen that for some commentators their very presence marks a move away from the Berle and Means model.[72] Scott produces evidence based on the ownership of shares in Barclays Bank in 1976 and 1977 to show that market transactions did not lead to instability in the short term; there had been changes in shareholdings but not in the overall structure. This can only tell us something about control by a constellation of interests; it says little about whether shareholders would be prepared to take profits in the short term if the opportunity arose or exercise the right to participate in the market for corporate control.[73] Exit[74] from the corporation by selling their shares is not always a viable option[75] if the company has a share price that reflects underperformance; the institutional investor is then thrown back on internally available mechanisms albeit armed with considerable knowledge about these borne out of experience. It could also be argued that it is inefficient to use the take-over mechanism if all that is required is a change of management. This can be achieved by using the mechanisms for internal governance offered by the Companies Acts.[76]

The anti-managerialists argue that these controls are ineffective as a

[72] See Scott, 'Corporate Control and Corporate Rule', (1990) *Brit. J. of Soc.* 351 at 363 where he provides a tabular breakdown of the twenty leading shareholders of Barclays Bank, the largest one of whom holds 1.98%. More recent figures are provided by Paul Davies in 'Institutional Investors in the UK' in Prentice and Holland, *Corporate Governance*, 83 at n. 45. The same growth in institutional investors is recorded as occurring in Australia, see Ramsey and Blair, 'Ownership Concentration, Institutional Investment and Corporate Governance: An Empirical Investigation of 100 Australian Companies', (1993) 19 *Mel. Univ. LR* 153.

[73] 'Corporate Control'.

[74] The term *exit*, and indeed *voice*, which is used later to examine the internal mechanisms for dissent open to investors, is borrowed rather crudely from Hirschman, *Exit Voice and Loyalty: Responses to Decline in Firms Organisations and States*, (Cambridge, Mass., 1970). Hirschman also offers us the idea that *voice* will only be exercised if there is a decline in the availability of *exit*. The veracity of this proposition is something which may be illuminated by the discussion in the text which follows this note.

[75] The taking of short-term profits by exiting from the company is controlled in some jurisdictions; this can be seen as an attack on the activities of institutional investors. See for example a Pennsylvania Statute which requires institutional investors who hold either as an individual entity or as a group structure 20% plus in a Pennsylvanian company to account for profits made if they exit and sell their shares within eighteen months, 15 PA Cons Stat Ann paras. 2573–5 (Purdun Sup. 1991).

[76] For an expression of this view see Charkham, 'Corporate Governance and the Market for Control of Companies', (1989) 25 *Bank of England Panel Paper* and 'Corporate Governance and the Market for Control of Companies: Aspects of the Shareholders' Role', (1989) 44 *Bank of England Discussion Paper*.

system of governance. Frug,[77] in particular, provides us with an anti-managerialist critique. His approach is to equate the power of the corporation with bureaucratic/administrative power. In his view, bureaucratic power now reigns unchecked, having left behind the models he believes are usually used to justify the existence and exercise of this type of power. He labels these models formalism (agency theory and managerialism), expertise, judicial review (corporate litigation in the form of derivative actions), and market/pluralist (shareholders can exist from the company by selling their shares). In a sense the anti-managerialists have won the day, as it is in part the apparent breakdown of the managerialist model of the exercise of power within corporations that has sparked off the current debate in the UK[78] and US[79] on corporate governance.

Corporate governance

The complaint of 'short-termism' has already been identified as one reason for the current interest in corporate governance. Another is the spectacular company collapses of the late 1980s and early 1990s. Oft-cited examples include Polly Peck, BCCI, and the Maxwell Corporation. The problems ranged from apparent lack of accurate audit information to failure by anyone internally or externally to act on audit information and an unwillingness or inability on the part of institutional investors to deal with powerful individuals within companies whose remit of action appeared to be virtually limitless. In this section we consider in more detail the Companies Act provisions and other legislative measures which deal with the processing and distribution of information from the company to its investors and any proposals for change in those areas. Then we examine the reactive mechanisms available to the company and the shareholder to deal with breaches of duty by management.

Information Dissemination

Audit is obviously the principal means for the dissemination to outsiders and insiders of information about the company's performance in the last

---

[77] 'The Ideology of Bureaucracy in American Law', (1984) 97 *Harv. LR* 1277.

[78] In May 1991 the Financial Reporting Council, the London Stock Exchange and the accounting profession set up the Cadbury Committee (so called after its chairman, Sir Adrian Cadbury) to examine aspects of corporate governance. The Committee produced its report and code of best practice on 1 December 1992 entitled 'The Financial Aspects of Corporate Governance'.

[79] For a discussion of the final draft of the American Law Institute proposals see the articles in a symposium issue of the *George Washington Law Review*, 61/4 (1993).

financial period. The literature on audit and corporate governance is too vast to be explored here[80] and the precise form and content of company accounts is a special subject in its own right.[81] This discussion will limit itself to identifying the key issues. The issue of the standardization of accounting practice has been dealt with to a large extent by the reforms contained in the Companies Act 1989.[82] It is now a requirement that company accounts state whether accounting standards have been followed and give reasons for non- compliance.[83] A larger problem is that of auditor liability for negligently prepared audited accounts. The House of Lords decision in *Caparo Industries Plc* v. *Dickman*[84] decided that there was normally no scope for a tortious action against auditors by shareholders and potential investors.[85] Any duty that auditors have is owed to the company in much the same way that directors owe their duty to the company. However, positing the auditor's duty to the company. However, positing the auditor's duty as one which the company rather than the shareholders individually[86] can litigate over has the result of calling into question the value of audit as an information providing device for shareholders. Aside from audit there are other devices for the dissemination of financial information, including interim reports which are required as a condition of stock exchange listing.

The Cadbury report is the most prominent reply yet in the UK to some of the questions raised about corporate governance. It produced a code of best practice, compliance with which is voluntary. It is recommended that all listed companies comply with the code and non-listed companies are encouraged to comply. The voluntary nature of the code is 'beefed-up' by the London Stock Exchange requirement that, as a

[80] See for example 23 *Accountancy and Business Research* Special Issue 23 (1993) and the references contained therein; Freedman, 'Accountancy and Corporate Governance: Filling a Legal Vacuum', (1993) 64 *Pol. Q.* 285 and Power, 'The Politics of Financial Auditing', (1993) 64 *Pol. Q.* 272.

[81] See Gower, *Principles*, 447–75.

[82] See CA 1985 sch. 4, para. 36A. Judicial recognition of accounting standards can be seen from the judgment of Hobhouse J. in *Berg Sons & Co.* v. *Adams* [1992] BCC 661.

[83] For two very different discussions see McBarnet and Whelan, 'The Elusive Spirit of the Law: Formalism and the Struggle for Legal Control', (1991) 54 *MLR* 848 and McGee, 'The "True and Fair View" Debate: A Study in the Legal Regulation of Accounting', (1991) 54 *MLR* 874.

[84] [1990] 1 All ER 568. For further comment see Freedman and Power, 'Law and Accounting: Transition and Transformation', (1991) 54 *MLR* 769.

[85] For an overview of the development of legal analysis in this area see O'Sullivan, 'Auditors' Liability: Its Role in the Corporate Governance Debate', 23 *Accountancy and Business Research* op. cit. n. 80, p. 413.

[86] See Lord Bridge's judgment at p. 580e.

condition of continued listing, companies supply a statement of compliance with the code or reasons for non-compliance in reports and accounts.[87] In essence, the report is in favour of self-regulation and regulation through the market for firms that do not comply.[88] The report takes as one of its main focuses the provision of financial information to shareholders. It encourages, for example, boards of directors to give an assessment of the company's financial position in the annual report.[89] It recommends the inclusion in interim reports of balance sheet information,[90] so enabling investors to have access to up-to-date information more readily. However, it does not recommend that shareholders should have any greater input to the appointment of directors or auditors by means of devices such as shareholder committees, as it was apparently impossible to ensure the representative nature of these committees among shareholders[91] and shareholders are in a better position to exercise their power directly presumably through the forum of shareholder meetings. The internal consistency of the first objection is hard to see, as the Report later comments that company strategies should be communicated to major shareholders;[92] here it seems there is no need for representative or equal access to information. The second point on the nature of shareholders' meetings will be evaluated below in a further discussion of these meetings. The Cadbury Report recommends no change to the *Caparo* v. *Dickman* decision on broadly similar grounds to those by which the House of Lords justified its original decision; it would make the scope of liability too wide and create an indeterminate class of potential plaintiffs.

The success of creating means for providing more information is dependent on its use. It is by no means clear that institutional investors want or will use more information.[93] The Cadbury Report endorses recommendations made by the Institutional Shareholders Committee[94] encouraging active ownership of shares evidenced by, *inter alia*, positive use of voting rights at shareholder meetings, positive interest in the composition of boards and regular contact with senior executives to exchange views and information on company performance. The idea behind this is

---

[87] Para. 3.7 of the Code.

[88] A detailed review of the Cadbury report and initial evaluation of its worth is to be found in Finch, 'Board Performance and Cadbury on Corporate Governance', [1992] *JBL* 576. There are references within this article to contemporary press comment on the report.

[89] Para. 4.41, a 'balanced and understandable assessment'.

[90] Para. 4.47.   [91] Para. 6.2.   [92] Para. 6.11.

[93] See Wittington, 'Corporate Governance and the Regulation of Financial Reporting', 23 *Accountancy and Business Research* op. cit. 313.

[94] *The Responsibilities of Institutional Shareholders in the UK*, Institutional Shareholders Committee (1991).

to encourage intervention to remedy poor performance rather than dealing with this through the sale of shares. It is too soon to evaluate the effects of these sorts of exhortations.

The encouragement to institutional investors to use their votes and to take an interest in the appointment of directors points towards the use of 'voice' at meetings. As pointed out earlier, articles in the form of Table A prevent shareholders from influencing management decisions directly at meetings. Nevertheless the shareholders in general meeting[95] have the power to dismiss directors,[96] change the company's constitution by altering the articles,[97] change its ownership base by issuing new shares[98] and authorizing the purchase by the company of its own shares,[99] and ratify transactions in which directors have an interest. Even without the authority to influence management decisions, these are wide-ranging powers indeed and present the shareholders as an alternative power block, within the company, which is separate to the board of directors.

However, against this has to be set the prevailing culture, which is for non-participation in shareholder meetings. There is no tradition in the UK of a concerted practice to identify fellow shareholders[100] and use the forum of the meeting in a pro-active way. Much voting at shareholder meetings is done by proxy.[101] Intervention by the Stock Exchange ensures that all listed companies supply members with proxy forms that enable them to appoint a proxy to vote for or against but this has done little to dispel the idea that shareholders who exercise their proxy in favour of management have done so out of habit. Gower[102] offers us a rather depressing overview of the exercise of shareholder voice:

It cannot be said, however, that these provisions have done much to curtail the tactical advantages posed by the directors. They still strike the first blow and their solicitation of proxy votes is likely to meet with a substantial response before the opposition is able to get under way. Even if their proxies are in the 'two-way' form, many members will complete and lodge them after hearing but one side of the case and only the most intelligent or obstinate are likely to withstand the impact of the, as yet, uncontradicted assertions of the directors. It is of course, true that once opposition is aroused members may be persuaded to cancel their proxies. . . . But in practice this rarely happens.

---

[95] For a fairly recent discussion of the rules concerning the conduct of shareholder meetings see *Byng* v. *London Life Association Ltd and another*, [1989] BCLC 400.

[96] CA 1985 s. 303 (ordinary resolution).   [97] CA 1985 s. 9 (special resolution).

[98] CA 1985 s. 80.   [99] CA 1985 s. 164.

[100] This is notwithstanding the apparent transparency of the shareholder register in the UK; it is publicly available to anyone who wishes to inspect it, see CA 1985 s. 356.

[101] CA 1985 s. 372.   [102] *Principles*, 514–16.

22   Sally Wheeler

In relation to public companies, although the result of any disputed resolution is in reality generally determined in advance through the system of proxy votes, the meeting still has to be held. At the meeting the board and the opposition will have an opportunity of repeating the arguments already expressed in their circulars . . . Nor are meetings merely a means of passing resolutions, they also give the members an opportunity of asking questions. . . . And, of course, meetings may be, and most often are, held when there is no battle at all, and here they afford an opportunity for the management to report to members. . . . Unhappily meetings are rarely attended by more than a handful of members unless there is some dispute, and then the only real excitement arises from attempts by the party that has lost the battle of the circulars to trap the other into some formal irregularity or into revealing information which may enable the validity of the notices to be attacked as misleading or incomplete.

It is interesting to compare the UK situation with regard to proxies with the account of US procedure provided by Eisenberg in his essay in this reader. The Cadbury Report does little to promote the meeting as a forum for discussion. Apart from its general endorsement of the Institutional Shareholders Committee Report, it suggests rather than recommends that 'shareholders and boards of directors should consider how the effectiveness of general meetings could be increased and, as a result, the accountability of boards to all their shareholders strengthened'.[103] This approach is unlikely to create incentives for voice rather than exist and is perhaps consistent with a report couched in terms of self-regulation and market discipline.

Reactive Measures

Litigation against wrongdoing directors is based, historically at least, on the derivative action—the idea that the true plaintiff is the company. If the wrongdoing directors are in control it is unlikely that they will resolve to sue themselves. It is possible for the shareholders in general meeting to compel the board to sue its wrongdoing members, if this power is reserved for shareholders under the Articles[104] of the company. If this power is not expressly reserved then shareholders who wish to litigate will have to remove the incumbent board by means of ordinary resolutions and appoint a new one that is prepared to litigate. There are two problems with this approach. One is that it appears that the custodians of the right to litigate are exactly those who are likely to be the subject of control and two it requires a degree of co-ordination within the share-

---

[103] Cadbury Report para. 6.5.
[104] See *Breckland Group Holdings Ltd* v. *London & Suffolk Property Ltd* [1989] BCLC 100.

holders meeting that is unlikely to be present. The only mechanism for company-driven action is the group of provisions dealing with the intervention of the DTI in the Companies Act 1985.[105] This is a sanction not used very often because of the difficulty of obtaining sufficient information to justify an investigation and because of the catastrophic effect such an investigation has on share prices. Of course this catastrophic effect is a symptom of rare use but there have been no suggestions as to how this cycle of consequences can be broken.

Minority shareholder action can take one of two routes. Again, the most important, traditionally, was the common law derivative action to remedy a wrong done to the company.[106] The company is the proper plaintiff but the minority shareholder can sue, joining the company as a defendant.[107] This is subject to the conditions that the wrongdoers are in control and so implicitly are barring the use of the company name wrongfully and that there is fraud on the minority—the so-called exceptions to the rule in *Foss* v. *Harbottle*.[108] It is possible to identify sound policy reasons for this approach to minority actions. The company has a legal responsibility of its own, and asserting that it is the proper plaintiff gives effect to this personality; it prevents multiplicity of actions from disaffected shareholders; and it preserves majority rule within the company while at the same time appearing to balance this with the needs of minority shareholders.[109] However, the derivative action is borne down with procedural and substantive difficulties that have already been alluded to, and, to this extent, it has lost its balancing function. Recent years have seen few derivative actions[110] and it seems fair to say that this type of litigation is unsuited to policing the activities of management and playing a role in corporate governance.

Statutory intervention has created two possible remedies for disaf-

---

[105] CA 1985 Part XIV (ss. 431–53).

[106] If an individual shareholder has suffered a wrong, as opposed to the company, for example, the company has not carried on its business in accordance with the company's articles, then the individual shareholder can sue in his own name in a personal action in which the defendant is the company.

[107] The company is joined as a defendant so that it is bound by the court's decision and can be awarded damages.

[108] Op. cit. n. 15.

[109] In some company constitutions this balance is achieved by creating a system of rights of veto for the minority over some corporate decisions taken by the majority. For a discussion of these devices see Riley, 'Vetoes and Voting Agreements: Some Problems of Consent and Knowledge', (1993) 44 *NILQ* 34.

[110] See the cases referred to in n. 15 above.

fected shareholders.[111] The Companies Act 1985 s. 459 provides for a minority petition complaining that the company is being conducted in 'an unfairly prejudicial manner to the interests of its members generally or some part of the members'. The second, which has a longer legislative history, is found in the Insolvency Act 1986 s. 122(10(*g*); an application under this section is an application to wind the company up, on the grounds that it is just and equitable to do so. The first statutory provision gives rise to a wide variety of remedies,[112] not least that the court allows a derivative action to be brought by the petitioners. There are numerous cases on CA 1985 s. 459 and while we can say that there appears to be no reason why this procedure cannot replace the complications of the derivative action, it is the case that almost without exception the decided cases concern small private companies and not listed companies. This has given rise to a perception that CA 1985 s. 459 applications are unsuitable for resolving problems within listed companies because aggrieved shareholders have the remedy of 'exit', which is less likely to be available to shareholders in private companies because of the difficulty in finding a purchaser other than those already involved in the company, who may not be willing to pay the price the shareholder is asking. This emphasis on the availability of exit displays a preoccupation with the market as a remedial force. What we do not know about CA 1985 s. 459 is the extent to which it is used as a bargaining counter by disaffected groups. It may be that its use in this way accounts for the decline in the use of the derivative action. A petition for winding-up on just and equitable grounds is a remedy of a rather different character: first, it does not offer the range of remedies that CA 1985 s. 459 offers and second, a winding-up petition can be sought in circumstances such as deadlock, a situation which is not remediable under CA 1985 s. 459.[113]

---

[111] A third legislative intervention may come about if the Fifth Directive on Company Law is enacted. The Directive would, amongst other things, give minority shareholders the right to bring an action in the company's name if they held 5% of the shares. It appears that this would be the case even if the act or acts in question had been ratified by the company but without the dissenting 5%. If enacted then this may well achieve the balancing of policy factors that the rule in *Foss* v. *Harbottle* and the exceptions to it has lost over the years. However, other proposals in the Fifth Directive are more controversial and it seems unlikely to be enacted. See the Fifth Directive Com (90) 629; OJ C7 11 Jan. 1991.

[112] See CA 1985 s. 461.

[113] See the Practice Direction issued in [1990] 1 WLR 490 which highlights the separate remedial nature of these two statutory sections by pointing out the undesirability of petitioning under each in the alternative.

Board Structure

Internal monitoring of management and company performance by the board of directors is not thought to be very effective, as in the UK the board of directors is made up in the main of executive directors; representatives of management and the very organ within the company that an effective board monitoring mechanism would be required to monitor. There are several alternatives available for creating at board level a unit capable of being perceived of as independent enough to be a monitor of management. The suggestion of the Cadbury Report is a separation of functions between the chairman of the board of directors and the chief executive[114] and an increased role for non-executive directors.[115] Every listed company is encouraged by the Cadbury Report to have at least three non-executive directors[116] on the board whose 'calibre . . . should be such that their views will carry significant weight in the board's decisions'.[117] These non-executive directors are exhorted by the report to be independent of management and 'free from any business and other relationships which could materially interfere with the exercise of their independent judgement'.[118] In order to preserve this independence and presumably to enable them to fulfil their role, it is recommended that non-executive directors should be able to obtain legal advice at the expense of the company. The Report recommends their appointment to sub-boards such as the audit committee and the remuneration committee. It is not clear from the Report whether non-executive directors have a role to play in management or whether they are to confine themselves solely to monitoring management, if these are indeed separate functions.[119] Clearly it is too soon to assess whether there is substantial

---

[114] The purpose of this is to prevent one individual having unfettered discretion: 'Chairmen should be able to stand sufficiently back from the day-to-day running of the business to ensure that their boards are in full control of the company's affairs and alert to their obligations to their shareholders', para. 4.9 of the report.

[115] Non-executive directors have become increasingly recognized as having a part to play within the enterprise see *A Code of Practice for the Non-Executive Director*, Institute of Directors (1982).

[116] Para. 4.11 of the Report.   [117] Ibid.   [118] Para. 4.12 of the Report.

[119] See Finch op. cit. n. 88, pp. 591–94 for a good discussion of non-executive directors and their role post the Cadbury Report and the Gilson and Roe essay in this volume at p. 000 for a further assessment of the value of independent directors.

[120] A recent study undertaken jointly by Arthur Anderson and Director Magazine, reported in the *New Law Journal* of 15 Oct. 1993, reported encouraging signs of compliance with Cadbury; new non-executive directors are 50% more likely to have a degree and speak a foreign language than before the Cadbury Report.

compliance with these recommendations, and to evaluate the effect of compliance on corporate governance.[120]

It is significant that the Cadbury Report recommendations are made in the context of preserving a unitary board structure. This illustrates that the emphasis of the Cadbury report is on the relationship between management and shareholders and strategies of internal governance and regulation. Little significance is attached to broader conceptions of the company as a social institution.[121] Two-tier board structures, including a supervisory board and a management board, are not uncommon in Europe.[122] This approach is perhaps strongest in Germany[123] where the two-tier structure is accompanied by employee representation on the supervisory board. Employees form half of the membership of this board but, in the event of voting deadlock, power rests with the shareholder representatives. The supervisory board has no management power and its involvement in management proposals is limited to that prescribed in the company's statutes. The supervisory board is under a duty to promote the best interests of the company

In comparison, the UK makes little attempt at employee participation or the consideration of employee interests in the running of the enterprise. The directors are instructed by statute[124] to have regard to the interests of employees but this is enforceable only as a duty owed to the company with all the consequent problems of enforcement that were highlighted above. Some companies have employee share ownership schemes but this only empowers employees in the same way as shareholders. Views of worker participation or co-determination have not

---

[121] The American Law Institute proposals do try to capture a model of corporate law that includes ideas drawn from the various different theories of the firm put forward in this collection. See Mitchell, 'Private Law, Public Interest? The ALI Principles of Corporate Governance', (1993) 61 *Univ. of Toronto LJ* 871.

[122] Belgium is an exception to this. In France the two-tier structure is optional. For a Europe-wide review see M. Gold and M. Hall, *Legal Regulation and the Practice of Employee Participation in the European Community* (Dublin, 1990) and E. Córdova, 'Workers Participation in Decisions within Enterprises: Recent Trends and Problems', (1982) 121 *Int. Labour Rev.* 125.

[123] See Schregle, 'Workers' Participation in the Federal Republic of Germany in an International Perspective', (1987) 126 *Int. Labour Rev.* 317; Wever and Allen, 'The Financial System and Corporate Governance in Germany: Institutions and the Diffusion of Innovations', 13 (1993) *Jnl. of Public Policy* 183.

[124] CA 1985 s. 309. See also CA 1985 s. 719, which permits the company, in the event of it not being constitutionally authorized otherwise, to make provision for employees on the cessation or transfer of business.

always been so lukewarm.[125] The Bullock Committee[126] undertook an extensive review of the policy alternatives and concluded that worker participation within a unitary board structure was preferable if employee directors were not to become so divorced from the management process that they would be unable to make any input. A subsequent government White Paper[127] favoured co-determination with a two-tier board structure but that has now disappeared from the policy agenda. The statutory provisions referred to above were, metaphorically speaking, the eventual response to the Bullock Report and the Bullock Report itself was a response to the first draft of the Fifth EC Directive.

The draft Directive was first issued in 1972[128] and contained proposals modelled on existing German legislation[129] for harmonization of the structure of public companies including compulsory co-determination within a two-tier board structure. The first draft was subjected to intense criticism and the resulting second draft of 1983 bore all the hallmarks of political compromise; it only applied to a limited number of companies and permitted member states to opt for a unitary board structure which included elements of employee representation on a separate body with consultation rights, so enabling compliance to occur with a minimum of real change. The Fifth Directive has encountered further opposition and seems unlikely to be enacted.[130] The latest draft, proposed in 1983, offered member states a variety of different mechanisms of worker participation, not all of which would have required the abandonment of the

---

[125] The involvement of workers in selecting management was favoured by Mill, BPP (1850) XIX qus 837 and 846, and was a standard creed of Christian Socialists of the time. For an account of its successes see B. Jones, *Co-operative Production* (Oxford, 1894).

[126] *Report of the Committee on Industrial Democracy* Cmnd. 6076 (1977).

[127] *Industrial Democracy* Cmnd. 7231 (1978).   [128] OJ 1972 C131/49.

[129] For a discussion of the German model and the Fifth Directive see Hopt, 'New Ways in Corporate Governance: European Experiments with Labour Representation on Corporate Boards' (1984) *Mich. Law Rev.* 1338. Hansmann, 'Worker Participation and Corporate Governance', (1993) 43 *Univ. of Toronto LJ*, provides a discussion of worker-controlled firms, in whole or in part, in the USA and contrasts this with the worker participation structure in Germany.

[130] Since the adoption by eleven member states (the UK dissenting) of the (declaratory) Community Social Charter in 1989, the emphasis in EC policy-making has changed. On the agenda now is a draft directive on European Works Councils, which would require large enterprises operating across more than one EC country to establish works councils for the consultation and information of employees (OJ 1989 C39; amended proposal OJ 1991 C336). Because of strong UK opposition to the measure, it is likely to be adopted, if at all, by the eleven other member states using the framework of the Social Policy Agreement, from which the UK obtained an opt-out under the Treaty of Maastricht. See generally on the various EC proposals for worker participation, Cressey, 'Employee Participation', in Gold (ed.), *The Social Dimension: Employment Policy in the European Community* (Basingstoke, 1993), 85.

unitary board structure. One of the problems with introducing worker participation models is the relative absence of empirical studies on the effects of this on decision-making within the enterprise.[131] Clearly the character of decision-making will change. Teubner[132] suggests that the distribution of power and influence within the company, the 'goal structure' of the company, and the structure of the capital–labour conflict will all be changed. Whether these changes are desirable or not depends, on one level, upon whether they will result in greater productive efficiency and whether, on another, there is a belief in social democracy[133] and the right to participation distinct from an ownership right. This second-level question involves looking at the position of the enterprise and the worker in the current political and economic culture within the state. The argument for participation was powerfully summarized[134] by Charles Handy[135] thus:

The principal purpose of a company is not to make a profit. It is to make a profit in order to continue to do things or to make things and to do so even better and more abundantly   Our concept of the company is out of step with the times. The myth of property gets in the way. It diverts the attention of top management from building the business to protecting its equity. It does not inspire the workforce who see little point in sweating for other people's profits. And it gives business the image of selfishness and greed in the surrounding world. . . . It may even be immoral, now that the principal assets in a company are not buildings and machines but people and people should not be anyone's property in a free society.

[131] An exception to this in the UK is Schuller and Hyam, 'Forms of Ownership and Control: Decision-Making within a Financial Institution', (1984) 18 *Sociology* 51. This was a piece of research on worker participation at board level within pension funds. The parameters of co-determination may well be different within institutions where the debate between ownership and social democracy is more marked. See also the empirical studies referred to by Teubner, 'Industrial Democracy through Law? Social Functions of Law in Institutional Innovations', in Daintith and Teubner (eds.), *Contract and Organisation: Legal Analysis in the Light of Economic and Social Theory* (Berlin, 1986), 261 at 263.

[132] 'Industrial Democracy'.

[133] A completely different form of business enterprise is the workers co-operative. For a discussion of this see Bartlett, 'The Evolution of Workers' Cooperatives in Southern Europe: A Comparative Perspective', in Karlsson, Johannisson, and Storey (eds.), *Small Business Dynamics* (London, 1993), and Turnbull, 'Re-Inventing Corporations', (1991) 10 *Human Systems Management* 169.

[134] See also Adamson, 'Economic Democracy and the Expediency of Worker Participation', (1990) 38 *Political Studies* 56 and Parkinson, *Corporate Power and Responsibility* (Oxford, 1993), 402–23.

[135] Speech given to the London Business School in 1990 as reported in the *Guardian* of 26 Nov. 1992. Handy expresses similar views in *The Empty Raincoat* (London, 1994).

The idea that a company has responsibilities to a wider group other than its shareholders does have a growing constituency not just in the context of employees[136] but in areas such as environmental liability.[137] However, there is no indication that this will translate into a concerted reassessment of power relations within the company and corporate responsibility to groups and interests outside the proprietary rights through ownership framework.

Corporate Governance in International Perspective

The corporate governance debate is framed rather differently in Europe and Japan as compared with the UK and the USA. Wymeersch[138] makes the point that the parameters of debate on corporate governance are framed by the 'cultural enterprise' of the jurisdiction in question. There is, for example, in addition to the possibility of co-determination, no real equivalent to the phenomena of the separation of ownership and control in France and Germany. Franks and Mayer[139] produced the finding that in Germany 'nearly 90% of the 200 hundred largest companies have at least one shareholder with a sharestake of at least 25% of the issued equity. In the UK in two-thirds of the largest 200 companies there is no single shareholder with a holding in excess of 10% of issued equity's'.[140] This difference is partly explicable by the very different role of investment capital in Germany; it is long-term investment finance from banks rather than speculative capital raised from the markets. The investment is controlled by the presence of bank representatives on the supervisory board rather than through accountability to them as shareholders or secured lenders as the case would be in the UK. The Japanese model of business organization, which is the subject of Mark Roe's essay in this volume, bears some similar characteristics. Its unitary board structure gives it the same starting-point as the UK but its capital raising activities and model for co-determination gives it more in common with mainland Europe. As in Germany, Japan has a culture of capital supplied from banks which then fulfil a monitoring role as capital providers distinct

---

[136] In 1992 the RSA launched an inquiry into the role of business in a changing world, one of the launch comments referred to the need for a company to have 'a clear purpose and a clear understanding of its obligations to all shareholders'.

[137] See the provisions of the Environmental Protection Act 1990.

[138] 'Corporate Governance in Europe', in Prentice and Holland, *Corporate Governance*, 10–12.

[139] Franks and Mayer, 'Corporate Ownership and Corporate Control: A Study of France, Germany, and the UK', (1990) *Economic Policy* 191.

[140] Jenkinson and Mayer, 'The Assessment: Corporate Governance and Corporate Control', (1992) 8 *Oxford Review of Economic Policy* 6.

from direct board involvement (see the figures given by Roe in his essay for inward investment from banks). As Roe explains, this is not the only distinctive feature of Japanese business organization. Considerable cross-holdings in Japanese corporations give the whole structure of enterprise an interlocking dependent characteristic that is absent in other economies.

According to Roe these factors effectively remove control over the decision-making process from management and place it in the hands of shareholding banks. On the basis of this analysis, the Japanese structure of the firm has more in common with Scott's 'constellation of interests' approach than with the Berle and Means paradigm. There is, however, no evidence that the enterprise benefits more from bank monitoring in Japan than it does from institutional shareholder input in the UK and the US or that the banks in Japan are any more willing to take a pro-active role in governance than their investor counterparts in the UK or the USA. Roe's championing of the Japanese enterprise structure is challenged by those who point out that when, in the 1980s, restrictions in Japan on finance supply were relaxed there was a large decrease in the supply of bank financing.[141] The concept of the bank as a major shareholder is not current in the USA, not least because US banks are prevented by statute[142] from holding more than 5 per cent of shares in any non-bank company. It is not possible to evaluate the lessons that one jurisdiction could learn from another in the context of corporate governance, any more than it is possible to effect an evaluation in other areas, without a lengthy examination of political institutions, culture, and economic structure. This is a theme that we touched on in the context of codetermination and to which we return when looking at the market for corporate charters and the issue of the creation of supra-national enterprise forms.

Economic theories of the firm

The Coase Theorem

The second great influence on academic thought in this field this century after Berle and Means was Coase.[143] Coase explained the firm as a way of reducing the transaction costs that the parties would incur if they used

---

[141] See Ramano, 'A Cautionary Note on Drawing Lessons from Comparative Corporate Law', (1993) 102 *Yale LJ* 2021 and MacDonald and Beattie, 'The Corporate Governance Jigsaw', (1993) 23 *Accounting and Business Research* 304.

[142] See the Glass Steagall Act of 1933 and the Bank Holding Company Act of 1956.

[143] 'The Nature of the Firm', (1937) NS 4 *Economica* 386.

the market as the forum for their exchange. 'Transaction costs' is used here as a term to describe the costs of bargaining over events like the terms of sale and supply of commodities. If, for example, these would be lower in a vertically integrated firm (i.e. a company or organization where different stages in the production process have been integrated together, see the examples provided by Perrow on p. 000 of his essay) then the market should be abandoned in favour of a hierarchical structure. Another example would be the supply of labour; if certain specialized labour is required to perform a particular task on a regular basis then it is more efficient to engage that labour on a permanent basis than rely on the market to supply it. The Coase theorem can be summarized thus:

principal interest here is internal organisation. Internal organisation is well-suited to transactions that involve recurrent exchange in the face of a nontrival degree of uncertainty [we can define uncertainty as changes in the market that participants may have no control over] and that incur transaction-specific investments. Since internal organization requires the development of specialised governance structure, the cost of which must be amortized across the transactions assigned to it, it is rarely economical to organize occasional investments internally. Likewise, transactions for which uncertainty is low require little adaptation, hence little governance, and thus can be organised by market contracting.[144]

The market test this approach offers is similar to the one propounded by Mill[145] some ninety years earlier. Coase's theory of the firm has now been developed into two distinct economic approaches to the firm, the neo-classical approach, whose proponents include Jensen, Meckling, Fama, Easterbrook, and Fischel,[146] and the institutional approach, whose principal exponent is Williamson.[147] It is possible to draw further subdivisions of approach within these broad categories.[148] However, our interest lies primarily in identifying the fundamental ethos and general theory of

---

[144] Williamson and Ouchim 'Markets-Hierarchies and Visible Hand Perspectives', in Van de Ven and Joyce (eds.) *Perspectives on Organisation Design and Behaviour* (New York, 1981), 347 at 352.

[145] John Stuart Mill, *Principles of Political Economy* (1848) v.i (New York, 1899).

[146] The literature is enormous. Both the Bratton essay and the Perrow essay carry extensive references to it, see Bratton pp. 000–0, 0000, 0000–00 and the accompanying notes and Perrow pp. 000–00 and accompanying notes. Bratton also provides a further critique in 'The Nexus of Contracts Corporation: A Critical Appraisal', (1989) 74 *Cornell Law Review* 407.

[147] Again see the Bratton essay pp. 000–00, 000, 000–00 with the accompanying notes, and the Perrow essay pp. 000–00 and the accompanying notes.

[148] See for example, O. Hart, 'An Economist's Perspective on the Theory of the Firm', (1989) 89 *Col. LR* 1757 where differences between various proponents of what I have broadly classified the neo-classicists are expounded.

these approaches and comparing them to existing and proposed models of corporate governance.

Institutional and Neo-classical Theories

The institutional approach reflects more closely the managerialist school of thought and builds directly on Coase by attempting to identify the particular transaction costs that are replaced by contracting within a firm. It is on this point that Perrow's criticisms slot in, as Perrow does not believe that the proponents of institutional or transaction cost theory show that the firm does have these advantages over the market.[149] Perrow also opposes Williamson's desire for authority and hierarchy to govern transactions. He would prefer bargaining and negotiation whatever the cost. It is a feature of both the institutional and neo-classical approach that neither offers empirical verification of its propositions: they are both based on assumptions about the requirements of private-ordering, when no significance is accorded to the exercise of control by shareholders and the need for accountability to shareholders. Like the managerialists institutional economists perceive the firm as a hierarchical structure; fiat or authority is present within the firm in the hands of management and for institutional economists represents the cheapest way of organizing exchanges.[150] The displacement of the forum for exchange from market to firm renders the idea of contract very important to institutional economists. This interest in contract provides a point of intersection with neo-classical economists. The role of contract is crucial in this approach as it involves perceiving the firm not as a hierarchical institution but as a series of contracts. Contract in this sense refers not only to relationships that are described as such by statute, for example the articles of association[151] of a company (which, aside from perhaps the initial incorporation, has few of the features of a traditional private law contract in terms of negotiation and formation but where we might use the tools of contract construction in dispute-solving), but also to the relationships between all factors of production within the firm. Some of these may be in the form of private law contracts (e.g. employee–employer relationships); others may considered as exchange relationships in a very broad sense of being voluntarily entered into with expectations on both sides of co-operation

---

[149] In addition to the essay contained in this reader see also Perrow, 'Market, Hierarchies and Hegemony' in Van de Ven and Joyce (eds.), *Perspectives on Organisation Design and Behaviour* (New York, 1981).

[150] T. Guinness, 'Markets and Managerial Hierarchies', in Thompson, Frances, Levacié, and Mitchell, *Markets Hierarchies and Networks: The Conduct of Social Life* (London, 1991).

[151] See n. 16.

and understanding (e.g. the relationship between management and investors). Management is merely part of this network of contract relationships. The relationship between investors and management is described as one of principal and agent in which managers are agents and shareholders are principals.[152] Management behaviour is seen in this context as resulting in agency costs which are twofold; one is the cost to shareholders of management decisions which do not enhance their interests and the second is the cost of controls imposed, such as monitoring to deal with divergence. In a free contract scenario such as this, agency costs will be minimized by selecting the most efficient package of controls from the range available, e.g. reliance on fiduciary rules or internally imposed hierarchies. The market price for shares in firms will reflect the agency costs current in that firm and the effectiveness of the controls imposed. So governance measures are not ownership or control driven, but market driven.

A critique of this position as a theory of organization is provided by Perrow in his essay. More specific as a critique of the effect on company law of the 'nexus of contracts' theory is Eisenberg's essay. For Eisenberg the idea of the corporation as a set of negotiated contracts is problematic because it gives insufficient weight to the rules-based nature of the corporation; although there are some rules that can be bargained out by the corporation and the actors involved, there is equally a large number of mandatory rules. The apparent Americo-centric nature of Eisenberg's essay belies what is in fact a useful characterization of corporate rules for UK purposes as well. In the same way that Eisenberg can point to statutory and judicial intervention in the area of closely held corporations (private companies is a more familiar term in the UK), UK lawyers would draw attention to CA 1985 s. 459 and the IA 1986 s. 122(1)(g)[153] as well as to the now less important common law remedies of derivative and personal actions. The division of rules into structural and distributional, on the one hand, and fiduciary, on the other, is a division which can be drawn up in relation to UK company law. The categorization of rules as enabling, default, and mandatory can also be applied to the statutory and common law framework of UK corporate law; Table A, for example, provides a set of default rules as do the statutory provisions dealing with the variation of class rights.[154] Fiduciary duties on the whole are mandatory

---

[152] The *locus classicus* of this position is found in Jensen and Meckling 'Theory of the Firm: Managerial Behaviour, Agency Costs and Ownership Structure', (1976) *J. Fin. Econ.* 305 at 312–19.

[153] See infra p. 000.   [154] CA 1985 ss. 125 and 127.

but as *Guiness* v. *Saunders*[155] shows, it is possible for rules to move from being apparently mandatory to the default category.

Whether Eisenberg's answer to the neo-classical conception of the firm goes above the level of rule categorization, and counters the theory in its own terms, is a matter of debate. Opponents of Eisenberg complain that he misunderstands their position, which is one of asserting that mandatory rules are unnecessary and not of arguing that they do not exist. Eisenberg, they say, does not expose any problems which require in actuality legal coercion as their solution.[156]

Legitimizing Corporate Power

In his essay Bratton considers whether contract can be the sole explanation for the corporation in terms of whether it is accepted by legal doctrine. The effect of attributing this label of contract to the corporation would be to label it a purely private concept where the state had no mandate for intervention and where the corporation existed as no more than a collection of contracting parties. Bratton carefully charts the rise, fall, and resurrection of contract-based explanations for the corporation in the legal treatises, but in the end points to historical influences to dispose of the suggestion that the enterprise from both a legal and economic viewpoint can be explained by contract. To this can be added the point that limited liability and separate personality are not features that can be explained through the matrix of private ordering—while we may be able to explain the internal structure of the corporation as a series of negotiated and standard form contracts, relations with the state are not so easily explained.

Earlier we rejected the concession theory as way of explaining the role of the state *vis-à-vis* the corporation and it now appears that the contract theory does not provide a convincing explanation either. A third approach to explaining corporate power may be the real entity theory. This allows us to view the company as an entity separate from its members; the members are acting together for a common purpose and their doing so creates the entity of the corporation.[157] This gives us a very mal-

---

[155] Op. cit. n. 12.

[156] For a detailed critique of Eisenberg's approach see McChesney, 'Economics, Law and Science in the Corporate Field: A Critique of Eisenberg', (1989) 89 *Col. LR* 1530. Further information can be obtained from examining the references contained therein.

[157] The best discussion of the real entity theory and its background in European philosophy occurs in Hagar, 'Bodies Politic: The Progressive History of Organisational "Real Entity" Theory', (1989) 50 *U. Pitt. LR* 575. An interesting contrast can be drawn between the approach taken here to corporate criminal liability and that found in Wells op. cit. n. 38.

leable theory. We can explain the existence of separate personality and limited liability as the terms offered by the state for the existence of this form of organization. We can in the same way justify state intervention in the realm of areas like financial reporting.[158] As Stokes points out (p. 85 of her essay) the fact that it is a theory which sees the corporation as separate from its members can be used to explain the separation between ownership by a diversified passive community of shareholders and the rise of control by management.

As a legitimation of corporate power, Stokes offers us a corporatist view of the company:

The more or less complete independence of corporate managers from their shareholders enables managers to pursue goals other than those of profit-maximization in the interests of the shareholders. Released from the constraints of both shareholders and any market, managers are free to become public servants, 'a purely neutral technocracy, balancing a variety of claims by various groups in the community and assigning to each a portion of the income stream on the basis of public policy rather than private cupidity'.[159]

For Stokes this corporatist approach can be observed in company law through the provisions on the interests of the employees which we mentioned in the discussion of co-determination. It is true that the approach to this issue in UK enterprise law does not cause any inter-group conflict but for all that the provisions are of little use to disaffected employees.

Teubner, at the end of his discussion of the self-reflexivity of law and the descriptive force of the 'unit' as a concept, makes the plea for the 'strengthening of the corporate actor' to make the pursuit of corporatist policies easier. It is not easy to see how a corporatist approach differs from real entity theory: a move by management towards corporatist policies would be encompassed by the real entity explanation of the corporation. The similarity of the Berle and Means concept of 'corporate conscience' is striking[160] and perhaps it is that similarity which mitigates against the real entity or corporatist explanation of corporate power. The criticisms of corporate conscience made earlier remain—it involves a reification of an inanimate body and tells us nothing about the ranking of

---

[158] See Laski, 'The Theory of Popular Sovereignty', (1919) 17 *Mich. Law Rev.* 201.

[159] Stokes at p. 159 quoting in part from Berle and Means op. cit. n. 56, p. 312.

[160] An indication of how difficult it is to categorize approaches into tight boxes is demonstrated by the fact that Bratton (p. 160) takes Berle and Means's support of the market for corporate control and the discrete exchanges consequent upon that as an opportunity to label them as endorsers of the contract approach. Other aspects of their work fit as well into other theories.

interests within the corporation, which group does or should have primacy, or the extent to which each group can enforce its interests against the company.

Multinational enterprise

To date this introduction has viewed the business enterprise as a single entity incorporated within a single state. In reality much of the power that corporations possess is derived from enterprises made up of group structures, operating in both a national and transnational perspective. The shift is explained in Figure 1. There are principally two issues to be examined in the context of this development. The first is to decide whether there is a theoretical perspective that explains the phenomenon of the multinational enterprise. The second issue is to examine the type of regulatory responses that can be made both to control and to facilitate multinational enterprise.

Multinationals: a theory of the firm or a theory of growth of the firm

The institutional approach of Williamson examined above can be used to explain the existence of multinational enterprise.[161] The unit of analysis remains the transaction cost but, in the context of the multinational, the transaction costs to be internalized concern events like the acquisition of technology. The driving force behind expansion into markets abroad is profit maximization not through collusion and the exclusion of competition but through increased efficiency. This then is the theory of the firm being used to explain multinational enterprise as an extension to its explanation of internal organization; it is not a theory which tries to explain why some firms expand to become multinational in form and others do not. Its focus is on the organization of firms at the expense of markets.

The transaction cost approach is not the only theory of the firm, as opposed to a theory of the growth of the firm, that can be used to explain multinational enterprise. The alternative to the transaction cost approach

---

[161] To explain the extension of his internal organization theory of the firm to the multinational Williamson draws on the historical contribution of Chandler and his work on the development of US firms from family-controlled enterprise to large management corporations: see Williamson, 'The Modern Corporation: Origins, Evolution, Attributes', (1981) *Journal of Economic Literature* 1537. Others have attempted to refine Williamson's approach within the paradigm of institutional economics and transaction costs, see for example Galbraith and Kay, 'Towards a Theory of Multinational Enterprise', (1986) 7 *J. of Econ. Beh. & Org.* 3; Teece, 'Transaction Cost Economics and the Multinational Enterprise', (1986) 7 *J. of Econ. Beh. & Org.* 21.

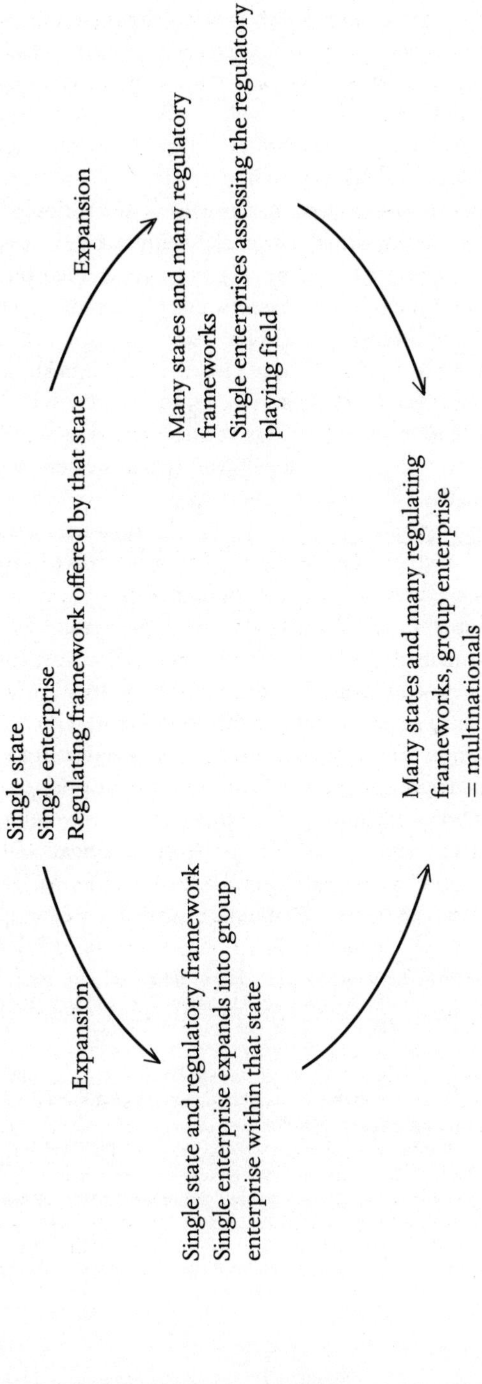

Expansion

Single state
Single enterprise
Regulating framework offered by that state

Many states and many regulatory frameworks
Single enterprises assessing the regulatory playing field

Expansion

Single state and regulatory framework
Single enterprise expands into group enterprise within that state

Many states and many regulating frameworks, group enterprise = multinationals

Fig. 1

is the market power approach perhaps best illustrated in the work of Hymer.[162] Hymer sought to show why firms moved outside their national seat of operations; it occurred when home markets, through the expansion of firms and the collusive behaviour of some, became oligopolistic markets (i.e. markets where there are a few relatively large firms which do not of themselves have a monopoly. The effect of this is that the firms have little or no incentive to compete with each other as it is impossible for the remaining firms to increase their market share. Further expansion can only take place to other states where similar behaviour will bring about saturation of these markets. For Hymer and other exponents of the market-power approach the key is collusive behaviour amongst firms leading to an expansion of market power, unlike the transaction cost theorists, efficiency of the firm is a secondary consideration.

Bornschier and Stamm's essay in this reader explains how Hymer's market-power theory has been developed from what is essentially a theory which explains the behaviour of the firm into one which supports theories of industrial organization. At this level it is no longer a theory of the firm but a theory which looks at the behaviour of firms towards each other.[163] The consequences of oligopoly are treated as things which firms move abroad to avoid; expansion overseas is not the result of collusion but the result of sustained rivalry. The consequences for host countries, often less developed countries, of this expansion are examined by Bornschier and Stamm in the context of the effects of imported technology and the change on industrial structures.[164] These effects can also be explained by using essentially macro-economic concepts of foreign direct investment and import substituting investment or a combination of the two methods.[165] These approaches seek to explain multinational expansion into other countries as reflecting the host country's own particular development to date. The work of Dunning[166] provides a third approach

---

[162] See for example Hymer, *The International Operations of National Firms: Study of Foreign Direct Investment* (Cambridge, Mass., 1976) and Hymer and Rawthorn, 'Multinational Corporations and International Oligopoly: The Non-American Challenge', in Kindleberger (ed.), *The International Corporation* (Cambridge, Mass., 1970), 57.

[163] This approach is described by Cantwell as 'meso-economic' i.e. industry-level approach: 'A Survey of Theories of International Production' in Pitelis and Sugden (eds.), *The Nature of the Transnational Firm* (London, 1991).

[164] An interesting historical perspective on this issue is provided by Wilkins, 'Comparative Hosts', (1994) 36 *Business History* 19.

[165] See Ozawa, 'Europe 1992 and Japanese Multinationals: Transplanting a Subcontracting System in the Expanded Market', in Burgenmeier and Mucchielli (eds.), *Multinationals and Europe 1992* (London, 1990).

[166] J. Dunning, *Industrial Production and the Multinational Enterprise* (London, 1981) and

to the growth of multinational enterprise. His contribution is not viewed as a theory in its own right but as a synthesis drawing on all the theories briefly summarized here. He explains the growth of the multinational as being based on ownership advantages; examples of these are the ability to invest and develop new technology and the ability to retain control over assets such as commercial property. In many ways this approach, although using ownership advantages to pull in industry-based theories, pleases no one. It offers an organizational system but does not take account of the very different approaches to the idea of ownership advantage taken by other theories. For example, for market-power theorists ownership advantage is something which encourages collusion and forces other firms out of the market, whereas for institutional theorists, the existence of ownership advantages is simply a reflection of the failure of markets and the ability of some firms to overcome this by internalizing transactions.

Regulatory Issues

Whether or not it is possible to discern a theory which explains the establishment and continued growth of multinational enterprise does not detract from the proposition that the existence of multinational enterprise raises regulatory issues for states. The sorts of area where the activities of multinational enterprise are a concern for states as issues of economic or political importance, and the empirical research contributions that have been made to illuminate these areas, are summarized by Bornschier and Stamm. The responses of states may occur at a purely national level, or states may group together and produce a response that is more transnational in character. Much economic activity is conducted on an international level and states when acting on their own see their sphere of regulatory control as being confined to their national boundaries—any attempts to regulate beyond territoriality are likely to result in conflicts between neighbouring states. This explains for example the existence of double taxation treaties.[167] In the absence of appropriate cross-jurisdictional enforcement mechanisms such attempts will be largely useless.

The prospects of states alone, without creating some type of

Casson, *The Firm and the Market: Studies on Multinational Enterprise and the Scope of the Firm* (Oxford, 1987), 32–6.

[167] See the discussion of the Model Double Taxation Convention in Income and Capital prepared by the Organization for Economic Co-operation and Development in 1977 in Picciotto, *International Business Taxation* (London, 1992), ch. 2.

supra-national body, being able to achieve a common approach to the issue of the regulation of corporate groups is unlikely for two reasons. First, economic activity is so truly international that the effectiveness of solely national responses has to be questioned[168] and second, different legal cultures do not necessarily engage in regulatory control from the same starting-point. For example, the UK and indeed the USA, rather formalistically, regard the place of incorporation of the business as the starting-point for regulation, even if the enterprise does not carry on any business activities in that jurisdiction. The civil law systems, in a rather more realist approach, see regulation centring on the place of business operation.[169] National regulation is hampered by the absence of a business form for corporate groups which is either nationally or internationally based; each national jurisdiction has to make the decision whether it will recognize the economic reality of the group situation and accord enterprise entity status to the group or whether it will confer separate legal personality on each member of the group. The response of the UK to this has been to reject, in the overwhelming majority of cases, the idea of group enterprise liability.[170] There are in the UK certain statutory provisions which take account of group liability. These are grouped in three areas: company accounts,[171] company guarantees and loans to directors,[172] and a company's purchase of its own shares.[173] This does not represent a change of heart as to the legitimacy of the economic entity argument—some of these developments came about through the need to comply with EC Directives.[174] The Companies Act 1989 inserted new

---

[168] However, see the comments of Hadden, 'Regulating Corporate Groups: An International Perspective', in McCahery, Picciotto, and Scott (eds.), *Corporate Control and Accountability* (Oxford, 1993), 367 on the demands of some states that shares in subsidiaries of multinationals operating within their jurisdictions be held by national or even local interests, further structural regulation can be achieved by insisting on the business involvement of the host state as a joint venture partner.

[169] This is necessarily a basic description—there are instances in most jurisdictions of the legislature creating statutory exceptions to the norm, see Vagts, 'The Multinational Enterprise: A New Challenge for Transnational Law', (1970) *Harv. L. Rev.* 739.

[170] Apart from a brief flirtation with the idea by the Court of Appeal in *DHN Food Distributors* v. *Tower Hamlets London Borough Council* [1976] 1 WLR 852 the judiciary have been implacably opposed to the idea of enterprise entity liability, see *Woolfson* v. *Strathclyde Regional Council* 1978 SC (HL) 90 and *Adams* v. *Cape Industries PLC* op. cit.

[171] See CA 1985 s. 227.

[172] CA 1985 s. 232(1) and sch. 6 require the disclosure in accounts of any arrangement made with directors which is regulated under CA 1985 s. 330 (the provision which deals with loans, guarantees, quasi-loans, and credit transactions).

[173] See CA 1985 s. 153(4) and 153(5).

[174] UK law has thus avoided the changes which would be necessitated if the Draft Ninth Directive were to be adopted. This was first proposed in the 1970s and would go some way

provisions into the Companies Act 1985 to take account of the requirements of the Seventh EC Directive of the EC[175] on group accounts.

The most developed international response to the issue of multinational enterprise is that offered by the EC.[176] In some ways EC regulatory
authorities have to make the same choice as those in other federal trading
blocks such as the US. There the choice is between state level measures
and federal measures; in the EC the choice is between community level
harmonization of existing regulations at national level and leaving
national laws unchanged. The EC has also considered the possibility of
pan-European legislation. In other ways the problems encountered by
the EC are more likely to mirror the problems encountered by other
supranational bodies such as the UN which has sought in a variety of
ways to control multinational enterprise,[177] in that in seeking to regulate
already nationally evolved economies,[178] underwritten by particular
political philosophies, it is bound to have to accept compromises over the
content of regulation as national interests bargain down any proposals
made.

We look next at four types of regulatory intervention that the EC has
embarked upon that have impacted on multinational enterprise. These
are not all intended by the EC as control measures; the EC is no different
from any nation-state in that it wishes to have both a facilative and a control relationship with multinational enterprise. The European Economic

towards addressing the issue of the parent company's liability for debts of subsidiary companies and the question of the relationship between the parent company and the shareholders
of its subsidiary companies. UK law has consistently refused to impute liability for subsidiary company debts to the parent company, see *Re Southard* [1979] 1 WLR 1198 and
Kleinwort Benson v. *Malaysia Mining Company* [1985] 1 WLR 193. Prentice in 'Some
Comments on the Law Relating to Corporate Groups', in McCahery, Picciotto, and Scott
(eds.) *Corporate Control and Accountability* (Oxford, 1993), 371 at 372 identifies five problems
with creating a debt accountability link between parent and subsidiary. These include the
question of exit and entry liability, i.e. the question of a subsidiary entering and leaving a
group with a debt liability, and the conceptual difficulties of distinguishing between
accountability for debts because a subsidiary company is dominated by its parent company
and the situation of a dominant individual shareholder who controls a company's activities—present reform suggestions do not deal with this issue which goes right to the heart of
the company's existence as a separate personality.

[175] Directive 83/349 OJ 1983 L 193/1.

[176] See for example the contributions in Young and Hamil (eds.), *Europe and the
Multinationals* (Aldershot, 1992).

[177] See the rather dated but nevertheless still interesting account in Nixson, 'Controlling
the Transnationals? Political Economy and the UN Code of Conduct' (1983) 11 *Int. J. of Soc.
of Law* 83.

[178] Robson and Wotton, 'The Transnational Enterprise and Regional Economic
Integration', (1993) 31 *J. of Comm. Mkt. Studies* 71.

Interest Grouping (EEIG)[179] is a good example of this. It is a device created to facilitate the creation of European co-operation between 'undertakings'.[180] Undertakings established in different member states can form a body, set up in any member state in which one of the parties has a business interest either through operation or incorporation, to carry on activities in which the undertakings have a common interest ancillary to their main activities. When, or perhaps if, the harmonization programme for corporate laws is complete, the EEIG will have little function in relation to enterprises incorporated as companies[181]—there will be no advantage to them in being able to choose their state of incorporation as all states will offer the same conditions. This fact, together with the current exemption of EEIG's from existing financial disclosure regulations, the restriction to 500 employees, and the downgrading of the profit motive,[182] makes the entire form look like a rhetorical political device for promoting the European economy and its receptiveness to and indeed encouragement of transnational business.

In September 1990 the EC Merger Control Regulation came into force.[183] It requires proposed mergers involving businesses of a certain minimum, which have a Community dimension, to be notified in advance to the European Commission for clearance. The role of the Commission is to decide whether the proposed merger is compatible with the Common Market or not. The Commission, for its part, undertakes to give a decision on compatibility within a maximum of five months of the date of notification. Compatibility is assessed by looking at factors like the market power of the undertakings concerned, the effect on competition, and the effect on consumers.[184] The Community dimension limitation is

---

[179] Regulation 2137/85, OJ 1985 L199/1 discussed by McBarnet and Whelan in their essay in this reader at pp. 000–00; see also Israel, 'The EEIG: A Major Step Forward for Community Law', (1988) 9 *Company Lawyer* 14 and Dine, 'The Harmonisation of Company Law in the EC', (1989) *YEL*.

[180] This is a term used by EC law generally to describe the business enterprise. It has been given a wide interpretation by the European Court of Justice to attach to any body, including the individual, which carries on an economic activity, see Case 170/83, *Hydrotherm* v. *Andreoli* [1984] ECR 2999. When discussing EC law it seems appropriate to use the term 'undertaking' in relation to the enterprise.

[181] Within the UK use has been made of this form by groups such as legal professionals, who as groups to whom incorporation is generally unavailable will derive little advantage from the harmonization of company laws.

[182] Art 3(1).

[183] Regulation 4064/89 OJ 1990 L 257/14. A review of the Regulation can be found in Whish, *Competition Law* (3rd edn., London, 1993). See also Parton, 'Merger Control in the EC: Federalism with a European Flavour', in Cafrung and Rosenthal (eds.), *The State of the European Community: The Maastricht Debates and Beyond* (Harlow, 1993), 285.

[184] See Art. 2.

designed to catch only large-scale mergers; it is currently defined in terms of world-wide turnover figures and Community turnover figures.[185] By catching large-scale mergers in this way, the EC is able to create a control/channelling device for mergers and a facilitative mechanism for developing the European economy, by removing the ability of national governments to block mergers or hold them up with lengthy procedures. It also ensures that uniform criteria are applied to all mergers above the threshold financial levels. In this way, the EC can create the sort of conditions in which European firms can achieve sufficient economies of scale to enable them to compete with the largest firms in other trading blocks, notably the USA and the Far East.[186] However, the real world scenario is that the partisan interests of member states are afforded some recognition under the Regulation; member states can seek EC intervention, in some circumstances, where the EC might otherwise disclaim an interest.[187] Member states can also attempt to oust EC jurisdiction by asserting that the proposed merger affects a defined national market.[188]

The EC has a continuing programme of harmonization of company law.[189] If we take the UK as an example the impact of the programme on domestic law has been in the area of technicalities rather than fundamental structure.[190] As McBarnet and Whelan's essay in this reader shows, even at the level of technical harmonization,[191] there are problems for the success of the process, not only with the responses of multinational

---

[185] See Art. 2.1. World-wide turnover of all undertakings involved has to be more than 5,000 m.ECU and the aggregate community turnover of at least two of the undertakings concerned has to be more than 250 m. ECU.

[186] The comparatively small size of the largest European-based corporations with the exceptions of the chemical and aerospace industries is highlighted by Rosenthal, 'Competition Policy' in Hufbauer (ed.), *European 1992: An American Perspective* (Washington DC, 1990).

[187] See Art. 22.

[188] Art. 21 allows member states to apply to the Commission for a referral to national merger authorities to protect the public interest generally or specifically in the area of public security, plurality of the media, and prudential rules. Art. 9.2 allows member states to apply to the Commission for a referral back to national merger authorities on the ground of the effect of the proposed merger on competition within a defined national market.

[189] See Dine op. cit. n. 175 for a list of the Directives that have adopted so far.

[190] The two Directives most likely to have a structural effect, the Fifth and the Ninth, have yet to be adopted.

[191] Note the different roles ascribed to technical harmonization by McBarnet and Whelan on the one hand and Charney on the other. Charney appears to dismiss the problems that the market may be caused in this area whereas McBarnet and Whelan's empirically based work, not only in their essay in this reader but also in other work, see 'Beyond Control: Law Management and Corporate Governance', paper presented at the International Workshop on Corporate Control and Accountability, Warwick 1991, indicates completely the opposite position.

enterprise to regulation, but also with cultural differences between states. A more ambitious proposed channelling instrument is the *Societas Europea*.[192] This would create a European company form, capable of incorporation under EC law and registered with a Community Institution. The facilitative effect is designed to be the same as the Merger Regulation—to create the climate for trans-European enterprise co-operation. The level of the proposed capital thresholds make it clear that this form would be available only to large-scale enterprise.[193] The practical difficulty for any proposal of this nature is that in the absence of harmonized national laws, background legal rules will still be drawn from differing national laws.

State, market, and enterprise

So far, the business enterprise has been looked at as a unit of production. The remainder of this essay will consider the use by the state of the concept of private enterprise in order to structure its economy. As Marsh's essay in this reader points out, we are now in a period of unparalleled privatization activity in the UK; the same is true; in particular of the countries of central and eastern Europe.[194] The explanations for this, as for the post-war nationalization policy and the municipal regulation policy of the Victorians,[195] are both political and economic. The policies of post-war nationalization were, in very general terms, to create an enhanced sense of state responsibility. In particular sectors where either technology or natural resource factors dictated that a monopoly would exist, this was to be transferred to public ownership. Once in public ownership the profit motive would be discarded and replaced by the public interest. So, from the outset, nationalized industries in the UK assumed a character that was not present in other mixed economy states that had a state industry

[192] COM (89) 268 as amended by COM (91) 174, see Wehlau, 'The *Societas Europea*: A Critique of the Commission's 1991 Amended Proposal', (1992) 29 *CMLR* 473. See also the recent proposal for Regulations establishing statutes for European associations, co-operative societies, and mutual societies, OJ 1992 C99.

[193] The proposed SE has always contained co-determination provisions which are now set out in a separate proposed Directive, which is similar in content to the draft Fifth Directive. This factor mitigates against its adoption in the near future. The three 1992 drafts on other enterprise forms also adopt this structure.

[194] Privatization is not solely a Thatcherite policy; the Conservative government of 1951 denationalized or privatized some of the industries taken into state ownership under postwar government. However there intervention was not on the same scale as post-1979 intervention has been.

[195] Foreman-Peck op. cit. n. 36.

and service sector; nationalized industries in the UK consisted almost exclusively of monopolies.[196] The constitutional structure of these nationalized bodies disappointed; the public interest was not given effect to in either systems of co-determination or in accountability at the consumer level; lack of statutory direction left relationships between these bodies and central government vague and so removed accountability in that direction.[197]

Most commentators agree that in the above respects nationalization policies failed. The privatization policies pursued by successive Conservative governments post-1979 have concentrated on several policy issues.[198] One is the retreat of the state behind the market; the idea is that the market allocates resources better than state intervention can.[199] Another is accountability: this is to be achieved by diverse share ownership and through regulation by quasi-government bodies. The effect of share ownership and exit by dissatisfied shareholders as an accountability and control mechanism in this context is subject to the same criticisms as those made earlier about the market for corporate control. For example, in practice, any accountability to shareholders is likely to be through the activity of institutional shareholders, not through any pressure applied by members of the new shareholding democracy. One of the methods adopted to achieve privatization has been to engage in asset sales[200] targeted at sectors of the public who had not previously been part of the share-owning community. The identity of these shareholders is one reason why we may have expected central government to enact provisions to offer some degree of market insulation for these new shareholders, rather than expecting them, rhetorically more than in reality, to fulfil a monitoring function. The inadequacies of shareholder accountability mechanisms will place the regulatory bodies created under privatization (e.g. OFGAS, OFTEL) under considerable strain; their very existence

---

[196] The 1970s saw the taking into the state sector of parts of the car industry that were suffering financial difficulties. Clearly these were not monopolies.

[197] For a detailed review of the structure of these bodies and the issues surrounding the definition and operation of the public interest criteria see Prosser, *Nationalised Industries and Public Control* (Oxford, 1986), chs. 7 and 8.

[198] For a general discussion of privatization as part of the wider political agenda see Gamble, 'Privatisation, Thatcherism and the British State', (1989) 16 *J. L&S Rev.* 1.

[199] Wolfe, 'State Power and Ideology in Britain: Mrs Thatcher's Privatisation Programme', (1991) 39 *Political Studies* 237.

[200] As indicated by Marsh's essay, asset sales are not the only method used to create the application of the market to previously nationalized industries. For a detailed review of the legal issues involved in these methods, see Graham and Prosser, 'Privatising Nationalised Industries: Constitutional Issues and New Legal Techniques', (1987) 50 *MLR* 16.

points away from the adequacy of market regulation for these industries. They will then have to demonstrate that they can be effective bodies in achieving a balance between consumers and the demands of the market in order for privatization to achieve anything more than nationalization did.[201] A characteristic of the privatization programme so far has been the absence of any competitive force in the market. This will increase the pressure on the regulatory bodies to prevent monopoly pricing occuring. Contract, which as a concept, has played a significant part in the development of explanations for the existence of the firm as a unit for production and as an entity, is also called into play as an important tool in privatization. In the same way that asset sales are used to create an enhanced culture of share ownership, so the use of the discourse of contract implies an an emphasis on individual rights, duties, and accountability and a move away from discretion-based power structures. Contract in the scheme of privatization is used both to 'contract out' services and to generate procurement markets in areas such as the NHS. Contracts in this sense often have none of the features normally associated with contract in the private law sense; they are not necessarily the product of voluntary exchange, as the resort to the market has been legislatively imposed and the contracts are generally, in the area of procurement markets, not enforceable in the courts.[202] The creation of the Citizens' Charter is, as with the regulatory agencies, a recognition of the fact that there is still a need to monitor the activities of procurement markets and service providers; the contract device is imperfect as the sole balancing weight in these activities.[203] The success of privatization in this context will be judged on the effectiveness of the Citizens' Charter to achieve this. However, as Harden points out[204] a more effective approach would have been to create a public law contract which specifically addressed the issues of enforceability etc. and which was clearly intended to be interpreted on the basis of 'shared values and purposes that go beyond those of—even long-term—commercial self-interest'.[205] The apparent disinclination to go down this route maybe that it mitigates against adherence to the model of accountability and involvement through ownership, and points in the direction of account-

---

[201] For suggestions as to how we can encapsulate a theory of public ownership which may go some way towards answering this problem, see Mayer, 'Public Ownership: Concepts and Applications', in Helm (ed.), *The Economic Orders of the State* (Oxford, 1989), 251.

[202] See Hughes, 'Reorganisation of the National Health Service: The Rhetoric and Reality of the Internal Market', (1991) 54 *MLR* 88.

[203] Barron and Scott, 'The Citizens' Charter Programme', (1992) 55 *MLR* 526.

[204] Harden, *The Contracting State* (Buckingham, 1992).   [205] Ibid. 75–7.

ability on the basis of broader social democracy principles, given effect to in policies of co-determination amongst other things.

The events in Eastern and Central Europe, which saw the demise of communism, have also led to the dash for marketization and ultimately privatization as the old command economies and external state-trading enterprises have collapsed. All of these states are moving towards private enterprise. Indeed the states in the Visegrad group—Hungary, Poland, and the Czech and Slovak Federal Republics—are committed to harmonizing their corporate laws to those of the EC.[206] but this is not to say that they have settled already their optimal forms of corporate governance. The final shape of these economies is not yet known or indeed even speculated upon to any great extent in the available literature.[207] What is significant is the speed with which the ideology of marketization and privatization has taken over in these states.[208] It appears that to be part of the international capital market in terms of obtaining inward investment, it is not possible to maintain any other system. The obvious third position between a command economy and a market economy is a system of worker managed co-operatives.[209] However, this does not create the same investment opportunity for the international capital markets. The consequence of this is that domestic economies have been severely disrupted by exposure to international capital. In practice, the actual process of privatization has taken rather longer[210] as the capital market has selected some enterprises as desirable investment opportunities, leaving others without investors. Opportunities have been created for enterprise capitalists and this will result in the rapid rise of a traditional capitalist class system.

---

[206] See Cremona, 'Community Relations within the Visegrad Group', (1993) 18 *ELR* 345.

[207] A great deal of literature concentrates on the constitutional processes involved, see *inter alia* Gabor, 'The Quest for Transformation to a Market Economy: Privatisation and Foreign Investment in Hungary', (1991) 24 *Vand. J. of Transnat. Law* 269 and Kluson, 'The Transformation of a State Enterprise into a Joint-Stock Company', (1991–2) 14 *Eastern Economics* 9. A notable exception is Frydman and Rapaczynski, *Privatisation in Eastern Europe: Is the State Withering Away* (London, 1994).

[208] See Ferguson, 'Privatisation Options for Eastern Europe: The Irrelevance of Western Experience', (1992) 15 *World Economy* 487.

[209] Clarke, 'Privatisation and the Development of Capitalism in Russia' (1992) 196 *New Left Rev.* 3.

[210] For an account of the progress of privatisation in various command economies see Frydman, Rapaczynski, Earle, *et al.*, *The Privatization Process in Russia, Ukraine and the Baltic States* (London, 1993) see also Hughes, 'Industrial Restructuring in Czechoslovakia and Hungary', (1993) 14 *Policy Studies* 14, and Stevens-Ströhmann, 'Privatisation and Restructuring: the German Experience', (1993) 14 *Policy Studies* 4.

Conclusions

The general objective of this introductory essay has been to provide an orientation guide to the vast and often complex literature on business enterprise. It has also sought to build bridges between the often theoretical and largely US-oriented literature, some of which is contained in this collection and the regulatory responses of the British state to issues of corporate governance and corporate power. Some of the issues addressed in this introduction are enduring features of any form of organization; others are more immediately linked to current political preoccupations. In sum, however, we gain a picture of a deeply complex but none the less vibrant form of business organization which stands at the hub of social and economic activity.

THEORIES OF THE COMPANY AND OF CORPORATE CONTROL

Enterprise Corporatism: New Industrial Policy and the 'Essence' of the Legal Person

GUNTHER TEUBNER

I. Persona mystica revisited

The legal person has become an inert person indeed. While in the 19th century it was a fiery fighter for political and economic freedom against government regulation, today it is no longer trusted with any role in major economic policy controversies. What can the legal person, of all persons, possibly contribute to current issues such as the 'new industrial divide', the European choice between 'Americanization' and 'Japanization' of industrial organization, the strategies of new flexibility, and the 'management of uncertainty'?[1] The search for the 'essence' of the legal person, which has fascinated whole generations of lawyers, has now been tacitly abandoned due to an everyday familiarity with this legal entity. Today the legal person is having to pay the price of success: nobody is interested in its essence any longer, and, despite warnings to the contrary, it is no longer taken seriously, not even when the issue involved is the famous 'piercing of the corporate veil' that so inflames the legal imagination.[2]

To be sure, there have been some recent attempts to rediscover the political dimensions of the legal person.[3] In an impressive reinterpretation, for instance, Claus Ott has described the old dispute over the 'essence' of the legal person as a political conflict over the function and legitimation of intermediary forces in society, raising the question of its political legitimation under present-day conditions.[4] But while a pluralist concept of corporate governance did emerge from Ott's analysis, it made no contribution to the theory of the legal person. And no wonder, for if Ott proposes to solve the corporate person's legitimation problems by

Gunther Teubner is Otto Kahn-Freund Professor of Comparative Law and Social Theory, London School of Economics.

establishing links to interest groups and regional parliaments, then the real achievement of the legal person—namely to increase organizational autonomy—has to take second place.

In order to rediscover the social dimension of the legal person, it would seem advisable to invert completely the approach adopted. It is not a reduction of organizational autonomy that is needed, but its expansion. If the legitimation of the first is sought primarily not in the consent of those involved, but in its overall social function and performance,[5] then the heightening of organizational autonomy *vis-à-vis* the persons and interest groups involved is not only compatible with this legitimation, but indeed its precondition. We can then start to see what the concept of the legal person might be able to contribute to industrial policy. Industrial policy might be able to find a viable alternative to the current strategies of contractual flexibility in the expanded autonomy of an action system which is independent *vis-à-vis* the groups involved and which is capable of reacting sensitively, in autonomous goal-seeking, to the demands of, threats to, and changes in the environment.[6] To achieve such flexibility through organization,[7] however, it is necessary, in the interest of society as a whole to strengthen the 'corporate actor'—a new-fangled term for the legal person—and its autonomy *vis-à-vis* the internal interest groups involved. This turns the current logic of legitimation entirely on its head. It is not pluralism within the firm that justifies the actions of the corporate actor, but the contrary: internal pluralism is legitimate only in so far as it is oriented towards the corporate actor's goals, which in turn must be legitimized by the firm's function and performance in society.

To give such pre-eminence to the collective identity of organizations is certainly problematic today.[8] With the spread of economic models adhering strictly to methodological individualism, collective actors have fallen into disrepute. The firm is dissolved into a network of contracts among the individuals involved, or into a 'transactional network' in which, while a 'central agent' does appear as a natural person, the legal person either does not feature at all, or does so only as a bizarre fiction of jurists.[9] Even sociologists, who by the nature of their discipline ought to develop a feeling for the reality of the collectivity, analyse the corporate actor out of existence by conceptualizing it as resource pooling by individuals.[10] Those who assert the social reality of collective units are liable to be suspected of a methodologically and politically doubtful holism/collectivism.

If instead a systems theory approach is chosen, the very distinction between individualism and collectivism becomes questionable.[11] This theory neither reduces collective action to individual action nor vice versa, but interprets both as different forms of social attribution of action. The theory of self-referential systems allows the legal person and its social reality to be understood without collectivist or organicist metaphors, without 'invoking some mystic entity, the social group, and endowing it with superorganic, self-sustaining powers'.[12] The thesis to be developed below is that the legal person is neither a fiction à la Savigny, nor has it as its substratum the 'physico-spiritual unity' of Gierke's *reale Verbands-persoenlichkeit* (real corporate personality), nor is it merely an autonomized pool of resources. Nor has a convincing social basis for the legal person yet been found in the social action system, not even with formal organization. Instead, I would suggest that the *social reality* of a legal person is to be found in the '*collectivity*': the socially binding self-description of an organized action system as a cyclical linkage of identity and action.

The compactness of this thesis admittedly makes it obscure and therefore in need of considerable amplification (given in Part II). This approach also has far-reaching implications for legal theory, legal doctrine, and legal policy, which certainly cannot be worked out fully in this article. Some of the legal theory implications will be touched upon in a discussion of the relationship between the social reality and the legal regulation of the legal person (in Part III): What degree of freedom does the legal person have *vis-à-vis* the corporate actor? What is the function of legal personification of collectivities? Some consequences of our thesis for legal doctrine (Part IV) will be treated, especially how the relationship between legal person and economic organization is to be conceptualized in law. Finally, some legal policy implications (Part V) will be discussed under the heading of 'enterprise corporatism': if a strategy of neo-corporatist producers' coalitions is developed as an industrial policy alternative to contractual flexibilization, how does this strategy relate to the impersonal order that the corporate actor represents?

II. Social substration of the legal person

The contemporary debate on the legal person seems content to accept its purely technically legal character,[13] but there are nevertheless views that stress its dynamic social reality.[14] The most advanced proponents of this position are prepared to 'award Gierke the palm', as long as his *reale Verbandspersoenlichkeit* is cleansed of collectivist and organicist metaphors. But a peculiar embarrassment makes itself felt when it comes to defining how thorough the cleansing should be. What is left, after this purge, of the 'physico-spiritual life-unit' of Gierke's 'real corporate personality?'[15] After Rittner's treatment, we still have the objective spirit: a 'special spiritual action centre of objectivity', which makes possible 'the supra-individual continuity of (in the broadest sense) cultural substances'.[16] Taking a suitable distance from neo-idealistic formulations, Wieacker in his turn has a go at social psychology. Then all that is left is the empirical reality of the legal person in 'group consciousness'.[17] Ott allows the legal person more of a political reality: as the power and action centre of 'private government'.[18] In a particularly thorough cleansing, finally, Flume reduces the hard reality of 'social entities' to Savigny's *ideale Ganze* (ideal whole), the more detailed definition of which, however, with wise self-restraint, he leaves open.[19] By contrast with the burgeoning fullness of Gierke's real corporate personality, such a cleansed and filleted legal entity looks rather thin. Considering the original grandiose concept, this present state of debate seems rather petty-minded. Is Jellinek's call to make the pre-legal reality of associations independent of organism theory[20] unfulfillable even today?

Gierke's cardinal error was to conceive of the components of the association as flesh and blood people.[21] When he called associations 'organisms whose parts are human beings',[22] he programmed the errors of organicist collectivism. Not only does this entail difficulties for the treatment of institutions, foundations, and one-man companies, but by taking actual human beings as the essential elements of an association, it bars access to the social reality of associations, for then collectivities can be seen only as 'supermen'. Methodological individualism is quite right to attack such mystifications of collective units as supra-individual entities linking separate individuals into new wholes. It is, however, quite wrong to reduce the specific dynamics of social processes to individuals' actions, and correspondingly to see collectivities such as the legal person only as mere abbreviations, shorthand expressions, or 'verbal symbols' for the complex aggregates of individual actions that are really involved.[23] The internal dynamics of the legal person's substratum can be better understood by viewing the substratum as an autonomous communicative process, with actual people simply being treated as part of this process's environment. If this step is not taken and yet the social reality of the legal person is nevertheless maintained, one falls into the trap of organicist collectivism—or else on escapes into neo-idealism, social psychology, or politics.

If, then, the substratum of the legal person does not consist of an assemblage of individuals, what is it? Is it a social relation, an aggregate of roles, a decision-making sequence, a chain of transactions or a resource pool? All these solutions have their advocates: Max Weber saw the associational reality as a 'relation';[24] Talcott Parsons conceived of 'actions' or 'roles' as the reality of social systems;[25] Chester Barnard dissolved the organization into 'activities',[26] Herbert Simon into 'decision premises',[27] Oliver E. Williamson into 'transactions';[28] James Coleman sees the reality of the corporate actor in 'pooled resources'.[29] These are just a few of the authorities that have done without actual individuals as the units of the pre-legal reality of legal persons. But which of these elements ought to take the place of actual people?

With unerring intuition, Gierke found the criterion by insisting on the 'livingness' of the association, on its internal dynamic and continual self-reproduction, concomitantly ridiculing the theories of *Zweckvermögen* (resource pools, special-purpose funds) because only 'organized associations of individuals with unitary associative will could have the animated body to which a genuine legal personality can be attributed, such as a mere purpose or a dead fund could never acquire'.[30]

This argument of course reveals the second major error of organicist collectivism. Social systems are in fact not constituted on a basis of life as 'real physico-spiritual units'. This does not mean, however, that they need necessarily be taken, as does Rittner, as substances of the objective spirit. One size smaller will still do. It is enough for social systems to be constituted as communicate units on the basis of social meaning, which in principle excludes both biologism and idealism. Nevertheless, if one abstracts from 'life' and 'meaning' in the direction of a theory of 'self-reproducing systems', then one has found the criterion, with Gierke. The social substratum to be personified is not simply a (static) social structure. Instead, it is an internal dynamics system, with selections of its own, and with a capacity for self-organization and self-reproduction. All that Gierke had available to express this dynamism was the misleading metaphor of 'life'. Today for this we have the cooler, remoter concept of an autopoietic social system: a system of actions/communications that reproduces itself by constantly producing from the network of its elements new communications/actions as elements.[31] Therein lies the dynamic social reality of the substratum: the legal person is based not on a mere social relation (Weber) or social structure (Parsons), but on a 'pulsating' sequence of meaningfully interrelated communicative events, that constantly reproduce themselves.[32]

From this position we can see that the purpose and pool theories of the legal person,[33] in their more recent versions of the *organisiertes Zweckvermögen* (organized special-purpose fund, or resource pooling)[34] are incomplete, applicable to only a partial aspect of the whole. Even if we ignore the less advanced purpose theories, which disqualify themselves by trivially defining the *Vermögen* as things or assembles of things, and consider only the more ambitious definition of *Vermögen* as a bundle of property rights, such theories are of only limited scope. For they apply only to a (relatively static) substructure of a whole dynamic system of action—Gierke's 'dead fund'. For this reason, the more recent legal theories which argue on a corporate actor basis are superior in principle to those which argue on a basis of a resource pool,[35] since they at least aim at the personification of the whole action system, and not merely of the partial aspect of the property rights structure.

Ought we, then, to take a self-reproducing action system as the social substratum of the legal person? No, for this, too, is accurate only in a very provisional, not to say misleading, sense. The term 'social action system' covers a multitude of social phenomena, from simple conversation and the group via law, the economy and politics, right up to the world society, far from all of which have any entitlement to legal personification. A qualifying characteristic must be added that justifies giving a social system the honorary title of 'collectivity' or 'corporate actor'.

The criterion which is frequently chosen for this today is formal organization.[36] The substratum of the legal person is said to be a formally organized social action system.[37] This certainly provides a plausible criterion, and at the same time covers the majority of empirical phenomena, namely formal organizations.

But however formal organization is defined, whether as a goal-oriented social system,[38] a relation of bureaucratic domination,[39] or a governance structure,[40] none of these definitions catches the reality of the corporate actor or the collectivity. An organization does not become capable of action (in a pre-legal sense) by merely constituting itself as a goal-oriented system.[41] Indeed, the social reality of the corporate actor is not located at all at the level of actual system operations (communications, actions, decisions). *The emergent quality of a 'corporate actor' arises from self-description in the action system itself.* It is reflexive communication in the action system, communication on its own identity and its capacity for action, that constitutes the corporate actor or the collectivity as a mere semantic artifact, as a linguistically condensed perception of group identity.[42] It is only to the extent that such a corporate actor becomes institutionalized, i.e. that organizational actions are actually oriented round this self-description, that the corporate actor takes on social reality.

Looking back from here once again at the old dispute on the nature of corporate personality, the ambivalence of the corporate actor, its remarkably fluctuating reality becomes clear. It is neither Savigny's pure fiction nor Gierke's real corporate personality—or else it is both at the same time. The corporate actor is 'fictional' because it is not identical with the real organization but only with the semantics of its self-description. It is 'real' because this fiction takes on structural effect and orients social actions by binding them collectively. Max Weber came closest to capturing this ambivalence by treating collectivities only as 'ideas' in the heads of judges, officials and the public, while at the same time assigning them 'a powerful, often a decisive, causal influence on the course of action of real individuals'.[43] Another who came close is Franz Wieacker, for whom 'the socio-empirical reality of the social group types 'association, corporation' . . . lies in the group consciousness of the members and their partners and in the specific nature of the group's behavior'.[44]

To be sure, both formulated only the psychic but not the social reality of the collectivity. It is not unexpressed ideas in the heads of those involved, but communicative self-descriptions in the organization as an action system that constitute the hard reality of the collectivity, the collective bond: 'collective action is adopted as a premise in the meaning of other system actions, thereby limiting possibilities'.[45]

An additional step further beyond Max Weber, who explicitly denied collective entities the capacity for action, is necessary in order to throw full light on the substratum of the legal person. For the social self-description of collective identity—'corporate identity'—only succeeds in conveying a half impression of the corporate actor. Only a first approximation of the collectivization of a group can be obtained from representing it as the institutionalization of collective identity, be it on the model of a human person or of an organism. To gain a full understanding, the collectivity must instead be seen as a dyadic relationship. This is, say, what Parsons does in construing it as a relationship between 'solidarity' and capacity for 'action in concert'.[46]

The key to understanding lies in the cyclical linkage of action and collective identity via mechanisms of attribution. Even in the case of simple interaction or of the group, the everyday understanding of acting individuals must be redirected so that events become system actions only once the communication network regards its participants or members as 'persons', i.e. only once individuals are constituted as social constructs, and particular events are then assigned to these self-created communicative realities.[47] Even at the level of interactions and groups, then, it is mechanisms of attribution that constitute system actions as actions of people *within* the system. It is only by taking this construction seriously that one can understand the process of collectivization. Collectivization means a shift in the attribution of an action from one social construct to another, from a 'natural' to a 'legal' person. *A self-description of the system as a whole is produced and to this construct actions are attributed as actions of the system.* This is a self-supporting construction: collective actions are the product of the corporate actor to which events are attributed, and the corporate actor is nothing but the product of these actions.

A first interim result might then be as follows: the social substratum of the legal person is neither an assemblage of people nor a pool of resources nor a mere organizational structure. Nor is it adequately characterized as an action system or as a formal organization. The substratum is conceived properly as a 'collectivity' or 'corporate actor', i.e. the self-description of a (usually formally) organized social action system that brings about a cyclical linkage of self-referentially constituted system identity and system elements.

III. Freedoms vis-à-vis the corporate actor

If we now know everything about the 'substratum' of the legal person, we still know nothing about its 'essence'. For the question of 'essence' changes the system reference from the organization to the law, bringing up the question of what room the legal system has for manœuvre in its external description of the self-description of an organized social system. What freedoms can the legal person assume *vis-à-vis* the corporate actor? All freedoms and every freedom, is the answer in good positivist language. Even if we no longer see the substratum merely diffusely as a 'social phenomenon', an 'action centre', an 'acting unit' and the like, but more precisely as a 'collectivity' in the sense defined above, there still remains a difference in principle between the social structures and the legal structure of corporate personality. There are no fixed objective relationships between pre-legal structures and legal construction. There is no sociological natural law of the legal person. If legal positivity is to be taken seriously here, too, then one would on the contrary have to expect a high degree of variability between law and social substratum. As Selznick says: '. . . the institutional perspective is quite compatible with a more selective policy-oriented concept of the corporation.'[48]

From the standpoint of the theory of self-referential systems, too, the autonomy of the law in the construction of its own environment and in the choice of its distinctions must be stressed. This is external observation of a self-observation: the legal system observes, using its own conceptualizations, how the organized social system observes itself as a 'collectivity', or else how it is observed as such by its environment. The legal system is in no way 'bound' by the self-observation, nor by other (e.g. psychological, sociological, or 'life world') external observations of this self-observation.[49] There is therefore no contradiction between on the one hand stressing the social reality of the substratum and on the other defending a positivist or constructivist concept of the legal person. The most decisive advocate of this position was perhaps Kelsen: the legal person is a partial legal suborder, a complex of norms relating to a particular legally defined entity (contract, corporation, association, federation, municipality, state). In the personification, the norm complex is nothing but a point of attribution.[50] Kelsen's problem, however, lies in his rigid separation of the social and the legal spheres, the interaction of which is set aside by erecting a conceptual barrier between them.

Accordingly, nothing prevents the legal system from taking any object whatever—divinities, saints, temples, plots of land, art objects—as points of attribution and giving them legal capacity.[51] Trees particularly are prominent candidates. In legal theory and legal policy discussion they are continually raised as potential legal subjects—quite rightly today. ('Should trees have standing?')[52]

It is amazing that, despite an extremely high degree of freedom and choice, there are nevertheless such great structural similarities between 'collectivity' and 'legal person'.[53] It is not only that the social and legal mechanisms of action attribution to constructs produced within the system (individual/collectivity in the social world, natural person/legal person in the legal world) are in principle structured in a parallel fashion. It is more striking that the law today makes practically no use of its positivist freedom and exclusively promotes 'collectivities' to the status of legal persons. (In the sense defined above, even a one-man-company is a 'collectivity'!) Flume has argued forcefully that it makes no sense to subsume the complex reality of the legal person under a 'unitary concept': 'What meaning is it supposed to have if one covers the reality of the state, of municipalities, of churches, of a corporation, of a foundation, of a sporting association, etc., in a unitary concept?'[54] But the concept of 'collectivity' or 'corporate actor' developed above (i.e. self-description of an organized social system as the link between identity and capacity for action) shows instead that it certainly does make sense to subsume these social phenomena under a unitary concept.

What are the objections to the unitary concept? Certainly not the fact of acting in different spheres (e.g. politics, economy, culture, religion, leisure). More problematic are the important differences that exist between associations, institutions and foundations. Because of these differences it is often believed that there can be no unitary concept of the substratum. For in the case of associations it can only consist of human beings, whereas for foundations and institutions it is only the resource pools that could be the real substratum.[55] But this is precisely the point at which collectivity and the corporate actor step in, supplying a more precise unitary concept of the substratum than, say, Rittner's and Flume's vague concepts of 'action unit' and 'social phenomenon' could do.

The thesis is that, without being normatively compelled to do so, the law regularly binds up legal capacity with a large set of prerequisites of a particular social reality, which can be described by a 'unitary concept'. These prerequisites are: (1) (formally) organized action system; (2) a self-description of a collective identity; and (3) a cyclical linkage of identity and action via mechanisms of attribution. And thus we return to the social system's unitary concept of the collectivity.

The reasons for this close correspondence between law and society, astonishing from the viewpoint of positivist freedoms, are neither of natural law nor of legal logic, but merely of legal policy. Giving legal capacity to social formations makes policy sense only when they have a highly developed internal order.[56] Social capacity for action, i.e. the capacity for attributing external effects to the social system as such, implies that actions entitling and obligating them. This calls for an order that has many social prerequisites: 'the development of leadership structures, the formation of media for transferring selections in the system, mainly of power, the legitimation of representation rules and distributive processes with external or internal effect, and, not least, a certain alleviation of personal attribution, plus provision, despite this, for motivation and responsibility.'[57]

These requirements can be summarized in the formula 'social capacity for collective action'. As a rule, it makes legal policy sense to grant legal capacity to social systems that already have social capacity for collective action. As the German example of the *nichtrechtsfähiger Verein* (association without legal capacity) or the Italian example of the *Mafia* shows, there may be powerful legal policy reasons which militate against the granting of legal capacity to certain social systems even though they are effectively capable of collective action. At the same time, the examples of political parties and trade unions show that once social capacity for collective action has been developed, the legal system is exposed to massive pressure to complete the social personification by legal personification.

The second reason supporting a correspondence between the social and legal structure lies deeper. It concerns the social function of legal personification. This is understood quite inadequately if only the advantages of limited liability are taken into consideration and if the disadvantages are partially compensated for by 'piercing the corporate veil'.[58] Much more important aspects are, for example, the saving in transaction costs and the coordination advantages of 'resource pooling';[59] efficiency gains deriving from the legal support of the capacity for action of the system as such;[60] the positional advantages for the organization in contacts with the environment;[61] or, last but not least, the well known 'legal immorality'.[62] The really interesting 'emergent property' lies, however, in the building up of a (second order) autopoietic system.[63] By the cyclical linkage of identity and action perfected in the legal person, the organization acquires a hitherto unachieved autonomy *vis-à-vis* its environment, both the external environment of market and politics and the internal environment of members and others involved in the organization. The legally supported personification is a decisive step towards complete operational closure, which at the same time means a new type of environmental openness, i.e. a step towards that linkage between closure and openness which is typical of autopoietic systems and is the basis of their evolutionary success.[64]

This clears the way for transferring the profit motive from shareholders to the *Unternehmen an sich* (enterprise in and of itself), and would make the criteria of social responsibility apply not only to the personal actors, but also to the organization in terms of 'corporate' social responsibility.[65] The development of autopoietic autonomy thereby also opens up far-reaching perspectives of economic and political control. As Mayntz recently rightly stressed, although autopoietic closure of formal organizations produces opaqueness and therefore control problems, it nevertheless at the same time also creates new opportunities for political and legal control.[66] On the whole, then, the self-description as 'collectivity' contributes to producing the 'unity' of the system. It allows for 'operational closure' of the self-referential information process and for 'structural coupling' to the needs and interests of the environment.

The second interim result could be formulated as follows: in the sense of positivist or constructivist theories of the legal person, the law has great freedom as to what social phenomena are to be given legal capacity. Nevertheless, in practice there exists a great correspondence between social structures and legal structures of corporate personality, which justifies a unitary concept of the substratum as collectivity or corporate actor. The basis for this is the linking of legal capacity to the social capacity for collective action. Its function is the building up of a second-order autopoietic system which allows a new combination of operational closure and environmental openness.

IV. Legal capacity of the enterprise?

Of what concern is all this to the practicing lawyer? A great deal, for apart from consequences in legal theory, this view of the 'essence' of the corporate personality also has implications for legal doctrine. If its 'essence' lies not in resources nor in people but in the legal reconstruction of a collectivized action system, this has immediately foreseeable consequences for such exotic legal phenomena as the one-man company, and the 'personless corporation'. The 'personless corporation' not only becomes conceivable, but is always presupposed.[67] But consequences then also have to be drawn for the legal conceptualization of corporate membership and of corporate bodies (*Organe*), since in the glaring light of systems theory corporate members and corporate bodies evaporate into mere bundles of roles.[68] When the issue of the disregard of the corporate entity is raised, the legal person is to be 'taken seriously' in a different sense than that recently proposed.[69] And the relationship between 'unity and multiplicity in the group enterprise' should be rethought in relation to the legal capacity for action of the group enterprise as a whole.[70] Obviously the new 'group theory' of German partnership law (*personengesellschaft*) developed by Flume would require critical examination specifically as to whether the distinctions still affirmed in the concept of 'group' between an association of persons and the person of the association can in fact be maintained.[71] Here, however, we shall consider only one legal problem in more detail, specifically because it lies at the crossing point of questions of legal theory, legal doctrine and legal policy: the 'legal nature' of the business enterprise, in particular the relationship between the enterprise and the legal person.[72]

On this issue Thomas Raiser's bold sortie has assured prolonged controversy, fuelled still further by its legal policy implications in the codermination debate. Raiser argued that *de lege lata* the enterprise as such (as opposed to the association of shareholders) was increasingly developing into the real point of attribution for legal rules, that it was 'pressing' for legal capacity, and that *de lege ferenda* the enterprise as such should be assigned legal capacity.[73]

This thesis has been challenged on many grounds, the most interesting of which for our purposes here are the legal theory arguments which purport to refute the 'suitable ideology'[74] from a seemingly higher standpoint. Rittner teaches that 'for logical reasons alone it is out of the question to declare that the enterprise itself is the "subject" (*Traeger*) of the enterprise'.[75] Flume caps this with: 'Muenchhausen jurisprudence!'[76] That is intended to discourage pursuit of the idea. Yet one's ears prick up when both scholars thereupon themselves start operating in the immediate vicinity of Muenchhausen. In the case of the stock corporation (*Aktiengesellschaft*), Flume 'identifies' (!) the enterprise with the legal person 'because it belongs (!) to it'.[77] Can something belong to itself? Rittner, too, builds a self-referential construction whose compatibility with the presupposed logic would require some checking, when he maintains that the 'enterprise in the broader sense' is the representative of the 'enterprise in the narrower sense'. Furthermore, in the area of overlap between the 'narrower' and 'broader' enterprise he does just what he previously said was out of the question, namely, he declares 'the enterprise to be the representative of the enterprise'.

It is striking how many arguments for and against Muenchhausen accumulate around the topic of the legal person. There is the time-honoured argument that the fiction theory is false because the State itself, as a legal person, would then have to be a fiction, whereas the State could not, like Muenchhausen, have erected itself by mere motion into a legal fiction.[78] Then, by contrast with Flume, who angrily rejects this argument as speculation, Hofstadter of Goedel-Escher-Bach would joyfully welcome it: 'Reflexivity of law!'[79] We also find that Kelsen's concept of legal person as legal suborder and point of attribution has been objected to on the grounds that the statement that the legal suborder is itself a bearer of norms is a tautology: the construction would have to support itself 'like the late Baron Muenchhausen'.[80] And in this same context we are confronted with the attempt of German corporation law to circumvent Muenchhausen by making the enterprise have a 'subject' (*Traeger*) different from itself, namely, the legal person, which in turn is supposed to have a substratum different from itself, namely, the association of persons or the resource pool.[81] Obviously this is an attempt to avoid such tautologies and circular arguments as that the firm 'represents' itself or that the legal person is 'based' on itself.

But perhaps the mendacious Baron was not so wrong after all? Perhaps there really are, in the area of the legal person, circular relationships. May not the legal person's function indeed consist in making self-reference possible and in increasing self-reference still further in the interest of organizational autonomy? This, at any rate, is what the theory of self-referential systems, which has been successfully applied in such varied fields as logic, computer science, neurophysiology, sociology, business organization and legal theory[82] would suggest.

This prompts the following two theses: (1) the traditional demarcations between the enterprise, the legal person, and its substratum are to be interpreted as attempts to avoid self-referentiality in corporation law. Under this smokescreen, however, self-referentiality was actually able to make its way into the reality of the enterprise: (2) If the taboo of self-referential circularity is broken, the view opens up on to a self-supporting construction: the 'subject' (*Träger*) of the enterprise is the collectivity, constituted as legal person; the 'substratum' of the legal person is the enterprise personified as collectivity.[83]

This formulation of a strictly circular relationship between the enterprise and the legal person seems tautological, incompatible with existing law and unconstitutional as expropriation.[84] But before condemning it out of hand, one ought to examine the formulation very closely, bearing in mind that in a systems-theory formulation both concepts—enterprise and legal person—are related to a third, that of the collectivity. They thus go through a change in meaning, able to transform the tautology into impure self-reference, the illegality into a defensible alternative interpretation and the expropriation into a legitimate state interference (*Sozialbindung*).

Let us clarify this against the two most advanced positions (Raiser and Flume). Raiser's definition of both terms—enterprise and legal person—is still too person-related and insufficiently systemic. While he does manage, as he himself rightly comments,[85] to reach a higher stage of academic reflection using the organization sociology approach (mainly Parsons and Mayntz) to expose the enterprise as an organized system of actions, he nevertheless frequently falls back on the current stage of formulations in the course of analysis. Thus, for instance, he argues that 'as the aggregate of its members', the enterprise is also a 'stock of material and personal resources'.[86] He thereby plays away the advantages of the systems-theory conception of the firm, according to which members and material resources constitute environment. When he goes on to see the workers as members of the organization in the legal sense, then he is, admittedly, forced to postulate the legal personification of the enterprise only *de lege ferenda*.

On the other hand, Raiser also conceives of the legal person too personalistically. He stresses its associational character and thereby 'internalizes' the shareholders into the legal person. The association of shareholder thereby implicitly becomes the legal person, while the other sub-associations, that of the workers and that of the managers, as well as the enterprise as the overall association that incorporates these sub-associations, are (still) denied the privilege of legal personification. This corresponds to current conceptions whereby the company of shareholders as a legal person is the subject of the enterprise;[87] but it nevertheless leads to group-specific asymmetries which do not at all originate in the legal person—even, indeed, in Savigny's classical conception. If the legal person is bound up to that extent with the group of shareholders, and no clear division of spheres is made between legal person and members,[88] then here too all one can do is call for changes *de lege ferenda*.

With two bold conceptual steps, Flume has overtaken Raiser and managed in the outcome to identify the enterprise, already *de lege lata*, with the legal person, at any rate for the case of the stock corporation. In all rigour, he brings about the separation, already begun in Savigny, between the sphere of the legal person and the sphere of the members.[89] He thereby disqualifies the identification of the shareholders' association with the legal person as the famous major error that 'identifies the totality of current members with the corporation itself'.[90] The sphere of the 'ideal whole', as if it were hovering free, can then be linked with the enterprise whereby 'both the enterprise with everything belonging to it, those working in it, the assets and liabilities and the members of the legal person'[91] are brought together as integral components of the 'ideal whole' of the legal person. Flume thereby goes a considerable step beyond Raiser. The latter, in strict obedience to *lex lata*, declares the firm to have legal capacity only in so far as rules of law in force positivize the enterprise explicitly as a point of attribution and sees the enterprise's full legal capacity as a task *de lege ferenda*. Flume, by contrast, takes a cavalier attitude towards the law and already identifies the enterprise with the legal person under the prevailing state of the law.

Yet for all the boldness of the construction, even Flume has still not gone far enough. He limits the identification explicitly to the stock corporation, remaining remarkably ambivalent as regards the limited liability company (*Gesellschaft mit beschränkter Haftung*).[92] He understands it substantively as a kind of partnership (*Personengesellschaft*) which is, however, autonomized as a legal person by virtue of its limited liability limitation alone. But he sees at the same time that this is untenable for the 'big' limited company. He takes refuge in the legal policy recommendation of making the legal form of the stock corporation compulsory in these cases.[93] There is a similar ambivalence about Flume's sharp distinction between corporations (*Kapitalgesellschaften*), where legal person and enterprise are supposed to be identical, and partnerships (*Personengesellschaften*), where the old notion that the partners are the 'subjects' of the firm is supposed to remain. Whether, without internal splits, it is possible on the one hand to transform the partnership into a quasi-collectivity, with the 'group' as the 'action center', and on the other to make a fundamental distinction between 'group' and legal person in their relationship to the enterprise, seems at least questionable.

The second objection is that Flume, although he consistently separates the sphere of the 'ideal whole' from that of the members, ultimately is not consistent enough to define the human individuals as the environment of the spheres of enterprise and legal person, but instead includes both the members (i.e. shareholders) and those working in the firm (i.e. management and employees) in the concept of the enterprise and that of the legal person.[94] This means that he inevitably gets bogged down again in a misconceived debate that links the relationship between legal person and enterprise with the membership question, i.e. the question whether only shareholders are members of the enterprise, or also managers and workers, or even major customers, consumers, etc.

That this debate is misconceived can be demonstrated on the basis of the third objection to Flume's theory. Flume falls for the current conceptual model which allows as the reference point for the legal person only the alternative between the shareholders' association or the enterprise. What has legal capacity, according to this model, is either the association comprising only the shareholders, or else the whole enterprise, including shareholders, management and others involved. *Tertium non datur?* Here the circuit to the systems-theory concepts developed above is closed, and at the same time it becomes clear that for all the 'technical' legal understanding, the question of the substratum cannot be foisted off on to sociology. Neither the shareholders' association nor the enterprise as a whole are identifiable with the legal person, but only the above defined corporate actor or the collectivity.

The point that, due to the clear separation of spheres, the association of shareholders and the legal person are not identical has been made adequately clear by Flume. Their spheres of action overlap only as regards the actions of corporate bodies. But to make the *whole* enterprise into the legal person instead, as Flume does, is to go far too far. For what acts as the 'centre of action' is not the whole action system of the enterprise, but only the subcomplex which above we called 'collectivity'. Legal capacity is given only to the extent that collective action is involved. All that is affected is the subset of action in the whole enterprise which is to be attributed to the system as a whole in the collective bond. The legal person covers not the whole action system of the enterprise, but only the subset of action called collectivity, i.e. only those actions covered by the attribution mechanisms of corporation law, agency law, and labour law. It may sound unusual to name these phenomena in one breath, but they have one function in common: they transform individual action (of 'members' or 'workers') *in* the system into collective action *by* the system.

This makes clear why the problem of the legal person *vis-à-vis* the enterprise is not to be bound up with the membership question, as keeps on happening. Put rather crudely, not the scope of the membership but the scope of the corporate organs (*Organe*) decides what actions belong to the legal person. Or, as Rittner puts it, the corporate organs (*Organe*) are 'parts of the legal person itself, through which alone the latter can come to life'.[95] It is important, however, not to forget the other two attribution mechanisms (agency law and labour law). The transformation processes that are decisive for the action area of the legal person accordingly take place not in the area of membership (expropriation!), but within the attribution mechanisms for collective action.

Both factual and legal transformations play a part here, as do private law-making and governmental regulation. The action area of the legal person expands through the private installation of new corporate bodies in the firm, particularly newly established consultative councils, committees, etc., through which environments of the firm are co-opted.[96] It likewise changes through the creation or alteration of corporate bodies by governmental regulation (corporate governance and codetermination). But factual transformation processes within the firm, notably decentralization, divisionalization, and functional democratization also change the action area of the legal person. The attribution mechanisms are changed: hierarchical attribution to the top of the organization gives place to an attribution to the action of autonomous decision-making centres within the firm based on its executive bodies (divisions, profit centres, autonomous working groups, and quality circles).

A further interim result might, thus, be added to the differentiation between enterprise and collectivity: it is an error to identify the legal person with the association of shareholders. Even *de lege lata*—Raiser would have to be reformulated—the enterprise personified as collectivity has legal capacity, and for all enterprises with legal capacity—Flume would have to be reformulated—the legal person is identical with the collectivity, as the personification of the enterprise.

V. Enterprise corporation as a legal policy

A new 'suitable ideology'? It has already been claimed about theories of the enterprise as a 'social association' (*Sozialverbandstorien*) that they were created in order to provide ideological support for codetermination.[97] The '*Unternehmen an sich*', enterprise in and of itself, too, is supposed to have been only an ideology aimed at helping managerial capitalism over the hurdles against financial capitalism.[98] This obviously prompts the search for political interests being pursued in a theory of the firm as a self-referential system. The systemic approach formally takes its distance from the models of financial, managerial, labour, and state capitalism. At most it could be said that it is pursuing the interests of an organizational capitalism. Or rather more seriously, a theory of the firm as a self-reproducing social system may suggest a legal policy of 'enterprise corporatism'.

This cautious formulation should ward off too much 'dietrologia' in advance. It would be rather unreasonable to maintain that neo-corporatism is the political consequence of the theory of self-referential systems.[99] For there are many versions of systems theory—'emancipatory', 'technocratic', and 'evolutionary'. And the systems theory analyses of enterprise, collectivity, and legal person attempted above still claim to be correct even if enterprise corporatism should prove to be a legal policy failure.

All the same, there is a link between systems theory analyses and legal policy recommendations, albeit a much looser one than the suspicion of a 'suitable ideology' supposes. On the one hand a theoretical apparatus always perceives reality only selectively (for instance, a systems theoretician sees only elements, structures, and processes, where other observers see flesh-and-blood people acting) and correspondingly makes legal policy recommendations directed only to this selected reality. Secondly, systems theory asserts quite specific evolutionary trends which only when formulated can be influenced through legal policy intervention. In economic enterprises a trend can be observed to the autonomization of an impersonal economic complex of action, consisting of the differentiation of the corporate actor with a sharp demarcation between those involved internally and externally. This trend is perceived as collectivization of an autopoietic social system. One may seek to combat this trend in legal policy through such concepts as shareholders' democracy, codetermination or government participation, or else one may see the autonomization of the organization as a promising development in the interest of society as a whole in guaranteeing need satisfaction for the future, following a direction that the law can to some extent help to influence.[100] The name for that direction is enterprise corporatism.

Neo-corporatist strategies are not in vogue at present. On the contrary, in a period of extremely rapid market changes, increased pressure of competition and weakening or collapse of governmental regulatory systems, industrial strategies are being pursued for which neo-corporatist arrangements appear rigid, centralist and immobile.[101] The new slogan is decentralization and flexibility through contractual arrangements, and this applies also to methods of finance, technologies, product range, customer relations, and labour relations.[103] The aim of recent industrial policy is flexibility as a value in itself: 'a general capacity of enterprises to reorganize in close response to fluctuations in their environment'.[103]

While flexibility through contract is the prevailing demand at the moment, there is also an alternative put forward in the heated debate on 'Americanization' or 'Japanization' of the European economy: flexibility through organization.[104] Its defenders can point out that flexibility can be brought about not only through contractual arrangements but also through decentralization of organization, and that a policy based on organization can additionally use the productivity advantages of a 'producers' coalition' (capital, management, labour, state), which in the conditions of the new industrial divide are becoming increasingly necessary.

This industrial policy position is close to the ideas developed here. In fact, to privilege one group, whether shareholders or management, that acquires flexibility through contractual arrangements would be bound to be sub-optimal in the interest of the corporate actor. Certainly, the advantage of contractual arrangements lies in the speed of reactions with which action systems can be built up and demolished in the short term, in accordance with the fluctuations of environmental pressures. The drawback, however, is that contractual solutions cannot exhaust the 'organizational surplus value'.[105] 'Organizational surplus value' arises (1) through the building up of long-term cooperative arrangements which would be continually destroyed by contractual flexibility; (2) through the diffuseness of 'commitments' in the organization which by comparison with rigid, sharply defined contractual obligations produce more situational flexibility; and finally (3) in the orientation towards the organization's interest, which provides stronger orientation than mere linkage to a contractual purpose.

This suggests a law of corporate governance based on a microcorporatist producers' coalition. According to this, none of the resource providers, neither the factor of capital, nor that of labour, or that of management, nor indeed the factor of state control, has any natural claim to 'sovereignty over the association'. In principle, the connection between resource provision and control rights is loosened, and all control rights over all resources are assigned to the corporate actor as such. The idea of 'organizationally bound property rights'[106] is diametrically opposed to the idea that the firm constitutes a mere 'contractual network'. The distribution of control rights within the firm is then made neither according to the primacy of one resource interest nor according to exchange logic in a contractual network, but according to efficiency considerations oriented towards the interest of the 'corporate actors', which is different from all of the participating interests.

Even if the external integration effects and internal motivation effects of microcorporatist arrangements are recognized, still the external disadvantages of producers' coalitions have to be pointed out, especially the fact that they may arrive at their agreements at the expense of third parties and even of the public interest.[107] Here is the real weak point of enterprise corporatism in the sense of a producers' coalition. However, the 'corporate actor', the existence of which is asserted against all methodological individualism, steps in to set the legal policy direction. Efforts should concentrate on the institutional strengthening of the corporate actor and the autonomization of an impersonal complex of action which imposes effective constraints on action upon the individual interests involved in the interest of the organization defined in terms of society as a whole.

Notes

1. Piore and Sabel, *The New Industrial Divide* (1984); Kern and Schumann, *Das Ende der Arbeitsteilung? Rationalisierung in der Industriellen Produktion* (1984); Streeck, 'The Management of Uncertainty and the Uncertainty of Management' (manuscript 1985).
2. Whilhelm calls for the legal person to be taken serious: *Rechtsform and Haftung bei der juristischen Person* (1981).

3. Joerges, 'Juristische Person', in Goerlitz, *Handlexikon zur Rechtswissenschaft*, 222 ff. (1972); Ott, *Recht und Realität der Unternehmenskorporation* 43 ff., 85 ff. (1977); Dan-Cohen, *Rights, Persons and Organizations* 26 ff., 163 ff. (1986). From a political science viewpoint, Mayntz, 'Corporate Actors in Public Policy: Changing Perspectives in Political Analysis' (manuscript 1986). From an economic viewpoint, see Hutter, *Die Produktion von Recht*, ch. 4D (1986). From a sociological view, see Simmanch, 'Der mangelnde Akteursbezug systemtheoretischer Eklärungen gesellschaftlicher Differenzierung', 6 *Zeitschrift für Soziologie* 421, 430 (1986); Japp, 'Kollektive Akteure als soziale Systeme', in Unverferth, *System und Selbstproduktion* 166 (1986).

4. Ott, *supra* n. 3 at 283 ff.; for the discussion in the US, see Horwitz, *supra* n. 3.

5. Buxbaum, 'Corporate Legitimacy, Economic Theory, and Legal Doctrine,' 45 *Ohio State J* 515 ff., 520 (1984); Teubner, 'Corporate Responsibility als Problem der Unternehmensverfassung', 1983 ZGR 34 ff.

6. Strauss, 'Industrial Relations: Times of Change', 23 *Industrial Relations* 1 ff. (1984).

7. Streeck, *supra* n. 1 at 21 ff.

8. On the individualism/collectivism debate, decisively influenced by Popper and Hayek, cf. Phillips, *Holistic Thought in Social Science* (1976); Vanberg, *Die zwei Soziologien: Individualismus und Kollektivismus in der Sozialtheorie* (1975); Bohnen, *Individualismus und Gesellschaftstheorie* (1975). Elster, *Making Sense of Marx* 34 ff. (1985); Teubner, 'Corporate Responsibility as a Problem of Company Constitution', EUI-Working Paper.

9. Alchian and Demsetz, 'Production, Information Costs and Economic Organization', 62 *Am. Econ. Rev.* 777 (1972); Jensen and Meckling, 'Theory of the Firm: Managerial Behavior, Agency Costs and Ownership Structures', 3 *Financial Econ.* 305 (1976); Fama, 'Agency Problems and the Theory of the Firm', 88 *J. Polit. Econ.* 288 (1980); Cheung, 'The Contractual Nature of the Firm', 26 *JL Econ.* 1 ff. (1983); for the transactional approach, see Williamson, *The Economic Institutions of Capitalism* (1985). For an interesting expansion of the network model, see Schanze, 'Potential and Limits of Economic Analysis', in Daintith and Teubner, *Contract and Organization* 204, 212 ff. (1986).

10. Coleman, *Power and Structure in Society* (1974); idem, *The Asymmetric Society* (1982); idem, 'Responsibility in Corporate Action: A Sociologist's View', in Hopt and Teubner, *Corporate Governance and Directors' Liabilities* 69 ff. (1985); Swanson, 'An Organizational Analysis of Collectivities', in Genevie, *Collective Behavior* 270 ff. (1978); Vanberg, *Markt und Organisation* 8 ff., 37 ff. (1982); idem, 'Das Unternehmen als Sozialverband', 1 *Jahrbuch für Neue Politische Oekonomie* 276 ff. (1982); also Krause, 'Corporate Social Responsibility: Interests and Goals', in Hopt and Teubner, *Corporate Governance* 99 ff., 102 f. (1985).

11. This must be explicitly stressed because systems theory has the reputation

of taking the stance of holism/collectivism. However, collectivism and individualism are 'over-hasty options' for system theory; cf. Luhmann, 'Wie ist soziale Ordnung möglich?', ibid., 2 *Gesellschaftsstruktur und Semantik* 245 ff. (1981).

12. This is a critique of the old Philadelphian Social epistemology; cf. Douglas, *How Institutions Think* 10 (1986). On the connection between self-reference and personification of the organization, see Teubner, '*Hypercycle in Law and Organization*' in *European Yearbook in the Sociology of Law* (1988).

13. For the older debate on the legal person, see in detail Wolff, I *Organshaft und juristische Person* 1–87 (1933); Hallis, *Corporate Personality* (1930). Kantorowicz, *The King's Two Bodies* (1957); Stein, 'Nineteenth Century English Company Law and Theories of Legal Personality', 12 *Quaderni Fiorentini* 502 (1983).

14. For the recent debate in the USA, see Dan-Cohen, *supra* n. 3. A survey of the recent German debate is in, for instance, Reuter, *MK* paras. 21, 1 ff.; Staudinger-Coing, Einleitung zu, paras. 21–89, 1 ff. Schmidt, *Verbandszweck und Rechtsfähigkeit im Vereinsrecht* 4 (1984); idem, *Gesellschaftsrecht* 142 ff. (1986).

15. Gierke, *Das Wesen der menschlichen Verbaende* 12 (1902). On the problems of the organism analogy, see Rottleuthner, 'Biological Metaphors in Legal Thought', in Teubner, *Autopoietic Law* (1988) and more generally, Dachler, 'Some Explanatory Boundaries of Organismic Analogies for the Understanding of Social Systems', in Probst and Ulrich, *Self-Organization and Management of Social Systems* 132 ff. (1984).

16. Rittner, *Die werdende juristische Person* 211, 214 *et passim* (1973). For a skeptical review, see Ulmer, 'Zu einer neuen Theorie der juristischen Person', 1976 *ZHR* 61 ff.; Reich, *Markt und Recht* 297 ff. (1977).

17. Wieacker, 'Zur Theorie der juristischen Person des Privatrechts', in *Festschrift für Huber* 339 ff., 367 (1973).

18. Ott, *supra* n. 3 at 85 ff.

19. Flume, *Die Juristische Person* 25 ff. (1983).

20. Jellinek, *Allgemeine Staatslehre* 170 (1920).

21. Gierke, III *Deutsches Genossenschaftsrecht* (1881); IV (1913) (English translation by Maitland, 1913, and Heiman, 1977) idem, *supra* n. 15; idem, I *Deutsches Privatrecht* 466 ff. (1895).

22. Gierke, *supra* n. 15 at 13.

23. For an extreme formulation, see, e.g., Radin, 'The Endless Problem of Corporate Personality', 32 *Colum. L. Rev.* 643 (1932).

24. Weber, *Economy and Society* 48 ff. (1978).

25. Parsons, *The System of Modern Societies* 4 ff. (1971); Parsons and Shils, *Toward a General Theory of Social Action* 190 (1981).

26. Barnard, *The Functions of the Executive* 73 ff. (1938).

27. Simon, *Administrative Behavior* XVII f. (3rd edn. 1976).

28. Williamson, *supra* n. 9 *passim*.

29. Coleman, *supra* n. 10.
30. Gierke, *Die Genossenschaftstheorie und die deutsche Rechtsprechung*, 11 ff. 91887). See also idem, I *Deutsches Privatrecht*, *supra* n. 21 at 472: '. . . a living being that wills and acts as such'. Today it is notably Selznick, *Law Society and Industrial Justice* 43 ff. (1969), who stresses the living, dynamic character of the 'corporate entity'.
31. Luhmann, *Soziale System* (1984), is basic. On the autopoietic nature of social systems, see the lively discussion in the collective volumes: Benseler, Hejl, and Koeck, *Autopoiesis, Communication and Society* (1980); Dumouchel and Dupuy, *L'auto-organisation. De la physique au politique* (1983); Ulrich and Probst, *Self-Organization and Management of Social Systems* (1984); Baecker, *et al.*, *Theorie als Passion* (1987); Haferkampt and Schmid. *supra* n. 12; Teubner, *supra* n. 15. For an assessment of the theory of self referential systems in its implications for law by a 'fascinated sceptic', see Wiethölter, 'Sanierungskonkurs der Juristenausbildung?' 1 *Kritische Vierteljahresschrift für Gesetzgebung und Rechtswissenschaft* 21 ff. (1986).
32. In this sense, Hutter, *supra* n. 3 at 112, defines persons as 'social systems to which communications are ascribed'. See also Ladeur, *Alternativkommentar Grundgesetz*, art. 19 III, 28 ('organized collectivities').
33. The founders are Brinz, I *Lehrbuch der Pandekten* ss. 60 f., III, ss. 432 ff. (3rd edn. 1884); Bekker, *System des heutigen Pandektenrechts* 1886, ss. 42 ff. (1886).
34. Wiedemann, 'Juristische Person and Gesemthand als Sondervermögen', 1975 *Wertpapiermitteilungen* Sonderbeilage Nr. 4; ibid., *Gesellschaftsrecht* I 195 ff. (1980); Coleman, *supra* n. 10; Vanberg, *supra* n. 10.
35. Rittner, *supra* n. 3 at 210 ff.; idem, 'Juristische Person', in *Staatslexikon* 267 ff. (1987); Ott, *supra* n. 18 at 85 ff.; Flume, *supra* n. 19; Schmidt *supra* n. 14.
36. For organization in a specifically legal sense, see John, *Die organisierte Rechtsperson passim* (1977). The more recent 'technical legal' definitions of the legal person also like to use the metaphor of 'organization'; see, e.g., 25 BGHZ 134, 144; Enneccerus and Nipperdey, *Lehrbuch des Bügerlichen Rechts* 1959, paras. 103; Soergel and Schulze-von Lassaulx, *BGB*, vor s. 21, 3; Reuter, *MK* vor s. 21, 3; Staudinger-Coing, Einleitung zu ss. 21–89, 5 ff.
37. For organization in a sociological sense, see Rotter, *Zur Funktion der juristischen Person in der Bundesrepublik und in der DDR* 30 ff. (1967); Raiser, *Das Unternehmen als Organisation* 93 ff., 166 ff. (1969); Ott, *supra* n. 3 at 85 ff.; Dan-Cohen, *supra* n. 3 at 26 ff.
38. Parsons, *Structure and Process in Modern Society* 17, 63 (1960); Mayntz, *Soziologie der Organisation* 40 (9th edn. 1977). Etzioni, *Complex Organizations* 1 (1961). Blau and Scott, *Formal Organizations* 5 (1962).
39. Weber, *supra* n. 24 at 48 ff., 720 ff. and the literature on 'private government'.
40. Williamson, *supra* n. 9 at 298 ff.
41. Luhmann, 'Einfache Sozialsysteme', in idem, 2 *Soziologische Aufklärung* 21 ff., 32 ff. (1975); idem, *supra* n. 31 at 270 ff. For Giddens, *The Constitution of Society*

200 (1986), it is reflexive monitoring of action 'which masks the decisive difference'.

42. On this, see Teubner, *supra* n. 12, which also gives more details on the connection between interaction, group and organization, seen as a cumulative rise in self-referentiality to the point of hypercyclical linkage. The view of the corporate actor as a semantic artifact of social communication is supported by the linguistic analysis; Schane, 'The Corporation is a Person: The Language of a Legal Fiction', 61 *Tulane LR* 563 ff., 609 (1987): 'The Law has been able to exploit to its advantage and to maximize for its needs conceptualizations that are deeply embedded within the structure of language.'

43. Weber, *supra* n. 24 at 13 ff.

44. Wieacker, *supra* n. 17 at 367. Dworkin, *Law's Empire* 168 ff. (1986) develops a concept of 'working personification': 'The personification is deep: it consists in taking the corporation seriously as a moral agent. But it is still a personification, not a discovery, because we recognize that the community has no independent metaphysical existence, that it is itself a creature of the practices of thought and language in which it figures' (at 171).

45. Luhmann, *supra* n. 31 at 273 f. The fact that this is supposed to be a merely psychological reality is seen by Wieacker, *supra* n. 17 at 369, as a problem, since the legal order has only an external (i.e., social) approach to the object. It is, then, all the more important to be able to analyze the social reality of the collective and the collective bond by comparison with the merely psychic one. On the emergent quality of collective *vis-à-vis* individual constructions of reality, see Dachler, *supra* n. 15 at 132 ff., 140.

46. Parsons, *The Social System* 41, 96 (1951); idem, *Societies* 187 (1966); idem, *supra* n. 25 at 6 ff., 23 ff. (1971); Parsons and Shils, *supra* n. 25 at 61, 192; Parsons and Smelser, *Economy and Society* 15 ff. (1956).

47. Luhmann, *supra* n. 31 at 155, 225 ff. The issue of 'personifying' human individuals and institutions is also stressed by Vining, *Legal Identity* (1978) 156 f.

48. Selznick, *supra* n. 30 at 48. On the parallel question of the 'Gesamthand', cf. Teubner, in *Alternativkommentar BGB* ss. 705 ff., 21 ff. Herein lies the relative justification for the present 'technical legal' understanding of the legal person, in e.g. Staudinger-Coing, Einleitung zu ss. 21 ff., 4 ff., in *Münchner Kommentar* vor s. 21, 2; John, *supra* n. 36 at 66 ff. Its problem is, however, to derive from the variability between legal concept and social phenomenon to the irrelevance of the social phenomenon for the legal concept. The legal system, as the debate on the legal concept of the firm decisively shows (see IV below), needs not only a legal concept of the legal person but also a legal concept of the substrate.

49. From this point of view one may sympathize with Hart, 'Definition and Theory in Jurisprudence', 70 *LQ Rev.* 37 (1954), when he calls for abandonment of the 'ever baffling question' of 'what is any association or organized group?' and its placement by the question 'Under what conditions do we

refer to numbers and sequences of men as aggregates of individuals and under what conditions do we adopt instead unifying phrases extended by analogy from individuals?'

50. Kelsen, *Allgemeine Staatslehre* 66 ff. (1925) (English translation, *General Theory of Law and State* 96 ff. (1954)); similarly Wolff, *supra* n. 13 at 170 ff.

51. Wieacker, *supra* n. 17 at 359.

52. Kohler, *Lehrbuch des buergerlichen Rechts* I 230 (1906); Wolff, *supra* n. 13 at 62; Stone, *Should Trees Have Standing? ;Toward Legal Rights for Natural Objects* (1974).

53. In the prevailing legal understanding, too, a 'regular linkage' between legal person and particular types of association is admitted, without, however, this putting the technical legal conception in question; e.g. Westermann, *Vertragsfreiheit und Typengesetzlichkeit im Recht der Personengesellschaften* 7 ff. (1970); Staudinger-Coing, Einleitung zu ss. 21 ff., 6. By contrast, e.g. Wieacker, *supra* n. 17 at 359 ff. and Ott, *supra* n. 3 at 50 ff., 69 ff. take this 'regular linkage' as a basis for more precise treatment of the connection between social structure and legal structure.

54. Flume, *supra* n. 19 at 25. Similarly, also Wolff, 'On the Nature of Legal Persons', 54 *LQ Rev.* 494 ff., 506 (1938), 'lawyers as a rule have no concern with the structural differences underlying the various kinds of legal persons, as that is a question of sociology'. Cf. also Staudinger-Coing, Einleitung zu ss. 21–89, 17.

55. The difficulties that authors that argue in *'Personal law'* terms have with institution and foundation make the advantages of thinking in systemic categories (system of action, collectivity) clear. Gierke's difficulties with institution and foundation are notorious: cf. Gierke, *supra* n. 30 at 9 ff.; see also Nobel, *Anstalt und Unternehmen* 174 ff. (1975). But Rittner and Flume have their problems too: Rittner, *supra* n. 16 at 232 ff., with the personal element so highly rated by him, without which the 'spirit freezes'; Flume, *supra* n. 19 at 29 ff., with the limits of the legal person, since because of his over-concrete understanding of 'social phenomena' he is forced to define individuals and special assets of the legal person as 'belonging' to it. On the relationship between the firm and institution, see the penetrating analyses in Nobel, *supra*.

56. This observation and the following ones are oversimplified to the extent that they take it that the legal system is 'building upon' particular social structures. For the moment, they leave socio-legal interactions out of account. In reality, of course, social capacity for action is regularly partly constituted through legal norms, indeed sometimes 'artificially' created by the law alone.

57. Luhmann, *supra* n. 41 at 33; idem, *supra* n. 31 at 271; cf. Parsons and Smelser, *supra* n. 46 at 15; Popitz, *Prozesse der Machtbildung* (1968); Moore, 'Legal Liability and Evolutionary Interpretation: Some Aspects of Strict Liability, Self-help and Collective Responsibility', in Gluckman, *The Allocation of Responsibility* 51 ff. (1972); Coleman, 'Loss of Power', 38 *Am. Sociol. Rev.* 1 ff.

(1973); idem, *supra* n. 10; Vaanberg, *supra* n. 10; French, *Collective and Corporate Responsibility* 48 ff. (1984).

58. This seems to be the prevailing trend, and not only in Germany: see the collective volume by Bastid, David and Luchaire, *La personnalitee morale et ses limites* (1960), with country by country reports; Fletcher, *Cyclopedia Corporations*, I, 92 ff. 1974; for the USA, see Blumberg, *The Law of Corporate Groups* Vol. 3, Substantive Law (1987); Fabritius, 'Parent and Subsidiary Corporations under U.S. Law—A Functional Analysis of Disregard-Criteria', EUI Working Paper (1986). A critique of this trend can be found in Flume, *supra* n. 19 at 24 f.

59. Williamson, *supra* n. 9; Coleman, *supra* n. 10; Vaberg, *supra* n. 10.

60. Raiser, *supra* n. 37 at 166 ff.

61. Luhmann, *supra* n. 31 at 270 ff.

62. Blackstone, *Commentaries on the Law of England* 467 ff. (1771).

63. On this, using the construction of the hypercycle, see Teubner, *supra* n. 12. On second-order autopoiesis, cf. Maturana and Varela, *Autopoiesis and Cognition* 107 ff. (1980) Mossakowski and Nettmann, 'Is There a Linear Hierarchy of Biological Systems?', in Roth and Schwegler, *Self-Organizing Systems* 39 ff. (1981); Jessop, 'Relative Autonomy and Autopoiesis in Economy, Law and State', in Teubner, *State, Law, Economy as Autopoietic Systems* (1988).

64. On the symmetry of closure and openness in autopoietic systems, see in particular, Varela, 'Autonomy and Autopoiesis', in Roth and Schwegler, *supra* n. 63 at 14 ff.; ibid., 'L'auto-organisation: de l'apparence au mechanisme', in Dumouchel and Dupuy, *L'auto-organisation* 147 ff. (1983); Luhmann, *supra* n. 31 *passim*; Gomez and Probst, 'Organisationelle Geschlossenheit im Management sozialer Institutionen', 5 *Delfin* 22 ff. 1985; Teubner, 'Social Order from Legislative Noise', in Teubner, *supra* n. 63; Dupuy, 'On the Supposed Closure of Normative Systems', in Teubner, *supra* n. 15. Zolo, 'The Epistemological Status of the Theory of Autopoiesis and its Application to the Social Sciences', in Teubner, *supra* n. 63.

65. Cf. Kübler, 'Verrechtlichung von Unternehmensstrukturen', in idem, *Verrechhtlichung von Wirtschaft, Arbeit und sozialer Solidarität* 214 ff. (1984); Teubner, *supra* n. 5; idem, 'Unternehmensinteresse—das gesellschaftliche Interesse des Unternehmens an sich?', 149 ZHR 470 (1985).

66. Mayntz, 'Steuerung, Steuerungsakteure und Steuerungsinstrumente', 70 *HIMON*, Universitaet Siegen (1986).

67. Kreutz, 'Von der Einmann-zur Keinmann-GmbH?', *Festschrift für Walter Stimpel* 379 ff. (1985); for a comparative view, see Ziebe, *Der Erwerb eigener Aktien und eigener GmbH-Geschäftsanteile in den Staaten der europäischen Gemeinschaft* (1981). On the debate in the US, cf. Dan-Cohen, *supra* n. 3 at 41 ff.

68. For a recent systematic approach to membership, see Lutter, 'Theorie der

Mitgliedschaft', 1980 *AcP* 84 (1980); on the concept of 'corporate body' (*Organ*), the absence of a theory is generally bewailed; see e.g. Coing, 65 ff. (1979); Wiedemann, *supra* n. 34 at 212 ff. (1980). For the present situation, see e.g. Ulmer, 'Zur Haftung der abordnenden Köperschaft nach ss. 31 BGB für Sorgfaltsvertösse des von ihr benannten Aufsichtsratsmitglieds', in *Festschrift für Stimpel* 705 ff. (1985).

69. Wilhelm, *supra* 2; for interesting suggestions, see Schanze, *Einmanngesellschaft und Durchgriffshaftung* 102 ff. (1975); Schmidt, *supra* n. 14 at 170 ff., 177 ff. (1986).

70. Ambitious formulations can be found in Baelz, 'Einheit und Vielheit im Konzern', in *Festschrift für L. Raiser* 287 ff. (1974); 'Groups of Companies—the German Approach: "Unternehmen" versus "Konzern"', EUI Working Paper (1985).

71. Flume, *Die Personengesellschaft* 1 ff. (1977); Ulmer, 'Die Lehre von der fehlerhaften Gesellschaft', in *Festschrift für Flume* 301 ff. (1978); for a (constructive) criticism, see Teubner, *Alternativkommentar BGB*, vor ss. 705 ff., 16 ff.; a tempting systematization in Baelz, 'Treuhandkommanditist, Treuhänder der Kommanditisten und Anlegerschutz', 1980 ZGR 1 ff., 37 ff.

72. The economic aspects of a legal concept of the firm are stressed by Koehler, 'Rechtsform und Unternehmensverfassung', 115 ZgStw 721 ff. (1959); Ballerstedt, 'GmbH-Reform, Mitbestimmung und Unternehmensrecht', 135 ZHR 184 (1971); Rittner, *supra* n. 16 at 282 ff.; Wiedemann, *supra* n. 34 at 307 ff. (1980); Flume, *supra* n. 19, at 48 ff.

   The aspect of a social association is stressed by Fechner, *Die Treubindungen des Aktionärs* 64 ff. (1943); Duden, 'Zur Methode der Entwicklung des Gesellschaftsrechts zum Unternehmensrecht', in *Festschrift für Schilling* 309 (1973); Kunze, 'Unternehmen und Gesellschaft', 147 ZHR 16 ff. (1983); Steinmann and Gerum, *Reform der Unternehmensverfassung* (1978); Steimann, 'The Enterprise as a Political System', in Hopt and Teubner, *Corporate Governance* 401 ff. (1985).

   The organization-theory perspective is stressed by Raiser, *supra* n. 37 at 166 ff. Baelz, *supra* n. 70 at 293 ff. (1974); Ott, *supra* n. 3; Brinkmann, *Unternehmensinteresse und Unternehmensrechtsstruktur* (1983); Teubner, *supra* n. 5; parallel approaches in the US are in Seeznick, *Law, Society and Industrial Justice* (1969); Stone, *Where the Law Ends* (1975); Dan-Cohen, *supra* n. 3.

73. Raiser, *supra* n. 37 at 166 ff.; idem, 'Die Zukunft des Unternehmensrechts', in *Festschrift für Robert Fischer*, 561 ff., 572 ff. (1979); Rittner, *supra* n. 16 at 306 f.; Wiedemann, *supra*, n. 34 at 308 ff. (1980).

74. Wiedemann, 'Grundfragen der Unternehmensverfassung', 1975 ZGR 402.

75. Rittner, *supra* n. 16 at 283 ff., 288.

76. Flume, *supra* n. 19, at 48.

77. Id.

78. 1 Beseler, *System des gemeinen deutschen Privatrechts* 236 (1847). Saleilles, *De la*

personnalité juridique 354 (1922); Wolff, *supra* n. 13 at 63 ff.; Flume, *supra* n. 19 at 13.

79. Hofstadter, *Goedel, Escher, Bach: An Eternal Golden Braid*, esp. 692 ff. (1979). About the connections between self-reference and paradox in law, see Suber, *The Paradox of Self-Amendment, Law, Omnipotence and Change* (1982); Fletcher, 'Paradoxes in Legal Thought', 85 *Colum. L. Rev.* 1263 ff. (1985).

80. Wolff, *supra* n. 13 at 69, with other references.

81. Rittner, *supra* n. 16 at 232 ff., 283 ff.

82. For example, see *supra* n. 31 and 64. Scepticism about the whole trend comes from Lüderssen, 'Wär der Gedank' nicht so verwünscht gescheit, man wär' versucht, ihn herzlich dumm zu nennen', 5 *Rechtshistorisches J.* 344 (1986); see also Teubner's reply, 'Münchhausen-Jurisprudenz', loc. cit. at 350 and Hejl, 'Autopoiesis-muss es das sein?', loc. cit. at 357.

83. This can be read as the attempt to clarify the (confusing) definition of Ott, *supra* n. 3 at 52: 'legal person and corporate structure, legal person, and corporation, coincide', which has frequently been criticized, e.g. Staudinger-Coing, Einleitung zu, ss. 21 ff., 18; Reuter in *Münchner Kommentar*, vor s. 21, 5 ff. Of course the expression 'corporate' is misleading here, and 'coincide' should be replaced by the formulation are in self-referential relationship to the self-description as collectivity'—another example of the difficulty of choosing between precision and comprehensibility in the formulation!

84. This anticipated criticism is based on Flume, *supra* n. 19 at 47 ff.

85. Raiser, *supra* n. 73 at 565 (1979).

86. Raiser, *supra* n. 37 at 168; idem, n. 73 at 565 (1979); idem, 'Unternehmensziele und Unternehmensbegriff', 1980 *ZHR* 231.

87. Raiser, *supra* n. 36 at 138 ff.

88. This is Savigny's great achievement, which, however, is constantly negated by attempts to 'internalize' the membership structure in the legal person: Savigny, *System des heutigen roemischen Rechts* II, 283 ff., 332 (1840).

89. On the other hand, he modifies it again later; Flume, *supra* n. 19 at 28 ff., when he stresses the 'involvement' of the members.

90. Savigny, *supra* n. 88 at 347.

91. Flume, *supra* n. 19 at 48 ff.; idem, 'Körperschaftliche juristische Person und Personenverband', in *Festschrift für Gerhard Kegel* 154 (1987).

92. Cf. also the criticism by John, 'Personrecht und Verbandsrecht im Allgemeinen Teil des Bürgerlichen Rechts', 1985 *AcP* 209 ff., 220 ff.; Raiser, 1981 *AcP* 245 ff.

93. Flume, *Um ein neues Unternehmensrecht* (1980).

94. Flume, *supra* n. 19 at 49.

95. Rittner, *supra* n. 16 at 255.

96. See Teubner, 'Der Beirat zwischen Verbandssouveränität und Mitbestimmung', 1986 *ZGR* 565.

97. Wiedemann, *supra* n. 74 at 402; idem, *supra* n. 34 at 309 (1980); Flume, *supra* n. 19 at 45.

98. Flume, *supra* n. 19 at 37 ff.; Horwitz, *supra* n. 3 at 183.
99. Or—to exhaust the whole of the political spectrum—neo-Liberalism or neo-Conservatism, see e.g. Bercusson, 'Juridification and Disorder', in Teubner, *Juridification of Social Spheres* 55 ff. (1987); Nahamowitz, 'Difficulties with Economic Law', in Teubner, *supra* n. 63.
100. Teubner, *supra* n. 5.
101. A realistic assessment can be found in Simitis, 'Justification of Labor Relations', in Teubner, *Juridification of Social Spheres* 113 ff., 134 ff. (1987); see Dittrich, *Mitbestimmung—eine korporatistische Strategie?* (1975).
102. Cf. Piore and Sabel, *supra* n. 1; Strauss, *supra* n. 6; Willman, *The Implications of Process and Product Innovations for Labor Relations* (1985).
103. Streeck, *supra* n. 1, at 11.
104. Gutchess, *Employment Security in Action: Strategies that Work* (1985); Streeck, *supra* n. 1 at 18 ff., 27 ff.
105. A stimulating comparison between contractual and organizational solutions to the flexibility problem can be found in Streeck, *supra* n. 1 at 14 ff. On this, cf. the 'classical' formulation in Selznick, *supra* n. 30 at 54 ff.
106. Krause, 'From Old to New Monism: An Approach to an Economic Theory of the Constitution of the Firm', in Daintith and Teubner, *Contract and Organisation* 219 ff., 225 (1986).
107. Cf. the interpretation of the empirical material in Hopt, 'New Ways of Corporate Governance', 82 *Mich. L. Rev.* 1338 (1984); Streeck, 'Co-determination: The Fourth Decade', *International Yearbook of Organizational Democracy* (1984); Krause, 'Mitbestimmung und Effizienz', 23 *Sociologica Internationalis* 148 ff. (1985); Teubner, 'Industrial Democracy Through Law?', in Daintith and Teubner, *Contract and Organisation, supra* n. 106 at 261 ff., 268 ff.

Company Law and Legal Theory

MARY STOKES

Students of company law very often complain that the subject is technical, difficult and dull. This is not without some justification. The reason
can perhaps be found in the fact that company law as an academic discipline boasts no long and distinguished pedigree. The result is that company lawyers lack an intellectual tradition which places the particular
rules and doctrines of their discipline within a broader theoretical framework which gives meaning and coherence to them.

One object of this essay will be to suggest such a theoretical framework. The framework aims to provide a tool for analysing and explaining
many of the fundamental rules of company law. It will be argued that
one of the central features of the business company is the way in which it
centralizes the authority to manage the capital which it aggregates from
its investors in the hands of corporate managers. Clearly the nature and
extent of the power thus vested in the management of a company vary
according to the type and size of the company. But whatever its extent
the power of corporate managers poses a problem of legitimacy. This
essay will seek to explain the nature of that problem. It will also endeav-
our to illustrate how much of company law can be understood as a
response to the problem of the legitimacy of corporate managerial
power. Thus the theoretical framework takes the legitimation of corporate managerial power to be one of the underlying and unifying themes
of company law.[1] More concretely, those areas of company law which
are best viewed as a response to the problem of the legitimacy of corporate managerial power will be examined. Thus it will be shown how the
changing popularity of a number of theoretical models of the company
can be linked to the need to offer an explanation for the power which the
company vests in corporate managers. Similarly, the rules allocating
power between shareholders and directors and those imposing fiduciary

The author is grateful to Hugh Collins, Dan Prentice and David Sugarman for their helpful
comments on an earlier draft of this article.

duties on directors will be analysed in terms of the need to confer legitimacy upon the power of corporate management.

A second object of this essay will be to show how the law's attempt to justify the power vested in corporate managers has failed.[2] This in turn will lead us to an examination of how corporate law scholars have sought to offer new ways of legitimating corporate managerial power and how these too prove to be unequal to the task. Finally, some fresh methods by which managerial power might be justified will be explored.

The problem of the legitimacy of corporate managerial power

The reason why company law should have been so concerned to legitimate the power of corporate managers is that this power potentially threatens the political-economic organization we associate with a liberal democracy.

We make a distinction between public and private power. This distinction reflects the separation of the state from the individual in a liberal society. Liberal democracy has been concerned most explicitly with legitimating the power of the state, or public power. This is because the assumption is made that all important power in society is concentrated in the hands of the state. The arguments used to justify public power are very familiar. They are that the system of representative democracy gives authority to the legislature to make law, and that the power conferred upon all administrative or public bodies is legitimate as it is derived from the legislature. However, in a liberal society a democratic system of government is not considered sufficient by itself to legitimate public power. Liberalism is hostile to the existence of centres of unbridled power, believing that power unless limited and controlled may threaten the liberty and the equality of the individual which are the two fundamental tenets of liberalism itself. Thus it is sought to subject public power to the Rule of Law. At its broadest the Rule of Law aims to impose limits, controls, and checks on the exercise of power. Power must be prevented from being used arbitrarily. Arbitrariness is a difficult concept to define. It will be used to mean the exercise of power for purposes alien to those for which it was conferred.

Notice the structure of the argument legitimating public power. It breaks down into two parts. We are concerned, first, to provide a justification for power being vested in the state; and then, secondly, we seek to demonstrate that there are constraints upon the exercise of that power which prevent it from being used to infringe the liberty or equality of individuals. As we have seen, the power vested in the state is justified by a system of democratic government; and the assurance that the state's power is subject to constraints which prevent it from being used arbitrarily is found in the adherence to the ideal of the Rule of Law. The structure of this argument is important because we find it repeated when we look at the traditional ways in which it is sought to legitimate private power.

Although the theory is that all important power is concentrated in the hands of the state, this has not meant that the individual has been regarded as powerless. It has always been acknowledged that a system of private property ownership confers upon the owners of property private economic (and perhaps political and social) power.

Indeed, one of the justifications of private property takes as its premiss the idea that property ownership confers power. This provides a necessary bulwark against the danger of an all-powerful state invading the individual's liberty. In other words private property serves to protect the individual's freedom. Private ownership is also justified because by permitting individual property owners to pursue their own self-interest in a competitive market it is argued that we achieve an optimal allocation of society's resources.

It is not enough simply to suggest justifications for the existence of private ownership. If private property is to be legitimate within the framework of a liberal society it is also necessary to show that there are constraints which prevent it from becoming a source of power which threatens the liberty of the individual or rivals the power of the state. Two arguments are used for this purpose.

First, it is claimed that the economic power associated with the ownership of property does not threaten liberty because it is not concentrated in the hands of an individual or small group of individuals. Everyone is entitled to own property. It is true that the actual distribution of property in society is far from equal; but it is not so skewed as to give any individual a monopoly of economic power. The power of each property owner is checked by the corresponding power of each other property owner. Thus the distribution of property is not so unequal that it can threaten the liberty of the individual. Private economic power differs in this respect from the public power of the state. The state has a monopoly over the use of coercion which is perceived to be legitimate only because those exercising such power have been democratically elected or derive their authority from a democratic legislature.

A second argument has traditionally been used to reassure us that the economic power derived from the ownership of property is subject to constraints. It is claimed that economic power is constrained by the competitive market.[3] In a competitive market the bargaining power of the owner of a particular commodity is limited. Because many others own identical commodities or commodities which are close substitutes which they are willing to sell, the owner will not be free to charge any price he chooses for his commodity. Rather the price will be determined by the demand for and the supply of that commodity. In addition, if a property owner is manufacturing and selling goods in a competitive market he will be obliged to produce any given level of output of those goods at the lowest cost possible. And the quantity of goods which he produces will be such that the marginal cost of production is the same as the price of the product. If he fails to follow these simple rules the consequence will be economic failure. This flows from the assumptions made by the model of perfect competition that the individual entrepreneur maximizes his profits, that there is a price taker and that there is freedom of entry and exit from the industry in which he is producing goods. It is true that this model does not purport to describe accurately the way in which the market economy actually functions. Nevertheless, the model of economic theory is often taken to embody in an ideal form many of the characteristics of the actual market economy. Because this market controls and disciplines the economic power associated with property ownership it serves to legitimate that power within the framework of liberalism.

An analogy can here be made between the market and the Rule of Law.[4] The market is the mechanism which has traditionally been invoked to limit, control and thereby legitimate private power, whereas the mechanism by which it has been sought to control and justify the exercise of public power has traditionally been the ideal of the Rule of Law. Both mechanisms can be viewed as part of the liberal response to the threat to freedom which it is believed is posed by the existence of untrammelled power, be it public or private.

The economic power of the company was not thought to pose any particular difficulty within this framework of legitimation. Although the corporate form together with limited liability enabled large sums of capital to be aggregated for a common purpose, this was not perceived as problematic. Economic theory assumed that the company, like the individual entrepreneur, behaved as a profit-maximizing unit. It was obliged to do so if it was to operate within a competitive market where there were a sufficient number of firms producing the same or a substitutable commodity so that each firm was incapable of influencing the price of the commodity by adjusting its output. Thus the firm in economic theory behaved identically and was subject to the same constraints whether it took the form of an individual proprietorship, a partnership or a company.

Theory was, however, divorced from reality. The reality was that the growth of corporate enterprise shattered three of the assumptions which underlay the belief that economic power of the company was regulated and thereby legitimated by the competitive market. First, the growth of corporate enterprise falsified the theory that in any given industry there were numerous small firms so that each firm had no market power but was obliged to accept the market price for its products. The company facilitated the aggregation of vast sums of capital from numerous small investors and this together with changes in technology and organizational techniques led to a vast expansion in the size of the firm and a reduction in the number of firms operating in any particular industry. As a result the market structure very often ceased to be purely competitive, becoming monopolistic or oligopolistic. The consequence was that the company no longer had to accept the market price for its products but could affect that price by varying the output of the product.

Secondly, the assumption that the company behaved as a profit-maximizing unit of production just like an individual entrepreneur or a partnership was manifestly open to doubt. One of the central features of the company is that it separates out the functions of ownership and management. Those who manage the company do not own the company. If the managers of the company display the characteristics which economic theory credits to all other individuals they will be concerned to maximize their own utility rather than the profits of the company. Adam Smith himself understood this problem. He was hostile to the joint-stock company as a medium through which to carry on business enterprise.

The directors of such companies being the managers rather of other people's money than of their own, it cannot well be expected that they should watch over it with the same anxious vigilance with which the partners in a private copartnery frequently watch over their own. . . . Negligence and profusion, therefore, must always prevail, more or less, in the management of the affairs of such a company.[5]

Of course, it was the oligopolistic character of product markets which gave those who ran the company discretion to pursue goals other than profit-maximization. In a world of perfect competition it would not be possible for managers to deviate from the profit-maximization norm for any length of time even if they were tempted to pursue their own rather than the shareholders' interests. The failure of the market due to imperfect competition to regulate the company as an economic unit is thus indissolubly linked with the increased and potentially unconstrained power of corporate managers. It is for this reason that we can treat both imperfect competition and the separation of ownership and management as creating a problem for the legitimacy of corporate managerial power.[6]

Thirdly, one of the cardinal features of the market model of legitimation was that economic power was exercised through exchange transactions in the market. Yet as the company grew in size it was plain that much economic activity was being withdrawn from the sphere of the market and being replaced by a hierarchical, bureaucratic organization within the company. The invisible hand was being replaced by the visible hand.[7]

The effect of these three changes brought about by the growth of corporate enterprise was that the market could no longer be viewed as regulating and thereby legitimating the exercise of corporate power. The power conferred upon corporate managers by the business company was potentially unchecked and hence illegitimate within the framework of liberal democracy.

At a deeper level the concentration of economic power brought about by the growth in the size of companies and the oligopolistic nature of product markets undermined some of the traditional justifications for private ownership itself. The concentration of power in the hands of the managers of the largest companies could not be seen as a necessary bulwark against the power of the state. Nor could it be argued that private property ensured an efficient allocation of resources since the market no longer resembled the model of perfect competition.

The response of the law to the problem of the legitimacy of corporate managerial power

How did the law respond to this crisis of legitimacy of the business company?

The first reason why the market could no longer be perceived as limiting economic power was that the structure of the market ceased to correspond even loosely with the model of perfect competition which required numerous firms operating in the same industry so that no firm was capable of affecting the price of its product by varying the level of the output of that product. Ultimately the law has responded to this problem by intervening to try to ensure that the market resembles as closely as possible the paradigm of perfect competition, outlawing monopoly and trade practices that deviate from that paradigm. Although it can be argued that the *ultra vires* doctrine in company law was originally used to try to prevent concentration in industry this task has fallen primarily to competition law.

Company law has instead focused its attention on the problems created by the second characteristic of corporate enterprise which undercut the ability of the market to regulate the exercise of economic power: the separation of ownership and management. This feature of the company together with the increasing substitution of the organization of economic activity within the company rather than through the market[8] suggested that there had been an enormous growth in the power of corporate management. Both characteristics also suggested that that power was relatively uncontrolled by the market. There are two ways in which company law set about tackling the problem of legitimacy of corporate managerial power which was thus posed. First, company law sought to explain and justify why broad discretionary authority was conferred upon corporate managers. And, secondly, company law set about the task of demonstrating that the power of corporate managers was not limited but was subject to checks and controls which ensured that it could not be used for the manager's own purposes or for any other arbitrary end. The discussion of the methods by which company law has sought to legitimate the power conferred upon corporate managers and an assessment of their efficacy will be broken into parts to reflect these two strategies. The two strategies echo the structure of the argument which we have already seen used to legitimate public power and private power associated with the ordinary ownership of property. This suggests that there has always been an underlying awareness that company law doctrine was engaged in a discourse about the legitimation of power.

I will also seek to show how many parallels can be drawn between the arguments used to legitimate corporate managerial power and the arguments used in administrative law to explain, control, and legitimate the power conferred upon administrative bodies.[9] Given that the market has ceased to be an effective mode of regulating the exercise of the economic power of the company it is hardly surprising that arguments employed to regulate the exercise of public power should have been drawn upon to regulate the private economic power of corporate managers.

Before proceeding with an elaboration of the two strategies invoked by company law to legitimate the power of corporate managers, I will give an overview of the traditional model of the company with the object of showing how its development is characterized both by an increasing centralization of the authority to manage the company in the hands of the directors of the company and by a concern to justify this vesting of broad discretionary power in corporate management.

The traditional legal model of the company

The traditional legal model of the company originally treated the directors of the company as agents of the company.[10] This meant that their authority was rather limited since it could at any moment be revoked by the shareholders. Furthermore, the shareholders as the principal were entitled to issue specific instructions to the directors which as agents they were obliged to implement.

The beginning of the twentieth century saw the abandonment of this theory of the relationship between the shareholders and the directors. Instead of being perceived simply as agents of the shareholders the board of directors came to be viewed as an organ of the company which for many purposes could be treated as the company. Directors were given the exclusive right to manage the day-to-day business of the company. Shareholders were precluded from intervening in the ordinary business of the company, no longer being entitled to issue instructions to the directors as to how to exercise their powers. The courts justified this vesting of managerial autonomy over the everyday business of the company in the hands of the directors by arguing that it flowed from the construction of a company's articles of association which formed a contract between the members of the company.[11]

Although the shareholders no longer exercised the direct control of principals over the directors as their agents, the model nevertheless asserts that any danger that the directors might use their considerable discretionary powers to manage the business in their own interest is precluded. It is precluded because the model gives power to the shareholders to appoint and dismiss the directors[12] and power to supervise them once they are in office. A system of indirect control and accountability is thereby established over the directors as those responsible for the management of the company. This system of indirect control through the internal division of power between shareholders and directors is strengthened by providing that the assistance of the courts can be called upon to enforce it.

The legal model has one further method by which it attempts to balance the desirability of giving to the managers of the company substantial discretionary power so that they have sufficient flexibility to act effectively, whilst at the same time minimizing the danger that the existence of such discretion creates, which is that it will be used arbitrarily. This further method is found in the imposition upon directors of fiduciary duties. Directors are treated as being in a position analogous to that of trustees, so powers conferred upon them are given to them in a fiduciary capacity. This means that directors are under a duty to act in the best interests of the shareholders. They cannot place their own interests above those of the shareholders. The fiduciary duties of directors are not merely abstract injunctions to act only in the interests of the shareholders for they are once again enforceable in the courts.[13]

In the following two sections the two strategies employed by this model to legitimate corporate managerial power will be examined more closely. First, the justification given by the model for vesting substantial managerial power in the hands of the directors will be investigated. Secondly, the nature of the controls imposed on management so as to assure us that their power cannot be used arbitrarily will be analysed and criticized.

The legal model's legitimation of the vesting of broad discretionary power to manage the company in the hands of the directors

In trying to analyse the reasons for conferring upon the management of the company substantial power to run the company the law has relied heavily on a variety of conceptions of the company. There is a tendency among corporate law scholars to dismiss the debate about the nature of the company and corporate personality as too rarefied and speculative an enquiry better left to properly qualified jurisprudential writers. This is a mistake. For the different theoretical conceptions of the company have been intimately embroiled in the effort of company law to justify the vesting of substantial power in corporate management.

Before trying to link the legal model of corporate managerial power to a particular conception of the company a sketch of three conceptions of the company which have vied at different periods for dominance in corporate law doctrine and scholarship will be given. The first and traditional conception of the company might be labelled the fiction/ concession theory.[14] This theory treats the company as an artificial entity whose separate legal personality is granted as a privilege by the state. It was a privilege which the state guarded jealously and which was made available to business enterprises whose purposes aimed to benefit the public in general as well as enrich the corporators. Thus many of the early joint-stock enterprises which were granted the privilege of corporate identity were concerned with building and operating canals and railways. What gave legitimacy to these companies was the theory that as creatures of the state they were supervised and regulated by the state. In the eighteenth and early nineteenth centuries the theory found its doctrinal expression in the *ultra vires* rule. The *ultra vires* doctrine was used by the courts to keep corporate bodies within the narrowly defined powers granted to them by the statute or charter of incorporation conferring corporate identity upon them. Clearly there is a very strong resemblance between this method of legitimating corporate power and that which still prevails today in respect of administrative bodies. Their powers are granted to them by the state and the courts ensure through the *ultra vires* or jurisdictional principle that they do not act outside their powers. However, the fiction/concession theory came under tension once incorporation became freely available on compliance with some simple formalities, for it no longer made sense then to treat the incorporation as a special privilege or concession from the state.[15] We have seen that the more modern legitimation of corporate power, which has prevailed since the demise of the fiction/concession theory, is based upon the discipline which the competitive market exerts over the economic power of the company.

The second theory of the nature of the company is the contractual one.[16] The company is a form created by the free agreement amongst the shareholders, much like an extended partnership. This view has long been linked with those who have argued that the company should not be specially regulated by the state since it owed its existence to nothing more than a contract between individual property owners. It is unsurprising that the lawyers in the nineteenth and early twentieth centuries should have been attracted by a contractual analysis of the company. Contract was once the greediest of legal categories intent on devouring as many areas of the law as possible (e.g. quasi-contract) and indeed was even invoked to explain the nature of the state itself.[17] This contractual vision of the company focuses on the internal relation of the members within the company. It does not say anything explicit about the legitimacy of corporate power in relation to society generally. This is because the more modern justification for corporate power is assumed. That justification is, as we have seen, that the competitive market disciplines the economic power of the company. So the company is regulated both internally and externally by contract.

The third view of the company is one which has prevailed in the academic literature rather more forcefully than in company law doctrine itself. It is that the company is a natural or real entity which exists separately and distinctly from the shareholders. In Dicey's words it meant that 'whenever men act in concert for a common purpose they tend to create a body, which from no fiction of law but from the very nature of things, differs from the individuals of whom it is constituted'.[18] Sometimes the natural entity theory has been called a 'group person' theory. This posits that the company or any group of individuals acting together for a common purpose creates a living organism, or a real person, capable of willing and acting through the people who are its organs just as a natural person wills and acts through their brain, mouth, and hands.[19] It was a theory originally popularized by the German realists who were not slow to make the connection between a natural-entity theory of the corporation and a theory of the state. It was enthusiastically adopted by academic writers in this country at the beginning of this century.[20]

Quite clearly the conception of the company explicitly adopted by the legal model is the contractual one. The company is simply treated as an organization constituted by the contract between its members. That contract confers power on the directors of the company to manage the company. This contractual analysis formed the basis of the early theory that the relationship between the shareholders and the directors was that of principal and agent. It also forms the key to the courts' justification of managerial autonomy in the model which superseded the agency theory at the beginning of this century. For the conclusion that the powers vested in directors are to be exercised exclusively by the directors is arrived at by a careful analysis of the wording of the article giving to the directors of the company general managerial powers which is found in the constitution of most companies.[21]

By adopting a contractual conception of the company the legal model gives as the reason for the vesting of centralized authority to manage the company in the board of directors the contractual agreement of the owners of the company. Thus by invoking the idea of the freedom of a property owner to make any contract with respect to his property the power accorded to corporate managers appears legitimate, being the outcome of ordinary principles of freedom of contract. It reassures us that the hierarchy created within the company does not threaten individual liberty because it is the outcome of a voluntary consensual arrangement. This model of the company is one which has proved very attractive to some commentators. Some of the features of the legal model which we have depicted such as the power of the shareholders to dismiss the directors and the fiduciary duties imposed upon the directors are provided for by the law rather than by the articles of association. Nevertheless, commentators have argued that the function of these legal rules is to provide a standard set of terms to govern the relationship between the shareholders and the directors, the object being to reduce the transaction costs involved in the parties negotiating a private bargain. In other words these legal rules simply reflect the agreement the parties would have reached if bargaining on these questions had taken place at arm's length.[22]

The use of the contractual conception of the company to give legitimacy to the vesting of managerial power in the directors of the company encountered two difficulties. The first was that this contractual conception of the company conflicted with the theory prevailing in the case-law that treated the company as an artificial entity, separate and distinct from its shareholders.[23] This traditional fiction/concession theory had been embraced by legal doctrine in order to make the limited liability of the company seem a natural and inevitable incident of corporate personality. Clearly this would only be the case if the company was perceived as an entity distinct from its shareholders so that it followed that the company and not the shareholders would be liable for any debts. If, by contrast, the company was viewed as no more than a contractual association between the members much like a partnership, it was difficult to explain why each shareholder should not be liable for the full extent of any debts, as was the case in a partnership.[24] In other words what had happened is that legal doctrine had drawn upon conflicting conceptions of the company to legitimate limited liability and to endorse the power conferred upon directors to manage the company. Legal doctrine was in danger of appearing incoherent unless some reconciliation could be found between these two visions of the company.

The second difficulty which arose as a result of the legal model's reliance on the contractual conception of the company was the increasing artificiality of this analysis as the size of companies grew and the shareholders became increasingly passive investors. Any notion that the internal division of power within a company was the result of a consensual arrangement between the shareholders seemed purely fictional.

The difficulties associated with the contractual model of the company led academics in the early decades of this century to adopt instead in their writing the natural-entity conception of the company.

The natural-entity theory had several advantages compared with the contractual and the fiction/concession models of the company. First, it viewed the company as distinct from its shareholders and therefore, unlike the contractual model, it could be seen to support the theory that it was the company which was liable for any debts. The limited liability of the shareholders then appeared as a sort of concession to the creditors of the company rather than an arbitrary limitation on the normal liability imposed on partners in a business association. Secondly, the fiction/concession theory could have supplied an image of the company as separate and distinct from its shareholders which would also have supported the institution of limited liability, but there were strong reasons for preferring the natural-entity model of the company. The fiction/concession theory saw the company as entirely the creature of the state and therefore potentially accorded to the state the power to regulate and control the company as it saw fit. These implications of the fiction/concession theory were neither compatible with the reality of free incorporation on compliance with some simple formalities nor congenial to academics who did not favour state intervention in corporate enterprise. By contrast the natural-entity theory fitted perfectly a world where there was free incorporation and where the general belief was that there was no particular need to regulate the business company. Thirdly, and most importantly for our purposes, the natural-entity theory overcame the problems of the artificiality in the case of large companies of analysing the directors' managerial power as being derived from the contractual agreement of the shareholders. Its conception of the company as a real person or living organism suggested that the corporate managers could be treated as the brain of the organism formulating the policy of the company and directing its implementation by corporate executives. The fact that the shareholders within the large company were increasingly becoming passive investors, irrelevant within the company except for their function in supplying the capital of the company, was entirely consonant with this image of the company. They could be viewed as the organ within the living organism whose task it was to supply the basic necessity of capital without any need to accord them a fuller role within the enterprise. The natural-entity theory thus legitimated the fact that in the large public company, as we shall see, the shareholders no longer controlled corporate management, so that control as well as management came to be separated from ownership.

The enthusiasm for the natural-entity model of the company can be linked with a new justification given for the vesting of very extensive discretionary power in corporate management which is independent of the contractual justification which appears so clearly in English case-law. This justification is that the managers of the company have the time, information, organizational skills, and other expertise to manage the business, which the shareholders themselves lack. It is this expertise of the managers which justifies their being treated as the brain of the company, formulating corporate policy to further the ends of the enterprise. This modern justification of the discretionary power of corporate managers has a parallel in administrative law where we find that one of the arguments used to legitimate conferring discretionary power on administrative agencies has been their expertise and special competence in a particular field.[25]

The legal model's attempt to legitimate corporate managerial power through subjecting it to checks preventing it from being exercised arbitrarily

The discussion thus far has focused on the reasons given in legal doctrine to support the legal model's centralization of the power to manage the company in the hands of the directors of the company. I have argued that company law in its attempt to establish the legitimacy of corporate managerial power has been concerned also to show that the power conferred on managers is subject to controls which prevent it from being used arbitrarily. These controls are necessary if the business company is not to threaten the traditional liberal distrust of unconstrained power normally encapsulated in the adherence to the Rule of Law.

As we have seen the legal model adopts two mechanisms for ensuring that the directors of the company are subject to the control of the shareholders. The directors are, first, made accountable to the shareholders by structuring the internal division of power within the company so that the shareholders have the power to appoint and dismiss directors and to supervise them whilst in office. Secondly, directors are treated as fiduciaries required to act in the best interests of the shareholders. These mechanisms share in common the following features. Both mechanisms accept and endorse the separation of the management of the company from its ownership. They accept that it is no longer plausible to assume that those operating the business have their freedom of action constrained by the competitive market or their own self-interest. It is more probable that the managers will seek to pursue their own goals rather than subject their decisions to the norm of profit-maximization. Thus the common aim of both legal mechanisms is to force managers to maximize profits for their company and prevent them from maximizing their own utility.[26] If this can be done successfully the company will once again correspond to the profit-maximizing firm of economic theory. Corporate managers' discretion will be legitimated since their power will be severely limited by the requirement that all their decisions must aim simply at profit-maximization.

The efficacy of each of the mechanisms will be examined in turn.

The Internal Division of Power within the Company as a Means of Controlling Managerial Power

The traditional legal model divides power within the company between the directors and the shareholders. The object is to organize the internal structure of the company so that, whilst the directors as the managers of the company are given ample discretionary power to operate the company effectively, they are nevertheless obliged to exercise that power in the interests of the owners of the company.

The legal model of the company is often treated as establishing a basic constitution for the company, defining the powers of the different organs of the company and regulating the relationship between them.[27] An analogy is drawn between the company and the state. The argument is that just as direct democracy is ruled out by the size of the modern state, so too once companies grow beyond a certain size it is no longer possible to involve all their members directly in the decisions concerning the running of the company. In both cases therefore a system of representative democracy is adopted. This system relies upon the ability of the electorate to elect and dismiss leaders at periodic intervals. It is this which establishes the control of the people over their political leaders or of the shareholders over their directors. Thus the shareholders in the company are treated as the electorate, and the directors are regarded as the legislature. The legal model envisages the board of directors as actually carrying on the day-to-day business of the company so that there is no separate executive organ within the legal model. But once the size of companies expanded further it was very easy to accommodate the fact that whilst directors remained responsible for the formulation of the overall policy of the company the ordinary management was entrusted to executives. For the corporate executives could be viewed (as their name suggests) as executives implementing the broad objectives set by the directors as the legislature.

The comparison drawn between the company and the state in no way detracts from the contractual conception of the company, which we have seen was originally adopted to legitimate the vesting of broad discretion to manage the company in the hands of the directors. The two are entirely compatible if it is remembered that one of the popular theories of the nature of the state itself has always been that it was founded on a contract between the individual members of a society.

The powers conferred by the legal model on the shareholders can be analysed neatly in terms of the analogy between the constitution of a company and the constitution of a nation-state. Shareholders as the electorate are given the power to elect and dismiss their leaders, the directors. They are also given power to vote on fundamental structural changes to the company, such as altering the memorandum[28] and articles of association[29] or merging with another company[30] or dissolving the enterprise[31] which are thought to resemble constitutional issues. In addition the received legal model of the company gives powers to the shareholders to ensure that the directors once in office do not use their powers for their own self-interest. Thus the law insists that a director who wishes to enter into a transaction where there is any possibility of a conflict between his own interest and his duty to act in the best interests of the company must disclose the transaction to the shareholders in general meeting and obtain their consent to it.[32] The shareholders are thereby given the power to judge for themselves whether the directors are using their managerial powers for their own benefit at the expense of the company and if this is so to veto the transaction or at least hold the director liable for any profits thereby made.

How effective is this constitutional structure of the company in ensuring that directors do not use their powers arbitrarily? The constitutional framework makes the shareholders responsible for monitoring and supervising the directors of the company. Its efficacy in providing adequate controls over the directors therefore depends on the shareholders performing this task. Yet the reality is that it is only in companies where each shareholder has a sufficiently substantial stake in the company to make it worth his or her while performing the tasks of monitoring and supervising the behaviour of the directors that this constitutional framework can hope to provide an adequate control on the behaviour of directors. In the large public company it is now accepted as part of conventional wisdom that the shareholding is so widely dispersed that each shareholder does not own a significant enough proportion of the company to perform any of the functions of monitoring and supervising the directors that the legal model casts upon him. The consequence in the terminology of Berle and Means[33] is that there is a separation between ownership and control. The managers become a self-selecting body and cease to be effectively monitored by the shareholders once in office. Control is vested in their hands rather than the shareholders'.

The legal model of the company which separates ownership and management but still asserts that ultimate control resides with the owners of the company no longer corresponds to the realities of the modern large public company. Yet company law doctrine has failed to acknowledge this. Indeed the obstinacy with which company law has clung to the traditional legal model of the division of power in the company between the managers and the shareholders has sometimes had the effect of concealing from us the fact that company law regulates a variety of different sorts of companies. It is only by looking outside legal doctrine itself that we are made aware that neither the small closely held company (where there is no separation of ownership and management) nor the large public company (where there is a separation of ownership and control) conform to the legal model. Because company law fails to differentiate in any consistent fashion between these different sorts of companies all are treated as regulated by the traditional framework which we have been examining. The result is that there is a tendency to assume that corporate management are adequately controlled by the shareholders in all companies, including the large public company. The problem of legitimacy posed for liberalism by the fact that in reality the managers of a large public company wield power which is unconstrained by the shareholders is quietly ignored by legal doctrine itself.

This point can perhaps also be illustrated by some of the recent legislative reforms of company law. The Companies Act 1980 (now consolidated in the Companies Act 1985) has extended the occasions when the consent of the shareholders to a transaction is required, so that, for example, before directors enter into long-term service agreements with their company,[34] or substantial property transactions with their company,[35] they must disclose the details of these transactions and obtain the consent of the shareholders. What these legislative reforms seem to be suggesting is that all is basically well with the traditional model where the directors of the company manage the company but are supervised in that task by the shareholders who, if given the requisite powers, can be relied upon to ensure that directors do not use their powers for their own purposes. All that is needed is to specify clearly those occasions when there is a strong danger that directors may be tempted to act in their own self-interest and then to make the shareholders' consent necessary in those circumstances. But the attempt to assure us that directors are controlled by their shareholders must fail, for no matter how far the law goes in strengthening the powers conferred upon shareholders to monitor the managers of their company the reality is that where each shareholder only holds a tiny proportion of the share capital of the company none of the shareholders will avail themselves of the powers given to them to monitor the management. The attempt to revitalize shareholder democracy in this fashion is doomed to failure in the large public company. Efforts to do so are misplaced and can positively mislead us into believing in the efficacy of the internal organization of the structure of the company as a means of legitimating corporate managerial power.

Outside legal doctrine itself there has been a greater willingness to accept that in the large public company the shareholders may not perform that task of monitoring and controlling the management of the company, so that the managers are potentially left in a position of unchecked power. Several attempts have been made, however, to breathe new life into the traditional model which relies on structuring the internal organization of the company appropriately to ensure that controls are exercised over corporate managers.

It is sometimes argued that the rise of institutional investment and the decline of individual direct investment in large public companies means that the traditional model of the shareholder controlling the directors of the company is once again a realistic one. Although each institutional investor may still only own a very small percentage of the issued share capital of the company, nevertheless, they have the requisite skills to monitor management effectively, and can act collectively to exert pressure on the managers of the company, thereby overcoming the problem that there is little incentive for the individual shareholder to spend the necessary time and money to inform himself of and perhaps challenge the actions of the directors as the managers of the company. The empirical evidence suggests, however, that the supervision which institutional investors exercise over the management of a company is minimal and cannot be regarded as a sufficient control over the managers of large public companies.[36]

Others have argued that the traditional legal model overlooks a significant development which has taken place in the large public company. The legal model assumes that the board of directors manages the ordinary business of the company. Yet the truth is that the board of directors will only very rarely be involved in the day-to-day running of the company which is instead usually entrusted to the officers and executives of the company. Even the policy-making functions will generally be carried out by the executives rather than the board itself. The role of the board within the company needs to be re-examined. Since it is not involved in the management of the company it is in a position to monitor and check the performance of the executives actually managing the company, to ensure that they act only in the interests of the shareholders. This role can best be fulfilled by the board if the majority of directors are independent of the executive over whom they exercise a supervisory, checking function.[37] This model of the internal structure of the company acknowledges that the shareholders do not control those who manage the company and instead entrusts this task to a reconstituted board. As a means of assuring us that the management of large public companies do not wield arbitrary power it is unsatisfactory. First, it represents no more than a proposal for reform of the internal structure of the public company and not an accurate description of how the board at present functions in such a company. Secondly, even if implemented, the question would arise as to whether adequate checks existed to prevent the reconstituted board from exercising its powers in an arbitrary fashion. Without such checks the old problem arises of who is to be responsible for monitoring and supervising the supervisors.

The conclusion that must be drawn is that corporate management in the large public company are not controlled by the shareholders exercising the powers accorded to them by law to appoint, dismiss, and monitor the directors of the company. Unless there are other effective ways in which the managers of the public company are constrained, it would seem that the power of corporate management threatens liberalism's ideal that all power should be limited or subjected to checks.

Fiduciary Duties as a Mechanism for Controlling Managerial Power

The second mechanism for controlling managerial power which was singled out in the legal model was the fiduciary duties imposed upon the directors and officers of the company. These duties can be formulated as three distinct rules. Directors owe a duty of care and skill; a duty of loyalty; and a duty to act bona fide in the best interests of the company and not for any improper purpose.

One analysis of the function of these duties is that they ensure that the directors of the *company* have sufficient discretion and flexibility to be able to manage the company efficiently, whilst precluding them from exercising this discretion contrary to the interests of the shareholders. Much the same problem has arisen in administrative law. Here the problem is one of balancing an administrative body's need for substantial discretion to make choices between different courses of action and the desirability of giving the courts power to intervene to prevent the discretion being exercised contrary to the intention of the legislature. Judicial review of the exercise of discretionary powers by administrative bodies has been self-consciously based on the need to ensure that the intention of the legislature is implemented and that discretionary power is subjected to some sort of control in the name of the Rule of Law. The review of directors' managerial decisions can be viewed as being motivated by a similar desire to ensure that directors exercise their powers only in accordance with the will of their constituents (the shareholders) and that they are subjected to the controls often associated with the Rule of Law to prevent them from using their power arbitrarily.

The idea that there is a strong parallel to be drawn between judicial review in administrative law and company law is further strengthened by the similarities between the standards of review used in these two fields. Where broad discretionary powers have been conferred upon public authorities the courts take it upon themselves to review the exercise of those powers to ensure that the body does not make decisions which are so unreasonable that no reasonable body could have come to such a decision; to ensure that the decision-makers are not biased and that decisions are not made *mala fide* or for any improper purpose. It can be suggested that the fiduciary duties imposed on directors subject them to similar standards of review by the courts. Thus the duty of care prevents directors from acting wholly unreasonably; the duty of loyalty ensures that their decisions are not biased; and the duty to act bona fide in the interests of the company and not for any improper purpose is almost identical in its formulation as a standard of review to the administrative law test striking down decisions which are taken for an improper purpose.[38]

In administrative law the theory is that the courts are simply implementing the will of the legislature by subjecting the exercise of discretionary power to these standards of review. In company law it can equally be argued that by casting trustee-like duties on directors so that they are required to act only in the interests of the shareholders the law aims to ensure that the will of the shareholders is implemented. If this is the object of imposing fiduciary duties on directors it fails. This is because in considering what are the interests of the shareholders the directors are not obliged actually to consider what the subjective desires of the shareholders might be. The interests of the shareholders become an objective standard to govern the actions of the directors. Yet it is an objective standard which the directors themselves define, and not one that is imposed upon them by the courts, who regard it as illegitimate to substitute their own view of what constitutes the best interests of the company or the shareholders for that of the directors of the company. So the injunction to directors is that they must act bona fide in what they, and not the court, thinks are the best interests of the company.

In conclusion, the argument that the duty of directors to act only in the interests of the shareholders operates to ensure that the will of the shareholders is implemented by the management of the company is fundamentally flawed because the directors have considerable discretion in defining exactly what the interests of the shareholders are. Sometimes it is argued that the interests of the shareholders can provide the directors of the company with a purely objective standard on which to base their decisions if the interests of the shareholders are equated with profit-maximization. Apart from the fact that this ignores the possibility that shareholders may have other objectives in investing (such as opposing investment in countries practising apartheid, or opposing the manufacture of armaments or cigarettes, etc.) the profit-maximization norm does not provide a hard guideline as to how directors should exercise their discretion. They still have discretion to determine whether it is long-term or short-term profitability that they should be striving to achieve and discretion as to how to go about realizing that goal. Thus even if we accept that the duty of directors to act in the best interests of shareholders can be equated with a duty to maximize profits this does not provide us with any real assurance that the wishes of the shareholders are being executed by the directors or that we have a satisfactory way of controlling the discretion accorded to directors in the name of the Rule of Law.[39]

Another analysis of the function of imposing fiduciary duties on directors is that these duties are designed to ensure that directors act only within the ambit of their special expertise.[40] It has been seen that the modern justification for conferring broad discretionary power upon both corporate managers and administrative agencies is their special expertise. Not only is expertise the justification for giving broad discretionary power to both corporate managers and administrative bodies, it also supposedly limits and controls the exercise of their power. The theory is that the range of decisions open to managers and administrative agencies is limited because a set of criteria derived from their expert background and training governs their decisions. The function of fiduciary duties is to provide the courts with standards of review that enable them to guarantee that corporate managers do not act outside the limits of their special competence. Once again a similar argument exists in administrative law—namely that the function of judicial review is to ensure that public bodies only take decisions which are within the scope of their expertise. Thus is can be argued that although the courts proclaim that in reviewing the decisions of an administrative body they are merely attempting to keep the body within the jurisdiction conferred upon it by Parliament, in fact they do sometimes explicitly justify their decisions by reference to the expertise or lack of expertise of the body whose decision it is sought to review.[41]

There is an ambivalence in the expertise theory. There are two views of the purposes for which corporate managers will use their expertise. One view is that the expertise of the managers will ensure that they use their broad discretionary power to maximize the profits of the company in the interests of the shareholders. By preventing management from straying outside their competence fiduciary duties act as an alternative mechanism to the internal organization of power within the company for forcing managers to maximize profits. The common aim is to bring the company back in line with the profit-maximizing firm of the model of perfect competition. An alternative to this view is that corporate managers use their expertise to help define and implement the broad purpose of the organization, which is assumed to be that of furthering the public interest. This view is part of the corporatist vision of the company which will be examined more fully later. The contrast I wish to draw here is between an image of the corporate manager as an expert profit-maximizer and an image of him as a trained public servant. It is the former image which the courts have tended to have before them when reviewing the decisions of corporate managers.

Both these versions of the expertise theory assure us that the special expertise of directors at once justifies conferring upon them the discretion to run the business and imposes a restraint on how they exercise that discretion. Directors will only act according to professional standards of behaviour and the range of decisions available to them will be indicated by their own expertise. In theory it would be possible to rely simply on the professional background and training of corporate managers to act as a self-imposed limit on their discretion. Instead, however, we rely on the courts to review managerial decisions as a means of double checking that the directors are acting professionally (that is impersonally and for ends related to that of their organization). The courts' own role in reviewing managerial decisions is in turn defined by their own expertise. They are not competent to make business judgments but they have a special skill in detecting and thwarting management self-dealing. Hence they will not substitute their views as to the proper management of a company but they are prepared to articulate standards of review which are designed to catch self-dealing on the part of managers. The duty of loyalty has generally been invoked to prevent directors from having a personal financial interest in a decision, whilst the duty to act not for any improper purpose has sometimes been invoked to rule out decisions where directors have some other sort of personal but not directly financial interest in the decision.

The difficulty encountered by the expertise theory in trying to demonstrate the legitimacy of corporate managerial power by showing that there are restraints on the discretion of the managers stems from its attempt to combine a deference to the judgments of business managers with an insistence that corporate managers are subject to fiduciary duties that prevent them from exercising their power for their own purposes or for other non-corporate ends. The problem is that there is no satisfactory way of drawing a line between decisions of corporate managers which ought to be respected because they are based solely on the expertise of the directors and those which should be challenged as based on personal considerations or other non-corporate purposes. This is well illustrated by the controversy in the case-law about the legitimacy of a company's board of directors taking defensive action against a threatened take-over bid by issuing shares to someone who can be relied upon to support the incumbent management. The Canadian position is that the board of directors, provided it is acting in what it considers to be the best interests of the company, must have the discretion to take defensive measures against an imminent take-over.[42] The assessment of the bidder's capacity to run the target company is, in other words, something which lies within the range of the directors' expertise. By contrast, the position ultimately reached in the English cases is that if the primary reason for issuing new shares is to fend off a potential bidder for the company then the decision of the directors will be one that the courts can overturn even if the directors are acting bona fide in the best interests of the company.[43] It can be argued that the English courts have concluded that the danger that the judgment of the directors might be swayed by their own personal interest in retaining control of the company takes the decision outside the province where we should defer to their skill and judgment. Thus there is enormous difficulty both in defining precisely what we mean by expertise and in marking out what decisions will be considered to be taken for personal or other non-organizational ends. This difficulty in drawing a line between those decisions that are based on expertise and those that are influenced by personal or other non-corporate considerations means that we become suspicious of legal argument. Arguments based on deference to the judgment of corporate managers or those based on the finding of a personal interest or a non-corporate purpose on the part of the directors have the appearance of mere slogans to justify either judicial restraint or intervention. This in turn can lead us to query the legitimacy of judicial review, since it appears to be an *ad hoc* affair rather than a process governed by any firm and coherent standards.[44]

There is one further practical consideration which suggests that fiduciary duties are ineffective in constraining the discretion of directors. Fiduciary duties depend for their enforcement on the shareholders taking action against the wrongdoing corporate managers. Yet we have seen that due to the dispersion of shareholding in the large public company they have no incentive to inform themselves of the actions of their managers or to seek a remedy against them.

We can conclude that so far the law's quest to subject the power conferred on corporate managers to controls to prevent it from being exercised arbitrarily has not been successful. The internal organization of the company does not provide an adequate safeguard against the power of the managers being used for their own ends; and the imposition of fiduciary duties does not ensure that the discretion of the managers is only exercised either in accordance with the wishes of the shareholders or in accordance only with the expertise of the managers, since both these concepts prove impossibly difficult to define. Added to this is the doubt whether, because of the wide dispersion of shareholding in the large public company, shareholders can be relied upon to invoke the legal remedies at their disposal.

The legal model's attempt to equate corporate managers with ordinary entrepreneurs acting so as to maximize the profits of the company should be recognized for what it is—a failure.

Implications for the study of company law

There are two types of response which can be made to the failure of company law to legitimate corporate managerial power.

Firstly, renewed efforts can be made to constrain the power of those who manage the large public company. Two basic strategies are employed for this purpose. Either attempts can be made to ensure that corporate managers behave as profit-maximizers by making them responsive once again to the market; or, alternatively, new life can be breathed into the legal model of the company so that managers are once again forced to act in the interests of the shareholders.

The market which is envisaged as capable of disciplining managers may be the product market;[45] the market for corporate control;[46] or the market for managerial talent.[47] Or it may be that the internal organization of the firm is such that it replicates a capital market so that middle managers are obliged to profit-maximize.[48] In recent years much energy and ingenuity has been poured into the task of showing that such markets do in fact exist and can be made to force managers to profit-maximize.

It is suggested that the aim of constraining the managers of the large public company by organizing the internal division of power in the company appropriately can be achieved in a variety of ways. Faith is very often placed either in institutional investors[49] or in redefining the role of the board of directors as that of monitoring executive management.[50]

Both the hunt for new forms of market constraints on corporate managers and the search for appropriate ways of revitalizing the internal structure of the company to limit the ability of managers to pursue goals other than those of profit-maximization clearly accept that the traditional method of legitimating corporate managerial power has failed. That method depended, as we have seen, on managerial power being limited in two ways. It was limited because the company and hence the managers running the company were seen to exercise no greater power than any other ordinary individual participant in the product market in which the company operated. This had the effect of limiting the power of corporate managers both *vis-à-vis* their shareholders within the company and externally *vis-à-vis* society in general. If the market could not always be relied upon, due to its increasingly imperfect character, to constrain the powers of corporate managers there was a second way in which corporate managerial power was limited. The legal model which allocated powers to manage to the directors but vested ultimate control in the shareholders ensured that managers were adequately constrained. The failure of the product market and the legal model of the company to impose any real limits on managerial power has been the point of departure of the two avenues of corporate law scholarship already outlined. Nevertheless, both avenues of research do not seek to break out of the basic structure adopted by the traditional method of legitimating the authority of corporate managers. Instead they prefer simply to tinker with the particular mechanisms advocated for controlling corporate managerial power. Thus alternative external market constraints on managerial behaviour are isolated; or proposals are made reasserting the potency of the internal structure of the company as a means of preventing abuse of the discretion exercised by corporate managers.

A second approach to the problem of the legitimacy of corporate managerial power might begin by showing that the response outlined so far is fundamentally misguided. It is misguided in believing that a solution to the problem of the legitimacy of corporate managerial power can ever be found by looking to either the market or the ordering of power within the company. The search for such solutions fails to draw out the full implications of the criticisms of the traditional method of legitimating corporate managerial power. I will illustrate this by looking, first, at the claim that some form of market can legitimate the power of corporate managers, and, secondly, at the argument that the internal structure of the company can be so designed and used as to legitimate corporate managerial power.

The idea that some form of market will act so as to restrain corporate managers from abusing their discretion by failing to serve the interests of the shareholders is flawed in two ways. First, if the argument is that any of the suggested markets—be they for products, corporate control or managerial talent—at present actually operates to constrain corporate managers, this is not something which is empirically demonstrated, and given the present nature of these markets it seems an implausible claim. Take, for instance, the market for corporate control. It is said to function through the mechanism of the take-over bid so as to allocate the assets of companies to those managers who can put them to their best use, thereby disciplining managers to maximize profits or face the threat of a take-over bid ousting them from their jobs. However, the rules which regulate take-over bids are so riddled with occasions when the managers of a target company can affect the outcome of the bid that the take-over bid ceases to act as the potent threat to self-serving or inefficient corporate managers which it is supposed to be.[51]

Secondly, if, instead of being treated as a claim about the actual functioning of the suggested markets, the argument is taken to mean that it is possible to design a set of rules such that the proposed markets do operate to restrain corporate managerial power, it encounters an overwhelming obstacle. It overlooks the fact that the very notion that the market is capable of legitimating power is widely acknowledged as being open to serious doubt today. There is no one institutional set of arrangements which implements the abstract ideal of the market. That ideal of a multiplicity of individuals bargaining freely is translated into social practice through the rules of property, contract, tort, and criminal law. But those rules can take an almost infinite variety of forms. The market cannot be seen to be a neutral, fair process whose structure simply permits participants to exercise free choice in negotiating and concluding exchange transactions. Rather the rules which constitute the market structure people's available range of choices and consequently themselves help to define the distribution of wealth and power in society, for which an independent justification is required. Thus, for example, the way in which it is proposed to structure the rules regulating take-over bids simply reflects a judgment about how far acquiring companies should, through the mechanism of the take-over bid, be given the opportunity of dislodging the managers of the target company—a judgment which cannot be justified simply by appealing to the ideal of a free market. This is not to deny that it is possible for the market (of whatever kind) to impose some form of restraint on corporate managers. The difficulty is that it is impossible to draw the line, by appealing to any abstract ideal of the market, between the degree of constraint and the degree of discretion which will be accorded to corporate managers through, for example, the device of the take-over bid.[52]

Equally flawed is the idea that it is possible to legitimate the power of corporate managers by structuring the internal division of power in the company so that the managers are prevented from deviating from the narrow path of profit-maximization. It has already been shown above that the argument cannot be taken to mean that either institutional investors or the board of directors do in reality constrain corporate managers to profit-maximize. This, as we have seen, is simply not borne out by the facts. Even if institutional investors could be persuaded to exercise the responsibilities of ownership by playing an alert and activist part in monitoring corporate managers, difficulties would remain. Who would monitor the management of financial institutions? Equally, if the board of directors could be restructured so that it effectively monitored the executive managers of the company, who would monitor the board itself?

The second response to the problem of the legitimacy of corporate managerial power thus rejects the traditional strategies of company law for legitimating corporate managerial power. Neither the market nor the internal structuring of power within the company is accepted as a viable means of constraining managerial power. As a consequence this response breaks with the traditional obsession of the mainstream of corporate law scholarship. It abandons any attempt to design market or internal controls over managers to ensure that their discretion is only exercised in the interests of shareholders.

The problem of how to legitimate managerial power must be tackled from an entirely new perspective. This perspective takes as its point of departure the discrepancy between the law's assertion that shareholders control corporate managers and the reality of their more or less total failure to exercise any of the responsibilities of ownership. Instead of viewing this development with hostility it celebrates the way in which the modern public company has reduced the shareholders to passive property owners, thus freeing the managers from having to act purely in the interests of shareholders. Equally the way in which economic activity has increasingly come to be organized within the company rather than through the market is something to be celebrated instead of feared. At the level of legal reasoning these developments cannot be accommodated within the traditional contractual conception of the company. Instead a means of legitimating the power of corporate managers can be found by drawing upon and transforming the deviations within current legal thought.[53] The rejection of the ruling mode of dealing with the problem of the legitimacy of corporate managerial power (through market constraints or the internal structure of the company) does not necessarily lead one into an inconclusive political debate about the merits of the capitalist system. This style of deviationist doctrine seeks to 'integrate into the standard doctrinal arguments the explicit controversies over the right and feasible structure of society'.[54]

The seeds of such an approach are already present within corporate law scholarship. They are found in the corporatist model of the company. It provides a countervision to the traditional contractual model, dominant within legal theory. Three important characteristics of this model need to be singled out. First, it is accepted that the modern public company has become an organization whose significance almost rivals that of the state. It is the primary institution for organizing and employing much of our capital and labour resources and the primary supplier of goods and services in our community.[55] The rise of the corporate economy is said to lead to a 'gradual approximation of the state and society, of the public and private sphere'.[56] Society comes to resemble 'a constellation of governments, rather than an association of individuals held together by a single government'.[57] The second characteristic of the corporatist vision of the company takes up the theme of the obliteration of the distinction between state and society and between public and private to supply a normative vision of the role of corporate management. The more or less complete independence of corporate managers from their shareholders enables managers to pursue goals other than those of profit-maximization in the interests of the shareholders. Released from the constraints of both shareholders and any market, managers are free to become public servants, 'a purely neutral technocracy, balancing a variety of claims by various groups in the community and assigning to each a portion of the income stream on the basis of public policy rather than private cupidity'.[58] Thus the power of corporate managers *vis-à-vis* society is legitimated because they are perceived as experts wielding power for the benefit of society generally. The third characteristic of the corporatist vision is that it views the company as an organic body which unifies the interests of the participants into a harmonious and common purpose under the direction of its leaders. Within the company the power of the managers is legitimated because they are seen simply to help formulate, articulate, and execute the common purpose of shareholders, creditors, employees, and the community.

Traces of this countervision of the company can be found embedded in the legal materials. At the level of legal theory the natural-entity model of the company attempts to encapsulate many of the features of the corporatist countervision. The company is viewed as an organic body, bound together by a common purpose under the direction of its expert managers. At the more concrete level of legal rules, we find that many of the difficulties which the law has faced in defining the duties of directors to act in the best interests of the company stem from a conflict between the traditional contractual model of the company and the corporatist countervision. The traditional view was that the interests of the company meant the interests of the shareholders. But increasingly the view is that the interests of the company include not only the interests of the shareholders but the interests of the company's creditors[59] and employees.[60] And if these groups' interests must be considered, why not also require the directors to consider the interests of the local community, the environment and consumers? In so far as English law requires the directors to take into account the interests of groups other than the shareholders it adopts the position that these interests do not fundamentally conflict with those of the shareholders and that it is therefore possible to arrive at a decision that balances all the relevant interests, subsuming them under or subordinating them to the vaguely defined collective goal of the organization. Thus s. 309 of the Companies Act 1985 does not regard the interests of the employees and the shareholders of the company as irreconcilably opposed, expecting the directors to be able to take the interests of the employees into account whilst performing their duties to the company, including the shareholders. To this extent the law can be considered to have endorsed the corporatist perspective.

The tendency of legal doctrine to permit and even require the directors of a company to weigh the interests of groups other than those of the shareholders is closely allied with the claims that a revolution is occurring in the goals which corporate enterprise sets itself and that corporate managers are assuming for their companies' social responsibilities. Their sole concern is no longer the maximization of the company's profits. This goal is tempered by the pursuit of other social goals, such as donating corporate funds to charity, supporting community projects, promoting the welfare of employees, and taking steps to prevent pollution beyond those required by straightforward compliance with the law. It is because the shareholders no longer control the management of a large public company and the product market is no longer perfectly competitive that the management are free to use their discretion for these socially worthwhile ends. The argument is that provided they do use their power for the benefit of the public rather than for their own personal gain that power is legitimate. This vision of the company as socially responsible can be interpreted as being very closely linked if not identical to the corporatist vision.

The corporatist countervision argues that corporate managers are obliged to weigh the interests of a whole range of different constituents. In so doing it rejects the classical vision of the company which defines the interests of the company as those of the shareholders, who are the only members of the company. The reason why the corporatist vision takes a different stance on the question of whose interests corporate managers ought to further is because it pursues to its logical conclusion the implication for the classical view of the company of the separation of ownership and control in the large public company. The classical view of the company is that shareholders as the property owners are entitled to all the profits of the enterprise and hence that the company should be run in their interests alone. That view rested, however, on the assumption that the shareholders exercised ultimate control and responsibility over their property, even if the function of managing the property had been delegated to corporate managers. Since shareholders controlled the company they should be entitled to the profits and the managers obliged to act in their interests, for this ensured that the shareholders had the incentive to exploit wealth-maximizing opportunities. In other words one of the traditional defences of private property which states that an optimal allocation of resources results from owners (who it is assumed control their property) pursuing their own self-interest could be invoked to justify insisting that the company was run in the interests of the shareholders alone.

Clearly that justification collapsed once it became clear that shareholders in large public companies no longer exercised any real control or responsibility over their property. Once the link between property ownership and control is severed there no longer seems to be any compelling reason why the shareholders should receive all the profits of the company or why corporate managers should run the company in their interest alone.[61] Indeed if the aim is to provide those who control corporate assets with an incentive for putting those assets to their best use it should be the managers who receive the profits of the company and in whose interests it should be run, a conclusion which no one has as yet advocated seriously.

Once it has been demonstrated how the logic behind the traditional fidelity to the interests of the shareholders is flawed in the context of the large public company, we are free to examine exactly the nature of the stake which shareholders and others have in the company. Clearly the shareholders' interest tends to be a purely financial one; employees have an interest in the security of their jobs and the type of life they lead within the workplace; consumers have an interest in the type and quality of the goods and services produced; and the local community has an interest in the company as a supplier of jobs and livelihoods and as a potential threat to the local environment. Having freed ourselves of the shackles of the classical conception of the company and its assertion that it is only the interest of the shareholders as property owners that the law should seek to protect, it becomes evident that a whole web of relationships of interdependence exist around and within the company. Although some of the relations between the company and these other groups are contractual it is clear that the formal contractual relationship does not always define and protect all facets of the relationship. The issue for company law is whether the law should protect these non-contractual expectations and relationships of trust and dependence. The corporatist view suggests that the interests of all these groups must be balanced against each other by the managers. They are placed in a position analogous to that of a government agency and must ultimately reach a decision on the basis of the public good.

It has been suggested that we have contradictory ideals of human association informing three areas of our lives which are kept separate and distinct from each other. The relationship of the citizen to the state is informed by the democratic ideal; contract and impersonal technical hierarchy are the principles which govern our work and exchange relationships; and the ideal of community informs and structures relations between friends and within the family.[62] The corporatist view, by perceiving the company as a unit which welds together the interests of its participants into a harmonious common purpose defined as the public good, seems to draw on the ideal of community and seeks to inject it into an area which the dominant legal ideology regulates through contract and hierarchy.

The ideal is attractive. Nevertheless, powerful objections can be made to it. The ideal of community can become warped in its actual implementation in the context of the family. The family becomes a structure of 'power ennobled by sentiment'.[63] Undoubtedly a similar danger exists if we seek to implement the corporatist goal of community in the corporation. We may find that the corporatist vision of the company is legitimating a structure of hierarchical managerial power by appealing to the purposes for which that power is exercised. The purposes are assumed to be the public good. Yet there is great difficulty in defining what we mean by the public benefit. In a liberal society we assume that it cannot be objectively defined. Permitting management to use their discretion to run a company for the public benefit may be tantamount to encouraging them to run it according to their own moral and political views about what constitutes the public benefit. That this can be dangerous is illustrated by the facts of *Medical Committee for Human Rights* v. *SEC*.[64] The management of Dow Chemical Company resolved during the Vietnam war to continue to manufacture napalm in order to support the US government's involvement in Vietnam. They believed that this course of action was morally and politically desirable despite the fact that the manufacture of napalm did not generate much profit, that the company's manufacturing facilities could have been more profitably employed in the manufacture of some other chemical, and that the company's public image and recruitment activities were being damaged by the continued manufacture of napalm. Is it really self-evident that the manufacture of napalm to be used in war is something for the benefit of the public? Even if we believed that the public interest could perhaps be equated with goals supported by a broad social consensus so that the spectre of management indulging its own personal moral and political preferences under the guise of pursuing socially worthwhile goals no longer haunted us difficulties would still remain. It is unlikely that corporate management has the information available to it to determine what social goals are supported by a broad consensus or what their order of priority might be. For example, how is management to determine whether the object of minimizing pollution to the environment or supporting scientific

research establishments are objectives supported by a general social consensus and if so which of these should take priority?

By ignoring these sorts of objections it is clear that the corporatist
vision of the company is attempting to break with some of the basic
assumptions of liberalism. If it is to be successful in this objective it needs
to articulate much more clearly the rival communitarian philosophy
which one senses underpins its practical proposals.

If we are troubled by the fact that the corporatist countervision we
find hinted at in the legal materials might become simply a mask behind
which corporate managers exercise unconstrained economic and social
power, an alternative avenue for research is available to us. We have
seen how the corporatist vision of the company draws upon the ideal of
community which within our present legal system and our everyday
thinking is generally allowed to operate only within the realm of family
and friendship. A different vision of the company might draw upon the
democratic ideal which inspires the relation of the citizen to the state.
The democratic ideal asserts that those who are substantially affected by
the decisions made by political and social institutions in our society
should be involved in the making of those decisions. If we take that ideal
seriously there seems no good reason why it should be excluded from an
important area of our lives, our relations within and to the workplace.
Within company law doctrine this idea has no real impact. But it often
provides the guiding principle for a series of proposals for putting representatives of employees,[65] consumers, environmentalists and the neighbouring community on the boards of companies. These proposals can
also be seen as a response to the weakening of the claims of the shareholders as property owners due to the separation of ownership and control in the large public company. The framework for legitimating
corporate managerial power is a novel one. It justifies managerial power
by showing that those who are affected by it are involved in making managerial decisions. A framework for justifying such transformations in the
power structure of the company could be developed from the available
set of legal ideas. In distributing power between the shareholders and the
directors it will be remembered that the legal model invoked a powerful
comparison between the company and the state. That comparison is
made even more potent given that the large company tends to collapse
the distinction between private and public power. The company can thus
plausibly be viewed as a miniature state. All those affected by its decisions
are citizens of that state and should therefore be involved in making
those decisions. Whether this view should lead us to endorse a fully par-

ticipatory style of democracy or to rest content with some form of interest-group pluralism should be one of the key issues on the agenda for corporate law research.

Conclusion

In teaching and thinking about company law one of the themes which we cannot afford to ignore is the way in which legal doctrine and scholarship provide a mode of legitimating corporate managerial power which draws on a set of background assumptions of political theory. The inadequacy of the current strategies of legitimation needs to be acknowledged so that company law scholars can focus their efforts on rethinking the legitimation of managerial power. Two potential avenues for this enterprise have been suggested: the corporatist and the democratic ideal of the company. It is suggested that these are not merely speculative lines of enquiry but can be developed from within the current body of legal materials. At the same time these avenues depend for their inspiration on a more abstract set of values of community and democracy which can be found in political theory.

Notes

1. Frug, 'The Ideology of Bureaucracy in American Law' (1984) 97 *Harvard Law Rev.* 1277. Frug believes that much of company law is concerned to justify large-scale bureaucratic power. I would argue that company law has been concerned to explain and legitimate all corporate managerial power.
2. Ibid.
3. e.g. A Chayes, 'The Modern Corporation and the Rule of Law' in *The Corporation in Modern Society* (1959; ed. E. Mason), 36.
4. Ibid.
5. A. Smith, *The Wealth of Nations* (1776; Everyman's Library edn.), ii. 229, quoted by A. Berle and G. Means, *The Modern Corporation and Private Property* (rev. edn.; 1967), 304.
6. This is not to deny that imperfect competition could be said to undermine the legitimacy of all corporate power, whether it is exercised by owners or managers. The reason is that imperfect competition undermines one of the traditional justifications for private property. In an imperfectly competitive market we can no longer assume that there is an optimal allocation of society's resources. Furthermore, imperfect competition undermines the constraints on the exercise of economic power, be it wielded by managers or owners. Nevertheless, the primary focus of company law has been on corporate managerial power. The theory is that, if corporate managers can be made to

operate the company as a profit-maximizing unit of production, market forces will control the power of the company in society. Hence if company law is successful in its objective not only will the power of the company in society. This warrants focusing on the strategies adopted by company law to legitimate corporate managerial power.

7. This observation has been amongst others by P. Baran and P. Sweezy, *Monopoly Capital* (1966), 337. It is the focus of the economic literature on the theory of the firm, including the seminal article of R. Coase, 'The Nature of the Firm', 4 *Economica* (NS) (1937) 386, and forms the point of departure of an examination of the growth of and changes in the organization of the firm by A. Chandler in *The Visible Hand, The Managerial Revolution in American Business* (1977).

8. Company law does not directly address the problem of the increasing organization of economic activity within a hierarchically structured firm rather than through the market. Competition law is concerned with the associated problem of vertical integration. Labour law might be said to address rather half-heartedly the problem created by the power of the head office of a multi-divisional company to determine the fate of the company's divisions. It imposes on the managers a duty to consult a recognized trade union before making employees of a division redundant or before selling one of the divisions.

9. Frug, op. cit.

10. e.g. *Isle of Wight Rly* v. *Tahourdin* [1883] 25 Ch.D 320.

11. *Automatic Self-Cleansing Filter Syndicate Co.* v. *Cuninghame* [1906] 2 Ch. 34.

12. See L. Gower, *The Principles of Modern Company Law* (4th edn.; 1979), 141, and Companies Act 1985, s. 303.

13. Gower, op. cit., pp. 571–613.

14. See e.g. Maitland's introduction to O. Gierke, *Political Theories of the Middle Ages* (1900); and the numerous jurisprudence treatises of the nineteenth century: e.g. W. Markby, *Elements of Law* (1871); T. E. Holland, *The Elements of Jurisprudence* (1880). The discussion of the conceptions of the corporation owes much to a seminar on the history of the business corporation given by Professor M. J. Horwitz at Harvard Law School in 1982.

15. Maitland's introduction to Gierke, op. cit., p. xxxviii.

16. This conception of the company is best articulated in the case-law itself. See e.g. *Riche* v. *Ashbury Rly Co. Ltd* [1874] LR 9 Ex. 224.

17. 'Contract, that greediest of legal categories, which once wanted to devour the State, resents being told that it cannot painlessly digest even a joint-stock company.' Maitland's introduction to Gierke, op. cit., pp. xxiv–xxv.

18. A. V. Dicey, *Law and Public Opinion* (1st edn.; 1905), 165.

19. Maitland's introduction to Gierke, op. cit., p. xxvi.

20. e.g. Pollock (1911) 27 *Law Quarterly Rev.* 219. The natural or organic theory of the nature of corporate personality also had some influence on company law

doctrine. It was first adopted in *Lennard's Carrying Co.* v. *Asiatic Petroleum Co. Ltd* [1915] AC 705. For further examples of its use in the case-law see Gower, op. cit., pp. 205–12.

21. e.g. *Automatic Self-Cleansing Filter Syndicate* v. *Cuninghame*, op. cit.

22. e.g. Winter, 'State Law, Shareholder Protection, and the Theory of the Corporation' (1977) 6 *J. Legal Studies* 251.

23. e.g. *Ashbury Rly Carriage & Iron Co.* v. *Riche* [1875] LR 7 HL 653; *Salomon* v. *Salomon & Co.* [1897] AC 22.

24. See M. Stokes, 'Frankenstein's Monster: A History of the Ultra Vires Rule in Nineteenth Century English Company Law', unpublished LL.M paper on file at Harvard Law School.

25. See e.g. P. Craig, *Administrative Law* (1983), 5–6.

26. Fiduciary duties are often seen to be the mechanism whereby the law seeks to catch blatant forms of self-dealing and cheating. They are seen as a negative restraint on directors rather than as requiring them positively to maximize profits. I would argue that an understanding of the problem which the separation of ownership and management creates for the traditional mode of legitimating private economic power suggests that the overall purpose of imposing fiduciary duties on corporate managers is the more positive one of requiring them to maximize profits. The fact that their function is often explained in terms of controlling the worst cases of managerial cheating is simply a reflection of their failure to achieve their objective.

27. See e.g. M. Eisenberg, *The Structure of the Corporation* (1976), 1; Chayes, op. cit., pp. 39; Gower, op. cit., pp. 17–21.

28. Companies Act 1985, s. 4.

29. Ibid., s. 9.

30. Ibid., ss. 425–7.

31. Ibid., s. 278.

32. e.g. *Regal (Hastings) Ltd* v. *Gulliver* [1967] 2 AC 134 n.; Companies Act 1985, ss. 80, 312–16, 319, 320–2.

33. Berle and Means, op. cit.

34. Companies Act 1985, s. 80.

35. Ibid., s. 319.

36. *The Committee to Review the Functioning of Financial Institutions* (The Wilson Committee) (1980; Cmnd. 7937), 249–53.

37. e.g. Eisenberg, op. cit., ch. 11.

38. Frug, op. cit., pp. 1307–11 and 1322–7.

39. Ibid., 1307–11.

40. Ibid., 1318–33.

41. e.g. *Anisminic Ltd* v. *Foreign Compensation Commission* [1968] 2 QB 862, Diplock LJ; [1969] 2 AC 147, in particular Lord Wilberforce.

42. *Teck Corp. Ltd* v. *Millar* [1972] 33 DLR (3d) 288.

43. *Howard Smith Ltd* v. *Ampol Petroleum Ltd* [1974] AC 821.

44. A similar argument has been made in the context of the very open-ended standards used by the courts to review administrative action. See Galligan, 'Judicial Review and the Textbook Writers' (1982) 2 *Oxford J. Legal Studies* 257.

45. e.g. Hart, 'The Market Mechanism as an Incentive Scheme' *Cambridge University Discussion Paper*, no. 53 (1982).

46. The literature is vast. The theory was first articulated by Manne, 'Mergers and the Market for Corporate Control' (1965) 73 *J. Pol. Economy* 110.

47. e.g. Fama, 'Agency Problems and the Theory of the Firm' (1980) 88 *J. Pol. Economy* 288; Jensen and Meckling, 'Theory of the Firm: Managerial Behaviour, Agency Costs and Ownership Structure' (1976) 3 *J. Fin. Economics* 305.

48. O. Williamson, *Markets and Hierarchies* (1975), 132–54.

49. *Supra*, n. 36.

50. *Supra*, n. 37.

51. e.g. rule 5 of *The City Code on Take-overs and Merger* (April 1985) permits the board of a target company to favour one bidder over another

52. Frug, op. cit., pp. 1361–8.

53. Unger, 'The Critical Legal Studies Movement' (1983) 96 *Harvard Law Rev.* 563.

54. Ibid., 578.

55. e.g. *Teck Corp.* v. *Millar*, op. cit.

56. R. M. Unger, *Law in Modern Society* (1976), 193.

57. Ibid.

58. Berle and Means, op. cit., p. 312.

59. *Lonrho Ltd* v. *Shell Petroleum Co. Ltd.* [1980] 1 WLR 627.

60. Companies Act 1985, s. 309.

61. Berle and Means, op. cit., book 4, ch. 2.

62. Unger, op. cit., n. 53.

63. Ibid., 624.

64. 139 US App. DC 226.

65. e.g. *The Committee of Inquiry on Industrial Democracy* (1977; Cmnd. 6706).

The New Economic Theory of the Firm: Critical Perspectives from History

WILLIAM W. BRATTON, JR.

Introduction

Theories of the firm inform and undergird corporate law,[1] but they only intermittently appear as principal points in corporate law discourse. They stayed in the background during the half-century ending in 1980, while a conception of the firm as a management power structure prevailed unchallenged in legal theory.[2] The situation changed around 1980, when a new theory of the firm[3] appeared, imported from economics. This 'new economic theory of the firm' asserted a contractual conception. The firm, said its leading text, is a legal fiction that serves as a nexus for a set of contractual relationships among individual factors of production.[4] According to the theory, corporate relationships and structures could be explained in terms of contracting parties and transaction costs. Law and economics writers restated corporate law in the new theory's terms[5] and successfully reoriented legal discourse on corporations.[6] The new theory already has sunk into the fabric of academic corporate law.[7] Now we have two paradigms, one managerialist, the other contractual.

The new theory's proponents made strong claims on its behalf. The economists who originated it proclaimed a major discovery: Professor Michael Jensen, for example, predicted that this infant 'science of organizations' will produce a 'revolution . . . in our knowledge about organizations' during 'the next decade or two'.[8] In the law schools, its enthusiasts moved aggressively for equal academic status (including representation

Professor of Law, Benjamin N. Cardozo School of Law, Yeshiva University. My thanks to Victor Brudney, Drucilla Cornell, Stephen Diamond, Michael Piore, Paul Shupack, Katherine Van Wezel Stone, David Sugarman, Peter Temin, Willam Wang, Elliott Weiss, and Charles Yablon or their comments on an earlier draft of this paper, and to Alan Baral and Joseph Tomkiewicz for research assistance. I am grateful for the support of the Samuel and Ronnie Heyman Corporate Governance Program of the Cardozo Law School.

among the drafters of the American Law Institute's Corporate Governance Project).[9] Even outside observers expressed enthusiasm about the new perspective's potential. Professor Bruce Ackerman saw 'the stage . . . being set for a complex, yet broad-based analysis of the way in which activist law, by controlling the legal forms provided to the parties, can shape the way they use their legal freedom to plan their activities'.[10]

Employing historical analysis, this article disputes these claims. History contains essential information about theories of the firm:[11] Lawyers and economists have formulated principles to describe and regulate the relationship between individuals and producing institutions on repeated past occasions.[12] This article recounts these exercises in American corporate legal history, fitting the new economic theory into the resulting pattern.

Once seen in historical context, the theory loses the revolutionary impact claimed by its proponents. It constitutes a significant innovation in neoclassical microeconomic theory. But, outside that limited methodological context, is is merely the latest in a long series of attempts to describe and justify the phenomenon of collective production in individualist terms. Such theories have followed from and responded to economic practice; they have not dominated and determined it.

History also shows that contract always has held a constitutive place in corporate legal theory. This helps explain the new theory's success in the law. Its microeconomic innovations resonate well because they reconfirm and highlight intecedent concepts. However, history also suggests that the new theory goes too far in demanding that corporate law privilege contract. Historically, contract has had an equal, or more often subordinate, position in corporate legal theory—a position closely grounded in and responsive to economic practice. Changes in economic practice during the past two decades, whilst substantial, have not been so fundamental as to mandate that corporate law become absolutely contractual.

These recent changes in economic practice have played a role in the new theory's appearance. Taking the theory as a phenomenon in history, this article demonstrates that particular economic and legal practices of the 1960s and 1970s enabled the new theory's formulation. The theory, thus viewed, becomes an academic by-product of practical changes in the governance of the management corporation.[13] It stems from and follows the events, repeating time-honoured concepts about large-scale production in a form responsive to contemporary ways of doing business. Thus bound to history, it seems a vehicle unsuited to the control and reconstruction of legal practice.

This article has five parts. Part I describes basic concepts. It sets out the elements of traditional legal theories of the firm, managerialism, and the new economic theory. Part II sets out a history of theory of the firm concepts in American corporate legal theory. This history relates economic, institutional, and doctrinal changes to changes in theories of the firm. More particularly, the account centers on the appearance, success, and endurance of the management corporation in the late nineteenth and early twentieth centuries and corresponding developments in corporate doctrine. It shows how these practical events caused the reformulation of traditional legal theories of the firm and shaped the long-prevalent managerialist conception of the corporation. The account emphasizes an ongoing conflict between practical developments and the theorists' political preferences. Production by corporate entities—a collective phenomenon—conflicted with these theorists' individualistic assumptions about society and economics. The theories, succeeding one another in history, embody variant solutions to this conflict.

Part III sets out a parallel history of the theory of the firm in corporate legal doctrine. This account isolates the theory of the firm concepts underlying the doctrine. Here, in contrast to the theoretical evolution described in part II, the story is non-evolutionary. The concepts instantiated in the doctrine have persisted with notable stability from the mid-nineteenth century to the present. This contrasting pattern follows from its different context. Theoretical tensions between individualistic values and collective production do not concern legal practitioners. These lawyers, judges, and legislators employ a capacious firm theory, sidestepping theoretical conflicts and resolving conflicts between individual autonomy and production imperatives piecemeal, on the level of the particular.

Part IV is a commentary. It relates the histories to the contemporary contest between managerialism and the new economic theory. It suggests that historically dominant concepts still inform the law, limiting the potential influence of the new theory. This part also comments on the thesis recently advanced by Professor Morton Horwitz that the theory of the firm played a causative role in the success of the management corporation at the turn of the century.[14] Horwitz's thesis, it is argued, is untenable in light of the non-evolutionary path of the doctrinal theory of the firm identified in this article.

Part V analyses the new economic theory as an event in contemporary history. It relates the theory's appearance and success to practical developments concerning the management corporation. It suggests that the theory would never have existed had finance capitalism not become a force in corporate governance through the operation of the market for corporate control.

I. Legal theories of the corporate firm and the new economic theory

This part sets out the concepts basic to discourse on corporate legal theory, both historical and contemporary. First, it describes the recurring questions that legal theories of the firm traditionally address—concepts central to this article's historical accounts. Then it introduces concepts informing discourse on the theory of the firm today. It describes the managerialist conception of the corporation that prevailed when the new economic theory of the firm appeared in legal theory around 1980. Then it describes the new economic theory as set forth in the economics literature in the 1970s and early 1980s.

A. Traditional Legal Theories of the Corporate Firm

Traditional legal theories of the corporation[15] pursue an essentialist enquiry into the corporation's nature and origins. This enquiry, whether academic or doctrinal, dwells on sets of recurring questions.

One set of questions asks about the corporation's being. Here one line of responses holds the corporation to be at most a reification—a construction of the minds of the persons connected with the firm and those who deal with them and their products. A conflicting line holds the corporate firm to be a real thing having an existence, like a spiritual being apart from the separate existences of the persons connected with it.

A related set of questions looks into distinctions between the corporate entity (whether real or reified) and the aggregate of separate individuals and transactions in and around it. This is the 'entity or aggregate' discussion. It concerns the placement of emphasis between the group and the individual. If the corporate entity has a cognizable existence, questions arise about the nature and origins of its separate characteristics. Here personification—the attribution of human characteristics—provides a metaphorical mode of isolating components of the entity's essence. On the other hand, if the notion of an entity lacks meaning, the nature and origins of the corporation are determined by the relationship of its aggregate parts. Historically, observers taking this latter view characterize corporate life as contractual.

There also is a political version of this essentialist enquiry into the corporation's nature and origins. Here the basic question is whether the corporation must derive positive authority from the state. The statist response is called concession theory; the contrary view is called contractual. Concession theory comes in degrees.[16] A strong version attributes the corporation's very existence to state sponsorship. A weaker version sets up state permission as a regulatory prerequisite to doing business. The contractual response locates the source of all firms' economic energy in individuals. Stated most strongly, this view holds that the individuals' freedom of contract implies a right to do business as a corporation without state interference. A variant of this discussion suggests that the corporation is not a suitable subject for regulation because its activities have a 'private' rather than a 'public' nature.

B. Managerialism

Speculation about the reality of corporations, their entity and aggregate characteristics, and their origins in concession or contract was commonplace in legal theory until around 1930. At that time, discourse in these terms largely ceased as the management-centred conception of large corporate entities took hold.[17] The managerialist consensus recently disappeared, due in part to the successful emergence of the new economic theory in the legal literature beginning around 1980.

The managerialist picture put corporate management groups at the large corporation's strategic centre.[18] Management possessed hierarchical power. This structural power, stemming from their expertise in organizing resources, had three aspects. First, management determined the processes of production and distribution. Second, management dominated enormous bureaucracies and exercised authority over the lives of all those lower down on the ladder. Third, management-dominated firms imposed externalities.[19]

This picture's accuracy was not an issue in corporate law. All participants, pro- or anti-managerialist, saw the firm as a 'structure'. All agreed that the structure gave rise to power relationships and that management dominated the structure. The issue was whether management held and exercised the power legitimately. Anti-managerialists charged that management exercised its power without accountability. This argument had three parts. First, legal doctrine vested governing power of the corporate entity in the board of directors subject to shareholder vote. Second, management in fact controlled the board. And third, the financial community supported management. Therefore, management groups were unaccountable to higher authority. Management's defenders countered with a two-part defence. First came utility—expertise legitimized management authority. Then followed assurances of social responsibility—managers were capable of statesmanship.[20]

C. *The New Economic Theory of the Firm*

Economists devised the new economy theory during the 1970s. It appeared in corporate legal theory, achieving wide currency and acceptance, after 1980.[21] The theory challenged the managerialist picture of the corporation and prompted renewed concern about the nature of the corporation among legal academics. Once again entities and aggregates, and concessions and contracts, appeared in corporate law discourse.

The new economic theory has two variants, one strong, the other weak. The strong variant has antecedents in neo-classical economics; the weak variant has closer ties to institutional economics.

The institutional variant appeared first. Its earliest antecedent is an essay Ronald Coase published in 1937. Coase explained firms and markets as alternative forms of contracting, identifying transaction costs as the determinants of the choice between the two.[22] This work, while seminal, had no noticeable influence among neo-classical economists until after 1970.[23] Even then, Coase's distinction between markets and firm hierarchies only influenced the institutionalists, who restate the received managerialist picture in contractual terms.

We can precisely date the advent of the neo-classical variant with the publication of a paper by Alchian and Demsetz in 1972.[24] The watershed year was 1976, when Jensen and Meckling's well-known analysis of the firm appeared.[25] These papers draw on neo-classical conceptions of contract to devise a radical rejection of the managerialist approach.

The following describes the two variants, taking the neo-classical rendering first.[26]

1. *The neo-classical variant*   The neo-classical variant's central point is that the firm is a legal fiction that serves as a nexus for a set of contracting relations among individual factors of production.[27] Applied to corporations, this assertion displaces the management-centred conception. The firm, taken as a neo-classical contracting nexus, is not necessarily a hierarchy in which authority determines terms by fiat. As Alchian and Demsetz said in their 1972 article, firms have 'no power of fiat, no authority, no disciplinary action'. They do not differ 'in the slightest degree from ordinary market contracting between any two people'. The neo-classical variant reconceives management as a continuous process of negotiation of

successive contracts. The dissatisfied party always can terminate its dealings with the firm.[28]

From this starting-point, the neo-classical theorists construct a model of the management corporation. They find parties and terms for their firm of contracts by drawing on economists' basic assumptions about the behaviour of market-place actors and the nature of market-place contracts. The actors are rational economic actors[29]—self-interested individuals with divergent interests.[30] The contracts are the equilibrium contracts that rational economic actors enter into when dealing in markets[31]—instantaneous exchanges between maximizing parties. The parties make complete choices, dealing with unknown factors in the exchange price.[32] The theorists further assume that effective competition exists among the contracting parties. They also apply the principle of natural selection. That is, rational economic actors, consciously or not, solve problems in the process of pursuing wealth maximization. Given the actors' capabilities and intense competition, only optimal contracting strategies survive.[33]

Within this framework, firm contracts take forms determined by the now well-known imperative of agency cost reduction. The process works as follows. Risk-allocating contracts have winners and losers. Maximizing losers tend to 'shirk'—that is, take actions to avoid having to perform their promises fully. Agency costs are the costs of shirking. Since rational economic actors know about shirking, they charge agency costs against their contracting partners ahead of time. Given competition, the party who most reduces agency costs has the edge. Again, applying the principle of natural selection, the lowest cost contract forms survive.[34]

With this model the theorists have rationalized, *inter alia*, the positive law of relations among shareholders, boards of directors, and officers; the internal decision-making structures, policies, and procedures of corporate bureaucracies; and the contracts firms make with employees, suppliers, and creditors. Jensen and Meckling set out the basic themes. Managers act as agents to shareholder principals. When securities are sold publicly by management groups to outside shareholder principals, the purchasing shareholders assume that the managers will maximize their own welfare; the purchasers therefore bid down the price of the securities accordingly. Management thereby bears the costs of its own misconduct and has an incentive to control its own behaviour.[35] It achieves self-control, increasing the selling price of its securities by offering monitoring devices. These include common features of the corporate landscape such as independent directors and accountants, and legal rules against self-dealing.[36]

Subsequent essays from within the school expand the picture, pointing out that pressures from the management labour market[37] and the market for corporate control also impel management to reduce agency costs. The received division of authority between officers and board is explained in terms of low-cost information flow.[38]

This picture's implications become apparent if we contrast it with the earlier managerialist picture. The managerialist picture set out a structure and placed management at the top in a position of power. Pro-managerialists asserted that expertise necessitated this; anti-managerialists asserted that the power arose due to the absence of market constraints. The neo-classical new economic theory brings market constraints back into the picture. The discipline of price competition in the product market is accompanied by pricing disciplines from the markets for corporate securities and the markets for managers and other labour. The firm springs out of contracts in all of these markets. Since the contracts are bilateral, management power and corporate hierarchy, as previously conceived, disappear. In a firm of bilateral contracts between free market actors, both parties possess equal power to contract somewhere else.

The neo-classical picture also implies a limited role for corporate law. Corporate law does not invest and legitimize power in hierarchical superiors; instead, it appears as just another term of the contract governing equity capital input. Given the model's basic assumption that the fittest arrangements survive, the contract presumably effects an optimal sharing of risk.[39] The model, then, affords no basis for intervention by government for the protection of shareholders.

2. *The institutional variant*   The institutional variant, like the neo-classical variant, announces that the firm is contract. However, noteworthy differences distinguish this approach. First, the institutionalists grant that the firm exists as a single maximizing unit, not simply as an artifact of transactions among maximizing individuals.[40] While comprised of contracts, this firm entity amounts to a hierarchy. It is a 'governance structure', distinguishable in a meaningful way from market contracting.[41] Following Coase, the institutionalists inquire into differences between market and firm organization.

Second, the institutionalists assume an economic actor possessing a wider repertoire of human traits than does neo-classical economic man. Specifically, the institutional contracting party suffers from 'bounded rationality' and engages in 'opportunistic conduct'.[42] The former refers to a actor's limited ability to solve problems and process information.

Bounded rationality prevents the institutionalist actor from achieving the neo-classical actor's concrete risk analysis and from making complete choices. Opportunistic conduct goes beyond the neo-classical actor's self-interested maximization to 'guile'—behaviour a lawyer would term 'culpable'.

These human failings inform the institutionalist picture of the firm contracting process. The parties know that they cannot achieve complete exchanges in all situations. They therefore leave terms open and consent to structures and processes to govern the relationship's future.[43] Parties choose these 'governance structures' over market exchanges where, for example, one or both parties' performance requires a transaction-specific investment susceptible to appropriation by the other. The parties design a transactional structure to prevent appropriation. Firm organization, along with most other forms of long-term contracting, is one of these transactional structures.[44]

Many other matters affect the institutionalists' transaction structures. Some, such as free rider problems and agency costs, also figure prominently in the neo-classical models.[45] But the institutionalists also mention non-rational phenomena, such as human attitudes.[46] Authority and relational values also enter into the parties' transactional solutions: For example, fiat may be the cheapest way to solve problems; co-operation and reciprocity may reduce uncertainties, and hence costs, by causing expectations to converge.[47]

These differences result in a more thickly textured picture of the firm than that presented by the neo-classicists. Moreover, it embodies one main tenet of managerialism—the occurrence of a meaningful firm entity amidst an aggregate of individual transactions. With its hierarchies, planning failures, and bad faith conduct, the institutional variant approximates the picture of the firm underlying corporate legal doctrine.

Differences between the neo-classical and institutional pictures should not be emphasized too much, however. If we view both variants of the new economic theory together against the universe of alternative possible explanations of the firm, they represent a common point of view for many purposes. The institutional theorists, like the neo-classicists, view the firm as a contract and explain its structural features as the cost-saving devices of transacting parties. They share with the neo-classicists a non-interventionist political perspective. Since their firm 'is contract', and since private actors do a better job at making contracts than do government officials,[48] they see little constructive role for public policy. In addition, the institutionalists, like the neo-classicists, employ a methodology that delimits the scope of their enquiry and analysis. This approach assumes that transaction cost reduction best explains private contracting patterns, and they explain firm phenomena only as means to that end. When their enquiry does not lead to an explanation within this functional paradigm, both institutionalists and neo-classicists either try again or abandon the search; neither looks to the world of political, social, and economic behaviour outside.

II. The historical evolution of legal theories of the corporate firm

The part recounts the evolution of theory of the firm concepts in American corporate law history. The account is divided into five stages: the early nineteenth century to 1850; the mid-nineteenth century to the 1880s; the turn of the century; the twentieth century to around 1980; and finally, the recent appearance of the new economic theory. For each of the first four stages the account sets out primary points from the economic history of corporations and from the history of corporate legal doctrine. It then relates these points to the period's theories of the firm. At the fifth stage, the account returns us to the contemporary end point introduced in part I—the conflict between managerialism and the new economic theory.

The story has a constant theme: The corporate entity rises, posing challenges to both economic and legal theory. Both types of theory are based on individualism. They employ models of economic life based on visions of production by individual producers and transactions between individuals, all of whom bear responsibility for their own actions. These models must be adjusted to account for group production. In the case of economic theory, with its construct of entrepreneurial, profit-maximizing behaviour by rational economic actors, the adjustment requires that the individuals' entrepreneurial behaviour patterns be reconstructed or replaced somewhere in the collective producing institution. An analogous adjustment takes place in the case of legal theory. The corporate unit must be integrated with a wider legal fabric that assumes individual actors, makes them responsible, and seeks to facilitate their development.[49] As the corporation's economic significance increases, it becomes harder to reconcile its size and power with this individual-based system.[50]

The historical story climaxes when the management corporation appears at the turn of the century. Production by great collective entities becomes a reality rather suddenly. As collective production becomes more successful, theoretical adjustments consonant with individualism become harder to formulate. Successive efforts to resolve this tension mark the twentieth-century history of the theory of the firm. The new economic theory is simply the latest exercise in the series.

A. The Early Nineteenth Century to 1850

Very little tension arose between economic practice and individualist economic and legal theory in the early nineteenth century.[51] The economy closely resembled the atomistic type described in Adam Smith's classical theory. Economic units tended to be individual rather than collective. Individuals produced goods for sale in the market. Individuals bought goods for consumption in the market. To the extent production was organized, the market did the organizing by co-ordinating prices.[52]

Classical economic thinking integrated production and distribution with the wider scheme of politics and society. People assumed that market competition would keep the incompetence and greed of owners of the means of production under control. Thus, the competitive market legitimized private economic power. People also assumed that profit-oriented investors closely scrutinized the managers of firms.[53] Thus, the figure of the rational profit maximizer legitimized the positions of decision-makers in individual firms.

This individual perspective undergirded business law. Actors in the economic system received legal support from a regime of individual possessory property rights.[54] People did not yet associate the corporate form with general business, and, in fact, few businesses took the corporate form. This was corporate law history's 'special charter' phase. Corporate doctrine, as received from Great Britain, held that the corporate form was instituted by the sovereign's grant of a charter. The American states tended to confer charters on businesses that received state franchises— e.g. public utilities, transport concerns, banks, insurers, and water works—and thus were perceived to require regulation outside the market system.[55]

The prevailing legal theories described the corporation as a legal fiction and an artificial entity.[56] Rephrased in modern terms, this meant that the corporation was an entity, and that the entity was a state-created reification. This operative 'concession' notion had been received from British law. With the special charter as the dominant mode of corporate creation, this concession-based corporate theory accurately described American corporate practice.

Contractualism also was part of the British inheritance. During the two centuries prior to the American Revolution, British lawyers had resisted the sovereign's assertions of authority to create new legal actors pursuant to concession doctrine. They maintained that only natural persons occupied the legal world, and they advanced contractual conceptions of the firm.[57] American law, with its 'artificial entity' and 'legal fiction' concepts, carried on this tradition of individualism,[58] even as it conceded the existence of state-created juridical persons. The American concepts denied economic reality to the juridical construct. Corporations were 'artificial' and 'fictive' in part because observers looked to the conduct of individuals for the economic substance of businesses.[59] Thus, American legal theory fastened the classical conception of the economy as a system of transactions among individuals onto a legal foundation of individual property rights.

This description must end on a complicating note, since, despite all the individualist concord, the legal foundations for later corporate collectivities were laid during this early period. Early American corporate practice was more extensive and more highly developed than any in contemporary Europe.[60] According to Hurst, the legal form of the corporation had the functional capability for centralized production as early as the 1850s—by then the doctrinal provisions of free transferability and unlimited life were in place. More important, the doctrine instantiated group values. Corporate law favoured strong central direction of assets, barred stockholders from a direct managerial voice, and accorded management considerable assurances of tenure.[61]

B. The Middle Period—the 1850s to the 1880s

This was a transitional period in corporate history. Increased production by incorporated businesses ended the harmony between economic practice and individualist modes of thinking. Individualists began to object to corporate institutions, and devices designed to meet their objections showed up in corporate doctrine.

A factory economy developed during this period, as entrepreneurs launched the first manufacturing corporations.[62] The corporation became a common legal form for doing business, including manufacturing and selling.[63] The first great management hierarchies also appeared during this period, but these governed only the railways. Manufacturing, while now corporate, continued under simple governance structures; substantial identity still existed between owners and managers.[64]

The states enacted 'general corporation laws' to assure equal access to the corporate form. These laws emerged in a relatively set pattern, including provisions, respecting corporate purposes, directors' powers, capital structure, dividends, amendments, and mergers.[65]

The proliferation of general corporation laws necessitated adjustments in the underlying theory of the firm. The 'legal fiction' and 'artificial entity' notions were questioned because new statutes impaired their base in concession theory. With equal access to the form assured, corporations no longer seemed a product of sovereign grace. Although many still saw a reified corporate entity, widespread use of the corporate form directed attention away from juridical constructs and toward the social reality of the business and the creative energy of the individuals conducting it.

Widespread use of the corporate form also aroused individualist criticism. Individual economic power seemed to decline as corporate manufacturing expanded. With factory owners managing production, workers and consumers lost some of the control they had exercised through employment and purchase transactions in the earlier, atomistic economy. Other commentators charged that corporations subverted market control of private economic power. As separate economic entities, corporations diluted individual moral and legal responsibility among groups of business people. Furthermore, the corporate mode of conducting business through agents was criticized as inefficient, since the agents would never display the zeal of individual entrepreneurs.[66]

The management structures of the mid-century railways presented the most striking departures from the classical economic model. Like later management corporations, these corporations had large managerial hierarchies and were financed by outside equity holders. But unlike later management corporations, which had large numbers of outside stockholders holding small blocks of stock,[67] these railways had small numbers of outside stockholders holding large blocks of stock. The railways outside equity investors sought an active role in their internal affairs. Outside investment bankers sat on the boards and exercised vetoes against management. Conflicts of interest arose because the financial interests wanted short-term profits while the managers took a long-term perspective.[68]

The classical economic model did not offer a solution for this conflict. It assumed that profit-maximizing, individual entrepreneurs both owned the means of production and directed production. With the railways, this basic assumption no longer obtained: Groups of managers and investors, rather than individual actors, became the players. Furthermore, their interests came into conflict as ownership and direction of the means of production began to separate.

To address individualist concerns, corporate doctrine developed restraints against corporate and managerial power. To keep managers under control, the doctrine confined corporate activities within the parameters of a stated purpose. To keep corporations small, the doctrine limited their capital.[69] Nevertheless, according to Hurst, descriptions of the middle period should not overemphasize this anti-corporate thinking and restrictive doctrine. Like the preceding and subsequent periods of corporate legal history, this one was kind to management. General corporation laws effectively defused egalitarian objections to the corporation. And corporate law legitimized broad authority to officers while it kept stockholders out of direct participation in the decision-making process.[70]

C. From the 1880s through the Turn of the Century—The Appearance of the Management Corporation

Management corporations appeared around 1890.[71] Before then, small firms, whether individually owned or incorporated, had performed single tasks of production or marketing. Now they were joined, and in many cases replaced, by large corporations performing multiple tasks of production *and* marketing.[72] The new corporations produced an array of goods cheaply and in quantity. People perceived them as a success.[73]

Hierarchies of salaried executives dominated these new corporations. Successful mass production required long-term policy commitments and substantial investment; professional, salaried managers were designated to make these formulations and to direct production. Actors on the capital markets withdrew from active participation in corporate management because they saw themselves as lacking in necessary expertise. The split in the classical entrepreneurial function, presaged by the experience of the mid-century railway companies, widened: ownership of capital and control of the firm became completely separate.[74]

Management corporations rapidly came to dominate the economy.[75] Their dominance occasioned a substantial relocation and reformulation of economic power. Corporate control of production partially displaced market control, causing power to flow from individuals to groups.

Recall that in the atomistic economy of the first part of the nineteenth century, the limited 'control' or 'co-ordination' that existed resulted from market forces. In such an economy, actors do not exercise power against one another unilaterally. Each individual decides for himself or herself what to produce or consume. Power relations are bilateral—one can affect another's conduct only indirectly, by refusing to contract.[76] Since no one can direct production and consumption decisions, the economic system remains unplanned.

With management corporations dominant, entities, rather than transactions between individuals, guided the flow of goods through the processes of production and distribution. Some of this management power was effectively unilateral—hierarchical superiors directed subordinates in the production and marketing processes. As to other economic actors—investors, suppliers, and consumers—management groups exercised varying degrees of dominance in the context of bilaterally structured relations.

Different explanations have been advanced for the management corporation's displacement of the market-controlled economy. Assume that increases in productivity depend on increasingly specialized use of resources and that, in the nineteenth century, the division of labour and the development of special purpose machinery made greater productivity possible.[77] Why did the management corporation become the institutional means to the end of greater productivity? Chandler offers an explanation from the perspective of cost economics. In his view, administrative co-ordination permitted greater productivity by lowering costs; corporations thus won out in the competitive market-place. The internalization of units of production lowered transaction and information costs, and permitted more intensive use of resources. Internalization required management.[78] Piore and Sabel offer a contrasting explanation centred on production. In their view, co-ordination of resources by the price system became impossible as industrial resources became highly specialized in the late nineteenth century. The new production technologies had high fixed costs, the recovery of which necessitated high levels of capacity utilization. To justify high utilization, markets had to be created. The price system could not, by itself, co-ordinate mass production and mass marketing, so the management corporation was devised to perform the task.[79]

During its 'liberal incorporation' phase, lasting from around 1890 to 1930, corporate law facilitated the management corporation's successful appearance. New Jersey, and then Delaware, enacted new general incorporation acts in an effort to attract the charters of the large corporations. These new acts facilitated managerial action by offering standardized corporate structures without ancillary regulation of business decisions. Although nineteenth-century forms of shareholder participation stayed in the statutes, shareholders did not invoke them to challenge management arrangements. Judge-made corporate law changed too. Mid-nineteenth century fiduciary strictures on managers disappeared rather suddenly.[80] The fiduciary principle survived in name, but, in practice, the system tolerated individual selfishness.

The legal theory of the firm became a topic of debate just at the time management corporations appeared. Both sides of the debate rejected the earlier doctrinal notions of the corporation as 'legal fiction' and 'artificial entity'. But they diverged in their responses to the management corporation. One side was individualist and hostile, hewing closely to classical economic notions. The other side abandoned individualism for 'corporate realism', a metaphysical theory that proved congenial to management interests.

The hostile, individualist side advanced a contractual theory of the corporation. This theory incorporated the classical ideals of a disaggregated producer universe and control through market pricing. It carried on the individualism of the earlier 'legal fiction' and 'artificial entity' conceptions, even as it rejected concession theory, replacing the sovereign with freely contracting individuals. This theory took an aggregate, rather than an entity, approach[81]—separate relationships comprised the corporation's ontological centre rather than the force of the collective effort. Awkwardly, this contract theory was hostile to state regulation and to the management corporation simultaneously. Choosing a lesser evil, its adherents supported state-imposed restrictions on corporate activities through corporate law restrictions on size and purpose.[82] At the same time, however, lawyers representing management interests drew on contractualism to oppose regulation. For example, in 1886, contractualism served as the vehicle for protecting corporations from government regulation under the equal protection clause.[83]

The competing theory, corporate realism, drew on European ideas about the spiritual reality of group life, principally those of Otto Gierke.[84] In the United States, its most prominent advocate was Ernst Freund, who advanced the theory in a book published in 1884.[85] The theory achieved in anti-regulatory accent without individualism. The corporate entity was real, and group dynamics were more significant than individual contributions. With a real corporate entity, no meaningful split in the entrepreneurial function could occur; the management corporation reconstituted the classical profit maximizer in collective form. Thus, the theory resolved the tension between individualism and group production by privileging the group. But when attention turned to state regulation, individuals returned to the fore: since individuals and not the state supplied the creative force that brought the group into existence, respect for indi-

viduals counseled against regulation. Corporate realism thus offered a
theory of group production without state control. It suited the new management interest.[86]

The debate between contractualism and corporate realism lasted for
only a brief period. Contractualism disappeared as a force in corporate
legal theory after the turn of the century. People abandoned its underlying classical economic conceptions in response to the new corporations'
success as producing entities,[87] and the failure of the classical model adequately to describe complex, capital-intensive corporate entities and the
oligopolistic economy in which they operated. After 1890, classical
notions no longer influenced the formation of corporate law; the emphasis in that discourse shifted to legitimization of the producing group.[88] In
contrast, corporate realism survived in law reviews into the 1920s[90]—it
offered a theory of groups.

In the mid-1920s, corporate realism also fell, the victim of a series of persuasive critiques, most prominently an essay by John Dewey. These critiques denied the existence of a real entity, putting forth a conclusive case
for the reified corporation.[91] After corporate realism disappeared, discussion of the nature of the firm in traditional legal terms nearly disappeared
as well.[92] Dewey asserted that the whole jurisprudence was pointless. The
concepts, he said, were indeterminate. The same theories of the firm
employed in advancing the case of management also advanced the case for
labour, and they could be turned against the interests of either group.[93]

In a recent article, Professor Morton Horwitz reviews the turn-of-the-
century debates on the theory of the firm and de-emphasizes Dewey's
indeterminacy point.[94] Horwitz acknowledges that Dewey correctly
recounted the deployment of the same theory of the firm concept in support of different interests. But he contends none the less that corporate
realism should be accorded some determinative significance in connection with the rise of the management corporation. Although theory of
the firm concepts were manipulable, he says, corporate realism better
legitimized the practices of the management corporation than any other
theory then current.[95] And he goes further: corporate realism was a
'major factor' in legitimizing the management corporation.[96] This article
returns to Horwitz's proposition in part IV.[97]

D. The Twentieth Century to 1980

Management corporations continued their rise during the first half of the
twentieth century. The image of the corporation as an entity rose with
them.

During this period, internal changes in corporate structure enhanced management discretion. Early management corporations had been single hierarchical units following a 'line and organization' structure; that is, operations managers and top executives worked in the same unit.[97] After the First World War, a new structure composed of multiple divisions appeared in a few leading corporations. The multi-divisional corporation contained more than one operating unit and had a top management group responsible for all the units. Top management became separate from operations management. This permitted long-term policy to be formulated more effectively as decision-makers were freed from localized biases stemming from ties to operating units.[98] This form of organization became widespread after the Second World War, reaching maturity with the conglomerate corporations of the late 1960s.[99]

Investment patterns also enhanced management discretion during this period. Shareholdings became widely dispersed as small investors joined the full-time capitalists as equity investors in management corporations.[100] By the 1920s and 1930s, management and these widespread equity investors reached an unspoken, working understanding about power and money. Managers of large firms 'agreed' to maintain stable dividends in return for the freedom to pursue a 'growth' strategy. A growth strategy would permit management to raise equity capital internally, thereby avoiding new issues of equity securities and accompanying market judgments about management performance. The capital markets, valuing corporate 'growth', went along.[101] The conventional wisdom, moreover, held that investors had to go along whether they liked it or not: there was a collective action problem. Under the 'Wall Street Rule', individual stockholders never found it cost-effective to challenge the tenure of an ineffective management group; selling the shares was the best course of action.[102] This unspoken understanding governed management/investor relations until the late 1970s.

Corporate law also continued to support management. The model of state corporate law originated by New Jersey and Delaware at the turn of the century became the national norm. In the 1930s, the federal government supplemented state law with the federal securities laws. These required public disclosure of material information for the benefit of investors and the securities markets. In contrast to state corporate law, the securities laws operated as a moderate constraint on management discretion.

Legal theories respecting the management corporation changed substantially around 1930. As already noted, Dewey's 1926 essay marked the end of the corporate realist discourse and of corporate theory articulated in traditional terms.[103] An early and prominent exercise in law and economics, Berle and Means's *The Modern Corporation and Private Property*,[104] marked the beginning of the new era. Berle and Means set out a paradigm based on managerialist concepts drawn from economics. In its day, corporate realism had surmounted the split in the entrepreneurial function by describing a transcendent corporate being akin to a profit-maximizing individual. With the abandonment of this notion, managerialism faced the problem of the corporation's inability to replicate exactly the individual economic actor's profit-maximizing behaviour pattern. Managerialism highlighted tensions between the individual and the corporate collective, departing from the previous discourse in that individual interests came to be represented in socialized form by government and other 'group' representatives. Berle and Means recognized that shares of stock no longer carried the traditional incidents of property ownership. They offered a substitute concept of shareholder/corporate relations built around intermediate securities markets. This was a contractual concept: shareholders supplied capital and took risks, but then looked to the securities markets for fulfilment of their essential expectations of liquidity and appraisal.[105] Failures in the operations of the market-place required legislative intervention.[106] But, even assuming successful technical correction of these failures, the shareholder interest could not be said contractually to control management.[107]

Given this picture, which locates corporate power in the hands of management, management legitimacy became an issue. Participants in the discussion chose to address the issue as one of policy—'social' policy—rather than one of legal theory or doctrine.[108] This approach seemed to obviate the need for further philosophical discussion of the nature of the corporation.

Economists and legal academics shared the managerialist conception[109] of corporate structure and productive capability.

1. Managerialist economics. Berle and Means's book popularized the basic points of institutional economics. Although these ideas already had been circulating in different forms for several decades,[110] an even more extensive literature came after Berle and Means. Institutional economics analysed the firm from outside of the assumptions and methodology of classical and neo-classical economics. It concluded that the classical model of efficient production, in which production occurs at prices tending toward producers' marginal costs, did not apply to corporate productive processes. Furthermore, market forces controlled neither the structure, the organization, nor the performance of management corporations. Within the management corporation, profit no longer was a motivating force.[111] With the separation of ownership and control, the entrepreneurial drive assumed in classical economics had become split between management and capital. Management, the group controlling the means of production, was not motivated primarily by profit-seeking, but by drives for power, prestige, and job security.[112]

The question was, absent behaviour in the classical profit-maximizing mode, what behaviour patterns and objectives characterized the management corporation? Institutionalists made many suggestions. The most famous replaced profit with 'growth' as the objective,[113] and maximizing with 'satisficing' as the behaviour pattern.[114]

While in some respects critical of management, institutionalist literature had a supportive aspect. It afforded a cost justification: the management corporation produced goods more cheaply than could disaggregated producers in a classical economic universe; management corporations produced and competed effectively, if not efficiently in the narrow sense.[115] The lack of direct controls on management, either by the price system or by the capital markets, did not necessarily present a serious problem. Growth was the mark of successful enterprise and successful managing. Managers sought it, and strong institutional pressures from investors and peers encouraged them to do so.[116] This 'growth bias' left managers close enough to classical profit maximizers.[117]

Economic theory also explained why the investment community viewed management's pursuit of the growth objective with equanimity. The theory of present value, advanced by Irving Fisher in 1930, aligned management's long-term investment perspectives with capital's often short-term investment perspectives. Since growth ultimately raised the level of dividend return, it manifested itself in present capital appreciation, that is, a higher stock price.[118] Thus, long-term industrial stability and short-term profit came into balance,[119] or so it seemed.[120]

Meanwhile, a separate discipline within economics—neo-classical economics—continued to operate in the classical tradition. Prior to the appearance of the new economic theory of the firm in the 1970s, however, neo-classical microeconomists declined to theorize about the internal operations of the management corporation, restricting their attention to the market.[121] Their models explained co-ordination of the use of resources and distribution of income by the price system.[122] They employed the received model of the single-product firm operating in a static but highly competitive environment. This firm was owned by a single proprietor who strived to maximize profits, using only output and price as strategic variables.[123] This approach reduced the firm to a 'black box'—a 'production function' deemed to follow profit considerations exclusively and behave as an entity in rational patterns no different from those of human actors. Managerial power, if it existed at all, was assumed to be effectively controlled by market forces.[124]

In the age of the management corporation, this limited enquiry made neo-classical microeconomics a discipline of obviously limited explanatory capabilities.[125] Yet microeconomists did not perceive a debilitating problem and rush to expand their models. They thought of actions inside firms as 'engineering'—functions of hierarchical structures—and therefore not a subject-matter suited to a discipline that studies markets.[126] The neo-classicists' hierarchical conception of internal firm affairs signified concurrence in the managerialist conception prevalent among the institutionalists and academic lawyers.[127]

2. Managerialist law.   Berle and Means also contributed a political picture of the management corporation which prevailed in academic legal discussions until the new economic theory of the firm appeared to challenge it around 1980. As already stated in part I,[128] this political picture identified management as a powerful group. This power stemmed from corporate structure: the traditional legal model of corporate ownership had combined with passive, widespread security-holding to leave management in a strategic position. The result was real power at the top of a dependent structure,[129] and the issue was management legitimacy.

The debate over management legitimacy included one issue stated in terms of traditional legal theory. This issue—whether the corporation was public or private—addressed the validity of government regulation. A century earlier, concession theory would have justified regulation. But concession had fallen out of currency; its imagery no longer made sense.[130] Accordingly, advocates of regulation reformulated the political assertions bound up in concession theory. They abandoned the sovereign creation story and accepted the primacy of individual creativity and energy in corporate life. But they characterized the product of all this individual activity as 'public' in nature. This characterization supported the position that uncontrolled management wielded its power illegitimately and should be subjected to additional legal controls. The contrary 'private' characterization affirmed the legitimacy of vesting in management substantial discretion.

Anti-managerialists demonstrated the firm's public nature by analogizing managerial power to governmental power. Like government, large corporations took actions important to those outside of the organization. Like government authorities, managers exercised their power by means of a rationalized system of control and administration. Like the government, the 'public' firm was a 'political' entity.[131] Political theories respecting government, such as interest group pluralism, therefore should be applied to it.[132]

The 'public' theme also figured into doctrinal fairness jurisprudence. Corporate doctrine follows the trust model in name only. In practice, it leaves substantial room for self-interested conduct by corporate managers. Anti-managerialists drew on the analogy to government in their criticism of the doctrine's managerialist bias. Our system normally treats public offices as trusts. We require public officers to show respect for others, even-handedness, and selflessness in situations in which we leave private persons unregulated.[133] Given these assumptions, a 'public' model of corporations implies strict scrutiny of the managerial actions affecting the interests of investors.[134]

E. The Contemporary Debate—The New Economic Theory Versus Managerialism

With the new economic theory, neo-classical microeconomists surmounted the conceptual barriers that prevented them from elaborating a modern theory of corporate structure.[135] The solution was simple. The new theory avoided direct consideration of hierarchies in management corporations, setting out a picture in which corporate entity and hierarchy were irrelevant. By describing all internal relationships as market transactions, the theory permitted large organizations to be discussed within the traditions of neo-classical microeconomics. No acknowledgment of 'engineering' sullied the theorists' hands.

The neo-classical new economic theory pronounced a new solution to the problem of the split entrepreneurial function. Where turn-of-the-century corporate realism patched over the split with a unified, real corporate being, the new economic theory offered the converse solution of a completely deconstructed corporate entity. Since no cognizable corporate collectivity appears amidst the nexus of contracts, no tension arises between collective and individual interests. The new theory does not look for corporate replication of individual profit-maximizing. The entrepreneurial function emerges in separate but unified pieces among the aggregated individuals. Ironically, this solution draws on the same classical tradition that originally stated the problem.

With this market-based solution, the neo-classicists rebutted both the managerialists' statement of the corporate problem and their regulatory solutions. The neo-classical picture privileges the firm's aggregate parts almost absolutely, deconstructing the hierarchy that the anti-managerialists attack. The managerialist corporate entity almost disappears, dissolving into disaggregated but interworking transactions among the participating actors. All of these interworking firm transactions resemble one another.[136] The 'separation of ownership and control', on which the managerialist picture based management power, no longer matters. 'Ownership' becomes as irrelevant a concept as 'firm entity'. The 'firm' is only a series of contracts covering inputs being joined so as to become output. 'Capital', and thus the traditional legal situs of ownership, devolves into one of the many types of inputs.[137]

Though the neo-classicists nominally made these moves for the purpose of explanation, their operative assumptions gave the theory a normative aspect. Treating hierarchy as if it does not exist offers wonderful support to those at the top of the hierarchy, so long as the treatment implies no concomitant reordering of the status quo. Moreover, by challenging the anti-managerialist critique of corporate law,[138] the neo-classicists in some respects challenge the status quo in management's favour. They rebut the anti-managerialists' 'public' characterization with a model of 'private' contracts among successfully contracting market actors. 'Concessions' of sovereign authority have no place in this picture of free contract.

By stripping the content from the firm entity and introducing the self-interested rational economic actor, the new theory also rebuts the concept of fiduciary duty. Legal duties of selflessness do not figure into the neoclassicists' conception of bilateral contract relations.[139] These market contracts implicitly justify what they depict: since they are priced to take management self-interest into account, extant customs of managerial self-dealing therefore must be all right, or cost competition would have caused them to disappear long ago. None of this was lost on participants in the corporate governance debates of the late 1970s and early 1980s. To one anti-managerialist observer, the new economic theory completes the twentieth-century trend toward loosened fiduciary restraints and enhanced management discretion.[140] In fact, management spokespersons did make dramatic use of the theory in the early 1980s[141] to protest the first draft of the American Law Institute's *Principles of Corporate Governance*.[142]

The institutionalists, with their roots in managerialism, developed a variant of contractualism which does not offer an absolute solution to the split in the entrepreneurial function. The opportunistic conduct and bounded rationality of their actors leave room for tensions between individuals and corporate collectives that do not self-resolve. None the less, like the neo-classicists, their work offers normative comfort to management interests. They legitimize the received hierarchical picture of the management corporation[143] as a contractual arrangement which minimizes transaction costs. Their picture also makes the corporation a 'private' phenomenon. They affirm the corporate structure and management's place in it, even as they admit the possibility of contract failure.

Some of the new economic theory's initial success in the legal academy may be attributable to this support of management. The new economic theory brought academic theory into line with the practices of corporate doctrine. The academic line had stressed managerial public duty and legal constraint. Corporate doctrine equivocated; it repeated the fiduciary principle and maintained a governmental presence even as it steadfastly protected the management corporation's private law bases and the discretionary authority of managers. Management power had supporters in academia as well as opponents. Supporters saw a voluntary side to individual relations with corporations, and the new economic theory articulated this perception.[144]

F. Summary

In the classical world of the early nineteenth century, economic practice and theory coexisted in peace. Corporate production was an anomalous feature of the economic landscape. The corporation was integrated into the classical picture by a limiting theory—it was a legal institution only. But as the century proceeded and corporate production became the norm, it became clear that the corporate firm was more than a legal institution. The entrepreneurial function became split in economic practice, and the classical peace ended. Legal theory offered two opposing solutions. One, contractualism, sought to minimize the split and protect the individual by suppressing the corporation. The other, realism, made the split irrelevant by transcending the individual interest with a spiritual firm entity. Neither solution wore well in the twentieth century.

In the twentieth century, the management corporation became a normal institution. But the classical reproach continued to influence theoretical perspectives. With managerialism, the split entrepreneurial function became the base point of both economic and legal theory. Nineteenth-century individualism, however, did not dominate managerialist responses to the classically stated problem. In the ongoing discourse of legitimization, individual, bilateral relations within corporate entities were obscured amidst the concepts and habits of social policymaking. In legal theory, the individualist impulse remained largely subordinated until the appearance of the new economic theory. With this new theory, twentieth-century individualists integrated classical theory and twentieth-century practice. This theory offered a return to a world of classical peace: It healed the split entrepreneurial function and returned the corporate entity to limited life as a legal institution.

III. The non-evolutionary history of the doctrinal theory of the corporate firm

A second, non-evolutionary history of the theory of the corporate firm parallels the foregoing evolutionary account. It deals with the same juridical concepts, but it shows that, when deployed to support corporate doctrine, these concepts have remained substantially constant in history. This account looks only to corporate doctrine, drawing on the definitions of the firm operative in treatises and other doctrinal work from the mid-nineteenth to the mid-twentieth century. These sources state a 'doctrinal theory of the corporate firm' was that formulated during the early period and lasted into the twentieth century. . . .

A. The Angell and Ames Definition

The doctrinal theory of the firm may be traced, in America, to Angell and Ames,[145] the leading *ante bellum* corporate law treatise.[146] Angell and Ames dealt with the problem of devising a theoretical characterization of the corporation by drawing on definitions from three prominent works.[147] One definition came from Kent's *Commentaries*,[148] but had origins going as far back as the writings of Pope Innocent IV.[149] The second came from Kyd's late eighteenth-century British treatise on corporate law.[150] The third was the famous description of the corporation in Chief Justice Marshall's opinion in the *Dartmouth College* case.[151] This section closely examines each of these three texts.

First, the definition Angell and Ames drew from Chancellor Kent:

A corporation is [an artificial and fictitious][152] body, created by law, composed of individuals united under a common name, the members of which succeed each other, so that the body continues the same, notwithstanding the change of individuals who compose it, and is, for certain purposes, considered as a natural person.[153]

This definition begins with an anti-realist conception of the nature of the corporation: artificial bodies[154] are reifications. The phrase 'created by law' brings in the notion that the corporate reification originates as a concession from the state; implicitly, the creating law is positive law. But the definition balances this implication with an anti-positivist conception of firm life: while the states creates the reification, the corporation is 'composed of individuals'. Here the definition also makes an oblique reference to the firm's aggregate aspect. The reference does not go so far as to ascribe 'contractual' origins to the corporation in a legal sense, but in an economic sense it can be taken to locate the source of creative energy in individuals, rather than in the state. The definition's image of the corporate body remaining the same while individual members succeed each other ascribes content to the firm reification; something separate from the individuals exists.

The definition's final, uncontroversial point—that the corporation is considered a natural person for certain purposes—is noteworthy for its careful anti-realism. The corporation is a person for doctrinal purposes only, being classified with individuals in some doctrinal contexts even though it is not a natural person. . . . .

Second, the Kyd definition:

A corporation, or a body politic, or body incorporate, is a collection of many individuals, united into one body, under a *special denomination*, having perpetual succession under an *artificial form*, and vested, by the policy of law, with the capacity of acting, in several respects, as an *individual*, particularly of taking and granting property, of contracting obligations, of suing and being sued, of enjoying privileges and immunities in *common*, and of exercising a variety of political rights, more or less extensive, according to the design of its institution, or the powers conferred upon it, either at the time of its creation, or at any subsequent period of its existence.[155]

Kyd leans to the corporation's aggregate aspect more than does Kent. We get the same image of united individuals, but Kyd fixes on the idea of a 'denomination' to describe the firm. He thus limits the firm entity's substance to the common name of the collection of individuals.[156] Kyd acknowledges positive law aspects of firm creation, but he de-emphasizes concession theory. His definition includes the point about contextual treatment of the corporation as if it were an individual. He then restates the point more broadly, leaving out any assertion that the state creates the firm reification. In sum, Kyd minimizes the significance of both the corporate entity and state participation in corporate life. His corporation is a legal device that facilitates common action. The substance lies with individual contributions.

Finally, Chief Justice Marshall's discussion:

A corporation is an artificial being, invisible, intangible, and existing only in contemplation of law. Being the mere creature of law, it possesses only those properties which the charter of its creation confers upon it, either expressly, or as incidental to its every existence. These are such as are supposed best calculated to effect the object for which it was created. Among the most important are immortality, and, if the expression may be allowed, individuality. . . . Its immortality no more confers on it political power, or a political character, than immortality would confer such power or character on a natural person. It is no more a state instrument, than a natural person exercising the same powers would be.[157]

Chief Justice Marshall's first sentence, the foundation citation for early nineteenth-century 'fiction theory', depicts the corporation as a reification and presents a concession theory of its origin. The second and third sentences, noting the corporation's limited power, set out the conception undergirding *ultra vires* doctrine. But the operative conception may be characterized more broadly. These sentences offer a functionalist conception of the corporation: its powers have purposes; they are means to ends. . . . .

Significant commonalities tie the three definitions together, despite their variant vocabularies and emphases. Each definition conceives of the corporation as a reification, finding reality in the actions of individual participants. Each simultaneously recognizes entity and aggregate characteristics, concession, and contractual origins, and public and private aspects. Which aspect proves relevant in a given situation depends on the facts and the particular observer's perspective. Kent and Chief Justice Marshall may be distinguished from Kyd for stronger emphasis on the entity. Kyd permits virtually nothing in the way of determinate thought structures inside his corporate entity, and Kyd's lesser emphasis on concession follows from his treatment of the entity: the less content in the entity, the less practical significance attaches to the state's act of creating it. . . . .

B. Usage of the Angell and Ames Definition Prior to 1930

The Angell and Ames definition, or in some cases one or two of its three components, became standard matter. The succeeding century's corporate law treatises repeated it again and again.[158] The definition even can be found, stated as living legal doctrine, in a treatise published in 1958.[159] . . . .

The writers adjusted the Angell and Ames formula as corporate doctrine changed. For example, the late nineteenth-century texts tended to drop the immortality point. Unlimited corporate life, presumably, had become an unremarkable doctrinal assumption.[160] The late nineteenth-century texts also mentioned the decline of concession theory and the passing of the fiction notion. . . . .

Modifications continued after the turn of the century. Writers included the governance model of the liberal incorporation statutes next to the historical definitions. This move provided the reified entity with some additional substance, but otherwise left the Angell and Ames conceptions unchanged.[161] . . . .

After the turn of the century, writers began to lose confidence in the Angell and Ames definition's effectiveness. The nineteenth-century emphases on fiction and concession had disappeared, but no new concepts came in to replace them and limit the definition's capacity. Rather than reformulate from the ground up on some new theoretical basis, writers supplemented the definition with a practical admonition. As one writer said: 'A full and complete definition of a corporation can only be given by telling what are its rights, powers, duties, and relations, and the legal and equitable principles which control it in all its parts and functions and how they operate.'[162] Hohfeld went farther in this direction. Parting company with the historical definitions, he described the corporation as an association of natural persons conducting business under legal forms, methods, and procedures.[163] This characterization dispensed with entity and aggregate theorizing and directed attention to doctrinal devices without looking further into them for meaning. These practical definitions, by referring inquiries to particulars of corporate law, said in effect that the legal corporation is the sum of the laws, and that the received theoretical characterizations of the whole lack something in meaning. They thus anticipated Dewey's indeterminacy assertion of twenty to thirty years later.

C. The Doctrinal Theory of the Corporate Firm after 1930

Theory of the firm had a bad reputation after the realist/anti-realist debate terminated in the late 1920s. Dewey's indeterminacy assertion became conventional wisdom.[164] By 1976, traditional theory of the firm concepts had fallen so far from view that theoretically ambitious works on corporate structure omitted any mention of them.[165] Discussion shifted to policy enquiries into management performance. Bayless Manning characterized the situation with a flourish in 1962: commercial images of the corporation had overshadowed the concept of the corporation; corporate law's underlying intellectual construct had rotted away.[166] Manning correctly identified the dominance of 'commercial images' of the corporation even as he overstated the latter point.

Treatise writers after Dewey, freed from transcendental 'corporate realism', practised the very different lessons of 'legal realism'. They deprecated historical theory of the firm concepts as outmoded 'conceptual approaches' to policy problems.[167] They avoided the whole bundle of past concepts. They even denied the relevance of an entity concept,[168] debunking it as metaphor, a device for ease of reference.[169]

These writers employed various substitute concepts, all of which had an antecedent in Hohfeld. One concept described the corporation as 'more nearly a method than a thing'[170]—a 'technique' for organizing relationships among individuals.[171] This approach stripped the fixed content from the entity concept, causing the entity to devolve into a rope tying together the bundle of relationships. Under this approach, each corporate relationship, whether a contract, or performance of a duty stemming from positive law, was analysed separately according to its own circumstances. The corporation emerged with a variable meaning. . . . .

Despite different terminology and modes of legal analysis, and despite assertive repudiation of past conceptions, these 'modern' reformulations in the end only recreated the historical definitions' picture of the firm. Gone, of course, were corporate realism and fiction theory. But the historical definition never incorporated the former, and it dropped the latter prior to the turn of the century. Consciousness of the concept's indeterminacy may have been new, but the historical definitions had effectively recognized the inevitability of indeterminacy all along. They built indeterminacy into the doctrine by providing for situational application of the entity and aggregate concepts. The twentieth-century writers only repeated this basic lesson when they insisted that the corporation be treated as a person, unit, entity, or group, depending on the context.[172]

The twentieth-century writers' various characterizations of the firm entity . . . . give us more or less the corporate entity envisioned by Kyd and respected in the treatises for a century.

IV. Comments from the history

Drawing on the foregoing historical accounts, this part comments critically on the principal contemporary assertions about the legal theory of the firm.

Horwitz's proposition that corporate realism was a determinative force in legitimizing the management corporation is addressed first. Horwitz does not take into account the doctrinal theory of the firm emphasized in this article. The discussion suggests that once the perspective opens up to encompass the doctrinal theory and its constant quality, Horwitz's point must be modified substantially.

Second, attention turns to the new economic theorists' assertion that the corporation 'is contract'. The discussion suggests that this point is unsuited to literal transfer from the narrow context of economic theory to the wider, more complex context of legal doctrine.

A. Horwitz's Proposition

Horwitz is right in asserting that corporate realism and the management corporation rose together. Corporate realism certainly offered a collectivist justification for the new mass-producing entities. Moreover, it appeared just as these entities worked past the hostile implications of classical economic concepts to secure a safe place in the harbour of corporate law. Implications of mutual assistance arise from such temporal confluences of theory and practice.

But Horwitz's point that corporate realism caused the management corporation's success can be turned around—the practice could have aided the theory more than the theory aided the practice. A counter picture of practice determining theory finds support in the relationships between economic changes at the turn of the century and the several levels of the theory of the corporate firm—the constant doctrinal theory, the opposed schools of corporate realism and contractualism, and superseding managerialist theory. The counter picture is neither more nor less falsifiable than Horwitz's picture.

First, consider the relationship between the doctrinal theory of the firm and the development of the management corporation. The management corporation changed the landscape that the corporate treatises described. The definitions reflected the change, albeit indirectly. The late nineteenth-century writers omitted the legal fiction concept. This omission had a doctrinal cause—the appearance of general incorporation laws—but it also may be inferred that the management corporation made the theory untenable. The legal fiction notion instantiated the classical economic perspective. Given the management corporation, more in the way of social reality had to be conceded to the firm. The historical definitions made this concession by dropping the limiting concept.

Next consider the relationship between the doctrinal theory of the firm and the debate over corporate realism and contractualism. Here the treatise-writers made a significant move. As the concession and fiction notions dropped out, the contractual and realist schools invited the doctrine in different directions. One offered contract and pure liberal individualism; the other offered realism and European organicism. The doctrinalists refused both invitations, choosing instead, as their predecessors had done, to balance the metapolitical alternatives. The doctrinal theory only changed in appearance when the writers abandoned the historical vocabulary around 1930. This change occurred just after corporate realism collapsed and at the same time that managerialism became the basis for discussion of the management corporation. Policy replaced doctrine as the mode of debate on corporate legitimacy, and the treatise-writers made conforming changes in their basic conceptions of the corporation.

Thus, when the managerialist era arrived, neither corporate realism nor contractualism had achieved a sufficiently deep level of acceptance to become the generally accepted basis for everyday corporate doctrine. Realism and contractualism were events of primarily academic interest. When academic theory changed course around 1930, corporate realism disappeared with hardly a trace.

The fragility of theory of the firm concepts permits the inference that practice had the primary causative role. The new management corporation necessitated considerable adjustment to ways of thinking about economic life.[173] It took some time before a settled bundle of concepts achieved general currency. The corporate realism debates occurred during the period of adjustment. Observers were generally favourable to the management corporation because of its apparent economic success, but lacked present explanatory and legitimizing theories. This uncertainty made corporate realism plausible for a time, but the realist explanation proved tentative. As the management corporation matured, a more suitable set of concepts achieved general currency. As a result, corporate realism fell out of currency rather abruptly.

The supplanting and enduring ideas came from contemporary American economics rather than from nineteenth-century European jurisprudence. These ideas were practical: management possessed expertise and performed its job effectively; therefore, it had the law's support.[174] To the extent management's performance failed to fit whatever scheme of social, political, or economic guidelines the particular observer applied, then some economic or legal adjustment was required.[175] As this practical picture of the management corporation was drawn, and pro- and anti-managerial positions staked out within its framework, corporate realism's basis in European speculation about group imperatives must have come to seem out of touch with practice.

Ever-present American individualism provides a deeper explanation for the change. Americans historically tend to be uncomfortable with theories—here termed 'organicist'—that accord the group intrinsic primacy over the individual.[176] Corporate realism was organicist; managerialism was not, even though it tended to socialize individual interests. Managerialism internalized individualism by conditioning its legitimization of collective corporate life on management performance. It acknowledged a significant, if not dominant, place for contract in the structure of the management corporation.[177] And it offered a firm conception consonant with the political alignment sought by both sides of the debate: with managerialism, individualists could be pro-managerialist at the same time that collectivists could be anti-managerialist.

B. The New Economic Theory of the Firm

The new economic theory presented something new to the world of neo-classical microeconomics when its neo-classical variant appeared in the 1970s. Its nexus of contracts assertion solved a century-old problem by offering a way around the conceptual barriers to a neo-classical theory of corporate structure. But transposed to a legal context, the assertion was less new than it looked. Contract always has figured into the legal theory of the firm. The new economic theory confirms and repeats legal history when it asserts that the corporation 'is contract'. It joins a tradition when it offers to resolve the tension between the ideals of classical economics and the institution of the management corporation. But the new theory also breaks with the historical pattern: it is absolutely contractual, while contract never has dominated legal theory.

This absolute contractualism makes problematic the new theory's practical application in the law. The new theory faces the same dilemma as much contemporary academic legal theory. It was received successfully into legal discourse because of its connection to the values that historically have informed corporate law. But this enhancement of historical values continues only so long as the discourse stays on a theoretical level. If the new economic theory were to achieve practical acceptance and become the basis of corporate doctrine, it would reconstruct the earlier values. Thus, the basis for its original acceptance would dissolve in the wake of its complete success.

To see the connection between historical values and the new economic theory's reception in the legal academy, one must take a broad view of the contemporary theoretical landscape. Two steps must be taken for this large picture to come into focus. First, juxtapose the two variants of the new economic theory with the managerialist picture of hierarchical structure. Second, consider the entire theoretical landscape: managerialist, institutionalist, and neo-classical conceptions coexist in contemporary corporate discourse. Taken together, these conceptions resemble the juxtaposition of conceptions in Angell and Ames. Like the Angell and Ames pictures, these pictures variously emphasize the entity and the aggregate, the sovereign and the contractual. Like Angell and Ames's pictures, all of these view the corporation as a reification, differing in the conceptions placed inside it. The broad view, then, shows a level at which the historical doctrinal theory continues to operate.

Significantly, modern academic theory reflected the doctrinal theory less clearly before the new economic theory appeared. The managerialist picture understated the presence of contract, particularly arms-length contract, in corporate arrangements. For decades, anti-managerialist commentators criticized corporate doctrine for insufficient recognition of fiduciary constraints. Not all observers shared this anti-managerialism, but supporters of managerial discretion had no well-articulated theoretical response. The new economic theory's contractualism gave them an answer, explaining and justifying the doctrine's pro-management recalcitrance. It thereby brought academic theory back into alignment with the doctrinal theory and its enduring base point of individualism.

The new theory also resonated well because it drew on elements already present in and around corporate doctrine. Twentieth-century corporations and corporate doctrine offered plenty of contracts around which to base a theory. The case law alternated between an entity-based structural conception in which the entity employs management, and a contractually based structural conception, in which management acts as the shareholders' agent.[179] The Berlian theoretical picture of the corporation featured contract prominently:[179] Managers, labourers, suppliers, creditors, and customers contracted into corporate relationships; corporate investors traded stocks and bonds by means of discrete contracts. No generally accepted doctrinal barrier had forced the theoretical subordination of contract, at least in the twentieth century. In addition, American jurisprudence had the individualist spirit requisite for a contractual theory.

Thus, the new theory articulated points and values already embedded in the doctrine but only faintly recognized in earlier academic theory. But the new theory broke sharply with another, equally significant strand of historical precedent: the relegation of contract to a supporting role in corporate legal theory and practice. Absolutely asserted contractual theories had appeared before—one during the late nineteenth century and a second with Coase's essay of 1937. Nineteenth-century contract theory failed to garner general acceptance, and Coase's 1937 discussion of the firm as a product of cost-effective contracting had limited influence, even among economists, for more than thirty years.

The new economic theory descends directly from Coase. It has a more collateral relation with the contractualism of nineteenth-century legal theory, but a cognizable tie binds the two. Fixing the new theory's relations with earlier corporate theory, and explaining the earlier theory's failure to achieve general acceptance, demonstrates limitations on the new theory's potential practical influence.

The new economic theory's tie to nineteenth-century contractualism arises from their common ancestry in the classical economic tradition. The theories bear significant familial resemblances: both strip the entity reification of nearly all content; Both use the phrase 'legal fiction' to describe the entity;[180] both view the relations of managers and corporations in terms of the problems of self-interested agents;[181] and both utilize the contract idea to forestall governmental restraint of the corporation.[182]

Despite these similarities, the two approaches have materially different goals. The nineteenth-century contractualists sought to protect a disaggregated economic system from the constraints of corporate hierarchies. The new economic theory abandons their goal even as it revives their concepts. The new theory accepts the management corporation and employs classical economic ideas—ideas originally derived from observation of a disaggregated economy—to justify its continuing presence.

This is a significant turn in the history of relations between corporate enterprise and American individualism. Before the turn of the century, individualists held to an atomistic social ideal and attacked all big organizations, public and private. Next came an uneasy coexistence, manifested in the neo-classicists' limited consideration of the firm. Finally, with the new economic theory, the heirs of the classical tradition surrender to the corporate hierarchy and embrace it. In so doing, the new theorists announce that corporate hierarchies had been composed of bilateral market contracts all along. But theirs is a different, more rearguard political action than that of their nineteenth-century predecessors. Today's contractualists limit their critique to the largest hierarchical institution, the government. To bolster opposition, they legitimize non-governmental institutions with a diluted version of the atomistic social ideal.[183]

To explain contract's long absence from academic theories of the corporate firm, we look to the appearance of power relationships in practice. Before the 1970s, legal academics and institutional economists emphasized hierarchies, while neo-classical economists turned a blind eye to the firm's interior, because contract, and particularly the discrete contract of academic contract law of this century's early decades,[184] did not seem to capture the institution's essence. The contracting process had a quiet dynamic; it did not appear actively to govern. Management seemed to be the catalyst that made the factors of production work successfully in the management corporation, and this catalytic capability stemmed from structural position. Management appeared to possess unilateral power—it directed production. The obvious complex of bilateral contracts in and around the firm failed to comprise the centre of gravity in the theory because they did not seem to affect the distribution of power in practice.

Had actors in the capital markets chosen to exercise a governance role, as they did during the middle period of the nineteenth century, the complex of contracts respecting stocks and bonds might have prompted formulation of a different, more contractual theory of the firm. Instead, a contractual event in practice—the implicit agreement between management and the financial community—kept investors and their stock and bond sales contracts from figuring actively in the power picture. Given this background, the anti-managerialists quite sensibly looked to public sources—the force of public opinion[185] or legal reform[108]—for controls on management discretion.

Recent practical changes, subsumed under the heading 'market for corporate control', have changed the corporate power picture. Stockholders and their contracts have taken a prominent place.[187] But the changes have not been sufficiently revolutionary to create a practice that mirrors the absolute contractualism held out by the new economic theory.

Anything being possible, the new theory's absolutist contractualism could find its way into corporate doctrine and effect a break with the historical pattern. But given past experience, such a fundamental change seems unlikely. In the past, theories that would close off the capacity of corporate law to facilitate transactions or their regulation have not made the transfer from commentary into doctrine. Single-minded adherence to the new economic theory is as out of touch with the values historically undergirding corporate law as some of the single-minded anti-managerialism of the 1970s was in its time.

To sum up, the doctrinal theory of the corporate firm refutes the assertion that the corporation 'is contract, and always has been contract and other things besides'. While the doctrinal theory always takes cognizance of contractual elements, it never makes contract the essence. The doctrinal theory balances contract against the corporate entity and a sovereign presence. If, as seems probable, corporate law continues to evolve in accordance with the historical pattern, decision-making will proceed with reference to the particulars of the corporate relationship in question. Selection of the applicable theoretical paradigm—managerialist or contractual—will occur in the particular context as a quasi-political decision. Contractual notions will be entertained, but any move to foreclose wider discussion by the assertion that contract should govern as a function of the intrinsic nature of the corporation will fail.

V. Contemporary history—the market for corporate control, the management corporation, and the new economic theory

The preceding discussion focused on recent changes in the theories describing power relationships in management corporations. Practical changes in these power relationships also have occurred recently. After 1960, corporate control became a more and more aggressively traded commodity. After 1980, trading became so extensive that it precipitated a widespread restructuring of management corporations.[188]

A substantial body of commentary connects these practical developments to the new economic theory. The commentators look to the new theory to explain the practice, and to the practice to prove or disprove the new theory's assertions. These connections tend to be ahistorical.

The following discussion connects the theory and the practice on a different level. It considers the practice, in history, as an explanation for the existence of the theory, and the theory, in history, as an explanation for changes in the practice.

A. The Early Market for Corporate Control and the Appearance of the New Economic Theory

As discussed in part IV, practical appearances of hierarchical power kept contract in a supporting role in corporate theory during most of this century. The market for corporate control has changed the practical picture materially. The hostile take-over makes it possible to remove corporate superiors by the exercise of stock market purchasing power. As take-overs have proliferated, changes have followed in the structure and internal affairs of management hierarchies. In effect, discrete contracts among stockholders take a significant place in the governance of the management corporation for the first time. The new economic theory parallels this practical change: it brings discrete contracting to a significant theoretical place in the governance of the management corporation for the first time. The histories of the theory and the practice invite interrelation.

Here is the proposition: the appearance of this aggressive mode of discrete contracting was necessary to make a contractual picture of the management corporation plausible. Although the new economic theory, particularly its neo-classical variant, tends to be stated ahistorically, its success, and possibly its very existence, meaningfully can be accounted for historically. Had the practical changes not occurred, the new theory probably never would have appeared, and it certainly would not have achieved general currency in the legal academy.[189] . . . .

The earliest hostile uses of the tender offer came in the 1950s, and this usage matured in the 1960s. . . . . Neo-classical observers saw the tie to their methodology right away. Henry Manne made the first theoretical assertion that the take-over phenomenon constituted market control of management conduct in an article published in 1965.[190] He introduced the phrase 'market for corporate control' and asserted that the market accorded shareholders practical power commensurate with their interests in the corporation.

Manne's neo-classical interpretation was not the only plausible view of the take-over phenomenon during the early period. Indeed, prior to 1980, Manne's probably was not the most widely accepted view. The early take-overs also fit into the institutional economists' picture. In their view, the take-over enhanced managerial power. The paradigm hostile take-over during the 1960s and 1970s was an aggressive act by the managers of a large corporation against the managers of a smaller corporation. This paradigm take-over was one of several means employed in building conglomerate corporations. Such take-overs served the managerialist growth objective. Although the managers of the losing target corporation lost their jobs, their removal came at the initiative of a more powerful, similarly situated group. Management's image of structural empowerment therefore remained in place even as some insecurity of tenure came into the picture.[191]

Williamson, writing in accord with this perspective, explained the appearance of take-overs after 1960 as a product of the spread of the multidivisional corporate structure. This new structure redirected management attention from running production lines to the collection of conglomerate portfolios of operating units. Take-overs then arose to facilitate portfolio construction.[192]

During the early take-over period, lawyers and legal academics, like most economists, continued to operate under the managerialist picture. Anti-managerialists viewed management growth by acquisition with suspicion. Most of this suspicion manifested itself in antitrust objections, but corporate law reasons for caution also existed. Anti-managerialists sought application of fiduciary duty concepts to restrain the conduct of management in defending against tender offers and to protect the interests of minority shareholders after take-over.[193] Furthermore, hostile take-overs tended to depress the price of the stock of the successful offeror, showing a market judgment that the take-overs aggrandized the managers of offeror corporations, and enriched target shareholders at the expense of the offeror's shareholders.[194]

B. The Contemporary Market for Corporate Control and the New Economic Theory

The new economic theory does not unequivocally support management interests. The theory's denial of hierarchy strengthens management's position, but only as long as it does not support any serious challenges to that position. During the 1980s, the market for corporate control created such challenges. Just as the new economic theory's contractualism supports management against statist challenges from the corporate governance movement, its contractualism also supports corporate control transactions against management objections.[195]

In the more aggressive market for corporate control that appeared after 1980, almost all corporations became potential subjects for attack. Trading extended to corporate reconstruction as well as corporate control. Even middle management began to suffer. In this new cast, the take-over challenged not only management's security of position, but also its discretionary power.

New actors and financing devices carried the market to this more aggressive posture. Independent financial entrepreneurs entered the market as hostile offerors.[196] The new entrepreneurs played a different game. Unlike the conglomerate-building managers of the earlier period, they did not use the devices of the corporate control market to enhance operational power positions. They simply sought to force large payments to equity holders.

Funds for the big premiums came through aggressive use of the oldest financing tool, debt. The target's assets supplied the borrowing base. Once target-based debt financing became a critical component in a tender offer's success, a structural position atop a corporate hierarchy ceased to be a prerequisite for participation in the market. An actor taking an aggressive posture needed only credibility in the capital markets. . . . .

Although the full implications of this corporate restructuring remain unclear, a few generalizations can be made. The restructurings materially alter the old managerialist picture of structural empowerment. First, their quantity, scope, and frequency has made management tenure generally insecure. Second, the long-standing implicit agreement between management and capital has dissolved. The investment community no longer passively accepts the growth objective. Thus, restructurings may be viewed as the capital markets' successful demand for the return of capital suboptimally invested in pursuit of growth.[197] By forcing the return of this capital, the investment community indirectly, but strongly, influences the shaping of investment policy. Because investment policy is the central discretionary function of the multidivisional corporate management group, capital's refusal to comply and co-operate denudes management of significant power.

For the first time since the brief appearance of finance capitalism in the nineteenth century,[198] then, actors in the capital markets critically influence investment policy. Capital's perspective still tends toward the short term. As a result, conflicts between the short- and long-term investment perspectives of investors and managers have become a problem once again.[199] Legal policy discussions have adjusted in response. Emphasis has shifted from management's abuse of power acquired by structural default, to management's inability to invest with a long view because of capital's power to terminate management at will.[200]

The restructurings also require conforming adjustments in the existing body of work under the new economic theory. The institutionalists explained the conglomerate corporation as a product of a contracting process driven by the competitive need to decrease costs.[201] The restructuring undo conglomerate combinations, eliminating layers of multidivisional form diversification and firing layers of management staff.[202] In effect, the financial community repudiates the proposition that conglomerates are cost effective.

The neo-classical model[203] also must be adjusted.[204] The model assumed that contracting actors adopted structures capable of bringing agency costs down to a competitive minimum. It then explained existing arrangements, including the relative passivity of the capital markets and the dominance of management, in those terms. When historical forces suddenly and materially rewrote the contacts, doubts arose about the validity of this ahistorical picture, and of the methodology that created it.

The restructurings manifest the capital markets judgment that previous market arrangements did not effectively minimize management agency costs. In response, Jensen has modified his picture of the firm to explain the massive replacement of equity by debt in terms of an efficient contracting device: management borrows at a high fixed rate to 'bond' its future performance.[205] But, as Coffee has pointed out, this prospective and ahistorical adjustment does not erase the model's previous failure to accommodate history.[206]

Despite these difficulties with particulars, the new economic theory may be connected with the appearance of the market for corporate reconstruction. To see the connection one must take a broad view. The new theory's contractual perspective assumes that people look closely and act firmly when money is at stake. It depicts a corporate structure in which rational investors work hard to circumvent managerial claims to non-reviewability due to differential expertise.[207] This approach consigns management to a reduced status.

The neo-classical picture contains additional, strong negative implications for management. The theory's minimal firm entity removes management from its former position as the essence of the firm. Management emerges in the picture as but one of many factors of production.[208] In the neo-classical world of discrete contracts, factors of production come and go as contracts continually are made, performed, and remade, or are made and broken. No relational values afford management a defence against attack by investors seeking to rewrite the next generation of contracts. No entity notions, no notion of professionalism, and no sense of the necessity of tenure protection enter into the picture.

Even the institutional variant implicitly recognizes managerial vulnerability. Its description of multidivisional structure demystifies the management process. Hands-on production skills no longer figure into management's strategic position. The multidivisional architect of a portfolio of operating divisions has no skills not possessed in rudimentary form by the latest crop of business school graduates. Like the neo-classicists' factors of production, the institutionalists' portfolio manager is replaceable in the active search for a higher return.[209]

Thus, the market practice of corporate restructuring generated by contract—sales of stock on or off the trading markets, and arms-length debt contracts[210]—demonstrates the theory's dynamic, if not every point of the extant models. The market practice follows the theory in time: in the 1970s, the theory asserted that the managerialist picture of unilateral power was inaccurate; in the 1980s, the market-place changed the picture and used the theory's primary tool, the discrete, bilateral contract, as the means of shifting power. Today's popular conception of the powerful business figure is not the managerialist chief executive officer but the capitalist deal maker—the financial entrepreneur or the investment banker.[211] Characterized in the vocabulary of the new economic theory, these figures acquire power as transaction cost engineers. They conceive and initiate transactions, depriving the managerial beneficiaries of the more costly existing contracts of power and wealth. . . . .

Even so, the new economic theory has a place in all this. The restructuring take-over has met little effective opposition,[212] and any number of legislative moves might have deterred it.[213] The theory persuasively manifests the wider anti-regulatory and contractualist environment in a respectable academic form specific to the context. The neo-classical variant, with its roots in classical economic theory, comes particularly well made to support money-making by independent entrepreneurs well made to support money-making by independent entrepreneurs through bilateral contracting.

Significantly, corporate legal doctrine performs a similar legitimizing role. The doctrine, despite its close association with managerialism throughout this century, has accommodated the resurgent capitalists without significant alteration. The received structure incorporates bilateral contracting and aggregate interests. The doctrine made available all of the contractual devices employed in the restructuring market, and the long-standing conceptual association of management and the corporate entity did not prevent their use.[214] Even as the restructuring take-over brought the continued validity of reams of managerialist literature into question, it left the doctrine nearly untouched.[215] The historical doctrinal theory of the firm and its facilitative and capacious qualities come to mind, providing the new economic theory with a 'place' in the legitimization of the recent restructuring.

C. Comments

The restructuring take-over does not return us to the world of Adam Smith. The number of managerial personnel may have declined; their identities may have changed; and conglomerate corporations may have become less bloated. But they still exist. Management retains a position of 'power by default'. Its basic operational authority over resources and people in the organization remains largely intact.[216] Restructuring take-overs do not threaten the hierarchy; they only replace one set of managers with another. And aside from single rounds of cost cutting, no creative interplay between the restructuring take-over and the production operations of the firm has appeared.

Assume that a chastened and more heavily monitored management emerges with its position otherwise left intact. It can, ironically, turn to contractualism to reconstruct a theory of the firm protective of its position. Legal theory offers more than one model of contract. Theories more relational than that employed by the neo-classical new theorists offer values protective of individuals who invest their labour and energies in business enterprises, including firms.[217]

Conclusion

This article's historical perspectives do not deny the legitimacy of the new economic theory's approach to corporations. Nor do these perspectives deny that contract holds a constitutive place in firm life or that the new economic theory isolates significant aspects of corporate relationships. By contextualizing this theory of the firm discourse in time, however, these perspectives do facilitate a more accurate appraisal of the new economic theory's contribution. The history prompts doubts as to the theorists' extreme essentialist claims: their new corporate contract becomes hard to accept either as an evolutionary climax or as an objectively correct edifice standing outside of time. Instead, the theory appears as an edifice partly built on enduring ontology, partly prompted by recent, perhaps transitory, trends in corporate practice, and partly shaped by the theorists' political dispositions.

These historical perspectives, it should be noted, do not support discrimination among theories of the firm. They do not single out the new economic theory for critical questioning. Instead, they counsel wariness of essentialist claims made for *any* academic theory of the firm. The history shows us that the pairs of opposing concepts that make up theories of the firm—entity and aggregate, contract and concession, public and private, discrete contract and relational contract—endure in opposition over time. Academic firm theories and corporate legal doctrine tend to handle these internal conflicts differently. Doctrinal firm theory lacks analytical integrity; the opposing concepts are synchronized as decision-makers make normative responses to unfolding events in business practice. If recognition of one of these contradictions results in analytical paralysis in a specific case, the doctrinalists deny the contradiction, mentioning one side only. Despite this lack of integrity, the doctrinal theory works well as it operates at close quarters with economic practice. Rather than trying to privilege one or another contradictory element, it builds the contradictions into a capacious structure that loosely contains real-world producing organizations. This legal structure accommodates economic change easily.

Practice also drives academic firm theory. But in an academic context, a theory that follows the doctrine and merely synchronizes contradictions in particular situations probably falls short of prevailing standards. Academics, free of the immediate problem of deciding cases, try to achieve analytical consistency; they attempt to transcend the contradictions. Academic theory of the firm, created in pursuit of this objective, has a more volatile, evolutionary pattern than does doctrinal theory. One tends to have to overstate things in order to achieve consistency and at the same time remain in touch with practice in a complex world. Wariness therefore is appropriate in considering new academic theories that purport to explain existing doctrine and at the same time satisfy academic standards. Such theories may have more reconstructive potential than their progenitors admit.

The new economic theory falls into this historical pattern of academic/doctrinal interplay. Introduced in the law as a critical supplement to managerialist theory, it succeeded because it recognized discrete contract as a constitutive part of firms. The recent appearance of discrete contract as an important corporate power tool made the theory especially welcome: it brought academic theory closer both to business practice and to legal doctrine. But the theorists, driven by the academic need to universalize, outstripped this ontological base by privileging narrow notions of contract.

Pressure builds up as the new theory's paradigm approaches hegemony in legal academic discussion. Some structure of thought will have to change. Two possible scenarios present themselves. Under one, the doctrine is reconstructed. The theory's influence causes the doctrine to be reformulated to eradicate strains that contradict the theory. Under the other scenario, the theory adapts. The contract paradigm expands to encompass the range of conflicting firm components. Given the history, the second scenario seems the more likely to occur. Doctrinal reconstruction tends to occur in response to practical, not theoretical, developments, legitimizing or inhibiting them as the case to reconstitute it as a means to the end of recognition of the latest academic theory.

Notes

1. Economic theories of the firm concern all producing units, no matter how organized. Legal theories of the firm, in contrast, tend to focus on the corporation.
2. See nn. 17–20 *infra* and accompanying text.
3. The theory's proponents refer to it as the 'modern' theory of the firm. I use 'new' theory of the firm for two reasons. First, as this article's historical exposition demonstrates, the ideas constituting the theory are not modern. However, the particular configuration is new both to microeconomics and to corporate law. Second, at least one opponent of the new economic theory claims the mantle of modernity for corporate law reform proposals criticized by proponents of the new economic theory. See Melvin Aron Eisenberg, 'New Modes of Discourse in the Corporate Law Literature', 52 *Geo. Wash. L. Rev.* 582, 582 (1984).
4. Michael C. Jensen and William H. Meckling, 'Theory of the Firm: Managerial Behavior, Agency Costs and Ownership Structure', 3 *J. Fin. Econ.* 305, 310 (1976). For literal restatements of this in the legal literature, see, for example, Robert Hessen, 'A New Concept of Corporations: A Contractual and Private Property Model', 30 *Hastings LJ* 1327, 1330 (1979); Reinier H. Kraakman, 'Corporate Liability Strategies and the Costs of Legal Controls', 93 *Yale LJ* 857, 862 (1984); Kenneth E. Scott, 'Corporation Law and the American Law Institute Corporate Governance Project', 35 *Stan. L. Rev.* 927, 930 0(1983).
5. For a survey, see text accompanying n. 21–5 *infra*.
6. See n. 21 *infra*.
7. A recent round of discussion on take-overs demonstrates this, assuming contractualism without applying the theory formally. See Jeffrey N. Gordon and Lewis A. Kornhauser, 'Takeover Defense Tactics: A Comment on Two Models', 96 *Yale LJ* 295 (1986); Jonathan R. Macey and Fred S. McChesney, *A Theoretical Analysis of Corporate Greenmail*, 95 *Yale LJ* 13 (1985).
8. Michael C. Jensen, 'Organization Theory and Methodology', 58 *Acct. Rev.* 319, 324 (1983). Professor Jensen is one of the originators and masters of the new theory.
9. Judge Ralph Winter attacks the American Law Institute Corporate Governance Project because the new economic theory, a 'large body of reputable academic opinion in major law schools', is 'astonishingly unrepresented' among its drafters. Ralph K. Winter, Jr., 'The Development of the Law of Corporate Governance', 9 *Del. J. Corp. L.* 524, 528–29 (1984).
10. Bruce A. Ackerman, *Reconstructing American Law* (1984), 62. Ackerman's 'activist' seeks to use the law 'to design a better form of accommodation between competing activities than the one thrown up by the invisible hand.' Ibid. at 31. Ackerman's statist perspective contrasts sharply with the anti-statism that prevails throughout the economic literature of the new theory of the firm. See text accompanying n. 16 *infra*.

11. History rarely tends to be pursued in corporate law contexts. Usually this has no ill effect, since lack of historical perspective only trivially impairs discussions of the latest technical regulatory problems. As the context of discussion becomes wider, however, relentlessly ahistorical perspectives become limiting and damaging.

12. Historical information is particularly useful in the evaluation of the new economic theory. Many of the theory's basic conceptual elements—for example, classical economic assumptions, political individualism, and anti-positivism— have figured into past legal theories of the firm.

13. I employ the phrase 'management corporation' rather than 'public corporation' to describe large mass-producing corporations and other large corporate entities, the shares of which are widely held.

14. Morton J. Horwitz, 'Santa Clara Revisited: The Developments of Corporate Theory', 88 *W. Va. L. Rev.* 173, 176 (1985).

15. Traditional legal theories of the corporation were a recognizable category of jurisprudence and a focal point of legal theory until around 1930. See text accompanying notes 81–92 *infra*.

16. See William W. Bratton, 'The "Nexus of Contracts" Corporation: A Critical Appraisal', 74 *Cornell L. Rev.* 407 (1989).

17. See text accompanying nn. 103–9 *infra*.

18. For a further discussion, see Bratton, *supra* n. 16.

19. For exemplars of this picture, see Adolf A. Berle, Jr., *The 20th Century Capitalist Revolution* 32–9 (1954); Ralph Nader, Mark Green and Joel Seligman, *Taming the Giant Corporation* 62–5 (1976).

20. See Gerald E. Frug, 'The Ideology of Bureaucracy in American Law', 97 *Harv. L. Rev.* 1276, 1328–34 (1984).

    Berle worked both sides of the fence. While anti-managerialist, he eventually conceded that public opinion effectively controlled management and optimistically preached responsibility to the managerial audience. See A. Berle, *supra* n. 19, at 35–7, 54.

21. See e.g. Barry D. Baysinger and Henry N. Butler, 'Revolution Versus Evolution in Corporation Law: The ALI's Project and the Independent Director', 52 *Geo. Wash. L. Rev.* 557 (1984); Lucian Arye Benchuk, 'Limiting Contractual Freedom in Corporate Law: The Desirable Constraints on Charter Amendments', 102 *Harv. L. Rev.* 1820 (1989); Frank H. Easterbrook and Daniel R. Fischel, 'Close Corporations and Agency Costs', 38 *Stan. L. Rev.* 271 (1986); Frank H. Easterbrook and Daniel R. Fischel, 'Limited Liability and the Corporation', 42 *U. Chi. L. Rev.* 89 (1985); Frank H. Easterbrook and Daniel R. Fischel, 'Voting on Corporate Law', 26 *JL & Econ.* 395 (1983); Frank H. Easterbrook and Daniel R. Fischel, 'Corporate Control Transactions', 91 *Yale LJ* 698 (1982); Daniel R. Fischel, 'The Appraisal Remedy in Corporate Law', 1983 *Am. B. Found. Res. J.* 875; Daniel R. Fischel, 'The Corporate Governance Movement', 35 *Vand. L. Rev.* 1259 (1982); Ronald J. Gilson,

'Evaluating Dual Class Common Stock: The Relevance of Substitutes', 73 *Va. L. Rev.* 807, 808–11 (1987); Kraakman, *supra* n. 4; Saul Levmore, 'Monitors and Freeriders in Commercial and Corporate Settings', 92 *Yale LJ* 49 (1982); Jonathan R. Macey, 'From Fairness to Contract: The New Direction of the Rules against Insider Trading', 13 *Hofstra L. Rev.* 9, 39–47 (1984); Scott, *supra* n. 4.

Critical commentaries have appeared. See Victor Brudney, 'Corporate Governance, Agency Costs, and the Rhetoric of Contract', 85 *Colum. L. Rev.* 1403 (1985); Richard M. Buxbaum, 'Corporate Legitimacy, Economic Theory, and Legal Doctrine', 45 *Ohio St. LJ* 515 (1984); Robert C. Clark, 'Agency Costs Versus Fiduciary Duties', in *Principals and Agents: The Structure of Business* 55 (J. Pratt and R. Zeckhauser eds. 1985); Deborah A. DeMott, 'Beyond Metaphor: An Analysis of Fiduciary Obligation', 1988 *Duke LJ* 879.

22. See Ronald H. Coase, 'The Nature of the Firm', 4 *Economica* 386, 390–4 (1937) (reprinted in *Readings in Price Theory* 331, 336–9 (G. Stigler and K. Boulding eds. 1952)).

23. Coase reflected in 1972 that his 1937 essay was 'much cited but little used'. Ronald H. Coase, 'Industrial Organization: A Proposal for Research', 3 *Economic Research: Retrospect and Prospect* 59, 62–63 (V. Fuchs ed. 1972); see also Ronald H. Coast, 'The Nature of the Firm: Meaning', 4 *JL Econ. & Org.* 19, 23 (1988).

   Other early work came from Oliver Williamson. See Oliver E. Williamson, 'Managerial Discretion and Business Behaviour', 53 *Am. Econ. Rev.* 1032 (1963).

24. Armen A. Alchian and Harold Demsetz, 'Production, Information Costs, and Economic Organization', 62 *Am. Econ. Rev.* 777 (1972).

25. Jensen and Meckling, *supra* n. 4. An important contemporaneous work was Oliver E. Williamson, *Markets and Hierarchies: Analysis and Antitrust Implications* (1975). Other early works include Kenneth J. Arrow, *The Limits of Organization* (1974); Vernon L. Smith, 'Economic Theory and its Discontents', 64 *Am. Econ. Rev.* 320 (1974).

   Anti-managerialists dominated legal discourse during these years. For example, see William L. Cary, 'Federalism and Corporate Law: Reflections upon Delaware', 83 *Yale LJ* 663 (1974).

26. For a further discussion, see Bratton, *supra* n. 6.

27. This formulation draws on the original language of Jensen and Meckling, *supra* n. 4, at 310; see also Eugene F. Fama and Michael C. Jensen, 'Separation of Ownership and Control', 26 *JL & Econ.* 301, 302 (1983); Jensen, *supra* n. 8, at 326. In the legal literature, see e.g. Fischel, 'The Corporate Governance Movement', *supra* n. 21 , at 1261–2; Scott, *supra* n. 4, at 930.

28. See Alchian and Demsetz, *supra* n. 24, at 777; see also ibid. at 794. In another essay, Demsetz admits that there are some people who derive utility from coercive relationships, but he cites only bullies and rapists as exemplars of the type. Harold Demsetz, 'Professor Michelman's Unnecessary and Futile

Search for the Philosopher's Touchstone', in 24 *Nomos: Ethics, Economics and the Law* 41, 44 (1982).

29. Eugene F. Fama, 'Agency Problems and the Theory of the Firm', 88 *J. Pol. Econ.* 288, 289 (1980).

30. See Jensen, *supra* n. 8, at 331; William H. Meckling, 'Values and the Choice of Method in the Social Sciences', 112 *Schweizerische Zeitschrift fuer Volkwirtschaft und Statistik* 545, 548–9 (176).

31. See Jensen, *supra* n. 8, at 327.

32. See Ian R. Macneil, 'Economic Analysis of Contractual Relations: Its Shortfalls and the Need for a "Rich Classificatory Apparatus"', 75 *Nw. U.L. Rev.* 1018, 1022–3, 1039–40 (1981).

33. Jensen, *supra* n. 8, at 322, 327.

34. See e.g. Jensen, *supra* n. 8, at 331; Fama and Jensen, *supra* n. 27, at 301.

35. In the Jensen and Meckling model, the public sale is a secondary offering by the management group. In more complex, real world situations, the incentive is less intense.

36. This story, see Jensen and Meckling, *supra* n. 4, at 314, has been often repeated in the law reviews. See e.g. Fischel, 'The Corporate Governance Movement', *supra* n. 21, at 1262–5.

    Preceding Jensen and Meckling, Alchian and Demsetz, *supra* n. 24, also explained corporate structure in terms of agency costs. But it painted a somewhat different picture. Jensen and Meckling took a governance perspective. They built their model around a hypothetical close corporation situation in which an owner management group sells equity to outsiders. Alchian and Demsetz emphasized the production process, focusing on shirking problems among individuals on production teams. The existence of management groups is explained as a function of shirking by input factors. Monitors (managers) must be accorded power to observe, but further arrangements are necessary since managers themselves will shirk. Residual income shares reduce this incentive. See Alchian and Demsetz, *supra* n. 24, at 781–2, 787–8.

    Jensen and Meckling criticized this picture as too narrowly focused. See Jensen and Meckling, *supra* n. 4, at 310. Interestingly, the Alchian and Demsetz picture has been repeated in eclectic law review commentary subsequent to the Jensen and Meckling repudiation of it. See Scott, *supra* n. 4, at 930–1; Ralph K. Winter, Jr., 'State Law, Shareholder Protection, and the Theory of the Corporation', 6 *J. Legal Std.* 251, 272–3 (1977).

37. For the suggestion that management labour markets provide the primary discipline, see Fama, *supra* n. 29, at 293–5. This is disputed in Benjamin Klein, 'Contracting Costs and Residual Claims: The Separation of Ownership and Control', 26 *JL & Econ.* 367, 368 (1983), which takes the position that wage discounts cannot be taken into account in wage contracts *ex ante*. For criticism of Fama's point that junior managers can be expected to monitor senior managers, see Eisenberg, *supra* n. 3, at 584.

38. See Fama and Jensen, *supra* n. 27, at 302–5.

39. Klein, *supra* n. 37, at 370.

40. See Macneil, *supra* n. 32, at 1022–3.

41. See Oliver E. Williamson, 'The Modern Corporation: Origins, Evolution, Attributes', 19 *J. Econ. Lit.* 1537 (1981). Williamson sees the distinction between the firm and the market as a matter of degree. See Oliver E. Williamson, 'Intellectual Foundations: The Need for a Broader View', 33 *J. Legal Educ.* 210, 214 (1983).

42. See Williamson, 'The Modern Corporation: Origins, Evolution, Attributes', *supra* n. 41, at 1544–5 (using 'opportunism' for 'opportunistic conduct').

43. See Macneil, *supra* n. 32, at 1043.

44. Benjamin Klein, Robert G. Crawford and Armen A. Alchian, 'Vertical Integration, Appropriable Rents, and the Competitive Contracting Process', 21 *JL & Econ.* 297, 298, 307–24 (1978), gives nice examples of firm-specific investments and transaction structures. For an analysis of corporate organization in terms of firm-specific investment, bounded rationality, and opportunistic conduct, see Oliver E. Williamson, 'Corporate Governance', 93 *Yale LJ* 1197 (1984).

45. See Williamson, 'The Modern Corporation: Origins, Evolution, Attributes', *supra* n. 41, at 1547–8.

46. O. Williamson, *supra* n. 25, at 256–7.

47. Ibid. at 30–40.

48. See Oliver Williamson, 'Organization Form, Residual Claimants and Corporate Control', 26 *JL & Econ.* 351, 361 (1983).

49. For a recent statement of a general theory, see Meir Dan-Cohen, *Rights, Persons and Organizations: A Legal Theory for a Bureaucratic Society* (1986).

50. Allen Kaufman and L. S. Zacharias 'The Problem of the Corporation and the Evolution of Social Values' (1987) (Management Research Center Working Paper, Univ. of Mass. School of Management, Amherst, Mass.) (on file with the *Stanford Law Review*), casts the history of theories of the firm in the framework of nineteenth-century ideological dualism, an approach currently popular among historians. 'Civic republicanism', on the one hand, was egalitarian and stressed personal development. It viewed property as a prerequisite for developing the moral character of the citizen and for establishing the market as a meeting-place for independent producers. Large corporations disrupted the civic republicans' economic assumption of widespread individual property ownership. 'Liberalism', on the other hand, viewed property as an instrument for individual prosperity and property rights as a means of individual protection against the outside world. The corporation challenged the liberals' assumption of private, individual market competition. Ibid. at 5–8.

51. This was true at least once the Jeffersonian and Jacksonian adherent of classical, political economy eliminated Federalist mercantilist policies. See Herbert

Hovenkamp, 'The Classical Corporation in American Legal Thought', 76 *Geo. LJ* 1593, 1605–12 (1988).

52. See Peter Temin, *The Jacksonian Economy* 177 (1969) (the American economy in the 1830s 'functioned to a large extent in the fashion described by what we now call classical economic theory'); Alfred D. Chandler, Jr., *The Visible Hand: The Managerial Revolution in American Business* 15–28 (1977).

53. See James Willard Hurst, *The Legitimacy of the Business Corporation in the Law of the United States 1780–1970*, at 82 (1970).

54. Adolf A. Berle, Jr., 'Coherency and the Social Sciences', in *People, Power and Politics* 6, 10 (L.J. Gould and E. W. Steele eds. 1961); cf. A. Berle, *supra* n. 19, at 34–5 (property rights remained unchanged while corporations aggregated the power to plan the course of the economy).

55. J. Hurst, *supra* n. 53, at 7–8.

56. See John Dewey, 'The Historic Background of Corporate Legal Personality', 35 *Yale LJ* 655, 667–78 (1926); Paul Vinogradoff, 'Juridical Persons', 24 *Colum. L. Rev.* 594, 601 (1924).

57. Arthur J. Jacobson, 'The Private Use of Public Authority: Sovereignty and Associations in the Common Law', 29 *Buffalo L. Rev.* 599, 662–3 (1980).

58. Horwitz, *supra* n. 14, at 181.

59. Chief Justice Marshall's opinion in the most famous corporate law case of the early period demonstrates this. The *Dartmouth College* case held that a 'corporation is an artificial being, invisible, intangible, and existing only in contemplation of law'. *Trustees of Dartmouth Collage* v. *Woodward*, 17 US (4 Wheat.) 518, 636 (1819).

   The charters themselves were viewed as contracts and not as equivalent to statutes. See Adolph A. Berle and Gardiner C. Means, *The Modern Corporation and Private Property* 121 (rev. edn. 1968).

60. Oscar Handlin and Mary F. Handlin, 'Origins of the American Business Corporation', in *Public Policy and the Modern Corporation* 3, 7, 23–4 (D. Grunewald and H. Bass eds. 1966).

61. J. Hurst, *supra* n. 53, at 25 (stating that this 'armed' management for 'vigorous maneuver').

62. See Robert Charles Clark, 'The Four Stages of Capitalism: Reflections on Investment Management Treatises', 94 *Harv. L. Rev.* 561, 562 (1981).

63. The corporate form ceased to be associated with 'public interest' enterprises. The new corporations were industrial concerns, and the pace of industrial incorporation increased significantly after 1870. Peter George, *The Emergence of Industrial America* 79 (1982); see also A. Chandler, *supra* n. 52, at 2345–9, 240–7 (discussing the appearance of mass distribution systems and factory system, and the disappearance of the putting-out system).

64. A. Chandler, *supra* n. 52, at 237–8.

65. J. Hurst, *supra* n. 53, at 37, 55–7, 69; see Gregory A. Mark, 'The Personification of the Business Corporation in American Law', 54 *U. Chi. L.*

Rev. 1441, 1455 (1987) (student author) ('The transformation of the private law of corporations from 1819 to the 1920s is best described as a move from a circumstance in which a corporation could do only those things specifically allowed by its charter to one in which a corporation could do anything not specifically prohibited by it.').

66. J. Hurst, *supra* n. 53, at 43, 48.
67. This pattern emerged after 1890.
68. See A. Chandler, *supra* n. 52, at 87, 120, 148; J. Hurst, *supra* n. 53, at 82.
69. See J. Hurst, *supra* n. 53, at 45, 55–7; Robert S. Stevens, *Handbook on the Law of Private Corporations* 224–7, 331–5 (2nd edn. 1949) (summarizing *ultra vires* doctrine); Horwitz, *supra* n. 14, at 186–8.
70. J. Hurst, *supra* n. 53, at 37, 45, 55–7. Corporate doctrine did facilitate some self-protection by stockholders through proportional voting rules and proportional rights to subscribe to new issues of stock. On the other hand, mismanagement was not actionable without a showing of gross negligence. Ibid. at 49. Although a corporate law of investor protection developed during this period, its beneficiaries were corporate creditors.
71. Means uses the term 'collective capitalism'. See Gardiner C. Means, *The Corporate Revolution in America* 50–1 (1962). I use 'management corporation' to avoid the particular political implications of Means's phrase.
72. A. Chandler, *supra* n. 52, at 14, 285–6.
73. Michael J. Piore and Charles F. Sabel, *The Second Industrial Divide* 72 (1984).

    Between 1899 and 1929, the population rose 62%, while industrial production rose 295% and power production rose 331%. In 1929, per capita production was 60% higher than in 1900. Robert Sobel, *The Age of Giant Corporations* 52–3 (2nd edn. 1984).

    The first great integrated enterprises appeared in the 1880s and 1890s. Firms consolidated manufacturing into larger plants and expanded into operations other than production, including marketing, distribution, and raw materials procurement. See P. George, *supra* n. 63, at 82. The result of their success was the decline of the older form of small, self-sufficient economic unit during the first decades of the twentieth century. R. Sobel, *supra* at 52–75.

    The desire for monopoly profits was a principal motivation for integration and combination during the 1890s, but other factors figured in. The formation of United States Steel, for example, also served the need for sources of raw materials—due to the increased size of plants—and the promoters' desire to reap profits in the financial markets. See Peter Temin, *Iron and Steel in Nineteenth-Century America* 190–3 (1964).

74. This is the famous point of A. Berle and G. Means, *supra* n. 59.
75. For the view that the management corporation need not dominate production in the future, see M. Piore and C. Sabel, *supra* n. 73.
76. Macneil originated the term 'bilateral power'. It is the possibility of an exchange whereby two persons release one another from some of the

restraints imposed by their respective unilateral powers. He defines unilateral power as any capacity a person has to subject another to some particular effect without the other's consent. Macneil, *supra* n. 32, at 1036.

77. See M. Piore and C. Sabel, *supra* n. 73, at 22–3.

78. A. Chandler, *supra* n. 52, at 6–8.

79. M. Piore and C. Sabel, *supra* n. 73, at 49–51.

80. See Robert Charles Clark, *Corporate Law*, 160–6 (1986); Howard Marsh, Jr., 'Are Directors Trustees? Conflict of Interest and Corporate Morality', 22 *Bus. Law*, 35, 39–40 (1966) (strict rules dropped by 1910).

81. See Charles Fisk Beach, *The Law of Private Corporations* 1–4 (1891); Victor Morawetz, *Private Corporations* 1–2 (2nd edn. 1886); Henry O. Taylor, *A Treatise on the Law of Private Corporations* iv (1884).

82. See Horwitz, *supra* n. 14, at 183, 204–5. A suit based on the contractual conception was brought against the Standard Oil Trust in *State* v. *Standard Oil Co.*, 49 Ohio St. 137, 30 NE 279 (1892).

83. *Santa Clara Country* v. *Southern Pac. R.R.*, 118 US 394 (1886). The court looked through the entity to the individual interests at stake and found something protectible. This is Professor Horwitz's thesis. He makes the case persuasively. See Horwitz, *supra* n. 14, at 173, 178; see also Mark, *supra* n. 65, at 1463.

84. Otto Gierke, *Das Deutsche Genossenschaftsrecht* (1887). Maitland advanced Gierke's ideas in the English-speaking world. See Otto Gierke, *Political Theory of the Middle Age* x–xlv (F. W. Maitland trans. 1900) (introduction by Maitland). For a summary, see Frederick Hallis, *Corporate Personality* 137–65 (1930); see also Mark, *supra* n. 65, at 1468–9.

85. Ernst Freund, *The Legal Nature of Corporations* (1884).

86. Horwitz, *supra* n. 14, at 176, 224; Mark, *supra* n. 65, at 1470.

87. Where, for a century, market competition and property law had legitimized power in individual hands, now management performance legitimized power in corporate organizations. J. Hurst, *supra* n. 53, at 59, 62, 70, 82.

88. See Mark, *supra* n. 65, at 1464–5. They survived as a restraining influence only in antitrust law.

89. See George F. Deiser, 'The Juristic Person' (pts. 1–3), 57, *U. Pa. L. Rev.* 131, 216, 300 (1908–9) (realist); Harold J. Laski, 'The Personality of Associations', 29 *Harv. L. Rev.* 404 (1916) (realist); Arthur W. Machen, Jr., 'Corporate Personality' (pts. 1–2), 24 *Harv. L. Rev.* 253, 347 (1911) (realist); George F. Canfield, 'The Scope and Limits of the Corporate Entity Theory', 17 *Colum. L. Rev.* 128 (1917) (strong entity approach); Wesley Newcomb Hohfeld, 'The Individual Liability of Stockholders and the Conflict of Laws', 10 *Colum. L. Rev.* 283 (1910) (anti-reality); Wesley Newcomb Hohfeld, 'Nature of Stockholders' Individual Liability for Corporation Debts', 9 *Colum. L. Rev.* 285 (1909) (anti-realist).

90. Dewey, *supra* n. 56; see also Morris Raphael Cohen, *Reason and Nature* 386–92 (Free Press ed. 1964); Max Radin, 'The Endless Problem of Corporate Personality', 32 *Col. L. Rev.* 643(1932); Vinogradoff, *supra* n. 56.

91. But see Sigmund Timberg, 'Corporate Fictions: Logical, Social and International Implications', 46 *Colum. L. Rev.* 533 (1946).

92. Dewey, *supra* n. 56, at 669–70 ('Each theory has been used to serve the same ends, and each has been used to serve opposing ends. . . . Unfortunately, the human mind tends toward fusion rather than discrimination, and the result is confusion.').

93. Horwitz, *supra* n. 14.

94. Ibid. at 224.

95. Ibid. at 176. 'In the jargon of the current Critical Legal Studies debate', Horwitz denies the infinite 'flippability' of legal concepts; he ascribed them 'tilt' in determining outcomes. Ibid.

    For a similar, but more cautiously stated view of the influence of corporate realism, see Mark, *supra* n. 65, at 1478.

96. See text accompanying nn. 173–7 *infra*.

97. The central office of United States Steel, a complex of many firms that merged over a short period in the late 1890s, did little more than collect accounting information for the company's first decade. Central office expansion occurred after 1910. P. Temi, *supra* n. 73, at 192.

98. A. Chandler, *supra* n. 53, at 462–3, 482. The new general executive had a beneficial psychological commitment to the enterprise as a whole. Ibid. at 463.

99. Williamson explains these developments with a cost efficiency model: Multidivisional structure facilitated strategic planning with a larger information set and better control and monitoring of operating units. The result was the direction of cash flows to higher yielding uses. The corporation thus internalized functions formerly performed by the capital market. Williamson, 'The Modern Corporation: Origins, Evolution, Attributes', *supra* n. 41, at 1556. Once again we can turn to Piore and Sabel for a contrasting view focused on production operations rather than management costs. They see the direction of management energies to the building of portfolios of operating companies after World War II as a symptom of larger macroeconomic problems. Massproducing corporations saturated their own markets without developing new products and new markets. Their risks increased as a result; diversification through conglomeration reduced the risk. M. Piore and C. Sabel, *supra* n. 73, at 194–7.

100. Widespread public purchases of shares provided the heavy capitalization required by the new firms that appeared at the turn of the century. P. Temin, *supra* n. 73, at 193.

101. A. Berle, *supra* n. 19, at 35, 54.

102. See J. A. Livingston, *The American Stockholder* 60–1, 66–7 (1958).

103. See text accompanying notes 90–2 *supra*.

104. A. Berle and G. Means, *supra* n. 59.

105. See ibid. at 245–50. For a discussion of the implications of this contractual side of Berle and Means, see Kaufman and Zacharias, *supra* n. 50, at 20.

106. A. Berle and G. Means, *supra* n. 59, at 255–90.

107. Berle and Means thus combined a contractual conception of the corporation with a Weberian bureaucratic conception: corporations in part were management controlled bureaucratic entities vested with power by positive law, and in part were the contractual arrangements of economic actors. See M. Dan-Cohen, *supra* n. 49, at 17–20.

108. Means, for example, promoted a new theory of the firm, a thickly textured analysis of the 'corporate collective', bringing to bear actual economic, political, psychological, and anthropological observations. G. Means, *supra* n. 71, at 63.

109. I use the term 'managerialist conception' broadly to encompass entity conceptions of the management corporation in which management occupies a position of structural power. A narrower usage denotes a subcategory of theory in which managers function as neutral technocrats, balancing the conflicting interests of groups connected to the firm. See Masahiko Aoki, *The Co-operative Game Theory of the Firm* 34–7 (1984).

110. Thorstein Veblen was the most prominent predecessor. See Thorstein Veblen, *Absentee Ownership* (1923); Thorstein Veblen, *The Theory of Business Enterprise* (1904). For a review of the thinking about management prior to Berle and Means, see Edward S. Herman, *Corporate Control, Corporate Power* 5–9 (1981).

111. A. Berle and G. Means, *supra* n. 59, at 299–308; see also G. Means, *supra* n. 71, at 16.

112. G. Means, *supra* n. 71, at 171.

113. William J. Baumol, 'On the Theory of the Expansion of the Firm', 52 *Am. Econ. Rev.* 1078 (1962).

114. Richard M. Cyert and James G. March, *A Behavioral Theory of the Firm* (1963). For a short summary of this literature, see M. Dan-Cohen, *supra* n. 49, at 20.

115. See generally William J. Baumol, *Business Behavior, Value and Growth* (1959); Robin Marris, *The Economic Theory of 'Managerial' Capitalism* (1964); Buxbaum, *supra* n. 21, at 522–4.

116. See A. Chandler, *supra* n. 52, at 484–500; Edward S. Herman, 'The Limits of the Market as a Discipline in Corporate Governance', 9 *Del. J. Corp. L.* 530, 533–4 (1984). Chandler finds a close relationship between the push for growth and the development of the multi-divisional firm. The desire for firm security from disruption of supplies or outlets results in growth through vertical integration. Multi-divisional growth also is productive: The conglomerate firm adding a unit of production causes better use of the new unit. A. Chandler, *supra* n. 53, at 486.

117. This is Herman's thesis. E. Herman, *supra* n. 110, at 106–13; Herman, *supra* n. 116, at 533.

118. Irving Fisher, *The Theory of Interest* (1930); see also A. Berle and G. Means, *supra* n. 59, at 247–8. On dividend policy, see John Lintner, 'Distributions of

Incomes of Corporations Among Dividends, Retained Earnings and Taxes',
46 *Am. Econ. Rev.* 97 (May 1956) (papers & proceedings); see also Richard A.
Brealy and Stewart C. Myers, *Principles of Corporate Finance* 10–15 (2d edn.
(1984).

119. See A. Chandler, *supra* n. 52, at 10, 473–3, 492; J. Hurst, *supra* n. 53, at 82.

120. For an account of the disruption of this balance in the 1980s, see text accompanying nn. 195–201 *infra*.

121. The neo-classical models' assumptions of costlessly created and enforced contracts and perfect information obviated the need to inquire into organizational structure. See Jensen, *supra* n. 8, at 325–6; see also Nathan Rosenberg, 'Comments on Robert Hessen, "The Modern Corporation and Private Property: A Reappraisal"', 26 *JL & Econ.* 291, 295 (1983).

122. See Steven N. S. Cheung, 'The Contractual Nature of the Firm, 26 *JL & Econ.* 1, 18 (1983).

   Following Adam Smith's dictum that the division of labour, and thus the firm, establishes the boundaries of the market for analytical purposes, see A. Chandler, *supra* n. 52, at 489–90, neo-classical economists did not look at production processes inside the firm or at the contracting arrangements underlying them. See Harold Demsetz, 'The Structure of Ownership and the Theory of the Firm', 26 *JL & Econ.* 375, 377–8 (1983).

123. Mark Blaug, *The Methodology of Economics* 175–86 (1980).

124. See Milton Friedman, *Capitalism and Freedom* 121, 135 (1962); see also Jensen and Meckling, *supra* n. 4, at 306; Williamson, *supra* n. 44, at 1220–1. Neoclassical models avoided taking entrepreneurship and its concomitant, profit, into account through single-minded adherence to the concept of marginal productivity. In perfect conditions, entrepreneurs theoretically have no function and receive no income. Profits thus were conceived in terms of imperfect competition and disequilibrium conditions, and explained either as payment for the assumption of uninsurable risks or as temporary windfalls. See Paul J. McNulty, 'On the Nature and Theory of Economic Organization: The Role of the Firm Reconsidered', 16 *Hist. Pol. Econ.* 240–1 (1984).

   Neo-classical theory valued production by small traditional enterprises subject to the invisible hand. Production by internal administrative coordination is suboptimal because of the absence of perfect competition. These values prove unexpectedly complementary to those reflected in the anti-managerialist discourse in the legal academy. Both accept the hierarchical nature of the corporation and both question the legitimacy of management power, albeit from different points of view.

125. For criticism of the neo-classical model, see M. Blaug, *supra* n. 123, at 176–8; A. Chandler, *supra* n. 52, at 489–91; Ronald Coase, *The Firm, the Market and the Law* 5–6 (1988); Harold Demsetz, 'Theory of the Firm Revisited', 4 *JL Econ. & Org.* 141, 142–4 (1988); McNulty, *supra* n. 124; Nordquist, 'The Breakup of the Maximization Principle' in *Readings in Microeconomics* 278

(D. Kamerschen ed. 1965); Sidney G. Winter, 'On Coase, Competence, and the Corporation', 4 *JL Econ. & Org.* 163, 165–71 (1988).

126. See Meckling, *supra* n. 30, at 557.

127. The widely differing perspectives clashed mostly over questions of antitrust policy and law.

128. See text accompanying notes 17–20 *supra*.

120. A. Berle and G. Means, *supra* n. 59, at 244–52, 309–13; see also Herman, *supra* n. 116, at 530–3.

130. Bratton, *supra* n. 16.

131. See Earl Latham, 'The Body Politic of the Corporation', in *The Corporation in Modern Society* 218 (E. Mason ed. 1966); R. Nader, M. Green and J. Seligman, *supra* n. 19, at 33, 36–7. Anti-managerialist commentary written instead in the post-Realist proceduralist tradition declines to make the 'public' and 'political' assertion. See Melvin Aron Eisenberg, *The Structure of the Corporation* 16 (1976) (corporate law is 'constitutional'—that is, it 'regulates the manner in which the corporate institution is constituted').

132. The analytical framework of interest group pluralism prevalent during the post-war period was so applied. Cf. Morton Horwitz, 'The History of the Public/Private Distinction', 130 *U. Pa. L. Rev.* 1423, 1427 (1982) (describing changing views of the public interest).

    The anti-managerialists underpinned their 'public' and 'political' assertions with a historical story. Generations of law students have been introduced to the subject of corporations through this study as retold in the first chapter of William L. Cary and Melvin Aron Eisenberg, *Cases and Materials on Corporations* 1–15 (5th edn. 1980); see also R. Nader, M. Green and J. Seligman, *supra* n. 19, at 36–7, 62–5 (a nice telling of the story). In the early 19th century, corporate formation was a matter of special chartering by state legislatures. In those days, legal doctrine treated corporate power as a concession of sovereignty. Then, during the course of the nineteenth century, special chartering waned and then disappeared. In-so-far as it promoted equal access to the corporate form, this was a salutary development. Unfortunately, dark forces took control around the turn of the century. States ceded legal control to management groups in exchange for tax dollars. These bad faith transactions permitted corporations to escape their historical duty to serve public ends, even as corporations continued to derive their constituent and legitimizing power from the state and to share its sovereignty. See Latham, *supra* n. 132, at 223; see generally Jacobson, *supra* n. 57.

133. See Christopher Stone, 'Corporate Vices and Corporate Virtues: Do Public/Private Distinctions Matter?', 130 *U. Pa. L. Rev.* 1441, 1449, 1480 (1982).

134. This movement gathered force in the 1960s, eclipsing the managerialist expertise-based approach. In the 1970s, anti-managerialists dominated the

law reviews. Despite this, state corporate law remained substantially pro-managerial into the 1980s.

The literature on transfers of control provides a good example of this phenomenon. Academics argued strongly against the legitimacy of managers exchanging control power for money. See e.g. William D. Andrews, 'The Stockholder's Right to Equal Opportunity in the Sale of Shares', 78 *Harv. L. Rev.* 505 (1965); Adolf A. Berle, Jr., '"Control" in Corporate Law', 58 *Colum. L. Rev.* 1212 (1958). A few cases took up the idea. See *Rosenfeld* v. *Black*, 445 F 2d 1337 (2d Cir. 1971); *Perlman* v. *Feldmann*, 219 F 2d 173 (2d Cir. 1955). But academic criticism was never fully incorporated into doctrine; most judges saw nothing wrong with the practice. See *Clagett* v. *Hutchison*, 583 F 2d 1259 (4th Cir. 1978); *Essex Universal* v. *Yates*, 305 F 2d 572 (2d Cir. 1962); *Honigman* v. *Green Giant Co.*, 208 F. Supp. 754 (D. Minn. 1961), *aff'd*, 309 F 2d 667 (8th Cir. 1962), *cert denied*, 372 US 941 (1963); Easterbrook and Fischel, 'Corporate Control Transactions', *supra* n. 21, at 716.

Despite this general trend, a few anti-managerial innovations have come into corporate doctrine during the present decade. See n. 213 *infra*.

135. See text accompanying nn. 121–7 *supra*.

136. Some transactions have the firm entity as a party, but only as a matter of convenience. The 'firm' in the picture has no precise boundaries—unlike legal academics, the neo-classicists have no interest in categorizing transactions as occurring 'inside' or 'outside' the firm. See Jensen and Meckling, *supra* n. 4, at 311; Klein, *supra* n. 37, at 373; Klein, Crawford and Alchian, *supra* n. 44, at 326.

137. See Alchian and Demsetz, *supra* n. 24, at 781–3, 789 n. 14 (owners contract for rights to anticipated residual awards).

138. See generally sources cited in n. 21 *supra*; Winter, *supra* n. 9; Nicholas Wolfson, 'A Critique of Corporate Law', 34 *U. Miami L. Rev.* 959 (1980).

139. See Bratton, *supra* n. 16.

140. Brudney, *supra* n. 21, at 1410.

141. See *Statement of the Business Roundtable on the American Law Institute's Proposed 'Principles of Corporate Governance and Structure: Restatement and Recommendations'* 3–5 (1983); Paul W. MacAvoy, Scott Cantor, Jim Dana and Sara Peck, 'ALI Proposals for Increased Control of the Corporation by the Board of Directors: An Economic Analysis', in ibid. at C-1 (Exhibit C).

142. *Principles of Corporate Governance and Structure: Restatement and Recommendations* (Tent. Draft No. 1, 1982). The ALI's draft was based on prevalent anti-managerialist assumptions.

143. Indeed, the institutionalist picture is derived from the historical work of Alfred Chandler. See generally Williamson, 'The Modern Corporation: Origins, Evolution, Attributes', *supra* n. 41.

144. This recognition of a historical contribution should not be taken as an assertion that the new economic theory accurately modelled corporate legal

practice. If we were to take the neo-classical variant as system and follow it as an absolute guide, we soon would be reconstructing rather than recreating the practice.

145. Joseph Angell and Samuel Ames, *Treatise on the Law of Private Corporations Aggregate* (9th edn. 1871).

146. See Horwitz, *supra* n. 14, at 215.

147. J. Angell and S. Ames, *supra* n. 147, at 1.

148. James Kent, *Commentaries on American Law* 303 (11th edn. 1866). Kent's definition had been incorporated into the Louisiana Civil Code from 1825 through 1987. *La. Civ. Code Ann.*, art. 427 (West 1942 & Supp. 1989) (repealed in 1987).

149. Timberg, *supra* n. 91, at 540. According to Conard, it may not have been Pope Innocent IV but rather one of his editors who recognized in an introduction that corporations are both material and immaterial, that they have individual members, but that corporations as a whole are not natural but intellectual. See Alfred Conard, *Corporations in Perspective* 417 & n. 5 (1976) (quoting Baldus Ubaldi, in 'Index' to Innocentius, *Commentaria*, sub. tit. *Universitas*, the text credited with the origination of fiction theory).

150. Stewart Kyd, *A Treatise on the Law of Corporations* 13 (1793).

151. *Trustees of Dartmouth College* v. *Woodward*, 17 US (4 Wheat.) 518, 636 (1819).

152. J. Kent, *supra* n. 148, at 303–4.

153. J. Angell and S. Ames, *supra* n. 145, at 1 (footnote added).

154. Ibid. at 4. Angell and Ames use this and other terms to capture Kent's point.

155. S. Kyd, *supra* n. 150, at 13.

156. The new economic theories of the firm make a similar move when they strip the entity down to a contracting nexus. See text accompanying notes 27–39 *supra*.

157. *Trustees of Dartmouth College* v. *Woodward* 17 US (4 Wheat.) 518, 636 (1819).

158. *Bouvier's Law Dictionary* 318 (7th edn. 1857); George Field, *Private Corporations* 1–4 (1877) (Kyd and Marshall variants); Platt Potter, *Treatise on the Law of Corporations* 1–4 (1879); C. Beach, *supra* n. 81, at 3–4 (1891); Carl Spelling, *Law of Private Corporations* 3–4 (1892); Henry Taylor, *Law of Private Corporations* (3rd edn. 1894); William Clark, *Handbook of the Law of Corporations* 4–5 (1897) (Kent variant); William Wilson Cook, *A Treatise on the Law of Corporations* (4th edn. 1898) (Marshall variant and cases); Herbert Marcus Adler, *A Summary of the Law Relating to Corporations* 1–4 (1903) (Kyd variant); Leslie Tompkins, *A Summary of the Law of Private Corporations* 6 (1904) (Kent, Marshall, and Kyd variants); Richard Harvey, *A Handbook of Corporation Law* 7–8 (1906); Jon T. Mulligan, *Law of Corporations* 7 (1913); Joseph France, *Principles of Corporation Law* 3–4 (2nd edn. 1914); Isaac Wormser, *Law of Private Corporations* 3–4 (1921); James Treat Carter, *The Nature of the Corporation as a Legal Entity* 37–8 (1919) (Doctoral thesis, Johns

Hopkins Univ.) (Marshall, Kyd, and Kent variants); Charles B. Elliott, *The Law of Private Corporations* (5th edn. 1923) (Kyd and Marshall variants); Henry Winthrop Ballantine, *Ballantine's Manual of Corporation Law and Practice* 6 (1930) (Kyd and Marshall variants); William Crow, *Formal Corporate Practice* (1931) (Marshall variant); *Black's Law Dictionary* 438 (3rd edn. 1933) (Kyd and Marshall variants).

159. Howard Oleck, *Modern Corporation Law* § 2 (1958).

160. C. Spelling, *supra* n. 158, at 3–4.

161. J. Mulligan, *supra* n. 158, at 7.

162. C. Spelling, *supra* n. 158, at 4; see also Maurice Condit Cross, *Types of Business Enterprise* 53 (1928); R. Harvey, *supra* n. 158, at 7–8; L. Tompkins, *supra* n. 158, at 6.

163. Wesley Newcomb Hohfeld, *Fundamental Legal Conceptions* 198 (W. Cook ed. 1923); C. Elliott, *supra* n. 158, at 2.

164. See text accompanying notes 90–92 *supra*.

165. M. Eisenberg, *supra* n. 131, at 1 (The 'general principles underpinning the legal structure of the corporation have not been well articulated.').

One contemporary anti-managerialist writer advocates returning to an entity conception of the corporation in the corporate governance discourse. See Robert L. Knauss, 'Corporate Governance—A Moving Target', 79 *Mich. L. Rev.* 478, 487 (1981). Knauss's point rests on a correct doctrinal assumption: entity views and duties of care and loyalty go together. But in a climate in which the entity concept is suspect one does better to go beneath it. Instead of exalting the bald reification, one should assert that the care and loyalty duties spring from the constituting parts of the relations that give rise to the entity concept. See Bratton, *supra* n. 17, at 000.

166. Bayless Manning, 'The Shareholders' Appraisal Remedy: An Essay for Frank Coker', 72 *Yale LJ* 223, 245 (1962).

167. A. Conrad, *supra* n. 159, at 419–20.

168. Walter H. Anderson, *Limitations of the Corporate Entity* 7 (1931); Henry Winthrop Ballantine, *Ballantine on Corporations* 2 (rev. edn. 1946).

169. H. Ballantine, *supra* n. 168, at 2.

170. W. Anderson, *supra* n. 168, at 7.

171. David L. Ratner, 'Corporations and the Constitution', 15 *USFL Rev.* 11, 12 (1980–1).

172. R. Stevens, *supra* n. 69, at 95.

173. See text accompanying nn. 75–9 *supra*.

174. See nn. 115–20 *supra* and accompanying text.

175. See nn. 130–3 *supra* and accompanying text.

176. See Roberta Romano, 'Metapolitics and Corporate Law Reform', 36 *Stan. L. Rev.* 923, 929–30, 934 (1984); see also Bratton, *supra* n. 16. Organicist rhetoric never disappears entirely, however. For a recent example, see Oliver E. Williamson, 'The Logic of Economic Organization', 4 *JL Econ. & Org.* 65, 86

(1988) (describing the contemporary corporate restructuring movement as organizational 'mitosis', a 'quasi-biological' process).

177. See text accompanying n. 179 *infra*.

178. The entity conception is employed, for example, in A. Berle and G. Means, *supra* n. 59, at 220–3; R. Stevens, *supra* n. 69, at 691–2. For an example of the interplay between entity and contractual approaches, see M. Eisenberg, *supra* n. 131, at 85–94.

179. Kaufman and Zacharias, *supra* n. 50, pointed this out recently. See notes 103–107 *supra* and accompanying text.

180. See text accompanying n. 4 *supra*.

181. See J. Hurst, *supra* n. 53, at 45–9 (the nineteenth-century critique).

182. This was the move made by the *Santa Clara* litigants. See text accompanying n. 83 *supra*.

183. Anti-individualist perspectives have gone through twists of their own during this century in their application to corporations. At the turn of the century, the theorists concentrating on group existence were the realists, and their work favoured management. In today's corporate law discussions, anti-managerialists take entities most seriously. See text accompanying notes 128–134 *supra*. Actually, the point is more complex. Early twentieth-century Progressives also took group existence seriously, and they opposed the corporate realists. See Horwitz, *supra* n. 14, at 223–4. Post-war institutional economists take corporate entities very seriously on management's behalf. See notes 113–17 *supra* and accompanying text. The institutionalist new theorists also take group existence seriously, even though they privilege the individual participant's role.

184. This is the formal, objectified contract law of Williston and the first *Restatement of Contracts* (1932).

185. A. Berle, *supra* n. 19, at 54.

186. See Cary, *supra* n. 25; R. Nader, M. Green and J. Seligman, *supra* n. 19, at 62–5, suggesting federal intervention.

187. These changes are discussed in detail at notes 189–94 *infra* and accompanying text.

188. See notes 195–201 *infra* and accompanying text.

189. One caveat should be entered here. While practice in this context facilitated the emergence of new theory by raising practical questions about the accuracy of the received managerialist picture, the theorists did not necessarily make primary reference to the practice. The neo-classical variant of the new economic theory draws heavily on neo-classical microeconomic assumptions. The classical market ideal from which these assumptions are drawn has been largely superseded in history. The theory's adherence to these assumptions attenuates its connection to practice.

190. Henry G. Manne, 'Mergers and the Market for Corporate Control', 73 J. Pol. Econ. 110, 113 (1965).

191. The take-over 'threat' also was considered a market mechanism for discipline of management conduct. It accordingly provided a response to the anti-managerialists' legitimacy point. See M. Aoki, *supra* n. 109, at 36–40.

192. Focusing on multidivisional structure reconstituted the firm as a governance structure rather than a production function. Williamson, *supra* n. 48, at 362; see also Williamson, 'The Modern Corporation: Origins, Evolution, and Attributes', *supra* n. 41.

193. Heavily criticized decisions permitting defensive tactics include: *Panter* v. *Marshall Field &Co.*, 646 F. 2d 271 (7th Cir. 1981); *Moran* v. *Household Int'l, Inc.* 500 A. 2d 1346 (Del. 1985); *Cheff* v. *Mathes*, 41 Del. Ch. 494, 199 A. 2d 548 (1964). Recently, the courts have begun to scrutinize more closely management decisions regarding the control market. See *Revlon, Inc.* v. *MacAndrews & Forbes Holdings, Inc.*, 506 A. 2d 173 (Del. 1986); *Hanson Trust PLC* v. *ML SCM Acquisition, Inc.*, 781 F. 2d 264 (2d Cir. 1986).

   In cases concerning the treatment of minority shareholder interests remaining in the acquired corporation after a take-over, the Delaware courts have made some famous anti-managerial rulings. See *Weinberger* v. *OUP, Inc.*, 457 A. 2d 701 (Del. 1983); *Singer* v. *Magnavox Co.*, 380 A. 2d 969 (Del. 1977).

194. Herman, *supra* n. 116, at 537; Paul H. Malatesta, 'The Wealth Effects of Merger Activity and the Objective Functions of Merging Firms', 11 *J. Fin. Econ.* 155, 177 (1983). *Contra* Michael C. Jensen and Richard S. Ruback, 'The Market for Corporate Control: The Scientific Evidence', 11 *J. Fin. Econ.* 5, 11, 16 (1983).

195. The theory's agency cost line comes to bear against management here. The tender offer is conceived as a traditional form of market control. It encourages devotion to the principal's interest in the agent. This idea can be traced to Manne, *supra* n. 190, at 112–14, and it reappears frequently in the contemporary literature on take-overs. See e.g. Lucian A. Babchuk, 'The Case for Facilitating Competing Tender Offers', 95 *Harv. L. Rev.* 1028, 1030–1 (1982); Frank H. Easterbrook and Daniel R. Fischel, 'The Proper Role of a Target's Management in Responding to a Tender Offer', 94 *Harv. L. Rev.* 1161, 1169–74 (1981); Ronald J. Gilson, 'A Structural Approach to Corporations: The Case Against Defensive Tactics in Tender Offers', 33 *Stan. L.Rev.* 819, 841 (1981).

196. John C. Coffee, Jr., 'Shareholders Versus Managers: The Strain in the Corporate Web', 85 *Mich. L. Rev.* 1, 2–3 (1986).

197. That is, the capital was invested in the corporation for a return at a rate less than its cost. There is statistical evidence that excessive earnings retention, a practice detrimental to shareholders, was common. See ibid. at 22 & n. 59.

198. See text accompanying n. 68 *supra*.

199. See generally Louis Lowenstein, *What's Wrong with Wall Street* (1988).

200. The contemporary discussions are well summarized in several articles in a

Business Week special report entitled, 'Deal Mania'. See Norman Jonas and Joan Berger, 'Do all these Deals Help or Hurt the U.S. Economy', *Bus. Wk.*, 24 Nov. 1986, at 86–8; Judith H. Bobrzynski, 'More than Ever, It's Management for the Short Term', *Bus. Wk.*, 24 Nov. 1986, at 92–3.

201. See notes 98–9 *supra* and accompanying text.
202. This is Coffee's critique of Williamson. See Coffee, *supra* n. 196, at 31–5. Williamson has responded by updating his historical account of the evolution of corporate organization. He accounts for restructuring as an outgrowth of the spread of the modern conglomerate structure. Because the benefits from an acquisition may not continue indefinitely, the M-form entity undergoes 'mitosis'—a 'quasi-biological' process likened to cell division in which the firm divests acquired activities, often in multidivisional units which are themselves M-form firms. Williamson, *supra* n. 176, at 86–7.
203. See text accompanying notes 27–39 *supra*.
204. This discussion draws extensively on Coffee, *supra* n. 196, at 25–8.
205. Michael C. Jensen, 'Agency Costs of Free Cash Flow, Corporate Finance and Takeovers', 76 *Am. Econ. Rev.* 323, 324–6 (May 1986) (papers & proceedings).
206. Coffee, *supra* n. 196, at 28.
207. Levmore, *supra* n. 21, at 70–2. Levmore, working within the paradigm, anticipated the interacting elements of later restructurings. He noted that shareholder and management interests diverge when the shareholder interest calls for dissolution of the corporation. He applied an institutionalist explanation: management had made a firm-specific investment; a shutdown would be contrary to its interests in recouping that investment. Ibid. at 71.

Levmore also noted a pertinent problem with the Jensen and Meckling model of the firm. In their model, management, by increasing its own stake in the enterprise, decreased its incentive to misbehave and the investors' need to monitor, thereby reducing agency costs. Drawing on finance theory, Levmore noted that management's investment interests also include a diversified portfolio, and that this interest would prevent it from making such an extensive investment in its own firm. Ibid. at 67.

Coffee has expanded on these points in an explanation of the bust-up takeover. Coffee sees management through the lens of finance theory and contends that management's inevitably outsized investment in its own firm makes rational diversification of its portfolio impossible. Management therefore is more risk averse than are investors in the financial community who can and do fully diversify their investment portfolios. As a result, management makes safe investments which are suboptimal from the point of view of investors. The current wave of corporate restructurings are an assertion by the investment community of the primacy of its own investment objectives. See Coffee, *supra* n. 196, at 15–21.

208. See Eugene F. Fama, 'Agency Problems and the Theory of the Firm', 88 *J. Pol. Econ.* 288, 290 (1980) (describing management as a 'type of labor but with a special role—coordinating the activities of inputs and carrying out the contracts agreed [upon] among [the] inputs').

209. Viewed retrospectively, management's invocation of the authority of the new economic theorists in the corporate governance debates of the early 1980s was precipitous. See notes 141–2 *supra* and accompanying text. The notions of entity and sovereign participation undergirding the anti-managerialist arguments contain much more defensive potential than does the new theory's contractualism. A comparison of the Delaware cases on tender offer defence tactics dramatically illustrates this point. The successful case incorporates protection of the entity. See *Cheff* v. *Mathes*, 41 Del. Ch. 494, 199 A. 2d 548 (1964). The management group that abandons an entity conception and reconstitutes its responses with contractual values weakens its case. See *Revlon* v. *MacAndrews & Forbes Holdings, Inc.*, 506 A. 2d 173 (Del. 1986).

210. For a review of changes in debt contracting patterns, see Morey W. McDaniel, 'Bondholders and Corporate Governance', 41 *Bus. Law.* 413 (1986).

211. See Anthony Bianco, 'America Has a New Kingdom: the Investment Banker', *Bus. Wk.*, 24 Nov. 1986, at 77. The character Gordon Gekko in the film *Wall Street* manifests the conception.

212. For criticism of congressional inaction, see L. Lowenstein, *supra* n. 200, at 156–8, 168–76. Talk of congressional intervention persists, fuelled by the stock market crash of October 1987, and the great food company restructurings of the fall of 1988. Intervention itself still seems unlikely. See Gregory Robb, 'Ruder Sees No Crisis in Buyouts', *NY Times*, 23 Dec. 1988, at D1, col. 3; see generally William W. Bratton, 'Corporate Debt Relationships: Legal Theory in a Time of Restructuring', 1989 *Duke LJ* 92.

The exception to the rule of nonintervention is the proliferation of state take-over statues. These have gone through several generations of form and have been the subject of two Supreme Court opinions. *Edgar* v. *Mite Corp.*, 457 US 624 (1982) (statute requiring disclosure by offeror beyond that required by federal law unconstitutionally burdens interstate commerce); *CTS Corp.* v. *Dynamics Corp. of America*, 481 US 69 (1987) (sustaining statute conditioning offeror's privilege to vote its shares on the approval of other shareholders); see Arthur R. Pinto, 'Takeover Statutes: The Dormant Commerce Clause and State Corporate Law', 41 *U. Miami L. Rev.* 473 (1987). Here again, despite a lot of sound and fury, take-over activity does not seem to have been discouraged materially.

213. For a recent manifestation of the new economic thinking, consider David Ruder, then the nominee for Chairman of the Securities and Exchange Commission, telling Congress that the benefits to the shareholders of take-over premiums outweigh loss of employment and other disruptions of the

local community. See Nathaniel Nash, 'A Hands-Off Takeover Stance', *NY Times*, 23 July 1987, at D1, col. 3.

Congress only recently began seriously to consider additional procedural barriers to tender offers. See 'Proxmire to Offer Bill to Require Prenotification of Bidders' Purchases', *BNA's Corp. Couns. Weekly*, 15 Apr. 1987, at 1.

214. One of the strongest examples of corporate law's continuing conceptual association of management and the corporate entity is that management is permitted to engage in self-defence in the name of the entity. See n. 193 *supra*. That these defence tactics have had only limited success shows the constant power of contract.

215. Some of the alterations protect management. See n. 213 *supra* (discussing state anti-take-over statutes).

Other developments result in intensified judicial scrutiny under the rubric of fiduciary duty. The old management expertise rationale carries less weight when the decision-making context is that the sale of the entire company. In these transactional contexts, courts feel more comfortable with close review for self-interested decisions. See e.g. *Revlon, Inc.* v. *MacAndrews & Forbes Holdings, Inc.*, 506 A. 2d 173 (Del. 1986); *Smith* v. *Van Gorkom*, 488 A. 2d 858 (Del. 1985).

216. Changes are beginning to appear here also, as management organization structures become looser and more flexible in emerging industries. See Michael J. Piore, 'Corporate Reform in American Manufacturing and the Challenge to Economic Theory' (paper presented at the conference on Economics of Organization at the Yale School of Organization and Management, 24–5 October, 1986) (on file with the *Stanford Law Review*).

217. See Bratton, *supra* n. 16. For an early example of contractual managerialism, see Coffee's suggestion of sharing of take-over gains, or 'premium sharing'. Coffee, *supra* n. 196, at 12. Coffee proposes a conception of corporate structure in which management and shareholders share the position of residual risk bearer and residual beneficiary. Ibid.

Corporate Control: Markets and Rules

CAROLINE BRADLEY

1. Introduction

It is likely that the impact of statutes on transactions in corporate control in the United Kingdom will increase in the near future, whether as a result of recent scandals or because of the introduction of legislation to harmonize rules within the EEC.[1] For these reasons it is appropriate to consider again the interests of those who are affected by the operation of the market for corporate control.

Traditionally, comment on, and regulation of, take-overs has focused on three issues: (1) the maintenance of proper balances between managerial and ownership interests within companies which are the targets of take-over attempts, (2) the maintenance of a balance between the interests of predators and shareholders in the target company, and (3) the protection of the public interest. The first issue can be traced to the identification by Berle and Means of a potential conflict between the interests of owners and the interests of controllers of large corporations. Since Berle and Means, much of the literature about corporations has concentrated on whether constraints on corporate managerial power are necessary in order to protect the interests of shareholders.[2] One of the most significant constraints on corporate managerial power seems to many commentators to be the market for corporate control, and the threat of displacement which it poses to corporate managements.[3] The idea of the market for corporate control seems to have originated with Berle and Means,[4] but has since been refined.[5] The second issue arises out of the concern of regulators that predators should not profit at the expense of target company shareholders,[6] and some of the refinements of the corporate control theory are relevant to this issue. In practice, the third issue, the protection of the public interest, usually involves questions of competition policy.[7]

These three issues all have different origins, but economic theory is

Law Department, London School of Economics and Political Science.

relevant in all cases, as it suggests that markets operate in the public inter-est, except where there is market failure, such as insufficient competition, or external social costs.[8] Recent suggestions that the traditional approach to take-overs does not take adequate account of the interests of predator company shareholders, employees and suppliers of the target company, the local community, and the public interest[9] are suggestions that take-overs involve external social costs, which should be eliminated or inter-nalized.

This article describes the market for corporate control theory, and the implications of this theory for the interests of investors in the target com-pany, and investors in the predator (if it is a company), and of other affected groups. Current rules which affect the interests of these various groups are described, and I suggest ways in which the current rules could be amended in order better to protect the interests of those who may be threatened by the operation of the market for corporate control. These issues are often ignored in the context of a regulatory system which has developed in response to perceived abuses in the market-place.[10]

2. The market for corporate control

The theory of the market for corporate control is that 'inefficient man-agers, if not responsible to, and subject to displacement by, owners directly, can be removed by stockholders' acceptance of take-over bids induced by poor performance and a consequent reduction in stock value'.[11] The market for corporate control is supposed to reduce the risk, identified by Berle and Means, that managers may satisfice or engage in non-profit maximizing behaviour[12] and to ensure that resources are allo-cated efficiently.[13]

The foundation of the market for corporate control theory is the rela-tionship between the activities of a company's management and the price of its shares.[14] Inefficient managers do not take feasible action to maxi-mize the price of the company's shares,[15] and where the management of a company is inefficient in this sense the price of shares in that company fails to reflect the company's true potential. This creates a 'control oppor-tunity', an opportunity for a predator to acquire control of the company and appoint a new management which will act to maximize the share price, and, in so doing, produce capital gains for the predator. The removal of the 'inefficient' management by the predator reinforces the threat of displacement to the managements of other companies which might be tempted to engage in inefficient behaviour.[16]

There are various explanations for the willingness of predators to pay large premiums for shares in target companies. They may be paying more than the shares are worth,[17] or the market price of the target's shares may underprice the underlying assets for some reason,[18] or the predator may have identified a more valuable use for the target's assets.[19]

If the predator is a company, its management may be seeking to acquire the target in order to promote its own interests. Despite this, most, if not all, of the arguments a predator could advance to promote a proposed acquisition if its proposal were challenged may be seen as varieties of the managerial inefficiency claim. For example, a predator which claims that an acquisition will create synergy and which is prepared to pay a premium over current market price for shares in the target is suggesting that the existing target management could have increased the target's share price by identifying the same synergy.[20]

Anything which makes the process of acquiring control more expensive, including regulation, interferes with the market for corporate control,[21] because a rational predator will balance the costs of a take-over against the prospective benefits to be derived from that take-over. In order for the market for corporate control to work, the predator must be able to acquire control of the target company for less than the profit it will make by remedying the existing management's inefficiency to the company.[22] Increasing the costs involved in implementing take-overs could, therefore, deprive society of the benefits associated with such transactions.

3. Drawbacks of the market for corporate control

The idea that the market for corporate control functions as a threat to the management of companies and therefore benefits shareholders, and society, by ensuring that management acts efficiently and maximizes profits is attractive. Although there is a lively debate as to the extent to which the market for corporate control functions as a effective discipline to corporate management, most discussion tends to focus on the fine tuning of the regulatory context in which the market operates. The debate as to the fine tuning has concentrated on two main areas, that of the defensive tactics a corporate manager may adopt, and that of equal treatment of shareholders in the target company. Other issues are also significant, however, such as the position of the shareholders in the predator company (if the predator is a corporate body, rather than an individual), and the effect of take-overs on other constituencies, such as employees of the target company, consumers, the local community, and society as a whole. I will consider the impact of the market for corporate control on three separate groups: target investors, predator investors, and others.

Target Investors

While the market for corporate control may provide an opportunity for some investors to sell out of a target company subject to an inefficient management at a price which reflects the potential profit available to the acquirer, the market for corporate control also creates an incentive for the management of a target company to act in certain ways which are not likely to benefit investors. A corporate management faced with either a remote, or an immediate, threat of take-over may respond either by taking action to maximize the price of shares in the target company, or by acting so as to inhibit a change of control. For example, in order to increase the price of shares in the company, the management may decide to change the gearing of the company.[23] Alternatively, action which would drastically increase the consideration a predator would need to pay in order to obtain control tends to inhibit a change of control. Both types of response may be characterized as defensive tactics, because both responses may be designed to protect management from the threat of displacement through take-over.

The question whether the management of a company which is subject to a hostile take-over bid should be prohibited from implementing defensive tactics in the face of that bid has received much attention.[24] An example of such tactics would be an issue of shares to a 'White Knight', who, the incumbent management hopes, will not sell them, made after a potential predator has been identified. The setting up of a new large shareholder interest of this nature will inhibit the ability of the predator to obtain control of the target. Commentators advocate the restriction of the ability of management to implement defensive tactics because they believe that the decision as to whether there is a change in the control of a company should be made by the shareholders in that company rather than by its management.[25]

Some commentators have considered whether a prohibition on the implementation of defensive tactics should extend to general defensive tactics as well as specific tactics.[26] I use the phrase 'general defensive tactics' to describe action which is designed to make a company unattractive to any potential predator, and which is taken before any specific potential predator has been identified.[27] An example of such tactics would be a provision in the company's constitution giving to the shareholders the right to be bought out at a substantial premium on a change of control.[28] Such tactics are thought by many commentators to be less objectionable than specific defensive tactics as they are usually adopted with the consent of a majority of the shareholders in the company concerned.[29]

Once a predator appears, a corporate management may act to ensure that an auction is initiated and control of the company is transferred to the highest bidder.[30] However, corporate managements could claim to be initiating an auction to benefit shareholders when, in fact, they were implementing defensive tactics to protect their own position. Even if a corporate management were genuinely promoting an auction, its actions could deprive shareholders of the opportunity to benefit from a share in the premium for the passing of control could remove the threat to the management of the company, and could also lead to a reduction of the number of offers in future.[31]

Conclusion

The market for corporate control should benefit investors in companies whose managements do not actively try to increase the price of shares in the company by offering to such investors the opportunity of escaping from the company or remaining in the company with a new management which will try to increase the share price. If a change of control could not take place, the investors could only escape from the company by selling their shares at a price depressed by the management's inaction. However, the existence of the market for corporate control may not adequately protect the interests of target investors if corporate managements are free to act in ways which, while protecting their own interests, harm the interests of some or all of the investors in the target.

Predator Investors

There is a limited recognition by commentators that all companies are potential targets. Predator behaviour is supposed, under the theory of the market for corporate control, to be the mechanism which disciplines inefficient managements. However, in practice it may be used by management as a means to ward off market discipline. Some empirical studies[32] suggest that the most effective defence against take-over is the attainment of great size, and it is possible to view the action of management in promoting a policy of growth through acquisition rather than pursuing organic growth as self-serving rather than serving the interests of investors in the company. The attraction of the advantages of managing a larger enterprise, coupled with the lure of insulation from the danger of displacement through take-over may suggest that management should not be regarded as competent to make this type of business decision.[33] One way of protecting the shareholders from the activities of managements keen on pursuing aggressive acquisition policies in order to improve their own position would be the adoption of a rule to disqualify management from making acquisition decisions without the consent of the shareholders.

There is some debate about whether take-overs do, in practice, benefit acquiring firms. Empirical studies of the reaction of share prices to announcements of take-over bids show that shareholders in predator companies do not lose when their companies are involved in take-overs.[34] However, there is other evidence to suggest that take-overs do not always produce the benefits they are alleged to produce.[35]

Not all commentators accept that take-overs involve management in a significant conflict of interest. Some take the view that the decision to implement an acquisition policy involves no more of a conflict between the interests of management and investors than any other business decision.[36] The weakness in this argument is that a management which tends to make bad or self-interested business decisions will not be disciplined by the market for corporate control if it makes business decisions putting it beyond the reach of the threat posed by the market for corporate control. The model of the market for corporate control assumes the existence of market discipline, but its existence may in fact increase the risk that management will act in its own interests, rather than reducing that risk.

In recent years evidence has been collected to suggest that large conglomerates are subject to a threat of break-up or demerger acquisitions.[37] Corporate managements seem to pursue acquisitions in order to protect their companies from the threat of take-over, but at some point the nature of the conglomerate, produced by these acquisitions, seems to render is vulnerable to the threat of take-over, so that it may be broken up. Where a conglomerate is subject to the threat of a demerger take-over, this suggests that acquisitions which produced the conglomerate in the first place failed to increase efficiency. The phenomenon of break-up take-overs seems to be desirable in the interests of increased efficiency: these transactions are an example of the market for corporate control reasserting itself. Take-overs do, however, involve transaction costs, and this process involves an increased number of take-overs, so it would be preferable if take-overs which fail to increase efficiency did not occur in the first place.

Social Costs of Take-overs

Private gains from take-overs may be made at the expense of groups not directly involved in the transactions.[38] The costs involved may be of two types: transition costs necessarily involved in the change from an inefficient use of resources to a more efficient use of resources, and other costs.

The activities of those involved in the market for corporate control may harm the interests of groups such as consumers, creditors and investors in the stock market. The public interest may also be affected, for example in relation to research which is not undertaken in the private sector as a result of the existence of the market for corporate control. Whether financial markets are excessively affected by short term considerations or not,[39] corporate managers may believe in short termism and decide not to invest in long term research projects because of the risk that such investment would have a negative impact on share price. A corporate predator which pays more for control of target companies than that control is worth increases the risk that it will either become insolvent and go into liquidation or that it will become a target for a 'break-up' take-over.[40] If the company becomes insolvent the interests of creditors may be adversely affected. A break-up take-over may remove some of the costs involved in a liquidation, but will involve other costs.

Although take-overs seem to involve some social costs, various factors do operate to limit the effect of these costs. The company is at a 'confluence of multiple markets',[41] and the operation of these markets will tend to constrain the activities of the managements of the predator and target. For example, in the absence of a monopoly situation, competition in the product market will operate to ensure the maintenance of the quality of the product, and that the price of the product does not increase excessively. Competition rules apply to protect the product markets, although such rules tend not to be applied to conglomerate mergers as stringently as to horizontal and vertical mergers.[42]

In practice, some acquisitions result in an increase in the level of debt of the combined enterprise.[43] An increase in the level of debt of an enterprise may increase the risk to existing creditors of that enterprise. Mervyn King recognizes this cost to third party creditors, but suggests such costs as exist are costs related to gearing, rather than costs related to highly leveraged take-overs.[44]

If the acquisition significantly increases the power of the combined entity in the markets in which it operates, the predator might engage in monopolistic practices. For example, it might manufacture goods of worse quality, increase the price it charges for goods or services, and increase the length of time it takes to pay its bills. In the short term such actions could be harmful to consumers and suppliers. Other actions the predator might take after the acquisition could include the centralization of the combined entity's operations in one site, or the reduction of investment in research and development.

The interests of groups other than investors in the target company and the predator company are likely to be affected by the predator's action. Is it, therefore, appropriate for the decision whether the acquisition should go ahead to be made by the shareholders in the target company who will be offered part of the predator's anticipated profit in return for their shares?

In addition to the effects of the predator's actions on groups other than the investors in the target and in the predator itself, we should consider the effects of action by a management which is trying to insulate itself from the threat of take-over on such groups. Herman has suggested that: 'managerial capitalism may yield social inefficiencies by its better integration into an efficient capital market that heavily discounts large but uncertain long term profits (and disregards the positive social externalities of the longer view and risk-taking)'.[45]

A management which feels subject to the threat of displacement through take-over is likely to be reluctant to invest in research and development or in any activity which is unlikely to generate profits in the near future, even if the activity in question were a sensible long-term strategy. If the market for corporate control does tend to discourage corporate managements from investing in projects which might result in large profit in the future in favour of projects which will result in small certain profits in the short term, the market may not be as effective in ensuring the efficient allocation of resources as is often suggested.

The market for corporate control encourages management to take all feasible action to maximize the price of shares in the company, and could encourage management to maximize the share price through the release of information to the market or by some other means. Managements may often tread the fine line between permissible action to maximize the price of shares in their companies and unlawful market manipulation.[46] Shareholders in the company would tend to benefit from manipulation geared to maximizing the company's share price, but investors in the market at large would tend to suffer as a result of such action, because market prices would not tend to reflect the true value of the shares.

4. The regulatory framework in the united kingdom

Market mechanisms, company law, and the quasi-legal provisions[47] which regulate take-overs all provide some protection of the interests of investors before and during a take-over, and, to some limited extent, protection of the interests of employees and creditors and others who may be affected by take-overs. Regulators and commentators on these various mechanisms and regulations emphasize investor protection.[48] However, the market for corporate control is, it is argued, itself a mechanism for protecting investors. In theory, the market should ensure the efficient allocation of resources: owners of capital would furnish that capital for the most efficient possible use, because the most efficient use would provide the best return for the owners of capital. In practice, no markets are unregulated. For example, the current regime applicable to take-overs in the United Kingdom involves regulation of defensive tactics[49] combined with complete lack of regulation of the 'financial or commercial advantages or disadvantages' of a change of control.[50] Financial and commercial issues are not regulated because such issues are thought to be a matter for the company and its shareholders, unless specific questions relating to the public interest, usually involving competition policy, are raised. The refusal to regulate financial and commercial issues indicates an acceptance of the market as an appropriate decision-making process. This reinforces the market for corporate control. On the other hand the regulation of defensive tactics indicates a recognition that the market for corporation control may act against the interests of shareholders.

Company Law

In a large company many of the directors will not be actively involved in management but will, in theory, perform the function of monitoring management.[51] In practice, directors of companies which are taken over as a result of hostile take-overs are likely to lose their directorships.[52] Although there may be a distinction between the seriousness of a threat of take-over to executive directors and to non-executive directors, in practice all directors are subject to the threat provided by the market for corporate control in the same way as other members of a company's management.

In legal theory, the fundamental duty imposed on a director is to act bona fide in what the director considers to be the best interests of the company and not for any collateral purpose.[53] In addition a director must avoid all conflicts of interest.[54] The law imposes duties on directors, rather than on management, largely because when the duties were developed there was no separation between direction and management.[55] Directors are subject to fiduciary duties,[56] duties of care and skill, and statutory duties. In addition, duties are imposed on directors by service contracts. For managers who are not directors, service contracts are the only basis for their duties to the company.

The basic duty of a director to act bona fide in the best interests of the company is formulated subjectively: the courts do not review directors' decisions in order to discover whether it was reasonable to consider that a particular course of action was in the interests of the company or not.[57] However, in exceptional circumstances, the directors' objectives may be taken into account in deciding whether they are exercising their powers for the proper purposes or not.[58]

The directors' objectives have been held to be a relevant consideration in relation to issues of shares the purpose of which was to prevent a change of control.[59] This doctrine, the 'proper purposes doctrine', which has so far been limited to the question of issues of shares to friendly third parties to inhibit a change of control could be extended to other defensive tactics.[60] For example, suppose a board of directors sought to ward off a potential predator by entering into onerous contracts with third parties, arguing that, in their opinion, the contracts were in the best interests of the company. If the directors were acting in good faith it would seem to be necessary to use the proper purposes doctrine in order to challenge their actions.[61] It is not clear, however, that such an action would be likely to succeed in relation to a company involved in a public market.[62] Shareholders in a target company would want to take action against the delinquent directors to prevent the use of defensive tactics, or to obtain a remedy if the directors' action were successful in preventing the takeover. However, in practice, shareholders are not likely to find out about proposed defensive tactics in time to prevent their use, and, in general, litigation about breaches of directors' duties is corporate litigation and thus usually controlled by the directors.

Even if the directors of the target company have breached their fiduciary duties in opposing a potential take-over, it is not clear that a minority shareholder will be entitled to bring an action in respect of a breach of duty owed to the company, as the company itself should sue in respect of a breach of a duty owed to the company unless one of the exceptions to the rule in *Foss* v. *Harbottle* applies.[63] A minority shareholder in a target company should be able to benefit from one of the exceptions to the rule in *Foss* v. *Harbottle* to prevent the directors of the company from engaging in illegal acts, for example, manipulating the market price of shares in the company.[64] The purchase or sale of large amounts of shares on the market may have significant effects on the price of such shares, and such action may amount to criminal offences such as market manipulation, purchase by a company of its own shares,[65] or financial assistance for the purchase of a company's own shares.[66] The main difficulty an investor would encounter in relation to such activity would be in discovering its existence; for example it appears that the Guinness bid for Distillers in 1987 involved a price support operation which was not discovered until well after the event, and then only by accident. Similar difficulties would arise if the directors of the company were, on the other hand, engaged in an attempt to manipulate the market by means of a selective release of information.

In addition to the difficulties of discovering what the directors were doing, a minority shareholder might find it difficult to pursue litigation during a take-over bid, partly because of the reluctance of the courts to interfere with the take-over process, and partly because it seems that the courts are reluctant to accept that litigation is an appropriate mechanism for resolving disputes within companies which are subject to public markets.[67]

Another problem created by the rule in *Foss* v. *Harbottle* is that directors' duties are owed to the company, and not, as a general rule, to shareholders in the company.[68] The fraud on the minority exception to the rule in *Foss* v. *Harbottle* is unlikely to apply where directors implement defensive tactics in order to preserve their position, unless the directors are involved in activities such as market manipulation. Even if a minority shareholder were held to be entitled to bring an action, other than a personal action, against directors for breach of their duties, and were to succeed in that action, any remedy would benefit the shareholder only indirectly. The remedy would go to the company, and, although an increase in the company's assets might be reflected in the market price of the company's shares, whether such an increase would compensate the minority shareholder for the loss she had sustained as a result of the directors' actions would depend on the market's perception of the adequacy of the remedy.[69]

The courts have recognized that in certain circumstances directors may owe duties directly to shareholders. For example, during a take-over offer, the duties owed by directors to shareholders include a duty to be honest, and a duty not to mislead.[70] It is conceivable that a minority shareholder could bring an action against directors who defeated a take-over attempt by means of misleading target company shareholders into believing that the offer would not provide sufficient consideration for their shares. The minority shareholder would, however, only be able to prove damage if she could show that the offer would have succeeded had it not been for the directors' misleading statements, that, apart from the statements the offer would have been accepted by holders of shares carrying at least 50 per cent of the voting rights in the company. In practice such an action would seem to be unlikely to succeed.

The position of shareholders in a predator company is no better. The subjective formulation of the director's duty to act bona fide in the best interests of the company suggests that directors who contemplate the acquisition of another company might rely on a claim that they believed the acquisition was in the best interests of the company. However, the threat of displacement by take-over, which is reduced by the decision to become a predator, suggests that directors should not be considered competent to make such decisions because of the potential conflict between their own personal interests and the interests of the shareholders. The impact of the proper purposes doctrine may extend to take-overs designed not to benefit the company but to entrench management in its position. If the directors were to argue that in their view the entrenchment of their position would be beneficial to the company, a shareholder who wished to challenge their actions would have to use arguments based on the proper purposes doctrine.

Minority shareholders in predator companies who wish to bring an action will be faced by significant procedural barriers, which are aggravated in relation to large companies. A minority shareholder in a large company will have substantial evidential and other problems in mounting litigation. After the decision of the Court of Appeal in *Prudential Assurance* v. *Newman Industries*[71] the 'fraud on the minority' exception to the rule in *Foss* v. *Harbottle* will not afford much assistance to a minority shareholder in a company involved in a take-over. An investor in a company which makes a take-over offer for another company because the directors believe that the take-over will increase their power, prestige, and remuneration (although in fact it will actually harm the acquiring company) is unlikely to be able to show that such action amounts to a fraud on the minority by those in control. Such action would not fall in the same category as cases involving an actual misappropriation of corporate property.[72] Unless there is an express provision requiring shareholder consent to proposed take-overs creating a personal right for shareholders, or the directors engage in some type of illegal activity in order to promote the take-over, a minority shareholder is therefore unlikely to be able to challenge such action.

Present rules fail to recognize that a minority shareholder in a predator does have an interest in whether a take-over attempt is pursued or not because a successful take-over will result in a transfer of wealth from the predator shareholders to the target shareholders.[73]

As things stand, a minority shareholder in a predator company is even less likely to be able to challenge actions of the directors in relation to take-overs than a minority shareholder in a target company. One way of reducing the impact of the rule in *Foss* v. *Harbottle* in this area would be to grant to shareholders personal rights to decide on particular types of action.[74] Amendment of the Articles of Association of a company to require shareholder approval by a special majority before particular actions such as making a take-over bid or implementing defensive tactics would allow minority shareholders to litigate if the requirement were not complied with,[75] at the cost of constraining the operation of the market for corporate control. Such a rule could enhance the ability of minority shareholders, if not to monitor management activity, at least to ensure that management took adequate account of the interests of minority shareholders during a take-over bid. On the other hand, such a solution would only be effective if the courts would recognize such a personal right, if shareholders were able and willing to litigate, and if management believed that litigation would be likely if they did not comply with the requirement.

The City Code on Take-overs and Mergers

Because, in practice, the impact of company law on take-overs is limited, the City Panel on Take-overs and Mergers developed the Code to regulate the conduct of take-overs. The aim of this body of quasi-legal rules is: 'to ensure fair and equal treatment of all shareholders in relation to take-overs'.[76] The General Principles contained in the Code emphasize this aim,[77] and the Code contains detailed requirements as to the procedures which must be followed during a take-over transaction,[78] and as to the information which must be provided to shareholders.[79] The requirements contained in the Code relating to the disclosure of information are subject to the criticisms which apply to any disclosure requirements, namely that it is not evident that the costs of imposing the requirements outweigh the benefits produced by the requirements and that the information required to be disclosed is not necessarily of use to shareholders.[80] Empirical measurement of the costs and benefits associated with such requirement is, of course, problematic.

One of the most important elements in the Code is the requirement that in certain circumstances a 'mandatory offer' be made.[81] The aim of this requirement is to ensure that all shareholders in the offeree company may share in the premium for control, by requiring a general offer to be made to shareholders in the target company on a change of control. The level of consideration offered to target shareholders must equal the highest price paid for shares of the same class in the target company in the twelve months preceding the bid.

It is possible that a requirement of this nature increases the cost to predators of acquiring the control of target companies. Although the aim of the rule is to ensure that the premium for control is not paid to one or more shareholders who actually transfer control, but is shared among all of the shareholders in the target company,[82] it is arguable that the expense incurred by predators in preparing formal offer documents exceeds the benefits provided to minority shareholders by the mandatory offer, and that the high cost of acquiring control may discourage many transactions which might benefit target company shareholders. Even if there were no rule requiring a predator to make a mandatory offer, minority shareholders in target companies would still seem to be in no worse position after a change of control than they were under the previous 'inefficient' management. Indeed, if the predator is to avoid future take-overs by other predators it will have to increase the company's share price, which presumably benefits minority shareholders.

So long as the target company remains part of a public market, therefore, minority shareholders in the target company are subject to no greater risk than they were before the change of control. By contrast, if the change of control involves a 'going private' transaction, minority shareholders whose position was adversely affected by a successful predator's actions can bring an action against the predator claiming that the predator's conduct was unfairly prejudicial to their interests.[83] The existence of this remedy should deter predators from acting in ways which prejudice the interests of minority shareholders.

The minority shareholders in the target company will suffer loss as a result of the change of control only if the predator is able to use its position to benefit itself at the expense of the minority shareholders. The predator could, for example, strip the assets of the target company and transfer the proceeds to itself, leaving the minority shareholders with an interest in a mere shell.[84] Rules which protect the right of shareholders to receive dividends,[85] which protect the holders of class rights from variation of their rights without their consent,[86] and which require new issues of shares to be made pro rata to existing shareholdings[87] reduce this risk. Such rules, if enforced, reduce the risk posed to minority shareholders in a target company.

The Code also deals with the question of directors' conflicts of interest. General Principle 9 provides that 'Directors of an offeror and the offeree company must always, in advising their shareholders, act only in their capacity as directors and not have regard to their personal or family shareholdings or to their personal relationships with the companies. It is the shareholders' interests taken as a whole, together with those of employees and creditors, which should be considered when the directors are giving advice to shareholders.' In addition to this general provision, the Code prohibits the directors of the offeree company from taking action 'which could effectively result in any bona fide offer being frustrated or in the shareholders being denied an opportunity to decide on its merits'.[88] The Code also contains specific examples of action which falls within the prohibition[89] but in the light of the Code's emphasis on the spirit rather than the letter of its provisions[90] the prohibition would seem to cover any possible defensive tactic which a board of directors might think of adopting in the face of a bid. The provisions of the Code do not, however, restrict the ability of companies to adopt general, as opposed to specific, defensive tactics because they apply only after the board 'has reason to believe that a bona fide offer might be imminent'.[91] A general policy of pursuing growth through acquisition to avoid becoming a target would not be affected by the rule. This rule is expressed sufficiently restrictively to prevent directors of target companies from acting to encourage auctions because such action 'could effectively result in' a 'bona fide offer being frustrated'.[92] This rule should protect shareholders in target companies from action by directors of target companies aimed to prevent a take-over from succeeding. In this way the rule reinforces the market for corporate control.

Shareholders in target companies have little legal protection against defensive mechanisms designed to defeat the operation of the market for corporate control. Although there is a continuing debate about whether the Code is an effective regulatory system,[93] the Code fills this gap by providing significant, if not excessive, benefits to such shareholders. Predator shareholders are not protected by the Code. On the other hand, the transaction costs imposed on predators by the Code may discourage transactions which might benefit target shareholders.

The Monopolies and Mergers Commission has recently suggested that 'the Department of Trade and Industry and the appropriate City regulatory authorities might consider whether any change is desirable in the rules in order to require the consent at a General Meeting of the shareholders of the bidding company before a bid may be completed.'[94] The Commission thought that the interests of shareholders in the bidding company were affected by highly leveraged bids.

The Response of Regulation to Social Costs

Although much of company law is geared to the protection of the interests of investors in companies other themes are discernible. For example, incorporation has been viewed as a privilege, or concession, one which gave rise to correlated obligations on the part of those involved in corporate enterprise.[95] In recent years commentators have emphasized the idea of the social responsibility of the corporation, and debate has focused on the question of the extent to which directors of a company should consider the interests of groups such as employees, consumers, and the local community in the area in which the company carries on its operations.[96] Corporate managements promote schemes to protect the environment or to increase employment opportunities, although such activities may result from a feeling that they will promote good public relations as often as from a feeling of responsibility to society. Indeed, it is possible for company law to impose limits on the right of corporate managements to work for the general good.[97]

In practice, directors of companies are rarely required to consider the interests of persons other than shareholders. Directors have a statutory duty to consider the interests of employees,[98] and judges have recently recognized a duty to consider the interests of creditors where the company is insolvent,[99] or even doubtfully solvent.[100] These duties are of limited value to those whom they are meant to benefit: the duty to consider the interests of employees is enforceable in the same way as are the other duties imposed on directors, and is therefore subject to the rule in *Foss* v. *Harbottle*. The duty to creditors will in any event be enforced as part of a liquidation.

The Code also suggests that directors should consider the interests of employees and creditors of the company in advising shareholders.[101] However, the provisions of the Code are generally geared to the protection of investors. The Code aims to ensure that the decision as to whether a take-over will succeed or not is taken by the target shareholders, a group which will have no further interest in the company' affairs if it decides to accept the offer—unless the consideration offered consists of shares in the offeror. This could be an argument in favour of a requirement that all offerors offer a consideration in shares rather than cash, to tie target company shareholders to the interests of the continuing entity to ensure that their decisions reflected the interests of that entity rather than their own personal interests. However, this suggestion conflicts with views that shareholders should be allowed to sell out so they are not forced to continue in an enterprise different from that in which they invested.[102] Moreover, a requirement that target shareholders remain involved in the combined entity could reduce the allocative efficiency of the market for corporate control.

Take-overs and mergers are subject to scrutiny by the Monopolies and Mergers Commission under the provisions of the Fair Trading Act 1973, and the Commission is able to block transactions which will operate 'against the public interest'.[103] The Director General of Fair Trading has said that 'in assessing the public interest, my primary concern (though not an exclusive concern) has been whether competition would be adversely affected'.[104]

It seems that when considering whether to recommend to the Secretary of State that a proposed merger be referred to the Monopolies and Mergers Commission for consideration the Director General of Fair Trading assesses the public interest on the basis of whether competition could be affected adversely. When the Monopolies and Mergers Commission considers proposed mergers many other considerations are included in the question of whether the merger will operate contrary to the public interest.

During 1986, of the fourteen reports of the Monopolies and Mergers Commission which were published and present to Parliament by the Secretary of State for Trade and Industry, six dealt with mergers.[105] The Monopolies and Mergers Commission decided that two out of the six proposed mergers might be expected to operate against the public interest.[106] In one of these cases the merger was allowed to proceed, subject to undertakings,[107] in the other case the merger was not allowed to proceed.[108]

The reports on these proposed mergers reveal that the Monopolies and Mergers Commission took various factors into account. For example, in the BET report, the Monopolies and Mergers Commission refers to effects on efficiency,[109] on research and development and product development,[110] on employment,[111] on safety and training,[112] and on imports.[113] In the Elders report, in addition to competition considerations,[114] the Monopolies and Mergers Commission took account of the potential effect on employment[115] and of the question of whether Elders might raid the surplus in the Allied-Lyons pension fund.[116] Other considerations involved the likelihood of the reverse situation being allowed in Australia.[117] In the report, the Monopolies and Mergers Commission considered the general question of highly leveraged bids,[118] and recommended that the Bank of England and the Stock Exchange should consider whether new controls were desirable to deal with such bids.[119]

In another case, the Monopolies and Mergers Commission considered a predator's financial position, and the effects that this might have on the target or the region in which the target operated. 'A company's activities might be subject to such risks that it would be contrary to the public interest for it to expand its business by acquisition because by doing so it would either increase the degree of that risk or widen the area of activity affected by the risk.'[120] In another report the Commission decided that a merger would be contrary to the public interest because the predator's past record showed that it appeared 'to have bought and sold subsidiaries with regard mainly to the immediate financial interests of the group'.[121] In yet another report the Commission considered the implications of foreign ownership of a British company.[122]

It is apparent that, despite the rhetoric of merger control, which emphasizes competition, regulators are prepared to consider other factors, and to prevent take-overs on the basis of other factors. The DTI has recently identified factors which will be taken into account in determining the effect of a merger on competition, although it has said that: '[i]t is not possible to set out rules of thumb which can be straightforwardly or mechanically applied to all cases'.[123] In the same report, the DTI expressed the government's view that the effects of mergers on employment, on the regions, and on research and development spending, and the effects of highly leveraged bids and foreign take-overs are matters where there is usually no divergence between the interests of private sector decision-makers.[124] It remains to be seen whether the Monopolies and Mergers Commission will ignore these matters in future.

5. Conclusion

Current regulation of take-overs in the United Kingdom concentrates on protection of shareholders in target companies, and on restriction of the adverse effects of take-overs on competition. Both systems of regulation are costly, involving the institutional costs of running the system and the transaction costs imposed on participants in take-overs. For this reason, it is important that regulation achieves its aims.

Three criticisms of the current system may be made: (1) greater legal protection should be provided to target company shareholders; (2) the interests of predator company shareholders should be recognized and protected; and (3) protection of the public interest should operate in a less haphazard and more predictable manner. In general, regulation of the way in which take-overs are effected, and regulation of public interest issues involved in take-overs should be co-ordinated in a single scheme, rather than by two regulatory bodies. It is not clear that issues involving the interests of target and predator company shareholders are sufficiently distinct from issues involving other interests to justify separate systems.

Notes

1. Statutes already affect transactions in corporate control. See, for example: The Fair Trading Act 1973; sections 146–53 of the Companies Act 1989. On suggestions that the system of regulation of take-overs will change, see, for example: Gower, 'Big Band and City Regulation' [1988] 51 *MLR* 1, 19–20; The Annual Report of the Takeover Panel for the year ended 31 March 1988; *EC Proposal for a Thirteenth Company Law Directive Concerning Takeovers. A Consultative Document* DTI, August 1989, pp. 7–12.
2. See, for example: Berle and Means *The Modern Corporation and Private Property* (New York: The MacMillan Company, 1933); Fama and Jensen, 'Separation of Ownership and Control' 26 *JL and Econ.* 301 (1983); Williamson, 'Organisation Form, Residual Claimants, and Corporate Control' 26 *JL and Econ.* 351 (1983); Victor Brudney, 'Corporate Governance, Agency Costs and the Rhetoric of Contract' 85 *Col. L. Rev.* 1403 (1985); Helm, 'Mergers, Take-overs, and the Enforcement of Profit Maximization' in Fairburn and Kay (eds.), *Mergers & Merger Policy* (Oxford: Oxford University Press, 1989).
3. 'The Government believe that the threat of take-over is a powerful spur towards efficiency in the management of UK Companies.' *Merger Policy. A Department of Trade and Industry Paper on the Policy and Procedures of Merger Control.* (1988) at para. 2.27.
4. See Berle and Means, n. 2 above, p. 287.
5. See, for example: Manne, 'Mergers and the Market for Corporate Control' (1965) *Journal of Political Economy* 110; Manne, 'Some Theoretical Aspects of Share Voting' 64 *Col. L. Rev.* 1427 (1964); Marris, *The Economic Theory of 'Managerial' Capitalism* (London: MacMillan & Co. Ltd., 1964); Easterbrook and Fischel, 'Corporate Control Transactions' 91 *Yale LJ* 698 (1982); Comment and Jarrell, 'Two-Tier and Negotiated Tender Offers. The Imprisonment of the Free-riding Shareholder', 19 *Journal of Financial Economics* 283 (1987).
6. See, for example: The Takeover Panel *Guinness PLC. The Distillers Company PLC*, 14 July 1989.

7. See text at n. 103 below.

8. See, for example: Stone *Regulation and its Alternatives* (Washington DC: Congressional Quarterly Press, 1982).

9. See, for example: Greene and Junewicz, 'A Reappraisal of Current Regulation of Mergers and Acquisitions', 132 *U. Pa. L. Rev.* 647–739 (1984), 732–5; Coffee, 'Shareholders Versus Managers: the Strain in the Corporate Web', 85 *Mich. L. Rev.* 1 (1986), 12; *Takeovers and Mergers. A GMB Plan for Action.* General, Municipal Boilermakers and Allied Trades Union, May 1987; *A Market with Rules: Regulating Takeovers, merges and Monopolies*, Labour Finance and Industry Group, 1988.

10. See, for example: Statement of the Panel on Take-overs and Mergers 'Guinness PLC' 30 January 1987; Joint Statement of The Stock Exchange and of the Panel on Take-overs and Mergers 30 January 1987.

11. Herman *Corporate Control, Corporate Power* (Cambridge: Cambridge University Press, 1981), p. 10.

12. See, for example, Manne, 'Some Theoretical Aspects of Share Voting', n. 5 above, p. 1432.

13. See, for example: Manne, 'Mergers and the Market for Corporate Control', n. 5 above at p. 119. Manne suggests that other benefits of the market for corporate control are the lessening of costly bankruptcy proceedings, more efficient management of corporations and protection to non-controlling corporate investors, and consequent impact on the liquidity of the market in shares.

   The Department of Trade and Industry has endorsed the role of the market in ensuring efficient allocation of resources. See: *Mergers Policy. A Department of Trade and Industry Paper on the Policy and Procedures of Merger Control*, n. 3 above, and *DTI—the Department for Enterprise* Cm. 278 (1988) para. 2.9.

14. See, for example: Manne, 'Mergers and the Market for Corporate Control', n. 5 above; Ryngaert, 'The Effect of Poison Pill Securities on Shareholder Wealth', 20 *Journal of Financial Economics* 377 (1988); Dann and De Angelo, 'Corporate Financial Policy and Corporate Control: A Study of Defensive Adjustments in Asset and Ownership Structure', 20 *Journal of Financial Economics* 87 (1988).

15. Manne, 'Some Theoretical Aspects of Share Voting', n. 5 above, p. 1431, n. 11. If efficiency is defined as the failure to take action to maximize the price of shares in a company it is not surprising if there is a correlation between management efficiency and share price.

16. See, for example: Easterbrook and Fischel, 'Limited Liability and the Corporation', 52 *U. Chi. L. Rev.* 89 (1985), 98; Chiplin and Wright, *The Logic of Mergers* (London: Institute of Economic Affairs, 1987), 26; and n. 3 above.

17. See, for example: Roll, 'The Hubris Hypothesis of Corporate Takeovers', 59 *Journal of Business* 197 (1986).

18. See, for example: Kraakman, 'Taking Discounts Seriously: The Implications of "Discounted" Share Prices as an Acquisition Motive', 88 *Col. L. Rev.* 891 (1988).

19. See, for example: Chiplin and Wright, *The Logic of Mergers*, n. 16 above, pp. 23–5.
20. On the synergy theory of take-overs, see, for example: Bradley, Desai, and Kim, 'Synergistic Gains from Corporate Acquisitions and their Division between Shareholders of Target and Acquiring Firms', 21 *Journal of Financial Economics* 3 (1988).
21. See, for example: Fischel, 'Efficient Capital Market Theory, the Market for Corporate Control, and the Regulation of Cash Tender Offers', 57 *Tex. L. Rev.* 1 (1978), p. 26; Jarrell and Bradley, 'The Economic Effects of Federal and State Regulations of Cash Tender Offers', 23 *JL & Econ.* 371 (1980); Ryngaert, 'The Effect of Poison Pill Securities on Shareholder Wealth', n. 13 above, p. 384.
22. On the calculation of the control premium see, for example: Leebron, 'Games Corporations Play: A Theory of Tender Offers' 61 *NYUL Rev.* 153 (1986), 163–5; Huang and Walkling, 'Target Abnormal Returns Associated with Acquisition Announcements: Payment, Acquisition Form and Managerial Resistance', 19 *Journal of Financial Economics* 329 (1987).
23. See, for example: Kraakman, 'Taking Discounts Seriously: The Implications of "Discounted" Share Prices as an Acquisition Motive', 88 *Col. L. Rev.* 891 (1988), 916–19; Dann and De Angelo, 'Corporate Financial Policy and Corporate Control', 20 *Journal of Financial Economics* 87 (1988).
24. The approaches adopted by commentators vary. See, for example: Lynch and Steinberg, 'The Legitimacy of Defensive Tactics in Tender Offers', 64 *Cornell L. Rev.* 901 (1978); Williamson, 'On the Governance of the Modern Corporation' 8 *Hofstra L. Rev.* 63 (1979); Benchuk, 'The Case for Facilitating Competing Tender Offers', 95 *Harv. L. Rev.* 1028 (1982); Easterbrook and Jarrell, 'Do Targets Gain from Defeating Tender Offers?' 59 *NYUL Rev.* 277 (1984); Jarrell, 'The Wealth Effects of Litigation by Targets: Do Interests Diverge in a Merge?' 28 *JL and Econ.* 151 (1985).
25. See, for example: Easterbrook and Fischel, 'The Proper Role of a Target's Management in Responding to a Tender Offer', 94 *Harv. L. Rev.* 1161 (1981), 1198.
26. See, for example: De Angelo and Rice, 'Antitakeover Charter Amendments and Stockholder Wealth', 11 *Journal of Financial Economics* 329 (1983); Linn and McConnell, 'An Empirical Investigation of the Impact of "Antitakeover" Amendments on Common Stock Prices', 11 *Journal of Financial Economics* 361 (1983); Malatesta and Walkling, 'Poison Pill Securities, Stockholder Wealth, Profitability and Ownership Structure', 20 *Journal of Financial Economics* 347 (1988); Jarrell and Poulsen, 'Dual Class Recapitalisations as Antitakeover Mechanisms: The Recent Evidence', 20 *Journal of Financial Economics* 129 (1988); Ruback 'Coercive Dual-Class Exchange Offers', 20 *Journal of Financial Economics* 153 (1988).
27. An example of such tactics would be the implementation of a poison pill

defence before a take-over is imminent. See Gilson, 'A Structural Approach to Corporations: The Case against Defensive Tactics in Tender Offers', 33 *Stan. L. Rev.* 819 (1981), 888.

28. Cf. Rule 9 of the City Code on Take-overs and Mergers (the 'Code').

29. Commentators and regulators who consider general defensive tactics to be less objectionable than specific defensive tactics do so because of the consent of shareholders, rather than because there is no immediate threat to the management of the company. Specific defensive tactics which are adopted in with the consent of a majority of the target company's shareholders are generally considered to be harmless. See, for example, the Code, Rule 21; Malatesta and Walkling, 'Poison Pill Securities: Stockholder Wealth, Profitability and Ownership Structure', 20 *Journal of Financial Economics* 347 (1988), 348–9; Jensen and Ruback, 'The Market for Corporate Control: The Scientific Evidence', 11 *Journal of Financial Economics* 5 (1988), 33; Brickley, Lease, and Smith Jr., 'Ownership Structure and Voting on Antitakeover Amendments', 20 *Journal of Financial Economics* 87 (1988), 96–7. But see, for example: Ruback. 'Coercive Dual-Class Exchange Offers', 20 *Journal of Financial Economics* 153 (1988), 154: 'Shareholders approve antitakeover provisions because such approval is the least costly alternative presented.'

30. See, for example: Bebchuk, 'The Case for Facilitating Competing Tender Offers', 95 *Harv. L. Rev.* 1028 (1985).

31. Easterbrook and Jarrell, 'Do Targets Gain from Defeating Tender Offers?' 59 *NYUL Rev.* 277 (1984); cf. Jarrell, 'The Wealth Effects of Litigation by Targets: Do Interests Diverge in a Merge?', 28 *JL and Econ.* 151 (1985).

32. See, for example: Singh, *Take-overs: Their Relevance to the Stock Market and the Theory of the Firm* (Cambridge: Cambridge University Press, 1971); Mueller, *The Determinants and Effects of Mergers: An International Comparison* (Cambridge, Mass.: Oelgeschlager, Gunn & Hain, Publishers, Inc., 1980); Mueller, *The Modern Corporation: Profits, Power, Growth and Performance* (Lincoln: University of Nebraska Press, 1986).

33. See, for example: Roll, 'The Hubris Hypothesis of Corporate Take-overs', n. 17 above; Dent Jr., 'Unprofitable Mergers: Towards a Market-Based Legal Response', 80 *NWUL Rev.* 777 (1986), 782.

34. See, for example: Asquith, Bruner, and Mullins Jr., 'The Gains to Bidding Firms from merger' 11 *Journal of Financial Economics* 121 (1983); Jensen and Ruback, 'The Market for Corporate Control: The Scientific Evidence', 11 *Journal of Financial Economics* 5 (1983), 16–22; Chiplin and Wright, *The Logic of Mergers*, n. 16 above, pp. 68–70.

35. See, for example: Roll, 'The Hubris Hypothesis of Corporate Takeovers', n. 17 above; Chipling and Wright, *The Logic of Mergers*, n. 16 above, pp. 65–8; *Mergers Policy: A Department of Trade and Industry Paper on the Policy and Procedures of Merger Control* (1988) at para. 2.10: 'The bulk of the evidence . . . is that the commercial performance of enterprises post-merger has, more

often than not, failed to live up to the claims of the acquiring firm at the time of the merger.'

36. Fischel, 'Efficient Capital Market Theory, The Market for Corporate Control and the Regulation of Cash Tender Offers', 57 *Tex. L. Rev.* 1 (1978), 43, n. 147.

37. See, for example: 'Takeover Activity in the 1980s', *Bank of England Quarterly Bulletin*, February 1989 78, 79; Cyne and Wright (eds.), *Divestment and Strategic Change* (Oxford: Philip Allan Publishers Limited, 1986); Wright, Chiplin, and Coyne, 'The Market for Corporate Control: The Divestment Option', in Fairburn and Kay (eds.), *Mergers & Mergers Policy*, n. 2 above.

38. On social costs, see, for example: Coase, 'The Problem of Social Cost', 3 *JL & Econ.* 1 (1960); Calabresi, 'Transaction Costs, Resource Allocation and Liability Rules—A Comment', 11 *JL & Econ.* 67 (1968); Buchanan and Faith, 'Entrepreneurship and the Internalization of Externalities', 24 *JL & Econ.* 95 (1981); Ullmann, 'The Structure of Social Costs', in Ullmann (ed.), *Social Costs and Modern Society* (Westport, Conn.: Quorum Books 1983).

39. See, for example: Chiplin and Wright, *The Logic of Mergers*, n. 16 above, pp. 53–5.

40. See, for example: Monopolies and Mergers Commission, *Lonrho Limited and House of Fraser Limited* HC 73 (1981) The Commission considered, at para. 7.52, that there was 'at least a very real and substantial risk that the efficiency of House of Fraser would deteriorate seriously as a result of the merger, and that it would be detrimental to the public interest that it should be exposed by the merger to such a risk'.

41. Coffee Jr., 'Shareholders versus Managers: The Strain in the Corporate Web', *Mich. L. Rev.* 1 (1986), 100.

42. See, for example: Monopolies and Mergers Commission, *Lonrho Limited and Scottish and Universal Investments Limited and House of Fraser Limited.* HC 261 (1979) at para. 8.18: because Lonrho and Scottish and Universal Investments were conglomerates no issues of restriction or distortion of competition arose. For comments on the issues raised by conglomerate mergers see Monopolies and Mergers Commission, *Blue Circle Industries Limited and Armitage Shanks Group Limited*, Cmnd. 8039 (1980) at paras. 8.29 to 8.34.

43. See for example King, 'Takeover Activity in the United Kingdom', in Fairburn and Kay (eds.), *Mergers & Merger Policy*, n. 2 above, pp. 108–10; Taggart Jr., 'The Growth of the "Junk" Bond Market and its Role in Financing Takeovers' in Auerbach (ed.), *Mergers and Acquisitions* (Chicago: University of Chicago Press, 1988).

44. King, 'Take-over Activity in the United Kingdom', in Fairburn and Kay (eds.), *Mergers & Merger Policy* n. 2 above, p. 110.

45. Herman, *Corporate Control, Corporate Power*, n. 10 above, p. 100.

46. Section 47 of the Financial Services Act 1986 prohibits market manipulation. However, the boundaries of the offence are uncertain. Could off-balance sheet financing amount to unlawful market manipulation? On off-balance

sheet finance see Weetman, 'Off-balance Sheet Finance: The Quest for an Accounting Solution', *The Investment Analyst*, 89 July 1988, 4.

47. I use the word 'quasi-legal' to refer to the rules promulgated by the Panel on Take-overs and Mergers because, although the Panel has no statutory authority to make law, and the Introduction to the Code emphasizes that it does not constitute law as such, the Code has had an impact on the development of the common law. See, for example: *Gething* v. *Kilner* [1972] 1 WLR 337: *R.* v. *Panel on Take-overs and Mergers ex.p. Datafin plc* [1987] 2 WLR 699; *R.* v. *Panel on Take-overs and Mergers ex.p. Guinness* [1989] 1 All ER 509; and McCrudden, 'Codes in a Cold Climate: Administrative Rule-making by the Commission for Racial Equality', (1988) 51 MLR 409.

48. For example: Paragraph 1(a) of the Introduction to the Code emphasizes that it 'represents the collective opinion of those professionally involved in the field of take-overs as to good business standards and as to how fairness to shareholders can be achieved.' The maintenance of such standards is thought to be important to the integrity of the financial markets in the United Kingdom.

49. See the Code, General Principle 7, Rule 21.

50. See the Introduction to the Code at section 1(a).

51. See, for example: Fama and Jensen, 'Agency Problems and Residual Claims', 26 *JL & Econ.* 327 (1983), 331; Axworthy, 'Corporate Directors—Who Need Them?', (1988) 51 *MLR* 273; Jensen and Ruback, 'The Market for Corporate Control: The Scientific Evidence', 11 *Journal of Financial Economics* 5 (1983), 43.

52. For judicial recognition of this threat see *Hogg* v. *Cramphorn* [167] 1 Ch 254, 265. See also David Lodge, *Nice Work* (Secker and Warburg, 1988) at 263: '"What you mean," said Vic bitterly, "is that by selling off Pringle's now, you can show a profit on this year's accounts at the next AGM," Stuart Baxter examined his nails, and said nothing. "I won't work under Norman Cole," said Vic. "Nobody's asking you to, Vic," said Baxter.'

53. *Re Smith and Fawcett* [1942] Ch 304.

54. *Bray* v. *Ford* [1896] AC 44. For consideration of the conflicts of interest involved in management buyouts, see, for example: Booth, 'Management Buyouts, Shareholder Welfare, and the Limits of Fiduciary Duty', 60 *NYUL Rev.* 630 (1985); Schleifer and Vishny, 'Management Buyouts as a Response to Market Pressure', in Auerbach (ed.), *Mergers and Acquisitions*, n. 43 above. The Take-over Panel introduced new rules to deal with management buyouts in January 1990.

55. See, for example: *In re Forest of Dean Coal Mining Company* (1878) 10 Ch. D. 450, 452: directors were 'commercial men managing a trading concern for the benefit of themselves and of all the other shareholders in it'.

56. Directors' fiduciary duties are often characterized as representing the terms of the contracts investors would make with the directors if they were to

negotiate such contracts. See, for example: Easterbrook and Fischel, 'Corporate Control Transactions', 91 *Yale LJ* 698 (1982), 701–2.

57. Cf. the operation of the 'business judgment rule' in the United States. See, for example: Greene and Junewicz, n. 9 above, p. 712; Stegemoeller, 'The Misapplication of the Business Judgement Rule in Contests for Corporate Control', 76 *NWUL Rev.* 980 (1982); Easterbrook and Fischel, 'The Proper Role of a Target's Management in Responding to a Tender Offer', n. 25 above, pp. 1194–8.

58. *Hogg* v. *Cramphorn* [1967] Ch 254; *Bamford* v. *Bamford* [1970] Ch 212; *Howard Smith* v. *Ampol Petroleum* [1974] AC 821; *Clemens* v. *Clemens* [1976] 2 All ER 268. The precise limits of the doctrine are unclear.

59. *Howard Smith* v. *Ampol Petroleum* [1974] AC 821, 837. Although the company in this case appears to have been involved in a public market (see pp. 827, 828, 838) the other cases in which the proper purposes doctrine has been applied in the United Kingdom have involved unquoted companies.

60. See, for example: Gelfond and Sebastian, 'Re-evaluating Duties of Target Management in a Hostile Tender Offer', 60 *BUL Rev.* 403 (1980) at 415; Lofthouse, 'Competition Policies as Take-over Defences', (1984) *JBL* 320, 333.

61. For a suggestion that shareholders have a personal right to prevent directors from acting for an improper purpose, see *Re A Company (005136 of 1986)* [1987] BCLC 82.

62. Courts in the United Kingdom are reluctant to interfere in the take-over process. See, for example: *R.* v. *Panel on Take-overs and Mergers ex p Guinness* [1989] 2 WLR 863, 868: *Re Ricardo Group plc* [1989] BCLC 566, 577.

63. (1843) 2 Hare 461.

64. This exception does not seem to extend to obtaining a remedy once an illegal act has occurred. See *Smith* v. *Croft* [1987] 3 WLR 405. But see also section 111A of the Companies Act 1985, introduced by section 131 of the Companies Act 1989 removing barriers to remedies in damages for shareholders. If a shareholder were to have a personal right not to have the value of her shareholding affected by unlawful acts of the directors, this provision might allow a remedy in damages.

65. *Trevor* v. *Whitworth* (1887) 12 App Cas 409, section 23 of the Companies Act 1985.

66. See section 151 of the Companies Act 1985.

67. See e.g. *Prudential Assurance* v. *Newman Industries* [1982] Ch 204 at 225: 'the Prudential, not being the proper plaintiffs, had no knowledge of what had gone on inside Newman'.

68. *Percival* v. *Wright* [1902] 2 Ch 421; although see *Re A Company* n. 61 above.

69. A minority shareholder in a quoted company is not entitled to recover damages for a decrease in the value of the investment: *Prudential Assurance* v. *Newman Industries (No. 2)* [1982] Ch 204, 222, because 'such a "loss" is merely

a reflection of the loss suffered by the company. The shareholder does not suffer any personal loss.'

70. *Gething* v. *Kilner* [1972] 1 All ER 1166, 1170.
71. [1982] Ch 204.
72. See, for example: *Cook* v. *Deeks* [1916] 1 AC 554.
73. Nor is there any recognition of this potential threat to predator shareholders in the Code, which assumes that take-overs threaten target shareholders, rather than predator shareholders.
74. An example of the application of the personal rights exception to the Rule is *Edwards* v. *Halliwell* [1950] 2 All ER 1064.
75. *Edwards* v. *Halliwell*, see n. 74 above, is also an example of the special procedure/special majority exception to the rule.
76. See the Introduction to the Code at Section 1(a).
77. See e.g. General Principles 1, 4, 5.
78. See e.g. Rules 1, 2, 9–11, 30–2.
79. See e.g. General Principles, 4, 5, and Rules 19, 23–9.
80. See, for example: Kripke, 'A Search for a Meaningful Securities Disclosure Policy', 31 *Business Lawyer* 293 (1975).
81. See Rule 9.
82. On equal treatment in sales of control see, for example: Leech, 'Transactions in Corporate Control', 104 *U. Pa. L. Rev.* 725 (1956); Jennings, 'Trading in Corporate Control', 44 *Calif. L. Rev.* 1 (1956); Brudney and Chirelstein, 'Fair Shares in Corporate Mergers and Takeovers', 88 *Harv. L. Rev.* 297 (1974); Cohn, 'Tender Offers and the Sale of Control: An Analogue to Determine the Validity of Target Management Defensive Measures', 66 *Iowa L. Rev.* 475 (1981); Bebchuk, 'Toward Undistorted Choice and Equal Treatment in Corporate Takeovers' 98 *Harv. L. Rev.* 1693 (1985).
83. See section 459 of the Companies Act 1985.
84. Regulators have developed rules to prevent asset stripping in order to maintain public confidence in the markets. However, to an economist, asset stripping is not necessarily an undesirable practice as it involves the transfer of resources to a more efficient use. See, for example: *Mergers Policy: A Department of Trade and Industry Paper on the Policy and Procedures of Merger Control*. (1988) at para. 2.25.
85. See, for example: *Re A Company (No. 00370 of 1987) ex p. Glossop* [1988] 1 WLR 1068.
86. See sections 125–9 Companies Act 1985.
87. See sections 89–96 Companies Act 1985.
88. General Principle 7.
89. See Rule 21.
90. See the introduction to the General Principles.
91. See General Principle 7.
92. See General Principle 7.

93. See, for example: Hurst, 'Self Regulation versus Legal Regulation', (1984) 5 *Co. Law.* 161.
94. *Elders IXL Ltd and Allied-Lyons plc*, Cmnd. 9892 (1986) at para. 8.54.
95. See, for example: Stokes, 'Company Law and Legal Theory', in Twining (ed.), *Legal Theory and Common Law* (Oxford: Basil Blackwell, 1986), 162.
96. See, for example: Hopt and Teubner (eds.), *Corporate Governance and Directors' Liabilities* (Berlin: Walter de Gruyter, 1985).
97. See, for example: *Rosemary Simmons* v. *UDT* [1986] 1 WLR 1440.
98. See section 309 of the Companies Act 1985.
99. *West Mercia Safetywear* v. *Dodd* [1988] BCLC 250.
100. *Brady* v. *Brady* (1987) 3 BCC 535, 552 (obiter) (CA). reversed [1988] 2 WLR 1308.
101. See General Principle 9.
102. See, for example: Bradley and Rosenzweig 'Defensive Stock Repurchases and the Appraisal Remedy', 96 *Yale LJ* 322 (1986), 331.
103. Sections 69(1)(b), 69(4), and 84 of the Fair Trading Act 1973; and see Craig, 'The Monopolies and Mergers Commission: Competition and Administrative Rationality', in Baldwin and McCrudden (eds.), *Regulation and Public Law* (London: Weidenfeld and Nicolson, 1987); Fairburn, 'The Evolution of Merger Policy in Britain', in Fairburn and Kay (eds.), *Mergers and Mergers Policy*, n. 2 above.
104. *Annual Report of the Director General of Fair Trading for the period January to December 1985 to the Secretary of State for Trade and Industry* HC 403 (1986). See also *DTI—The Department for Enterprise* CM 278 (1988) at para. 2.10, indicating that in the future decisions as to whether to refer mergers, and the assessment of mergers by the Monopolies and Mergers Commission, will continue to be based mainly on the likely effect of the merger on competition, although other issues may occasionally be considered.
105. *British Telecommunications PLC and Mitel Corporation*, Cmnd. 9715 (1986) ('BT'); *BET Public Limited Company and SGGB Group plc*, Cmnd. 9795 (1986) ('BET'); *The General Electric Company plc and The Plessey Company PLC* Cmnd. 9867 (1986) ('GEC'); *Elders IXL Ltd and Allied-Lyons PLC* Cmnd. 9892 (1986) ('Elders'); *Norton Opax PLC and McCorquodale PLC* Cmnd. 9904 (1986) ('Norton'); *The Peninsular and Oriental Steam Navigation Company and European Ferries Group PLC* Cm. 31 (1986) ('P&O').
106. BT and GEC, n. 105 above.
107. BT, n. 105 above, at para. 10.77.
108. GEC, n. 105 above.
109. At para. 7.38.
110. At para. 7.40.
111. At para. 7.41.
112. At para. 7.43.
113. At para. 7.45.

114. At paras. 8.5 to 8.9.
115. At paras. 8.10 to 8.12.
116. At para. 8.13.
117. At paras. 8.14–8.17.
118. At paras. 8.50–8.54.
119. At para. 8.54.
120. *Lonrho Limited and Scottish and Universal Investments Limited and House of Fraser Limited.* HC 261 (1979) at para. 8.27.
121. *Amalgamated Industrials Limited and Herbert Morris Limited.* HC 434 (1976) at para. 127.
122. *Enserch Corporation and Davy Corporation Limited.* Cmnd. 8360 (1981) at paras. 9.16–9.24.
123. *Mergers Policy* n. 3 above, at para. 2.15.
124. At paras. 2.20–2.28.

Economic Theories of Organization

CHARLES PERROW

Until the last ten years or so the relationship between economics and organizational analysis has been a quite distant one. Most economic theorists treated the organization as an entrepreneur in a field of entrepreneurs, and saw little need to enquire into the nature of the organization itself. On the other hand, organizational analysts paid relatively little attention to the interaction of organizations, even less to industry characteristics, and virtually none to the role of organizations in the economy as a whole. The organization responded to an environment, and its response was the focus of interest, not the environment. This has changed. Two closely related bodies of theory in economics—agency theory and transaction-cost analysis—have taken the internal operation of the firm as problematical and have investigated it. Agency theory has focused upon the problem the 'principal' has in controlling the employee ('agent'), and transaction-cost analysis has focused upon the advantages of eliminating market contracts by incorporating suppliers and distributers into one's own firm—the replacement of the market by a hierarchy. Organizational analysts, on the other hand, have begun to develop the notion of the environment in a variety of ways, some of which involve networks of organizations, others take account of industry characteristics (but as yet none has studied the dynamics of the economy as a whole). These ventures by the two disciplines, if I may speak of organizational analysis as a discipline, are, of course, to be welcomed for a variety of obvious reasons. The two disciplines have much to learn from each other. A less obvious reason for welcoming the developments will concern me in this article, and it is a somewhat perverse one. I find the formulations regarding human behaviour and organizations by the economists to be not only wrong but dangerous. However, I find my own field of organizational analysis, and sociology in general, to be insufficiently developed to convincingly demonstrate the full measure of error. Therein resides the danger. But it is also an opportunity.

We are forced to develop an adequate answer to the characterization of human behaviour as pre-eminently the self-interested maximization of utilities, and forced to make a discriminating analysis of the rise of large corporations. The first, self-interested behaviour, has been a controversial view of human nature since the first marginalist doctrines two centuries ago, and our contribution to that intractable debate will be largely to try to keep alive alternative notions of human nature. The second, the rise of giant bureaucracies, is of more recent origin, and we have a chance of making a somewhat larger contribution there. I will start with agency theory, but spend most of this essay on transaction-cost analysis.

Agency theory

Agency theory refers to a contract in which one party is designated as the principal, and the other, the agent. The agent contracts to carry out certain activities for the principal, and the principal contracts to reward the agent accordingly.[1] Three assumptions are at the core of agency theory. The first is the one common to most economists: individuals maximize their own self-interest. The second is more specific to agency theory: social life is a series of contracts, or exchanges, governed by competitive self-interest. The third applies to internal organizational analysis: monitoring contracts is costly and somewhat ineffective, especially in organizations, thus encouraging self-interested behaviour, shirking, and especially opportunism with guile, or to put it more simply—cheating. Contracts *will* be violated because of self-interest, and *can* be violated because of the costs and ineffectiveness of surveillance. The theory then attempts to build models, almost always without empirical data, regarding the most effective ways to write and monitor contracts to minimize their violations.

If these assumptions sound extreme, note that they are widely shared. We invoke them when we blame unpleasant results on others, rather than ourselves or the situation. We say 'he was supposed to do that and didn't', or 'she should have known', or 'he works for me and I told him not to do that'. All assume either the difficulty of controlling subordinates or agents, or the opportunism of subordinates, or both when dealing with team efforts. We all invoke agency theory. We can all point to people who did do their share and thus got more rewards than they deserved—the 'free rider' problem celebrated by Mancur Olson.[2]

For agency theorists, even if the deception that occurs is unintended, without guile, and merely due to the slippage that occurs in social life, such as in missed signals, forgetfulness, or chance serendipity, the rational individual will turn it to his or her self-interest if that is possible. There is no occasion when behaviour will intendedly be other-regarding, rather than self-regarding, on any predictable basis or to any significant degree. Presumably there might be behaviour that is neither self- or other-regarding, but is neutral in its consequences, but this is never discussed and would probably be regarded as unmotivated or even non-rational behaviour. Agency theory, along with transaction-cost analysis, assumes that 'human nature as we know it', as Oliver Williamson puts it, is prone to opportunism with guile.

This condition accounts for capitalism. Alchian and Demsetz give us the scenario.[3] Four people performing a co-operative task, say loading trucks, find that the risk of any one of them slacking is such that they hire a fifth to monitor their work. The monitor has to have the power to hire and fire, thus we have a manager. She also appropriates a part of the income of the group, in the form of a salary. In order to motivate her to do the difficult job of watching the others work, she also gets any residual income or profit left over after paying the wages and her salary. (Measuring the work of others and watching them is universally regarded by these theorists as requiring more rewards than doing the work itself.) If she or the team decide to purchase equipment to increase their performance, say a fork-lift truck, they go to the money lenders. The level of trust being what it is, the money lenders set up a monitor to monitor the manager so as to assure them that their investment is protected. *They* then appropriate the residual income or profit. We now have stockholders, a board of directors, a CEO, management, workers, and capital equipment—in short, capitalism. It all started because four workers could not trust one another.

At least one heroic assumption is at work in agency theory—that human nature as we know it is ruled only or primarily by self-interest. Combined with the problems and costs of monitoring it means that people, being prone to cheating, will get the chance to do so. But human nature as I know it signifies primarily a *lack of instinctual responses*, compared to non-human nature, and this means humans are highly adaptive (as well as inventive and variable and so on). If so, the setting in which interactions or contracts occur is the most important thing to consider in explaining behaviour. Some settings, or organizational structures, as I shall argue shortly, will promote self-interested behaviour, others will promote other-regarding behaviour, and still others will be neutral. Furthermore, I follow Herbert Simon[4] and assume that rationality is bounded, or limited. If so, even where self-interest is encouraged by the context of behaviour, humans (1) do not have clear utilities to maximize, (2) do not have much of the information needed to maximize utilities, and (3) do not know of cause-effect relations regarding maximization. Agency theorists do not model the context of behaviour, nor the slippage occasioned by limited rationality, even though both of these should account for most of any observed variance in behaviour.

A second problem is less with the model than its application, though I believe the model builders nearly intend a biased application. When dealing with principal-agent relationships within organizations they almost invariably assume that it is the agent that is opportunistic, even to the point of cheating, rather than the principal. This may stem from unrealistic assumptions about an unimpacted (i.e. highly fluid) market for labour: the assumption that there is no authority relationship within firms, but only a series of contracts, because if the principal cheats, the agent is free to go elsewhere. Because agents (employees) generally don't go elsewhere, theorists assume any contract violations must be on their part rather than the principal's part. Were an authority relationship admitted (even the simple one that suggests the boss is free to fire employees, and maintain the firm by hiring others, while employees are not free to fire the boss and maintain the firm),[5] then the unequal power of the parties to the contract would have to be admitted. Once unequal power is entertained, it becomes obvious that, given self-interested behaviour, the boss has more occasions for cheating on employees than the reverse. He may exploit them, either by breaking the contract, or not including in the contract matters that violate their self-interest.

This focus upon agent opportunism to the exclusion of principal opportunism extends to the agency theory work on 'adverse selection'—hiring a poorly qualified agent. The principal has a problem, they say: the agent may misrepresent her 'type', that is, her training, skills, and character, when seeking employment. Elaborate models deal with this form of cheating.[6] But I could find no model in the literature that considered that the principal also has a 'type' and might misrepresent it to the prospective agent, e.g. in terms of hazardous working conditions, production pressures, adequacy of equipment, fairness of supervision, advancement possibilities, amount of compulsory overtime, etc. Agency theorists might argue that the principal who misrepresents himself will suffer a loss of reputation and thus not get agents, but prospective agents probably cannot determine the reputation accurately beforehand, will bear the costs of seeking a new job and perhaps relocation, and may simply find that 'elsewhere' also exploits. The employment relationship is an asymmetrical one; this is neglected by the theory, just as is the possibility that the principal's type may be represented. Agency theory appears to be ideologically incapable of keeping an eye on both ends of the contract, and incapable of noting any permanent asymmetry of resources and power stemming from the context.

Why, then, bother with it? First, because it, along with transaction-cost economics, is experiencing an amazing growth in popularity among organizational theorists,[7] possibly because it is so simple as to promise to cut through the complexities most of us are entangled in, and because it touches upon something we all like to do—blame our fellow workers or particularly our subordinates for failures that may well be a result of the situation or even our own behaviour. It is also in keeping with a recent presidential campaign theme of self-interest: are *you* better off today, not your community, city or nation, and not the less fortunate members of the community, city or nation, and not the prospects for the next generation—just you. There appears to be a basic cultural shift over the last two hundred or so years toward the celebration of self-interest.

The second reason we should bother with it is that it highlights the varying degree to which the major organizational theories recognize the asymmetry of power in organizations. Briefly, agency theory comes close to zero in this respect; in fact I suspect it may be designed to distract us from the existence of power differences. Human-relations theory does better; it recognizes the responsibility of masters to use their power wisely and humanely.[8] As such, it recognizes, to at least a limited extent, that behaviour is structurally determined and leaders are responsible for that structure. Classical bureaucratic theory pursues power and structure further, finding that power operates through such structural devices such as specialization, formalization, centralization, and hierarchy. It assumes that while shirking and deceptive representation of one's type will be problems, employment status is evidence that employees accept the necessity of unequal power relations, and can do little, other than shirk, to maximize their utilities at the expense of owners. The major problems of organization with both the human relations and bureaucratic model are not shirking by agents, but establishing routines, innovation when needed, and the co-ordination of the output of diverse units. Under the conditions of wage dependency and profit maximization, employee utilities are likely to be limited to continual employment, interesting work, opportunity to use and develop skills, safe work, some autonomy, and some influence in decisions that affect the efficiency of the organization.

What I have referred to as the neo-Weberian model goes even further in recognizing power differences and undercutting agency theory. It makes a central point of the fact that groups legitimately vie for power, as in the contest of sales and production; they seek to use the organization for their own ends, but these are rarely maximizing leisure or even income; because of bounded rationality one's interests are problematical at best, and the role of premiss-setting and unobtrusive controls in capitalist societies overrides the simple determination of interest. Thus, agency theory, by anchoring extreme assumptions about power and preferences, gives us a scale for judging theories.

But the best reason to pay attention to agency theory is that if forces us to consider the conditions under which organizations may promote competitive self-interested behaviour, and when they will promote other-regarding behaviour. I will consider only short-run consequences of behaviour where some immediate self-interest such as status, power, or income appears to be sacrificed in order to either not harm another, or to actually help another. In the world of organizations competitive self-regarding behaviour appears to be favoured by such conditions as the following:

1. *Self-interested behaviour is favoured when continuing interactions are minimized.* Some examples: a highly fluid ('unimpacted') labour market where job seekers are not constrained by personal or family ties to friends and the community when they seek work locations; 'spot contracting' in a labour market as with migrant workers, temporary help, high turnover fast food franchises, all of which maximize free movement of labour; heavy emphasis upon individual promotions or individual, rather than group, job rotations; rewarding loyalty to the firm rather than more proximate groups such as your own group and the other groups it interacts with.

2. *Self-interested behaviour is favoured where storage of rewards and surpluses by individuals is encouraged.* The tax structure favours individual rather than group rewards; organizational hierarchy promotes it, steep salary structures reinforce it; a stable class system (minimal redistribution of wealth) provides the context for it.

3. *Self-interested behaviour is favoured where the measurement of individual effort or contribution is encouraged.* This is done through personnel evaluations, promotions, piece rates, and the celebration of leadership; it is a continuing legacy of nineteenth-century individualism, celebrating individual rather than co-operative effort.

4. *Self-interested behaviour is favoured where we minimize interdependent*

effort through design of work flow and equipment. Work flow and equipment can minimize co-operative effort and responsibility by breaking up tasks and favouring assembly lines; precise contractual relationships promote this; so does the presumption that shirking is potentially rampant and that installing surveillance systems thwarts it.

5. *Self-interested behaviour is favoured where there is a preference for leadership stability and generalized authority.* This occurs when leaders are held to be all-competent and the position held continuously. Instead, we could alternate leadership tasks according to the skills of the individuals, thus avoiding stable patterns of dependency in subordinates and self-fulfilling assumptions of expertise in leaders. This is possibly a legacy of individualism and private ownership rights.

6. *Self-interested behaviour is favoured where tall hierarchies are favoured.* These are based upon unequal rewards and notions that co-ordination must be imperatively achieved.

It might be argued that I have just described capitalist organizations in the United States, and thus agency theory is appropriate. There are several responses. First, while capitalist organizations do encourage self-interested behaviour, this does not mean that human nature is self-interested; it may be the situation or context, that is, the organizational structures fostered by capitalism, that encourages it. The counter argument then would be that public organizations also have these characteristics, and even most organizations in the so-called socialist states. I would still resist the agency-theory formulation on the grounds that once what I call 'factory bureaucracy' (specialization, formalizations, centralization, and hierarchy) is made possible by creating a wage-dependent population, only extraordinary resistance to economic and political élites will prevent factory bureaucracy from spreading to non-economic organizations and to other nations. Next I would note that even in factory bureaucracy the overwhelming preponderance of behaviour is co-operative and 'neutral-regarding', and some is even other-regarding. Many have argued that social life would be impossible without other-regarding and neutral forms of behaviour.

Finally, I would argue that the task is to create structures that minimize self-regarding behaviour, and there is evidence that organizations vary considerably in this respect. Indeed there are some recognized firms which appear to minimize self-interested behaviour. Joyce Rothschilde-Witte describes many in her work, though they are small and unstable; Rosabeth Kanter and others argue that large ones can be designed in this way; Japanese firms, while far from ideal in many respects, do minimize some of the six characteristics that encourage self-interested behaviour. It may be that some small, innovative, high-technology firms require some to be successful, and Scandinavian societies, in particular, Sweden, have successfully developed some alternative structures, and in a shorter period than it took most Western countries to develop capitalist structures.[9]

Agency theory, then, forces us to recognize the extent to which we are all agency theorists in our worse moments, blaming others when the structure or ourselves should be blamed; forces us to examine the structures that evoke different kinds of behaviour; reminds us that, easy as it is to say so, human behaviour is not rooted in some vague notion of 'human nature as we find it', but depends upon the contexts that we create. Each generation of organizational analysts should be reminded of these key points, and be forced to continually explore them. For this, we might be grateful for agency theory, despite its very conservative political bias.

Transaction-cost economies

Transaction-cost economies (TCE), largely the creation of economist Oliver Williamson following early work of John Commons and Ronald Coase, is less politically conservative than agency theory.[10] In contrast to most agency theory it recognizes authority relations, denies that it is useful to consider the organization as nothing more than a series of contracts between parties, and recognizes some of the societal problems associated with giant corporations. it is also far more attentive to bounded rationality and sociological and structural variables. It has received much acclaim in the organizational literature, and indeed it claims to supplant most existing organizational theories. Like agency theory, however, it is based upon a self-interest model of human behaviour, and is relentlessly and explicitly an efficiency argument. Its appearance should prompt organization theorists, especially left-leaning ones, into some vigorous work, and for this reason we should welcome it.

The theory raises many issues that need discussion by organizational analysts. I will make the following arguments: we need a better formulation of some of our fuzzy notions of trust, and it provides one; we need more awareness of the economic concepts regarding industries and market characteristics, and TCE provides this; we have not explored issues of mergers sufficiently, such as the effect upon complexity and tight coupling, and a critique of TCE will encourage this; discussion of market concentration, monopoly power, and the growth of huge organizations needs to include standard economic concepts more than has been the practice; TCE concepts provide a way of bridging inter- and intraorganizational analysis more than has been our practice; the issue of markets versus hierarchies is falsely posed by this theory and we can use this opportunity to reconceptualize an important area of interorganizational analysis; and, perhaps most important, Williamson does not ask simply why there are so many big firms, but asks where will big firms fail to appear, a question even left-leaning organizational theorists have failed to ask. Thus, though I think TCE is a wrong theory, it forces us to address questions we have tended to neglect or improperly pose. This part of my essay will range widely and necessarily briefly over these several issues; each could be an essay in its own right. I hope it will stimulate more searching essays by others.

The theory

Transaction-costs economics is an efficiency argument for the present state of affairs, as most mainstream economic theories are, arguing that the appearance of giant organizations in some industries represents the most efficient way of producing goods for an industrial society. Distortions are acknowledged, and that the government should get out of this or that, but in general capitalism and the free market produce the most efficient economic system, apparently despite the fact that the market is supplanted by hierarchies. Williamson is explicit regarding efficiency, by which he means the efficiency of organizational forms, not the efficiency of specific practices or machines or sales techniques or transportation devices, though the efficiently run organization will seek out these other operating efficiencies. Discussing the shift from many organizations to a few large ones over the century, he says 'I argue that efficiency is the main and only systematic factor responsible for the organizational changes that have occurred.'[11]

There are four components in his theory: uncertainty, small-numbers bargaining, bounded rationality, and opportunism. Bounded rationality and opportunism are ever present, but will only result in large firms where there is uncertainty and small-numbers bargaining.

Uncertainty refers to changes in the environment that the owner cannot foresee or control; it provides the dynamic element that makes equilibrium of the market unstable.

Small-numbers bargaining means that once a long-term contract has been signed, with suppliers, or workers or customers, the normal market situation is disturbed. The parties to the contract have privileged positions because they have more experience with the other party, and more specialized resources to serve it, than those in the market that sought but did not get the contract.

For example, if you find that your supplier's quality is slipping, you may be reluctant to break the contract and find another because you are set up to deal with that supplier; you have made an investment in routines and have experience with that firm's supplies and procedures and idiosyncrasies, and that investment will be lost. Or, within the firm, after employees have worked for you for awhile, they gain experience and skills, and if they threaten to quit or strike you cannot simply hire others that will immediately be as productive.

A related concept is *asset specificity*. If, by working for a firm at a specialized job, one develops specific skills that job seekers outside the organization don't have, one has specific assets, and this gives one some bargaining power. The employer has to think twice about firing the person, or about refusing a demand for a raise. While I think this concept is useful, the bilateral nature of exchange renders it opaque: because these assets are specific to this firm, it gives the boss some power too—the employee's specific skills will give him or her no bargaining advantage over another potential employer because the skills are specific to this one organization. This is rarely acknowledged by Williamson. A similar bilateral relationship occurs between supplier and customer, which Williamson does acknowledge.

Bounded rationality creates a problem because of *opportunism*. Lacking perfect information about suppliers or workers allows them to behave opportunistically. You cannot judge the claim of the supplier that labour problems or raw material problems delay deliveries, and you cannot costlessly turn to another supplier. Similarly, the customer may misrepresent his problems to the supplier, and fail to honour the contract. But an alternative customer is not always available. Such situations are called 'market failures'; uncertainty about labour or supplies or demand, when combined with small-numbers bargaining, and the lack of adequate information and the chance of opportunism all disrupt the normal market relationships. In the normal, neo-classical market, a large number of suppliers and producers bargain daily over prices. The market assures the lowest possible prices, adjusts to changes in demand immediately and discourages opportunism because opportunists will not find people to trade with the next day. Instead, we find uncertainty, small numbers, bounded rationality, and opportunism, that is, a failure to achieve the classical market.

Well, that's serious. (It is also the rule of our economy; the markets of neo-classical theory are few in number and small in impact.) What is to be done? Williamson and capitalists have the solution: vertical integration. One can integrate forward by buying out the person one sells to (or setting up one's own distribution services) or integrate backwards by buying out one's supplier (or building one's own source of supply). If the supplier is part of your firm you can control her. It eliminates the leverage she had as one of a handful of suppliers that you had to depend upon. She won't dare lie about labour problems or raw material problems because you can check the books (controlling opportunism). And you will not have to write all those contracts with her, trying to specify complex future contingencies, and have your people checking to see that all the promises are fulfilled. This way you reduce the costs of transacting business, hence the term transaction-cost economics. There will be other economies, such as economies of scale though they are not stressed by Williamson, but these economies are likely to be quite small. For Williamson, minimizing transaction costs is the key to efficiency, and it explains concentration of production in large firms better than several competing theories, including Marxist and other power theories, historian Alfred Chandler's theory of co-ordination and throughput speed, technological arguments, and those that deal with the strategic use of finance.[12]

The development of large firms, so evident in our twentieth-century economic history, does not occur in all areas, however, and the ability to explain why markets will persist in some areas while they disappear in others would indicate the power of his theory. The question has often been asked, why, if giant firms are more efficient, do we not have just one giant firm? Here the potential pay-off of TCE becomes apparent.

Markets, argues Williamson, will continue to exist if spot contracts will do the job efficiently. The market for supplies is cleared each day, so to speak, if transactions are one-shot, so no long-term contacts need to be written. The firm that wishes to buy some furniture asks for bids and selects the lowest, just as a person shops for a television. There is no opportunity for cheating on long-term delivery contracts, no 'first mover advantages' (where the first firm to get the contract has an inside track on all future contracts because of small-numbers bargaining). Markets can also survive if there is little uncertainty in price, volume, production costs, labour relations, and the like, even if the market is not a spot one. Standard supplies (toilet paper, business forms, batteries, picks and shovels) are available from many sources, have clear prices, and the quality is readily judged. Markets will also survive if the costs of entry (starting up a production facility) are low; entrepreneurs will see that existing producers are making a lot of money and so they will come in and thus bring the price down because of competition. The cost of entry will be more likely to be low if the technology is well known. Predictable high-volume demand also reduces uncertainty and favours market transactions instead of vertical integration. Thus, hierarchy replaces markets when there are long-term contracts in an uncertain environment and the barriers to entry are reasonably high, because the costs of opportunism are reduced by substituting an authority relationship ('you now work for me') for a contractual one.

The value of the theory

Williamson's work highlights a number of variables that organizational theorists unfortunately neglect. Take the notion of 'asset specificity'. We are wont to invoke vague terms such as tradition, or trust, when we encounter long-term relationships between firms and suppliers, or firms and customers, or even a supervisor and workers. A good part of that tradition or trust may lie in the bilateral dependency of each of the parties. The supplier is as dependent upon the customer as he is upon her, because of asset specificity. The assets of the supplier are highly specific in order to meet the specific demands of the customer, and the customer's products are made more specific or inflexible because of the specificity of the supplier's components. (Note, though, that using this concept with its clear bilateral implications reduces any efficiency difference between markets and hierarchies because relationships in both will tend towards an equilibrium. Because hierarchies have replaced some markets, Williamson must explain the disappearance of bilaterality and the trust it implies on other than efficiency grounds.)

A similar argument can be made regarding the tasks the supervisor wants done, and the skills the workers have developed. Asset specificity, in a sense, demands the continuity that we call tradition, and produces the repeated interactions that we call trust. Locating the source of tradition and trust in an economic relationship need not remove the sociological concern with the social and cultural content of these transactions. One reason trust may appear in bilateral exchanges is that the parties get to know crucial non-economic aspects of each other and of their interdependency. Political, ethical, and cultural values are exchanged and modified. The economic relationship becomes 'embedded' (as Granovetter terms it, in his important essays on economics and sociology)[13] in social and cultural exchanges, and the strictly economic and strictly self-interested nature of the exchange is modified and overlaid. But Williamson reminds us that it cannot be ignored, and economic concepts help us to see it.

The bilateral relationship may not be equal, we should note. Generally, the larger firm has the greatest leverage. If the larger firm is the buyer its purchasing power allows it to find another source of supply, and probably do it more readily than the supplier can develop another customer. Similarly, the employer would prefer to retain the experienced employee, but can replace her, while she will have more trouble finding another employer, unless unusual skills or an unusual labour market exists. But any analysis of the concepts of trust and tradition had best be aware of Williamson's discussion of small numbers bargaining and asset specificity.

Nor have organizational theorists paid much attention to the characteristics of market transactions. Distinguishing spot from long-term contracts, many bargainers from small numbers of them, degrees of substitutability of goods or services and stability and instability of demand, technologies, and so on may not appear to be a signal contribution. In one form or another these ideas are used by many theorists. But Williamson links them together, makes them explicit, and demands that issues of market concentration, monopoly power, the growth of huge organizations, and the like be addressed with these considerations in mind. In particular, formalizing the argument about transactions allows us to focus on the important question of why hierarchies replace markets.

Furthermore, because the concepts can be applied both to the relations between organizations, and to relationships within organizations, we get a fruitful link between the nature of markets (interorganizational relationships) and the nature of firms (intraorganizational relationships). By allowing us to make the link Williamson also brings into organizational analysis a field that it has neglected—industrial economics, which deals with the characteristics of industries (concentration, size, rates of change, characteristics of customers, and so on), though the literature has left the firms themselves as empty shells. Williamson provides us with some of the most relevant aspects of industrial economics, packaged for organizational theory.

Finally, Williamson restates the problem 'why so many big firms?' as: why do we get big firms (hierarchies) in some areas and not in others. This is a more interesting and more tractable problem. (The historian Alfred DuPont Chandler also raises it in this form and treats it as the main question a historian of business organizations should answer.[14]) Marxists have an answer of a sort for the first question: the disappearance of small firms and the growth of big ones is the product of the dynamics of capitalism—a ceaseless search for ever more profits, wherein the big fish gobble up the small. But they have no answer for the second question: when will markets (small firms) persist, despite the existence of powerful organizations nearby that seek ever more profits. These are questions that an organizational theory that has finally met the environment should be preoccupied with; we deal with them at the margins of our work, but we have not directly confronted them. Williamson has.

The criticisms

An extended example will illustrate some major criticisms one can make of TCE, and then we will review the criticisms of other scholars. My example is intended to explore a variety of issues regarding the costs of integration; I argue that the costs are born because the advantages are not efficiency, but appropriating profitable businesses and establishing market control. I do not believe that the costs of vertical integration have been systematically assessed in the literature; if not, and if my fictional example rings true, we owe this assessment to the challenge of Williamson's argument. In general, the criticisms of Williamson are likely to enrich the field more than his theory has.

TCE would have us explain why firms are not engaged in only one single function, such as grinding valves, which are sent to another firm that puts them in an engine block that a third has made, and so on. But systems with that much specialization disappeared one or two centuries ago, for the most part. The real question is why does a firm that is *already* large, buy up another good sized firm: Why merge *two hierarchies*, rather than why move from a bunch of tiny firms to a few big ones?

Consider this hypothetical account of a firm called Engines, Inc. It has about a thousand employees producing engines for air conditioning systems. It then buys out a firm, Radiators, Inc., with three hundred employees, that supplies radiators for these engines. Engines, reflecting its new acquisition, renames itself the ACE Company (for air conditioning equipment). TCE would have us believe that the costs of long-term contracts between Engines and Radiators were too high, so Engines bought Radiators in 1980. ACE now controls all the people that were owners and employees of Radiators and can reduce opportunism on the part of these people and save on lawyers who write contracts and accountants that monitor them. But is there really a saving?

Prior to 1980, there were two sets of transaction costs: writing and monitoring the contracts between Radiators and Engines, and the costs that each of the firms had in dealing with other parts of its environment. The second costs are not reduced. When Engines buys Radiators out, it must continue to deal with the environment that Radiators had to deal with, for example, buying metal and other supplies, dealing with the government, with labour, the community and so on. As we shall see these costs may actually rise because the form of transactions will change somewhat under the new ownership. The transaction costs associated with the Radiators-Engines relationship will certain change, but I will argue that they are actually likely to rise, rather than fall, as far as Engines is concerned.

If the market for air conditioning equipment declines, the new firm, ACE, cannot simply tell its supplier of radiators that it is cancelling its order (with due notice, or even a penalty), or cutting the size of a new one, thus making Radiators suffer all or most of the loss. ACE itself has to absorb the loss of business (fixed capital lying idle, layoffs with unemployment insurance costs, excess managerial staff, and loss of profit-generating activity). The sum total of transaction costs remain; their location is different. (One of the problems with TCE is that the definition of a transaction cost is altogether too flexible for a convincing test of the theory; but shutting down facilities and laying off experienced employees seem to qualify as transaction costs.)

Suppose the opposite happened, and the demand for its product soared. The radiator division within ACE can build new facilities to expand its production no faster than Radiators could (though it might get capital a bit faster if ACE had some lying around); there is no saving here. In fact, there might be a loss. Radiators might have added facilities to meet the new demand, calculating that if the rise in demand by Engines turned out to be temporary, they still might be able to sell their excess to other engine companies. But ACE might find it awkward to become a supplier to its own competitors (though it happens regularly in a few industries such as electronics), and the competitors would probably prefer to buy from suppliers they can control rather than from a competitor. Thus ACE is less likely to risk an expansion of facilities. Some flexibility is lost in the acquisition.

Well, what about opportunism? Ms Radoe, once the head of Radiators is now the General Manager of the Radiator division of ACE. According to TCE she can now be watched much more carefully (ACE has the information on her behaviour) and any disputes between her and, say, the Chief Operating Officer, Mr Enginee (the former head of Engines who now oversees the radiator and engines divisions) can be settled 'by fiat', that is, a direct order. Before, there were transactions costs— contract writing, bargaining, legal actions, and so on. If Mr Enginee needs support for disciplining Ms Radoe if fiat is resisted, he can turn to the Chief Executive Officer of ACE, Mr Banke. Mr Banke was an officer of the bank that provided the loan for buying up the radiator company. As a condition of that loan, he was made CEO of the company. (He need not know anything about air conditioning, but he must know about transaction costs, according to TCE, because these efficiencies count the most. He does, as a finance man and banker.)

But what is Ms Radoe likely to be doing in her new position? Here we will use the assumptions about opportunism and competitive self-interest that Williamson shares with agency theory. We will assume that the firm is structured, as most are, to encourage competitive self-interest. When Ms Radoe headed up Radiators she worked extremely hard because she owned the company and got the profits from it. No motivation to shirk, or slack, on her part. But at ACE she gets a salary (and perhaps a bonus) rather than direct profits. She has less incentive to work hard, and indeed, more to shirk, or even steal. Reflecting the incentives problem, ACE may develop an elaborate bonus plan based in part on the performance of Ms Radoe's division and in part on the performance of the firm as a whole, as other companies have done. Such plans have led to fierce controversy over internal pricing decisions within firms—a substantial transaction cost. Is the radiator division being charged more than its share of the overhead, and thus its internal profits are set lower than they would be if it were independent? Robert Eccles details the extensive transactions costs and political problems of internal pricing schemes, necessary once the market no longer exists. He concludes from extensive research that firms perceive the costs of *internal* transactions to be higher than external ones, and did not find TCE useful in understanding the transfer pricing problem.[15]

No doubt, given the emphasis upon opportunism in TCE, Ms Radoe will also be required to monitor it in her subordinates, just as she did when she owned the firm. But if there is no bonus plan she has less incentive to do so; their slacking or stealing will have a trivial effect upon her income, though it should not become so gross as to invite an inspection from Mr Enginee or Mr Banke. If there is a bonus plan she will take up her superior's time by arguing about internal pricing, as Eccles documents.

Furthermore, Mr Enginee, who used to watch her intermittently from a distance when she was his supplier, now has to watch her continually as her superior. Her division draws upon the resources of ACE and affects its accounting and personnel practices. Another set of transaction costs have increased. If she allowed rampant opportunism on the part of her employees when she headed up Radiators it was of no concern to Mr Enginee. It just meant she got less out of them and thus less profits; perhaps if she treated them well and they worked hard she made more profits, though we could have reservations about that. But the price to Mr Enginee was not affected, so he did not need to bother about it. He was only concerned with the contract, not her whole firm. Now he is held accountable for the whole division; if they slack, the profits to ACE are reduced. (Setting the radiator division up as a 'profit centre' is of little help. Contracts must still be written. If it is made maximally independent, with no more interactions than when it was a supplier of radiators to Engines, it may as well have remained a separate firm because there are no transaction cost savings—with one very important difference: as a separate firm ACE would not 'appropriate its profit stream', as economists put it. That is, the profits now go to ACE, not to Ms Radoe. We will later count this as possibly the primary motive for acquisitions.)

One can imagine Mr Enginee going home one night to tell Mrs Enginee, 'What a mistake. I read Oliver Williamson and it looked as if Engines was ripe for savings on transactions costs. You know, he is the one that called Perrow's theory "bankrupt" in that book where Perrow criticized Williamson.[16] Well, we had this small-numbers bargaining situation with big Ms Radoe, and long-term contracts, uncertainty about product demand, and all the rest including opportunism on her part—she claimed those leaky radiators were the result of poor handling by us and threatened to sue us if we refused to pay. So I decided to buy her out. She was working eighty hours a week and she didn't like her reputation for driving her employees, so she was willing to come to work for us.'

'But I had to let Mr Banke come in as CEO in order to get capital for the buyout. Williamson never mentioned that there are large costs in acquiring even small firms. It was profitable, so we could raise the money, and it should increase our profits—Mr Banke and the stockholders will get them and not Ms Radoe. But it saddled us with three hundred employees and all kinds of commitments at a time when sales were falling. We are losing money, not her.' (Or, 'Now that sales are booming it is we that have to pay for the increase in overtime and other special production costs, whereas before she would have had to take less profit on each item because of the contract, at no cost to us.') [TCE neglects to consider all transaction costs. Flexibility in response to changes is reduced.]

'Furthermore,' he continues, turning up his custom-built air conditioner as he gets more heated, 'I have had a hell of a time getting their accounting and information-management system to link up with ours. Theirs was fine for their product and volume, while ours doesn't work well for them. But we have to have an integrated financial statement by law and the bankers demand certain kinds of reports, personnel needed to standardize and so on. So I had to hire more accountants, and Ms Radoe complains that she can't watch performances and budgets as closely now.' [Internal co-ordinating costs rise when different operations must be combined. Accounting and surveillance systems must be standardized while variable, tailor-made systems would be more effective; there are costs to decentralizing large, complex systems that do not appear in smaller, simpler ones.]

'It's even worse. In 1979, before we bought them, I used to call up two or three other radiator firms and find out what they were charging for various models, and she knew it, so she kept her prices in line. Now I don't have a good idea of the costs of our radiators because of internal-pricing problems. The accountants say the radiator division is a profit centre, but it has to contribute to the firm's overhead and advertising costs, some personnel costs, a lot of staff running back and forth to her city, and we just don't know if the prices they charge us for radiators are fair or not. It would cost us a lot to find out if they are fair.' [Internal pricing and internal cost systems are unreliable and expensive; the market provides comparatively cheap and reliable information.]

'When Radoe had labour trouble before the merger we just invoked the contract and it cost her plenty to fight that union, but it was her money (and her temper). We gave a little of course, we couldn't hang a good supplier, and buying elsewhere was expensive. But all in all it only cost us about 10 per cent in profits for the quarter. But now we have to bear the total cost. Our industrial relations manager doesn't know that union. The union is mad because of the strike two years ago. (It's very hard to put a price on the quality of labour relations when you buy a firm. Those agency theorists call it reputation and think that it can be priced like radiators, but it is hard to verify and easy for a firm to exaggerate with a bit of strategic public relations, classy accounting, and mimicry of leading firms in the field. The people at Radiators mislead us and I think we should have paid less because of the labour problem.) Any settlement they get will rev up our other union. And while Radoe was willing to do battle with the union and take the losses when she headed the firm, now I don't really think she sees the urgency of the labour problem as much as when she owned Radiators.' [Costs of acquisitions are poorly estimated and subject to opportunism. Reputation is subject to 'isomorphic pressure', that is, firms come to look alike by imitating superficial attributes of leading firms.[17] Unexpected interactions are increased in large systems.]

'We are still having problems with leaky radiators and the squabbling and charges between the radiator division and the engine division is worse than before the acquisition because personality clashes now make it more difficult. Not only are there problems with getting information about who is really responsible in the market (Williamson calls the problem 'information impactedness') but it can be worse in your own firm, especially when you try to do two different things, such as making stationery engines *and* radiators; the two processes, and the organizations and the personnel are just different.' [Information and control within the firm is subject to political and personality problems that may make it more expensive and less reliable than in the market. Co-ordination of diverse activities within a firm is expensive; such co-ordination is not needed in the market.]

'I would like to sell the division, but the transactions cost of selling it, after all those of buying it (which Williamson never mentioned), would just be too great. I agree with Perrow. You only should integrate forward or backward when it means you can get more market control, or get your hands on a very profitable piece of property and keep those profits for yourself.'[18] Mrs Enginee's only comment was, 'Dear, you read too many books.'

As light-hearted as this vignette may sound, it contains some important points. As Williamson himself notes in one chapter of his book on TCE, there are transaction costs within the firm as well as between firms, and his examples suggest that some are higher in hierarchies than in markets.[19] We should also note that markets can be efficient in establishing prices, whereas firms find 'internal pricing' (the allocation of costs to various units) difficult and a highly politicized process. The incentive structure is artificial and politicized in hierarchies as compared to markets.

Settling disputes by 'fiat' is difficult because of the very things Williamson has made us aware of—asset specificity and small numbers bargaining *within* the firm. Not all transaction costs are counted in Williamson's argument. Uncertainty affects internalized units as severely as it affects independent firms in the market; fluctuation in demand and supplies, labour problems, problems with competitors and so on do not disappear, and their resolution may be more difficult in a large firm. Opportunism, to the extent that it is a problem, will accompany the acquired firm because it is a hierarchy itself, and persist within the acquiring firm. Costs that could be externalized, and risks that could be born by the independent firm must be internalized by the acquiring firm, and it may have less flexibility in dealing with them because of long-term commitments and the power of groups with specific assets within the firm. Finally, while my account at several points favours markets over hierarchy, it does not assume a neo-classical perfect market. These rarely exist. Markets tends to be concentrated, rigged, protected, and inefficient. However, I would still give two cheers for markets, and only one for hierarchies, if only because of the power of giant firms to shape our premises to their own ends. (Three cheers for the market socialism described by Branko Horvat.[20]) But in any case the TCE argument is markets versus hierarchies, so the comparison has to be in these terms.

Lying behind my fiction is a more general point that goes beyond the critique of TCE: there is an advantage to decoupled units in a system, and a disadvantage to tight coupling. For instances, Radiators devised accounting and information management systems that were tailored to its specific operations; integrating it with the systems that were good for Engines entailed changes that made the new systems less efficient. The labour relations of Radiators may have been bad from some points of view, but they were not entangled with those of Engines. In the combined firm, ACE, any settlement for the radiator division will have an impact upon the engine division. Engines was buffered from changes in demand by Radiators, which absorbed some of the shock; ACE had to absorb all the shock.

Furthermore, Engines had the people and offices that knew how to deal with large suppliers, and thus could move quickly if demand was up; ACE lost some of that expertise, raising its transaction costs. When demand was down, Radiators suffered, but at least it could look for other customers, lowering its price (and profits). But as a division of ACE, it will find it more difficult to sell radiators to ACE's competitors. As a division, it probably can't trim its overhead during slack times as well as it could as an independent firm; some of the overhead costs assigned to it in

ACE are 'lumpy', that is, not divisible; overhead is a difficult thing to cut in large firms during retrenchment because of structural problems; it impacts all divisions regardless of their individual needs.

Finally, it is possible (though hardly inevitable) that Radiators could more easily change its production methods and incorporate new technologies than the division within ACE. As an independent firm, it can do what it wants with production as long as it meets the quality standards of the customer, Engines. As a division it interferes with the rest of the organization at many points, and changes may be resisted by people at some of those points who see disadvantages in the changes. (Were ACE to provide significant research and development services for the division, this might change, but there is evidence to suggest that smaller firms are the more innovative.)

These are arguments for loosely linked components of a system where there are likely to be uncertainties or shocks from the environment or from within. Tightly coupled systems have advantages, certainly; resources can often be more efficiently used, there is less redundancy and waste, and the processes are faster. But these advantages only appear if there is little uncertainty in the system—few 'exogenous' shocks (those coming from without the system); few endogenous shocks (those coming from within), plenty of time to recover from shocks, and many different paths to recovery. Most industries do not have these luxuries, and thus loose coupling is likely to be a more efficient system property than tight coupling. Loose coupling is associated with a large number of small units engaged in straight forward bilateral exchanges.[21]

Causes of hierarchy

Efficiency, as realized by the reduction of transaction costs, is thus an uncertain accompaniment of vertical integration, and some flexibility and buffering may be lost in the process. Clearly, in a comparison of two firms in the same industry with the same market power, political ties, etc. the more efficient will prosper and survive, and reducing transaction costs will make some unknown contribution to efficiency. But comparing firms with efficient internal operations is not the issue; it is the grounds for vertical and horizontal integration in parts of the economy that must be explained. I will sketch a possible explanation that relies primarily on the gross size of potential profits as realized through three factors: appropriation of 'profit streams' of other companies, market control, and government tolerance or support.

A firm requires various 'factors of production' such as land, labour, capital, supplies, technologies, and outlets. Advantages in any of these by one firm will lead to its growth relative to its competitors. Growth also requires at least tolerance on the part of the government, though it will benefit from a variety of state enabling factors (anti-union legislation, limits on liabilities, tax policies, tariffs) and from state resources (contracts, loans, access to minerals on public property). Many of these will favour a whole industry, allowing it to prosper and grow, and thus provide an incentive for some in the industry to take over other firms. There is little incentive for absorbing enterprises in a low-profit or low-growth industry; while the purchase price will reflect the stock market's evaluation of the industry and the firm, to the extent that future growth possibilities are good and greater market control over pricing and competitive products is possible, firms will reap advantages from attractive industries net of the existing stock price.

For the firm to grow there must be market growth, through the discovery or creation of new markets or expanding existing ones. Because firm growth will be challenged by the growth of other firms, and markets are not infinite, it must keep competitors out entirely, or failing that, limit or reduce the number of competitors. An illustration in the music recording industry provides an example of the *growth* of transaction costs with concentration, and their probable decline with competition.[22] Under oligopolistic conditions prevailing until the 1950s, transactions costs for the major firms were high, not low, because they had to maintain stables of recording stars on long-term contracts, control all outlets, and keep producers and manufacturing units on their payrolls. When intense competition set in because of technological changes that lowered entry costs and allowed numerous small firms to enter the market and expand it (by catering to untapped tastes for unconventional popular music), the transaction costs were probably greatly reduced. Companies established spot contracts with producers, stars, and manufacturers, and let them bear the risks of market uncertainty. But this also meant that the small firms could reap the profits when they were lucky, so the concentration ratio plummeted, and the profits of the majors did not grow as fast as the industry profits. The major firms managed to get control of the market again through various devices, appropriating the industry profit streams, but incurring the increased costs of internalizing risks and market fluctuations, controlling outlets, financing 'payola', and standardizing tastes once more.

Another example provides specific evidence of the irrelevancy of narrow efficiency, and a critique of both Williamson and Alfred DuPont

Chandler's 'visible hand' theory.[23] At the end of the nineteenth century, the iron and steel company of Andrew Carnegie grew phenomenally (and later became the basis of US Steel). An associate of Carnegie, James Howard Bridges, addressed the issue of transaction costs. It is particularly relevant because Carnegie was a fanatic on cost cutting in production areas and developed sophisticated bookkeeping devices to keep his transaction and production costs low. However, Bridges stated that 'it was other considerations than increased efficiency and economy that promoted the first and perfect combination of the Carnegie properties,' that is, the growth of his empire. There was no plan to the acquisitions, he flatly states. Instead, as Bridges details, there was the coveting of the high profits of other corporations; manœuvring to get rid of an officer; eliminating a competitor by getting the railroad pool to cut it out of the deals to provide a cheap freight, until he could buy the competitor at distress prices (Carnegie was paying dividends of 40 per cent at the time), and so on. He found the profits of the ore companies to be very large, so he moved in and through a combination of financial power and threats acquired a good bit of the Mesabi range, and when the ore boat companies would not reduce their prices, set up his own. His company was immensely rich and powerful. He did not have to worry about transaction costs, and they did not motivate his actions.[24]

Because of the factors of production it is unwise to consider strategies of market growth and competition only in terms of the firm; other organizations in the environment are crucial. Perhaps of most importance is the source of investment capital, a competitive but still concentrated system of banks, insurance companies, investment houses, and venture capital firms. Holding liquid (readily available) assets, they can provide the means for one firm to buy out competitors (with no efficiency gain), to finance price wars that force out competition, to buy up and destroy competitive goods or services (as the DuPont and General Motors interests were able to destroy much of public city transport in the United States in order to increase the demand for cars, and force the construction, through taxes, of roadways for them to run on[25]), or for firms to move to low-wage areas. Banks, insurance companies, and investment firms can make legal or illegal donations to politicians and political parties here and abroad to influence government actions that will tend to increase concentration in industries and reduce competition. They are not particularly concerned with the efficiency of a loan applicant, but with the opportunities the industry provides and the applicant's ability to exploit opportunities in it.

Firms, generally with resources from the financial community, may also use the patent system and other devices, legal and illegal, to gain control of new technologies and in some cases perhaps restrict their development in order to increase market control, and thus size. (Charges of suppressing innovations are common, but hard to prove. Industrial espionage is widespread and acknowledged, however.) Firms may conspire with suppliers or customers to undercut competitors and drive them out with illegal rebates, espionage, and defamation; concentrated industries can benefit all concerned: suppliers, producers, and distributors. Of course, fraud and force can be used to gain market control or other advantages, and our industrial history right up to the present is replete with examples. Some of our largest firms have fraud and force as active ingredients in their early history, quite possibly contributing significantly to their present dominance. The age of the 'robber barons' coincided with the great vertical and horizontal concentrations of industrial power.

As a few firms eliminate the competition and as they integrate vertically many opportunities for exercising power appear. Prices can be increased, and thus profits. With larger and fewer firms, the cost of entry for potential competitors goes up even though there is the attraction of large profits; new firms must start large. Market domination also slows the rate of innovation, limiting expensive changes and prolonging the returns on expensive capital investments. Fewer producers can also mean more co-ordinated lobbying activity regarding tariff protection, subsidized research, investment tax creditors, and so on; more concentrated economic power with regard to labour, more plant location incentives from local government, and local tax abatements. These are a few of the benefits of size in our economy. Thus, even if the acquired facility is not highly profitable in itself, it may add to the power and thus the profits of the acquiring firm.

I apologize for an account that will be obvious to many readers, but the above account is necessary to raise the more difficult question: why do we not have a few large firms dominating each industry? Why is steel concentrated but furniture not? Traditionally, factors such as size of capital investment, transportation costs, perishability of goods, and so forth have explained the differences in concentration rates. (A high concentration ratio is equivalent to the degree of hierarchy; technically hierarchy is a feature of organizational forms, not of industries, but if a decent-sized industry has over, say, 50 per cent of its capacity in the hands of four firms, the firms will be very large and in almost all cases hierarchical firms). I would like to put these explanations in a somewhat different light and argue that markets persist where large profits are not available, and in some cases where government policy prevents concentration.

Until recently, when financial considerations prompted the growth of conglomerates—firms that incorporated unrelated activities—most profit-seeking acquisitions were in closely related fields, such as suppliers, competitors, or distributors. The acquiring firm simply had more information about these types of firms, and had experience with the product. There may be economies of scale and benefits from smoother co-ordination of the enlarged input-throughput-output cycle achieved by acquisitions of closely related firms, but I believe these were secondary motives. Firms with resources will attempt to buy firms that are making good profits; transaction-costs savings or scale economies are of little importance if the profits to be gained are small. The purchase price will reflect the profitability of the firm, of course, profitable firms will have high stock values and cost more. But future profits are to be realized by the market power and political power that comes with increased size; neither unprofitable firms nor unprofitable industries favour the realization of such power.

Of course, the target firm must have sufficient amounts of profits (regardless of the rate of profits) to offset the costs of acquisition and integration. A very large firm will not usually be very interested in a tiny one no matter how profitable, though it does happen. A moderate-sized firm, however, would be interested. Note that the increased profits of the acquiring firm do not mean that the acquisition is more profitably run or that transaction costs have been saved, only that its profits have been appropriated, that is, assumed by the acquiring firm. (This is important in judging efficiency questions; increased profits or rates of profit after acquisition do not necessarily mean more efficiency; they can mean less competitive pricing and tax advantages.)

There are many highly profitable small firms that are not targets for acquisition. They can exist where there are small or localized markets. For example, the market for specialized luxury goods is small. The market for ethnic goods or foods is generally localized. Some items have small markets because they are unique or idiosyncratic. We speak of such markets as 'niches', small crevices in the economy where a few producers can make a lot of money, but the demand is fairly inelastic (it won't grow much because it is so specialized), thus there is no possibility for increased market control (too small a market) or expanding the market. The large firm has no interest in such firms; though the rate of profit in some niches is large, its absolute amount can be small; additionally, its absolute amount must be great enough to offset the substantial costs of integrating small, diverse businesses into a large firm. Acquisitions are not costless; there are transaction costs and organizational redesign costs, as illustrated in the case of the ACE firm.

Industries need not be forever unprofitable or fragmented into niches. In the nineteenth century the modest profits of the hundreds of small flour mills hardly made them a target for acquisitions, because they sold to middlemen and grocers who dumped the flour into a bin labelled 'flour'. By promoting branded flour through advertising ('as pure as the drifted snow') market control was achieved and a few large milling companies soon dominated the industry and still do. Much the same thing has happened with restaurants serving limited, quickly prepared meals, though here we must admit the importance of organizational efficiencies including reduced transaction costs. Small restaurants always existed, and were mom-and-pop operations requiring long hours and generating low profits. As the demand for quick meals out increased, heavily advertised chains moved in and took over the market. By combining the advantages of centralized control with nominal local ownership, they have been able to reap the advantages of low-paid local labour with high turnover, and nominal owners who work the long hours of mom and pop. Centralized buying, heavy advertising, and rigid procedures have no doubt contributed to the profitability of these chains, so in this one case we might say that profits may stem from efficiencies, including centralized control of transactions costs.

In addition to market control and acquiring profitable investments, financial 'manipulation' plays a role in mergers. In some cases the profit rate of acquired subsidiaries will actually decline after the merger, but capital accumulation by investors and officers through financial manipulations, rather than firm profit, is then the goal. This occurred when US Steel was formed by buying up many steel firms. Much money was made through issues of watered stock, making it a very profitable move for the investors, even though operating efficiencies declined. The decline was offset by enormous market power by the new combine. Today, stock manipulation, appropriation of cash flows (milking the profitable acquisition without reinvestment), and buying footholds in new markets figure prominently in merger and acquisition strategies, so prominently that it has become a national scandal. Lower transaction costs presumably play no role in these manipulations; indeed, transaction costs are greatly increased, but fortunes are made anyway.[26]

Though it is somewhat less apparent today because of the weakness of unions, control of labour has also been a motivation for acquisitions, resulting in increased profits though no increase in production efficiency. Acquiring facilities in low-wage areas; acquiring non-union facilities and using this as a means of attacking the unions in the existing facilities; and absorbing a sufficient proportion of the local work force to be able to control local wage rates are some of the tactics.

The creation of large, market-dominating firms also requires the acquiescence of the federal government. Large firms flourish in the national defence industry because the government favours them for military defence reasons. In fact, such firms are occasionally 'bailed out' by awarding handsome government contracts because letting them go under would remove resources the government feels we need. One does not start up a giant aircraft and missile firm easily or quickly. Their 'efficiency' is of secondary importance.[27] State banking laws have restricted the centralization of banking in the United States; a change in laws could produce a movement towards 'hierarchy' that would not caused by transaction costs efficiencies, but rather, market control and the acquisition of profitable properties. Thus, the absence of federal enabling actions will help account for the persistence of markets.

A final concern that can lead to the persistence of at least some degree of market phenomena rather than very high concentration ratios in an industry is a recognition that some degree of loose coupling is efficient. This appears to be the reason why the big three automobile companies control, but do not own, their distributors.[28] Though the manufacturing of autos is highly concentrated, the distribution system appears to be a market with many small dealers. But I would count this as a 'controlled market'; the manufacturers exercise great control over it. The retail dealers sign long-term contracts that govern the number and type of cars they are *allowed* to receive (a problem when a model turns out to be a 'hot' seller and the contract cannot be revised), and the number and type of cars they *must* receive (a problem for disposing of the poor sellers, the 'dogs'). These long-term contracts favour the seller. Contracts also cover how much of the cost of failures the dealer must bear under the warranty, how much they can charge for repairs in some cases, how much advertising they must do and so on. The dealer has discretion only on trade-in prices or preparation prices or other deals that make the final selling price somewhat flexible. Otherwise, the dealer is quite constrained; indeed, the manufacturer may unilaterally and without warning raise the wholesale price to the dealer without posting a higher retail price, thus cutting the dealer's rate of profit. The argument is sometimes made that car dealers represent flexible adaptations to local markets, and thus are more efficient than if owned and controlled outright by the manufacturers. This does not appear to be so; they cannot order just the makes and volume they wish, the prices can be changed, warranty work is tightly regulated by complex contracts written by the manufacturer, and advertising is regulated. They can be flexible and adaptive only in their used-car line.

The effect of this is to require the dealers to absorb the market declines (they have to cut their profit to get rid of the quota of cars they must buy) even though they cannot fully participate in market rises (they cannot get all the hot selling models they want). Cost of entry is not large for them, but as small businesspeople they do invest their own capital. They are forced to ride out poor times making little or no profit. A few dealerships do very well indeed, but most do not. Yet there are always small businesspeople willing to take the risk. Thus, the manufacturers are buffered from fluctuations in the market for cars and from the yearly gamble on model changes and new models. Because the profitability of dealerships overall is only modest and subject to much uncertainty, it is not worthwhile for the manufacturers to integrate forward into a business over which they already have considerable control.

While we have many dealer firms, we really have a controlled market with many small firms rather than either a hierarchy or a market. Most franchises, as in fast foods, are devices to spread risks and buffer the headquarters from uncertainties. Given the limited occasions for entrepreneurship in our economy for people without wealth or highly unique skills, there are always many who are willing to work very hard for low and risky returns. Though controlled, they have more autonomy than employees of large corporations.

Thus, we would expect to find small firms persisting in areas of the economy that show low overall industry profitability (unless the industry can be restructured to promote branded products or other forms of market control—there is always a drive to do that); where there are idiosyncratic factors despite high profits (local markets, niches); where the market cannot grow despite profitability (inelastic demand); or where government restrictions obtain. Finally, hierarchies are probably self-limiting; at some point, which varies according to technologies, capital requirements, and the shape of the market, firms probably lose control over some of their subsidiaries and the complex, internal interactions, and the ability to respond to external shocks, and lose out. The subsidiaries are sold off, or their efficiency declines to the point where they lose money despite substantial market control and other advantages of size, and someone else moves in. Some minimal efficiency *is* necessary, of course, but transaction costs rarely play a significant role.

This brief sketch of some of the forces contributing to hierarchy and economic concentration in our society stands in marked contrast to economic motives of efficiency in the face of opportunism and transaction costs. It is neither original or novel, but suggests the range of structural variables that are neglected by economic interpretations of organizational behaviour.[29]

Beyond markets and hierarchy

The distinction between markets and hierarchies is an old one in economics, though Williamson has given it new life. It is a useful one because it frames questions we might not otherwise ask. But there is increasing evidence that this formulation hides as much as it reveals. Scholars are beginning to note that some markets are quite hierarchically organized, and that some hierarchies have many phenomena associated with markets. This suggests that we might abandon the distinction for some purposes and seek other ways to characterize interdependent behaviour within and between organizations, or even to attack, once again, the recalcitrant conceptual problem of boundaries—what is the boundary between a supplier and a customer, the government and a firm, or between two industries. Rapid industrial change since the 1950s has made these questions pressing. I cannot even suggest answers to the problem of characterizing interdependencies and questioning formal definitions of boundaries here, but only conclude by mentioning some of the more interesting research that raises these questions. To a considerable degree this research and theorizing has either been stimulated by Williamson's work, or at least posed as a critique of it. It is one of the reasons we should be thankful for TCE. The general point is that large firms may be so large as to operate like markets, and markets appear to be hierarchically, diagonally and horizontally so organized as to make the notion of independent, autonomous price givers and takers questionable. These 'markets' may be governed by forces that most economists would not recognize as plausible.

A striking piece by Ronald Dore, a British sociologist familiar with Japanese history and industry, argues that Japanese industry is more efficient, over all, because the contracting involves a significant degree of goodwill, give-and-take, long-term horizons, and in general, an avoidance of opportunism. The classical market of economists is only efficient in allocating goods (if that). Citing the work of renegade economist Harvey Liebenstein for support, Dore argues that there are a number of efficiencies other than allocating goods that are more important, and they are realized by trust, non-competitive relations, and mutual assistance in time of need. These other efficiencies include rapid spread of innovation; shared information on changing market situations and consumer choices; aggressive search for new uses of labour and capital if old markets decline; flexibility in task assignments; and the disaggregation of industry when desirable (for example, he cites the move from hierarchy to small firms in the textile industry in Japan). Finally, he questions whether this is necessarily a product of Japanese culture; much more cut-throat, self-interested practices prevailed *in Japan* during the 1920s and again immediately after World War II. He also finds evidence for goodwill and suspension of self-interest in the United States and England, especially in industries or in firms noted for their emphasis upon quality, rather than quantity. There is a mine of research projects in this attractive essay.[30]

Arthur Stinchcombe considers several industries such as defence contracting, large civil engineering firms, and franchise networks, noting how their relations with their customers tend to be hierarchically organized, even though these would seem to be examples of markets.[31] In defence contracting the Department of Defence is very intimate with the contractors, putting inspectors and accountants in their firms, much as a multidivisional corporation puts inspectors and accountants into each of its divisions. This is true of consumer-goods industries too. Chevrolet treats its supposedly independent suppliers almost as profit centres and risk bearers, controlling much of what they do. On the other hand, hierarchies develop profit centres and divisions that bargain with each other and the main office in a market-like arrangement, encountering the large costs of simulating a market with 'shadow prices' and numerous complex accounting practices that simulate a market relationship.

Harrison White argues, in a suggestive paper that blurs the distinction between markets and hierarchy, that the principal-agent model is misleading. He describes the principal-agent relationship as a reflexive one that oscillates, dissolves, and is born again, making it difficult and arbitrary to designate who is agent and who is principal. Ranging from the ancient Roman empire to high-technology industries, it is an effective though not very explicit criticism of TCE.[32] More generally, I think the interdependencies among economic units and among principals and agents should be analysed in terms of such contextual influences that I argued will influence the degree of self-regarding and other-regarding behaviour that is encouraged—such contexts as the length and durability of relationships, the distribution or centralized storage of surpluses, calculation of group efforts, rotation of authority, and extent of surveillance.

Sociologists and other organizational theorists are positioned to explore these problems because they embrace a more system-wide viewpoint than economists, with attendant developments in network theory, evolutionary models, and attention to the environment in general. Their work is not disabled by assumptions of rational or primarily self-interested behaviour, but look at the contexts that call our rational, non-rational, self-regarding, and other-regarding behaviour. This broader enquiry is, in part occasioned by the challenge that economists have presented by their foray into the world of organizations, a challenge that resembles the theme of the novel and movie *The Invasion of the Body-Snatchers*, where human forms are retained but all that we value about human behaviour—its spontaneity, unpredictability, selflessness, plurality of values, reciprocal influence, and resentment of domination—has disappeared.

Acknowledgements

This article draws heavily on chapter 7 of the third edition of my book *Complex Organizations: A Critical Essay* (New York: Random House, 1986), where the issues are discussed at somewhat greater length.

Notes

1. My primary sources for agency theory are Armen A. Alchian and Harold Demsetz, 'Production, Information Cost, and Economic Organization', *American Economic Review* (1972), 777–95, 795; Eugene F. Fama, 'Agency Problems and the Theory of the Firm', *Journal of Political Economy*, 88 (1980), 288–305; Eugene Fama and Michael Jensen, 'Separation of Ownership and Control', *Journal of Law and Economics*, 26 (June 1983), 301–25, and Michael Jensen and William Meckling, 'Theory of the Firm: Managerial Behavior, Agency Costs, and Ownership Structure', *Journal of Financial Economics*, 3 (October 1976), 305–60, 309. The best exposition of the theory I have seen is by political scientist Terry Moe, 'The New Economics of Organization', *American Journal of Political Science*, 28/4 (November 1984), 739–77, 741.
2. Mancur Olson, Jr., *The Logic of Collective Action*, revised edition (New York: Schocken Books, 1971).

3. Alcian and Demsetz, 'Production'. I have elaborated their example.

4. James March and Herbert Simon, *Organizations* (New York: Wiley, 1958). I have discussed bounded rationality and its link to domination in Charles Perrow, *Complex Organizations: A Critical Essay*, third edition (New York: Random House, 1986), chapter 4.

5. See the review of Terry Moe, 'The New Economics'.

6. Louis Putterman 'On Some Recent Explanations of Why Capital Hires Labor', *Economic Inquiry*, 33 (April 1984), 171–87.

7. For the popularity of agency theory see Moe, 'The New Economics'; for the popularity of closely related transaction-cost economics see William Ouchi, 'Markets, Bureaucracies and Clans', *Administrative Science Quarterly*, 25 (March 1980), 129–41. Citations to both theories are mounting in the journals, such as *Administrative Science Quarterly*, and books discussing them are appearing, e.g. Arthur Francis, Jeremy Turk, and Paul Willman (eds.), *Power, Efficiency and Institutions* (London: Heinemann, 1983).

8. For a discussion of human relations, bureaucratic, and neo-Weberian theories see chapters 1, 3, and 4 of Perrow, *Complex Organizations*.

9. Joyce Rothschild-Witt, 'The Collectivist Organization: An Alternative to Rational Bureaucratic Models', *American Sociological Review*, 44 (1979), 509–27; Rosabeth Kanter, *The Change Masters* (New York: Simon and Schuster, 1983), Branko Horvat, *The Political Economy of Socialism* (1982).

10. The basic work is Oliver Williamson, *Markets and Hierarchies: Analysis and Antitrust Implications* (New York: The Free Press, 1975). A new volume under preparation by Williamson incorporates more organizational and sociological variables, and attacks a wide range of problems from the markets and hierarchies viewpoint.

11. Oliver Williamson, 'Organizational Innovation: The Transaction-cost Approach', in J. Ronen (ed.), *Entrepreneurship* (Lexington, Mass.: Heath Lexington, 1983), 101–34. Quote from 125.

12. Ibid. 125.

13. Mark Granovetter, 'Economic Action and Social Structure', and Mark Granovetter, 'Labor Mobility, Internal Markets and Job Matching: A Comparison of the Sociological and Economic Approaches', both unpublished manuscripts (Department of Sociology, State University of New York at Stony Brook, n.d.). The first was published in a shorter version that suffers from strict copy-editing in *American Journal of Sociology* 91/3 (November 1985), 481–510.

14. Alfred D. Chandler, *The Visible Hand: The Managerial Revolution in American Business* (Cambridge, Mass.: Harvard University Press, 1977).

15. Robert G. Eccles, 'Control with Fairness in Transfer Pricing', *Harvard Business Review* (November–December 1983), 149–61, and 'Transfer Pricing as a Problem of Agency', unpublished manuscript (Harvard Business School, February 1984), and *The Transfer Pricing Problem: A Theory for Practice* (Boston: Lexington Books, 1984).

16. Olivier Williamson and William Ouchi, 'A Rejoinder', in Andrew Van de Ven and William Joyce (eds.), *Perspectives on Organization Design and Behavior* (New York: Wiley Interscience, 1981), 390.

17. Paul J. DiMaggio and Walter W. Powell, 'The Iron Case Revisited: Institutional Isomorphism and Collective Rationality in Organizational Fields', *American Sociological Review*, 48 (1983), 147–60.

18. Charles Perrow, 'Markets, Hierarchies and Hegemony: A Critique of Chandler and Williamson', in Van de Ven and Joyce, *Perspectives*, 371–86, 403–4.

19. Williamson, *Markets and Hierarchies*, chapter 7. In a new work, *The Economic Institutions of Capitalism* (New York: The Free Press, 1985), he emphasizes this even more. Because transactions costs have not been operationalized, which would make measurement possible, the fundamental issue of whether they are higher between firms or higher within them will probably never be settled. See my comments on this issue in 'Markets, Hierarchies and Hegemony: A Critique of Chandler and Williamson', in Van de Ven and Joyce, *Perspectives*, 371–86.

20. Horvat, *Political Economy*.

21. Charles Perrow, *Normal Accidents: Living with High Risk Technologies* (Basic Books, 1984), chapters 3, 9.

22. Perrow, *Complex Organizations*, chapter 6.

23. See the discussion in Perrow, 'Markets, Hierarchies and Hegemony', in Van de Ven and Joyce, *Perspectives*.

24. J. H. Bridges, *The Inside History of the Carnegie Steel Company* (New York: Aldine Press, 1903), 135, 168, *passim*. For a survey of industries and their history of aggressive market control written by industrial economists—a breed apart from the 'new institutional economists' we are dealing with and ignored by the latter—see: Adams, Walter, and Scherer, *Industrial Market Structure and Economic Performance*, second edn. (1980), especially chapter 6.

25. Glen Yago, *The Decline of Transit* (Cambridge, Mass.: Cambridge University Press, 1983).

26. While it is not conclusive, the evidence on the performance of acquired units should induce skepticism regarding the efficiency of acquisition policies. Birch followed 6,400 firms that were acquired during 1972–1974, and compared their before and after growth rates with the 1.3 million firms that were not acquired. He found that, in Rothschild-Witt's summary, 'conglomerates tend to acquire fast-growing, profitable, well-managed businesses, contrary to the theory that they seek out poorly managed, inefficient firms', that is, those that might have, among other things, high transaction costs internally or with the environment. However, growth is not speeded up after the acquisition; in fact, 'firms that remain independent grow faster than acquired firm'. A congressional study found that firms that were acquired subsequently had lower rates of job creation, productivity, and innovation. David Birch, 'The Job

Creation Process', (Cambridge, Mass.: MIT Program on Neighborhood Regional Change, 1979). See also, Committee on Small Business, U.S. House Representatives, 'Conglomerate Mergers—Their Effects on Small Business and Local Communities' (Washington, DC: US Government Printing Office (House Document No. 96–343), 2 October 1980). Both are discussed in Rothschild-Witt, Joyce, 'Worker Ownership: Collective Response to an Elite-Generated Crisis', *Research in Social Movements, Conflict and Change*, 6, 1984, JAI Press, 67–94, a sobering, informative review of worker-ownership developments.

27. Seymour Melman, *Pentagon Capitalism: The Political Economy of War* (New York: McGraw Hill Book Co., 1970).

28. Kenneth McNeil and Richard Miller, 'The Profitability of Consumer Practices Warranty Policies in the Auto Industry', *Administrative Science Quarterly*, 25 (1980), 407–26; and J. Patrick Wright, *On A Clear Day You Can See General Motors* (New York: Avon Books, 1979), and Harvey Farberman, 'Criminogenic Market Structures: The Auto Industry', *Sociological Quarterly*, 16 (1975), 438–57.

29. There are other criticisms of Williamson's work, and the related work of Alfred Chandler. Williamson explored the early history of capitalism, arguing that hierarchies proved to be more efficient than co-operatives and inside contracting, but the economic historian S. R. H. Jones wrote a devastating critique of Williamson's evidence and interpretation. Richard DuBoff, a historian, and Edward Herman, an economist, reviewed the work of Chandler very critically, presenting evidence that the emergence of several of the hierarchies Chandler described had much more to do with market power than co-ordinating efficiencies (and I have made a similar criticism with more modest evidence). In a volume devoted to Williamson's work, Arthur Francis has a perceptive essay on the issue of efficiency versus market power. See S. R. H. Jones, 'The Organization of Work: A Historical Dimension', *Journal of Economic Behavior and Organization*, 3: 2–3 (1982), 117–37, replying to Oliver Williamson, 'The Organization of Work: A Comparative Institutional Assessment', *Journal of Economic Behavior and Organization*, 1 (1980), 5–38 (with a further exchange in volume 4: 57–68). Richard B. Du Boff and Edward S. Herman, 'Alfred Chandler's New Business History: A Review', *Politics and Society* 10: 2 (1980), 87–110, and Perrow, 'Markets, Hierarchies and Hegemony' in Van de Ven and Joyce, *Perspectives*; Arthur Francis, 'Markets and Hierarchies: Efficiency or Domination?', in Arthur Francis, Jeremy Turk, and Paul Willman (eds), *Power, Efficiency and Institutions* (London: Heineman, 1983), 105–116.

30. Ronald Dore, 'Goodwill and the Spirit of Market Capitalism', *British Journal of Sociology*, 34 (December 1983), 459–82. Harvey Liebenstein, *Beyond Economic Man: A New Foundation for Microeconomics* (Cambridge, Mass.: Harvard University Press, 1976).

31. Arthur Stinchcombe, 'Contracts as Hierarchical Documents', Work Report 65, Institute of Industrial Economics (Bergen, 1984).
32. Harrison White, 'Agency as Control', unpub. (Cambridge, Mass.: Harvard University, 1983), and Robert G. Feeles and Harrison White, 'Firm and Market Interfaces of Profit Center Control', unpub. (Cambridge, Mass.: Harvard University, February 1984). See also, for an industry study, W. Graham Astley and Charles J. Fombrun, 'Technological Innovation and Industrial Structure: The Case of Tele-Communications', in *Advances in Strategic Management* 1, 205–9 (1983), JAI Press. See also the interesting discussion of industrial markets in Sweden, developing the notion of heterogenous markets, in contrast to homogenous ones found in neo-classical economic theory, and of 'nets', those parts of the industrial 'network' where strong complementary pervails, in Ingemund Hagg and Jan Johanson, *Firms in Networks: New Perspectives on Competitive Power* (Stockholm, Sweden: Business and Social Research Institute, September 1983).

The Structure of Corporation Law

MELVIN ARON EISENBERG

A corporation is a profit-seeking enterprise of persons and assets organized by rules. Most of these rules are determined by the unilateral determined by market forces. Some are determined by contract or other forms
of agreement. Some are determined by law.

This article will consider the legal rules that directly concern the internal organization of the corporation and the conduct of corporate actors.[1]
Viewed in terms of their form, these rules fall into three basic categories.
Enabling rules give legal effect to rules that corporate actors adopt in a
specified manner. *Suppletory* or *default rules* govern defined issues unless
corporate actors adopt other rules in a specified manner. *Mandatory rules*
govern defined issues in a manner that cannot be varied by corporate
actors.[2]

The major purpose of this article is to develop the normative principles that determine which of the legal rules that concern the internal
organization of the corporation and the conduct of corporate actors
should be enabling or suppletory, and which should be mandatory.
Because the corporation is an economic institution that is owned and
managed by human actors, the development of these principles rests for
the most part on economic analysis, quantitative data, and the insights of
psychology.

In practice, the application of these elements depends largely on the
subject-matter of the rule and the nature of the institutional setting. In
terms of the nature of the institutional setting, I will distinguish between
closely held corporations, publicly held corporations, and corporations
that are about to go public. In terms of subject-matter, I will distinguish

Koret Professor of Law, University of California, Berkeley. BA Columbia University, 1956;
LL.B., Harvard University, 1959.
I thank Bernard Black, Bob Cooter, Merritt Fox, Ron Gilson, Bill Klein, Lewis Kornhauser,
Roberta Romano, Dan Rubinfeld, Marshall Small, and Oliver Williamson for extremely
helpful comments on drafts of this Article. An early version of this Article was presented as
a comment at a Conference on the Economics of Corporation Law at Harvard Law School
in December 1986.

between structural, distributional, and fiduciary rules. *Structural rules* govern the allocation of decision-making power among various corporate organs and agents and the conditions for the exercise of decision-making power; the allocation of control over corporate organs and agents; and the flow of information concerning the actions of corporate organs and agents. *Distributional rules* govern the distribution of assets (including earnings) to shareholders. *Fiduciary rules* govern the duties of managers and controlling shareholders. These three types of rules will be referred to collectively as *constitutive rules*, and that term will include both rules determined by law and rules determined by private action.

Part I will consider closely held corporations. In such corporations, constitutive rules are often determined by bargain. Whether the legal rules that govern such corporations should be enabling or suppletory on the one hand, or mandatory on the other, therefore depends in large part on the force and limits of the bargain principle. Given the force of that principle, structural and distributional rules should be enabling or suppletory at the core. Given the limits of that principle, fiduciary rules should be mandatory at the core.

Part II will consider publicly held corporations. In such corporations, constitutive rules are seldom determined by bargain. Whether the legal rules that govern such corporations should be enabling and suppletory on the one hand, or mandatory on the other, therefore depends in large part on the force and limits of non-contractual private ordering. Non-contractual private ordering may have considerable force in the absence of a conflict of interest. Accordingly, top managers should have power to determine the constitutive rules that govern the conduct of the corporation below their level, because it is in both their interests and the shareholders' interest to set such rules in an optimal fashion. In contrast, non-contractual private ordering by agents who have a conflict of interest is normally undesirable. Therefore, top managers in publicly held corporations should not have power to determine or materially vary the core fiduciary and structural rules that govern matters in which their interests may materially diverge from those of the shareholders. Furthermore, because of the defects in the proxy-voting process and the control over that process exercised by top managers, the core fiduciary and structural rules should not be subject to determination or material variation even with shareholder approval. . . . .

I. Closely held corporations

I begin with closely held corporations—corporations that have a small number of shareholders, most of whom either participate in or directly monitor corporate management.

A. Structural and Distributional Rules

In closely held corporations, shareholders often will bargain out at least some structural and distributional rules. It is a general principle of law that a bargain should normally be enforced according to its terms, without regard to whether it is reasonable or fair. One reason for this principle is that bargains have social utility because they create joint value through trade. Another reason is that a fully informed party is normally the best judge of his own utility or interest and, therefore, of the value to him of a bargained-for performance. The reasons for the bargain principle usually apply to bargains among the shareholders in a closely held corporation concerning the corporation's structural and distributional rules. Accordingly, at its core the law governing structural and distributional rules in closely held corporations should be enabling and suppletory, rather than mandatory.

This is essentially the position taken by modern corporate law. Modern case law has moved in the direction of enabling shareholders in closely held corporations to bargain out their own structural and distributional rules.[3] Many of the modern statutes explicitly validate such rules for those closely held corporations that elect special statutory treatment.[4]

At the periphery, however, a special type of mandatory legal rule should apply. The bargain principle is based partly on the proposition that a fully informed party is the best judge of his own utility. If a party is not fully informed, or lacks the sophistication to understand the implications of his bargain, the bargain principle loses some or all of its force. For example, the courts have traditionally refused to apply the bargain principle to liquidated-damages provisions, and instead have reviewed such provisions to determine whether they provided a reasonable forecast of the amount of damages foreseeable at the time the contract was made.[5] One major reason for this special treatment is that a contracting party will often fail to give his full attention to liquidated-damages provisions because he will focus on the contract terms governing his performance, which he expects to render, not on the contract terms governing breach, which he does not expect to commit. Furthermore, even if a contracting party does give such a provisions his full attention, he will often fail to understand its implications because every contingency under which breach may occur cannot efficiently be conceived of (and indeed may not be conceivable) when a contract is made.

Within the last forty years, contract law has also developed and elaborated the principle of unconscionability, which serves as a limit on the bargain principle where one party's lack of information or sophistication is exploited by the other.[6] . . . .

Another problem, which contract law has only begun to address, involves long-term contracts.[7] John Stuart Mill, who argued that 'laisser faire . . . should be the general practice and 'that every departure from it, unless required by some great good, is a certain evil,'[8] nevertheless singled out long-term contracts as appropriate for judicial invention:

[An] exception to the doctrine that individuals are the best judges of their own interest, is when an individual attempts to decide irrevocably now what will be best for his interest at some future and distant time. The presumption in favor of individual judgement is only legitimate, where the judgement is grounded on actual, and especially on present, personal experience; not where it is formed antecedently to experience, and not suffered to be reversed even after experience has condemned it. When persons have bound themselves by a contract, not simply to do some one thing, but to continue doing something . . . for a prolonged period, without any power of revoking the engagement . . . [any] presumption which can be grounded on their having voluntarily entered into the contract . . . is commonly next to null.[9]

Mill's analysis is now further supported by evidence that there is a tendency to make systematic errors when comparing the value of present benefits and costs with future benefits and costs, and in particular, that there is a tendency to systematically underestimate risks.[10] Based on a review of the empirical evidence, Kenneth Arrow concluded, '[i]t is a plausible hypothesis that individuals are unable to recognize that there will be many surprises in the future; in short, as much . . . evidence tends to confirm, there is a tendency to underestimate uncertainties'.[11] One reason for this is the representativeness heuristic, a characteristic judgment process in which small samples are often wrongly taken to be representative.[12] In particular, evidence based on the sample consisting of present events is often wrongly taken to be representative of future events. 'The individual judges the likelihood of a future event by the similarity of the *present* evidence to it. There is a tendency to ignore both prior information . . . and the quality of the present evidence, for example, the size of the sample used to present evidence.'[13] Another reason is that pallid evidence, such as a statement of probability, is unduly discounted in favour of vivid evidence, such as present events.[14]

These problems of systematic error apply with special force to bargains concerning closely held corporations. It is almost impossible for contracting parties to assess adequately the future costs and benefits in a fluid long-term relationship, because of tree of events will branch far beyond the ideas of the future that will be conceived when the contract is made. Furthermore, corporations by their nature involve a form of activity in which uncertainty plays an essential role. Because of the difficulty of predicting and planning for future events and their impact on a business enterprise, an opportunistic shareholder who controls one or more aspects of a closely held corporation will often find ways to exploit bargained-out structural and distributional rules that seemed both fair and complete at the time of bargain.[15] It is almost impossible to deal adequately with this potential for *ex post* opportunism by *ex ante* contracting. Therefore, although the purpose of enforcing bargains is to protect expectations, the full enforcement of bargained-out structural and distributional rules in a closely held corporation may actually violate fair expectations. Accordingly, while the law governing the structural and distributional elements of closely held corporations should be largely enabling and suppletory, corporation law should also provide mandatory rules that empower the courts to override bargains concerning structural and distributional terms when necessary to prevent opportunism and protect probable fair expectations.

Modern corporation law has taken just this position. Both the courts and the legislatures have fashioned mandatory rules that limit the full force of bargains concerning structural and distributional rules in closely held corporations. . . . .

A more widespread approach, reflected in both case and statutes, provides for judicial intervention when enforcement of bargained-out structural and distributional rules would defeat a shareholder's fair expectations. The case law approaches this problem through the use of fiduciary principles. For example, in *Donahue* v. *Rodd Electrotype Co. of New England*,[16] the Massachusetts Supreme Judicial Court held that majority shareholders in a close corporation cannot use their voting power to authorize the purchase of shares from one of their number when an equal opportunity is not offered to the minority.[17] In *Wilkes* v. *Springside Nursing Home, Inc.*,[24] the same court held that majority shareholders in a close corporation cannot use their voting power to take a business action that disadvantages the minority if the purpose of the action could be achieved through an alternative course of action that is less harmful to the minority.[19] In *Smith* v. *Atlantic Properties, Inc.*,[20] a Massachusetts appellate court held that if shareholders in a close corporation abuse a power of control over matters such as dividends or capital improvements, the court can determine the policies that will govern these matters.[21]

The statutes are equally far-reaching. A number of statutes give the courts authority to dissolve a corporation—and, thereby, any bargains concerning its constitutive rules—if those in control have acted oppressively or unfairly. Under the New York statute, for example, the court can order dissolution if those in control have been guilty of oppressive actions.[22] The statute directs the court to take into account whether liquidation is the only feasible means by which the complaining shareholders can reasonably expect to obtain a fair return on their investment.[23] In *In re Judicial Dissolution of Kemp & Beatley, Inc.*,[24] the New York Court of Appeals said that 'oppression', in the context of such a statute, means 'conduct that substantially defeats the "reasonable expectations" held by minority shareholders in committing their capital to the particular enterprise'.[25] . . . .

Under corporation law, the court may derive fair expectations not only from a written agreement but from a broad range of circumstances, and may dissolve rather than enforce the shareholder's contract. For example, under the North Carolina statute the courts have power to liquidate a corporation if it 'is reasonably necessary for the protection of the rights or interests of [a] complaining shareholder'.[26] In *Meiselman* v. *Meiselman*,[27] the court held that a complaining shareholder's 'reasonable expectations' are to be ascertained by examining the entire history of the participants' relationship. According to the Court, '[t]hat history will include the "reasonable expectations" created at the inception of the participants' relationship; those "reasonable expectations" as altered over time; and the "reasonable expectations" which develop as the participants engage in a course of dealing in conducting the affairs of the corporation.'[28]

Moreover, although the relevant statutes are rooted in the remedy of dissolution, the courts usually have the power to impose, as an alternative remedy, a revision of constitutive rules that the parties clearly agreed to. In some cases, the statutes explicitly grant such power. The California statute, for example, provides that the court 'may make such orders and decrees and issue such injunctions in the case as justice and equity require'.[29] The North Carolina statute provides that in an action for dissolution the court may cancel or alter any provision in the corporation's articles of incorporation or by-laws.[30] Even where such power is not explicitly granted, it may be held to be implied. For example, in *Baker v. Commercial Body Builders*,[31] the Oregon court held that although the Oregon statute in terms authorized only the remedy of dissolution, a court also had authority to grant other forms of relief, such as a decree reducing and distributing capital, ordering the declaration of a dividend, or empowering minority shareholders to purchase additional stock on terms set by the court.[32] In *In re Judicial Dissolution of Kemp & Beatley, Inc.*,[33] the New York court construed the comparable New York statute in a similar way.[34]

B. Fiduciary Rules

Structural and distributional legal rules for closely held corporations should be enabling and suppletory at the core but mandatory at the periphery. In contrast, fiduciary legal rules for closely held corporations should be mandatory at the core but enabling and suppletory at the periphery. The reasons behind these principles are straightforward. The bargain principle assumes that contracting parties are fully informed, or at least not systematically underinformed. Parties who bargain over structural and distributional rules are likely to understand the consequences of their bargain in most cases, at least over the short term, and mandatory rules are therefore needed only as a backstop. However, bargains to relax materially the fiduciary rules set by law would likely be systematically underinformed even over the short term. Even if the shareholders understood the content of the rules whose protection they attempted to waive—which is unlikely—they still could not begin to foresee the varying circumstances to which such a waiver would be applicable. Any such waiver would therefore inevitably permit unanticipated opportunistic behaviour.

Some bargained-out fiduciary rules do not present the dangers of systematic error and exploitation. Bargains to change a legal rule that is not congruent with current concepts of fairness or that does not afford any real protection to shareholders, such as the old rules that interested transactions were voidable without regard to fairness or that interested directors could not be counted in determining a quorum, fall into this category.[35] In some cases, a bargained-out fiduciary rule is specific, easily understood, and not easily susceptible to exploitation. A rule that clearly specifies a type of business venture that will not be considered a corporate opportunity may fall in this category.[36] Similarly, shareholder approval of a specific conflict-of-interest transaction usually does not present the dangers of systematically underinformed consent and exploitation, because the approval relates to a specific event rather than to an unknowable future. In these peripheral cases, bargained-out fiduciary rules should be enforceable.

The law reflects these principles. The core fiduciary rules which govern the close corporation are mandatory,[37] but private rules that do not present the dangers of systematic unforseeability and exploitation—such as rules that allow an interested director to be counted toward a quorum—normally will be given effect.[38]

II. Publicly held corporations

I turn now to publicly held corporations, by which I mean corporations that have a large number of shareholders, most of whom neither participate in the management of the corporation nor directly monitor corporate management. Typically, the number of managerial and non-managerial agents is also large, and for reasons of efficiency the business of the corporation is controlled and conducted by these agents. Under these conditions, bargaining among the shareholders, or between managers and the shareholders as a body, is virtually impossible. Accordingly, most of the constitutive rules of such corporations are determined not by contract, but by law or by private bureaucratic rulemaking—for example, by managerial orders, by board or committee resolutions, by board-adopted by-laws, or by board determination of governance terms in preferred stock, stock rights, or debt instruments.

In such corporations, therefore, the principles that determine which legal rules should be enabling or suppletory and which should be mandatory depend on the force and limits of forms of private ordering other than bargain and contract. The force and limits of these forms of private ordering in publicly held corporations, in turn, depend very largely on the impact of the potential self-interest of top managers of such corporations and on the extent to which this impact is controlled by market forces other than bargain and contract.

A. Divergencies of Interest

The interests of the shareholders and managers in publicly held corporations converge in many respects: in general, if the shareholders do well, so will the managers. As in any principal-agent relationship, however, the interests of shareholders and managers also diverge. All agents have a potential interest in working at a slack pace and in avoiding the effort and discomfort involved in adapting to changed circumstances, such as the emergence of new technologies. This is the problem knowing as *shirking*. All agents have a potential interest in diverting the principal's assets to their own use through unfair self-dealing. This is the problem of *traditional conflicts of interest*.

Top corporate managers differ from most other agents, however, in that they are legally and factually autonomous for many purposes. For example, under corporate law the shareholders normally cannot make ordinary business decisions and cannot make major structural decisions unless the directors concur. . . . . Because of this relative autonomy, and the range of discretion that it leads to, top corporate managers have the power to give expression to still a third potential divergence of interest: an interest in maintaining and enhancing their positions even at the shareholders' expense. I will refer to instances of this type of divergence of interest as *positional conflicts*.[39]

Positional conflicts may be expressed in a great variety of ways. For example, top managers may make it particularly difficult for anyone to objectively monitor their performance. They may impose high barriers to their own removal for inefficiency or other reasons. They may seek to increase corporate size as a way to maximize their power, prestige, and salary, even if an increase in corporate size does not increase shareholder wealth. They may seek to maximize the cash and other resources that they command, even when distributions to the shareholders would be more efficient. They may diversify the firm as a means to reduce the riskiness of their human-capital investments, even when diversification of the firm is not in the interest of shareholders because shareholders can diversify their own risks through portfolio management.[40]

In the real world, positional conflicts are much more important than either shirking or traditional conflicts of interest. Mot top managers will probably refrain from shirking simply because their self-esteem is tied to hard work and accomplishment. Most top managers will probably refrain from unfair self-dealing simply because they have internalized the rules of social morality. However, self-esteem and morality may often be inadequate to curb positional conflicts.[41] The top manager's self-esteem often crucially depends on the maintenance and enhancement of his position, and conduct designed to maintain and enhance one's position may not be immoral in any obvious sense.

Of course, many top managers will not act in a manner that reflects positional conflicts, just as they will not work at a slack pace or engage in unfair self-dealing. However, top managers may fail even to recognize that positional conflicts exist. Inefficient top managers are unlikely to believe themselves to be inefficient. Top managers who enhance their positions through corporate growth, diversification, or the like, usually believe (often, but not always, correctly) that their actions are in the interest of the shareholders. Finally, top managers may have more difficulty in taming a taste for maintaining and enhancing their positions than in taming a taste for shirking or unfair self-dealing. It is at least in part through the appetite for position that top managers have achieved their place atop the corporate hierarchy. Thus, not only are moral restraints normally weaker in the case of positional conflicts than in the case of shirking or unfair self-dealing, but avoiding the expression of such conflicts may require the manager to control the very characteristics that put him where he is.

The divergencies of interest between corporate agents and shareholders, and the special problem of positional conflicts, explain why some constitutive rules that govern publicly held corporations should be enabling or suppletory while others should be mandatory. The legal rules that govern the internal organization of the corporation and the conduct of corporate actors *below the level of top managers* should by and large be enabling or suppletory. Top managers have both the self-interest and the power to install constitutive rules that will efficiently determine the roles, coordination, supervision, and monitoring of lower corporate agents and constrain those agents from giving expression to their own interests in preference to the interests of the shareholders.

In contrast, top managers of publicly held corporations have little incentive to adopt rules that put constraints on their own positions. On the contrary, the incentive of top managers may be to insulate themselves from such constraints. The core fiduciary and structural rules that govern material divergencies of interest of top managers in publicly held corporations, therefore, should be neither determined nor subject to material variation by the action of managers or managerial organs.[42] The reason for this principle is not that legislatures or judges know more about such rules than top managers; they may or may not. Rather, the reason is that in this as in other areas of law, agents whose interests may materially diverge from the interests of their principals should not have the power to unilaterally determine or materially vary the rules that govern those divergencies of interest.

B. *The Limits of Shareholder Consent*

This first principle—that the core fiduciary and structural rules that govern material divergencies of interest of top managers in publicly held corporations should be neither determined nor subject to material variation by managers or managerial organs—spills into a second. Such rules should also normally not be subject to determination or material variation even with shareholder approval. Allowing such rules to be determined or materially varied on the basis of shareholder approval would effectively undercut the first principle, because, under current law and practice, shareholder consent to rules proposed by top managers in publicly held corporations may be either nominal, tainted by a conflict of interest, coerced or impoverished.

1. *Nominal consent.*—Under current law and practice, an action proposed by managers may be legally deemed approved by shareholders who never consented to it in fact. . . . . For many shareholders, the cost of reading and understanding each proposal in the proxy materials will exceed the likely economic effect of any given proposal. For such shareholders, it is rational not to read any proposals.[43] Shareholders receive a number of management proposals in proxy statements. Because the interests of managers and shareholders converge to a significant extent, and because many proposals relate to housekeeping details (such as approval of auditors), shareholders have reason to believe that the typical management proposal will be value-increasing. Therefore, unless a shareholder holds a very large amount of a given corporation's stock, he will probably conclude that the expected gains from analysing all the management proposals he receives will be less than the expected costs. . . . .

2. *Consent that is tainted by a conflict of interest.*—Shareholder consent that is not nominal may nevertheless be tainted by a conflict of interest. Approximately 50 per cent of the stock in publicly held corporations is owned by institutional investors.[44] Many institutional investors have ties to management that inhibit voting against a management proposal.[45] For example, if the trust department of a bank holds the stock of C Corporation in a pension portfolio, and C is also a client of the bank's commercial department, a trust officer will think long and hard before voting against a proposal made by C's management. Indeed, some corporate managers have begun to explicitly request their counterparts in other corporations to pressure pension-fund trustees to take a pro-management stance in casting their votes.[46] The same problem arises for insurance companies, which, like banks, often have extensive commercial contacts with corporations whose stock they hold in their investment portfolios.[47] Undoubtedly, institutional investors often vote in the interests of their beneficiaries despite such conflicts, but it seems equally clear that institutional investors often succumb to a conflict of interest in their voting decisions.[48]

Frequently, shareholder voting decisions are based on an even more direct conflict of interest. Managers often have significant holdings in their own corporations, and they are seldom if ever prohibited from voting their holdings in favour of a proposal that advances their own interests.[49] Even more to the point, in many corporations a controlling block is held by one or more corporate or individual shareholders whose interests may diverge from those of the non-controlling shareholders. In theory, voting by a controlling shareholder can be reviewed on a case-by-case basis under a fairness test.[50] In practice, however, the costs of bringing a suit based on fairness, and the difficulty of applying that test in this context, would make a case-by-case review of the fairness of votes cast by controlling shareholders an inadequate tool for regulating the conflicts of interest of controlling shareholders voting on variations in core fiduciary or structural rules that they have proposed.

3. *Coerced consent.*—Shareholder consent that is neither nominal nor tainted by a conflict of interest may nevertheless be coerced. For example, management may threaten to withhold approval of an action that is in the shareholders' best interests, such as an increase in dividends, unless the shareholders approve an unrelated management proposal.[51] Or, management may tie a proposal that shareholders might vote down if it stood alone to a proposal that shareholders will clearly favour.[52]

4. *Impoverished consent,*—Finally, and perhaps most importantly, shareholder consent that is neither nominal, tainted by a conflict of interest, nor coercive may nevertheless be impoverished. For example, shareholders may vote for a rule proposed by management even though they would prefer a different rule, because the proposed rule is better than the rule it replaces and management's control over the agenda effectively limits the shareholders' choice to the existing rule or the proposed rule. . . . .

More fundamentally, shareholder approval may be impoverished because many shareholders may have a weak, incomplete, or non-existent understanding of a proposal for which they vote. To begin with, under the Proxy Rules, management can present proposals to the shareholders with a one-sided argument. The Proxy Rules do not enable a shareholder who opposes a management proposal to present the other side of the matter in the corporate proxy statement.[53] Of course, the management argument cannot be misleading,[54] but an argument that is not misleading may nevertheless be very one-sided.[55]

Even if the argument for a management proposal is balanced, many shareholders will rationally decide not to read it, for reasons that have already been canvassed.[56] And even if a shareholder does analyse a particular management proposal and does determine that the proposal would be value-decreasing, he is unlikely to mount a counter-solicitation unless his stake in the corporation is extremely large, because if he prevails other shareholders would not bear any of the costs of the counter-solicitation but would free-ride on most of its benefits.

Of course, the free-rider problem could be addressed by collective action, but the barriers to collective action are extremely high. A communication by a shareholder who seeks to alleviate the free-rider problem by forming a group to share the costs of a solicitation will probably itself be a solicitation subject to the Proxy Rules, unless the shareholder solicits less than eleven other persons to join his group.[57] Even if a group is successfully formed, shareholders who do not join the group will free-ride on its efforts and will therefore have an incentive not to join.[58] . . . .

Even changes that can be accomplished without a certificate amendment face substantial impediments. Management can solicit proxies against a proposed change in the corporation's constitutive rules at no cost to itself, because it can charge the expenses of its soliciting activity to the corporation.[59] In contrast, a shareholder who proposes to solicit for a change must bear his own expenses, and will encounter the same free-rider problem and barriers to collective action that confront a shareholder who is considering a counter-solicitation.[60] Accordingly, even a very large shareholder in a publicly held corporation is unlikely to solicit for a change in the corporation's constitutive rules unless the change would be exceptionally wealth-maximizing for the shareholders of the individual corporation (for example, the elimination of a poison pill) or would have some sort of precedential value for other corporations in which he holds major investments.

The many limits on the meaningfulness of shareholder consent do not compel the conclusion that shareholder voting is never meaningful. Some individual holders may read the proxy statement and vote their own stock. Some institutional holders have no conflicting ties to management. Many institutional holders that do have conflicts of interest will nevertheless vote in the interests of their beneficiaries, either because of a sense of moral duty or because of legal pressures or pressures to maximize their returns. As a result, management proposals that will have obvious and very large value-decreasing effects are unlikely to be adopted by shareholders, and even proposals that have smaller negative effects may not always be adopted. Furthermore, it is entirely conceivable that with further increases in institutional ownership, and changes in the moral, legal, and financial pressures that affect voting by institutional owners, the significance of shareholder voting will change in the future. Under prevailing conditions, however, the limits on the meaningfulness of shareholder consent are so substantial that allowing those rules to be determined or materially varied by top managers with shareholder approval often would be functionally equivalent to allowing those rules to be unilaterally determined or materially varied by top managers.

C. The Structure of the Law Governing Publicly Held Corporations

The general principle, then, is that in publicly held corporations, mandatory legal rules should govern those core fiduciary and structural areas in which the interests of shareholders and top managers may materially diverge. The content of these rules should reflect the basic types of potential divergence. To deal with traditional conflicts of interest, mandatory rules should impose a duty of fair dealing, should provide for disclosure of self-interested transactions, and should establish an effective enforcement mechanism. To deal with the problem of shirking, mandatory rules should impose a duty of care. As to these matters, the principle that governs publicly held corporations is the same as the principle that governs closely held corporations: fiduciary rules should be mandatory at the core.

In the case of publicly held corporations, however, an additional principle comes into play to deal with positional conflicts, which involve the most serious of the divergencies of interest between top managers and shareholders. In such corporations, core structural rules double as fiduciary rules, because it is structural rules that address positional conflicts. Accordingly, in publicly held corporations core structural rules as well as core fiduciary rules should be mandatory.

These core structural rules fall into several categories. One set of mandatory structural rules should provide for the appointment and monitoring of senior executives by a governing organ (that is, a board of directors) that is elected by shareholders for a limited term of office, a majority of which is composed of members who are independent of the senior executives. A second set should require periodic disclosure of detailed financial data and information concerning material business and legal developments and should provide for institutional mechanisms to ensure that the financial data is reliable. A third set should concern the approval of, and dissent from, transactions that tend to raise positional conflicts. In general, shareholder approval should be required for any transaction in control to which the corporation is a party—that is, any corporate transaction that causes a change in control of the corporation, its assets, or its business. In the case of major transactions that character-istically involve either traditional or positional conflicts, create a signifi-cant potential for overreaching by controlling shareholders, or radically alter the structure of the corporation, dissenting shareholders should have the right to require the corporation to purchase their shares at fair value. A final set of mandatory structural rules should protect the integrity of shareholder voting.

The core mandatory rules should operate to check positional conflicts without preventing advantageous corporate transactions. To this end, the core structural rules should require mechanisms for accountability and disclosure for top executives, shareholder approval of certain transac-tions, and appraisal rights for certain transactions, but they should not regulate the content of corporate transactions. Because mandatory rules generally should not regulate the content of transactions, distributional rules should generally be enabling, except as required to protect the inter-ests of creditors.

The legal rules that actually govern publicly held corporations corre-spond reasonably well to the legal rules that should govern such corpora-tions.

Assume, for example, that a given corporation is publicly held, but has less than 500 shareholders and is not required to register its stock under Section 12(g) of the Securities Exchange Act.[61] Call such a corporation a small publicly held corporation. Suppose first that the corporation is incorporated in Delaware. Although Delaware is usually taken as the apotheoisis of enabling states, and indeed has the least regulatory of the major corporations statutes, even under Delaware law the corporation will be governed by a number of mandatory legal rules. For example, the corporation's directors and officers have a duty of loyalty to the corpora-tion that cannot be substantially altered.[62] The officers have a duty of care to the corporation that cannot be substantially altered.[63] Any share-holder who owned stock at the time of a breach of the duties of care or loyalty can bring suit against the wrongdoer on the corporation's behalf.[64] The corporation is required to have a board of directors or some comparable organ.[65] The term for which a director serves may not be longer than three years, and if the board is classified, one class must come up for election every year.[66] The corporation must have an annual meet-ing of shareholders for the election of directors.[67] The shareholders have a right to inspect a shareholder list within the ten days preceding a share-holders' meeting,[68] and a right to inspect the corporation's books and records at any time for a proper purpose.[69] The corporation's certificate of incorporation may be amended only with the approval of a majority of the outstanding shares.[70] Under a variety of circumstances, such an amendment must also be approved by separate classes of shareholders— even classes not entitled to vote under the certificate of incorporation.[71] The corporation may dissolve or sell substantially all of its assets only with the approval of a majority of the outstanding shares.[72] Shareholders who dissent from a merger generally have a right to be paid the fair value of their shares.[73] The shareholders have the power to amend the corporation's by-laws.[74] And so forth.[75]

In short, a small publicly held corporation will be governed by very extensive mandatory legal rules even in Delaware, which is probably the least regulatory of states. Furthermore, most small publicly held corporations will be incorporated not in Delaware, but in the state in which their principal office is located, because out-of-state incorporation will normally entail somewhat higher costs than local incorporation.[76] Since most states are more regulatory than Delaware, most small publicly held corporations will be governed by an even more extensive mandatory legal regime than that just described. . . . .

So much for the small publicly held corporation. Assume now that a corporation has 500 holders of a class of equity securities and more than $5 million in assets and thus must register under Section 12(g) of the Securities Exchange Act.[77] It will then be subject to a further and very extensive layer of mandatory rules concerning traditional and positional conflicts. For example, the corporation's directors, officers, and other employees may not trade in the corporation's securities on the basis of material undisclosed information.[78] Its directors, officers, and shareholders owning at least 10 per cent of the voting securities must give up any profits from short-swing trades even if the trades were not based on inside information.[79] The corporation must file annual reports that include annual financial statements audited by an independent public accountant, a management report on the corporation's financial condition and results of operations, and additional disclosures concerning specified matters.[80] It must file quarterly reports that include quarterly financial data prepared in accordance with generally accepted accounting principles, a management report, and additional disclosures concerning specified matters.[81] It must file current reports that describe the occurrence of specified events.[82] Proxies may not be solicited by management unless the shareholders are furnished with a written proxy statement containing specified information concerning the transaction to be acted upon.[83] The proxy statement for an annual meeting at which directors are to be elected must make extensive disclosure concerning conflict-of-interest transactions and executive compensation.[84] Such a proxy statement must be accompanied by an annual report that includes audited balance sheets for the corporation's last two fiscal years, audited income statements and statements of change in financial condition for its last three fiscal years, and other specified information.[85] Shareholders must be permitted to include a wide variety of proposals in the corporate proxy statement.[86] The corporation's form of proxy must identify clearly and impartially each matter or group of related matters intended to be acted upon.[87] Shareholders must be afforded an opportunity to specify in the proxy a choice between approval, disapproval, or abstention with respect to each matter or group of related matters, and to withhold authority to vote for directorial nominees.[88] A proxy normally may not confer discretionary authority to vote on an issue unless it states in boldface type how the shares represented by the proxy will be voted on the issue.[89] A proxy may not confer authority to vote at any annual meeting other than the next annual meeting.[90] And so forth.[91]

Finally, most very large publicly held corporations are listed on the New York Stock Exchange, which has had a virtual monopoly in the liquid trading market for the stock of such corporations and imposes a variety of constitutive rules on listed corporations. Among other things, corporations listed on that Exchange must have at least two outside directors, must have an audit committee composed of independent directors, and must obtain shareholder approval for most economically significant corporate combinations.[92]

In short, corporation law taken as a whole—that is, taken to include state law and federal law, and the rules of the New York Stock Exchange as a *de facto* legislator by virtue of its monopolistic power—contains a significant number of core mandatory rules to govern divergencies of interest between top managers and shareholders. And to a significant extent, these are just the mandatory rules that corporation law should contain.

D. Alternative Descriptions of Corporation Law and the Corporation

Three classes of argument may be made against the principle that the fiduciary and structural rules governing material divergencies in interests between top managers and shareholders in publicly held corporations should be and for the most part are mandatory. The first argument, which will be considered in this section, is that both corporation law and the corporation are essentially contractual in nature. One branch of this argument is that *corporation law* is essentially enabling and suppletory—or, as it has been put by Professor Fischel, that 'corporate statutes provide a set of standard-form terms, but firms are generally free to alter these terms in their charters or by-laws'.[93] The second branch of the argument is that the *corporation* is a 'nexus of contracts'.[94] Both branches of the argument are descriptively erroneous.

The characterization of corporation law as a standard-form contract whose terms each firm is generally free to vary is belied by the great number of mandatory rules of corporation law.[95] It is true that most of a corporation's constitutive rules will be adopted by private action. That is because most of a corporation's constitutive rules concern the roles, co-ordination, supervision, and monitoring of corporate agents below the level of top managers, and such rules should and will be determined by private ordering. (Indeed, many or most of the constitutive rules that define and co-ordinate the tasks of top managers also should and will be determined by private ordering, because many or most such rules do not involve divergencies of interest between top managers and shareholders.) It is also true that many rules of corporation law are enabling or suppletory rather than mandatory.

What is not true is that corporations are 'generally free' to vary the rules of corporation law. Many of the most important rules of corporation law—such as those dealing with unfair self-dealing, insider trading, proxy voting, and disclosure—are largely mandatory, at least for publicly held corporations. It is descriptively inaccurate to characterize corporation law as essentially either enabling and suppletory on the one hand, or mandatory on the other. Furthermore, for reasons already discussed,[96] a body of corporation law that *was* essentially enabling and suppletory would be normatively undesirable.

The characterization of the corporation as a nexus of contracts is also inaccurate. A corporation is a profit-seeking enterprise of persons and assets organized by rules. Some of these rules are determined by contract or other forms of agreement, but some are determined by law, and most are determined by the unilateral action of corporate organs or officials.

The problem with the nexus-of-contracts conception transcends its inaccuracy. For some commentators, the view of the corporation as a nexus of contracts carries heavy normative freight, because, having premissed that the corporation is a nexus of contracts, they then argue that mandatory rules are anti-contractarian.[97] Once it is understood that the premiss of this argument is incorrect, because the corporation is not a nexus of contracts but an enterprise organized by rules, many or most of which are adopted by the unilateral action of managers, the argument that mandatory rules are anti-contractarian falls of its own weight.

To make up for the paucity of real contracts, it is sometimes argued that the corporation consists of a web of 'implicit contracts'.[98] The term 'implicit contracts' is extremely misleading. It is borrowed from labour economics, and as used in that discipline it refers to relationships that are neither contracts nor bargains.[99] A contract is a legally enforceable bargain, or, at least, a legally enforceable promise.[100] In contrast, in labour economics the term *implicit contract* refers to a state of affairs in which a worker chooses to accept a lower wage rate from Firm A than he could get from Firm B, with the expectation that for reasons of self-interest, fairness, or altruism—that is, for reasons other than the sanction of a contract or other legally enforceable obligation—Firm A will provide an advantage that Firm B would not. For example, workers may accept a lesser wage rate at Firm A because they believe, based on past practice, that there is a lower probability of being laid off at Firm A than at Firm B. More generally, 'implicit contracts' are relationships that are marked *not* by a real bargain, let alone a legally enforceable commitment, but by a tacit expectation, or at most a tacit understanding. Such relationships are not unique to business; indeed, such relationships are ubiquitous in intimate settings like marriage and friendship. They are relationships in which for some reason—often, some very good reason—legal enforceability and explicit bargaining is deliberately avoided.

It is true that sometimes tacit understandings slide into implied-in-fact promises that do give rise to legally enforceable contracts,[101] and that sometimes tacit understandings provide a basis for legally enforceable fiduciary obligations.[102] These cases, however, involve a metamorphosis of the relationship, because it is a central characteristic of 'implicit contracts' that they are *not* legally enforceable.[103] The use of 'implicit contract' terminology in the corporate context screens out real and important differences between laid-down rules and real contracts. Contracts and bargains are forms of private ordering, but they are not the only such forms. 'Implicit contracts' are forms of private ordering, but they are not contracts. Most of a corporation's constitutive rules are not determined by law, but neither are they determined by contract.

E. *The Effect of Markets and Other Forms of Private Ordering*

A second class of arguments that might be made against the principles developed so far is that market forces so adequately align the interests of top managers and shareholders and so adequately address the problem of managerial inefficiency that mandatory legal rules to address these issues are unnecessary and indeed undesirable.[104]

Arguments of this type are on their face both descriptive and normative. They are descriptive in so far as they purport to set forth the outcomes of actual market forces. They are normative in so far as they claim that mandatory rules to govern divergencies of interest are undesirable because dependence solely on market forces would result in more efficient outcomes. None of the most prominent arguments that have been or may be made are persuasive in the present world.

1. *Product Markets.*—At the outset, it is occasionally argued that managers are severely inhibited from pursuing their own interests or acting inefficiently because product markets often will render insolvent any firm that does not minimize costs.[105] This argument seriously overstates the power of product markets.[106] Although a highly competitive market may have this effect, an imperfectly competitive market will not quickly convert unfair self-dealing or inefficiency into insolvency.[107] Most publicly held corporations have sufficient resources and market power to absorb substantial losses resulting from inefficiency, gross miscalculations, or unfair self-dealing.

2. *Management Compensation.*—A more weighty argument is that the interests of managers and shareholders are adequately aligned by executive compensation, because such compensation is closely tied to shareholder gain.[108] It seems likely that compensation has some alignment effect. Empirical studies have shown that there is indeed a statistically significant relationship on average between shareholder gain, measured by returns to common stock, and executive salaries and bonuses.[109] However, 'significance' in statistics bears no necessary relationship to the ordinary meaning of significance—that something is important.[110] Although the relationship between compensation and corporate performance is *statistically* significant, it is not *economically* significant. Based on a study of 2,214 chief executive officers during 1974–86, Jensen and Murphy determined that on average the chief executive's salary and bonus changed only 1.4 cents for each change of 1000 dollars in shareholder wealth.[111] They illustrate the trivial nature of this relationship as follows:

The [data implies] that a CEO receives an average pay increase of $31,700 in years when shareholders earn a zero return, and receives on average an additional 1.35 cents for each $1,000 increase in shareholder wealth. The median annual standard deviation of shareholder-wealth changes for firms in our sample is about $200 million, so the average pay change associated with a stockholder-wealth change two standard deviations above or below the normal (a gain or loss of $400 million) is $5,400. Thus, the average pay increase for a CEO whose shareholders gain $400 million is $37,300, compared to an average pay increase of $26,500 for a CEO whose shareholders lose $400 million.[112]

Jensen and Murphy also measured the relation between salary and bonus, and change in shareholder wealth based on stock performance, for the present and preceding year, rather than only the present year. This relationship was slightly stronger, but still trivial—2.2 cents, rather than 1.4 cents, for each change of 1,000 dollars in shareholder wealth.[113] If all benefits (other than those related to stock options) are taken into account, and the measurement is based on two years of lagged shareholder wealth rather than one, the relationship still amounts to only 3.3 cents in compensation per 1,000 dollars of change in shareholder wealth.[114]

Salary, bonus, and benefits are so little related to shareholder gain because managers want it that way. In theory, a chief executive's compensation is determined by the board on the recommendation of an independent compensation committee, which in turn acts on the recommendation of an independent personnel department and (often) an independent outside consulting firm, all without the chief executive's participation. In practice, however, 'the chief executive often has his hand in the pay-setting process almost from the first step'.[115] Personnel executives who don't recommend what the chief executive officer wants may find that their jobs are at risk; consultants who don't recommend what the chief executive wants are likely to be invited back.[116]

The value of executive stock options is also related to shareholder gain measured by returns on common stock. Here again, however, the dollar significance of the relationship is virtually immaterial—a change of 15 cents in the value of the chief executive's stock options for each change of 1,000 dollars in shareholder wealth.[117] The value of stock options as a mechanism to align adequately the interests of shareholders and top managers is further limited by the fact that while shareholders invariably lose wealth if the stock price decreases, top managers with stock options may not, because when the price of the stock goes down the board often reduces the option price to match the fall in the market.[118]

In short, the argument that the interests of managers and shareholders are adequately aligned by executive compensation is descriptively inaccurate because the dollar amounts involved are trivial or immaterial. Moreover, this argument is based on a fallacy. The fallacy, which runs through a great deal of the literature on the alignment effect of market forces, is that mandatory rules are unnecessary because *on average* the interests of managers and shareholders are adequately aligned by market forces. I shall call this the average-manager fallacy.

The average-manager fallacy reflects a fundamental misunderstanding of the use of statistical evidence in determining whether mandatory legal rules are desirable. A statistically significant relationship between two variables, such as compensation and corporate performance, occurs when there is a high correlation between the two variables. The presence of a material number of cases that are not consistent with the overall relationship will not necessarily preclude a finding of statistical significance. Accordingly, a finding that a relationship between two groups of data is statistically significant—that there is a relationship between the two variables 'on average'—may often mask the fact that many members of each group are not related in a manner consistent with the underlying relationship. This may not be a problem when statistical techniques are intended to *describe* certain social phenomena, or when prediction is an important objective. However, in determining whether conduct should be *prescribed* or *prohibited* by a mandatory legal rule, it is not enough to say that there is a significant overall relationship. Rather, all cases, including those that are not consistent with the observed relationship, must be taken into account. Conduct may be legally prescribed or prohibited *just because* not all conduct clusters around the norm. For example, even though most parents would send their children to school even in the absence of a legal rule, we prescribe mandatory education for children because some parents will not. Similarly, we make perjury a crime even though most witnesses would tell the truth in any event, because in the absence of a sanction some witnesses would not. Whether conduct should be prescribed or prohibited on the one hand, or left unregulated on the other, depends on a prudential, case-by-case judgment whether the cost of adopting a mandatory rule to govern the conduct of those who will not voluntarily conform to a desired norm exceeds the cost of failing to adopt the rule, and, in that connection, whether a mandatory legal rule will increase voluntary self-regulation by emphasizing the weight that society gives to the norm. This equation cannot be solved by looking only at average conduct.

Applying these principles to corporate law, even if a given market mechanism does align the interests of most top managers and shareholders in a statistically significant and material way, such a relationship does not in itself tell us that mandatory rules are unnecessary. For example, even if the correlation between executive compensation and shareholder

gain was both very high and material (which it is not), that would provide only limited help in determining the shape of corporate law unless
we also know the extent to which the relationship holds throughout the
executive population.

3. *Inside Stock Ownership.*—Closely related to the argument that the
interests of shareholders and managers are adequately aligned by executive compensation is the argument that those interests are adequately
aligned by managers' inside stock ownership, that is ownership of stock
in their own corporations. It is true that managers, or at least chief executive officers, do tend to hold significant dollar amounts of stock in their
own corporations. For example, Jensen and Murphy studied 73 chief
executive officers of manufacturing companies and found that the officers' inside stock ownership averaged $4.8 million, or $8.8 million if
shares held as a trustee and by members of the chief executive's family
were taken into account.[119] Jensen and Murphy concluded that the value
of inside stock held by the average chief executive would change $1.31 or
$2.40 (depending on the sample) for each $1,000 change in shareholder
wealth.[120]

Certainly this data establishes that inside stock ownership is often large
enough to have some alignment effect. What it does not establish is that
inside stock ownership so adequately aligns the interests of the shareholders and managers that mandatory legal rules to control divergencies of
those interests are unnecessary. For one thing, the median value of inside
stockholdings has been decreasing dramatically. Based on the sample of
73 chief executive officers mentioned above, Jensen and Murphy found
that the median value of chief executive officers' inside holdings had
dropped from $3,531,000 in 1969–73 to $1,178,000 in 1979–83, while the
median percentage of the firm owned by the chief executive officer
(including members of his family and trusts) fell from .21% to .11%.[121]
Similarly, a study comparing the inside holdings of the chief executive
officers of the 120 largest corporations in 1938 and 1984 showed a drop in
the average percentage of the firm owned by the chief executive officer
from .30% to .03%.[122]

Much more importantly, the argument that inside holdings have the
effect of adequately aligning the interests of shareholders and managers,
like the argument that executive compensation has that effect, reflects
the average-manager fallacy. The relevant questions include not simply
the magnitude of average or median inside holdings, but the extent to
which the relationship holds throughout the population. In fact, the relationship is extremely variable. A study by Jensen and Murphy of the

inside holdings of 746 chief executives and their family members found that 40% had inside holdings worth less than $2.5 million, 20% had inside holdings of less than $700,000, and some had inside holdings worth less than $100,000.[123]

Moreover, even relatively significant inside holdings will have only a limited alignment effect in the three major areas in which the interests of top managers may diverge from those of shareholders. Take first the problem of unfair self-dealing. Assume that a manager who contemplates unfair self-dealing has a large inside holding. The manager's gain from the unfair self-dealing will nevertheless almost invariably swamp the resulting loss in the value in his stock, because the manager will normally realize the full value of the unfair self-dealing, but will lose only a fraction of the value of his stock. For example, suppose Corporation C has a net worth of $1 billion, and Manager M owns C stock worth $10 million. If M unfairly appropriates a corporate opportunity worth $1 million, he will net $990,000 even after taking into account the impact of his action on the value of his inside holdings.

Inside holdings also will have little or no effect on efficiency. Few if any inefficient managers are likely to believe themselves inefficient. Accordingly, even the most inefficient managers will typically believe that their actions will increase the value of their inside holdings.[124]

Finally, inside holdings will have little or no effect on positional conflicts. Financial gain is only one incentive for top managers. Other and often far more important incentives include the sense of accomplishment, the self-esteem, and the power that accompany a top management position.[125] The combined financial and non-financial value that a top manager places on his position is almost certain to swamp any possible loss in his inside holdings that results from actions he take to maintain and enhance that position, even in the unlikely event that he believes those actions to be value-decreasing.

4. *The Market for Managers, the Prospect of Promotion, and the Risk of Discharge.*—Still another device that is said to adequately align the interests of managers and shareholders, and adequately address the problem of managerial inefficiency, is the market for managers.[126] The idea here is that managers who perform poorly will find it difficult to market themselves.

There is in fact a market for middle and lower managers, although it is somewhat limited because of skill specificity and asymmetric information.[127] However, it is top managers with whom corporation law should be and is concerned, and for these actors the market for managers, such as it is, is of limited relevance. That market is not relevant to the chief executive officer, because he is almost invariably in his final period as a manager.[128] It is of limited relevance to top executives other than the chief executive officer, because their major concern is satisfying the chief executive. It is not relevant to outside directors, because outside directorships are normally sideline activities.

A mechanism related to the market for managers is the prospect of promotion. This prospect, however, has no effect on directors or chief executive officers, because they cannot be promoted.

Another mechanism related to the market for managers is the risk of discharge. There is evidence that suggests a relationship between corporate performance and the discharge of chief executives,[129] and undoubtedly the risk of discharge has an alignment effect. However, the relationship between corporate performance and risk of discharge is weak. Because the discharge of a chief executive is usually masked as a voluntary separation, there is little or no evidence concerning discharge as such, but only aggregate evidence on departures for all reasons, including poor health, retirement, death, and takeover. A study by Weisbach of departures for all reasons of chief executives younger than age 64 concluded that in the highest-performing decile of corporations, 3% of chief executives probably would depart in any given year, while in the lowest-performing decile 6% would depart—a difference of only 3 percentiles.[130] Similarly, the difference between probable departures for all reasons in corporations whose performance was in the top and bottom quintiles was only two percentiles.[131] The difference between the median corporation and corporations in the lowest decile was also only two percentiles.[132]

Not only is the relation between departures and corporate performance weak, but the uniformity of the relationship is very low. The relation is apparently strongest for chief executives under age 50. For chief executives age 50–5 there is no significant relation.[133] For chief executives age 55–60 or past age 64 the relation is only marginally significant.[134] There is also no significant relation between departures and corporate performance in corporations in which 60% or more of the directors are either insiders or have significant relationships to management.[135] . . . .

5. *The Market for Corporate Control.*—Another market mechanism that has been claimed adequately to align the interests of shareholders and managers, and adequately to address the problem of managerial inefficiency, is the market for corporate control—that is, the take-over market. The now-familiar idea is that if the managers of a corporation act in their

own interests rather than the shareholders' interests, or are inefficient, a third party can make gains by bidding for the corporation's stock at a price that is above the market price, but below the value the stock would have if the corporation was properly managed.[136]

It seems clear that some take-overs are motivated by the inefficiency of the target's management.[137] Therefore, at least some completed take-overs undoubtedly result in a substitution of more efficient managers for less efficient managers, or of more efficient allocations of resources for less efficient allocations. It also seems likely, although not uncontroversial that the threat of take-over makes some managers more efficient, or causes some managers to allocate resources more efficiently than they otherwise would.[138] Nevertheless, the take-over market neither adequately aligns the interests of managers and shareholders, nor adequately addresses the problem of managerial inefficiency.

To begin with, the take-over market has very little impact on traditional conflicts of interest. A hostile take-over bid cannot succeed unless it includes a premium that is significantly above the market price, partly because all existing shareholders value their stock at a price higher than the market price,[139] and partly because the target's managers can create formidable obstacles to a take-over that can be overcome only by a substantial premium over market price. The premium for all take-overs runs between 30 and 50 per cent over market price.,[140] and in most cases it is probably impossible to make a successful hostile bid at less than a 30 per cent premium. A hostile bidder must also pay very large fees to investment bankers, lawyers, and other professionals. Because of the need to expend these large premiums and fees, a takeover bid will almost never be economically justified if the bidder's only strategy is to end unfair self-dealing by incumbent managers. Furthermore, if a bidder acquires most of a target's stock, and the financial impact of past unfair self-dealing was reflected in the target's financial statements, the target will normally be barred by law from recovering the managers' gains from unfair self-dealing.[141]

The take-over market also has only a limited effect on positional conflicts. The threat of take-over will not cause managers to avoid taking actions to maintain and enhance their positions at the shareholders' expense. Indeed, just the reverse has occurred. The threat of take-over has led many managers to cause the adoption of constitutive rules that make their ouster even more difficult than it would otherwise have been. Furthermore, the central problem posed by positional conflicts is the problem of inefficient managers who do not realize they are inefficient, and do their best as they see it. The threat of take-over will not affect the behaviour of such managers: they are already doing all they can.[142]

Even a manager who knows he is inefficient may not have too much to fear from the threat of a take-over. Take-overs are motivated by a variety of economic factors, of which inefficient management is only one, and not necessarily the most important.[143] As Jensen points out, '[m]ore than a dozen separate forces drive takeover activity, including such factors as deregulation, synergies, economies of scale and scope, taxes, the level of managerial competence, and increasing globalization of U.S. markets'.[144] A significant portion of the resources devoted to take-overs seems to be directed not at taking over poorly managed corporations, but rather at taking over well-managed corporations. Indeed, it seems likely that in some take-overs the target is better managed than the bidder.[145] Those resources that are directed at poorly managed corporations will probably not be directed at corporations that are managed in only a moderately inefficient way, because replacing a management that is only moderately inefficient will normally not produce sufficient gains to justify the huge premium and out-of-pocket costs required to mount a successful take-over.

In a well-known article,[146] Easterbrook and Fischel argued that managers should be prohibited from engaging in defensive actions against take-overs even if the purpose of the actions was to create an auction and thereby increase the premiums paid to the shareholders, on the ground that the need to pay high premiums interferes with the operation of the take-over market as an interest-alignment and efficiency-monitoring device.[147] This argument has not been accepted by either courts or legislatures. The courts have approved a variety of defences and the promotion of bidding contests,[148] and state legislatures have made take-overs harder rather than easier.[149] Nevertheless, the argument is instructive. The premiss of the argument is that if high premiums were eliminated, the take-over market would adequately align the interests of managers and shareholders and adequately address the problem of managerial inefficiency, and would thereby render mandatory legal rules to control these problems unnecessary. The negative implication is that if legal and business conditions result in a regime of high premiums, which they do, the divergencies of interests between managers and shareholders, and the problem of managerial inefficiency, will not be adequately dealt with by the market for managerial control. Instead, these issues must be addressed, at least in part, by mandatory legal rules. Indeed, mandatory rules that help prevent positional conflicts from interfering with the operation of the market for corporate control can be justified on the ground that they act to *protect* the operation of the market.

6. *The Market for Capital.*—Another market-forces argument is that the market for capital will adequately constrain managers from adopting constitutive rules that are in the managers' interests but against the shareholders' interests.[150] I shall refer to such rules as managerial rules. The idea of the argument is as follows: the adoption of a managerial rule would reduce the price of the corporation's stock. Reducing the price of the corporation's stock would increase the cost of the corporation's capital. Increasing the cost of the corporation's capital will lead either to bankruptcy of the corporation through the operation of the product market or ouster of management through the operation of the take-over market.

An analysis of the effect of the adoption of a managerial rule on the product and the capital markets shows that the capital market is unlikely to adequately align managerial and shareholder interests.

a. *Effect on the Product Market.*—To begin with, a corporation's ability to compete in the product market will not be impaired at all by the adoption of a managerial rule unless its out-of-pocket expenses are increased or its cash flow is reduced. However, many managerial rules are value-decreasing not because they increase cash flow, but because they may lead to reduced profits at some point in the future or create the possibility of a future redistribution of corporate profits from shareholders to managers. Poison pills, for example, are normally value-decreasing only for these reasons. Adoption of a managerial rule may therefore have no present impact on out-of-pocket expenses or cash flow. . . . .

b. *Effect on the Take-over Market.*—Although a managerial rule that has no impact on expenses or current cash flow may have no effect on the corporation's ability to compete in the product market, such a rule may cause the price of the corporation's stock to fall, which in turn could have an effect in the take-over market. But any decrease in the value of a corporation's stock that results from the adoption of a managerial rule will be typically either not measurable or relatively small[151] and relatively small effects on the market price of a corporation's stock will not trigger a hostile take-over because they will be swamped by the huge premium and fees required. Therefore, the capital market, operating through either the product or take-over markets, will seldom if ever prevent managers from adopting managerial rules.

That the financial effects of the market mechanisms considered so far will not in themselves adequately align the interest of managers and shareholders does not mean that managers will act only in their own interest except so far as constrained by law. Many or most managers will probably act in the shareholders' interests, even if not constrained to do so by market mechanisms, because they have internalized the moral principles of corporate stewardship. Those principles, however, have been significantly elaborated and supported by the legal rules that concern the powers and duties of corporate managers. Treating these rules as merely default rules would inevitably weaken the force of the principles they now support. . . . .

Conclusion

The efficacy of enabling and suppletory rules depends on the institutions of private ordering. These institutions have substantial force. Often, however, they have substantial limits as well, sometimes subsumed under the heading of market failure. Mandatory rules also have substantial limits, sometimes subsumed under the heading of regulatory failure. Determining the balance between the costs and benefits of private ordering and mandatory rules in any given case is a matter for the exercise of prudential judgment, informed by economic analysis, quantitative data, the insights of psychology, and other empirical propositions.

In the case of closely held corporations, where constitutive rules are often determined by bargaining, prudential judgment suggests that the shareholders should be allowed to determine their own rules, subject to the limits on the bargain principle in areas where consent is likely to be systematically underinformed and even bargained-out rules would be subject to opportunistic exploitation.

In the case of publicly held corporations, where private ordering seldom takes the form of bargains, a different calculus prevails. Publicly held corporations have survived and prospered in this country, despite the potential divergencies of interests of top managers and shareholders, because these divergencies have been constrained by market forces, moral principles, and legal rules. Mandatory legal rules do double duty in this regard. They are important not only in themselves, but because they serve to emphasize and make particular the general moral principles of stewardship. It would be a descriptive mistake to think that either corporate law or the corporation is contractual in nature. It would be a normative mistake to think that under prevailing circumstances (including the current rules and practices concerning shareholder voting and the structure of share ownership), publicly held corporations would continue at their present level of success if the legal constraints on traditional and positional conflicts that have contributed to that success were removed.

It is sometimes said that arguments for mandatory rules reflect the Nirvana Fallacy, which consists of believing that just because markets are not perfect, mandatory rules would be better. It is of course true that just because markets are imperfect does not mean that mandatory rules would be better. However, the converse proposition is also true: just because mandatory rules are imperfect does not mean that markets would be better. Commentators who stress the Nirvana Fallacy are almost invariably themselves guilty of a mirror-image mistake which might be called the Heavenly Market Fallacy. This is the erroneous belief that because regulation is imperfect, any market, no matter how terribly flawed, is heavenly, and therefore to be preferred to a mandatory legal rule. The brute facts are that most markets are not perfect and most mandatory rules are perfect; that even imperfect markets and legal rules may have positive effects; and that the question in any given case is to determine which of these imperfect mechanisms is better, or, if possible, to determine how these two imperfect mechanisms can be shaped to reinforce each other. Taken separately, neither markets, morals, nor law are in themselves sufficient to curb traditional and positional conflicts. Taken together, however, markets, morals, and law have shown themselves capable of achieving that objective.

Notes

1. These rules do not exhaust corporation law. For example, some rules of corporation law concern the relationship between the corporation and its organs on the one hand, and the outside world on the other. A leading example is the rule that shareholders have limited liability. Rules of this type often have an indirect effect on the internal organization of the corporation, but will not be considered in this Article.
2. I do not consider in this article the question which rules that are not mandatory should be enabling rules, and which should be suppletory or default rules. I also do not consider the principles that should govern the content of suppletory or default rules, and what form such rules should take. On these issues, see generally Ayres and Gertner, 'Filling Gaps in Incomplete Contracts: An Economic Theory of Default Rules' (forthcoming 99 *Yale LJ* (1989)).
3. See e.g. *Glazer* v. *Glazer*, 374 F. 2d 390, 411 (5th Cir.), cert. denied, 389 US 831 (1967); *Galler* v. *Galler*, 32 Ill. 2d 16, 25, 203 NE 2d 577, 583 (1964); *Tschirgi* v. *Merchants Nat'l Bank*, 253 Iowa 682, 690, 113 NW 2d 226, 232 (1962); *Peck* v. *Horst*, 175 Kan. 479, 486, 264 (P. 2d 888, 893 (1953), aff'd on rehearing, 176 Kan.

581, 272 P. 2d 1061 (1954); *Petruzzi* v. *Peduka Constr.*, 263 Mass. 190, 193, 285 NE 2d 101, 102 (1972); *Henderson* v. *Joplin*, 191 Neb. 827, 831–2, 217 NW ed 920, 923–4 (1974); *Sternheimer* v. *Sternheimer*, 208 Va. 89, 98–9, 155 SE 2d 41, 48 (1967).

4. See e.g. Cal. Corp. Code §§ 158, 300(b), 706(a) (West 1977 & Supp. 1989); Del. Code Ann. tit. 8, §§ 341–56 (1983 & Supp. 1988); Model Statutory Close Corp. Supp. §§ 3, 31 (1988), reprinted in 4 Model Business Corp. Act Ann. §§ 1803, 1810, 1845 (3rd edn. Supple. 1989).

5. See Restatement (Second) of Contracts § 356 (1981).

6. See Eisenberg, 'The Bargain Principle and its Limits', 95 *Harv. L. Rev.* 741, 769–73 (1982).

7. See *A Schroeder Music Publishing Co.* v. *Macaulay*, [1974] 3 All ER 616, 622 (five-to-ten-year assignment of copyright to music publisher with no corresponding obligation to publish is unenforceable).

8. J. Mill, *Principles of Political Economy* 950 (W. Ashley ed., 1961).

9. Ibid. at 959–60.

10. See T. Jackson, *The Logic and Limits of Bankruptcy Law* 232–40 (1986) (reviewing and synthesizing the literature).

11. Arrow, 'Risk Perception in Psychology and Economics', 20 *Econ. Inquiry* 1, 5 (1982).

12. Tversky and Kahneman, 'Belief in the Law of Small Numbers' in *Judgment Under Uncertainty: Heuristics and Biases* 23 (D. Kahneman, P. Slovic and A. Tversky eds., 1982).

13. Arrow, *supra* n. 11, at 15.

14. See R. Nisbett and L. Ross, *Human Inference: Strategies and Shortcomings of Social Judgment* 55–9 (1980).

15. Moreover, closely held corporations involve personal relationships, which give rise to a special type of systematic error:

    Typically, [closely held corporations] are founded by individuals who have a virtually complete identity of interests and strong feelings of trust and confidence for one another.

    Time and human nature may cause a divergence of interests and a breakdown in consensus, however. The nature of the enterprise may change so that the once-valued contributions of a shareholder-employee become irrelevant. The shareholder may become incapacitated. Personal relations with dominant shareholders may become strained to such an extent that the minority finds itself ignored. The interest of a deceased shareholder may pass to an heir who is unwilling or unable to participate actively in the business. Or a shareholder may simply come to believe that his talents and capital can be more profitably invested elsewhere.

    Hetherington and Dooley, 'Illiquidity and Exploitation: A Proposed Statutory Solution to the Remaining Close Corporation Problem', 63 *Va. L. Rev.* 1, 2–3 (1977); see also Hillman, 'Private Ordering Within Partnerships',

41 *U. Miami L. Rev.* 425, 434–5 (1987) (discussing difficulty of anticipating future events in business relationships).

16. 367 Mass. 578, 328 NE 2d 505 (1975).

17. Ibid. at 600-, 328 NE 2d at 519.

18. 370 Mass. 842, 353 NE 2d 657 (1976).

19. Ibid. at 851–2, 353 NE 2d at 663.

20. 12 Mass. App. Ct. 201, 422 NE 2d 798 (1981).

21. Ibid. at 210, 422 NE 2d at 804. For additional cases holding that close corporation shareholders owe each other a fiduciary obligation, see *Comolli* v. *Comolli*, 241 Ga. 471, 475, 246 SE 2d 278, 281 (1978); *Cressy* v. *Shannon Continental Corp.*, 177 Ind. App. 224, 229–30, 378 NE 2d 941, 945 (1978); *68th St. Apts., Inc.* v. *Lauricella*, 142 NJ Super. 546, 559, 362 A 2d 78, 85 (1976), aff'd *per curiam*, 150 NJ Super. 47, 374 A 2d 1222 (1977).

22. NY Bus. Corp. Law § 1104-a (McKinney 1986); see also Cal. Corp. Code §§ 1800(a)2), (b)(4), 1804 (West 1977). Under the California statue, the courts are authorized to dissolve a corporation on the ground that those in control have knowingly countenanced persistent unfairness toward any shareholders. A petition can be brought on this ground by (i) shareholders who hold at least one-third of the corporation's shares, exclusive of those owned by persons who have personally participated in the actions under attack, or (ii) any shareholder of a statutory close corporation.

23. NY Bus. Corp. Law § 1104-a(b)(1) (McKinney 1986). The section is confined to unlisted corporations, and a petition for dissolution under the action can be brought only by holders of 20% or more of the corporation's stock. Ibid. § 1104-a(a).

   Many of the involuntary-dissolution statutes permit the corporation or the non-complaining shareholders to avoid dissolution by purchasing the shares owned by the complainants at their fair value. See e.g. Cal. Corp. Code § 2000(a) (West Supp. 1989); NY Bus. Corp. Law § 1118(a) (McKinney Supp. 1989).

24. 64 NY 2d 63, 473 NE 2d 1173, 484 NYS 2d 799 (1984).

25. Ibid. at 72, 473 NE 2d at 1179, 484 NYS 2d at 805 (citations omitted). The court continued:

   A shareholder who reasonably expected that ownership in the corporation would entitle him or her to a job, a share of corporate earnings, a place in corporate management, or some other form of security, would be oppressed in a very real sense when others in the corporation seek to defeat those expectations and there exists no effective means of salvaging the investment.

   Ibid. at 72–3, 473 NE 2d at 1179, 484 NYS 2d at 805; see also *Stefano* v. *Coppock*, 705 P. 2d 443, 446 n.3 (Alaska 1985); *Fox* v. *7L Bar Ranch Co.*, 198 Mont. 201, 209–10, 645 P. 2d 929, 933 (1982); cf. *Meiselman* v. *Meiselman*, 309 NC 279, 298, 307 SE 2d 551, 563 (1983) (dissolution allowed where 'rights and interests of minority shareholders' were violated by majority shareholder);

Masinter v. *WEBCO*, 164 W. Va. 241, 251–2, 262 SE 2d 433, 440 (1980) (breach of fiduciary duty is "'oppressive conduct'"). See generally Thompson, 'Corporate Dissolution and Shareholders' Reasonable Expectations', 66 *Wash. ULQ* 193, 237–8 (1988) (remedy of dissolution and the reasonable expectations standard form effective substitute for private ordering).

26. N.C. Gen. Stat. § 55–125(a)(4) (1982); see also NY Bus. Corp. Law § 1104-a(b)(2) (McKinney 1986) ('[T]he court . . . shall take into account . . . [w]hether liquidation of the corporation is reasonably necessary for the protection of the rights and interests of any substantial number of shareholders . . . .'); Minn. Stat. Ann. § 302A.751, Subd. 3a (West Supp. 1989) ('In determining whether to order . . . dissolution . . . the Court shall take into consideration the duty which all shareholders . . . owe one another to act in an honest, fair, and reasonable manner . . . and the reasonable expectations of the shareholders . . .'); ND Cent. Code § 10.91.1–115.3 (1985) (same).

27. 309 NC 279, 307 SE 2d 551 (1983).

28. Ibid. at 298, 307 SE 2d at 563; see also *Fox* v. *7L Bar Ranch Co.*, 198 Mont. 201, 210, 645 P. 2d 929, 933 (1982) ('[C]ourts must determine the expectations of the shareholders concerning their respective roles in corporate affairs.'); Thompson, *supra* note 25, at 218–19.

29. Cal. Corp. Code § 1804 (West 1977 & Supp. 1989).

30. NC Gen. Stat. § 55–125.1(a)(1) (1982) (court may cancel or alter 'any provision contained in charter or the bylaws'); see also Me. Rev. Stat. Ann. tit. 13-A, § 1123(3)(D) (1981) (same); S.C. Code Ann. § 33–14–310(d)(1) (Law. Co-op. 1976 & Supp. 1988) (same).

31. 264 Or. 614, 507 P. 2d 387 (1973).

32. Ibid. at 631–3, 507 P. 2d at 395–96.

33. 64 NY 2d 63, 473 NE 2d 1173, 484 NYS 2d 799 (1984).

34. Ibid. at 73, 473 NE 2d at 1180, 484 NYS 2d at 806. But see *White* v. *Perkins* 213 Va. 129, 135, 189 SE 2d 315, 320 (1972) (dissolution or appointment of custodian are exclusive remedies available to a minority shareholder under the Virginia dissolution statute).

35. See Marsh, 'Are Directors Trustees?—Conflict of Interest and Corporate Morality', 22 *Bus. Law*. 35, 39–43 (1966).

36. See Principles of Corporate Governance: Analysis and Recommendations § 5.09(c) (Tent. Draft No. 7, 1987). On the other hand, a rule that permitted directors or officers to take opportunities that were derived from corporate information would present the dangers of unforeseeability and exploitation and, therefore, should be unenforceable. See ibid.

37. See *Pappas* v. *Moss*, 393 F. 2d 865, 867–8 (3d Cir. 1968); *Irwin* v. *West End Dev. Co.*, 342 F. Supp. 687, 701 (D. Colo. 1972), aff'd in part and rev'd in part on other grounds, 481 F. 2d 34 (10th Cir. 1973), cert. denied, 414 US 158 (1974); *Sterling* v. *Mayflower Hotel Corp.*, 33 Del. Ch. 293, 313–14, 93 A. 2d 107, 118 (S. Ct. 1952); *Abeles* v. *Adams Eng'g Co.*, 35 NJ 411, 428–30, 173 A. 2d 246, 255 (1961).

A number of recent statutes permit the certificate of incorporation to limit or eliminate personal liability of directors for simple duty-of-care violations. See e.g. Del. Code Ann. tit. 8, § 102(b)(7) (Supp. 1988). Almost all of these statutes, however, are explicitly inapplicable to duty-of-care violations by officers and duty-of-loyalty violations by either directors or officers. See Principles of Corporate Governance: Analysis and Recommendations § 7.17, reporter's note 6 (Tent. Draft No. 9, 1989).

38. See *Picard* v. *Sperry Corp.*, 48 F. Supp. 465, 469 (SDNY 1943), aff'd *per curiam*, 152 F. 2d 462 (2d Cir.), cert. denied, 328 US 845 (1946); *Sterling* v. *Mayflower Hotel Corp.*, 33 Del. Ch. at 313–14, 93 A. 2d at 118; *Hackett* v. *Diversified Chem., Inc.*, 180 So. 2d 831, 834–5 (La. Ct. App. 1965); *Everett* v. *Phillips*, 288 NY 227, 233, 236–7, 43 NE 2d 18, 20–2 (1942); *Adams* v. *Mid-West Chevrolet Corp.*, 198 Okla. 461, 473, 179 P. 2d 147, 160 (1947).

39. The take-over movement is based in part on the results of positional conflicts. A bidder may be able to offer an above-market price for a target because the target's managers have prevented the installation of internal monitoring and removal devices, so that the target is being run by inefficient managers. Or the target's managers may have stressed growth over profits, so that a sell-off of the corporation's business (a bust-up take-over) will yield more value than its continued operation. On the other side of the equation, the bidder's management may be motivated by its own taste for size, as evidenced by the fact that bidders appear to make little or perhaps even no gains on acquisitions. See Jarrell, Brickley, and Netter, 'The Market for Corporate Control: The Empirical Evidence Since 1980', *J. Econ. Persp.* (Winter 1988), at 49, 53; Roll, 'The Hubris Hypothesis of Corporate Takeovers', 59 *J. Bus.* 197, 198 (1986).

40. See Shleifer and Fishny, 'Value Maximization and the Acquisition Process', *J. Econ. Persp.* (Winter 1988), at 7, 7–9:

Like the rest of us, corporate managers have many personal goals and ambitions, only one of which is to get rich. The way they try to run their companies reflects these personal goals. . . . Much corporate behavior seems best understood in terms of managers running the show largely as they please. . . . [I]n practice, non-value-maximizing behavior seems vastly to exceed what one would expect to observe under optimal incomplete information contracts. A wealth of evidence suggests that managers often take actions that dramatically reduce the value of the firm. . . . [I]t is important to recognize that a manager is likely to take whatever actions he can to make himself more valuable to the firm, and more costly to remove.

41. Market forces are also inadequate, as demonstrated below. See Part II.E. *infra*.

42. This does not mean that all constitutive rules that concern top managers should be mandatory. Many or most of the constitutive rules that define and co-ordinate the tasks of top managers should be determined by private order-

ing, because many or most such rules do not involve divergencies of interest between top managers and shareholders.

43. See R. Clark, *Corporate Law* § 9.5.1. (1986); Easterbrook and Fischel, 'The Corporate Contract', 89 *Colum. L. Rev.* 1416, 1443 (1989); Gordon, 'Ties That Bond: Dual Class Common Stock and the Problem of Shareholder Choice', 76 *Calif. L. Rev.* 1, 43–4 (1988).

44. See W. Cary and M. Eisenberg, *Cases and Materials on Corporations* 195–6 (6th edn. 1988) (in 1986, 54% of total equity holdings held by institutional investors).

45. See generally Herman, 'Commercial Bank Trust Departments', in *Abuse on Wall Street: Conflict of Interest in the Securities Markets* 23, 72 (Twentieth Century Fund ed. 1980).

46. See J. Heard and H. Sherman, *Conflicts of Interest in the Proxy Voting System* 90 (1987).

47. See ibid. at 54.

48. See ibid. at 40–67.

49. The mean inside holding (including options that could be exercised within 60 days) of chief executive officers and their immediate families in 746 corporations, as published in the 1987 Forbes Executive Compensation Survey, was 2.42 per cent, although the median holding was only 0.25 per cent. *What the Boss Makes: The People in Power*, Forbes, June 15, 1987, at 162, discussed in M. Jensen and K. Murphy, *Performance Pay and Top-Management Incentives*, University of Rochester Managerial Economics Research Center Working Paper No. 89–98, at 14–15 (1989). Obviously, however, many chief executive officers own significantly more than the mean, and many top officers other than the chief executive also have significant inside holdings.

50. Cf. *Sterling* v. *Mayflower Hotel Corp.*, 33 Del. Ch. 293, 298, 93 A.2d 107, 110–11 (Sup. Ct. 1952) (review of self-interested merger for fairness).

51. This tactic has been especially prevalent in dual-class voting. See *Lacos Land Co.* v. *Arden Group, Inc.*, 517 A. 2d 271, 276–9 (Del. Ch. 1986); Gordon, *supra* note 43, at 48–53. For an analysis of the coercive effect of this tactic, see Ruback, 'Coercive Dual-Class Exchange Offers', 20 *J. Fin. Econ.* 153, 157 (1988).

52. See e.g. 'Inco "Poison Pill" Tested in Canada', *NY Times*, 7 Dec. 1988, at D8, col. 3 (poison pill and special $10 dividend combined in a single proposal).

53. See Rule 14a–8(c)(9), 17 CFR § 240, 14a–8(c)(9) (1988).

54. Rule 14a–9, 17 CFR § 240, 14a–9 (1988).

55. See e.g. the proxy statements of Schering Plough Corporation and RCA Corporation, excerpts from which are reprinted in M. Lipton and E. Steinberger, *Takeovers & Freezeouts* G-3, G-20 (1989).

56. See *supra* note 43 and accompanying text.

57. Rules 14a–1(k)(iii), 14a–2(b)(6), 17 CFR § 240, 14a–1(i)(iii), 14a–2(b)(6) (1988).

58. Even if a shareholder's stake is large enough, and the expected negative

impact is great enough, rationally to justify some expenditure against the proposal, the expenditure will be less than the optimum amount. See Gordon, *supra* note 43, at 44 n. 143.

59. See M. Eisenberg, 'The Structure of the Corporation' (1976) 102–10.
60. Rule 14a–8, 17 CFR § 240.14a–8 (1988), gives shareholders the right to require certain kinds of proposals to be included in the corporate proxy statement. However, the Rule is subject to a number of important exceptions that drastically limit its usefulness to shareholders who propose to solicit for significant changes. For example, under state law, mergers, sales of substantially all assets, amendments to the certificate of incorporation, and dissolution must normally be initiated by the board. Shareholder proposals to effectuate any such transactions would therefore normally be excludable from the proxy statement under Rule 14a–8(c)(1), 17 CFR § 240.14a–8(c)(1) (1988), which permits exclusion of a proposal that is not a proper subject for action by shareholders under state law.
61. Securities Exchange Act § 12(g)(1)(B), 15 USC § 78l(g)(1)(B) (1982).
62. See authorities cited at *supra* note 37.
63. Ibid.
64. Del. Code Ann. tit. 8, § 327 (1982).
65. Ibid. § 141(a).
66. Ibid. § 141(d) (Supp. 1988).
67. Ibid. § 211 (1983).
68. Ibid. § 219(a).
69. Ibid. § 220.
70. Ibid. § 242(b).
71. Ibid.
72. Ibid. §§ 271, 275 (1983 & Supp. 1988).
73. Ibid. § 262.
74. Ibid. § 109(a) (1983).
75. For example, the power to manage the business of the corporation or to supervise its management must be confided in a board or a comparable organ, and cannot be exercised by the shareholders. Ibid. § 141(a). A quorum for directors' meetings may not be less than one-third of the whole broad. Ibid. § 141(b). A committee of the board may not be given power or authority to amend the certificate of incorporation or adopt an agreement of merger, may not recommend to the shareholders a dissolution or a sale of substantially all assets; and may not amend the by-laws. Ibid. § 141(c) (Supp. 1988). A quorum for shareholders' meetings may not be less than one-third of the shares entitled to vote. Ibid. § 216. A proxy to vote shares in the corporation may not be made irrevocable unless accompanied by an interest. Ibid. § 212(c) (1983). A voting trust of the corporation's stock may not exceed ten years in duration. Ibid. § 218. Restrictions on the transferability of stock may not be imposed on previously issued shared without the consent of the

holder. Ibid. § 202(b). Shareholders are not liable for the corporation's debts. Ibid. § 102(b)(6) (Supp. 1988). Distributions are regulated within broad limits. Ibid. § 170 (1983).

I do not claim that all the rules that are presently embodied in the corporate statutes should be viewed as mandatory, or that all the rules that are presently mandatory should be so. For an exploration of this issue, see Coffee, 'The Mandatory/Enabling Balance in Corporate Law: An Essay on the Judicial Role', 89 *Colum. L. Rev.* 1618, 1618 n.1 (1989).

76. See W. Cary and M. Eisenberg, *supra* note 44, at 98.
77. Securities Exchange Act § 12(g)(1)(B), 15 USC § 78(g)(1)(B) (1982); Rule 12g-1, 17 CFR § 240.12g-1 (1988).
78. Securities Exchange Act § 10(b), 15 USC § 78j(b) (1982); Rule 10b-5, 17 CFR § 240.10b-5 (1988).
79. Securities Exchange Act § 16(b), 15 USC § 78p(b) (1982).
80. Rule 13a-13, 17 CFR § 240.13a-13 (1988), and Form 10-K, 17 CFR § 249.310 (1988). The specified matters include legal proceedings and defaults on senior securities. See 4 Fed. Sec. L. Rep. (CCH) ¶ 31,102 (5 Apr. 1989).
81. Rule 13a-1, 17 CFR § 240.13a-1 (1988), and Form 10-Q 17 CFR § 249.308a (1988). The specified matters include legal proceedings, executive compensation, and conflict-of-interest transactions. See 4 Fed. Sec. L. Rep. (CCH) ¶ 31,032 (5 Apr. 1989).
82. Rule 13a-11, 17 CFR § 240.13a-11 (1988), and Form 8-K, 17 CFR § 249.308 (1988). The specified events include a change in control of the corporation, an acquisition or disposition of a significant amount of assets, and a change of accountants.
83. Rules 14a-2, 14a-3(a), 17 CFR §§ 240.14a-2, 240.14a-3(a) (1988).
84. Schedule 14A, 17 CFR § 240.14a-101 (1988). The proxy statement for such a meeting must also disclose whether the corporation has audit, nominating, and compensation committees, and if so, the number of meetings each committee held during the last fiscal year and the functions it performs. Ibid. Item 7.
85. Rule 14a-3(b), 17 CFR § 240.14a-3(b) (1988).
86. Rule 14a-8, 17 CFR § 240.14a-8 (1988).
87. Rule 14a-4, 17 CFR § 240.14a-4 (1988).
88. Ibid. § 240.14a-4(b)(1) (1988).
89. Ibid.
90. Ibid. § 240.14a-4(d)(2) (1988).
91. For example, under Securities Exchange Act § 14(c), 78 USC § 78n(c) (1982), Regulation 14C, 17 CFR § 240.14c-1–7 (1988), and Schedule 14C, 17 CFR§ 240.14c-101 (1988), a corporation that is registered under Securities Exchange Act § 12(g) must distribute an information statement and an annual report in connection with an annual meeting at which directors are to be elected, even if the corporation is not soliciting proxies.

92. New York Stock Exchange Listed Company Manual ¶¶ 303.00, 312.00 (1983). The monopoly position of the New York Stock Exchange, and with it the Exchange's power to impose constitutive rules, has been weakened, but not yet eliminated, by the development of NASDAQ.

93. Fischel, 'Labor Markets and Labor Law Compared with Capital Markets and Corporate Law', 51 *U. Chi. L. Rev.* 1061, 1063 (1984); see also Easterbrook and Fischel, 'Voting in Corporate Law', 26 *JL Econ.* 395, 401 (1983) ('The code of corporate law is a standard form contract for issues of corporate structure'); Fischel, 'The Corporate Governance Movement', 35 *Vand. L. Rev.* 1259, 1264 (1982) ('Fiduciary duties serve . . . as a standard form contractual term . . .').

94. See e.g. Fama and Jensen, 'Separation of Ownership and Control', 26 *JL & Econ.* 301, 302 (1983); Jensen and Meckling, 'Theory of the Firm: Managerial Behavior, Agency Costs and Ownership Structure', 3 *J. Fin. Econ.* 305, 310 (1976).

95. See supra text accompanying notes 5–25, 35–7, 62–92 (setting out some of these rules).

In his comment on this Article, Professor McChesney (like many other contractarians) recognizes that corporation law has many mandatory elements. McChesney, 'Economics, Law, and Science in the Corporate Field: A Critique of Eisenberg', 89 *Colum. L. Rev.* 1530, 1537 (1989). Having said that, however, he makes the following two wholly inconsistent arguments: (1) Corporation law should be radically reformed, by making it completely enabling and suppletory. Ibid. at 1534–5. (2) Those who propose reforms in corporation law have failed to demonstrate the existence of any problems in corporation law. Ibid. at 1539–40 & n. 33 (quoting Fischel, 'The Corporate Governance Movement', supra n. 93, at 1265).

96. See *supra* Parts II.A, II.B.

97. See McChesney, *supra* n. 95, at 1536.

98. See e.g. 'Coffee, Shareholders Versus Managers: The Strain in the Corporate Web', in *Knights, Raiders, & Targets* 77, 85, 107, 110–12 (J. Coffee, L. Lowenstein, and s. Rose-Ackerman eds. 1988).

99. See Rosen, 'Implicit Contracts: A Survey', 23 *J. Econ. Lit.* 1144, 1149 (1985) ('an implicit contract must be interpreted in the "as if" sense of an explicit one').

100. See Restatement (Second) of Contracts § 1 (1981) ('A contract is a promise or a set of promises for the breach of which the law gives a remedy, or the performance of which the law in some way recognizes as a duty.').

101. One unfortunate aspects of the term 'implicit contract' is that it phonetically resembles the term 'implied contract', while in fact the two terms describe two entirely different concepts. An implied contract may be either a real contract (a contract implied in fact) or a legal obligation that is not contractual but is denominated contractual for purely historical reasons (a contract-

implied in law). In contrast, an 'implicit contract' is neither a real contract nor a legal obligation.

102. See e.g. *Meiselman* v. *Meiselman*, 309 NC 279, 307–11, 307 SE 2d 551, 567–70 (1983).

103. I owe this point to Ron Gilson.

104. Those commentators who argue that market forces make mandatory legal rules unnecessary do not claim that such forces completely eliminate the divergencies of interest between managers and shareholders. Rather, they claim that such forces so greatly reduce the divergence of interest between investors and managers that any attempt to reduce the remaining divergence even further by the use of mandatory legal rules would not be worth the costs. See e.g. Fischel, 'The Corporate Governance Movement', *supra* n. 93, at 1265.

Those who make such arguments are often somewhat ambiguous about the role of law. For example, Fischel claims that '[t]he combination of direct monitoring, market forces, *and legal rules* operate greatly to reduce the divergence of interests between investors and managers.' Ibid. at 1265 (emphasis added). However, Fischel characterizes the legal rules as 'a standard form contractual term', which 'serves as an alternative or a supplement to . . . writing lengthy and complicated contracts.' Ibid. at 1264. Presumably, this characterization is intended to mean that the legal rules, like the rules in other standard form contracts, are merely suppletory or default rules. See the statement by Fischel quoted *supra*, text accompanying n. 93. If Fischel and other commentators who characterize legal rules as standard form contracts believe that legal rules are mandatory, their characterization is incorrect but their view of the rules would then be comparable to mine.

105. See Butler, 'The Contractual Theory of the Corporation', 11 *Geo. Mason UL Rev.*, Summer 1989, at 99, 114; Dooley and Veasey, 'The Role of the Board in Derivative Litigation: Delaware Law and the Current ALI Proposals Compared', 44 *Bus. Law.*, 503, 526 (1989); Fischel, 'The Corporate Governance Movement', *supra* n. 93, at 1264.

106. Cf. Jensen and Meckling, *supra* n. 94, at 330 ('[T]he existence of competition in product . . . markets will not eliminate the agency costs due to managerial control problems. . . . If my competitors all incur agency costs equal to or greater than mine I will not be eliminated from the market by their competition.').

107. See J. Tirole, *The Theory of Industrial Organization* 277–303 (1988).

108. See e.g. Coughlan and Schmidt, 'Executive Compensation, Management Turnover, and Firm Performance: An Empirical Investigation', 7 *J. Acct. & Econ.* 43, 46 (1985):

> [T]he existence of competition in capital markets makes the survival of corporations depend on the construction of incentive arrangements which encourage top management to act in the shareholders' interest. Firms which fail to compensate managers in this way will face higher costs and thus will not compete successfully with firms whose managers act in the shareholders' interest.

See also Fischel, 'The "Race to the Bottom" Revisited: Reflections on Recent Developments in Delaware's Corporation Law', 76 *Nw. UL Rev.* 913, 919 (1982) ('Various compensation packages such as stock option plans, which cause managers to share the risk bearing function with shareholders, provide managers with an incentive to maximize shareholders' wealth and keep stock prices high.').

109. See Coughlan and Schmidt, *supra* n. 108, at 53–60; M. Jensen and K. Murphy, *supra* n. 49, at 5; Murphy, 'Corporate Performance and Managerial Remuneration: An Empirical Analysis', 7 *J. Acct. & Econ.* 11, 32–7 (1985).

110. See Gould, 'Through a Lens Darkly', *Nat. Hist.*, Sept. 1989, at 16. Gould illustrates: 'Mouse tails may be "significantly" longer in Mississippi than in Michigan—meaning only that average lengths are not the same at some level of confidence—but the difference may be so small that no one would argue for significance in the ordinary sense.' Ibid. at 16.

111. M. Jensen and K. Murphy, *supra* n. 49, at 5–6.

112. Ibid. at 5–6.

113. Ibid. at 5–7. The relationship between salary and bonus, and three years of lagged shareholder wealth, was little different from the relationship for two years of lagged shareholder wealth. Ibid. at 7.

114. Ibid. at 5, 7.

If it is assumed that all increments in salary and bonus are permanent and that all CEOs will receive the increments until age 70, the average present value of the cash flow resulting from the sum of the change in salary and bonus from the present year until the year of retirement would add or subtract 30 cents per 1,000 dollars to the average chief executive's wealth. Ibid. at 8–9. For present purposes, however, these assumptions seem both inaccurate and inappropriate. The assumptions seem inaccurate because bonuses are supposed to be dependent on performance, and a change in bonus therefore should be transitory, not permanent. (Jensen and Murphy recognize this, but were forced to adopt the assumption because their data source aggregated salary and bonuses.) The assumptions seem inappropriate, because they produce only an average present value for all chief executives and are therefore of no relevance for chief executives who are about to retire, and of limited relevance for chief executives who are close to retirement.

See also Shleifer and Vishny, *supra* n. 40, at 10 ('No study we know of indicates that the incentives provided by extant compensation contracts effectively discourage most non-value-maximizing behavior.').

115. Williams, 'Why Chief Executives' Pay Keeps Rising', *Fortune*, 1 April 1985, at 66, 67, see also ibid. (The CEO 'generally approves, or at least knows about, the recommendation of his personnel executive *before* it goes to the compensation committee, and may take a similar pregame pass at the consultant's recommendations too'); Louis, 'Business is Bungling Long-Term Compen-

sation, *Fortune*, 23 July 1984, at 64, 65 ('[T]he reality at most companies is that top management itself usually devises the executive compensation plan—hiring the consultants whose scheme is then ratified by the board of directors and shareholders . . .').

Cf. Crystal, 'Where's the Risk in CEOs' Rewards?', *fortune*, 19 Dec. 1988, at 62, 62–3:

> The implicit message of every broad-based incentive pay plan is, 'We're all in this together. When the company prospers, we all do—and when it suffers, we suffer.' Trouble is, in many companies that statement is obviously false. With a few notable exceptions, the CEOs suffer little or not at all no matter what happens to the company. . . .
>
> . . . .
>
> How did this odd situation develop? Mainly as a result of several factors operating together:
>
> Many CEOs receive huge base salaries. Remember that base salary is part of the CEO's aggregate remuneration, the part that, for practical purposes, is inert. . . .
>
> Many companies' short-term incentive plans begin to generate bonus pools at levels of performance that are ridiculously puny. This writer's study of 100 major companies' bonus plans conducted a few years back showed that the typical company began to generate bonus money once it achieved a triflingly low 6% return on equity. (Last year the median [return on equity] of the FORTUNE 500 was 14.4%.)
>
> Most executive bonus plans allow far too much discretion—and with discretion comes rationalization. It is amazing to see the clarity of vision demonstrated by CEOs and board compensation committees when it comes to spotting uncontrollable events that trigger downturns in company performance—events like rising oil prices, rising interest rates, hurricanes, and so forth. Yet is is equally amazing to see the cloudiness of vision demonstrated by the same CEOs and board compensation committees when it comes to spotting external events that spark upturns in company performance—events like falling oil prices, falling interest rates, and a booming economy. In the first case, compensation committees almost always cushion the CEO's pay from events that he arguably cannot control. But in the second case, those committees seem to assume that great performance is always a result of CEO brilliance: Therefore pay moves sharply upward.

116. Williams, *supra* n. 115, at 66–7.

117. M. Jensen and K. Murphy, *supra* n. 49, at 10–1, 45.

118. See e.g. *Cohen v. Ayers*, 596 F. 2d 733, 735–43 (7th Cir. 1979) (board of directors' decision to terminate and reissue overpriced options does not constitute waste); *Michelson v. Duncan*, 407 A. 2d 211, 219–22 (Del. 1979) (shareholder ratification of plan to issue stock options was adequate to sustain directors' cancellation and reissue of options following sharp decline in stock price); Coffee, 'No Exit?: Opting Out, the Contractual Theory of the Corporation, and the Special Case of Remedies', 53 *Brooklyn L. Rev.* 919, 943 (1988).

119. M. Jensen and K. Murphy, *supra* n. 49, at 12.

120. Ibid. at 11, 13, 45.

121. Ibid. at 40–1. The measurement is in constant dollars.

122. Ibid.

123. Ibid. at 14; M. Jensen and K. Murphy, 'Are Executive Compensation Contracts Structured Properly?' 28 (14 Oct. 1987) (unpublished draft).

124. It is sometimes argued that the mere fact that managers invest in their own corporation indicates that they do not intend to exploit investors in the corporation, because if they did, they would invest somewhere else. This argument is one more reflection of the average-manager fallacy, because it assumes that all managers own substantial amounts of stock in the corporations they manage. Furthermore, a manager could exploit a corporation without damaging its essential profitability. Finally, the argument fails to address unfair self-dealing that managers convince themselves is fair, inefficient conduct by managers who believe themselves efficient, and conduct that gives expression to positional conflicts.

125. Cf. the Shleifer and Vishny passage quoted *supra* n. 40.

126. See Dooley and Veasey, *supra* n. 105, at 526; Fama, 'Agency Problems and the Theory of the Firm', 88 *J. Pol. Econ.* 288 (1980).

127. The limited mobility of managers is suggested by the fact that the typical chief executive has had only one other corporate employer. M. Jensen and K. Murphy, *supra* n. 123, at 33.

128. See ibid. at 31 (most chief executives leave office only after reaching normal retirement age).

129. See Coughlan and Schmidt, *supra* note 108, at 60–5; Warner, Watts and Wruck, 'Stock Prices and Top Management Changes', 20 *J. Fin. Econ.* 461 (1988); see also Weisbach, 'Outside Directors and CEO Turnover', 20 *J. Fin Econ.* 431 (1988) (boards dominated by outsiders more likely to remove CEO for poor performance than boards dominated by insiders).

130. Weisbach, *supra* n. 129, at 440. Warner, Watts, and Wruck, *supra* n. 129, at 477–9, predicted a difference of 5.3 percentiles between top and bottom deciles, 2.55 percentiles between top and bottom quintiles, and 1.35 percentiles between the median and the bottom deciles. Coughlan and Schmidt, *supra* n. 108, at 60–5, found higher spreads—8 percentiles between top and bottom deciles, 5 percentiles between the median and the bottom decile, and 5 percentiles between top and bottom quintiles. See also M. Jensen and K. Murphy, *supra* n. 49, at 12–21.

131. Weisbach, *supra* n. 129, at 443.

132. Ibid.

133. M. Jensen and K. Murphy, *supra* n. 49, at 16–17.

134. Ibid.

135. Weisbach, *supra* n. 129, at 435–41.

136. See e.g. Easterbrook and Fischel, 'The Proper Role of a Target's Management in Responding to a Tender Offer', 94 *Harv. L. Rev.* 1161, 1173–82 (1981); Manne, 'Mergers and the Market for Corporate Control', 73 *J. Pol. Econ.* 110, 113 (1965).

137. See Jensen, 'Takeovers: Their Causes and Consequences', 2 *J. Econ. Persp.*, Winter 1988, at 21, 28.

138. The effects of takeovers on managerial efficiency are discussed in Jarrell, Brickley, and Netter, *supra* n. 39; Shleifer and Vishny, *supra* n. 40, at 7, 18; Jensen, *supra* n. 137; Scherer, 'Corporate Takeovers: The Efficiency Arguments', *J. Econ. Persp.*, Winter 1988, at 69, 76.

139. See Coffee, 'Regulating the Market for Corporate Control: A Critical Assessment of the Tender Offer's Role in Corporate Governance', 84 *Colum. L. Rev.* 1145, 1187–8 (1984).

140. See Jensen, *supra* n. 137, at 22.

141. See *Bangor Punta Operations, Inc.* v. *Bangor & Aroostook R.R.*, 417 US 703, 710–11 (1974).

142. A distinction may be drawn between operating and resource efficiency. By *operating* efficiency, I mean the ability to manage the resources that the corporation holds in such a manner as to maximize the profits derived from those resources. By *resource* efficiency, I mean the ability to determine what resources the corporation should hold, and how those resources should be financed. The pressure of take-overs normally will not increase a manager's ability to operate the resources that the corporation holds, but it may force him to increase resource efficiency, as by selling off resources the corporation should not hold or refinancing the resources it continues to hold. I use the term 'inefficient' in the text to mean operating inefficiency, that is, a failure to manage a corporation's existing resources so as to wring out maximum profits.

143. See Jensen, *supra* n. 137, at 28; see also Shleifer and Vishny, *supra* n. 40, at 16.

144. Jensen, *supra* n. 170, at 28.

145. See Herman, 'The Limits of the Market as a Discipline in Corporate Governance', 9 *Del. J. Corp. L.* 530, 536–7 (1984).

146. Easterbrook and Fischel, *supra* n. 136.

147. Ibid. at 1174–80.

148. See e.g. *Moran* v. *Household Int'l, Inc.*, 500 A. 2d 1346, 1350 (Del. 1985) (defensive action against take-over threat upheld); *Unocal Corp.* v. *Mesa Petroleum Co.*, 493 A. 2d 946, 955 (Del. 1985) (same).

149. See e.g. Del. Code Ann. tit. 8, § 203 (1983 & Supp. 1988); Ind. Code Ann. § 23-12-42 (Burns Supp. 1989); NY Bus. Corp. Law § 912 (McKinney 1986 & Supp. 1989); Wis. Stat. Ann. § 180.726 (West Supp. 1988).

150. See Easterbrook, 'Managers' Discretion and Investors' Welfare: Theories and Evidence', 9 *Del. J. Corp. L.* 540, 556–7 (1984); Fischel, 'The Corporate Governance Movement', *supra* n. 93, at 1264; Winter, 'State Law, Shareholder Protection, and the Theory of the Corporation, 7 *J. Leg. Stud.* 251, 275–5 (1977).

151. Merritt Fox, in a comment on an earlier draft of this Article, worked out the effect of a small but measurable change on the price of a new issue as follows:

> [S]uppose a corporation has assets that would produce a permanent cash flow available for shareholders of $500,000 per year (in other words its gross cash flow is

sufficiently large to leave $500,000 after payment of operating expenses, interest on debt and the cost of purchasing new productive assets to replace those that have worn out during the year). The discount rate is 10%. The value of the equity of this firm, absent the managerial rule, would thus be $5 million. If there are 100,000 shares, they would be priced in an efficient market at $50 each. Imposition of the managerial rule reduces the net cash flow to $490,000, the value of the equity to $4.9 million and the share price to $49. If the cash flow is certain in this example, the corporation can continue operating under the managerial rule without the slightest risk of bankruptcy and would have no need to reenter the capital markets. . . .

[A]ssume that the corporation wishes to raise $500,000 to invest in a project that will produce a net cash flow of $50,000 (i.e., a market rate of return) and with respect to which the managerial rule will not be imposed. . . . The net cash flow of the corporation after the expansion will be $540,000 and the value of the equity will be $5.4 million. If the corporation proposes to raise the $500,000 by offering 10,204 shares at $49, the public will willingly pay the price. The value of the equity will be $5.4 million and $5.4 million/110204 = $49.00.

[A]ssume now that the corporation wishes to raise the $500,000 to invest in [a new] project but that it plans to extend the managerial rule to these new operations. . . . The net cash flow of the corporation after the expansion will be $539,000 and thus the value of the equity will be $5.39 million. . . . Set $E = $5.39 million (the value of the equity after the investment), $i = $500,000 (the amount that must be raised for the new project) and $S = 100,000 (the number of shares initially outstanding). Take p as the price at which the shares will be offered and [let] n be the number of shares that must be issued at p in order to raise i. An efficient capital market imposes the following conditions:

$$p \times n = I$$
$$E/(n + S) = p \text{ (so that } p \text{ is a market clearing price)}$$

These conditions can be manipulated to get the value of p and n in terns of E, I, and S:

$$E/(n + S) = p = 1/n$$
$$(n + S)/E = n/I$$
$$(I/E) \times (n + S) = n$$
$$(I/E) \times S = n \times (1 - (I/E))$$
$$\frac{(I/E)}{1 - (I/E)} \times S = n$$

Filling in the actual values of E, I, and S, $n = 10,224$ shares. Correspondingly, $p = $48.90, which is a market clearing price because $5.39 million/110,224 = $48.90.

Letter from Merritt B. Fox to author (12 December 1988) (copy on file at the Columbia Law Review).

Understanding the Japanese Keiretsu: Overlaps between Corporate Governance and Industrial Organization

RONALD J. GILSON AND MARK J. ROE

We aim here for a better understanding of the Japanese keiretsu. Our essential claim is that to understand the Japanese system—banks with extensive investment in industry and industry with extensive cross-ownership—we must understand the problems of industrial organization, not just the problems of corporate governance. The Japanese system, we assert, functions not only to harmonize the relationships among the corporation, its shareholders, and its senior managers, but also to facilitate productive efficiency.

Comparative corporate governance, once an academic backwater, now enjoys important government and scholarly attention. US government reports attribute Japan's competitive success in part to features of the Japanese system.[1] Harvard Business School's major, multi-disciplinary study of American management's time horizons recommends, as a way to combat 'short-termism' among US managers, restructuring American corporate governance so that it resembles Japan's more closely.[2]

This new-found interest derives from two changes, one domestic and one international. The domestic change is evident in scholars' new understanding of America's corporate governance system; during a short

Ronald J. Gilson is Charles J. Meyers Professor of Law and Business, Stanford University, and Professor of Law, Columbia University. Mark J. Roe is Professor of Law, Columbia University. We are grateful to Bernard Black, John C. Coffee, Jr., Victor Goldberg, Jeffrey Gordon, Henry Hansmann, Hideki Kanda, Steven N. Kaplan, W. Carl Kester, Louis Lowenstein, Roberta Romano, Mark Wolfson, and participants at the Conference on Corporate Governance: New Problems and New Solutions, Center for Economic Policy Research, Stanford University, 16–17 April 1992, and at the University of Michigan Law School Law and Economic Workshop, for helpful comments on earlier drafts of this article. An informal seminar series on comparative corporate governance sponsored by Columbia University's Law and Economics Center led to our collaboration on this article.

period of time, the basic paradigm has shifted. The 'traditional' model of American corporate governance presented the Berle–Means corporation—characterized by a separation of ownership and management resulting from the need of growing enterprises for capital and the specialization of management—as the pinnacle in the evolution of organizational forms. Given this model's dominance, the study of comparative corporate governance was peripheral; governance systems differing from the American paradigm were dismissed as mere intermediate steps on the path to perfection, or as evolutionary dead-ends, the neanderthals of corporate governance. Neither laggards nor dead-ends made compelling objects of study.

More recent scholarship challenges the 'traditional' view, arguing that the separation of ownership and management—and the absence of substantial shareholders or lenders to monitor professional management—is historically and politically contingent. In particular, in the United States, populism, federalism, and interest group conflicts combined to restrict the growth of large financial intermediaries, especially banks, and constrained other efforts to oversee management, through a regulatory web of banking, insurance, tax, and securities laws.[3] The American system may be the product of an evolutionary process, but its development has been affected by features of our politics, some of which are fundamental to democracy, some peculiar to American democracy. Nothing in that process assures the American system's productive superiority to systems that evolved under different conditions.

The second change—heightened international competition—has made it important to understand the contingency of American corporate governance. The globalization of commerce and the post-war re-emergence of the Japanese and European economies has required American corporations to compete with organizations having dramatically different governance systems. In this new environment, competition exists not only among products, but also among governance systems, and American firms are not always winning. Thus, real world competition has obliged business scholarship to focus on comparative corporate governance. Because the American system is now seen as contingent, and other systems seemed in the 1980s to be doing better, understanding the differences has become urgent.[4]

Yet, we shall argue here, our system's characteristics colour the lens through which the first comparative studies viewed the rest of the world. Analysis of American corporate governance has always sought to solve the problem of separation of ownership and control: who will monitor management in light of dispersed shareholdings. Favoured candidates for this monitoring role have shifted from outside directors[5] to the market for corporate control, and, most recently, to institutional investors. As a result, the primary focus in comparative studies of Japanese corporate governance has been the role of the main bank. Conventional wisdom among American scholars has been that the Japanese system solves the corporate governance problem—who monitors management—through continuous monitoring by a financial intermediary, rather than through intermittent and often disruptive monitoring by capital markets.[6] Relying on this analysis, reform proposals have identified institutional investors as having the potential to provide Japanese-style monitoring in the American system.[7]

To date, comparative analyses of the Japanese corporate governance system have assumed that the central *purpose* of the Japanese system, like that of the American system, is solving the Berle–Means monitoring problem. We argue that the Japanese system serves a function in addition to the monitoring of management. Our Japanese model reflects not only the need for *corporate governance*, the traditional factor American scholars have identified as shaping corporate structures, but also the need to support production and exchange—what we will call *contractual governance*.[8] To be sure, complex multi-level monitoring is part of the production process, but this monitoring is motivated not just by financial institutions seeking a return on capital, but also by product market competition. Bank monitoring thus should not be seen in isolation, but as one specific (although important) kind of a wide range of contractual monitoring types in Japan. An empirical observation informs this perspective: although financial institutions hold one-half of Japanese public firm stock, often in highly-concentrated blocks, another quarter of Japanese stock is held by other corporations, often suppliers or customers.[9]

Our claims are modest. We do not contend that our model fully describes the Japanese system; we do not seek to *displace* the main-bank-as-monitor paradigm. Indeed, we doubt that any single model fully captures the system's complexity. Rather, we mean to show only that (1) our model captures an important element missed thus far, and that (2) intermediary monitoring is only one part of a larger Japanese system of contractual governance. We also do not seek to discredit proposals that would reform American corporate governance by enabling intermediaries to monitor management more effectively. The path-dependent development of the American Berle–Means corporation might well indicate that intermediary monitoring is now the best solution for the

American corporation's deeper governance problems. But the broader contractual governance structure characteristic of large Japanese firms, having taken another evolutionary path, cannot be duplicated exactly in the United States by changing only the role of financial intermediaries.[10] . . . .

In Part I, we sketch the development of the traditional Berle–Means conception of American corporate governance and the succession of potential monitors that have led to a comparative focus on Japan. In Part II, we briefly summarize the dominant theme of current comparative analysis of Japanese corporate governance: the monitoring role of the main bank. In Part III, we set out our contractual governance model of the Japanese corporate system, and, in Part IV, we explore the model's implications both for comparative corporate governance analysis of the Japanese system and for reforming America's corporate governance system.

I. The Berle–Means model of American corporate governance

In 1932, Adolf Berle and Gardiner Means announced the separation of ownership and control in American industry. *The Modern Corporation and Private Property*,[11] a book that for some sixty years has defined the intellectual mission of American corporate governance, reported that owners of major corporations had become atomistic shareholders lacking the ability, skill, information, and often the incentives to monitor the performance of specialized managers.[12] Thereafter, the corporate governance debate became a search for the organizational Holy Grail: a mechanism to bridge the separation of ownership and control by holding managers accountable for their performance.

The modern corporate governance literature has treated this separation as the efficient response to economic forces. Specialization of risk bearing increased the availability of capital by opening investment to individuals who would not be active in the firm's operations, and reduced the cost of capital by allowing diversification.[13] Efficiency became the standard in the corporate governance debate. To increase the value of the corporation, control is delegated to managers with specialized skills. But this delegation also gives managers the discretion to advance their own agenda at the shareholders' expense. The purpose of corporate governance, thus, became minimizing the sum of the costs involved in aligning managers and shareholders' incentives and in unavoidable self-interested managerial behaviour.[14]

The most enduring institution for minimizing agency cost has been the independent director. The concept—that shareholders would bridge their separation from managers by electing non-employee directors to monitor management performance—has reached the status of conventional wisdom. The Business Roundtable,[15] the Conference Board,[16] the American Bar Association,[17] the American Law Institute,[18] and the Delaware courts[19] have all come to accord independent directors the primary monitoring role. Substantial doubt remains, however, as to independent directors' effectiveness. They typically are chosen by management and perceive themselves as 'serving at the pleasure of the CEO-Chairman'.[20] In addition, most are chief executive officers of other large companies[21] who are unlikely to monitor more energetically than they would want to be monitored by their own boards.[22]

Hostile take-overs during the late 1970s and 1980s provided another technique for minimizing agency costs. Here the external monitor—the market—replaced the internal monitor. When the market price of a company's stock signalled poor managerial performance, those who thought they could do better paid the shareholders a premium—reflecting some sharing of the potential gain—for the privilege of improving the target company's performance. But owing in no small part to the discretion that the Delaware courts and other states' legislatures gave target management, take-overs grew more expensive, and some states made many take-overs too costly to attempt.[23] Moreover, take-overs were reactive at best: they attacked much bad management but did not directly prevent it. Finally, at least the 1980s generation of take-overs depended on debt financing, which dried up at the beginning of the 1990s. Many such take-overs have resulted in costly recapitalizations, often in Chapter 11. By 1992, the market for corporate control was quiet.

The take-over market's decline coincided with a realization among commentators that perhaps the premiss underlying the Berle and Means analysis no longer held. While no one was looking, shareholders had reaggregated somewhat; institutional investors held half the stock of the largest American corporations, although in small blocks.[24] The blocks were never as concentrated as those now found in Japan, but the number of layers was often sufficiently small so that concerted investor action could be considered—or at least prescribed by academics. While a take-over's governance benefits rested on an *outsider* buying enough stock to become a large stockholder, the new aggregation raised the possibility that *existing* large stockholders could provide those benefits without take-overs. Some institutions—usually public pension funds—began to act somewhat like monitors, making proposals concerning take-over defences, shareholder advisory committees, and director independence.[25] Emboldened by this activity, reformers even suggested that institutional investors had the power to make the outside director concept viable,[26] or to set forth the changes necessary to make it viable.[27]

Once it became clear (1) that the Berle–Means corporation was historically and politically contingent and (2) that intermediaries *could* play a role, other patterns of corporate governance became plausible alternatives, including foreign patterns in which intermediaries have long played a more important role than they have played in the United States.[28] Foreign structures no longer seem to be laggards struggling to catch up to America's advanced capital markets; instead, they have become alternatives to our own structures. Even if we would never use the foreign structures as a blueprint for American reform, they might help us chart a new course for the large American public corporation.

II. The Japanese main bank as the missing monitor

Japan, it appeared, had developed a solution to the Berle–Means monitoring problem: the main bank. A Japanese corporation had a single bank that provided the largest share of its borrowings and also held a substantial equity position.[29] Moreover, the main bank spoke with more than its own authority. Each main bank seemed to act as the delegated monitor for other banks lending to its client corporation, so that, in effect, the creditors spoke with a single voice.[30] The main bank required review of a client corporation's business plans[31] and, in the event of poor performance, intervened to impose new management or strategies. It often bailed out a troubled company.[32] Thus, the main bank was said to provide 'an important substitute mechanism for what in effect is a "missing" take-over market in Japan; or to put it somewhat differently the main bank system serves to internalize the market for corporate control.'[33]

It is hardly surprising that American commentators were drawn to this picture of a monitoring paragon,[34] the Japanese main bank confirmed the historical and political contingency of American arrangements. American political history prevented American financial intermediaries from directly monitoring management.[35] America never had widespread main banks, but where financial intermediaries were not so severely limited, as in Japan, they helped bridge the separation of ownership and management.

The standard Japanese bank monitoring story needs qualifications in two respects. To the extent that a monopoly control of credit in the

Japanese banks was critical to their power, the rise of alternative credit sources and the growth of corporate retained earnings diminished it.[36] While banks—which remain as stockholders—might still intervene in the event of a crisis,[37] and large blocks, even if normally passive, might motivate managers to avoid a crisis, crisis intervention is a more limited role than that of an ongoing monitor of business strategy. The primary active role of the banks' large stockholdings would not be to improve normal corporate governance before crisis—the primary American goal—but to facilitate financial and managerial restructuring when big problem arose—an important but secondary American goal.

Second, characterizations of the main bank as 'internaliz[ing] the market for corporate control'[38] need clarification. Displacing inefficient management—management that is performing so poorly as to threaten the corporation's economic viability—is one function of take-overs. But it is neither the only function[39] nor, over lengthy periods, necessarily the most important one. During the 1980s, the dominant acquisition motive appears not to have been to remove management whose operational performance threatened to bankrupt the company, but instead to dismantle ineffective conglomerates that were in danger only of continuing to throw away their free cash flow.[40] Managers were inefficient in using an unwieldy structure, but once the (bad) decision had been made to keep the structure and invest free cash flow in it, they did as good a job as could be done. The prototypical target was RJR Nabisco, not Chrysler. If the Japanese main bank has served thus far primarily as a crisis manager, allocator of capital, and gatekeeper to bankruptcy, it has not yet shown itself to be a complete substitute for America's 1980s takeovers. A complete monitor must (at least) reduce poor use of free cash flow, a problem Japan is only beginning to face.

Moreover, our point is not to criticize the limits of the Japanese main bank system. Indeed, the very limits are said by Professors Aoki and Sheard to be central to the system's genius. The limits allow managers freedom from outside pressure except in crisis so that they can respect commitments to employees. In times of crisis, the main bank provides a safety net—the funds and expertise to bail the employees out—although at some personal cost to the employees and with some positive probability of liquidation. Avoiding bank intervention gives both management and employees an incentive for team performance.[41]

Our point is instead that the Japanese corporate governance system is not only about Berle–Means corporate governance. It also may be an effort to link the structural features of the corporation directly to the efficiency of the corporation's actual production; it is about industrial organization, not just corporate governance. Viewing the Japanese system through Berle–Means blinkers, in the belief that it reflects only an effort to bridge the separation of ownership and control, will cause us to misunderstand it and, as a result, to miss the lessons that comparative analysis can offer.

Recent work by economists is consistent with a model of Japanese contractual governance. Much of it has focused on the Japanese firms' ability to provide incentives making the interests of owners and employees compatible and on enforcing implicit contracts among related firms.[42] In the next Part, we seek to extend this work by explaining the keiretsu as a form of industrial organization motivated by the need to support multi-lateral relation-specific investment. Then we explore the circumstances, notably competition in the product market, under which such an organization can flourish.

III. The Japanese system as global contractual governance of which specific corporate governance is a subset

One-third of Japanese corporate cross-holdings is not held by financial institutions, but by industrial companies, which are often suppliers or customers of the portfolio company.[43] What is the function of this one-third of the cross-holdings? Can the Japanese system be partly understood as a form of industrial organization, as a means to integrate customers and suppliers, different pieces in the production process, of which capital suppliers are only one component? In this Part, we develop a simple model of the Japanese system in which cross-ownership's primary purpose is to foster efficient production, not directly to provide monitoring by the residual equity holder. The inquiry here focuses less on corporate governance than on industrial organization.[44]

Two introductory points should be made, one substantive and one methodological. The substantive point is that we take as the Japanese structure not a single Japanese corporation in isolation, but the keiretsu structure—the interlocking webs of firms, which loom so large in the Japanese economy.[45] The study of American corporate governance concentrates on the structure of a single firm, say, General Motors; a Japanese keiretsu may include the equivalent of GM, GE, US Steel (now USX), and IBM, as separate firms. A keiretsu might have a car assembler, a steel company (which supplies steel sheets for cars and buys furnaces for its factories from the electrical machinery company), and a computer firm (which supplies microprocessors for the cars, appliances, machines, and factory).[46] Each company would have some separate existence, but through extensive cross-ownership,[47] these quasi-firms would blend at the edges. We take the entire structure—all these quasi-firms, in Japan, the keiretsu—as the meta-firm, the object of our study.[48] In the United States, we would typically view these as separate firms that interconnect only via contract. Americans would define the 'firm' as including only the wholly-owned subsidiaries of the core firm; GM's Fisher body plant and EDS's computer operation—once separate companies—would now be seen as part of a single, GM firm.

Although about 50 per cent of the stock in large Japanese firms is held by banks and insurers, often in large blocks, other corporations own about 25 per cent of the large-firm stock. Often these other firms have supplier-customer relations.[49] Banks and insurers are not the only large block stockholders: steelmakers, for example, own blocks of the leading automakers, their customers.[50] This is our point of departure: although we do not need to displace the bank monitoring theories, focusing on bank monitoring alone could blind us to a potentially critical feature of the Japanese ownership structure. We hypothesize that fostering relational contracting is the function of the one-third of corporate cross-ownership not held by the banks.

We offer only a model, not a rich, institutional description of the various keiretsu structures. As with any model, ours carries with it familiar limitations: to highlight the importance and operation of a complex system, we must necessarily make simplifying assumptions.

A. A Stylized Model of the Japanese System

1. The Continuum: Contract Versus Organization Imagine factors of production for a product—say, five parties consisting of a distributor, two parts suppliers, a bank, and an assembler—which sit down to negotiate a co-operative structure for producing the good.[51] Efficient production requires all the parties to make substantial investments in relation-specific capital. Labour at the assembly firm must learn flexible production methods and skills peculiar to this enterprise and its team of co-workers.[52] The suppliers have to locate their production close to the assembler. They must develop, with the assembler, design and quality standards and procedures and a just-in-time delivery system, all specific to the parties and the product. The assembler, in turn, must invest jointly with the parts suppliers in the development of standards and procedures and, in turn, must specialize its assembly facilities for the suppliers' parts. Finally, the supplier of capital assures that short-term swings in the business cycle do not leave the venture short of funds, insuring against the business cycle for those who cannot diversify their relation-specific investments.[53] But the benefits of relation-specific investment come with a cost: once a factor so invests, the other factors could appropriate the gains from cooperation. The industrial organization challenge, then, is to design a structure that provides the parties incentives to make the optimal investment in relation-specific assets. Efficiency requires loose, long-term, relational investments, which create the risk of opportunism. Maximizing productive efficiency and minimizing opportunism are the goals of contractual governance.

But what type of arrangement will maximize efficiency and minimize opportunism? The continuum of possible structures is anchored by two extremes, one pure contract, the other pure organization. On the idealized *contractual* end of the continuum, one factor becomes the entrepreneur and uses highly specific contracts to organize production; these contracts specify the terms on which the entrepreneur can acquire goods and services from the other factors under all possible future circumstances, thereby preventing all involved from acting opportunistically. Every contingency is anticipated and dealt with in this perfect contract, whose terms will be judicially enforced without significant friction.[54] This 'firm' is a loose connection of factors that are linked through a nexus of arm's-length contracts. On the idealized *organizational* end of the continuum, few arm's-length contracts are specified: the entrepreneurial factor buys up, or establishes by itself, the other factors. This firm vertically integrates.[55]

These two idealized extremes capture much of the tension that has motivated American academic debate over contractual governance. Limited foresight and the threat opportunism presents to relation-specific investment render neo-classical contracting incapable of providing a complete structure for organizing production. Perfect contractual governance is impossible. But the other extreme, vertical integration, presents its own problems. Organizing production solely within a firm increases the capital and managerial expertise required and creates the Berle–Means problem. The substitution of ownership for market procurement—making rather than buying—requires effective internal incentives and monitoring to avoid organizational opportunism.

2. Japan: A Hybrid Between Contract and Organization   Our model puts the Japanese keiretsu in the middle of the continuum, a region that has perceived inadequate attention in the American corporate governance debate.[56] Partial vertical integration through partial cross-ownership, combined with market contracting, incorporates features of both contract and organization.[57]

Suppose our factors of production seek to avoid both the bounded rationality that limits neo-classical contracting and the agency costs that limit corporate governance. They deliberately use an open-ended relational contract—one committing the parties to a long-term affiliation for the production of the good, but consigning to the parties' good intentions the way in which the terms of trade for relation-specific assets will respond to unexpected changes in conditions. Kester, for example, describes the basic agreement between supplier and assembler in the Japanese auto industry: 'The buyer and seller will operate on a basis of mutual respect for each other's autonomy and undertake to establish and maintain an atmosphere of mutual trust in business dealings.'[58]

While this intermediate solution has the surface appeal of steering a course between the Scylla of neo-classical contracting and the Charybdis of vertical integration, without more, the covenant of future good faith is illusory. What assures the factor providers that one of them will not take advantage of the others tomorrow when exploitation is possible? In the absence of an effective barrier to opportunism, the corrosive effect of anticipated misbehaviour will cause mid-range solutions to devolve into either vertical integration or short-term contracting.[59]

Cross-ownership of equity among factor providers—a central feature of the Japanese system—helps reduce this opportunism.[60] Suppose that in our hypothetical organizational design problem, each of the five factor providers supports its investment in relation-specific assets by exchanging equity interests so that each owns 20 per cent of the other four.[61] In this setting, the cross-holdings help enforce the commitment to a good faith determination of new terms of trade for relation-specific assets following the occurrence of an unexpected state of the world. Cross-ownership prevents the party having the chance to act opportunistically from doing so.[62] With stock ownership, the other factors could coalesce to replace the opportunistic factor provider's managers, or threaten to sell the stock, which would leave the recalcitrant managers without 'protection' from market havoc (or even a take-over).[63] So long as partners making a relation-specific investment do not expect any one party systematically to be advantaged over time—that is, the expectation of states favouring a factor is random—cross-holdings of equity help to support long-term productive exchange, reducing the opportunism of neo-classical contracting and the agency costs of vertical integration.[64]

The critical insight of our stylized model of the Japanese system is that equity serves a larger purpose than in the Berle–Means corporate governance model. In the Berle–Means corporation, equity has governance rights because the holder of the residual profits interest has the best incentive to reduce agency costs; the right to control rests with those who stand to gain the most from efficient production.[65] In contrast, in our Japanese model, a big slice of equity serves not just to encourage monitoring through ownership of the residual profits interest, but also to encourage relation-specific investment by reducing opportunism as well.[66]

Traditional main bank monitoring can be reconfigured to fit this system. Creditors may invest through long-term relation-specific loans just as steelmakers will invest in a car factory by investing in machinery and at locations most useful for auto steel; both the creditor and the steelmaker will take stock positions in the automaker. An automaker that behaves badly will induce bank intervention. This may appear as American-style intervention of the residual equity holder to some, but we believe that the relationship is more complex, because it is deeply embedded in a system of contractual governance. The bank may deal with an opportunistic portfolio company. It does so, however, not just to maximize the returns of the residual equity holder—the American model—but also to protect the bank as a factor of production and provider of credit, and to protect the other industrial factors, in which the bank is a stockholder.

Even bank crisis intervention or actions as an ongoing monitor are partly acts of contractual governance, occurring in two dimensions. First, the bank is protecting its loan position, just as the steel company protects its long-term investment in machinery tailored to a customer's needs. Second, the bank, as an owner of stock in the related factors, is acting as their 'agent'. Main bank monitoring is not precisely analogous to monitoring by the residual equity holder, even when the bank *is* the residual equity holder, because the bank is also a factor provider and owns stock in other factor providers. The factor providers receive their returns on investment from the terms on which they provide their input, not just from the residual performance of the collective enterprise.[67] In the Berle–Means model, corporate governance serves to assure that someone has the right incentives to monitor. In our stylized Japanese model, corporate governance serves to support contractual exchange. The multiple relationships—stockholder *and* creditor, stockholder *and* supplier—increase the incentives to intervene (by bundling up two advantages in the relationship) and decrease the costs (information flows through supplier contacts and stockholder contacts) when a related firm has problems.[68]

3. *Illustration: General Motors and Fisher Body* An example from America's vertical integration literature will illustrate our model.[69] In 1919, GM needed auto bodies. Fisher Bodies needed a customer for its auto bodies. To build the kind that GM needed, Fisher had to invest in specific body-building assets. Fisher was unwilling to do this without assured purchases from GM. Without contract protection, GM could threaten to abandon Fisher once Fisher built the GM-specific plants unless Fisher lowered its price, making the GM-specific assets worthless. Once Fisher made the specific investments for GM auto bodies, GM could squeeze Fisher's price down to its variable costs (plus the value of Fisher's assets that could be redeployed away from GM's bodies). To protect Fisher, GM agreed to purchase its requirements of the specific body type for ten years from Fisher. This agreement opened up GM to the risk of exploitation by Fisher: GM was making an openended commitment to buy its requirements of the specified auto body *only* from Fisher. What would stop Fisher from raising its price? Price might be specified in a contract, but over ten years costs could change, making a specified price impossible. So, to protect GM, Fisher agreed to a formula by which the price would be calculated at Fisher's variable costs plus 17.6 per cent, with the 17.6 per cent presumably representing the expected value of the specific assets to which Fisher was committing.

An unexpectedly rapid run-up in demand for the specified type of auto bodies made it worthwhile for Fisher to exploit the contract's formula to hold up GM. The unexpected run-up in demand for Fisher-type bodies made it worthwhile (from an integrated perspective) for Fisher to build new capital-intensive plants and locate them next to GM, but Fisher refused to do so and wanted to be paid under the contract formula. With expanded demand, capital-intensive plants would have been cheaper than the labour-intensive means Fisher used, but capital-intensive production disfavoured Fisher under the contract. Eventually GM solved its problem by buying up all of Fisher's stock.

In our abstract model, Fisher's unexpected ability to exploit GM might have been mitigated by extensive cross-ownership. Fisher would have been 5 per cent owned by GM, 5 per cent owned by a steel firm, 5 per cent owned by an automotive paint and fabric firm (DuPont), and 20 per cent owned by a coalition of banks, one of which would have been a 'main bank' for this network. In such a setting, Fisher could not have readily exploited the unexpected loophole because a coalition of owners could displace Fisher's senior management. *Ex ante*, GM and Fisher might not have been bothered with the detail they put into the contract, a contract that *ex post* turned out to be insufficiently detailed.

The end result for the GM-Fisher Body problem was complete vertical integration, raising a serious problem for our model: why is vertical integration not a general solution for investments in relation-specific assets? Shouldn't the factors always choose vertical integration—complete, not partial ownership—as the full solution?

We take this point seriously and do not have a complete answer. Our hypothesis—suggested by GM's subsequent history—is that something else must be traded off. First, complete vertical integration raises the agency problems of large organizational structures, requiring costly investments in internal monitoring. GM's bloated bureaucracy and recent poor performance may be the result of 'excess' vertical integration. Second, the cross-holding/cross-exchange structure differs from complete vertical integration. There is some resort to contract. The trading relationship between members of even a vertical keiretsu is not exclusive. The Japanese corporate governance system is said to be

an attempt to secure the best of two worlds. By tying themselves to one another in groups, yet eschewing outright ownership and control, Japanese corporations have been able to exploit some of the high-powered incentives of the market that derive from independent ownership of assets, while relying on selective intervention by key equity owners to adapt contracts to new circumstances as needed.[70]

The ability of even the completely vertically integrated firm to use outside suppliers to test the internal division somewhat weakens the distinction. If the internal division does not measure up, it can be disbanded. One weakness of complete vertical integration, however, is that if the relational failure goes the other way—the *division* performs, but the enterprise as a whole slackens—the division cannot easily detach itself from the slackers and migrate to a high-performance company.[71] With keiretsu partial cross-ownership, that kind of migration—and the incentives it provides others in the organization—is possible.[72]

B. But What About Monitoring? Product Market Competition as the Catalyst that Makes the Hybrid Work

Our stylized model of the Japanese corporate system, in which cross-holdings of equity serve to support exchange rather than to provide incentives for minimizing agency costs, is not yet complete. By reducing opportunism, cross-holdings may support the investment in relation-specific assets necessary to efficient production. Acquisition of these assets, however, will not guarantee efficient production. Even an optimal amount of relation-specific assets must be effectively employed. And here, the skeptic will remark, is where the contractual governance model falls short. Monitoring—a corporate governance system directed at reducing agency costs—could still be necessary to assure that those in charge of employing the relation-specific assets work hard enough to maximize the return on investment. Without it, the co-operative arrangement supported by cross-holdings may cease to support efficient production, instead deteriorating into a co-operative arrangement to protect a collective decision by the various factor providers to live the good life: I won't monitor you if you won't monitor me.[73]

In the corporate governance model, monitoring is conducted, albeit imperfectly, by the residual owners. And in the absence of an alternative to a residual owner at the centre of the corporate governance model, a contractual governance model also will not work. Thus, the contractual governance model we have proffered could lead to everyone working hard or no on working hard, or any point in between. Understanding the success of the Japanese model requires that we understand what helps prevent co-operative shirking.[74]

1. Competition as Catalyst The most elegant monitoring mechanism is intense product market competition. We hypothesize that product market competition and relation-specific investment could interact to generate a powerful monitoring structure.

Each factor provider has made a substantial relation-specific investment and must bear a substantial non-diversifiable risk in that investment. Everyone suffers if the joint effort does not succeed in the product market. Thus, competition with producers outside the keiretsu gives each factor provider an incentive to perform effectively.[75] Additionally, the joint character of the production creates an incentive for factor providers to cross-monitor each other as a check on free riding. Because a joint product's success in the product market depends on the quality of each factor, each provider's relation-specific investment is hostage to each of the other's performance; shirking by any factor provider endangers all. Each factor provider, therefore, has an intense interest in the other providers' performance.

Product market competition, then, gives each factor provider an incentive both to perform and to monitor the others' performance. In addition, the factor providers occupy a unique informational position. Because each factor monitor is also a producer with relational contacts, it need not invest significant new resources in information when acting as monitor: it already knows (or almost knows) what the target is doing by interacting in the production process. Joint production—of information and goods—yields factor providers real time information about their co-venturers' performance. A factor provider using another provider's parts quickly identifies any decrease in quality. Similarly, a just-in-time inventory system, while economizing on storage space and capital costs, also measures factor performance on a daily basis; the supplier's or assembler's inability to perform quickly becomes apparent.[76] Moreover, an opportunist seeking to shirk at a supplier's expense cannot capture the full benefit of its opportunism; because it owns a slice of the supplier's stock, it will bear some of the cost, thereby reducing opportunistic incentives. Finally, the movement of executives among factor providers, said to be commonplace within the keiretsu,[77] also provides for monitoring.

In our model, these aspects of the Japanese system do not exist for the primary purpose of monitoring may help them survive.[78] Rather, cross-ownership and contractual relations facilitate monitoring if competition in the product market provides the incentive to monitor. In this view, monitoring is not only an intermittent phenomenon, carried out by a board of directors or even a financial intermediary when the situation so deteriorates that those at the top of the structure learn of the crisis. Instead, inter-factor monitoring is woven into the fabric of production.[79] Put differently, product market competition and relation-specific investment transform the production process into a low cost monitoring process. Joint production yields information about performance, and thus performance monitoring.

Thus, product market competition is central to our stylized model of the Japanese system as one of contractual governance.[80] In the presence of competition, the system encourages investment in relation-specific assets which, in turn, provides both the incentive and the information for inter-factor monitoring. Centralized monitors, such as a board of directors or, as we will argue shortly, even a financial institution, cannot always get this information as quickly.[81]

This critical role of product market competition to the success of the Japanese contractual governance model suggests a means of testing our stylized model's consistency with observed facts. For our model to be consistent with the actual Japanese system, superior Japanese industrial performance should depend on the presence of product market competition rather than on the existence of a few dominant companies: Japanese companies should succeed internationally in industries with substantial competition and fail in industries when competition is less vigorous. This appears to be the case. Michael Porter reports that '[v]irtually every significant industry in which Japan has achieved international competitive advantage is populated by several and often a dozen or more competitors'.[82] The converse is also true: 'While domestic rivalry is intense in virtually every industry in which Japan is internationally successful, however, it is *all but absent in large sectors of the economy*. . . . Almost none of these . . . industries ha[s] ever achieved international success.'[83]

2. Vertical and Horizontal Keiretsu: Helping to Explain Some Performance Differences Taxonomists divide Japanese keiretsu into vertical and horizontal types. Our contractual governance story best fits the vertical keiretsu, in which companies tend to be related, such as suppliers to an end-producer. Companies in the horizontal keiretsu are more often unrelated, with looser supplier-customer relations. Since there is cross-selling even in the horizontal keiretsu, however, our story has a role to play there as well.

Our contractual governance model could also help explain a recurrent puzzle among those observing the large Japanese firm: the new firms of the vertical keiretsu—sometimes called the independents—have slightly better measures of performance than the old-line horizontal keiretsu.[84] Some might suggest that the banks' role is detrimental. This does not seem to be so, however, since banks' blocks of independents' stock are slightly *larger* than their old-line keiretsu blocks.[85] Differing main bank ownership levels cannot explain the slightly different performance levels. One explanation is that vertical keiretsu are new firms in new, initially profitable industries and have not yet reached their long-run equilibrium. Another is that the vertical independents have had families with significant ownership stakes—the Toyoda family in Toyota, the Matsushita family in Matsushita, Akio Morita in Sony. Family ownership and financial ownership give these firms two hierarchical monitors.

We offer a third explanation. These independents are not free-standing corporations, like GM or IBM. As members of vertical keiretsu, consisting primarily of companies in related industries, suppliers, and customers,[86] they should exhibit the productive features we examine here better than old-line horizontal keiretsu. With completely unrelated keiretsu firms, monitoring would be slower, from the top, not rapid as among related production factors. Vertical keiretsu should provide more rapid monitoring. Thus in our story, vertical keiretsu have three strong brands of monitoring: top-down by institutional shareholders, top-down by family shareholders (sometimes), and across companies via contracting. Old-line companies will be weaker in the third. The strengthened form of contractual governance in the independents may explain their slightly superior performance.

3. Is Competition Enough?   If competition triggers good performance in the keiretsu and reduces shirking, the next question a skeptical reader might ask is, why isn't competition enough? Why wouldn't competition without cross-ownership induce superior performance?

To a large extent, of course, it does. Firms losing customers eventually react. Some slower reacting firms disappear. We have no way of measuring how much competition acts directly and how much it acts through the organizational features we analyse. The point, however, is that cross-ownership can speed up and deepen the organizational changes that competition induces.

A deteriorating firm loses customers. But with many long-lived assets in place, no particular need to access capital markets, and senior managers who seek a quiet life in the three years until their retirement, a firm facing only competitive constraints does nothing. A group of owner-suppliers or owner-customers, however, is not yet slothful. Such a group wants a shirking firm to produce quality components for the group. A group of owner-customers has two incentives to prevent a slothful supplier from deteriorating: first, the group wants a good component, now; second, it wants to protect the value of its investment in the decaying firm. Moreover, the group's stock investment gives it another method to bring about quick change: it can withdraw its purchases (the pure competitive solution) *and* it can use its sock to bring about management changes. It has, in the standard terminology, the options of exit *and* voice.[87]

IV. Implications for comparative corporate governance analysis

The measure of an analytic model is whether it helps us better understand the world we observe. In this Part, we consider (1) the implications our contractual governance conception of the Japanese corporate system has for understanding the main bank's role, (2) the significance of the antitake-over role of cross-holdings, (3) the public shareholder's role in companies with significant cross-holdings, and (4) the stability of the Japanese corporate structure. We then turn to the American corporate governance system. Does this perspective on Japanese governance help us evaluate current proposals seeking to reform the American system by incorporating institutional features considered characteristically Japanese?

A. Implications for Understanding the Japanese Corporate Governance System

1. Understanding the Role of the Main Bank The Japanese main bank is often seen as a monitoring paragon: solving the Berle–Means quest to bridge the separation of ownership and control, and internalizing the market for corporate control by intervening in its client firm's operations when it detects deterioration in performance that threatens the firm's economic viability. Our model of a Japanese contractual governance system, in contrast, allows a more limited role for the bank, as residual owner. It need not be the first line monitor; factor providers conduct real time monitoring during the production process.[88]

This account of main bank monitoring's fit with our model's production-based monitoring is consistent with Professors Aoki and Sheard's main-bank-centred view of Japanese corporate governance.[89] They recently argued that the main bank operates primarily in financial crisis, giving management and employees an incentive to perform efficiently: the bank frees management from capital market discipline and *efficient performance* frees management from bank discipline. The mere existence of a coalition of banks with large stockholdings may motivate managers to avoid a crisis that will trigger bank intervention. In addition, the cross-holdings among factors of production may help managers avoid falling behind competitors and the bank action such a lag would precipitate.

The main bank system has also been heralded as a substitute for take-overs. We do not challenge the view that institutional influence, if structured properly, could be a replacement for, or indeed be superior to, take-overs. And by inducing managerial change, main bank crisis intervention replicates some of take-overs' desired effects. Also, Japanese managers may work hard to avoid a crisis that would trigger activity from an otherwise inactive group of stockowning banks, similar to the serious efforts of some American managers to avoid triggering a take-over offer. The Japanese managers' goal of keeping banks quiet could induce good management even without hands-on bank monitoring.

That said, we believe that the main bank system has yet to be shown as a close, proven substitute for much of the 1980s antitake-over activity in the United States. The US take-over market of the 1980s primarily broke up the conglomerates of the 1960s and early 1970s, whose principal problem was not financial peril but the misspending of free cash flow. In contrast, the Japanese main bank of the 1950s, 1960s, and 1970s had little experience in overseeing the effective utilization of free cash flow. Few Japanese companies had free cash flow: they were expanding their core business, reinvesting profits in that core business, and seeking financing for further expansion. In this sense, the main bank had an easy job; the hard job is only now beginning, as more large Japanese firms acquire enough cash to be free of dependence on bank lenders. Whether the banks' dual role—as stockholder of and lender to Japanese firms—will induce firms to fall less deeply into free cash flow pitfalls remains as a fuller test of the claim that main banks internalize the market for corporate control.[90] Our point here is not that the main bank failed as cash flow monitor in Japan; our point is that Japan only now is confronting the problem.

2. Understanding the Significance of Cross-Holdings' Antitakeover Rule

Keiretsu cross-holdings are also an antitake-over device.[91] Cross-holdings make an external take-over impossible, and the 'possibility of bank takeover'[92] is said to substitute for the corporate control market in enforcing managerial discipline.

Our model treats cross-holdings as a means to prevent one factor provider's opportunistic behaviour following relation-specific capital investment by others. An external take-over threat has no role in this explanation. What accounts for the conflict?

Part of the original motivation for cross-holdings was to secure protection from take-overs. Cross-holdings increased in response to the sale, from 1967 through 1969, of stock in 'Kyodo Shoken'—a company established by the Japanese government to acquire stock held as inventory by financially troubled brokerage houses. Depressed stock prices and the Kyoda Shoken overhang created take-over fears. Increased cross-holdings were said to be the response.[93] The motivation for acquiring cross-holdings, however, may differ from the function the holdings came to perform. The contractual benefits of cross-holdings might not be obvious or easy to construct. A catalyst—fear of take-overs—might have been the impetus for cross-holdings; thereafter, the positive functions were seen, or survived.

The pattern of contractual governance that our model represents did not spring forth, fully-formed, at a single point. For example, our model assumes a production process in which efficiency requires substantial relation-specific investment by all parties. Both Aoki[94] and Piore and Sabel[95] associate the Japanese system's success with a shift in demand, leading to a responsive shift in the production process that in turn requires greater relational specificity with respect to both industrial and human capital. Multiple products and shorter product cycles necessitate flexible production machinery and more flexible, highly trained workers; the combination leads to relation-specific investment. It makes little difference, however, why the cross-holdings were acquired; once the character of the production process began to change in the direction of greater investment in relation-specific assets by all parties, cross-holdings helped to support it.

Observers of the American corporate governance system should not be surprised that environmental change can dramatically alter the governance function of a corporation's structural features. It is now commonplace to stress the important role institutional investors, especially pension funds, will play in future corporate governance; the extraordinary growth in institutional holdings could, some say, help bridge the separation of ownership and control by reaggregating shareholdings.[96] It is clear, however, that a desire to improve corporate governance did not motivate the growth of pension funds. Rather, that growth reflects both a post-World War II decision in the United States to provide for retirement security through private pension funds instead of through an expansion of Social Security,[97] and the substantial tax incentives for individuals to use pensions for savings.[98] But whatever the original motivation behind the growth of pension funds in the post-War United States, their present function is central to the current corporate governance system.

The original motivation for cross-holdings may be beside the point. Our model hypothesizes what their current economic function may be.

3. Understanding Japanese Contract   In our view, there may be a more fruitful area of historical inquiry than Japan's take-over history. We hypothesize that Japan's path of development led it to rely more on relational cross-investments than on contingent contracts. Our hypothesis depends on our finding either weak law enforcement or a reluctance to use the courts. At the turn of the nineteenth century, when large scale enterprise became technologically possible, Japan imported key elements of its legal system from Prussia and France.[99] Perhaps the Japanese were reluctant to use the imported system tenaciously. If so, vertical integration, rather than contract, could have guided large enterprises. And indeed there were large vertical organizations, the zaibatsu. Moreover, Japanese culture is said to resist the use of legal action[100] and to resist discussing unharmonious conflict—a discussion that writing a contingent contract requires. These cultural traits handicap the effective use of a detailed contract.

If law is weak, then alternatives must be found. The zaibatsu helped, and after their post-war prohibition, the partial relationships of the keiretsu also help. An alternative to the bond indenture of hundred-page supply contract is partial stock ownership.

We posit three contractual problems for modern economies to solve: debt governance, supply contract governance, and corporate equity governance. In the United States, a well-developed legal system makes it possible to achieve passable debt and supply contract governance through explicit contracts. Although the completely contingent contract is unattainable, a passable contract—the bond indenture, the loan agreement, the hundred-page supply contract—can be written and enforced without impinging cultural norms. Two contractual governance problems are tolerably controlled in America; only viable corporate equity governance contracts cannot be written.

Contrast Japan. If neither the bond indenture nor the supply contract can be effective because of the nature of the Japanese legal system or culture, some mechanism to foster long-term relations must be constructed. In the course of constructing such a mechanism, Japan also reduces the corporate governance problem.[101]

4. Understanding the Role of Public Shareholders in Japan   In our model of a contractual governance system, factor providers' shared control, accomplished through cross-holdings, does not diminish the returns to any other party. This simple depiction of the system contemplates that *only* factor providers are shareholders. In actuality, keiretsu members also have public shareholders, holding about one-quarter of the stock. This has caused some commentators to question whether factor providers' demand for higher than market-clearing wages—growth more than price maximization with the pay-off to creditor-stockholders in excessive debt—comes at the expense of individual stockholders.[102]

Our model suggests an explanation other than exploitation for the implicit difference between the value of controlling factor provider shares and the value of non-controlling public shares. Shareholders will unanimously favour maximizing the corporation's share value when separation applies: that is, when the corporation's decisions affect shareholder wealth only through their impact on the value of its shares. In our model, however, separation does not apply for factor providers making relation-specific investment. In order for factor providers to receive a return that reflects the specificity of their investment, the firm by definition must maximize something other than share value. Simply put, the factor providers make an additional investment for which they expect an additional return, a return not provided by maximizing shareholder return.

An additional step is necessary to complete the argument: non-controlling shareholders may well approve of the non-maximizing behaviour. So long as the 'extra' return to factor providers is less than the increased productivity resulting from the relation-specific investment, non-controlling shareholders are better off than if factor providers maximized share value but did not make the investment. Moreover, if public shareholders hold pieces, directly or indirectly, of each factor, they will want to maximize aggregate productive efficiency, net of costs to non-stockholding factors (like employees). Thus, our model suggests that to demonstrate exploitation of public shareholders requires more than the observation that keiretsu companies do not maximize share value; it requires the stronger claim that share value is lower than if the relation-specific investments were not made at all. In other words, public shareholders are only exploited when they receive no return from the increased productivity resulting from the factor providers' investment. This showing has yet to be attempted.[103]

5. Understanding the Stability of the Contractual Governance Model The familiar account of the Japanese corporate governance system seems to assume that the implicit contract it describes—assured employment, protected by cross-holdings from breach by take-over, and monitored by the main bank to assure viability—is stable. No party will break the covenant because some unspecified implicit remedy—perhaps reputation—deters it. Our model suggests a more precise analysis.

In Part III, we described cross-holdings as protecting against opportunism when, in an unexpected state of the world, fortune randomly sets up a factor provider with an opportunity to exploit. What happens, however, when an event occurs that *permanently* devalues a factor provider's relation-specific investment? In that circumstance, the factor providers in our model *will* unfavourably alter the participation of the unlucky provider. While the coalition will prevent one lucky factor provider from exploiting the group, it will not protect a single unlucky provider from the consequences of a long-term shift in fortunes.

This analysis calls into question the claim that American antitake-over protection (or the Japanese main bank) is necessary to support factor providers' relation-specific investment. Imagine that a hostile bidder confronts a target whose factor providers receive a return on relation-specific investment. If continued relation-specific investment by a particular factor provider is no longer valuable—that is, if the factor provider's special contribution has been *permanently* devalued—the hostile bidder will cut it off. *But so will participants in a contractual governance system.* A contractual governance perspective thus suggests that an implicit contract justification for antitake-over protection requires more careful specification.[104]

B. Evaluating Reform Proposals for the US Corporate Governance System

In recent years, the Japanese corporate governance system has captured the vision of those seeking to reform American corporate governance. Japan appeared to have solved the Berle–Means problem.[105] Yet quick, complete institutional imitations are difficult.[106] We next consider one such reform effort—the LBO ['leveraged buy out'] association, said to be arising in the shadow cast by the eclipse of the public corporation— whose proponents hold out the Japanese system as evidence of their effort's promise. We also briefly consider the segments of the US economy identified by our model as potentially suitable recipients of a contractual governance transplant.

Our model suggests that the Japanese system differs from the LBO association in its specifics; as a result, it offers less support for the reform effort than is claimed. It is important to stress, however, that we do not meant to reject the reforms themselves. Rather, we argue only that the reforms must be justified by their fit with our system, not by their limited resemblance to a very different Japanese system.

1. The Keiretsu and the LBO Association   Michael Jensen has advanced the LBO association as a successor to the public corporation.[107] Jensen describes LBO associations as having three components: (1) a sponsoring partnership that organizes highly leveraged going-private transactions and advises and monitors post-transaction target management on a co-operative and ongoing basis; (2) target company managers who remain post-transaction and who receive a substantial equity stake to 'incentivize' their performance; and (3) institutional investors who provide the limited partnership with the debt and equity to make the acquisition.[108] These entities, Jensen argues,

> have a fundamental affinity with Japanese groups of firms called 'keiretsu'. LBO partnerships play a dual funding and oversight role that is similar in many ways to that of the main banks in the Japanese keiretsu. Like the main banks, which typically hold significant equity stakes in their corporate borrowers, the leaders of the LBO partnerships hold substantial amounts of equity in their companies and control access to the rest of the capital. Further like the Japanese banks, the LBO partners are actively involved in the monitoring and strategic direction of these firms.[109]

> Finally, like the Japanese banks, the LBO association privatizes bankruptcy.[110]

In our view, the LBO and keiretsu have one similarity, but two significant differences. Jensen identifies the similarity: financial institutions play a large role in both. One difference, however, is that the Japanese bank's role is embedded in a deeper system of relational cross-holdings. Industrial companies with relation-specific investments provide much of the monitoring and one-third of the cross-ownership in the keiretsu. In contrast, they provide none of the monitoring or cross-ownership in the LBO. The *contractual* governance structure among factors of production, and its dependence on product market competition, is critical to the keiretsu, but absent in the LBO.[111]

Secondly, they differ in that the LBO association is best suited to companies with substantial shares in mature markets that generate free cash flow. This is precisely the opposite of the product market conditions that, we argue, are critical to the success of a contractual governance system dependent on *new* relational investments, and precisely the opposite of the crisis conditions under which Professors Aoki and Sheard claim the main bank has so far played its real role.[112] The main bank's active role appears now to be crisis intervention;[113] its primary non-crisis role is to hold a large block of stock that will become active *if* managers allow a crisis to develop. We do not want to demean the political effectiveness of large but usually passive shareholders—as the main banks may be when their credit-monitoring dissipates—if managers fear their actions may activate such shareholders.[114] But this type of monitoring differs quite substantially from the LBO association's hands-on real time monitoring. In our view, the main bank's crisis role is more analogous to that of Warren Buffett's Berkshire Hathaway—large stakes but major action only in crisis—than to the LBO association.[115] Finally, the amount of stock that the main banks own appears to be considerably less than the amount the LBO association owns. The main bank typically owns 5 per cent and can usually put together a small coalition of other financial institutions that will reach 20 per cent or so. In contrast, the LBO association frequently owns all of the company's stock.

The point of this analysis is not to enter the debate over Jensen's claim that the LBO association should replace the public corporation.[116] Rather, the point is that an analysis comparing the LBO and the keiretsu is not directly illuminating, because such an analysis implicitly relies on the belief that the Japanese corporate governance system is a response only to the Berle–Means problem. The LBO association's efficiency as a governance structure depends on its fit with the American system of weak financial intermediaries, weak cross-holdings among factors of production, and strong enforcement of contracts. The success of the Japanese main bank, which operates in circumstances very different from those in the United States, only illuminates the American inquiry to the extent that it suggests that the American system of corporate governance is not inevitable.

2. *Where Might the Japanese Model Provide Guidance?*   Though not perfectly transferable, the Japanese contractual governance model is nevertheless relevant to American problems. Three conditions are central to our model of contractual governance: a productive relationship among the participants; the need for relation-specific investment; and the presence of substantial product market competition. The first condition provides the context; the second creates the problem; and the third causes the coalition formed by corss-holdings among factor providers to reject a shared commitment to the quiet life. America's high technology industry seems an obvious candidate for contractual governance initiatives. Joint venture and equity participation have already become familiar,[117] and the difficulty of technology transfer makes relation-specific investment important.[118] Moreover, an established group of venture capital investors already play roles similar to Japanese main banks, in particular those of crisis monitoring and privatization of bankruptcy, by facilitating a single voice for numerous suppliers of capital.[119] Finally, competition among products and between technologies is vigorous.

We realize that high technology is currently one of the American economy's best performers, for which contractual or corporate governance improvements may now be unnecessary. Heavy industries—like autos and steel—are in worse condition and seem to have serious governance problems. Here too our prescriptions might fit. If each is slow to develop new technologies and production methods, cross-ownership among relational suppliers might speed adaptation. So, if new steel technologies—say, the mini-mills—are to be located near new auto plants having innovative production technologies, cross-ownership might function in a manner similar to that which we hypothesize for Japan. Each will double up their interest in the other's prosperity: steel firms will want a better customer and a better portfolio firm. Information that the firms will gather about each other while adapting the production process together may make each a more valuable stockholder to the other. Moreover, competition, which we hypothesize is necessary to prevent mutual shirking, is today generally present in both industries (to the extent that import restrictions are not severe).

Our point is neither that the existing organizational structure in high technology industries mirrors Japanese contractual governance nor that parallel technological changes in related industries like autos and steel make them ripe for cross-ownership; we have not undertaken this inquiry, and our views are not so deterministic. Nor do we claim that American legal, tax, and financial structures are ready to support cross-ownership. We do suggest, however, that comparative analysis of the Japanese contractual governance model may lead to the instrumental use of such a governance structure in the United States, transplanted to where the structural economic preconditions to successful domestication are in place.

V. Conclusion

Too many efforts to understand the Japanese system have suffered from Berle–Means blinders. Hidden by the focus on main banks is the fact that one-third of the cross-ownership is held by industrial companies.[120] We hypothesize that cross-ownership reduces the risk of opportunism when parties make large relational investments. The management of any factor that defects, by trying to raise price inordinately, to skimp on quality, or to miss the next technological step in the industry, will face a coalition of stockholders. Fear of such a confrontation deters defection. Product market competition keeps the system from lapsing into a conspiracy of passivity.

Industrial cross-ownership has not previously been emphasized as a key element of the Japanese corporate system, and we believe this connection is important. Indeed, we suspect that some of the main bank interventions can and should be seen not just as the pure intervention of the residual equity holder (or large creditor) to protect its investment—the American model—but as the intervention of factor providers. The bank monitors directly by providing credit and indirectly by serving as agent for the other factors. The bank assumes this agency role partly because of its stock ownership in the other factors.

The existence and persistence of such a system strongly supports the view that the American system of corporate governance is not inevitable, but is instead contingent on the accidents of American financial organization and political history. The newfound activism of some financial intermediaries and the rise of the LBO association also support this general proposition. But neither the newly active intermediary nor the LBO replicates the Japanese system in its specifics. Finally, although the Japanese system may provide general deterrence to keep managers faithful, this system has not yet shown itself to be an effective substitute for the American take-over of the 1980s. The Japanese main banks have yet to face the widespread cash flow and conglomerate problems that pervaded the targets of these take-overs. The Japanese system tells us generally that there is more than one way to build a large corporation. It tells us little, however, about whether and how American financial intermediaries should be unleashed.

Notes

1. See e.g. Report of the Subcomm. on Financial Institutions Supervision, Regulation and Insurance, Task Force on the International Competitiveness of US Financial Institutions of the House Comm. on Banking, Finance and Urban Affairs, H.R. Rep. No. 7, 101st Cong., 2d Sess. 7–8, 66, 189–90, 193–4 (1990) [hereinafter Task Force Report] (Japanese 'cross-shareholding arrangements create real linkages with real advantages'; 'the "keiretsu" system [is] a very effective system designed to maintain Japanese business competitiveness').

2. Michael Porter, Remarks at the US Securities and Exchange Commission Forum on Corporate Governance and American Economic Competitiveness: The Role of Shareholders, Directors and Management 41–62 (20 Mar. 1992) (transcript on file with authors).

3. See Mark J. Roe, 'A Political Theory of American Corporate Finance', 91 *Colum. L. Rev.* 10 (1991) [hereinafter Roe, 'A Political Theory']; Mark J. Roe, 'Political and Legal Restraints on Ownership and Control of Public Companies', 27 *J. Fin. Econ.* 7 (1990); Joseph A. Grundfest, 'Subordination of American Capital', 27 *J. Fin. Econ.* 89 (1990). See generally Michael C. Jensen, 'Eclipse of the Public Corporation', *Harv. Bus. Rev.*, Sept.–Oct. 1989, at 61.

4. Business Roundtable, 'Corporate Governance and American Competitiveness', 46 *Bus. Law.* 241, 242–3 (1990); see sources cited *supra* nn. 2–3.
5. See *infra* text accompanying nn. 15–22.
6. See *infra* text accompanying nn. 29–34.
7. See e.g. Bernard S. Black, 'Agents Watching Agents: The Promise of Institutional Investor Voice', 39 *UCLA L. Rev.* 811 (1992) [hereinafter Black, 'Agents Watching Agents']; Bernard S. Black, 'The Value of Institutional Investor Monitoring: The Empirical Evidence', 39 *UCLA L. Rev.* 895 (1992) [hereinafter Black, 'Value of Institutional Investor Monitoring']; Ronald J. Gilson and Reinier Kraakman, 'Reinventing the Outside Director: An Agenda for Institutional Investors', 43 *Stan. L. Rev.* 863 (1991); Jensen, *supra* n. 3.
8. While Carl Kester does not draw this distinction, his work, together with that of Professor Masahiko Aoki, is unusual in its focus on the relationship between the production process and corporate governance. See W. Carl Kester, *Japanese Takeovers: The Global Contest for Corporate Control* 53 (1991) [hereinafter Kester, *Japanese Takeovers*] ('The overall effect of Japanese corporate governance is to foster tremendous efficiencies in the execution of business transactions by making it easier to build and maintain long-term relationships'); Masahiko Aoki, 'Toward an Economic Model of the Japanese Firm', 28 *J. Econ. Literature* 1 (1990) [hereinafter Aoki, 'Toward an Economic Model']; Masahiko Aoki, *The Japanese Firm As A System of Attributes: A Survey and Research Agenda* (Center for Economic Policy Research Working Paper No. 288, 1992) [hereinafter Aoki, *A System of Attributes*]; W. Carl Kester, *Governance, Contracting, and Investment Time Horizons* (Harvard Business School Working Paper No. 92–003, 1991) [hereinafter Kester, *Governance*].
9. Stephen D. Prowse, 'The Structure of Corporate Ownership in Japan', 48 *J. Fin.* 1121, 1123 (1992); Yasaku Futatsugi, 'What Share Cross-Holdings Mean for Corporate Management', *Econ. Eye* Spring 1990, at 17, 18.
10. See Mark J. Roe, 'Some Differences in Corporate Governance in Germany, Japan, and America', 102 *Yale LJ* (June 1993).
11. Adolf A. Berle, Jr. and Gardiner C. Means, *The Modern Corporation and Private Property* (1933).
12. Ibid. at 47–68.
13. Alfred Chandler argues that the increasing complexity of business was a more important cause of separation than the dispersion of stock holdings. Alfred D. Chandler, Jr., *Scale and Scope: The Dynamics of Industrial Capitalism* 232 (1990). Existing owners lacked the skills and information necessary either to run modern corporations themselves or to monitor the decisions of those who did. Ibid.
14. See Michael C. Jensen and William H. Meckling, 'Theory of the Firm: Managerial Behavior, Agency Costs and Ownership Structure', 3 *J. Fin. Econ.* 305 (1976).
15. See Business Roundtable, *supra* n. 4, at 247–8; Business Roundtable, 'The

Role and Composition of the Board of Directors of the Large Publicly Owned Corporation', 33 *Bus. Law* 2083, 2108 (1978) ('We note the strong tendency of U.S. business corporations to move toward a board structure based on a majority of outside directors—and we endorse it').

16. See Jeremy Bacon and James K. Brown, *The Conference Board, Corporate Directorship Practices: Role, Selection and Legal Status of the Board* (1975).

17. See Committee on Corporate Laws, Section of Corporation, Banking and Business Law, American Bar Association, 'Corporate Director's Guidebook', 33 *Bus. Law.* 1595, 1619–21 (1978).

18. See American Law Institute, *Principles of Corporate Governance: Analysis and Recommendations* § 3A.01 (Proposed Final Draft 1992).

19. The Delaware courts have assigned special weight to outside directors' decisions. See *Weinberger* v. *UOP, Inc.*, 457 A. 2d 701 (Del. 1983) (finding merger failed fairness test where feasibility study not shown to outside directors); *Zapata Corp.* v. *Maldonado*, 430 A. 2d 779 (De. 1981) (dismissing derivative suits where self-interested board members delegated litigation decision to independent committee of disinterested board members); William T. Allen, 'Independent Directors In MBO Transactions: Are They Fact or Fantasy?', 45 *Bus. Law.* 2055 (1990) (arguing that special committees of outside directors may, if used properly, protect shareholder interests) (Allen is Chancellor of the Delaware Court of Chancery).

20. Jay W. Lorsch, *Pawns or Potentates: The Reality of America's Corporate Boards* 17 (1989).

21. Ibid. at 18 (63% of outside directors are CEO's of other companies).

22. See generally Gilson and Kraakman, *supra* n. 7, at 872–6 (analysing failings of outside director concept).

23. See Mark J. Rose, 'Takeover Politics', in *The Deal Decade* (Margaret Blair ed., 1993).

24. Carolyn Kay Brancato, 'The Pivotal Role of Institutional Investors in Capital Markets', in *Institutional Investing: The Challenges and Responsibilities of the 21st Century* 3, 21, Table 1-7 (Arnold W. Sametz ed., 1991); Carolyn Kay Brancato, Institutional Investors and Capital Markets: 1991 Update 18 (1991) (unpublished manuscript, on file with authors).

25. See Gilson and Kraakman, *supra* n. 7, at 867–76 (reviewing strategies).

26. See ibid.: see also Ronald J. Gilson, Lilli A. Gordon, and John Pound, 'How the Proxy Rules Discourage constructive Engagement: Regulatory Barriers to Electing a Minority of Directors', 17 *J. Corp. L.* 29, 30–4 (1992).

27. See e.g. Bernard S. Black, 'Shareholder Passivity Reexamined', 89 *Mich. L. Rev.* 520 (1990) (reviewing regulatory barriers to institutional shareholders actively participating in corporate governance); John C. Coffee, Jr., 'Liquidity Versus Control: The Institutional Investor as Corporate Monitor', 91 *Colum. L. Rev.* 1277 (1991) (asserting those seeking influence should forego liquidity). As Louis Lowenstein points out, index funds, with tiny management fees of

two basis points, lack the resources to monitor. Louis Lowenstein, *Sense and Nonsense in Corporate Finance* 220 (1991). They are the ultimate Berle–Means free riders, capable of acting but depending on others to monitor for them.

28. This argument parallels a similar one made by Michael Piore and Charles Sabel that the American system of industrial organization is historically and politically contingent. Michael J. Piore and Charles F. Sabel, *The Second Industrial Divide: Possibilities for Prosperity* 19–48 (1984). The parallel is especially interesting in light of our suggestion that the Japanese system can be understood as one of industrial organization as much as corporate governance. See *infra* Part III.

29. See e.g. Paul Sheard, 'The Main Bank System and Corporate Monitoring and Control in Japan', 11 *J. Econ. Behav. & Org.* 399 (1989). Sheard reports that for corporations listed on the Tokyo Stock Exchange, the main bank was the largest or second largest shareholder in 29% of the cases in his sample and among the top five shareholders in 72% of the cases. Ibid. at 402. Similarly, a recent study reports that a Japanese corporation's largest lender owned on average 6.2% of equity, its five largest lenders owned on average 18.2% of equity, and in 57 of the 133 sample corporations, the largest lender was the largest shareholder. Stephen D. Prowse, 'Institutional Investment Patterns and Corporate Financial Behavior in the United States and Japan', 27 *J. Fin. Econ.* 43, 46–7 (1990).

30. See Sheard, *supra* n. 29, at 401–3; Paul Sheard, *Delegated Monitoring Among Delegated Monitors: Principal-Agent Aspects of the Japanese Main Bank System* (Australian National University and Osaka University Working Paper, 1992). Such a co-operative allocation of monitoring responsibility minimizes duplication and, because other banks act as first-line monitors with respect to other companies, reduces incentives to free ride.

31. 'In a "good" main bank relationship, the firm will consult the bank closely when drawing up its business plans and will provide regular reports on its performance.' Sheard, *supra* n. 29, at 403.

32. See e.g. Takeo Hoshi, Anil Kashyap and David Scharfstein, 'The Role of Banks in Reducing the Costs of Financial Distress in Japan', 27 *J. Fin.Econ.* 67 (1990). For descriptions of active main bank intervention in crises, see Kester, *Japanese Takeovers, supra* n. 8, at 70–3; Paul Sheard, 'The Economics of Interlocking Shareholding in Japan', 45 *Ricerche Economiche* 421, 436–8 (1991).

33. Sheard, *supra* n. 29, at 407.

34. For example, Michael Jensen stressed that 'LBO partnerships play a dual funding and oversight role that is similar in many ways to that of the main banks in the Japanese keiretsu.'Michael C. Jensen, 'Corporate Control and the Politics of Finance', *J. Applied Corp. Fin.*, Summer 991, at 13, 22. Gilson and Kraakman stated the corporate governance challenge as designing 'a new structure that duplicates the monitoring capabilities of the LBO and [Japanese] banker models'. Gilson and Kraakman, *supra* n. 7, at 879. We

return to Jensen's comparative analysis of the LBO association later. See *infra* text accompanying notes 107–16.

35. See Roe, 'A Political Theory', *supra* n. 3.

36. Kester tells us:

> Financial managers at manufacturing companies generally concur with this description of the [lessening] degree of monitoring and control exerted over their companies by their traditional main banks. Whereas all but one of the companies in the field sample indicated that their corporate plans and investments were closely examined by banks during the 1950–1980 period, none reported being subject to such scrutiny today. Although meetings with lenders are still held semi-annually or at least annually to discuss performance, these have apparently evolved into largely perfunctory presentations of past performance rather than substantive discussions of future capital investment.

> Kester, *Japanese Takeovers*, *supra* n. 8, at 197. Other commentators offer similar observations. See e.g. James C. Abeglen and George Stalk, Jr., Kaisha, *The Japanese Corporation* 189 (1985) ('The conclusion is that dependence on a bank is no more to the liking of Japanese management than management in other countries, and for leading Japanese companies no longer a significant issue'); J. Mark Ramseyer, 'Legal Rules in Repeated Deals: Banking in the Shadow of Defection in Japan', 20 *J. Leg. Stud.* 91, 98 (1991). Available data show a decreased role for banks. In the early 1970s, listed Japanese companies generated internally only 36% of their net increase in funds; by the early 1980s, internally generated funds accounted for 71% of the increase. The data with respect to bank borrowings are consistent. In the early 1970s, 41% of the net increase in funds came from bank borrowings. By the mid-1980s, the bank share had dropped to 6%. Paul Sheard, 'Japanese Corporate Finance and Behaviour: Recent Developments and the Impact of Deregulation', in *Japanese Financial Markets and the Role of the Yen* 55, 56 (Colin McKenzie and Michael Stutchbery eds., 1992). A slowing Japanese economy may well lead industrial firms short of cash to restore main bank relationships.

37. Professor Aoki states: 'In the normal course of events . . . the main bank exercises *explicit control* neither in the selection of management nor in corporate policy making.' Aoki, 'Toward an Economic Model', *supra* n. 8, at 14 (emphasis added). 'Financial control by bank cum stockholders concerning corporate direction is exercised only in a business crisis.' Ibid. at 16.

38. Sheard,*supra* n. 29, at 407.

39. For efforts to identify what proportion of hostile take-overs are made to displace inefficient management as opposed to synergy or other strategies, see e.g. Kenneth Martin and John McConnell, 'Corporate Performance, Corporate Takeovers, and Management Turnover', 46 *J. Fin.* 671 (1991); Randall Morck, Andrei Shleifer, and Robert W. Vishny, 'Alternative Mechanisms for Corporate Control', 79 *Am. Econ. Rev.* 842 (1989); Randall Morck, Andrei Shleifer, and Robert W. Vishny, 'Characteristics of Targets of Hostile and Friendly Takeovers', in *Corporate Takeovers: Causes and*

Consequences 101 (Alan J. Auerbach ed., 1988); see also Ronald J. Gilson and Bernard S. Black, *The Law and Finance of Corporate Acquisitions: 1991 Supp.* 37–86 (1991) (summarizing literature).

40. See Sanjai Bhagat, Andrei Shleifer, and Robert W. Vishny, 'Hostile Takeovers in the 1980s: The Return to Corporate Specialization', in *Brookings Papers on Economic Activity: Microeconomics* 1 (Martin N. Baily and Clifford Winston eds., 1990); Amar Bhide, 'The Causes and Consequences of Hostile Takeovers', *J. Applied Corp. Fin.*, Summer 1989, at 36, 52 ('real source of gains in hostile takeovers lies in splitting up diversified companies'); Randall Morck, Andrei Shleifer, and Robert W. Vishny, 'Do Managerial Objectives Drive Bad Acquisitions?', 45 *J. Fin.* 31, 47 (1990) (evidence 'that the source of bust-up gains in the 1980s is the reversal of the unrelated diversification of the 1960s and the 1970s').

41. See Aoki, 'Toward an Economic Model', *supra* n. 8, at 14–15; Masahiko Aoki, 'Ex Post Monitoring by the Main Bank' (1992) (unpublished manuscript, on file with authors) [hereinafter Aoki, 'Ex Post Monitoring']; Masahiko Aoki and Paul Sheard, 'The Role of the Japanese Main Bank in the Corporate Governance Structure in Japan (1991) (unpublished manuscript, on file with authors).

42. Professor Aoki may be the most explicit in identifying these links. Concentrating on the structure of a single corporation, his three Duality principles—between a firm's co-ordination and incentive modes, its decision hierarchy and incentive-ranking hierarchy, and the interests of ownership and employees—link the Japanese corporation's success to a particular economic environment and a particular type of production. Aoki, *A System of Attributes*, *supra* n. 8, at 10–20. See Kester, *Japanese Takeovers*, *supra* n. 8, at 53–82 (treating, most ambitiously, overall structure of keiretsu as designed to support exchange among member corporations, as system of contractual, not corporate, governance); Kester, *Governance*, *supra* n. 8, at 14–31 (same); Gerald T. Garvey and Peter L. Swan, *The Interaction between Financial and Employment Contracts: A Formal Model of Japanese Corporate Governance* (Australian Graduate School of Management, University of New South Wales Working Paper, 1991) (linking main bank and keiretsu cross-holding features of Japanese system to structure of employee incentives); Paul Sheard, *The Economic of Interlocking Shareholdings in Japan* 21–2 (Center for Economic Policy Research, Stanford University Working Paper No. 259, 1991); Erik Berglof and Enrico Perotti, 'The Japanese Keiretsu as a Collective Enforcement Mechanism' (Jan. 1989) (unpublished manuscript, on file with authors) (modelling keiretsu as technique for enforcement of implicit contracts among member firms).

43. Futatsugi, *supra* n. 9, at 17, 18.

44. Traditional theory of the firm was not a theory of the firm at all, but rather described how firms behaved under different competitive conditions. See e.g.

R. H. Coase, 'The Nature of the Firm', 4 *Economica* 386 (1937); R. H. Coase, 'The Institutional Structure of Production', 82 *Am. Econ. Rev.* 713 (1992) (Nobel lecture). The firm itself remained a black box. An agency-based theory of the firm opened the box to find a nexus of contracts. More recent comparative corporate governance scholarship seeks to move the analysis down yet another level and examine how firm structure—the *particular* pattern of contracts whose nexus is the firm—relates to the actual productive activities of the firm. Like the early physicists, we are finding boxes within boxes.

45. While only one-tenth of 1% of Japanese corporations belong to a keiretsu, member firms account for approximately one-quarter of total corporate sales and represent one-half of all listed Japanese corporations. Kester, *Japanese Takeovers, supra* n. 8, at 55.

46. Japanese keiretsu are of two general types, vertical and horizontal (intermarket). Vertical keiretsu comprise suppliers, distributors and capital providers of an industry-specific manufacturing concern. In contrast, horizontal keiretsu include a number of manufacturers across different industries, a trading company, a large bank, and insurance companies. Some vertical keiretsu overlap with horizontal keiretsu. See Michael Gerlach, 'Alliance Capitalism: The Social Organization of Japanese Business' 12–13 (1992) (unpublished manuscript, on file with authors); Ulrike Schaede, 'Corporate Governance in Japan: Institutional Investors, Management Monitoring and Corporate Stakeholders' (Aug. 1992) (unpublished manuscript, on file with authors) (developing typology for distinguishing between the two forms of groups).

47. To be sure, two-thirds of the cross-ownership would be held by financial institutions, but because the financial institutions are partly owned (although at a lower level) by industrial companies, we could exaggerate and make the financial institution transparent as a gateway for industrial cross-ownership.

48. In so doing we pass over a core problem in the theory of the firm: defining the object of enquiry. One might conceive of a theory of the firm as encompassing three questions: (1) what is the firm, that is, how do we define the boundary between market and hierarchy?; (2) what is the efficient boundary of the firm, that is, given that we know a firm when we see one, what activities should be undertaken within it?; and (3) how are decisions made and monitored within the firm?, that is, the traditional corporate governance problem. It is interesting to note that although the second and third questions plainly depend on the answer to the first, the vertical integration and corporate governance literatures—responses to the second and third questions—are far more developed than efforts to understand the first. For example, is Silicon Valley a firm? In this Article, we assume the answer to the first question: the firm relevant to our enquiry is the keiretsu.

49. Futatsugi, *supra* n. 9, at 17.

50. Ibid. at 18.

51. Our stylized model most closely resembled a vertical keiretsu. There are,

however, substantial intra-keiretsu purchases and sales even within an inter-market, horizontal keiretsu. See *infra* n. 68.

52. See Aoki, *A System of Attributes*, *supra* n. 8, at 8; Hideshi Itoh, *Japanese Human Resource Management from the Viewpoint of Incentive Theory* (Center for Economic Policy Research, Stanford University Working Paper No. 258, 1991) (reviewing economic structure of Japanese employment patterns); Sheard, *supra* n. 42, at 24–6.

53. See e.g. Sheard, *supra* n. 42, at 21–4.

54. See Oliver E. Williamson, *The Economic Institutions of Capitalism* 69 (1985).

55. See Oliver D. Hart, 'Incomplete Contracts and the Theory of the Firm', 4 *JL Econ. & Org.* 119, 120 (1988); Benjamin Klein, Robert G. Crawford, and Armen A. Alchian, 'Vertical Integration, Appropriable Rents, and the Competitive Contracting Process', 21 *JL & Econ.* 297 (1978).

56. The lack of attention to intermediate forms of organization in the United States may reflect the character of production during the debate. As Piore and Sabel show, the pattern of US manufacturing prior to 1980 stressed special-ized machinery and unspecialized labour as a means of creating and exhaust-ing scale economies in a period of relative economic calm. Piore and Sabel, *supra* n. 28, at 27. Intermediate solutions work well where greater numbers of products produced, and lower product life-spans, increase returns from flexi-ble human-capital investment yet decrease economies of scale resulting from specialized machinery. See Aoki, 'Toward an Economic Model', *supra* n. 8, at 7–10.

57. On this point, our strongest precursor is Kester. Kester, *Japanese Takeovers*, *supra* n. 8, at 80–1. Some of what seem to American eyes to be corporate gov-ernance matters are really corporate arrangements that facilitate relational contracting.

58. Kester, *Governance*, *supra* n. 8, at 19. This mode of contracting is not limited to the automobile industry. Kester refers more generally to claims 'that a typ-ical Japanese contract does not even state definitely the transactions at stake so as not to restrict the flexibility considered necessary for good perfor-mance.' Ibid. at 19 n. 7. Similarly, Akio Morita, chairman of Sony, explains that all Japanese contracts contain a provision to the effect that 'in the event of disagreement, both parties to the contract agree[ ] to sit down together in good faith and work out their differences.' Akio Morita, 'Do Companies Need Lawyers? Sony's Experiences in the United States', 30 *Japan Q.* 2, 3 (1983).

59. Note how closely the description of Japanese contracting parallels Oliver Williamson's description of the simple form of contract that would suffice in a world in which opportunism was somehow impossible: 'A general clause, to which both parties would agree, to the effect that "I will behave responsi-bly rather than seek individual advantage when an occasion to adapt arises" . . . .' Oliver E. Williamson, 'Transaction-Cost Economics: The Governance

of Contractual Relations', 22 *JL & Econ.* 233, 241 (1979). See generally Anthony T. Kronman, 'Contract Law and the State of Nature', 1 *JL Econ. & Org.* 5 (1985). For an effort to understand barriers to opportunism in dealings between Japanese firms, see Ronald J. Gilson, 'Value Creation by Business Lawyers: Legal Skills and Asset Pricing', 94 *Yale LJ* 239, 308–10 (1984).

60. This protection is a hybrid of spontaneous and intentional governance techniques, that is, invisible hand techniques as well as a conscious contractual protective governance structure. See Oliver Williamson, 'Economic Institutions: Spontaneous and Intentional Governance', 7 *JL Econ. & Org.* 159 (1991) (Special Issue). The literature also contains models of spontaneous techniques falling on both the neo-classical contracting and organizational ends of the continuum. See Drew Fudenberg, Bengt Holmstrom and Paul Milgrom, 'Short-Term Contracts and Long-Term Agency Relationships', 51 *J. Econ. Theory* 1 (1990) (succession of short-term contracts is equivalent of first-best long-term contract); David Kreps, 'Corporate Culture and Economic Theory', in *Perspectives on Positive Political Economy* 90–143 (James E. Alt and Kenneth A. Shepsle eds., 1990) (corporate reputation model). We do not consider these models here.

61. We recognize that (1) Japanese cross-ownership rarely rises above 5%; (2) the keiretsu groupings have more than five members; and (3) there are public stockholders. We use five members and 20% to simplify the model, not to describe the typical cross-ownership in Japan.

62. On also might formulate the arrangement as a means of enforcing an *ex ante* risk sharing agreement, in effect assuring that any good fortune is shared among the participants. See Sheard, *supra* n. 42, at 13–14.

63. Dumping stock seems to be the implicit threat in Japan. See Roe, *supra* n. 10.

64. In this regard, our model is similar to that of Berglof and Perotti, *supra* n. 42; see also Williamson, *supra* n. 54, at 158–9; Gary P. Pisano, 'Using Equity Participation to Support Exchange: Evidence from the Biotechnology Industry', 5 *JL Econ. & Org.* 109 (1989). However, we extend the insight, albeit informally, to include a determination of what substantive arrangement is enforced—hard work or shirking—and the market circumstances necessary for the technique's success. See *infra* Part III(B)(1).

65. As one of us stated 10 years ago:

> [The] description of shareholders as the 'owners' of the corporation does not suggest that [their] role . . . flows, normatively, from their 'ownership.' It derives, rather, from the need for those holding the residual interest in corporate profits to have the means to displace management which performs poorly. . . . [T]his position is based on matters other than a preconception of the rights associated with 'ownership'; indeed, if the statute did not provide for shareholders we would have to invent them.

> Ronald J. Gilson, 'A Structural Approach to Corporations: The Case Against Defensive Tactics in Tender Offers', 33 *Stan. L. Rev.* 819, 834 n. 56 (1981); see also Frank H. Easterbrook and Daniel R. Fischel, 'Voting in Corporate Law,

26 *JL & Econ.* 395 (1983); Eugene F. Fama and Michael C. Jensen, 'Agency Problems and Residual Claims', 26 *JL & Econ.* 327 (1983); Henry Hansmann, 'Ownership of the Firm', 4 *JL Econ. & Org.* 267 (1988).

66. Note that this treatment of the Japanese system contemplates the crisis intervention role that Aoki and Sheard assign the main bank. See *supra* text accompanying n. 41. In particular, our model assumes not only the familiar fact that main banks will own blocks of stock in their large borrowers, but also that the large borrowers will in turn own stock in the bank to assure that the bank does not behave opportunistically. This latter assumption appears to be consistent with the facts. For example, Sumitomo Bank is the largest lender to 11 of its 21 largest corporate shareholders and is a major lender in most other cases. Importantly, these borrower-shareholders control some of the bank's stock. Roe, *supra* n. 10.

67. See *infra* text accompanying n. 103.

68. A similar theme is developed in Ito, Nezukuka Nihon-Ban M&A to Kabushiki Mochiai-no Honshi Tsu, Kin-yu, Dec. 1989; see Michael Gerlach, 'Business Alliances and the Strategy of the Japanese Frim', *Cal. Mgmt. Rev.*, Fall 1987, at 126, 133 (cross-holdings 'create a structure of stable, mutual relationships among trading partners'); Kester, *Governance*, *supra* n. 8, at 26 (cross-holdings '"cement" business relationships among companies and serve as indicators of mutual long-term commitments').

Our model assumes complete cross-holdings and virtually complete intra-group trade. The reality is much less extreme. With respect to cross-holdings, Kester reports the percentage of reciprocally owned shares in the six inter-market keiretsu as follows:

Mitsui group	18.0%
Mitsubishi group	25.3%
Sumitomo group	24.5%
Fuyo group	18.2%
DKB group	14.6%
Sanwa group	10.9%

Ibid. at Exhibit 6 (1987 data). However, if the denominator is limited to the total shares held by the top 20 shareholders in a company, the percentage of reciprocally owned shares increases substantially:

Mitsui	55.2%
Mitsubishi	74.2%
Sumitomo	68.6%
Fuyo	49.2%
DKB	42.3%
Sanwa	32.8%

Gerlach, *supra*, at 133 (Table I). Additionally, large bank borrowers appear to own stock in their main banks.

With respect to intragroup sales and procurement, Kester reports average intragroup sales among all group industrial companies in 1981 as 20.4% (29% among original zaibatsu groups) and average intragroup procurement as 12.4% (18.6% among original zaibatsu groups), with a variance of between 8% and 30%. Kester, *Governance, supra* n. 8, at 17, Exhibit 4. Gerlach notes that such figures may understate actual intragroup sales and procurement by excluding transactions within vertical groups inside the intermarket keiretsu. Gerlach, *supra* n. 46, at 12–13, 185–91.

69. We draw this example from Benjamin Klein's description. See Benjamin Klein, 'Vertical Integration as Organizational Ownership: The Fisher Body-General Motor Relationship Revisited', 4 *JL Econ. & Org.* 199, 200–2 (1988).

70. Kester, *Japanese Takeovers, supra* n. 8, at 80. Roe argues that the Japanese cross-ownership flattens authority in the large firms compared to the hierarchical pyramid in the large American firm. Flat authority may sometimes perform better than a pyramid of authority. See Roe, *supra* n. 10.

71. There is surprising mobility from one keiretsu to another. See Roe, *supra* n. 10.

72. We do not for our purposes here need to identify and quantify the exact value of hybridization of contract and organization in Japan. It is indeed possible that the difference is one of form (although we doubt it), arising solely from the Japanese ban on pure holding companies after World War II. For present purposes we only claim that the Japanese form is a hybrid between contract and organization, which *may* have some efficiency advantages.

73. Coffee makes a similar point:

   [T]he very structure of the *keiretsu* seems designed to ensure weak monitoring. Because the main bank holds an ownership level that is below five percent by definition, it must secure the consent of its fellow *keiretsu* members before it can take disciplinary action or remove senior management. Yet these other members share a common interest in restricting main bank interventions in the internal affairs of each member to occasions in which the demonstrated delinquency of a member firm threatens the *keiretsu* as a whole.

   Coffee, *supra* n. 27, at 1300.

   As developed in the remainder of this section, the critical issue is identifying why the structure of the keiretsu does not ensure weak monitoring.

74. One of us encountered the multiple equilibria problem years ago when he left his two daughters home without a babysitter for the first time. The children were told that each would babysit the other, the parents assuming that a monitoring equilibrium would result. As the children later recounted, almost immediately after the parents left, one child asked the other if she could have a sweet. The other child answered in the affirmative and made a reciprocal request—a shirking equilibrium.

75. It is a familiar pattern in the principal-agent literature that an agent must bear non-diversifiable risk to create an incentive, but that the very act of creating the incentive shifts risk to an inefficient bearer.

76. We realize that much just-in-time production often involves delivery by smaller, closely held firms to larger publicly held firms. In such a relationship, the smaller supplier probably does not own stock in the assembler.

77. See Gerlach, *supra* n. 46, at 173–4.

78. The just-in-time inventory system, for example, is said to have been a response to the 1973 energy shock. See Takao Komine, 'Structural Change of Japanese Firms', 19 *Japan J. Econ. Stud.* 79, 780 (1991). Similarly, cross-ownership increased to prevent takeovers. See *infra* text accompanying notes 91–3.

79. Professors Aoki and Sheard also stress the importance of monitoring as a by-product of a primary commercial relationship in connection with main bank crisis monitoring. They note that a company's main bank also carries its principal payment settlement accounts, the primary method of payment for inter-company transactions in Japan. By observing levels in these accounts, the bank can monitor day-to-day cash flows of bank borrowers, including their dealings with suppliers and distributors. See Aoki, 'Ex Post Monitoring', *supra* n. 43; Aoki and Sheard, *supra* n. 41.

80. Some have observed that in the American corporate governance system, product market competition may substitute for the market for corporate control in providing an incentive for efficient performance. Of the companies that proposed dual class recapitalizations, which, by placing absolute voting control in the hands of management or a dominant shareholder group, eliminated the influence of the market for corporate control, over half were relatively young companies in fast growing markets with negative cash flows—that is, companies facing strong product market competition. See Ronald J. Gilson, 'Evaluating Dual Class Common Stock: The Relevance of Substitutes', 73 *Va. L. Rev.* 807, 824–32 (1987); Kenneth Lehn, Jeffry Netter, and Annette Poulson, 'Consolidating Corporate Control: Dual-Class Recapitalizations Versus Leveraged Buyouts', 27 *J. Fin. Econ.* 557 (1990) (empirical test of Gilson hypothesis).

81. We do not mean that inter-factor monitoring is *always* faster. Inter-factor monitoring of serious breaches will require transmission up through the factor's organization to the board (or its equivalent). Then that board—or senior management—will deal with the breaching factor's senior management. This transmission will, we suppose, usually be as slow as the board's monitoring of internal problems. The difference we see is that *sometimes* inter-factor monitoring is faster and transmission up to the board is unnecessary. The assembler's mid-level foreman sees bad parts and tells the supplier's mid-level foreman that the rejection rate is rising, leading the supplier to investigate and change. No one contacts any board of directors.

82. Michael E. Porter, *The Competitive Advantage of Nations* 411–12 (1990). We realize that competition could directly spur superior performance, without going through the organizational mechanisms we model here.

83. Ibid. at 413. Komine also stresses the importance of domestic competition to Japan's international success. Komine, *supra* n. 78, at 82–4. For our purposes, it matters little whether the competition is domestic or international, as Japanese firms seek export markets and must compete. The point is that competition activates the model, pushing the firms away from mutual protection of slothfulness.

84. See Coffee, *supra* n. 27, at 1301.

85. See Roe, *supra* n. 10, at app.

86. See Gerlach, *supra* n. 48, at 12–13.

87. See generally Albert O. Hirschman, *Exit, Voice, and Loyalty—Responses to Decline in Firms, Organizations, and States* (1970).

88. Professor Aoki notes that some 400 banks had extended credit to Chrysler at the time of its near bankruptcy. In the absence of delegated monitoring, no bank had the incentive to gather information necessary to intervene early. Moreover, an enormous co-ordination problem impeded capturing the lenders' attention before disaster was imminent. Aoki, 'Toward an Economic Model', *supra* n. 8, at 15 n.7. A focused group of lender-stockholders constantly interacting with Chrysler's senior managers, suppliers, and customers might have intervened earlier and more effectively.

89. See Aoki, 'Ex Post Monitoring', *supra* n. 43; Aoki and Sheard, *supra* n. 41.

90. Indeed, cross-holdings may have perverse effects when business is, or should be, contracting. First, the presence of free cash flow can reflect reduced product market competition, thereby lowering a barrier to mutually accepted shirking. In addition, customer and supplier shareholders may be more willing to accept expansion during a business decline than pure shareholders. Perhaps the financial shareholders (banks and insurers) will intervene in a role approaching a pure Berle–Means monitor, but that is in fact the question to be seen.

91. See e.g. Sheard, *supra* n. 34, at 425; Jack McDonald, *Origins and Implications of Cross-Holdings in Japanese Companies* (Graduate School of Business, Stanford University Technical Note No. 79, 1991).

92. See Aoki, 'Toward an Economic Model', *supra* n. 8, at 15.

93. McDonald, *supra* n. 91, at 3–4.

94. Aoki, 'Toward an Economic Model', *supra* n. 8, at 7–10.

95. Piore and Sabel, *supra* n. 28, at 223–6.

96. See *supra* text accompanying notes 26–9; Black, 'Agents Watching Agents', *supra* n. 7, at 813–14; Black, 'Value of Institutional Investor Monitoring', *supra* n. 7, at 896; Gilson and Kraakman, *supra* n. 7, at 892–4.

97. See William Graebner, *A History of Retirement* 215–21 (1980).

98. See e.g. Deborah M. Weiss, 'Paternalistic Pension Policy: Psychological Evidence and Economic Theory', 58 *U. Chi. L. Rev.* 1275 (1991).

99. Karel Wolferen, *The Enigma of Japanese Power* 208 (1991).

100. Ibid. at 315.

101. This is an economy-of-scale argument. Japan has three contractual governance problems to solve with cross-ownership. Cross-ownership may have costs, like illiquidity, see Coffee, *supra* n. 27, at 1918–21, but in Japan the gains are in three dimensions. In America, the costs loom larger, because the gains come primarily in one dimension.

     Without well-developed relational contracting doctrines, enforcement costs may be high in Japan. If the standard approach is to enforce the four corners of the document without interpretive understanding, contracting parties may be forced to choose between the rigidities of the four-corners contract and the looseness of the relational structure. American contract law may give American suppliers and customers an alternative. We also recognize that these legally-determined results could explain not only the origin of the cross-holdings, but also part of their continuing rationale.

102. See e.g. Ryutaro Komiya, *The Japanese Economy: Trade, Industry, and Government* 167–70, 172–3, 177, 180 (1990); see Coffee, *supra* n. 27, at 1298. Contrary to the commentators, we believe that the 'higher' in higher than market-clearing wages must be judged in terms of productivity. If 'higher' wages yield greater productivity, or are a needed component in a system yielding productivity, then the 'higher' wages may benefit stockholders. We leave pursuit of this analysis for others, who might begin with George A. Akerlof and Janet L. Yellen, 'The Fair Wage-Effort Hypothesis and Unemployment', 105 *QJ Econ.* 255 (1990). In the text we generalize this labour productivity argument.

103. Professors Coffee and Ramseyer argue that the main banks' co-insurance role cannot be valuable to the non-controlling shareholders 'because shareholders can diversify to protect themselves from losses and so would not want expensive insurance purchased from banks at the price of above-market interest rates'. Coffee, *supra* n. 27, at 1298; see Ramseyer, *supra* n. 36, at 112 n. 66. But shareholders *ought not* to be the beneficiary of the insurance; it is the *other* providers of relation-specific investment who are protected. Shareholders can diversify risk; these providers cannot. Insurance induces the proper level of relation-specific investment which, in turn, benefits non-controlling shareholders so long as their share of the productivity gain from the investment exceeds the above market portion of the interest rate.

104. See Ronald J. Gilson, 'The Political Ecology of Takeovers: Thoughts on Harmonizing the European Corporate Governance Environment', 61 *Fordham L. Rev.* 101, 129–31 (1992) (providing more detailed criticism of implicit contract arguments against take-overs).

105. See Task Force Report, *supra* n. 1, at 7–8, 66, 189–90, 193–94, 286; Porter, *supra* n. 2.

106. See Roe, *supra* n. 10; Coffee, *supra* n. 27, at 1318–19, 1324–7. Roe emphasizes that the bank as monitor—whether through residual equity-holding or as part of a contractual governance system—cannot easily be constructed in

the United States. Due to historical (and some current) product and geo-graphic restrictions, American banks are too weak and too small compared to Japanese banks. Deposit insurance is too deeply embedded in the American system; massive bank ownership cannot work well without solv-ing problems arising from deposit insurance. But since we have had many more compelling reasons than corporate governance to solve these deposit insurance problems and have not done so, there is little reason to be opti-mistic about unleashing banking institutions. There are possibilities, Roe argues, for *other* financial institutions. Coffee believes that the current reward systems for institutional fund managers do not reward superior long-run performance; he believes institutions as currently structured need so much liquidity that they could not undertake the long-term investments said to be commonplace in Japan.

107. See Jensen, *supra* n. 3, at 61.
108. Ibid. at 68.
109. Michael C. Jensen, 'Corporate Control and the Politics of Finance', *J. Applied Corp. Fin.*, Summer 1991, at 13, 22.
110. Michael C. Jensen, 'Active Investors, LBOs and the Privatization of Bankruptcy', *J. Applied Corp. Fin.* Spring 1989, at 35 (statement before House Ways and Means Committee, 1 February, 1989); Jensen, *supra* n. 3, at 73.
111. At least for pre-1986 transactions, the LBO association did appear to priva-tize bankruptcy. Transactions occurring after 1985 reflected changes in structure that made such privatization more tenuous. First, publicly held debt replaced privately placed debt, increasing the negotiating costs of con-sensual reorganizations. See Mark J. Rose, 'The Voting Prohibition in Bond Workouts', 97 *Yale LJ* 232, 236–43 (1987). Second, strip finance, which miti-gated intrafirm bargaining in the event of distress, also declined after 1985; and, finally, principal payments on senior bank debt were accelerated. See William F. Long and David J. Ravenscraft, 'Decade of Debt: Lessons from LBOs in the 1980s', in *The Deal Decade* (Margaret Blair ed., forthcoming 1993); Steve N. Kaplan and Jeremy C. Stein, *The Evolution of Buyout Pricing and Financial Structure in the 1980s* (Center for Research in Security Prices, Graduate School of Business, University of Chicago Working Paper No. 327, 1991).
112. See *supra* text accompanying n. 41.
113. Ibid. The reason for the difference in monitoring roles maybe found in the source of the power to monitor; unlike the main bank, which owns no more than 5% of a client company, the LBO association has absolute voting con-trol over its operating entities.
114. Kester reports semiannual meetings between managers and bankers where the managers report on recent performance but do not submit budget and future plans to banks. Kester, *Japanese Takeovers*, *supra* n. 8, at 194–7.
115. Berkshire Hathaway takes large stock positions. While Berkshire's senior

managers often become members of the portfolio companies' boards, their visible activity has been limited to times of crisis, as at Salomon Brothers after the Treasury bidding scandal.

116. For a rejoinder to Jensen, see Alfred Rappaport, 'The Staying Power of the Public Corporation', *Harv. Bus. Rev.*, Jan.–Feb. 1990, at 96.

117. See Williamson, *supra* n. 54, at 158–9; Pisano, *supra* n. 64.

118. See Williamson, *supra* n. 54, at 293–4; David J. Teece, 'Economies of Scope and the Scope of the Enterprise', 1 *J. Econ. Behav. & Org.* 223 (1980).

119. See Christopher B. Barry, Chris J. Muscarella, John W. Peavy III and Michael R. Vetsuypens, 'The Role of Venture Capital in the Creation of Public Companies: Evidence from the Going-Public Process', 27 *J. Fin. Econ.* 447, 449–51 (1990); William A. Sahlman, 'The Structure and Governance of Venture-Capital Organizations', 27 *J. Fin. Econ.* 473, 475–87 (1990).

120. This amount increases when one attributes the bank's industrial portfolio to the other members of the keiretsu.

THE BUSINESS ENTERPRISE IN INTERNATIONAL PERSPECTIVE

Transnational Corporations

VOLKER BORNSCHIER
and HANSPETER STAMM

Introduction

What is specific about transnational corporations (TNCs), what is their 'distinctive nature' (Dunning 1981)? Aren't they simply firms like the many others that flourish in the capitalist world? Maybe TNCs are simply bigger and command more economic resources than the others, but do not represent a species of their own. Obviously, the business of TNCs is highly concentrated, but so is business in many economic fields that are organized only nationally. For example, the eight leading world manufacturers of passenger cars—all TNCs according to the standard specification (see below)—accounted for 75 per cent of the world output of passenger cars in 1980. But it is not difficult to find higher concentration ratios of supply in more local or regional markets. Thus, neither size nor concentration, nor the command over technology *as such* represents any specificity on its own. . . . . TNCs represent organizations designed for capital accumulation on a world scale. This fact is also reflected in the most simple definition of TNCs: decision-making centres owning income-generating assets in at least two countries. Many researchers in the field suggest the more stringent criterion of owning income generating assets in six or more countries.[1]

Accumulation on a world scale implies that there exists a system and social processes beyond individual societies organized as (nation) states in the modern world. Joseph A. Schumpeter was an early proponent of such a conceptualization, arguing that 'capitalism itself is, both in the economic and sociological sense, essentially one process, with the whole earth as its stage' (1939, ii. 666). . . . . The modern world system does not simply consist of a great number of societies. Beyond these coexisting societies there are economic processes at the level of the world economy that affect all these societies and their states. At the same time, the rather

This chapter was prepared in the spring of 1987.

decentralized social and political structure of the world system shapes the very logic of the overarching world economy, too.[2]

Transnational capital accumulation as the *differentia specifica*, however, is by no means a modern phenomenon. Various types of transnational business have existed throughout the course of history. First, the trade diasporas of ethnic groups must be mentioned as early organizers of exchange in world economies which seem to be traceable back to the Mesopotamian systems and were still of importance in recent times (Curtin 1984). Second, the big chartered companies of the early centuries of the modern world system should be noted. These companies produced their own protection (Lane 1979), built their own colonies and were active throughout all three main economic sectors: primary, secondary, and distribution. They were especially important outside the domain of the emerging national states in Europe. Third, the transnational corporations of the nineteenth and twentieth centuries, with which we will deal here, came to the fore.

Thus, the specific feature about TNCs is their double nature: the combination of transnational business—which itself is nothing new—with a certain organizational form. The scholar who elaborated this organizational feature of the phenomenon and directed the research community to it was the late Stephen Hymer, to whom contemporary theory of TNCs owes a lot.

Theoretical views on transnational corporations

Theoretical investigations of TNCs can be seen as closely related to the perception of their phenomenal growth and the problems arising from their activities. While up to the 1950s the (neo-)classical theories of trade and direct investment[3] (Ricardo, Ohlin, and others) seemed to be adequate for the treatment of the phenomenon of TNCs, the situation changed radically in the early 1960s. In 1960 a new era in the discussion of TNCs was triggered by Stephen Hymer's seminal dissertation thesis 'The International Operations of National Firms'.[4] Hymer, inspired by the work of Bain (1956) and Dunning (1958), pointed, for the first time, to the specific features of TNCs. Among these he identified monopolistic advantages, which allow TNCs to survive in foreign markets where domestic firms have—other things being equal—advantages. The advantages of TNCs—stemming, for example, from economies of scale in production or the control over resources and patents—help them to overcome barriers to entry in foreign markets as well as to protect their market position *vis-à-vis* local or TNC competitors once they have got hold in a foreign market. So monopolistic advantages allow TNCs to create and exploit imperfect markets.

Especially in economic theory, Hymer's ideas have been widely acknowledged, improved, and refined, which has led to the emergence of a variety of more or less original and autonomous theories of TNCs, generally stressing the economically positive side of their activities. At the same time, researchers outside the classical economic sciences became aware of the growing weight of TNCs in the world economy and consequently included this phenomenon in the broader framework of theories of development and underdevelopment. Therefore, the present body of theory can quite simply be classified according to two main orientations, 'neo-conventional' and 'critical' (Biersteker 1978). Although the critical perspective does not represent a homogeneous theoretical body, it still owes much to the Latin American *dependencia* approach, which itself cannot be described as one uniform theory. The *dependencia* approach suggests an answer to explanatory shortcomings of older theories of modernization in Latin America. It offers a 'broad set of contemporary discussions about imperialism, global inequality and underdevelopment, that focus on the economic, social and political distortions of peripheral societies' (Duvall *et al.* 1981), which have their roots in the writings of such authors as Marx, Baran, and Prebisch. It must be stressed that critical approaches in general are not theories of TNCs; rather, they represent more encompassing historical-structurally oriented approaches, aimed at explaining the 'development of underdevelopment' (Amin 1974). Development thereby is not understood simply in terms of economic growth but also as social and political progress.

One of the common features of the critical perspective is its division of the world into a (developed) core and an underdeveloped periphery, which are entangled in a network of unequal, capitalist exchange relations.[5] This interdependence, however, leads to a permanent reproduction of dependence, which in turn hinders or even blocks development in the periphery. A great deal of the differences between various critical theories arise from their perception of the degree of possible development in this situation. While some authors believe 'associated-dependent development' to be possible (Cardoso 1973), the stagnationists see the only solution for the periphery as revolutionary change (see for example Dos Santos 1970 or Frank 1969) and/or radical withdrawal from the capitalist world economy and 'autocentric development' (see for example, Amin 1974; Senghaas and Menzel 1976).[6] Within those theoretical perspectives TNCs become important as mediators of capitalist dependency relations. It is difficult to derive explicit hypotheses about their activities and effects from those general frameworks. Nevertheless, with reference to the conceptualization of Theodore Moran (1978), three broad hypotheses can be set out.

1. The advantages of transnational direct investments are unequally distributed between TNCs and host countries, because TNCs have the ability to absorb gains that could otherwise be reinvested.[7]

2. TNCs create distortions in the economy by displacing domestic production, utilizing inappropriate technology, and distorting consumer tastes. In addition their behaviour leads to a worsening of income distribution.

3. TNCs may pervert or undermine the political system of host countries.

While in the *dependencia* approach the nation-state stood at the centre of analysis—external dependence was therefore taken more or less as given—in some new theoretical perspectives more weight is attached to the unity of the world system. In this perspective there is no distinction between processes internal and external to the system as they are all internal to the overarching world system.[8] So this approach allows a more general interpretation of the processes and the dynamics of the capitalist world system than the geographically limited framework of other approaches. Within such a framework TNCs, too, have been studied in more detail (see for example Bornschier and Chase-Dunn 1985).

Some other approaches have further stimulated discussion in recent years, as for example the concept of the 'new international division of labour', which regards differential labour costs between centre and periphery as the most important determinant of dependence (Froebel *et al.* 1981). At this point one should also mention the more recent contributions of Stephen Hymer (1979), who at the beginning of the 1970s turned to a Marxist view of the problems attached to TNCs and addressed his theory of monopolistic advantages more and more to questions of underdevelopment. Those contributions, however, were quite sparsely noticed by other authors.

The line of argument against the critical perspective was often directed towards the conceptual shortcomings of the various approaches, which have prevented their systematic empirical testing. But in current research there have been some attempts at conceptualizing and testing critical perspectives as a whole (Moran 1978; Duvall *et al.* 1981) and with special regard to TNCs (see Biersteker 1978; Bornschier and Chase-Dunn 1985; Gereffi 1983; Newfarmer and Topik 1982; Newfarmer 1985).

One of the more important disadvantages of critical research lies in its absolute orientation to development problems at the periphery. Implicitly assuming a balancing of effects in the core, critical writers seem to forget that the overwhelming part of foreign direct investment takes place in the core zone.[9] Even where research is concerned with less developed countries (LDCs), the simple zero-sum contention that if TNCs are to win, other actors—for example the host country—have to lose may not hold true (Biersteker 1978).

The extensive criticism of TNCs arising in the 1960s and early 1970s brought many replies, mainly from business schools and the TNCs themselves. As stated earlier, economic theorizing on TNCs had begun in the early 1960s. As opposed to critical theories, 'neo-conventional' writings offer a large variety of directly testable hypotheses on various issues. Their disadvantage lies in the preoccupation with purely economic questions such as growth, efficiency or organization of activities, and their confinement to the micro-level.

Since it is impossible to describe the development of neo-conventional theories in detail, the following paragraphs name only the most influential contributions to the stream of theorizing. One is Raymond Vernon's seminal product cycle model which links the internationalization of firms to the developmental sequence of their products. New products (innovations) emerge in highly developed countries and spread from there all over the world through exports. This development is accompanied by a process of diffusion of the know-how of production: similar products are developed and sold by other firms, in turn lowering the profitability of investments. However, as production becomes standardized, its shift to more peripheral areas allows the maintenance of profits (Vernon 1971, 1973).

For some time this theory was one of the most important instruments for explaining foreign direct investment by US firms. But as German and Japanese TNCs became able to reduce the technological gap between themselves and US TNCs in the late 1970s, Vernon's model showed some explanatory shortcomings, which at last led Vernon himself to doubt the viability of his product cycle model for the 1980s (Vernon 1979, 1985).

During the 1970s, an influential group of economists around John H. Dunning refined and extended Hymer's concepts. Their effort resulted in a number of theories, which for Charles P. Kindleberger (1984b) are all more or less unoriginal replicas of Hymer's ideas—a fact that makes it rather difficult to distinguish between them.

Various approaches in industrial organization theory emerged in direct succession to Hymer's ideas. They treat questions of imperfect markets, oligopolistic competition and reaction (Caves 1971, 1974; Knickerbocker 1973). Theories which emphasize internalization of market functions as the central feature of TNCs (Buckley and Casson 1976) aim in a similar direction. Such theories argue that internalization—that is, the vertical and horizontal integration of operations—and markets represent alternative ways of organizing economic activities (Hennart 1982). It is argued that internalization of activities lowers transaction costs in imperfect markets.[10] Yet internalization may in turn lead to even more imperfect markets, for example where it is put into effect by mergers or unfriendly take-overs. In this context, location theory also received some consideration. Unlike other approaches, it is closely related to the classical theory of trade and explains foreign investment by pointing to features of host countries.[11]

For the present, the discussion seems to end with Dunning's (1981; Black and Dunning 1982) integration of those different approaches into his 'eclectic theory', which combines owner-specific advantages, location theory, and internalization-specific advantages[12] in an impressive mix, which now apparently belongs to the standard research equipment of economists interested in the study of TNCs.

Reviewing the theoretical discussion reveals the interesting fact that the vehement exchange of arguments between critical and neo-conventional researchers of the late 1960s and the early 1970s has significantly calmed down. There may be different reasons for this. To begin with, public interest in TNCs seems to have declined[13] and it is not difficult to conclude that academic interest correlates considerably with this. Furthermore, some resignation among scholars in the critical camp may be observed. This is paralleled by the recent development towards theoretical perfectionism that has occurred in the neo-conventional camp. Although the neo-conventionalists have turned away from discussions with theorists of other schools of thought, even among the neo-conventionals there have recently been signs of theoretical stagnation (Schlupp 1985).

Stagnation, however, does not mean that the theories offered are already perfect. And in fact there are some avenues for possible further development and improvement. Apart from the long overdue integration of critical and neo-conventional knowledge, as has for example been suggested by Biersteker (1978) or Newfarmer (1985), there are some other interesting ideas which surely deserve more attention. For example,

Robert Gilpin, a political scientists, points to one fundamental problem in theorizing: 'the fact that economists don't believe in power; political scientists, for their part, do not really believe in markets' (Gilpin 1976: 5). As a consequence he offers a politico-economic model postulating interdependent relationships of political and economic (TNCs) actors. Within this model, Gilpin is able to explain the growth of US TNCs as a result of favourable factors, both in the US and abroad, that is, the establishing of the Bretton Woods system and the rise of the United States to hegemony. The work of Stephen Krasner and others on international regimes also draws attention to global political conditions that favour or hinder world economic processes (Krasner 1983). In addition, the contributions of economic historians, such as Mira Wilkins, Alfred D. Chandler Jr, Stephen J. Nicholas, or Oliver E. Williamson, should be mentioned. Some of those approaches allow a possible reconciliation of the different theories. Economic historians generally point to the institutional and organizational roots of the foreign expansion of industrial firms, and in doing so they sometimes draw heavily on the writings of already mentioned neo-conventional authors. The concepts of Williamson (1981) and Nicholas (1982, 1983), for example, are inspired by Caves's (1982) transaction-cost approach. The work of Alfred D. Chandler Jr points in somewhat the same direction (1969, 1977, 1980). In his approach, national growth of firms is a consequence of vertical integration and the formation of a multidivisional structure among the leading business firms. In this process, administrative activities are centralized and production is rationalized, which leads to the emergence of managerial hierarchies that are able to replace the classical family entrepreneur. This transition from family to managerial capitalism is also stressed in the later writings of Hymer (1979: 58 ff.) and Bornschier (1976). The concept of managerial capitalism, however, has been challenged on theoretical and empirical grounds lately (Nyman and Silberston 1978, see also Mizruchi 1982), which in some instances has led to an integration of managerial capitalism in the framework of corporate élite approaches (Useem 1980; Fennema 1982).

Closely related to Chandler's theory is Mira Wilkins's (1974) interpretation of the expansion of US TNCs as a three-step process. The first step is characterized by foreign investments with little complexity. With the growing number of affiliates the establishment of an administrative supervising organization becomes necessary. In the second phase, the original monocentric approach is replaced by a polycentric system in whose setting the affiliates get (back) a certain autonomy which allows them to begin expansion on their own.[14] The growth of the affiliates and their own partial internationalization generate an even more complicated structure in the third phase: the conglomerate entangled structure. According to Wilkins, the model holds for TNCs in different sectors and times.

Findings

Transnational Business over Time

Although the extraordinary growth of the modern TNC represents a relatively new phenomenon, the historical roots of direct control over the production of goods and services in foreign countries can be traced back several hundred years. In historical perspective, TNCs are merely a new organizational form of the capitalist world economy, the origin of which has been dated to the long sixteenth century (1450–1640) by several authors (see, for example, Wallerstein 1974, and other scholars in the world system perspective). Initially, exchange in this system of world-wide division of labour was confined to trade relations in the first place. Historical analyses, however, show that even under merchant capitalism big chartered companies, for example the British East India Company in the seventeenth century, already exercised some direct control of production processes (Choudhuri 1978). In the eighteenth century big trading companies began founding foreign agencies, but most of the responsibility was in the hands of family members or independent agents (Wilkins 1970). With the growth of world trade and industrial production—and the simultaneously growing importance of technological know-how—in the nineteenth century, the pressure to found affiliates increased, due to the need to open up new attractive markets and to secure access to raw materials. Independent agents played a major role in such activities, too, but as they were often unreliable they were replaced more and more by directly controlled affiliates (Nicholas 1983; Williamson 1981; Wilkins 1970: 207).

British capital exports in connection with the construction of railways in Britain's colonies and in Latin America boomed in the second half of the last century. Yet these capital exports consisted in large part of portfolio investment which does not involve direct control (Edelstein 1982). Direct investment by industrial enterprises in the US and Europe dates back in some cases to the early nineteenth century, but it was, with some exceptions,[15] restricted to small family entrepreneurs or licence arrangements with independent firms (Wilkins 1970: 15 ff.).

The emergence of TNCs in the modern sense can only be traced back to the late nineteenth century. The lead was taken by big industrial enterprises in the US and Germany and in some smaller continental European countries, like The Netherlands, Belgium, and Switzerland (Wilkins 1970, 1974; Chandler 1977, 1980; Franko 1976). Transnationalization in Great Britain and several other European countries began somewhat more slowly, a fact that Chandler (1980) explains as the hesitating transformation of family to managerial enterprises. Apart from internalization of national operations and the emergence of the multidivisional structure as a result of the growth of the domestic market (Wilkins 1974: 436; Chandler 1977, 1980),[16] external factors have also been important. Export opportunities as well as the threat of loss of established export outlets, the desire to secure access to raw materials and the growth prospect of foreign markets have been fundamental preconditions for transnationalization; in addition, improved international transport and communication facilities have been favourable to the decision to go abroad (Wilkins 1974; Nicholas 1982, 1983; Chandler 1977, 1980). All in all, 'aggressive and innovative enterprises' (Wilkins 1974) and firms from highly concentrated sectors (Nicholas 1982; Chandler 1980; Bornschier 1976) generally took a marked lead in going transnational.

While the already mentioned model of Mira Wilkins (1974) seems to have some validity in explaining the growth of American TNCs, the development of continental European TNCs shows, according to Franko (1976: 187 ff.) a somewhat different pattern. Here, the monocentric structure—Franko calls it the 'mother–daughter structure'—was maintained longer because of personal or familial relationships between presidents of parent companies and affiliates, and the more personally structured pattern was only slowly given up in favour of impersonal managerial hierarchies because of the success of the US corporate structure.

The importance of transnationalization at the turn of the century can be illustrated with figures for the stock of US foreign direct investment in 1914. Although total stock was only about $2.65 billion, this figure equals about 7 per cent of the US GNP at that time—a share that was only slightly higher in 1966 (Wilkins 1970: 201–7).[17] While the foreign activities of mining, agriculture, and petroleum corporations were concentrated in underdeveloped areas, manufacturing industry had its operations in Europe and Canada. Nevertheless, it seems necessary to point out that—at the turn of the century—a large number of foreign affiliates were still merely sales companies.

Contrary to the widespread opinion, US TNCs by no means had a monopoly of transnationalization in this early phase. Of the estimated total stock of direct investments of $14.3 billion in 1914 about $11 billion were held by firms in European countries, with Britain in a dominant position in terms of stocks (Dunning 1983).[18] A look at the number of European TNCs in manufacturing shows that in 1914 a total of 37 mostly chemical or electrical enterprises had affiliates in at least one foreign country.[19] Contrary to US TNCs, European firms were almost exclusively confined to the European market and only hesitatingly ventured into other areas, especially into the USA (Franko 1976). Nevertheless, for that early time Franko (1976: 8) concludes that German TNCs in manufacturing had a competitive edge over US TNCs.[20]

As noted earlier, transnationalization was not always successful. Examples like that of Dunlop, whose American affiliate operated only one year without loss between 1923 and 1936 (Jones 1984), also reveal aspects neglected by the 'success story' (Nicholas 1982: 630). In addition, the expansion of transnational business did not take a continuous course. There is a close relationship between waves of transnationalization, merger waves, and economic stagnation (Bornschier 1976: 482–91), and Franko (1976: 10) has pointed to the cyclical pattern in the founding of foreign affiliates by European TNCs. The generally more continuous evolution of US TNCs—favoured by European self-destruction in two wars and the shift of hegemony in the world system over the Atlantic—has made them the leaders in international direct investments over time: their share in the total stock of direct investments increased from 19.5 per cent in 1914 and 30.4 per cent in 1938 to 56 per cent in 1960. At the same time the share of Western European TNCs dropped from 76.9 per cent in 1914 to 39.8 per cent in 1960 (Dunning 1983). Since the early 1970s, however, this trend has been reversed again. The share of the US in the total stock of $386.2 billion in 1978 not only decreased to 47 per cent (with the European share recovering somewhat to 41 per cent), but also their share in the 50 largest industrial corporations went down drastically from 43 in the late 1950s to 21 in the late 1970s (Bergesen and Sahoo 1985). During the 1980s the 50 largest industrials of the world distribute among head-quarter regions as follows: 21 are US, 20 European, 5 Japanese and about 4 from semiperipheral countries.[21] This indicates a marked loss of the former US position. Furthermore, during the world recession the US turned from the leading capital exporter to an important importer of foreign capital. While only 2.6 per cent of world capital flows between 1961 and 1967 went to the US, this share rose to about one-third in the period 1978–80 (OECD 1981: 13; UN 1983: 18 ff.). With regard to capital exports,

West Germany and Japan have markedly increased their shares[22] and other European countries have either increased (France) or at least stabilized (United Kingdom) their shares. In addition, TNCs from developing countries are now appearing on stage (see Lall 1983; Wells 1983). Yet, the operations of those (mainly Indian, South-East Asian, and South American) firms are still of modest size and almost exclusively limited to investments in other LDCs.[23] The data on the changing relative shares of headquarter countries in total TNC business, should not obscure, however, the general growth of TNC activities in the post-Second World War period. The quite modest initial growth rates virtually 'exploded' in the 1960s, but declined again from the mid-1970s on. The sharp increase in foreign direct investment around the 1960s can largely be explained by an interaction of push, pull, and rivalry factors, and this constellation was bolstered by the generally favourable economic and political environment as established for example by the Bretton Woods system, the functioning of which also reached its peak in the 1960s. While push forces arise from the concern of TNCs for new market outlets, which cannot be serviced easily by exports, pull forces stem from host countries' policies of industrialization. The last factor—rivalry—is a consequence of oligopolistic reaction among TNCs, that is, a follow-the-leader effect, as analysed by Knickerbocker (1973, see also p. 208).

The annual growth rate of total foreign direct investment from 13 OECD countries amounted to an average of 12 per cent between 1960 and 1973 (OECD 1981: 6). That figure approximately equals the growth of world trade and is about one and a half times larger than the GNP growth rate of the capital-exporting countries. Although the growth rates remained of this order up to the mid-1970s, real growth has slowed down due to increasing inflation (OECD 1981: 12; UN 1983: 18).

Capital flows to LDCs stand out against this world pattern. Between 1960 and 1968 flows from Development Assistance Committee (DAC) countries to LDCs grew at an average annual rate of only about 7 per cent. This figure increased sharply to 19.4 per cent p.a. in the period 1973–8 (OECD 1981: 43). This increase of foreign direct investment in LDCs did not, however, affect the share of the LDCs in the total stock of foreign direct investment. At the end of the 1970s, this share amounted to about 30 per cent, a figure similar to that at the beginning of the 1960s (Dunning 1983). Although the LDCs do not play an overwhelming role in the transnational network, one still has to stress the comparatively more important role of TNCs in LDCs. This is manifested by the fact that in 1966–7 LDCs produced only 15 per cent of world GNP, but hosted 30 per cent of the total stock of foreign direct investment (Bornschier 1976: 349).[24] Even more important is the LDC share in world payments for foreign direct investment (dividends, royalties and fees, and related categories). The annual figure for such payments from LDCs was about $12.8 billion, which was about half of the world total of such payments, and these annual outflows were larger than the annual figures for fresh capital inflows, which amounted to about $8 billion per year (see UN 1983: 19 ff.).

In talking about capital flows, one should also mention the growing importance of reinvested earnings—which provide about 50 per cent of the increase in the stock of foreign investment—and the financing of TNC activities with loans in host countries (about a quarter of the total increase in capital: see Vernon 1973: 69; Niedermayer 1979: 51 ff.; UN 1983: 19 ff.). In addition, one has to mention a tendency, which has recently been observed, away from wholly owned affiliates to majority or minority participations, joint ventures, and licence agreements. The kind of engagement, however, seems to differ according to technology (UN 1978: 229; UN 1983: 40–6; OECD 1981: 31–5). Such observations reveal that a mere examination of international capital flows and stock measures underestimates the real impact of TNCs in the world as well as in the host country economy.

The sectoral distribution of TNC operations has also been subject to some changes. At the beginning of the 1970s, raw materials and services each held about a quarter of all foreign direct investment, with the rest being made up by manufacturing. Since then, the trend to investments in the services sector has continued while in manufacturing there is a tendency to divide production into separate production steps which may even be located in different geographical regions (Helleiner 1973, 1975). Assembly production has become important in some low-wage countries of South-East Asia and Central America and leads—according to some authors—to a new form of dependence (Grunwald and Flamm 1985: Froebel *et al.* 1981).

In global figures, the importance of transnational business is documented by a growing share of foreign affiliates in the overall sales of TNCs. By 1980 this figure had amounted to 40 per cent of total sales (UN 1983). In general, the foreign activities of TNCs have grown much faster than their activities in their country of origin.

The importance of TNCs as organizers of world trade has also increased. Trade between affiliates and the parent firm (intra-firm trade) has become more important, but estimates of its share in total world trade differ between various sources. Yet, one may at least impute about one-quarter to one-third of total world trade to intra-firm transactions (Berthold 1980; Lall and Streeten 1977).

There has been a growing number of small and medium-sized firms taking part in the process of transnationalization lately, yet the largest TNCs have a high and increasing share in total transnational business. The overall concentration is shown by the fact that the largest 350 TNCs of the world owned about a quarter of the total of about 100,000 foreign affiliates. These largest 350 had approximately 25 million employees worldwide. Their world sales were about $2635 billion, according to the UN (1983: 46 ff.), a figure that equals 28 per cent of the GDP of developed and less developed countries together. Furthermore, the largest hundred TNCs are growing even faster—at about 17 per cent a year 1971–80—than the rest of the TNCs (UN 1983: 47; Dunning and Pearce 1981). Finally, there is a growing number of public enterprises which have also started to go transnational.

This short overview of the development and size of TNCs shows only part of their economic significance and their considerable power in the modern world. In order to obtain a more complete picture we must now turn to some particular questions.

Analytical Questions and Empirical Studies

Over the past twenty years a vast number of empirical studies addressing various subjects has been published. It is thus almost impossible to present an overview in a short chapter. Credit is due here to Peter B. Evans (1981), who did an excellent job in reviewing the vast literature that had appeared up to the late 1970s. As it is not possible to plunge as deep into the material as he did, it seems adequate to divide the empirical material into four, partly overlapping subject areas: 'TNCs and development', 'TNCs and labour', 'TNCs and the nation-state' and 'TNCs as organizations and control within TNCs'.

As already mentioned, research has been especially preoccupied with LDCs, a fact that limits the possibilities of generalizing several of the following findings. Whenever possible and of interest, however, we try to mention empirical material pertinent to core countries, too.

TNCs and development.   Questions concerning the developmental impact of TNCs have received special interest from researchers in the past. Regardless of the underlying concept of development, studies addressing the growth effects of TNCs seem to be an adequate starting-point in the discussion of development problems in general.

A large body of studies address the impact of TNCs on overall economic growth. An overview of these studies seems to suggest, however, contradictory results.[25] Yet many of these differences can be reconciled since they are in part due to insufficient design, lack of adequate control variables and differences in indicators and samples used in the various analyses.[26] The lack of distinction between short-term and long-term effects on growth is of particular importance for reconciling discrepant findings. A detailed look at all available studies and a reanalysis by Bornschier and Chase-Dunn (1985)[27] with an improved design and using large country samples (101 countries) confirm the evidence and conclusion of several earlier studies—that penetration by TNCs adds to overall economic growth in the short run while it reduces growth performance in the long run. This holds for world samples and for LDCs, while the effect for core countries is small or absent. In more technical terms, this finding is established as follows: if growth rates of GNP per capita over six to twenty years are regressed together with several control variables on weighted stocks of TNC capital at the beginning of the growth period and on TNC investment during the growth period, one observes a significant negative effect of stocks on subsequent growth and a significant positive one for investment on growth. The design to disentangle short-term TNC effects on growth was suggested independently by researchers in Great Britain, the United States and Switzerland, in 1975. Meanwhile these different effects on overall growth belong to what may be called a fairly consolidated finding for growth periods from 1950 to the mid-1970s. During the world recession starting in 1975 almost all previous predictors of growth in cross-national studies lost their predictive power, and so did TNC variables (Bornschier 1985).

Negative effects of TNCs on growth in industrialized countries have been found by Hammer and Gartrell (1986) in their time series analysis of Canada. They suggest that Canada is a special case of 'mature dependency', since it is characterized by a long-lasting penetration, mainly by US firms. More research, however, is necessary in order to clarify the issue of whether and why effects of TNCs differ in core countries.

The impact of TNCs on changes in the industrial structure which may have effects on the performance of the economy as a whole has been repeatedly studied. The issue under debate is whether or not TNCs increase market concentration and/or competition. From the observation that TNC prevail in highly concentrated sectors in their home markets (Buckley and Dunning 1980; Bornschier 1976; Caves 1974) it has been concluded that they will also be active in highly concentrated indus-

tries of host countries. This contention seems to hold true for both industrial (Fishwick 1982) and less developed countries (Newfarmer and Marsh
1981; Lall 1978, see also Newfarmer 1985). Yet it remains unclear
whether TNCs are only attracted by oligopolistic markets, which does
not preclude that they may enhance competition once they have pene-
trated these industries or if they themselves increase concentration leading to negative effects as, for example, by means of oligopolistic pricing
(Biersteker 1978; Dunning 1981; Caves 1982). Empirically it seems difficult to establish a causal relationship which could allow one to evaluate
the balance of negative and positive effects (Fishwick 1982). Yet, on the
whole, TNC activities seem to lead to higher industrial concentration.
This is illustrated for example by Blomström's (1986) analysis of the manufacturing sector in Mexico or the various sector studies in Newfarmer's
1985 volume on South America, which, in addition, points out important
differences between sectors. Data on the market entry behaviour of
TNCs fits into this picture. Often entry takes place by the acquisition of
existing domestic firms, and later acquisition of domestic firms is also
quite common (Evans 1977; Lall 1978; Newfarmer 1985). Nevertheless,
for the method of entry the literature also reports differences according
to industrial sector.

The question of displacement of domestic production and employment enters here. But still we have little conclusive evidence. Biersteker
(1978: 103–18) finds only weak displacement effects in his case study of
Nigeria, but points to an important relationship between displacement of
domestic production and imported consumption patterns.[28] Closely
related to these problems are questions of whether and to what extent
local backward linkages are created by TNC investment, and of the influence of TNCs on entrepreneurial capabilities in the population of the
host country. One may argue that growth-stimulating effects of TNCs in
segments of the host economy do not add to balanced overall growth as
long as backward linkages in the economy are lacking. Under such conditions, growth spurred by TNC investment may even lead to greater
dependence and distortions in the structure of society (Biersteker 1978).
Again there are sectoral differences. Assembly production is a special case
in so far as linkage and displacement effects are rarely associated with it
(Helleiner 1973, 1975), while in certain other branches of manufacturing
industry linkage effects rarely seem to occur (Lim and Fong 1982).

Related problems are technological dependence (Meyer-Fehr 1980) and
inappropriate technologies that may be introduced by TNCs in LDCs.
The lack of systematic evidence seems to preclude any generalization

(Lall 1978). Effects of TNCs on trade and on trade dependence, and the question of decapitalization of host countries due to TNC activities have also received some attention. One of the main arguments in favour of TNCs is their alleged positive contribution to the trade and capital accounts of LDCs. Yet various studies (Reuber 1973: 162; Lall and Streeten 1977: 134 ff., 142 ff.; Bornschier 1976: 384) have reported a negative overall effect on the balance of trade and the balance of payments of host countries, even if one restricts the analysis to export-oriented TNCs (Reuber 1973). This unfavourable effect may be largely due to two syndromes: (*a*) the affiliates' high propensity to import factor inputs, and (*b*) the possibilities of using transfer pricing mechanisms within TNCs across countries. Conclusive findings on the extent of transfer pricing devices are still lacking. While Müller and Morgenstern (1974) and Niedermayer (1979) find significant transfer pricing effects, Biersteker (1978: 87 ff.) and Lall and Streeten (1977: 153 ff.) are not able to establish the systematic use of this mechanism to shift income across countries, except in the pharmaceutical industry.[29]

The previously mentioned observations combined with findings for effects of TNCs on capital imports and exports strengthen the point of the decapitalization hypothesis (Ochel 1982; Bornschier 1976, 1980; Committee on Finance 1973; Biersteker 1978; Lall and Streeten 1977). The relationship between foreign direct investment and foreign borrowing has been analysed, too (Rothgeb 1984; Pfister and Suter 1986; Bornschier 1982*a*). These studies suggest that capital penetration by TNCs adds to the increase in foreign debt of host countries (which may differ according to regions, as Rothgeb suggests). Such a relationship is indirectly supported by findings in an analysis by Schneider and Frey (1985), who identify the extent of bilateral and multilateral aid as important determinants of TNC investment.

The catalogue of questions relating to the influence of TNCs on growth could easily be extended, but we prefer to turn attention to some of the 'social effects' which are, however, related to growth problems, and, at the same time establish a link to the next section (TNCs and labour). Income inequality and development have received considerable attention (see Gagliani 1987, for a recent review). Numerous studies have analysed the effect of TNCs on income distribution.

A review of fifteen studies on the question of the effect of TNCs on income inequality reveals that all except one report a positive relationship between TNC penetration and income inequality (see Bornschier and Chase-Dunn 1985). A reanalysis by Bornschier and Chase-Dunn

(1985) confirms these earlier findings in a sample of seventy-two countries. But while TNCs are associated with higher income inequality in LDCs, the opposite holds for core countries. Moreover, sectoral differences again seem to be important to the relationship in LDCs. TNC penetration of the manufacturing sector is significantly related to higher overall income inequality in LDCs, while no such relationship exist for the penetration of agriculture (see also Sullivan 1983). The findings for TNCs and income distribution do not permit causal conclusions since sufficient cases for cross-national time series analyses on distribution data are lacking. One has to note also that in some theoretical approaches income inequality may be both a consequence and a precondition for TNC investment in LDCs. Other aspects of social structure have also been studied. TNCs were found to have an influence on overurbanization (Timberlake and Kentor 1983). This may be related to the fact that TNCs operate in core areas of host countries (Blackburn 1982). The unbalanced growth this implies is connected with a growing marginalization of broad segments of the population (Evans and Timberlake 1980; Michel 1983). Effects on gender inequality have been found in empirical studies, too (Michel 1983; Froebel *et al.* 1981).

In theoretical contributions, distorting effects of TNCs on traditional cultural are often mentioned. The problems extend from imported, inappropriate consumption patterns—often mediated by the international advertising industry—to influence by the international media business (Mattelart 1983; Reiffers *et al.* 1982). Systematic empirical studies that address such problems are still lacking.

TNCs and labour. It is often argued that one of the most important incentives to invest abroad is labour cost differences between countries. This may hold true in the case of assembly production and related labour-intensive manufacturing activities, but not necessarily in more capital-intensive sectors. The observation that TNCs on average seem to pay somewhat higher wages than domestic firms applies for LDCs as well as for industrialized countries (Dunning 1981: 272–303). This finding can largely be attributed to the fact that TNCs generally operate in modern industrial sectors. Yet high wages in the leading sector do not imply more social equality in the society as a whole. Higher wages paid by TNCs may strengthen the segmentation of the labour market, and a mere comparison of wages neglects the question of total employment. Actually, the already mentioned figure of 25 million people employed by the largest 350 TNCs worldwide seems quite modest when compared to their contribution to world production. According to estimates of the ILO (1981*a*, 1981*b*) about 45 million people work for TNCs, of whom only about 10 per cent are employed in LDCs,[30] mainly in the semi-periphery. Although employment by TNCs has increased two and a half times between 1960 and 1977 (ILO 1981*a*), a complete evaluation of their labour market effects must also take into account indirect effects which can arise from linkage and displacement processes (see p. 347). In an overview of existing studies the ILO (1976) is unable to suggest a conclusive answer to the employment effects, although positive effects may exist in some sectors (for example in the food industry). Similar conclusions are drawn by Meller and Mizala (1982) for South America and by Enderwick (1985), who reviews different studies. Positive employment effects, however, may be outweighed by distortions of the traditional labour market structure. Evans and Timberlake (1980), for example, suggest that according to their findings the negative effect of TNCs on equality is mediated by a disproportionate growth of the tertiary sector. Sullivan (1983) points to the negative consequences of sectoral income differences and Bornschier and Ballmer-Cao (1979) mention structural unemployment.

While these questions address LDCs, some research has been inspired by the so-called job export debate in core countries. The central issue here is whether the shift of production to other countries lowers domestic employment or, indeed, increases it by indirect feedback effects. Such studies are necessarily tied to various (sometimes rather problematic) assumptions. It is thus not astonishing that the evidence is mixed. In his sophisticated analysis of West Germany covering the period 1975–80, Olle (1983) estimates a net loss of 300,000–400,000 jobs caused by TNCs investing abroad, while estimates for the US reach from a gain of 279,000 to a loss of 660,000 jobs (ILO 1976).

In connection with problems of the labour market, the bargaining position of labour unions deserves attention. Unions normally take a rather critical stance towards TNCs because they have no adequate organizational structure to cope with transnational business. Lately, however, one has observed a certain internationalization of the labour movement (Baumer and von Gleich 1982) together with an intensification of the dialogue between unions and TNCs in industrialized countries (De Vos 1981). But in some instances TNCs are still able to pursue explicit policies against labour unions (Hood and Young 1983).[31]

TNCs and the nation-state. Researchers usually assume a conflictual relationship between TNCs and the nation-state which arises from the contradictions of national (development) policies and global profit-maximizing strategies pursued by TNCs (see for example Vernon 1973; Barnet and Müller 1974). A more thorough analysis of power structures, however, reveals possible alliances between TNCs, official and local élites (Evans 1979). Thus a state's actions may be limited by the selfish interests of its own élites. Yet, this perspective does not contradict the observation that conflicts and hard bargaining between TNCs and state officials are relatively frequent because alliances of actors and the distribution of the gains between them are different things. Furthermore, alliances of the state and local capital against TNCs may also be possible (Evans 1986).[32] Alliances between TNCs and local élites tend to favour the political exclusion of the masses. In cross-national studies there seems to be a positive empirical relationship between the dependence on TNCs and political exclusion (Timberlake and Williams 1984), and social conflicts and political instability are higher when TNCs have a stronghold in a society (Ballmer-Cao 1979).[33] Although political instability may be the consequence of a social setting to which TNCs contributed, it represents at the same time an important factor in the relocation decision of TNCs. In cross-national research one has observed that fresh foreign direct investment is negatively affected by political instability (Schneider and Frey 1985), while contrary to common expectations the ideology of governments does not play an important role in the worldwide process of allocation TNC investment (Schneider and Frey 1985).

The last few years have witnessed an improvement in the bargaining position of states *vis-à-vis* TNCs, which is reflected in more stringent codes of conduct regulations and tougher contractual terms as well as in the numerous nationalizations that have occurred (UN 1978, 1983). Nevertheless, we have concluded from corss-national research over the 1960–76 time span that restrictive government policies against TNCs have often been contradictory (stop-and-go interventionism) and thus government measures in LDCs in general have not been very successful; indeed, the immediate impact of restrictive policies has been disadvantageous to overall growth (Bornschier and Hoby 1981; Berweger and Hoby 1980; Bornschier 1982b). Although 'sovereignty at bay' (Vernon 1971) has not become a reality, the ability of TNCs to shift their activities from one country to another still imposes severe restrictions on the policy alternatives of LCDs. The actual policy mix in LDCs may thus be contradictory.

TNCs as organizations and the control within TNCs. We have already mentioned important organizational changes that are suggested as necessary preconditions for the growth and the internationalization of firms. The literature has pointed to the emerging separation of ownership and control in large corporations since the 1920s (Berle and Means 1967; Useem 1980). Hence the problem of control in TNCs has at least two dimensions: first, one must ask who owns the shares of TNCs, and second, who actually decides on their business activities. Research in this field rarely considers TNCs explicitly; rather, it is concerned with large business firms. But, as we have seen, the correlation between size and transnationalization is very strong (Bornschier 1976; Dunning and Pearce 1981).

It has often been argued that, with the increasing dispersion of the ownership of corporate shares, top management has gained control over large firms at the expense of the classical family entrepreneur. In this line of reasoning, the separation of ownership and control has been accompanied by a transition from short-run profit maximization goals to long-run growth strategies. Recently the hypothesis of managerial control has been subject to criticism on various grounds. First, the question has been raised whether managers really act differently from family entrepreneurs who have certainly no less interest in securing the long-run existence of the firm. Furthermore, it has been possible to show that managers themselves obtain a growing proportion of their income in the form of company shares and dividends. Thus, they also earn elements of classical entrepreneurial income (Useem 1980; Allen 1981).[34]

Other challenges to the separation thesis (family versus managerial capitalism) stress the concept of financial capitalism.[35] Financial control exercised through the shareholdings of financial institutions (mainly large banks) is likely to limit the sovereign decision-making capability of managers similarly to the way in which big private shareholders are supposed to. In their analysis of the 224 largest British firms, Nyman and Silberston (1978) found only a very small proportion of firms that could not be labelled as owner controlled, that is, controlled by families, by other firms or by financial institutions. The importance of financial capitalism has also been stressed by other authors. In his research Mizruchi (1982) furthermore found a cyclical pattern of shifts between managerial and financial control in the United States since the turn of the century that was influenced by political conditions.[36] With regard to control patterns, the work of Grou (1983) points to national differences. While American, British and, to a smaller extent, German firms are able to finance themselves on their own, Japanese firms are directly linked to big financial conglomerates. Contrary to this, many large Swiss firms are still under direct family control.

Apart from formal capital participation which is obvious in interlocking directorates (Fennema 1982; Ornstein 1984; Stokman *et al.* 1985) informal and personally based networks have also been identified in the research. This has been termed a 'corporate élite'. It is constituted by family ties, and by membership of business associations and exclusive social clubs, and it exhibits features of a new capitalist class (Useem 1980). Recently research has gone a step further, also studying articulations between this corporate and the political élite (Useem 1984). This brings research back to the already mentioned question of the relationship of state, local and transnational capital.

Concluding remarks

Having reviewed the research on TNCs over the last decades we would like to add some general observations which may also point to future areas of research not satisfactorily dealt with in the past.

The perspective opened by Stephen Hymer left unanswered an important question in his research as well as in that of his colleagues and followers. Some corporations command monopolistic advantages, but why should they not exploit them simply by exporting from one country to another? One conventional answer is to stress labour cost differentials. Yet this is limited, at least in general. Low labour costs do not necessarily imply low costs of labour per unit of production. John H. Dunning goes further in his integration of location theory into the eclectic approach, although not far enough. What we suggest as a future area of research is to look at the spread of TNCs as a joint result of two sets of monopolistic strategies: one pursued by corporations and the other by states. The interface of these two strategies seems to be the most fertile ground for the spread of TNCs.

Unfortunately there are several arguments against monopolistic practices, even among liberal economists. Thus the interaction of *two* monopolistic practices may be particularly unfavourable since they involve the risk of accumulating the disadvantages of both types of monopoly. Thus the claim of TNCs to bring progress to the world and the claim of the nation-state to be the natural and legitimate organizer of society—although they may have some truth—are frustrated by the very existence of this modern marriage.

Yet the problems involved may be especially pertinent to LDCs, where the rent-seeking character of the state seems to have produced problems of development that interact with the TNC as organizer of world production.

Obviously TNCs did not prevent economic development at the periphery. Having extended the layer of the semiperiphery, they may be considered to have introduced a more continuous ladder of levels of development. But, overall, development gaps in the post-Second World War world system have remained relatively stable.

For world development as a whole, however, and especially for Western core societies, TNCs may be looked at as a progressive force in the emergence and evolution of the capitalist state, a complementary institution to accumulation on a world scale. Thus, Raymond Vernon's vision of 'Sovereignty at Bay' may appear to be mistaken. In a sense, TNCs have made states stronger as supporters of capital accumulation. Whether TNCs have made states stronger at the periphery remains unclear, but there the subordination of states to the capitalist logic of accumulation remains more problematic.

If one looks at the world system in terms of a conflictual merger of two logics—the states' and corporations'—the role of TNCs in the rise and decline of countries as well as industries needs further study. Thus more studies over longer period of time seem necessary, also in order to put current big business into perspective. TNCs after all are mortal, even if John K. Galbraith argued the contrary. In the long run, the once prospering steel giants, for example, have become weak and almost dying bodies that yearn for public subsidies.

While problems of overcoming underdevelopment have received much attention in the literature on TNCs, looking at world development and at core countries remains a vast field for future research.

Notes

1. There are other, more specific definitions of TNCs as well, which will not be discussed here. For an overview see for example Dunning (1981) or Lall and Streeten (1977).
2. One of the most widely known writers who stress this structure of the 'world system' is Immanuel Wallerstein (1984 and various of his other writings).
3. The term *direct* investment refers to the direct control associated with the ownership of income-generating assets, i.e. it involves direct control of the entrepreneurial decision-making process. Foreign direct investment is then the term to characterize cross-national acquisition of income-generating assets by TNCs.
4. The doctoral thesis (on microfilm) was, despite its theoretical impact, not published until 1976. Charles Kindleberger, who supervised the thesis, was the popularizer of Hymer's ideas.

5. The concept of 'unequal exchange' has been elaborated in depth by A. Emmanuel (1972).

6. For this classification see Evans (1981) and Bornschier and Chase-Dunn (1985: 4).

7. This leads to the creation of a redistributive economy on a world scale.

8. The most prominent author in the world systems approach is certainly Immanuel Wallerstein (1974, 1979, 1980), but others such as Charles-Albert Michalet (1976) or Samir Amin *et al.* (1982) have also made important contributions to this kind of analysis.

9. One exception is the world system perspective, which suggests a further structural differentiation, the stratification inside the code which, however, fluctuates between periods of hegemony and periods of a more equal distribution of power among core states. Yet a lot of work in this theoretical tradition is still concerned with the periphery or with core-periphery relations.

10. See for example Rugman (1981), who especially stresses the financial diversification of firms and Caves (1982) who offers a good overview of the transaction-cost approach, which states that market functions are increasingly internalized as the new organizations turn out to be more efficient and less costly in transactions.

11. For a more detailed overview of economic theories see for example Buckley and Casson (1985), Dunning (1974), and Black and Dunning (1982).

12. The combination of the first letters of those three concepts leads to another term for the eclectic theory: OLI paradigm.

13. In addition, Cotteret *et al.* (1984), for example, show a significant improvement in public opinion towards TNCs between 1976 and 1982 in France.

14. This process can be described as the implementation of the multidivisional firm structure at the international level.

15. The earliest 'real affiliate' in manufacturing seems to be the Prussian daughter of the Belgian firm Cockerill, which was established in 1815 (Franko 1976: 3). The first affiliate of an American firm was the—unsuccessful—London affiliate (1882) of Colt (Wilkins, 1970: 30). It must be pointed out that—following the information on France given by Kindleberger (1984a: 118–45)—enterprises engaged in the services sector originally took a certain lead in transnationalization, which later turned into a lag. Only recently has the service sector again become very prominent in TNC business.

16. See also Fligstein (1985) for recent findings on the reasons for implementation of the multidivisional structure.

17. The geographical distribution of this amount was concentrated in the closely neighbouring countries of Canada, Mexico and the Caribbean and the Central American area (in total about $1.6 billion), but also Latin America ($323 million), Europe ($573 million) and Asia ($120 million) had substantial shares. Looked at by industrial sectors, raw materials (mining, agriculture and oil) were by far most important ($1.5 billion). The rising oil industry was especially important, with a stock of $343 million.

18. For Great Britain Svedberg (1978) estimates the share of direct investments in the stock of total foreign investments before the First World War at 53 per cent.

19. The importance of European TNCs is illustrated furthermore by a comparison of the number of affiliates in manufacturing: up to the First World War American TNCs had founded 122 affiliates, continental European TNCs 167 and British TNCs 60 (Franko 1976: 10).

20. See also the contributions in Chandler and Daems (1980), in which the common organizational features of American and German firms are stressed.

21. *Informationen über Multinationale Konzerne* (periodical appearing in Austria), various issues.

22. The share of West Germany in the flows of direct investments has increased from 7.2 per cent (1961–7) to 17 per cent (1974–9). The figures for Japan look quite similar: they increased from 2.4 per cent to 13 per cent during the same period (OECD 1981: 11 ff.).

23. UN data (1983: 19, 31) estimate the share of TNCs from LDCs as about 2 per cent of total direct investment flows. Dunning (1983) calculates their share in the stock of direct investments in 1978 as 3.8 per cent.

24. If one takes the stock of investment of TNCs in their home countries into account—a figure normally not included in TNC-statistics—the share of LDCs in total TNC-controlled capital is reduced and corresponds to the LDC share in world production.

25. Bornschier and Chase-Dunn (1985) review and reanalyse 28 studies that appeared between 1972 and 1983.

26. Especially important seems to be the distinction between stock and flow measures as well as regional differences. The latter, however, turn out to be affected by different weights of very poor countries in regional samples.

27. This reanalysis includes, apart from an indicator for TNC-penetration, measures of the per capita income, the domestic investment rate, exports and internal market size.

28. Biersteker (1978) distinguishes four possible ways of displacement: (1) displacement of small, artisan firms; (2) displacement of manufacturing firms by TNCs which produce similar goods; (3) change (shrinking) of market shares by indigenous firms; and (4) anticipated displacement in the sense that barriers to entry are raised by TNCs.

29. On the special role of the pharmaceutical industry see Helleiner (1981), Gereffi (1978, 1983), and Kirim (1986).

30. Again there are important differences between industrial sectors: the employment effects of TNCs in the mining sector are generally very limited, but in manufacturing they can be significant, depending on the technology applied.

31. In their analysis of the United Kingdom, Hood and Young (1983) find this behaviour especially relevant for American TNCs.

32. See also the vast literature on the protection of indigenous industries against foreign competitors (Krueger and Tuncer 1982; Lall 1978).

33. In addition Bollen (1983) demonstrates a negative relationship between economic dependence and political democracy.
34. The article by Useem (1980) represents one of the best overviews of the state of the art in this field of research.
35. This concept dates back to Marxist theorists (like Hilferding) and has recently experienced a renaissance.
36. He demonstrates a drastic increase in managerial control at the beginning of the century, following the implementation of very stringent antitrust laws. The share of managerial control, however, has dropped since.

References

ALLEN, M. P. (1981), 'Power and privilege in the large corporation: corporate control and managerial compensation', *American Journal of Sociology* 86: 1112–23.

AMIN, S. (1974), *Accumulation on a World Scale: A Critique of the Theory of Underdevelopment*. New York: Monthly Review Press.

AMIN, S., G. ARRIGHI, A. GUNDER FRANK, and I. WALLERSTEIN (1982), *Dynamics of Global Crisis*. New York: Monthly Review Press.

BAIN, J. S. (1956), *Barriers to New Competition*. Cambridge, Mass.: Harvard University press.

BALLMER-CAO, T.-H. (1979), 'Système politique, repartition des revenues et pénétration des enterprises multinationales', pp. 153–79 in *Annuaire suisse de science politique*.

BARNET, R., and R. MÜLLER (1974), *Global Reach: the Power of Multinational Corporations*. New York: Simon and Schuster.

BAUMER, J.-M., and A. VON GLEICH (1982), *Transnational Corporations in Latin America*. Dissenhofen: Rueggger.

BERGESEN, A., and C. SAHOO (1985), 'Evidence of the decline of American hegemony in world production', *Review* 8 (Spring): 595–611.

BERLE, A. A., and G. C. MEANS (1967), *The Modern Corporation and Private Property* revised edition. New York: Macmillan.

BERTHOLD, N. (1980), *Multinationale Unternehmen und nationale Währungspolitik*. Freiburg im Breisgau: Haufe.

BERWEGER, G., and J.-P. HOBY (1980), 'Nationale Wirtschaftspolitik und multinationale Konzerne', pp. 263–302 in V. Bornschier (ed.), *Multinationale Konzerne, Wirtschaftspolitik und nationale Entwicklung*. Frankfurt: Campus.

BIERSTEKER, T. J. (1978), *Distortion or Development?* Cambridge, Mass.: MIT Press.

BLACK, J., and J. H. DUNNING (eds.) (1982), *International Capital Movements*. London: Macmillan.

BLACKBURN (1982), 'The impact of multinational corporations on the spacial organization of developed nations: a review', pp. 147–57 in M. Taylor and N. Thrift (eds.), *The Geography of Multinationals*. London: Croom Helm.

BLOMSTRÖM, M. (1986), 'Multinationals and market structure in Mexico', *World Development* 14(4): 523–30.

BOLLEN, K. (1983), 'World system position, dependency and democracy: the cross-national evidence', *American Sociological Review* 48(4): 468–79.

BORNSCHIER, V. (1976), *Wachstum, Konzentration und Multinationalisierung von Industgrieunternehmen*. Frauenfeld/Stuttgart: Huber.

—— (1980), 'Multinational corporations and economic growth: a test of the decapitalization hypothesis', *Journal of Development Economics* 7 (June): 191–210.

—— (1982*a*), 'The world economy in the world-system: structure, dependence and change', *International Social Science Journal* 34 (1): 38–59.

—— (1982*b*), 'World economic integration and policy responses: some developmental impacts', in H. Makler, A. Martinelli and N. Smelser (eds.), *The New International Economy*. Newbury Park, CA:SAGE publications.

—— (1985), 'World social structure in the long economic wave'. Paper presented at the Annual International Studies Association meeting, 5–9 March, Washington DC.

—— and T.-H. BALLMER-CAO (1979), 'Income inequality: a cross-national study of the relationships between MNC penetration, dimensions of power structure and income distribution', *American Sociological Review* 44 (3): 487–506.

—— and C. CHASE-DUNN (1985), *Transnational Corporations and Underdevelopment*. New York: Praeger.

—— and J.-P. HOBY (1981), 'Economic policy and multinational corporations in development: the measurable impact in cross-national perspective', *Social Problems* 28 (4): 363–77.

BUCKLEY, P. I., and M. CASSON (1976), *The Future of Multinational Enterprise*. London: Macmillan.

—— and J. H. DUNNING (1980), 'The industrial structure of US direct investment in the United Kingdom', *Journal of International Business Studies*, 5–13.

CARDOSO, F. H. (1973), 'Associated dependent development: theoretical and practical implications', in S. Alfred (ed.), *Authoritarian Brazil: Origins, Policies and Future*. New Haven, Conn.: Yale University Press.

CAVES, R. E. (1971), 'International corporations: the industrial economics of foreign investment', *Economica* 38: 1–2.

—— (1974), 'Multinational firms, competition and productivity in host-country markets', *Economica* 41: 176–93.

—— (1982), *Multinational Enterprise and Economic Analysis*. Cambridge: Cambridge University Press.

CHANDLER, Jr., A. D. (1969), *Strategy and Structure: Chapters in the History of the American Enterprise*. Cambridge, Mass.: MIT Press.

—— (1977), *The Visible Hand: the Managerial Revolution in American Business*. Cambridge/London: The Belknap Press of Harvard University Press.

—— (1980), 'The growth of the transnational industrial firm in the United States and the United Kingdom: a comparative analysis', *The Economic History Review* 33: 396–410.

—— and H. DAEMS (eds.) (1980), *Managerial Hierarchies: Comparative Perspectives on the Rise of the Modern Industrial Enterprise.* Cambridge/London: Harvard University Press.

CHOUDHURI, K. N. (1978), *The Trading World of Asia and the English East India Company 1660–1760.* Cambridge: Cambridge University Press.

Committee on Finance (1973) *US Senate: Implications of Multinational Firms for World Trade and Investment and for US Trade and Labor.* Washington, DC: US Government Printing Office.

COTTERET, J.-M., G. AYACHE, and J. DUX (1984), *L'image des multinationales en France dans la presse et l'opinion publique.* Geneva/Paris: Institut de recherche et d'information sur les multinationales.

CURTIN, P. D. (1984), *Cross-cultural Trade in World History.* Cambridge: Cambridge University Press.

DE VOS, T. (1981), *U.S. Multinationals and Worker Participation in Management: the American experience in the European community.* London: Aldwych Press.

DOS SANTOS, T. (1970), 'The structure of dependence', *American Economic Review* (Papers and Proceedings) 60: 231–6.

DUNNING, J. H. (1958), *American Investment in British Manufacturing Industry.* London: George Allen and Unwin.

—— (ed.) (1974), *Economic Analysis and the Multinational enterprise.* London: George Allen and Unwin.

—— (1981), *International Production and the Multinational Enterprise.* London: George Allen and Unwin.

—— (1983), 'Changes in the level and structure of international production: the last one hundred years', pp. 84–139 in M. Casson (ed.), *The Growth of International Business.* London: Allen and Unwin.

—— and PEARCE, R. D. (1981), *The World's Largest Industrial Enterprises.* New York: St Martin's Press.

DUVALL, R., S. JACKSON, B. M. RUSSETT, D. SNIDAL, and D. SYLVAN (1981), 'A formal model of "dependencia theory": structure and measurement', pp. 312–50 in R. L. Merritt and B. Russett (eds.), *From National Development to Global Community.* London: George Allen and Unwin.

EDELSTEIN, M. (1982), *Overseas Investment in the Age of High Imperialism.* London: Methuen.

EMMANUEL, A. (1972), *Unequal Exchange: a Study of the Imperialism of Trade.* New York: Monthly Review Press.

ENDERWICK, P. (1985), *Multinational Business and Labor.* New York: St Martin's Pres.

EVANS, P. B. (1977), 'Direct investment and industrial concentration', *Journal of Development Studies* 13: 373–86.

—— (1979), *Dependent Development. The Alliance of Multinational, State and Local Capital in Brazil.* Princeton, NJ: Princeton University Press.

Evans, P. B. (1981), 'Recent research on multinational corporations', *Annual Review of Sociology* 7: 199–223.

—— (1986), 'State, capital and the transformation of dependence: the Brazilian computer case', *World Development* 14(7): 791–808.

—— and M. Timberlake (1980), 'Dependence, inequality and the growth of the tertiary: a comparative analysis of less developed countries', *American Sociological Review* 45: 531–52.

Finnema, M. (1982), *International Networks of Banks and Industry*. The Hague: Martinus Nijhoff.

Fishwick, F. (1982), *Multinational Companies and Economic Concentration in Europe*. Aldershot: Gower.

Fligstein, N. (1985), 'The spread of the multidivisional form among large firms 1919–1979', *American Sociological Review* 50(3): 377–91.

Frank, A. G. (1969), *Latin America: Underdevelopment or Revolution?* New York: Monthly Review Press.

Franko, L. G. (1976), *The European Multinationals: A Renewed Challenge to American and British Big Business*. London: Harper and Row.

Froebel, F., J. Heinrichs, and O. Kreye (1981), *The New International Division of Labour: Structural Unemployment in Industrialized Countries and Industrialization in Developing Countries*. Cambridge: Cambridge University Press.

Gagliani, G. (1987), 'Income distribution and economic development', *Annual Review of Sociology* 13: 313–34.

Gereffi, G. (1978), 'Drug firms and dependency in Mexico: the case of the steroid hormone industry', *International Organization* 32: 237–86.

—— (1983), *The Pharmaceutical Industry and Dependency in the Third World*. Princeton, NJ: Princeton University Press.

Gilpin, R. (1976), *US Power and the Multinational Corporation—the Political Economy of Foreign Direct Investment*. London: Macmillan.

Grou, P. (1983), *La structure financière du capitalisme multinational*. Paris: Presses de la fondation nationale des sciences politiques.

Grunwald, J. and K. Flamm (1985), *The Global Factory*. Washington DC: The Brookings Institution.

Hammer, H.-J., and J. W. Gartrell (1986), 'American penetration and Canadian development: a case study of mature dependency', *American Sociological Review* 51 (2): 201–13.

Helleiner, G. K. (1973), 'Manufactured exports from less-developed countries and multinational firms', *The Economic Journal* 83: 21–47.

—— (1975), 'Transnational enterprises in the manufacturing sector of the less-developed countries', *World Development* 3 (9): 641–50.

—— (1981), *Intra-firm Trade and the Developing Countries*. London: Macmillan.

Hennart, J.-F. (1982), *A Theory of Multinational Enterprise*, Ann Arbor: University of Michigan Press.

HOOD, N., and S. YOUNG (1983), *Multinational Investment Strategies in the British Isles*. London: Her Majesty's Stationery Office.

HYMER, S. (1979), *The Multinational Corporation: a Radical Approach. Papers by Stephen Herbert Hymer*. Cambridge: Cambridge University Press.

ILO (International Labour Office) (1976), *The Impact of Multinational Enterprises on Employment and Training*. Geneva: ILO.

ILO (1981*a*), *Employment Effects of Multinational Enterprises in Development Countries*. Geneva: ILO.

ILO (1981*b*), *Employment Effects of Multinational Enterprises in Industrialised Countries*. Geneva: ILO.

JONES, G. (1984), 'The growth and performance of British multinational firms before 1939: the case of Dunlop', *The Economic History Review* 37: 35–53.

KINDLEBERGER, C. P. (1984*a*), *Multinational Excursions*. Cambridge, MA: MIT Press.

KINDLEBERGER, C. P. (1984*b*), *A Financial History of Western Europe*. London: George Allen and Unwin.

KIRIM, A. S. (1986), 'Transnational corporations and local capital: comparative conduct and performance in the Turkish pharmaceutical industry', *World Development* 14 (4): 503–21.

KNICKERBOCKER, F. T. (1973), *Oligopolistic Reaction and the Multinational Enterprise*. Cambridge, Mass.: Harvard University Press.

KRASNER, S. D. (ed.) (1983), *International Regimes*. Ithaca/London: Cornell University Press.

KRUEGER, A. O. and B. TUNCER (1982), 'An empirical test of the infant industry argument', *The American Economic Review* 72 (5): 1142–52.

LALL, S. (1978), 'Transnationals, domestic enterprises and industrial structure in hot LCDs: a survey', *Oxford Economic Papers* 30(2): 217–48.

—— (ed.) (1983), *The New Multinationals: The Spread of Third World Enterprises*. Chichester: Wiley.

—— and P. STREETEN (1977), *Foreign Investment, Transnationals and Developing Countries*. Boulder, Col.: Westview Press.

LANE, F. C. (1979), *Profits from Power: Readings in protection Rent and Violence-controlling Enterprises*. Albany: State University of New York Press.

LIM, L. Y. C., and PANG ENG FONG (1982), 'Vertical linkages and multinational enterprises in developing countries', *World Development* 10(7): 585–95.

MATTELART, A. (1983), *Transnationals and the Third World: The Struggle for Culture*. South Hadley, MA: Bergin & Garvey.

MELLER, P., and A. MIZALA (1982), 'US multinationals and Latin American manufacturing employment absorption', *World Development* 10(2): 115–26.

MEYER-FEHR, P. (1980), 'Technologische Kontrolle durch multinationale Konzerne und Wirtschaftswachstum, pp. 106–28 in V. Bornschier (ed.), *Multinationale Konzerne, Wirtschaftspolitik und nationale Entwicklung im Weltsystem*. Frankfurt: Campus.

362 *Volker Bornschier and Hanspeter Stamm*

MICHALET, C.-A. (1976), *Le capitalisme mondial*. Paris: Presses Universitaires de France.

MICHEL, A. (1983), 'Multinationales et inégalités de classe et de sèxe', *Current Sociology* 31 (1): 1–211.

MIZRUCHI, M. S. (1982), *The American Corporate Network 1904–1974*. Newbury Park, SA: SAGE Publications.

MORAN, T. H. (1978), 'Multinational corporations and dependency: a dialogue for dependentistas and non-dependentistas', *International Organization* (Special issue on 'Dependence and dependency in the global system') 32: 79–100.

MÜLLER, R., and R. D. MORGENSTERN (1974), 'Multinational corporations and balance of payment impacts in LDCs: an econometric analysis of export pricing behaviour', *Kyklos* 27: 304–12.

NEWFARMER, R. S. (ed.) (1985), *Profits, Progress and Poverty*. Notre Dame, IN: University of Notre Dame Press.

—— and MARSH (1981), 'Foreign ownership, market structure and industrial performance: Brazil's electrical industry', *Journal of Development Economics* 8: 47–75.

—— and S. TOPIK (1982), 'Testing dependency theory: a case study of Brazil's electrical industry', in M. Taylor and N. Thrift (eds.), *The Geography of Multinationals*. London: Croom Helm.

NICHOLAS, S. J. (1982), 'British multinational investment before 1939', *The Journal of European Economic History* 11(3): 605–30.

—— (1983), 'Agency contracts, institutional modes and the transition to foreign direct investment by British multinationals before 1939', *Journal of Economic History* 143(3): 675–86.

NIEDERMAYER, O. (1979), *Multinationale Konzerne und Entwicklungsländer*. Königstein: Hain.

NYMAN, S., and A. SILBERSTON (1978), 'The ownership and control of industry', *Oxford Economic Papers* 30: 74–101.

OCHEL, W. (1982), *Die Entwicklungsländer in der Weltwirtschaft*. Cologne: Bund Verlag.

OECD (1981), *International Investment and Multinational Enterprises: Recent International Direct Investment Trends*. Paris: OECD.

OLLE, W. (1983), *Strukturveränderung der internationalen Direktinvestitionen und inländischer Arbeitsmarkt*. Munich: Minerva.

ORNSTEIN, M. (1984), 'Interlocking directorates in Canada: intercorporate or class alliance', *Administrative Science Quarterly* 29: 210–31.

PFISTER, U., and C. SUTER (1986), 'Verschuldung im Weltsystem: eine systemtheoretische Analyse der internationalen Finanzbeziehungen, Schlussbericht zum Nationalfondsprojekt" Zu Struktur und Wandel des Weltsystems seit 1960'. Zurich: Sociological Institute (mimeo).

REIFFERS, J.-L., A. CARTAPANIS, W. EXPERTON, and J.-L. FUGUET (1982), *Transnational Corporations and Endogenous Development: Effects on Culture, Communication, Education and Science and Technology*. Paris: Unesco.

REUBER, G. L. (1973), *Private Foreign Investment in Development*. Oxford: Clarendon Press.

ROTHGEB Jr., J. M. (1984), 'Investment penetration in manufacturing and extraction and external public debt in the third world states', *World Development* 12 (11/12): 1063–76.

RUGMAN, A. M. (1981), *Inside the Multinationals*. London: Croom Helm.

SCHLUPP, F. (1985), 'Geschichte, Stand und Tendenzen der Diskussion über Multinational Konzerne', pp. A1–A18 in P. H. Mettler (ed.), *Multinationale Konzerne in der Bundesrepublik Deutschland*. Frankfurt am Maine: Haag & Herchen.

SCHNEIDER, F., and B. S. FREY (1985), 'Economic and political determinants of foreign direct investment', *World Development* 13(2): 161–75.

SCHUMPETER, J. (1939), *Business Cycles: A Theoretical, Historical and Statistical Analysis of the Capitalist Process*. New York: McGraw-Hill.

SENGHAAS, D., and U. MENZEL (eds.) (1976), *Multinationale Konzerne und Dritte Welt*. Opladen: Westdeutsche Verlag.

STOKMAN, F. N., R. ZIEGLER, and J. SCOTT (eds.) (1985), *Networks of Corporate Power: A Comparative Analysis of Ten Countries*. Cambridge: Polity Press.

SULLIVAN, G. (1983), 'Uneven development and national income inequality in third world countries: a cross-national study of the effects of external economic dependence', *Sociological Perspectives* 26 (2): 201–31.

SVEDBERG, P. (1978), 'The portfolio: direct composition of private foreign investment in 1914 revisited', *Economic Journal* 88: 763–77.

TIMBERLAKE, M. and J. KENTOR (1983), 'Economic dependence, overurbanization and economic growth: a study of less developed countries', *Sociological Quarterly* 24 (4): 489–508.

TIMBERLAKE, M., and K. R. WILLIAMS (1984), 'Dependence, political exclusion and government repression: some cross-national evidence', *American Sociological Review* 9 (1): 141–6.

United `nations (1978), *Transnational Corporations in Development: a Re-examination*. New York: UNCTNC.

—— (1983), *Transnational Corporations in World Development, 3rd Survey*. New York: UNCTNC.

USEEM, M. (1980), 'Corporations and the corporate elite', *Annual Review of Sociology* 6: 41–77.

—— (1984), *The Inner Circle: Large Corporations and the Rise of Business Political Activity in the U.S. and the United Kingdom*. New York: Oxford University Press.

VERNON, R. (1971), *Sovereignty at Bay: The Multinational Spread of U.S. Enterprises*. New York/ London: Basic Books.

—— (1973), *The Economic and Political Consequences of Multinational Enterprise* second edition. Boston, Mass.: Graduate School of Business Administration, Harvard University.

—— (1979), 'The product cycle hypothesis in a new international environment', *Oxford Bulletin of Economics and Statistics* 41 (4): 255–67.

VERNON, R. (1985), *Exploring the Global Economy*. Lanham, Md.: University Press of America.

WALLERSTEIN, I. (1974) (1980), *The Modern World-system* volumes i. and ii. New York: Academic Press.

—— (1979), *The Capitalist World Economy*. Cambridge: Cambridge University Press.

—— (1980), *The Modern World Systems II: Mercantilism and the Consolidation of the European World Economy 1600–1750*. New York: Academic Press.

—— (1984), *The Politics of the World Economy: The States, the Movements and the Civilizations*. Cambridge: Cambridge University Press.

WELLS, L. T., Jr. (1983), *Third World Multinationals: The Rise of Foreign Investment from Developing Countries*. Cambridge, Mass.: MIT Press.

WILKINS, M. (1970), *The Emergence of Multinational Enterprise: American Business Abroad from the Colonial Era to 1914*. Cambridge, Mass.: Harvard University Press.

—— (1974), *The Maturing of Multinational Enterprise: American Business Abroad from 1914 to 1970*. Cambridge, Mass.: Harvard University Press.

WILLIAMS, O. E. (1981), 'The modern corporation: origins, evolution, attributes', *Journal of Economic Literature* 19 (December): 1537–68.

Competition among Jurisdictions in Formulating Corporate Law Rules: An American Perspective on the 'Race to the Bottom' in the European Communities

DAVID CHARNY

I. Introduction

The ongoing formation of a single European market in 1992 has raised again the difficult issue of the 'race to the bottom'—more elegantly termed the problem of the 'lowest common denominator', or more fearsomely, the prospect of 'regulatory meltdown'.[1] Simply put, the concern is that the increasing ease of corporate activity across the boundaries of EC Member States will enable corporations to incorporate in the state with the laxest set of corporate rules. The paradigmatic case is taken to be the US state of Delaware, haven for corporations due to its lax corporate laws. European lawyers referred particularly to the American experience when they embarked upon the project of harmonization. As Clive Schmitthoff wrote in 1973:

[U]nless the national company laws in the Community are identical in all essential aspects, a movement of companies to the state with the laxest company law will take place in the Community. If it may be said without giving offense to our friends in the U.S.A., the Community cannot tolerate the establishment of a Delaware in its territory.[2]

More recently, Professor Walter Kolvenbach, former President of the European Company Lawyers Association, observed:[3]

[T]he . . . goal [of] harmonization of the company laws of the Member States . . . presents continuing difficulties. Citizens of a Member State (including business associations formed under its laws) are generally able to extend their business

Professor of Law, Harvard Law School.

into the territory of any other Member States. A 'market' thereby arises for company laws[,] which offers the business the greatest degree of latitude. On the other hand, 'Company law Delawares' were to be avoided.[4]

Nonetheless, from the perspective of American corporate theory—the methodological perspective that will provide the basis for my analysis—the European[5] effort to harmonize corporate laws seems at first to be a process in search of a justification.[6] To be sure, harmonization of company law among Member States will facilitate development of the single European internal market. On one view, however, such harmonization of corporate rules, to the extent desirable, is the natural outcome of competition among jurisdictions offering competing sets of rules. Individual managers make jurisdictional choices that, in the aggregate, achieve the right level of jurisdictional diversity and unification. On this view, harmonization at present is proceeding in precisely the wrong way. Rather than bureaucratically adjusting the rules of the different states to achieve a common standard, the European states should simply free themselves to offer whatever corporate rules they wish. Each corporation will incorporate in the jurisdiction that offers the most appealing set of rules.[7]

Indeed, as commentators have observed, we seem to lack any theory of the proper allocation of responsibility between local and centralized rulemakers[8] for developing corporate law rules.[9] Such improvisation places lawyers back in familiar terrain, but naturally raises concerns that decisions will be made, without guiding principle, on the basis of parochial interests and prejudice. To understand the processes by which rational legal actors allocate rule-making responsibilities, a more systematic understanding of the advantages and disadvantages of various rule-making schemes is a necessary first step.

The present article outlines some basic principles for constructing a theory about how to allocate corporate rule-making responsibility among jurisdictional levels. The article proposes a basic model for analysing the problem substantially different from any now used. It then applies that model to explain past experience with harmonization and to propose strategies for harmonization of rules that have not yet been fully addressed.

In particular, my analysis here supplements extant work in three respects. First, I will systematically introduce into the jurisdictional analysis recent work on the process of corporate charter formation and on the public-goods nature of many corporate law rules. I will suggest that these bodies of theory provide the main source of our understanding of how rule 'quality' is affected by centralization and decentralization. Second, I will then place the question of the 'lowest common denominator' in the context of fundamental considerations regarding centralization of rule-making. Clearly, concern with the 'quality' of rules—the outputs of the decision-making process—ought to be only one factor in selecting the appropriate decision-maker. Other costs—the administrative costs of uniformity or duplication, both in formulation and compliance—may prove equally important. The American obsession with the 'Delaware' phenomenon has, until recently, eclipsed an adequate concern for these other costs. Third, I will consider the role of institutions beyond state legislatures and courts in accomplishing 'harmonization' of laws among diverse jurisdictions.

Part II of the article begins by comparing the past experiences of the United States and western Europe with interjurisdictional competition for incorporations. It then surveys the literature on interjurisdictional competition. Inevitably, this portion of the article focuses on the present analytical literature in the United States. United States corporate lawyers have wrestled with the incorporation problem for over a century, facing a situation like that to which the EC aspires—a single capital market, enjoying relatively free mobility of capital among jurisdictions, but exhibiting a diverse set of corporate regulatory regimes—at least for the near future.

Part III presents a normative framework, arguing that decision-makers should consider which types of corporate rules are most likely to be evaded through interjurisdictional competition for incorporations or through interjurisdictional mobility of capital. These rules should be the primary check against a 'lowest common denominator' regime by setting minimum or uniform standards. Further, this part argues that it would be advantageous to centralize a number of types of rules, even though they should not be given priority in harmonization. The development of the analysis begins at a high level of abstraction: it envisions a global decision-maker and the multiple local decision-makers, without specifying much about their characteristics or the constitutional relationships between them.

Part IV argues that this analysis permits one to identify desirable targets for harmonization in terms of two sets of variables: (1) the role and content of the rules; and (2) the incentives for managers to comply with, or attempt to evade, the rules. This analysis, in itself, proves relatively powerful in generating recommendations about the types of rules for which harmonization is important. There are a substantial number of rules for which harmonization is desirable: accounting, disclosure, control transactions, capitalization and veil-piercing. In many cases, harmonization does not prevent a 'race to the bottom', but simply affords the convenience of a uniform set of rules to transactors who must deal with a large number of different corporations. The transition to such a body of rules is relatively straightforward, and has already been substantially accomplished in the EC. More difficult, but also demanding harmonization, are rules that provide 'public goods' rather than directly protect investors or other market participants. A race to the bottom is likely for these rules because investors, as well as managers, will countenance jurisdictional evasion. But substantive conflicts are inevitably part of the harmonization process for such rules, because corporate regulation in these areas reflects different national policies toward the 'public goods' that are generated by corporate regulation in these areas.

Finally, in part V, I make some suggestions about placing the relatively abstract analytic framework developed here in the context of the institutional frameworks for corporate rule-making in the United States and the EC.

I. Competition among jurisdictions: the 'market for incorporations'

A. The Emergence of 'Markets for Incorporations'

Both European and US legal history support the view that the laws offered by jurisdictions led them to emerge as favoured sites of incorporation because of the laws that they offer. In the United States, New Jersey came to the fore during the first great merger wave of the late nineteenth century with a set of rules that favoured the formation of 'trusts'. New Jersey's corporate doctrine emerged from an active—and, at least from a business viewpoint, fruitful—collaboration among entrepreneurs (affectionately known as 'robber barons'), the New York bar,[10] and the New Jersey legislature, which adopted laws drafted by the bar and collected enormous revenues from incorporation fees.[11]

The second wave of incorporation came in the second and third decade of the twentieth century. After New Jersey's progressives, led by Woodrow Wilson, tightened that state's corporate law, corporations in large numbers reincorporated in Delaware, whose law—drafted under the auspices of the DuPont family to protect their managerial and shareholder interests[12]—appeared relatively favourable to managers-shareholders of other corporations as well.[13] Delaware remains to this day the leading state of incorporation. Over 40 per cent of New York Stock Exchange-listed companies, and over 50 per cent of the Fortune 500 companies, are incorporated in Delaware. 82 per cent of the firms that reincorporate move to Delaware.[14]

The pattern of incorporation in Western Europe is substantially different. But the fundamental phenomenon—reincorporation in search of more favourable rules—recurs among European jurisdictions as it has among the United States. In the 1840s, for example, French corporations were first attracted to England. But after Gladstone's leadership provided the impetus for reform of British company law, French corporations moved to Belgium.[15] In Europe, the sovereign states have responded to protect the integrity of their corporate regimes; European corporate doctrines, unlike those of the American states, have given them the tools with which to do so. In the 1840s, in response to the movement of French corporations to reincorporate abroad, the French state used the *siège* doctrine—the rule that the law governing the corporation is that of its actual seat of business, not simply that of a state in which it has filed appropriate papers or keeps a mailing address—to force corporations that were 'French' in fact to remain 'French' in law as well.

As in the United States, the situation reached a rough equilibrium in the late nineteenth and early twentieth centuries, but with a greater diversity of regulatory approaches. The Netherlands, the United Kingdom, Ireland, and Denmark recognize the corporation as created and governed by the laws of its state of incorporation, even if the corporation operates primarily or exclusively in a different host state.[16] Under the alternative system of '*siège réel*—which prevails in the other Member States—the laws of the host state are applied if the actual centre of the company's activities has moved to the host state.[17] In short, the law of the place of management—the real seat or headquarters of the company—governs.[18] The *siège réel* doctrine requires, in practical terms, that a company create a subsidiary company or branch in accordance with the laws of the host country.[19]

Despite possible fundamental differences in treatment of foreign corporations, however, the spectre of a 'race to the bottom' haunts European as well as US jurisdictions. Indeed, events in the European corporate community have illustrated the extent to which corporations will go to qualify to be governed by one set of corporate rules rather than another. Corporations may relocate their 'seat of operations', as well as their jurisdiction of formal incorporation, if necessary to maintain their national status: the Netherlands, for example, has been said to benefit from this practice, especially due to its pro-managerial rules on share ownership and mergers.[20]

Most fundamentally, the goal of a single European market with free movement of capital and non-discriminatory treatment of domestic and foreign business enterprises raises substantial problems. The shift would seem to require that corporations doing business in different countries be permitted to operate freely whether they govern their internal corporate affairs under the law of the one Member State in which they do substantial business or another in which they are already incorporated. Indeed, it may be that the more exclusionary aspects of the *siège* doctrine may conflict with the Treaty of Rome. In particular, recent cases require that a Member State not discriminate against corporations 'formed in accordance with the laws of [another] Member State and . . . hav[ing] a registered office or principal place of business within the Community', even where 'the company pursues its activities exclusively through an agency, branch or subsidiary' outside the state of incorporation[21]—a requirement that some commentators read as incompatible with the *siège réel* system.[22] But it is not clear—and no cases have held—that it would be discriminatory to impose further regulatory requirements on the company's activities under the *siège réel* doctrine in the state where those activities are conducted.

The prospect of the single European market in 1992 intensifies the problem in other respects as well. Creation of a single European market heightens the threat of a 'race to the bottom' to the extent that companies from outside Europe, now entering the increasingly attractive European market, may be able to choose any state as the seat of their European business. Further, the internationalization of the financial markets, and the growing trade in financial services, increases the pressure for a unitary set of laws, as well as increasing the possibility for regulatory evasion by transferring the jurisdiction of the seat of incorporation or the locus of a securities transaction.

B. Assessing Competition among Jurisdictions: The Debate in American Corporate Theory

Three interpretations of interjurisdictional competition for incorporations have dominated the debate in American corporate law. The first view criticizes interjurisdictional competition as creating corporate rules that are overly lax on managers—the 'race to the bottom' among state legislatures.[23] The key to the critique is the observation that corporate *managers* generally decide where the corporation will be incorporated.

The state with the laxest (most pro-management) corporate rules will attract the most incorporations. Thus, states—which can charge substantial fees for issuance of a corporate charter—face irresistible financial inducements to adopt lax corporate laws. Delaware, the state where a preponderance of public corporations are incorporated, has won the race for now, but other states cannot afford to lag far behind. Exponents of this position have pointed to the traditional laxity of Delaware law, particularly on basic questions of fiduciary law central to managers' concerns: the business judgment rule, the corporate opportunity doctrine, standards for validiating self-dealing transactions, and review of parent-subsidiary mergers. Although recent Delaware decisions are occasionally seen as more' stringent', they have been, on the whole, easily explained by a 'reregulatory' or 'pro-managerial' view of Delaware law.[24]

A second, revisionist view of decentralized corporate law-making has established itself in the law-and-economics corporate scholarship (and, more tentatively, in judicial opinions) over the past two decades.[25] The revisionist position has two premisses. First, managers will choose to incorporate in the state whose corporate laws are most efficient from the shareholders' point of view. As Judge Easterbrook explained in *Amanda Acquisition Corp.* v. *Universal Foods Corp.*,[26] 'When entrepreneurs want to raise capital for a corporate venture, they must decide where to incorporate. The choice of where to incorporate in turn affects the price investors are willing to pay for shares. . . . State that enact laws that are harmful to investors will cause entrepreneurs to incorporate elsewhere'.[27] On this view, Delaware attracts incorporations not because its laws are lax, but because they are efficient. In essence, the laws are designed to maximize the total value of outstanding shares of the Delaware corporation. The revisionists' second premiss is that this 'market for incorporation' creates an incentive for each state to offer the most efficient laws: the state thereby increases its revenues from incorporation fees, and indirectly, from the income of lawyers in the state who specialize in that state's corporate law.[28]

Consensus among corporate lawyers has begun to form around a third, compromise view. The seminal work was done by Professor Roberta Romano.[29] The compromise position accepts the revisionists' basic point—that managers will be deterred by market pressures from opting for corporate rules that are overly lax. Further, Romano's work emphasized the formal advantages of the Delaware system: Delaware offered comprehensive statutes and case law; Delaware's courts of chancery provided an experienced judiciary specialized in corporate matters; Delaware's large population of corporations quickly generated legal controversies, and thereby new precedents and rules; Delaware's reliance on incorporation fees as a large percentage of state revenues, as well as private investment in providing services linked to Delaware's prominence in corporate law 'bonded' the Delaware system to maintain the stability and serviceability of its system.[30] Thus, a system emerges whose basic rules and procedural aspects probably maximize shareholder value. None the less, managers' direct gains from some pro-managerial state statutes may outweigh the losses. Most importantly, managers may benefit from antitake-over statutes[31] and from only cursory scrutiny of their merger and recapitalization decisions. Further, the Delaware bar may exploit its monopoly position by adopting some pro-interest group rules.[32] The compromise view leaves the decentralization question to *ad hoc* analysis: for some types of rules, interjurisdictional competition is desirable; for others, harmful.[33]

How can lawyers assess the plausibility of these three competing positions? Most obviously, one can simply try to decide whether one likes Delaware's laws—the question for which the slogan 'race to the bottom' provides an easy formula.[34] But more sophisticated empirical work has attempted to circumvent the inevitably contentious and *ad hoc* quality of this approach by seeking more direct indications of a managerialist bias in states' decision-making procedures or legislation. One approach is the direct observation of the processes of reincorporation and corporate law formation. For example, surveys of the managers or corporate counsels of reincorporating firms have provided powerful indications of the reasons for reincorporation. Most often, managers who reincorporate in Delaware indicate that they find the legal climate favourable for a particular corporate transaction they are contemplating for the near future. Usually, the transaction involves corporate control—a planned merger, a spinoff, adoption of a target defence, and so forth.[35] These survey results bode ill for the European context, for they again show that corporations see reincorporation as a feasible tool to be used in acquisitions or financial strategies.

Analysis of the legislative process also suggests that corporate law is tailored to fit managerial priorities. Before adopting legislation, law-makers carefully consult the state corporate bar and corporate representatives of managerial groups. The Delaware statute permitting opt-out from negligence liability was drafted in a local law office and was marched through the legislature without significant change in response to pressures from local counsel representing national firms incorporated in

Delaware.[36] To the cynical, the process will appear to be simply a more genteel version of the robber barons' dictation of the law of New Jersey a century ago.

Most ambitiously, students of the problem have tried to assess the market impacts of particular jurisdictional enactments or of corporations' decisions to incorporate or reincorporate. If Delaware tends to enact laws that help managers but harm shareholders, then event studies should show that the market price for shares in Delaware companies dropped after enactment of such laws. For example, if Delaware's amendment to permit opt-outs from negligence liability were 'managerialist', then event studies should detect a drop in share prices after the statute was passed. Investigators have already searched unsuccessfully for evidence of statistically significant abnormal returns earned by Delaware firms after announcement of Delaware opinions that could be characterized as reversals or departures from existing corporate law rules.[37] Somewhat less equivocal are the data on the market impact of decisions to reincorporate.[38]

Aside from disappointingly inconclusive statistical outcomes, however, several methodological difficulties undermine this approach. It is hard to determine what should count as the date of passage of the statute: the market presumably informs itself about legal trends in a state such as Delaware, and may gradually anticipate passage of the statute, making it harder to identify a cause-and-effect relationship. Further, the passage of a statute, or corporations' reactions to it, may have a 'signalling' effect independent of the actual desirability of the statute. For example, passage of the statute may signal (but not cause) an anticipated drop-off in merger activity and heightened managerial resistance to take-overs. None the less, event studies on the passage of state antitake-over statutes have shown that states have adopted provisions harmful to shareholders.[39]

C. The Approach of the Present Article

In short, the state of the evidence leaves the debate at a stalemate. It is clear that the process of US corporate law-making is by design responsive to managerial concerns, and that the decisions about reincorporation and legislation are fine-tuned to managerial plans and interests. But the evidence of the relative 'efficiency' of the process, as we have seen, is attenuated. Further, even more unequivocal data, gathered on the paths of research now trodden, would leave essential questions unanswered. The focus on the incentives of decentralized and centralized rule-makers has distracted attention from the more general issue of the relative costs and benefits of using these different sources of rules. The debate has yet to consider the large body of recent theoretical and empirical work on such issues as the formulation and amendment of corporate charters and the impact on shareholders of various state laws. A more useful general framework would consider, as well, variables that are important in the European context, while more muted in the US context—different standards and procedures for corporate governance in Europe, the higher costs of 'reincorporation' in the face of a *siège* doctrine, the problem of new corporate entities from outside the EC nations, and the greater regulatory burdens imposed by European as contrasted to American law. The next part of the article proposes such a framework.

II. Analysing interjurisdictional competition: identifying costs and benefits of centralized and decentralized rule-making

To lay the groundwork for identifying the types of corporate rules most profitably subject to harmonization, this part considers the benefits and costs of centralized rule-making. Most important, the part considers systematically the implications of recent work on 'opt-outs' from corporate rules, particularly by charter amendment, for the process of reincorporation—an analytic task that has not been undertaken.

A. Analytic Framework

1. *The Case for Centralized Rule-making*   Presumptively, well-informed transactors should be free without restriction to determine the set of rules that will govern their transactions. In corporate law, this would mean that managers and shareholders could, under whatever terms seemed proper, formulate the investment contract between shareholders and the firm. It is generally acknowledged, however, that shareholders do not have the knowledge or the drafting capacity to create for their transactions a body of corporate law *ab initio*. Even commentators who endorse a large degree of freedom to opt out emphasize the need for a well-developed set of background terms.[40] Further, shareholder ignorance and information externalities would plague shareholders' private formulation of rules for corporate investment. For these reasons, many features of fundamental importance to the investor—capitalization rules, legal duties of managers, managerial decision-making procedures, treatment of the firm's liabilities and assets on merger or dissolution, and disclosure to investors—must be determined in the first instance by

background law. Furthermore, at least some of these background rules should be mandatory.

When the law establishes a set of rules for transactors, it would seem presumptively efficient to mandate a single set of uniform rules that would govern *all* transactions, regardless of the jurisdiction in which they occur. Particularly for the corporate context, where numerous corporations transact with numerous shareholders within a single jurisdiction and across jurisdictional boundaries, it appears desirable to have a single set of ground rules observed by all shareholders investing and corporations raising capital in a single common capital market.

Uniformity offers several familiar advantages.[41] Most clearly, it saves the decision-makers and transactors the costs of having to develop and learn a multiplicity of rules. With a single set of rules for corporations from different jurisdictions, shareholders do not have to know the impact of differences in rules on the comparative risks and returns of different corporate investments. Similarly, they need not be concerned that where or with whom they transact will influence the rules that govern them. By contrast, if disclosure for securities sales was entirely governed by the rules of fifty states, rational investors would have to account in some way for the fact that the amount of information disclosed would depend on the state of incorporation, and, perhaps, on the location of the sale as well.

More important, uniformity protects against evasion of regulation by rule-shopping. In particular, it must be emphasized that the Panglossian view of rule-shopping—that managers always shop for the pro-shareholder rule—is analytically oversimplified. The problem is best understood from the perspective of recent research on managerial incentives in drafting and amending corporate charters.[42] This research shows that when managers *form* the corporation, they want the rules that are best from the shareholders' point of view, since the incorporators bear the cost of any deviation from optimality in the form of lower share values. But this assumes that shareholders are well informed, an assumption implausible for the entire range of corporate rules. The most important variable in distinguishing between benign and harmful interjurisdictional competition is whether the long-term harm to shareholders from laxer rules could be priced by the market.

Consider, on the one hand, a jurisdiction that over a substantial period of time routinely applies a 'lax' regime of conflict-of-interest rules, which thereby systematically permits managers to appropriate funds from shareholders. Shareholders who see that this is the case will correspondingly discount *ex ante* the value of investments in corporations that are formed in that state. In this instance, entrepreneurs who form corporations simply cannot gain at the expense of shareholders by choosing the lax state of incorporation. Whatever entrepreneurs could gain *ex post* from theft or otherwise taking advantage of the shareholders will be lost *ex ante* when they raise capital in the initial public offering.

Where there are corporations with different opportunity sets for theft, or different propensities for thievery by managers, then investors who can acquire the information will correspondingly discount the shares differently for different corporations. To the extent that they cannot acquire the relevant information about the corporations, its managers or the impact of legal rules, then a 'lemons' problem develops: entrepreneurs of more-than-average honesty will incorporate in other jurisdictions; prospective investors will raise the amount by which they discount the value of their investments to account for future managerial depredations; accordingly, the next-most-honest set of entrepreneurs will move to other jurisdictions. Eventually, no one will incorporate in the jurisdiction at all. Again, the attempt to 'race to the bottom' becomes self-defeating: entrepreneur-managers cannot gain from incorporation in the lax regime.

A similar analysis might apply to reincorporations. The reincorporation to the laxer state will accomplish a one-time drop in share values equal to the prospective future gains to the managers from theft. None the less, midstream changes in rules—the standard case of reincorporation—are even more troubling than the possibility of managers' opportunistic choice of the jurisdiction of initial incorporation. For midstream rule changes, it is clear that managers may profit from changes that harm shareholders. They will have an incentive to adopt any change that accrues a net benefit to *them*, even if it harms shareholders. Generally, the managers hold a relatively small fraction of the corporation's shares, and so bear directly only a small part of the total costs that a midstream change might impose on shareholders.[43] Further, the indirect effects of a small decrease in share values (and a correspondingly small increase in the cost of raising capital) is not sufficient to deter managers from adopting rule changes that harm shareholders. The corporation may not need to go back to the capital markets to raise capital. If it does, it can compensate for decreased share value by simply selling more shares. The reputational harm to managers from reincorporation generally is small, as the decrease in share value will be small and may be masked by other market fluctuations.

Although rational shareholders will not approve a proposed reincorporation, rationally apathetic shareholders may approve a reincorporation, as they would a charter amendment, that decreases share value because they are ill-informed about its impact.[44] Further, approving shareholders may have divergent interests, such as a direct link with the management group that permits them to gain sidepayments from future thefts, or a sufficiently large voting stake to have the clout to extract such sidepayments.

Thus, the 'race to the bottom' becomes a serious problem under several conditions. First, where there is a class of potential investors who are poorly informed about the effects of the jurisdiction's rules for a given type of company, then managers may incorporate that type in a jurisdiction which suboptimal rules that permit thievery. Investors do not discount for future thievery, and so the managers raise a pool of capital from which thievery can occur. Similarly, midstream changes may occur because of shareholders' rational apathy. The empirical evidence is inconclusive because it cannot separate the loss of value from reincorporation from gains in value from the signalling effects of the reincorporation.[45]

In the European corporate setting, more than the American, application of this model is complicated by other market and social pressures that influence corporate managerial decision-making. Particularly in the German corporate environment, corporate employees[46] and bank creditors[47] exert more powerful influences on managerial decision-making, either through direct board representation or more indirect business ties. Often, the major bank creditor is a substantial shareholder as well—an arrangement still prohibited by American law.[48] In this regime of stakeholder control, the stakeholder has sufficient incentives—because of its shareholdings or its direct contractual ties to the business—to monitor the directors' reincorporation decisions. For these firms, the prospect of suboptimal reincorporation, though real, seems less of a danger than the competition that they face in capital and product markets from firms that are incorporated in laxer jurisdictions.

2. Advantages of Decentralization A general presumption that uniformity is desirable—because it saves on information costs or prevents managers' opportunistic choice of jurisdiction—cuts the Gordian knot. But, for all of its surface plausibility, it is inconsistent with observed legal conditions in both the United States and Europe, where considerable political struggle accompanies the adoption of centralized rule systems. What, then, would justify the fragmentation, among multiple and territorially differentiated decision-makers, of authority to promulgate rules governing corporate transactions?

One factor, clearly, is history—or, as some analytic theorists prefer to call it, 'path dependencies'.[49] As we have seen, an account of the current multiplicity of corporate rules begins with jurisdictional fragmentation during the period when modern business law developed. This creates a situation of 'high transition costs' to a unified regime of corporate governance. New rules must be formulated, interpreted, and mastered by many practitioners; incorporation documents, corporate charters, bylaws, indentures, and other corporate documents, if based on older rules, must be revised. Given that our legal order has evolved so that there are many fragmented sources of rules, it is easier to maintain the status quo than to try to get consensus on a single set of transactional rules. Transactors' interested conduct reinforces this inertia. In part, decentralized rule-making persists because of xenophobia and self-protectiveness: local élites fear interference from outsiders and gain substantial advantage from maintaining the authority to create their own local rules.[50]

But the rule formulation and learning costs of a shift to new rules, and a prejudiced or self-interested affection for the well-established, are clearly only part of the story. Other costs of harmonization reflect the substantive advantages that accrue with decentralization and are lost when a uniform set of rules is mandated for multiple jurisdictions. Although the advantages of decentralization are generally familiar, a brief survey of the aspects most important to corporate law will provide a grounding for the analysis of specific corporate rules undertaken in the next part.

The consideration that has predominated in the debates to date is the incentive created by jurisdictional competition. Decentralization, as we have seen, may encourage local decision-makers to offer the best rules in order to attract transactors to that jurisdiction. The phenomenon is particularly important in a 'rational actor' model of legislative decision-making. Legislation that represents bargains struck among special interest groups is not likely to be efficient; and so, on this view, it is particularly salutary to pressure the legislature to act efficiently. The 'market for incorporations' may do just that. In contrast, a US federal corporate law, formulated by either Congress or an administrative agency relatively free compared to the states from pressures of reincorporation, would become fair game for the interests of special groups, including managers, the corporate bar, and professional securities traders.

Second, decentralization facilitates adaptation to local conditions. In the corporate context, local 'transactional cultures' call for rules fitted to the local culture. Local decision-makers are better informed about the culture than a centralized decision-maker, and may face better incentives to accommodate the local culture. Of particular importance are what one might call 'integrated' or 'embedded' rules: rules that make sense because of the way they fit into other rules or practices adopted by the community. As discussed in more detail below, rules about such basic corporate matters as disclosure or managers' responses to tender offers reflect a diverse range of such cultural conditions.[51]

Third, decentralization permits localized experimentation and reduces the impact of errors in the rule-making of any one jurisdiction. For many types of rules, decision-makers may be uncertain what the best rule is. For that reason, it is arguably good to have many jurisdictions promulgating rules. From experience we can learn which rule is best; and the impact of a mistake by any one rule-maker is limited to the jurisdiction in which its decisions are authoritative. For example, in the corporate context, the recent proliferation of diverse tender offer regimes has provided the opportunity to assess the impacts of those different regimes.

III. A typology of corporate rules

An appealing analytic strategy, then, is to balance the relative costs and benefits of centralized and decentralized rule-making. I shall argue that the analysis best proceeds by considering *types of corporate rules*. The comparative advantage of one type of rule-making over another varies with different types of rules. For some rules, the advantages of localized experimentation or adaptation may be few; for others, experimentation or adaptation may be an important part of any process to develop a suitable rule. Similarly, for some rules, the need for uniformity among different corporations within a single capital market may be great; for other rules, uniformity may be relatively unimportant. By classifying rule types, the analyst can begin to determine the appropriate decision-making authority of central and local rule-makers. This section offers such a classification.

In this part, I will proceed by considering four types of rules. First, there are 'focal point rules'—rules that should be centrally promulgated because of the overwhelming importance of uniformity among transactions. Second, there are rules whose formulation should be centralized because of managerial opportunism—managerial choice of jurisdictions of incorporation that offer pro-managerial rules. As the argument shall explain, the analysis offered above indicates that setting minimal standards may be useful for these types of rules. Finally, there are two types of rules that create 'public goods'.[52] First, some rules benefit shareholders as a group, although shareholders of any single corporation would opt out of the rule for their corporation, if they were given a chance to do so (a rule banning resistance to take-overs is a familiar example). Second, other rules benefit non-shareholder groups, such as workers or tort victims, who are prevented from bargaining for those rules by high contracting costs or collective action problems.

A. Centralization to Foster Uniformity: Focal Point Rules

In terms of the comparative advantages of centralization and decentralization, the easiest corporate rules to analyse are 'conventional' or 'focal point' rules. For these rules, the *content* of the rules is less important than their uniformity. Like any given word in a language[53] or a simple convention like driving on the right side of the road, the content of each stipulated rule is less important than (1) that everyone follows the same rule: uses the same word for the same thing, or drives on the same side of the road;[54] and (2) that the rule system as a whole be clear and coherent.

Many corporate rules are conventional or focal. For example, numerous accounting conventions can be used accurately to represent the firm's financial position. Indeed, for many accounting variables, such as inventory values, it is well documented that a firm's changes in accounting conventions has no significant impact on the market value of the firm's shares. The market is not fooled by cosmetic accounting changes: it sees through superficial differences among the results recorded by different conventions. In that sense, the choice among conventions is arbitrary; one is no more informative than another, and sophisticated market analysts have no more difficulty in deciphering one type of accounting convention than another (within the range of conventions among which firms can choose).

This is not to say, however, that accounting rules 'don't matter'. To the contrary, one can infer that the uniformity among the conventions that corporations follow does matter, in at least two respects pertinent to the debate on interjurisdictional co-ordination. First, market analysts are bearing substantial costs in figuring out what various conventions mean, and making the conversions that permit them to compare the values of corporations that are using different accounting conventions. Second, it may be important that the meaning of each convention is fixed: there is a uniform language, but a choice of several dialects.

Another, somewhat different example is provided by the 'rules of the road' for corporate decision-making: rules on such matters as annual elections of directors, periodic board meetings, majority rule on boards, and so forth. Such rules are fixed and mandatory, that is, they cannot be varied by individual corporate charters. Why not permit variation in these rules? Somewhat counterintuitively, perhaps, the answer is that these are very similar to accounting rules. The important task of a fixed rule is to spare parties the costs of verifying what any given corporation is actually doing, and of trying to decide whether reported differences among corporations actually reflect differences in the fundamental value of their shares. With respect to procedural varieties in corporate charters, the problem arises in the form of investment analysts' decoding the managerial machinations that various imaginative charter provisions might permit. Rather than put the analysts to these costs, legal decision-makers should simply specify a uniform rule.

To be sure, what counts as a 'focal point' rule may not be obvious. For example, one set of rules subject to early harmonization addressed the scope of authority of agents and the duties of corporations to inform others of the scope of agency by filing appropriate documents. Clearly, a uniform set of rules reduces the costs for third parties transacting with corporations. They know that they can follow the same procedure for verifying the scope of agency for all companies. But a number of different rules are possible, and some may accomplish substantial savings over others. For example, overly stringent filing requirements may impose substantial costs on corporations while gaining no corresponding advantage for third parties who deal with corporate agents. Generally, the problem is the familiar one of allocating the risk of agents' depredations between two parties—a balance which is struck on familiar information-gathering and risk-bearing grounds. None the less, it seems likely that only small cost differences were involved in the choice among the different rules governing the European states. Harmonization was primarily a matter not of making a complex or controversial choice among diverse rules but simply choosing a single rule set and making it stick for all transactors.

The hard question is whether a *mandatory* rule is required. Often, conventions emerge 'spontaneously' by imitation. Transactors simply follow the lead of a prominent initiator of a standard; or they adopt a common standard after collective deliberation.[55] In both the United States and Europe, however, uniformity of accounting standards, basic corporate decision-making, and share-transfer procedures have been accomplished by a strong element of centralized public or quasi-public rule-making by third parties.[56] Spontaneous generation would be unreliable or unduly costly. First, the standards to be developed are often quite complex. This means that no single initiator can bear all of the costs of setting the standard: there is a 'public goods' problem that only collective decision-making can solve. The complexity of standards implies, as well, that propagation through imitation would be unreliable: imitators would get things wrong, and, as in the simple childhood game of 'Telephone', repeated informal communication of the standards would repeatedly introduce errors and distortions. Second, and more fundamentally, 'spontaneously generated' standards impose on parties at least one of the costs that a uniform standard is designed to avoid: the cost of verifying that a given corporation is complying with the standard. For basic procedural rules, for example, investment analysts would have to check each corporate charter to make sure that the corporation was not deviating from the 'voluntary' or spontaneous corporate standard—just as we need policemen to assure that the occasional driver does not seek the advantage of driving on the wrong side of the road.

None the less, the *process* of harmonization may not be correspondingly straightforward. Distinct transactional cultures may spawn diverse transactional rules—particularly for focal-point rules—even though they appear similar in many respects. The problem reflects what biologists call the 'founders' effect'. That is, when the choice of rule is arbitrary—so that many different possible rules may be roughly comparable in effect—independent cultures, like independent organizations, may begin by choosing arbitrarily different rules from among the menu of possibilities and then sticking with that choice simply because it was the first chosen. Hence, different national business practices incorporate different accounting rules, and although accounting rules may seem technical and arbitrary, there would none the less be strong resistance to changing rules in order to move to a common standard. Because rule differences reflect the 'founders' effect', the fact that the rules differ does not indicate that any one set of rules was superior to another; nor does the resistance to standardization indicate that the move to a common set of rules involves sacrificing the advantages of the rules that are abandoned. None the less, there will be large transitional costs. Harmonization disrupts the investment that parties have made in current transactional practices: accountants, as well as investors, creditors, and regulators who consult prospectuses or balance sheets, must learn new rules. This is, however, a transitional cost incurred only once. Further, it is inevitably less costly for a group of transactors to learn a new set of rules than once it would be for the group continuously to apply several different, inconsistent rule sets. From this perspective, the advantages of harmonization are clear.[57]

The key feature of focal-point rules, then, is that consensus about a rule is more important than the substance of the rule adopted. Thus, experimentation to search out different rules is of little value; there is no need for diversity of rules, and local transactional practices (among firms or jurisdictions) can adopt readily to whatever rules are in place. With focal-point rules, the argument for harmonization arises from the transactors' advantage of having a uniform set of rules. Harmonization facilitates an evolution that might occur spontaneously—though perhaps very slowly—in any event. Further, harmonization prevents opportunistic opt-out by managers. Managers cannot exploit the assumption by transactors that one rule applies, by substituting a different rule more favourable to themselves. But the content of the rule weighs less in the case for harmonization than the advantages of a uniform and mandatory rule. While some corporate lawyers may object to the depiction of their field as 'a body of law largely technical and arbitrary in character,'[58] clearly a large number of corporate rules are focal-point rules. Indeed, the early successes of harmonization were largely with rules—like the accounting and agency rules discussed above—that apparently have this character.

B. Exploiting Opportunities for Opportunistic Reincorporation: The Problem of Downward Creep in Basic Fiduciary Norms

In instances where social welfare can be identified with the rule that maximizes the wealth of the shareholders of the particular corporation, a divergence of interest may occur because managers can enrich themselves with an anti-shareholder rule. An important example is the general phenomenon of 'downward pressure' or 'downward creep' in basic fiduciary norms regulating managerial conduct. The reason to suspect 'downward creep' is apparent from the analysis that has been presented above. As we have seen, managers of some corporations will be able to obtain shareholder approval to reincorporate in jurisdictions that have rules that favour managers more than would be optimal from a wealth-maximizing perspective. The managers earn more in opportunistically gained wealth than they lose from the firm's decrease in value under the suboptimal set of rules. Thus, over time, established corporations will drift into a jurisdiction with suboptimal rules.

To be sure, there are institutional and market limits on *how* suboptimal the rules can be. Imagine a 'super-Delaware' or a 'Lichtenstein' whose laws basically permitted managers to confiscate much of the value of the firm through unreviewed self-dealing transactions or unfair freeze-out mergers. Clearly, it would be hard for an entrepreneur to raise capital by initially incorporating in such a state. Further, various constraints would prevent managers from flocking to reincorporate there. If the laws were egregiously permissive, shareholders could probably block reincorporation either by vote or possibly by lawsuit; and there will be market and social pressures on managers not to reincorporate to a super-Delaware, particularly for those managers who want to remain in the market for high-level jobs at other companies. Finally, the threat of intervention from the centralized decision-maker may keep local laws from going too far out of line.[59] . . . . .

What are the implications for the European framework? Downward creep should be less of a problem in the European than the US context. The problem is most pronounced where there is a single clearly identified 'haven for corporations'—a small state with a powerful commitment to maximizing the number of corporations that it serves. With large states, however, a variety of political considerations are likely to counteract the temptation to weaken gradually the corporate law's regulatory force. It is unlikely that franchise fees for corporations would be sufficiently important to the revenues of France or Germany that they would degrade fiduciary standards to attract or keep corporations. This pressure aside, there is no reason why legislatures or courts would foster or develop biases to adopt pro-manager, anti-shareholder rules. To the contrary, one would expect that shareholder groups will be at least as influential in the political process, and that roughly wealth-maximizing rules would emerge. In short, as long as the EC can vigilantly rule out the manifest forms of the 'Delaware' phenomenon—as it can by setting minimal standards for fiduciary conduct for all member states—fiduciary standards can safely be left in the hands of the member states.

C. Centralization to Create 'Public Goods' among Transactors in Capital Markets

In the cases to which we now turn, properly selected rules may maximize the wealth of investors *taken as a group*, but not the wealth of shareholders of the particular companies to which the rules apply. For example, rules that prohibit tender offer auctions may maximize total investor wealth, but would probably prevent managers from using auctions to maximize returns to the shareholders of their particular companies. Here, managers whose interests coincide with those of the companies' particular shareholders may wish to evade the rules, as would the share-holders whose wealth is decreased by the rule.[60] In these cases, analysis of the costs and benefits of centralization differs from that for focal-point rules. Because of the possibility of more or less efficient rules, experimentation is desirable. Further, sorting of corporations among different rules (and the concomitant incentives for decision-makers) might also be desirable. Jurisdictional multiplicity invites 'managerialist' rule-shopping, however, so uniformity is needed to prevent opt-out by reincorporation.

1. Takeover Regulation   Capital markets regulation—rules for take-overs and for disclosure to investors—usefully illustrate these generalizations. In the United States, rules governing management's response to a tender offer provide a familiar, if controversial, example. In the take-over setting, managers gain enormously from tactics that entrench them in their current positions at the firm. Recent corporate conduct in the United States makes clear that managers will adopt such tactics even when they harm shareholders taken as a group.[61] In this environment, jurisdictional diversity provides clear opportunities for evasion. If one jurisdiction attempts stringently to limit managers' opportunistic resistance to hostile take-overs, the managers can simply reincorporate in a jurisdiction more permissive of resistance tactics.

Further, take-over regulation raises problems of public goods. Rules that foster resistance to take-overs have a powerful impact on the take-over market as a whole: resistance decreases both the likelihood of a take-over and the expected profits from successful take-overs. These rules diminish the incentive to search for take-over targets, dilute the monitoring effects of the market for corporate control, and thereby foster lax management.[62] Because many of these detrimental effects fall outside the jurisdiction that adopts a given take-over rule,[63] the jurisdiction gives less weight to the detriments than would be optimal from a social point of view. In addition, take-over rules protect managers and local stakeholders, who are politically powerful inside the jurisdiction, to the detriment of shareholders, inside or outside the jurisdiction, who are politically less powerful.[64]

The US experience with take-over regulation points to the value both of limited experimentation and of national authority to adopt a single rule. The tender-offer experience illustrates directly the 'laboratory' value of a multitude of state rules. Suggestive evidence for the harmful impact of resistance tactics and manager-protective rules, has come from event studies of the impact on share values of enactments by the various state legislatures.[65] Each enactment provides a controlled experiment of the capital market's assessment of the new rule; the controls are provided by comparing one state's corporations' share values with those of the corporations of other states. But as the evidence accumulates, the experimental value of jurisdictional diversity wanes, and the costs from pro-management law-making increase. Centralized rule-making is then in order.

The challenge in the European context is equally striking.[66] Rules regarding take-overs and control transactions—as well as transactional practices and understandings—are, if anything, even more diverse among members of the EC than among the American states. In nations such as Germany, where the stakeholder-monitoring model of corporate governance predominates, take-overs are uncommon.[67] Stakeholders aligned with management control sufficiently large share holdings to block the efforts of any hostile bidder. Further, relatively lax disclosure rules and a thin stock market pose indirect obstacles to an active take-over market. In Britain, by contrast, an active take-over market is in place, and is enhanced through City rules designed to assure fairness in the bidding process and to require hostile bidders to bid for large stakes.[68] In France, as well, the transactional foundations for an active market have been laid, although relatively permissive attitudes toward limiting alienability and the voting of shares readily facilitate managerial defensive tactics.

Clearly, differences in the relative feasibility of conducting a hostile takeover are linked to a broad range of public policies *vis-à-vis* managerial monitoring and control. The German 'stakeholder' model encourages stakeholders, like workers and managers, to invest directly and indirectly in the firm and to adopt policies of long-term firm development. The prospect that managers will be displaced, and managerial policies radically altered, clearly disrupts these ties and incentives—as demonstrated in British and US firms over the past decades.[69] Conversely, the existence of firms resistant to take-overs dampens activity in the European take-over market while legal rules that facilitate resistance attract managers eager to secure their corporate sinecures.

A capital market in which firms are monitored neither by an effective take-over mechanism, nor by well-motivated stakeholders clearly presents the worst of both worlds. But EC member states committed to the stakeholder model might equally object to being forced to adopt a regime of take-over rules that would disturb established—and effective—institutional practices. The challenge to harmonization, then, is whether a uniform set of take-over rules can be grafted onto diverse institutional structures.

Clearly, there must be flexibility in some rule-making. The British rule that obstructs acquisition of large but minority blocks of shares (in order to force any-and-all offers) is inconsistent with the capital structures of many continental firms, where creditors or affiliated firms hold such blocks. Stringent mandatory disclosure and equal-sharing requirements in control transactions may similarly be inconsistent with the ready transfer of large blocks of shares among stakeholders and corporate groups. But it is not clear that the full panoply of British takeover regulation is required to sustain a well-functioning take-over market: the US market has thrived with relatively loose rules (until recently) about the size of acquired blocks of shares. Further, once the take-over market is in place, its operation can be reconciled with the stakeholder model by permitting tender-offer defences upon a showing of business justification. In large measure, the costs of harmonization would then lie, in this more *ad hoc* scrutiny of the justifications for establishing corporate structures that impede take-overs.[70]

2. Mandatory Disclosure and Anti-fraud Regulation The justifications for mandatory disclosure are several. First, the mandatory standards provide focal points—convenient uniformity for comparison among shareholders.[71] Second, and more importantly,[72] disclosure by each firm is a public good. Disclosure confers value not only on the firm that discloses, but also on all other firms, because information about one firm enables investment analysts to analyse the value of other firms more intelligently. For that reason, purely voluntary disclosure provides inefficiently low amounts of information.[73]

EC attempts to strengthen disclosure requirements for publicly traded stock, however, have met substantial resistance.[74] The resistance has two sources. First, it is feared that extensive regulation of EC exchanges will drive transactors to non-regulated exchanges elsewhere. For example, the International Primary Market Association, representing Eurosecurities traders, argues that the prospectus review and delivery requirements would cause issuers to move transactions to unregulated markets in non-EC states, such as Switzerland.[75] Second, permitting EC exchanges to opt out of EC standards would in effect drive all markets to the 'lowest common denominator' of permissible regulation. Consequently, as the US Securities and Exchange Commission has observed, harmonization thus creates a strong pressure for a 'leveling down' of disclosure requirements to preserve the competitiveness of markets.[76]

At first cut, resistance by sophisticated market intermediaries to more extensive disclosure might appear to be decisive evidence against the welfare argument for further regulation. After all, sophisticated players apparently believe that more extensive disclosure is not cost-justified and are therefore willing to incur the relocation costs to avoid disclosure costs.[77] None the less, the prospect of relocation does not resolve the issue. First, firms that relocate to jurisdictions with lenient disclosure rules may be getting a 'free ride' from the higher levels of disclosure required to be made of other firms: investors are willing to take the risk of investing in more 'covert' firms because of the extensive information they have from the more highly regulated ones.[78] Second, firms may relocate to exploit transactors who mistakenly believe that they can dispense with disclosure requirements; in effect, the losses suffered by these naive transactors would subsidize the unregulated transactions of more sophisticated players.[79]

A second set of difficulties arises because disclosures systems engender different costs and benefits to firms operating under varying governance structures. Diverging disclosure systems are compatible with different market structures—central exchange vs. over-the-counter, in particular. For example, it appears that the extensive SEC-style disclosure system favours large over small firms and forces firms to adopt a more open style of corporate decision-making than is favoured even among larger European firms. A decision about the scope and format of disclosure is thus a decision to favour one type of firm over another. A second public good thus enters the picture: each state may decide, for any number of reasons, that it has public policy grounds for favouring one type of firm over another.

The uniform system forced upon the states by the US federal government in the 1930s favoured the emergence of corporate structures on what became the characteristically American model: dispersed shareholders holding small stakes for short terms and trading in well-developed markets; managers without well-defined loyalties or responsibilities to recognized shareholder or stakeholder groups; a board that is relatively passive or non-interventionist even in the face of substantial firm difficulties; and—in the 1970s and 1980s—managers vulnerable to an active market for corporate control. As we have seen, a different model prevails in many European firms, where large shareholder-stakeholders exert a strong influence on a correspondingly active, but otherwise relatively secure, managerial group. More important for the question of harmonization, however, are the different policy goals among member states, or among particular groups within the European corporate economy.[80] In France and Germany particularly, corporate lawyers have expressed concern that more extensive disclosure requirements would penalize small firms and disrupt intracorporate relationships. States and entities that wish to foster international capital markets, however, will tend to favour a more extensive disclosure system.

D. Rules to Create Public Goods or Correct Information Problems among Stakeholders or Third-party Transactors

In examining these rules, the desirable rule from a social point of view may be different from the rule that maximizes shareholder wealth. In that case, shareholders as well as managers have an incentive to seek incorporation in jurisdictions adopting a socially suboptimal rule.[81] This is the case for rules of corporate governance that consider third parties' interests—for example, a rule that required representatives of environmental interests to sit on boards of directors.

1. Board Structure: Codetermination Codetermination[82] offers an analytically simple, though politically intractable case of the costs and benefits of centralized rule-making. The need to prevent jurisdictional competition is clear. The rule primarily serves a public good: it either corrects for contracting failures among workers or provides externalities in terms of pro-worker policies that benefit the community though reduce the value of the firm. The requirement is apparently understood to impose a burden on the shareholders, as well as making life more difficult for managers. Either way, profit-maximizing, as well as opportunistic, managers will seek to reincorporate to avoid codetermination requirements. Thus, global rule-making is in order.

But global rule-making runs up against the claims for decentralization. Most important is the need to adapt to local transactional cultures; the structure of labour regulation, the established modes of contracting between workers and firms (particularly, whether union or non-union, and whether unions are firm- or industry-wide), and possible conflicts of interest among different types of workers. Given complex interactions with an array of regulatory and transactional factors, the transitional costs to a new regime are high. Further, given the ever-changing dynamics of labour relations, with changes in technology, and workers' wealth and preferences, local experimentation might seem desirable. Of course, I do not propose to resolve the conflict here: codetermination is an especially complex, politically charged issue—one that involves deep questions about the self-understandings of workers and managers, and conceptions of the fair sharing of wealth and power.

2. Mandatory Capitalization Requirements and Liability Rules for Corporate Groups   Capitalization requirements and liability rules protect tort victims and creditors by assuring that adequate funds will be available to satisfy enterprise liabilities. Again, the challenge to the notion of optimal jurisdictional competition lies in several sources. First, the constitutive rules serve the interests of third parties to the shareholder-manager relationship. If managers made incorporation decisions that maximized share value, then they would choose a jurisdiction with rules that were socially undesirable, taking into account the welfare of the jurisdictions in which the corporation operated, as well as the jurisdictions of incorporation. Essentially, shareholders benefit from rules that shield them from tort liability for the corporation's operations[83] and permit them to operate a relatively under-capitalized corporation.[84] Further, both shareholders and managers benefit from rules that shield assets of parent and affiliated corporations from subsidiary and affiliated liabilities.

With liability to creditors, multiple contractual relationships complicate the problem. If creditors often bargain for shareholder liability, shareholders might incur lower transaction costs under an unlimited liability rule. Even then, might managers prefer a limited liability rule? Although bankruptcy of the corporation would leave managers poorly situated whether or not further claims were assessed against individual shareholders, manager-shareholders might be less willing to bear this risk than other shareholders, because it would leave their asset portfolio (including human capital) even less well-diversified than were their assets protected from personal liability as shareholders. This intra-shareholder group conflict also encourages managers to seek permissive capitalization and limited liability rules. Further, creditors have no incentive to bargain to protect tort victims and creditors too naive to bargain for themselves, except in a jurisdiction with priority rules in bankruptcy that are designed to force contract creditors to protect tort creditors' interests.

V. Conclusion

'Harmonization'—the process of a 'central' authority's promulgating rules to be applied to corporations in numerous 'local' jurisdictions—usefully serves three functions. First, it can co-ordinate agreement upon a single set of rules, where uniformity facilitates transactions. Second, it can set minimal standards for jurisdictions, to assure that managers do not opportunistically 'opt out' of the optimal standards by reincorporating in a jurisdiction with laxer, more pro-managerial rules. Third, it can impose rules that benefit shareholders as a group—or, more generally, transactors as a group—in circumstances where shareholders of any single corporation would choose to 'opt out' of the wealth-maximizing rule by reincorporation.

I have in this article analysed rules that exemplify each function of harmonization. The article is thus meant to fill a gap in our understanding of the harmonization process by presenting a basic framework for determining what types of rules are candidates for centralized rule-making in a system where corporations can choose to incorporate in one of a number of 'local' jurisdictions. Clearly, a full comparison of the harmonization process must consider the enormous institutional differences between the United States and the EC—between a system of federal states subordinate to a national authority and bound by a common history, culture, language, and economic system, and a system of independent states attempting to create a set of common regulatory policies.[85] As the analysis explains, appropriate designation of centralized or decentralized responsibility for rule-making depends in part on the institutional features of the different rule-makers—the information to which they have access, the incentives which direct their conduct, and their authority to enforce decisions. In particular, the EC process inevitably consigns to states implementation of rules that might otherwise be candidates for full implementation by a central authority—as with the regulation of disclosure requirements in capital markets. Conversely, a comparison of the processes of harmonization in the United States and the EC reflects the comparatively rich profusion of decentralized sources of rules in the United States—not only state legislatures, but the American Law Institute, bar and professional (e.g. national accounting) associations, and self-regulatory organizations. In many respects, the centralized rule formulation functions of the Commission substitute for the more diffuse, but none the less powerful forces for harmonization in the US corporate system.

Notes

1 For a vivid description of regulatory meltdown, see e.g. Manning G. Warren III, 'Regulatory Harmony in the European Communities: The Common Market Prospectus', 16 *Brooklyn J. Int'l. L.* 19, 50–1 (1990). Two closely related phenomena can be distinguished. First, jurisdictions may adopt lax rules in order to *attract* incorporations. Second, jurisdictions may adopt rules to *protect* their own companies. If a regime of mutual recognition benefits companies

operating under less stringent regulatory regimes, the more stringent regimes may loosen their rules to protect the competitiveness of their companies.

2. Clive M. Schmitthoff, 'The Future of the European Company Law', in *The Harmonization of European Company law 3, 9* (Schmitthoff 2nd edn. 1973).

3. Walter Kolvenbach, 'EEC Company Law Harmonization and Worker Participation', 11 *U. Pa. J. Int'l Bus. Law* 709, 711–12 (1990). See also Inne Cath, 'Freedom of Establishment of Companies: A New Step Towards Completion of the Internal Market', 6 *YB Eur. L.* 246, 260 (1986) (arguing that article 56 of the Treaty of Rome is construed to prevent 'the "Delaware" effect' that would arise from 'an excessively broad application of articles 52–58 with respect to cross-border establishments of companies. . . .').

4. Kolvenbach continues: 'The European scheme of harmonizing company laws is based on a "federal" approach; in other words, the harmonization results in little influence by the Member States in these matters. The safeguards contained in national regulations are politically sensitive and/or in evolution. The process of harmonization is as much political in character as it is technical.' Kolvenbach, *supra* n. 3, at 712.

   For other general treatments, see Marcus Lutter, 'Europea und das Unternehmensrecht', in *Vorträge, Reden und Berichte aus dem Europa-Institut der Universität des Saarlandes* 118 (1988); Thomas E. Abeltshauser, 'Strukturalternativen für eine europäische Unternehmensverfassung', in *Europäische Integration als Herausforderung des Rechts: Mehr Marktrecht, weniger Einzelgesetz* 10 (1990).

5. For stylistic convenience, I will use 'European' as an adjectival reference for the EC.

6. The rationales for harmonization offered in the various EC directives are diverse and not entirely consistent. See Richard Buxbaum and Klaus Hopt, 'Legal Harmonization and the Business Enterprise: Corporate and Capital Market Law Harmonization Policy in Europe and the U.S.A.', in 4 *Integration Through Law: Europe and the American Federal Experience* 1, 196–7 (1988). The directives refer to concerns such as extrajurisdictional impacts of corporate enterprise law, the need for regulations to accommodate multinational corporations subject to a range of national laws; equal protection of creditors and partners of companies in different member states; the desirability of consistency; and, perhaps most persistently, the endeavours to 'bring about within the Community equal minimum legal conditions for companies competing with each other' (Fourth and Fifth Directives). Professor Hopt's own formulation is found ibid. at 197–204.

7. A few European commentators have advocated this approach. See e.g. H. Krekeler, *Wirtschaftliche Integration und Gesellschaftsrecht—Amerikanische Erfahrungen und europäische Irrwege* 171 (1973) (analysing efforts at corporate law harmonization); Hauschka, 'Entwicklungslinien und Integrationsfragen der gesellschaftsrechtlichen Akttypen des europäischen Gemeinschaftsrechts',

in 1990 *Die Aktiengesellschaft* 85, 94 (analysing the proposal for a *societas europas*); Kallmeyer, 'Die europäische Aktiengesllschaft—Praktischer Nutzen und Mangel des Statuts', in 1990 *Die Aktiengesellschaft* 103 (1990). In Krekeler's view, harmonization can be confined to the minimal degree of common regulation, essentially, requirements that each member-state recognize the corporate personality and rights of companies incorporated in other member states. The consensus approach seems to endorse the goal of harmonization but divides over the range of rules for which harmonization is feasible or desirable—what Thomas E. Abeltshauser calls 'problem-oriented harmonization'. Abeltshauser, 'European Constitution of the Firm', 11 *Mich. J. Int'l. Law* 1235, 1264 (1990). The analysis here seeks to shed light on the minimalist and the problem-oriented perspectives from the viewpoint of the theory of the corporation.

8. I shall use the term 'local rule-makers' to refer to the states of the US and the Member States of the EC; and 'centralized rule-maker' to refer to the US federal government and the complex legislative apparatus of the EC. Much of the analytic framework here could probably be transferred to other structures of centralization and decentralization as well. Of course, this is not to deny the importance of the vast differences among different types of federal or transnational systems; none the less, for the comparatively austere policy-making problems of corporate law, it is possible to present a basic framework that prescinds from many of these institutional differences.

9. See Richard A. Buxbaum and Klaus J. Hopt, *Legal Harmonization and the Business Enterprise* 15 (1988) (noting inadequacies of current theories of integration); Eric M. Stein, 'Company Law in Divided-Power Systems', 38 *Am. J. Comp. L.* 171, 173, 189 (1990) (agreeing with Buxbaum and Hopt).

10. Because of New Jersey's proximity to the commercial centres of Manhattan, and the New York bar's active role in proposing formulations of New Jersey law, no independent New Jersey corporate bar emerged. In contrast, the contemporary Delaware bar is an independent force in formulating modern corporate law.

11. See generally Lawrence M. Friedman, *A History of American Law* 523–5 (2nd edn. 1985); Henry N. Butler, 'Nineteenth Century Jurisdictional Competition in the Granting of Corporate Privileges', 14 *J. Legal Stud.* 129 (1985).

12. Although the extent of direct DuPont influence is debated, it seems naive to attribute great weight to local historical accounts that deprecate this influence and emphasize the 'public good' accomplished by corporate reform. See Roberta Romano, 'The State Competition Debate in Corporate Law', 8 *Cardozo L. Rev.* 709, at n. 60 (1987) (espousing the view that reforms were adopted for the public good).

13. Delaware first entered the race in the 1890s. See Note, 'Little Delaware Makes a Bid for the Organization of Trusts', 33 *Am. L. Rev.* 418 (1899).

14. Data provided by Joseph Grundfest, SEC Commissioner, to the Council of

the Corporate Law Section of the Delaware State Bar Ass'n, reprinted in Craig B. Smith and Clark W. Furlow, *Corporate Practice Series: Guide to the Takeover Law of Delaware* app. E, at 162 (1988). For data on reincorporations, see Roberta Romano, 'Law as a Product: Some Pieces of the Incorporation Puzzle', 1 *JL Econ. & Org.* 225, 244 (1985).

15. See Buxbaum and Hopt, *supra* n. 6, at 176.

16. See Carsten T. Ebenroth and Uwe Eyles, 'Die innereuropäische Verlegung des Gesellschaftssitzes als Ausfluss der Niederlassungsfreibeit', 42 *Der Betrieb* 363, 366 (1989).

17. See Inne G. F. Cath, 'Freedom of Establishment of Companies: A New Step towards Completion of the Internal Market', 6 *YB of European Law* 246, 250 (1986); Peter Behrens, 'Identitäswährende Sitverlegung einer Kapitalgesell-schaft von Luxemburg in die Bundesrepublik Deutschland', 32 *Recht der internationalen Wirtschaft* 590, 591 (1986). In an intermediate system, the doctrine of social priorities, certain essential rules—*règles d'application immédiate*—are applied as well even though the state recognizes the foreign incorporation. This system is developed in Dutch private international law and used in the UK under the Companies Act 1985, sections 691–703, which impose certain requirements upon foreign companies with a place of business in the UK. Going further than the minimal registration requirements for foreign corporations in US jurisdictions, this approach is somewhat analogous to the California doctrine of 'quasi-domestic' corporations, foreign corporations that become subject to some California requirements if they do substantial business in the state.

18. For a comparison of European and US approaches, see Richard A. Buxbaum, 'The Origins of the American "Internal Affairs" Rule in the Corporate Conflict of Laws', in *Festschrift für Gerhard Kegel zum 75. Geburtstag 75*, 88 (H.-J. Musiak and K. Schurig eds. 1987); for comparison of the two approaches within Europe, see generally Bernhard Grossfeld, 'Die Entwicklung der Anerkennungstheorien im internationalen Gesellschaftsrecht', in *Festschrift für Harry Westermann* 199, 200 (W. Hefermehl, R. Gmor, and H. Brox eds. 1974).

19. It appears, however, that application of the doctrine may conflict with the Treaty of Rome. In particular, recent cases require that a member state not discriminate against corporations 'formed in accordance with the laws of [another] Member State and . . . hav[ing] a registered office or principal place of business within the Community,' even where 'the company pursues its activities exclusively through an agency, branch or subsidiary' outside of the state of incorporation. *Segers* v. *K. Bedrijfsvereniging voor Bank en Verzekeringwezen, Groothandel en Frije Beropen,* Case 79/85, [1986] ECR 2375. Some commentators regard this requirement as incompatible with the *siège réel* system. See Cath, *supra* n. 2, at 259–61. But it is not clear—and no cases have held—that it would be discriminatory to impose further regulatory

requirements on the company's activities, in the state where those activities are conducted, under the *siège réel* doctrine.

20. For example, Dutch corporate law permits managers to control large blocks of voting stock by placing such stock in the hands of company-owned trusts—an arrangement generally forbidden in most jurisdictions' corporate law, and only recently available, *de facto*, to US managers with the emergence of the employee stock ownership trust, whose trustees may be effectively controlled by management.

    Analogously, in Germany, it appears that corporations structure themselves to limit their size and thereby to avoid the stringent regulatory requirements attached to the Aktiengesellschaft. Hopt, 'European Attempts to Harmonize Company and Capital Market Law', in 4 *Integration through Law* 167, 171 (1987). Quite simply, manages will manipulate legal forms to avoid the types of regulatory burdens—on corporate structure or accounts—that are contemplated under the harmonized regimes.

21. *Segers* v. *Bedrijfsvereniging, supra* n. 19.

22. See Cath, *supra* n. 2, at 259–61.

23. The metaphor was apparently coined by Justice Brandeis. See *Liggett* v. *Lee*, 288 US 517, 557–60 (1933) (Brandeis, J., dissenting). The influential modern formulation calling for federal chartering of corporations is due to William Cary. Cary, 'Federalism and Corporate Law: Reflections Upon Delaware', 83 *Yale LJ* 663 (1974). See also Joel Seligman, 'The Case for a Federal Corporate Charter', 49 *Md. L. Rev.* 947 (1990) (reviving a 'modest' form of Cary's proposal in light of recent corporate developments).

24. An example is the discussion of the controversial *Trans Union* decision found in Jonathan R. Macey and Geoffrey P. Miller, 'Toward an Interest-Group Theory of Delaware Corporate Law', 65 *Tex. L. Rev.* 469, 517–19 (1987).

25. Landmarks of the substantial literature include William J. Carney, 'Toward a More Perfect Market for Corporate Control', 9 *Del. J. Corp. L.* 593 (1984); Daniel R. Fischel, 'The "Race to the Bottom" Revisited: Reflections on Recent Developments in Delaware's Corporation Law', 76 *Nw. UL Rev.* 913, 944 (1982); Peter Dodd and Richard Leftwich, 'The Market for Corporate Charters: "Unhealthy Competition" versus Federal Regulation', *J. Bus. L.* 259, 275 (1980) (positive abnormal returns after reincorporation); Ralph Winter, 'State Law, Shareholder Protection, and the Theory of the Corporation', 7 *J. Leg. Stud.* 251 (1977); David A. Drexler, 'Federalism and Corporate Law: A Misguided Missile', 3 *Sec. Reg. LJ* 374 (1976).

26. 877 F. 2d 496 (7th Cir. 1989).

27. Ibid. at 507. See Fischel, *supra* n. 25, at 919–20. Fischel purported to find empirical evidence for the argument in Dodd and Leftwich, *supra* n. 25, at 275, 281–2 (finding that firms reincorporating in Delaware earn positive abnormal returns over the 25-month period preceding and including the reincorporation).

28. See Roberta Romana, 'Law as a Product: Some Pieces of the Incorporation Puzzle', 1 *JL Econ. & Org.* 225, 240 (1985) (documenting importance of corporate franchise revenues to Delaware). The New Jersey Corporation Law Revision Commission explicitly endorsed as 'sound public policy' the view that a 'flexible and permissive' corporation code should be adopted in order to attract and keep enterprises incorporated in the state. See Preface to NJ Stat. Ann. § 14A at xi (1969). See also Jonathan Macey and Geoffrey Miller, 'Toward an Interest-Group Theory of Delaware Corporate Law', 65 *Tex. L. Rev.* 469 (1987) (arguing that Delaware corporate bar is major beneficiary of incorporations in Delaware).

29. See Roberta Romano, 'The Political Economy of Takeover Statutes', 73 *Va. L. Rev.* 111 (1987); 'The State Competition Debate in Corporate Law', *supra* n. 11; 'Law as a Product: Some Pieces of the Incorporation Puzzle', *supra* n. 27.

30. The Delaware advantage extends to such routine matters as speed of processing incorporation papers and documents of verification. See Curtis Alva, 'Delaware and the Market for Corporate Charters: History and Agency', 15 *Del. J. Corp. L.* 885, 901–2 (1990). Alva's illuminating and entertaining survey of local bar attitudes and participation in the legal process adds two further elements: the absence of anti-managerial judges and of anti-managerial interest groups in the legislative process.

31. See *infra* n. 39.

32. See Macey and Miller, *supra* n. 28. I note in passing a difficulty with this theory: Delaware lawyers could more profitably exploit their monopoly position simply by charging higher fees for their services, rather than by inducing the Delaware legislature to adopt suboptimal, pro-lawyer rules. It may be that the rules transfer additional surplus from corporations that do not directly pay lawyers' fees, but at first cut it is not clear how this would be the case.

33. See Romano, *supra* n. 11, at 251–3 (suggesting lines of further research).

34. This was William Cary's approach. See Cary, *supra* n. 23.

35. Survey data are reported in Romano, *supra* n. 26, at 250, 272–3.

36. See David S. Schaffer, Jr., 'Delaware's Limit on Director Liability: How the Market for Incorporation Shapes Corporate Law', 10 *Harv. JL & Pub. Pol'y* 665, 683–4 (1987). See also Alva, *supra* n. 30, at 904–15 (reviewing history of the control share acquisition statute, the involuntary redemption statute, the limitation of corporate directors' liability, and several miscellaneous amendments, and finding that key to process is drafting by the Corporate Law Section of the Delaware State Bar Association).

37. Elliot J. Weiss and Lawrence J. White, 'Of Econometrics and Indeterminacy: A Study of Investors Reactions to "Changes" in Corporate Law', 75 *Calif. L. Rev.* 551 (1987).

38. Romano, *supra* n. 28, found that reincorporation is sometimes associated with positive abnormal returns for shareholders, but noted that the results may be affected by the association of announced reincorporation with acqui-

sitions programme. See also Peter Dodd and Richard Leftwich, 'The Market for Corporate Charters Unhealthy Competition versus Federal Regulation', 53 *J. Bus.* 259, 282 (1980) (reporting positive abnormal returns of 20.25% over 25-month period preceding and including the month of reincorporation, and finding no evidence of negative market reaction); Barry D. Baysinger and Henry N. Butler, 'Race for the Bottom Versus Climb to the Top: The ALI Project and Uniformity in Corporate Law', 10 *J. Corp. L.* 431, 459–61 (1985) (finding no significant difference between financial performance among corporations in strict and liberal states).

39. E.g. Michael Ryngaert and Jeffry M. Netter, 'Shareholder Wealth Effects of the Ohio Antitakeover Law', 4 *JL Econ. & Org.* 373, 373–83 (1988); Laurence Schumann, 'State Regulation of Takeovers and Shareholder Wealth: The Case of New York's 1985 Takeover Statutes', 19 *Rand J. Econ.* 557, 557–65 (1988). These effects appear analogous to the adoption of antitake-over charter amendments to which state take-over statutes bear a strong resemblance. See e.g. Harry DeAngelo and Edward M. Rice, 'Antitake-over Charter Amendments and Stockholder Wealth', 11 *J. Fin. Econ.* 329 (1983); Gregg A. Jarrell and Annette B. Poulsen, 'Shark Repellents and Stock Prices: The Effects of Antitakeover Amendments Since 1980', 19 *J. Fin. Econ.* 127 (1987). For further debate on the evidence regarding state statutes, see Donald G. Margotta, Thomas P. McWilliams, and Victoria B. McWilliams, 'An Analysis of the Stock Price Effect of the 1986 Ohio Takeover Legislation, 6 *J. L. Econ. & Org.* 235, 235–50 (1990); Michael Ryngaert and Jeffry Netter, 'Shareholder Wealth Effects of the 1986 Ohio Antitakeover Law Revisited: Its Real Effects', 6 *J. L. Econ. & Org.* 253, 253–61 (1990).

40. See e.g. Frank Easterbrook and Daniel R. Fischel, 'The Corporate Contract', 89 *Colum. L. Rev.* 1416, 1444–6 (1989). The relative efficiency of a background set of 'off the rack' terms should, of course, be distinguished from the desirability of permitting parties to 'opt out' of the background rules.

41. In addition to the two advantages mentioned in text, it prevents jurisdictions from adopting rules that discriminate against outsiders (as many state tender-offer statutes may do) or that create interjurisdictional externalities. I will return to these points below.

42. Lucian A. Bebchuk, 'Limiting Contractual Freedom in Corporate Law: The Desirable Constraints on Charter Amendments', 102 *Harv. L. Rev.* 1820 (1989); Lucian A. Bebchuk, 'Freedom of Contract and the Corporation: An Essay on the Mandatory Role of Corporate Law (1990) (Harvard Law and Economics Program Working Paper).

43. See Melvin Aron Eisenberg, 'The Structure of Corporation Law', 89 *Colum. L. Rev.* 1461, 1493–5 (1989).

44. Bebchuk, 'Limiting Contractual Freedom', *supra* n. 42, at 1840–51.

45. Curiously, Romano does not particularly emphasize the signalling effects, which assuredly are of great importance in this context.

46. German, Dutch, and French law mandate supervisory board representation for workers in at least some large corporations. While the impact of workers' representatives on board decisions is controversial, the ability to gather information and to exert moral suasion on the arguments made at board deliberations has force even when workers' representatives can be outvoted.

47. For an historical account, see Alfred D. Chandler, *Scale and Scope: The Dynamics of Industrial Capitalism* 506–13, 587–92 (1990). Currently, banks exert authority through control of voting rights conferred on them, by custody of bearer shares of individual investors, as well as through direct board representation and influence as creditors.

48. Mark Roe, 'A Political Theory of American Corporate Finance', 91 *Colum. L. Rev.* (Jan. 1991), argues for the substantial impact of American banking regulation on the patterns of share holding and on corporate governance structures.

49. See Jon Elster, *Sour Grapes* 93 (1983).

50. For example, some commentators attribute the difficulties with developing a unified set of ground rules for capital markets to the interest of members of particular exchanges in maintaining the market for their exchanges or in discouraging new members. See Wolf, 'EC is Expected to Clear Proposals on Securities and Bank Base Capital', *Wall St. J.*, 12 Dec. 1988, at 11, col. 1.

51. Matching of rules and transactional characteristics also occurs by a reverse process. Instead of local rule-makers, adapting to transactional conditions, transactors migrate to find the rules best suited for them. With consensual transactions, migration may be virtually costless, because parties can 'migrate' simply by stipulating the law to govern the transaction (via reincorporation or choice of law clauses).

52. Of course, in a sense, all of the rules considered here create 'public goods'. By using the term for the last two classifications of rules only, I wish to emphasize this distinction: that for the first two types of rules as discussed in the text, the shareholders of any single corporation, if it were feasible, would contract to have the 'harmonized' or optimal rule apply to them. In the latter two types of rule, by contrast, shareholders of any single corporation would favour evasion by reincorporation of their particular corporation.

53. Indeed, agreements to use a common language play an important role in facilitating trade, and help to account for the modern (post-15th-century) impetus toward formation of 'national' cultures based on uniform linguistic usage throughout a single political entity. See Ernest Gellner, *Nations and Nationalism* 19–62 (1983); Jose Ortega y Gasset, *La Rebelión de las Masas* 156–91, in 2 *Obras de José Ortega y Gasset* (Paulino Garagorri ed. 1979).

54. Michael Adams, 'Norms, Standards, Rights' 9–22 (Discussion Paper 79, Harvard Law School Program in Law and Economics) (Nov. 1990), provides a general description of the role of legal rules in establishing compatible standards, although the paper does not analyse corporate law rules. See also Katz

and Shapiro, 'Network Externalities, Competition and Compatibility, 75 *Amer. Econ. Rev.* 424 (1985) (presenting basic theory of compatibility).

55. Cf. Robert C. Clark, 'Contracts, Elites, and Traditions in the Making of Corporate Law', 89 *Colum. L. Rev.* 1703, 1728–30 (1989) (describing process of developing 'traditional' rules through imitation).

56. A related question beyond the scope of the present analysis is the appropriate *coercive powers* to be given to the centralized rule-making organization. In the US, of course, the SEC exercises its well-known panoply of criminal and civil coercive remedies to enforce disclosure, accounting, and procedural standards (on matters such as proxy voting). The Financial Accounting Standards Board is 'quasi public'. Its various rulings on accounting procedures and techniques are enforced by a mix of sanctions: standards of professional training and accreditation; incorporation of professional standards into the civil liability rules of tort and contract; incorporation into SEC rules; and reputational pressures exerted by the capital markets, particularly through the 'gatekeeping' function of accountants. See generally David Charny, 'Nonlegal Sanctions in Commercial Transactions', 104 *Harv. L. Rev.* 373, 412–20(1990). By contrast, the EC lacks a centralized rule-making organization with coercive powers (a European 'SEC') or a central European Stock Exchange with rule-making authority. Instead, harmonization operates through EC directives implemented by Member States or indirectly by the influence of quasi-public European-wide organizations.

57. Harmonization also sacrifices the benefits of experimentation by diverse sets of local rule-makers. But in the context of focal point rules, where the content of the rule is largely arbitrary, it seems unlikely that substantial improvements can be achieved by continued experimentation.

58. Detlev Vagts, 'Company Law Harmonization in the European Community', in *Emerging Standards of International Trade and Investment: Multinational Codes and Corporate Conduct* 17, 28 (Seymour J. Rubin and Gary Clyde Hufbauer eds. 1982).

59. For example, the Delaware courts' sharp tightening of fiduciary norms in the late 1970s, in *Singer* v. *Magnavoc*, 380 A. 2d 969 (Del. 1977), and its progeny, is sometimes attributed to fears of an SEC crackdown on Delaware's lax rules governing mergers among affiliated corporations. From this perspective, the EC directives on fiduciary norms can be seen as attempts prospectively to prevent this downward creep or race to the bottom, by specifying minimal levels below which no jurisdictions can crawl. In the US context, the looming spectre of SEC intervention provided a more informal and less highly articulated sense that there were indeed minimal standards for state regulation of corporate fiduciaries.

60. To be sure, if a shareholder holds a diversified portfolio, he or she would desire rules that maximize total shareholder wealth. However, this perspective would not govern the shareholder's conduct if opportunities for

subsequent evasion of the rule would mean an increase in personal wealth. Rather, the shareholder would then seek to seize these opportunities, even though he or she normally favours the same ruling being evaded. Large shareholders in a target firm would want to use an auction to maximize their payout in the take-over; they would just hope that the rules will prevent every one else from doing so, so that in general they can get the benefits of the wealth-maximizing auction ban. (Of course, my example here simply assumes that the ban on auctions maximizes wealth.)

61. Numerous event studies demonstrate that managers' defensive tactics harm the corporation's shareholders. See sources cited at n. 38 *supra*.

62. Cf. Alan Schwartz, 'Search Theory and the Tender Offer Auction', 2 *JL Econ. & Org.* 229 (1986) (describing the impact of auctions on incentive to search).

63. Cf. Easterbrook and Fischel, *supra* n. 40, at 1438–40 (noting that target shareholders have an incentive to adopt defences excessive from a social point of view, though not extending the analysis to jurisdictions' choice of rules).

64. Romano, 'The Political Economy of Takeover Statutes', *supra* n. 29, provides evidence for an interest-group account of take-over statutes.

65. See text at n. 38, *supra*.

66. The Commission's proposed take-over rules are reported at 21 *Fed. Sec. Reg. R.* 26 (1989). The rules are 'minimum standards', and comprise a ban on partial take-overs and some types of recapitalizations and poison pills, and a requirement that each Member State establish a regulatory authority for supervising compliance.

67. Julian Franks and Colin Mayer, 'Capital Markets and Corporate Control: A Study of France, Germany and the UK', 10 *Econ. Pol'y* 189, 195–9 (April 1990) (citing data from France, Germany, and Great Britain). There are no overtly hostile take-overs in Germany, and most control transactions are acquisitions of majority stakes rather than full acquisitions.

68. Ibid. at 209–10. Praise for the British regulatory system can be found in Lucian A. Bebchuk, 'The Pressure to Tender: An Analysis and Proposed Remedy', 12 *Del. J. Corp. Law* 911 (1985).

69. See Robert Schleifer and Lawrence Summers, 'Breach of Trust in Hostile Takeovers', in *Corporate Takeovers: Causes and Consequences* 33, 45–6 (A. Auerbach ed. 1989). Joshua G. Rosett, 'Do Union Wealth Concessions Explain Takeover Premiums? The Evidence on Contract Wages', 27 *J. Fin. Econ.* 247 (1990), provides some empirical data on the size of redistributions from union workers. For discussion of the normative implications of the Schleifer and Summers analysis, see Charny, *supra* n. 57, at 442–4.

70. It seems that effective resistance of German corporations to take-overs is accomplished more through informal co-operation among shareholders— facilitated by various social ties and pressures among businesspersons—rather than by the availability of legal mechanisms for warding off hostile bids. Pirelli's ill-fated attempt to take over Continental recently has stimulated

analysis along these lines. See 'Our Crowd: Corporate Governance in Germany', *The Economist*, 23 Feb. 1991, at 66–7 (attributing Pirelli's failure to concerned share-buying and voting by corporations whose managers had links to Continental); Hans-Jochen Otto, 'German Takeover Barriers: Obstacles to Foreigners are Nothing but a Myth', *Fin. Times*, 20 Feb. 1991, at 15, col. 6 (arguing that legal restrictions do not prevent hostile bids and that defensive devices are easily circumvented).

71. See text at notes 53–8, *supra*.

72. The focal-points argument for regulation is relatively weak because disclosure represents an area where conventions would readily emerge by spontaneous processes. See text at notes 55–6, *supra*.

73. See e.g. Frank Easterbrook and Daniel R. Fischel, 'Mandatory Disclosure and the Protection of Investors', 70 *Va. L. Rev.* 668, 680–96 (1984).

74. The relevant directives are: (1) Council Directive Coordinating the Requirements for Drawing Up, Scrutiny and Distribution of the Listing Particulars to be Published for the Admission of Securities to Official Stock Exchange Listing (Directive No. 80/390), OJ Eur. Comm. (No. L 100) (17 Mar. 1980), 1 Comm. Mkt. L. Rep. (CCH) para. 1731 (30 Aug. 1983) [the 'Listing Particulars Directive']; (2) Council Directive Coordinating the Requirements for the Drawing Up, Scrutiny and Distribution of the Prospectus to be Published When Transferable Securities Are Offered to the Public (Directive No. 89/298), OJ Eur. Comm. (No. L 124) 17 Apr. 1989); (3) the Interim Reports Directive, Directive No. 82/121, OJ Eur. Comm. (No. L 48) 26 (20 Feb. 1982), 1 Comm. Mkt. L. Rep. (CCH) para. 1741 (30 Aug. 1983); the Insider Trading Directive, Council Directive of 13 November 1989 Coordinating Regulations on Insider Trading (Directive No. 89/592), OJ Eur. Comm. (No. L 334) 39 (18 Nov. 1989). For a comparison of EC and US disclosure requirements, see Patrick Merloe, 'Internationalization of Securities Markets: A Critical Survey of U.S. and EEC Disclosure Requirements', 8 *J. Comp. Bus. and Cap. Market L.*249 (1986). The insider-trading directive (see Council Directive Coordinating Regulations on Insider Dealing (Directive No. 89/592), OJ Eur. Comm. (No. L334) (18 Nov. 1989)) similarly imposes regulations on insider trading more stringent than those of member states, some of whom had no extant regulation of such conduct.

75. See Rules Requiring Detailed Prospectuses Adopted by EC, will be effective 1991, 20 Sec. Reg. L. Rep. (BNA) 1975 (23 Dec. 1988).

76. SEC Release No. 6568 [1984–1985 Transfer Binder] Fed. Sec. L. Rep. (CCH) para. 83,743 (6 Mar. 1985); see also Securities and Exchange Commission, *Summary of Comments on Concept Release, Request for Comments on Issues Concerning Facilitation of Multinational Securities Offerings*, SEC File no. S76-9-85, Fed. Reg. (1986).

77. In particular, the resistance of European market intermediaries to more extensive regulation sharply contrasts with the attitude of US brokers and

investment bankers in the 1930s, who apparently favoured the move to stricter disclosure requirements. In effect, the securities laws provided intermediaries with an effective way of bonding themselves to a higher disclosure standard and of adopting a single disclosure format.

78. The possibility of such free-riding is a simple corollary of the public-goods argument for disclosure.

79. For a general analysis, see Charny *supra* n. 57, at 429–33, 439–41.

80. Klaus Hopt, 'European Attempts to Harmonize Company and Capital Market Law', *supra* n. 20, at 255–7, 280–2, summarizes the debate.

81. The manager's incentives would be derivative of whatever incentive they have to maximize shareholder wealth. Ironically, managerial 'slack' may serve the social good in cases where the managers diverge from shareholder wealth-maximization by complying with other social norms—as might be the case, for example, with some 'socially responsible' corporate conduct.

82. 'Codetermination' refers to the legally required appointment of workers' representatives to the board of directors. Germany and the Netherlands (and, among countries now applying to join the EC, Sweden and Austria) have adopted codetermination for some types of corporations. See generally Klaus Hopt, 'New Ways in Corporate Governance: European Experiments with Labor Representation on Corporate Boards', 82 *Mich. L. Rev.* 1338 (1984). For a thorough review of the obstacles to harmonization of codetermination rules, see Thomas E. Abeltshauser, 'Towards a European Constitution of the Firm', *supra* n. 7, at 1237–60.

83. The discussion in the text draws on the provocative rethinking of corporate limited liability proposed by Henry Hansmann and Reinier Kraakman, 'The Uneasy Case for Limiting Shareholder Liability for Corporate Torts', *Yale LJ* (1991), and David Leebron, Limited Liability Tort Victims and Creditors (Columbia University School of Law Center for Law and Economic Studies) (working paper number 48) (1990).

84. For discussion of the particular issues that arise with bank capitalization requirements, see Sydney Key and Hal Scott, 'International Trade in Banking Services: A Conceptual Framework' (draft 8 Oct. 1990). As Key and Scott argue, safety and soundness rules, such as capitalization requirements, require harmonization of rules among jurisdictions, with enforcement by the 'home' country (analogously, for corporations generally, the jurisdiction of incorporation).

85. Joseph Weiler, *Il sistema communitario europeo: Struttura giuridica e processo politico* 41–53 (1985), provides an elegant exposition of the conceptual difficulties with the 'supranational' regulatory enterprise.

International Corporate Finance and the Challenge of Creative Compliance

DOREEN MCBARNET
and CHRISTOPHER WHELAN

Regulation and the internationalization of capital markets

Internationalization of capital markets has underlined two key interrelated issues in the regulation of corporate finance. First, demands for access to reliable financial information have escalated as international financial risks have grown. The sums involved in corporate deals grew exponentially in the 1980s. The leveraged buyout of RJR Nabisco in 1988 cost $25.08 billion, resulting in borrowings for the new RJR of $22.08 billion, more than the combined national debts of Bolivia, Uruguay, Costa Rica, Honduras, and Jamaica.[1] The need for transparency in financial reporting has been further highlighted by recent major corporate and banking crashes, such as the Bank of Credit and Commerce International, British and Commonwealth, Rush and Tompkins, Polly Peck, Bond Corporation, and Maxwell Communications Corporation.

Subsequent analysis of some of these has revealed that the reliability of the financial information disclosed prior to collapse was suspect while the transparency of corporate financial activity was undermined by the use of 'havens' throughout the world where secrecy rather than disclosure is the norm. The suddenness, at least as far as the public was concerned, of many of these crashes, as well as the 'mega' sums involved, both testify to the fact that, in practice, investors are not always properly informed of the real financial risk to which they are exposed.

Secondly, calls for international harmonization of the rules governing disclosure have increased as markets have opened up to international capital. The demand is for harmonization which allows the players in capital markets to genuinely compare the financial results disclosed by different companies in different countries, and creates a 'level playing field', in which all the players are subject to the same rules. In an international capital market, the argument runs, there are dangers in differences

This chapter is based on research in the UK, France, Germany, and Brussels. We are grateful for the funding contributions of the European Commission, French Commissariat du Plan, and Jacob Burns Socio-legal Fund.

in national rules, dangers, for example of creating what has been called a 'Delaware effect'. In the USA, the advantageous rules of the state of Delaware attract corporate registration of companies which actually operate elsewhere—at the time of our research only one major US corporation operated out of Delaware but 56 per cent of the top 500 US corporations, and 45 per cent of all companies whose shares were listed on the New York Stock Exchange, were registered there.[2]

Concern has been expressed that in an international market, different national rules can likewise create competitive advantage. Companies in one country might attract investment on the basis of high profitability or net value which is a product of advantageous rules on financial reporting and disclosure rather than genuine superiority of performance. The Securities and Exchange Commission recently announced a review of US accounting standards to determine whether they were 'adversely affecting the ability of US companies to compete internationally with foreign companies whose home country's accounting rules may be less stringent than US standards'.[3]

Different rules in different regimes may well distort the level playing field as when UK accounting rules have given UK companies an edge in take-overs, allowing them to offer higher bids for acquisitions than otherwise equally placed competitors. So, for example the spate of take-overs in the 1980s of US corporations by UK companies, often large US companies by smaller UK companies, has been put down in part to the comparative advantage given to UK companies by rules on accounting for goodwill. When Blue Arrow acquired the US corporation, Manpower, it could, under UK accounting rules, project annual profits of $30.1 million. A US bidder operating under US rules would have had to deduct at least $30 million each year from profits to write off goodwill, allowing a projected profit of only $1.1 million. This could make it harder to sell the bid to shareholders and to raise finance.

How advantageous this competitive advantage was, might with hindsight be questioned, where overbidding and major financial difficulties have resulted.[4] However differences in rules have provided fuel for complaints and for the rhetoric of the need for harmonized rules and a level playing field in international capital markets. Can harmonization and comparability, and the perhaps more fundamental goals of transparency and reliability, be achieved? This chapter addresses the issue by drawing on our research on law and accounting in the Single European Market.[5]

The creation of the Single European Market (SEM) provides us with a case study in regulation aimed at harmonization. Fundamental to its idea of a free competitive market is the removal of those rule-based competitive advantages which act as prohibited trade barriers and their replacement with single community rules. The harmonization programme of the SEM is a regulatory response to the problem of divergent rules within an international market. The tool being used in this strategy is European Community law. The SEM is thus a prime example of an attempt at using law to achieve international integration into a single market based on a level playing field. How successful has it been? How successful can it be?

In practice there have been major problems in the EC's programme of integration and regulation. Some are familiar problems with any regulation, although they are exacerbated by the international context. We will explore these in the specific context of the regulation of the financial reporting, briefly reviewing the familiar problems of legislation and enforcement, then focusing on the particular challenge we identify as 'creative compliance'.

Controlling competitive advantage: the case of the Single European Market

Harmonization of disclosure of financial information in the SEM has been tackled via the company law directives, particularly the fourth directive on company accounts and the seventh directive on group accounts. It has been no easy task.

The process of political compromise which has marked EC legislation generally has led to problems. There is the problem of settling for the lowest common denominator in standardization. While the playing field may then be level, the EC rules are too weak. Worse, they may have been substituted for strong national regulations. Thus, fears have been frequently been expressed that high standards of protection—for investors, employees, consumers, etc.—in particular member states will be 'jeopardised in pursuit of economic integration'.[6] Then there is the tolerance of options within apparently harmonized rules. This can take the form of permission for member states to derogate from or to choose whether to implement certain terms of the measure. It seems, for example, that only the UK has implemented the option in the Seventh Directive which declares a parent–subsidiary relationship to exist where there is a participating interest and the actual exercise of dominant influence (discussed further below).

Compromise can also lead to gaps. It has been argued that a mergers regulation has been possible only on the basis that it concentrates on the competition aspects and ignores the social effects of mergers.[7] There is also the problem of delay with the result that by the time old problems are sorted out new ones have appeared. In an accounting context, the new practice of transferring goodwill to intangibles such as brands is possible 'as a result of the absence of any requirement to the contrary within EC directives'.[8] Such problems of the political and legislative process have undermined the quality of the rules themselves and their value as an instrument of genuine harmonization. In short, while EC Directives are binding on all member states as to the end to be achieved and uniform standards may be mandated, significant deviations in the actual rules of member states remain in practice.

In the particular context of the disclosure of financial information, the European Community was confronted with marked differences in the basic purposes and philosophies of accounting in different countries. Indeed, even after the implementation of the fourth directive there remain considerable variations between member states, as Touche Ross's recent study[9] indicates.

This study demonstrated how a hypothetical company's performance could be reported in line with the national rules of different European Community countries. The reported profits for the same company undertaking the same transactions in the course of a year could vary from a lowest achievable ECU 27 million under German rules to a highest achievable ECU 194 million under UK rules. The most likely German result was only two thirds of the UK's (ECU 133 million in Germany, compared with ECU 192 million in the UK). Yet this was the same company reporting exactly the same business. This is a striking example of the difficulties involved in making international comparisons of company performance on the basis of disclosed financial information when the rules governing that disclosure are so diverse.

The Touche Ross study attributed a key role in this to the different orientations of member states to accounting for the capital market or accounting for tax. Where UK and Netherlands accounting separates tax and market accounts, in other countries, such as Germany, tax and market accounts are the same so that companies wishing to claim tax allowances must present the market with accounts with the appropriate claims deducted from profits. This leads to an inbuilt conservatism in German accounts which distorts comparability.

One can see just how difficult comparison can be by considering the accounts of German motor manufacturer BMW at the time of our research of Germany. BMW was taking full advantage of tax benefits such as the 100% first year allowances for investments in West Berlin, involving accelerated depreciation, which appeared as such on the accounts. The result is that one could not even sensibly compare a Berlin company's financial accounts with those of a Hamburg company. Yet even for the international market, BMW did not (and was not required to) disclose the effect this had on profits, noting merely that 'full advantage is taken of tax concessions regarding depreciation charges'.[10] As one (then) Big 8 accountant observed: 'this tells you they are extremely prudent but does not tell you much else'. How then are investors to compare BMW's performance with that of companies based elsewhere in Europe, or for that matter in the world? Continued variation in rules, and in accounting purposes and philosophy, undermines comparability.

This situation has been compounded by problems of enforcement and non-compliance even with compromised rules. Enforcement of law is a perennial problem even within the nation-state. Effective enforcement is constrained by organizational problems, by lack of resources, by problems in detecting violation or non-compliance. Enforcing *international* regulation is more complex still.

In the European Community there are policing problems at two levels. First there is the problem of ensuring member states who have agreed to the substance of specific directives in fact implement them. European Community law comes in different forms. While 'regulations' are directly applicable in member states, the more frequently used 'directives', have, for the most part, to be implemented into their own domestic law by member states before they take effect. The organization of the European Commission has been focused more on making than on enforcing legislation.

Then there is the problem of how closely member states themselves police compliance among companies falling under new regulations. Politics can play a part here too. Implementing law, but failing to enforce it, can result in the 'law in the books' bearing no relation to actual practice, and reduce the appearance of regulation and harmonization to the merely symbolic.

In Germany, for example, the fourth directive was extremely unpopular. Many small and medium sized companies had not hitherto been required to produce public accounts. The implementation of the fourth directive meant 340,000 companies would now have to do so for the first time, this in a country where in 1985 there were only about 6,000 and in 1990 only 12,000 qualified auditors (Wirtschaftsprufer and Vereidigte

Buchprufer).[11] Germany was five years late in implementing the directive and has throughout lobbied (successfully)[12] for a change in the directive to exempt many of these companies. In the meantime enforcement appears to have been somewhat ineffective. Less than 10% of German companies complied with the requirement to register company accounts in the prescribed time.[13] Harmonization of member state legislation did not necessarily mean harmonization—or transparency—in practice.

What are the solutions to such problems? The routine reaction is to demand a regulatory response, calling for better rules, better enforcement to achieve more effective rules and real compliance. Yet even if they could be achieved, better rules, better enforcement may not produce transparency or comparability. A great deal of effort—in policymaking, enforcement, and research—is expended routinely on the objective of securing compliance. But even achieving this objective may not solve the problem. Securing compliance may not be enough.[14]

Formal compliance by those subject to regulation with even tough rules, cannot necessarily be equated with effective achievement of declared regulatory goals. Compliance far from being a solution to a regulatory problem may itself pose a regulatory problem. This is what we see as the paradox of compliance. Regulatory problems have been defined for too long as problems of non-compliance. The problem we focus on is the problem of compliance, and particularly the problem of 'creative compliance'.

Focusing on compliance as a problem involves a switch of perspective, from the regulatory response, to the response of the regulated. After all, those on the receiving end of rules do not simply receive them passively; they react and respond. They can respond by lobbying for change or by non-compliance, taking the risk of sanctions if law is enforced.

But the regulated can also respond in another way, setting lawyers and other advisers to work to develop responses to regulation, which do not simply accept the impact of the rules but which circumvent them. This involves using the rules themselves in innovative ways to avoid and manage regulation. This is why we have to switch perspective in another way too, from issues of politics and enforcement, to closer scrutiny of the nature and role of law and regulation. Law and regulatory rules are amenable to use not only as instruments for implementing regulation but as instruments for resisting it. Such resistance to law through law is epitomised in the strategy of 'creative compliance'.

Creative compliance

Creative compliance means complying with rules in form without complying in substance, meeting the letter but not the spirit of the law. This is not an enforcement problem. On the contrary enforcement is preempted because control is avoided without breaking the rules. Creative compliance means operating within loopholes in the law, beyond the reach of the law, or using the fabric of the law itself to create loopholes or innovative techniques which comply totally with the requirements of the rules but none the less completely undermine the policy behind it.

So for example when Germany implemented the fourth directive requiring disclosure of financial information for many companies for the first time, one response for the companies concerned was to lobby for change; another was simply not to comply. These strategies posed practical enforcement problems and political problems for regulators. There was, however, another response possible, and it posed a more fundamentally legal problem. That was to change the legal structure of the business to remain outside the ambit of the law, and so avoid disclosure by creative use of law.

In Germany there are a number of different legal forms available for the conduct of business. Those affected by the 1987 implementation of the fourth directive were mainly GmbHs. However, those who wished to escape the requirement of the directive to disclose financial information could reorganize into a different legal form, into a GmbH & Co. or a GmbH & Co. KG, often via highly complex legal routes.[15] The advantage lay in the fact that the GmbH & Co. and GmbH & Co. KG were commercial partnerships which were not required to disclose financial information like other German corporate structures (Aktiengesellschaft, Kommanditgesellschaft auf Aktien, and GmbH). Disclosure could thus be escaped without non-compliance, via legal lateral thinking, via creative compliance.

This particular loophole has been closed by new rules,[16] not least because of EC fears that what was defined at the time as a local German problem might be used more widely, fear indeed of a Delaware effect, despite apparent legislative harmonization by regulators. As a senior European Commission official put it: 'It would be iniquitous and contrary to the spirit and aims of the Fourth and Seventh Directive to allow those particular kinds of partnerships and unlimited companies to evade the accounting requirements applicable to other undertakings having limited liability.'[17] The regulatory response was not enough; the regulated could respond in turn to find new sources of rule-based competitive advantage, requiring further regulatory response in a cat and mouse game which is repeated in tax avoidance, the regulation of financial institutions and elsewhere.[18] And the game is not yet over, European Community law has itself provided other business structures which, we would suggest, might in turn be used to avoid disclosure. Certainly, even where such structures are set up for other reasons, non-disclosure of financial information is one consequence.

So, when Airbus criticizes British Airways (BA) for being anti-European by buying its engines from America and even hints that 'sweeteners' may have underpinned its decision-making,[19] BA cannot easily retaliate. Airbus is a French Groupe d'Intérêts Économique (GIE). As such it does not have to publish accounts. Its liabilities, its sweeteners, government subsidies or whatever are hidden, legally, from view.

The GIE is only available in France. But it was the model for the new business structure available since July 1989, throughout the EC known as the European Economic Interest Grouping (EEIG).[20] The EC Regulation on EEIGs was designed to facilitate cross-border business co-operation within the Community by removing the need to operate in an unfamiliar system of law. But the EEIG is not only freed from legal obstacles, it is also freed from the obligation to disclose financial information. An EEIG has the advantage of flexible forms of funding. There is no capital requirement and liabilities can be hidden. The EEIG may thus offer route to escape from harmonized disclosure rules.

It is paradox enough that the 'strongest' form of EC law, a Regulation,[21] can be used as a means of escaping from EC Directives, but there is more. While the Regulation provides for a uniform framework throughout the EC, it leaves to national law a number of matters it could not cover without seeking to impose a uniform system of private law. EEIG members are free to register it in any member state where it has a business presence or where it has its central administration. It will then be subject to the law of that state. The perceived and actual differences in national law, such as tax provisions, and in national legal systems—common law/adversarial versus civil/inquidistorial—re-emerge then as factors in determining where to register the EEIG. The effect of the Regulation may thus be that the choice of location will be distorted, 'Delaware' fashion, to the most favourable state. This may be the least regulated. Whether this will pose a significant problem remains to be seen.

Escaping disclosure requirements altogether is one way to throw transparency and comparability, but of course if a company wants to enter the market it may have to disclose information. Indeed, in practice there may be more harmonization than the formal rules would imply. French companies often voluntarily produce accounts following US GAAP (Generally Accepted Accounting Principles) for the simple reason that they want to enter the US market. Companies may produce multiple accounts for different markets or show how accounts prepared under one set of rules would have to be adjusted in another context.

But that is where we come to the underlying sense of the reliability of the information that is being disclosed. Creative compliance affects the reliability of financial information and, in doing so, it also affects its comparability. One area of creative compliance currently attracting regulatory attention is that of off-balance sheet financing (OBSF). This refers to the raising of finance in ways which do not appear in the accounts at all or do appear in the accounts but fail to make clear the real exposure involved.

OBSF can take many forms. It can involve the creation and use of complex and innovative financial instruments, which have posed a challenge for accounting rules worldwide. It is often unclear just how they should be accounted, measured or categorized, and this provides an opportunity for creative accounting. But OBSF can also involve the use of legal structures which avoid disclosure of awkward information. One UK example which has stimulated extensive regulatory response is the 'quasi-subsidiary'.

In the UK, and with the implementation of the seventh directive throughout the European Community, groups of companies are required to produce consolidated accounts showing the assets and liabilities of the group as a whole. However the techniques known as the non-subsidiary subsidiary, quasi-subsidiary or orphan subsidiary, have been used to avoid the requirement to consolidate financial information, thus hiding liabilities, manipulating performance indicators such as earnings per share, and, according to the reported figures, making the company stronger on the market, more creditworthy to lenders, and more powerful in the take-over market, in short, creating a potential competitive advantage based on manipulation of rules rather than performance or value.

The form used depends on the rules in play. In the UK under the rules of company law prior to the 1989 Companies Act, a subsidiary's accounts had to be included in the group's accounts (subject to some exceptions) if the parent company owned more than 50 per cent of the shares and controlled more than half of the board of directors. A number of legal structures were created with varying degrees of complexity to retain control of a company while avoiding meeting those two requirements and so avoiding the need to include the quasi-subsidiary in the group's accounts. With the quasi-subsidiary safely off the balance sheet it could be used to carry debts or other awkward financial information in *its* accounts without affecting the balance sheet or earnings per share ratios of the group.

Such vehicles were used for many purposes by many household name companies including Cadbury Schweppes, Dixons, Burton, Storehouse, Habitat, S & W Berisford, and Beazer.[22] Maxwell Corporation's acquisition of Macmillan and the Official Airlines Guide (OAG) for $2.6 billion and $750 million respectively, in 1988, used off-balance sheet structures. Macmillan was bought through shell company Mills Acquisition. OAG was bought by Pergamon, which as a private company, was not included in Maxwell Corporation's balance sheet. If the companies had been bought directly by MCC and included in the group's balance sheet there would have been seriously adverse effects on the earnings per share ratios of the group with possible knock on effects on share prices. The interest costs involved in servicing the enormous debt incurred would also have affected MCC's pre-tax profits.

Purchasing through an off-balance sheet structure provided a window in which to try to sell off assets to reduce the enormous burden of debt before bringing the acquisitions onto MCC's accounts. MCC's broker was reported in the press offering reassurance that the timing of the transfer of ownership of MacMillan would ensure there was no dilution of group earnings per share.[23] In reality, neither the debt nor the interest costs went away. But they were kept off MCC's reported assets and profits, even though MCC remained ultimately exposed to the financial risks involved.

The quasi-subsidiary in the particular forms constructed in the 1980s is no longer possible. These have been caught by new rules in the Companies Act 1989. However, the form employed is dictated by the rules in play at any given time. New rules can simply mean adaptation and new techniques. Even before the 1989 Act was on the statute book, the practitioners we were interviewing claimed to be constructing new techniques with the express purpose of meeting the requirements of the new rules yet still avoiding consolidation of riskier ventures in group accounts.

The deadlocked joint venture is one of several current techniques, carefully designed in a bid to escape the new law. The criteria for consolidation of a company's results in the larger group's accounts moved in the 1989 Act towards broader criteria, aimed more at capturing the economic substance of corporate relationships and not just their formal legal structures.[24] The new criteria were, first, participating interest (which was broadly but clearly defined) and second, control defined more vaguely in terms of 'actual dominant influence'.

The deadlocked joint venture is geared to avoiding this criterion of control, being based on a 50–50 partnership with neither partner controlling. Deadlocked joint venture companies have been used as vehicles for property development, and the discovery, after its sudden collapse, of a claimed £700 million of debt in joint ventures involving construction/property development group Rush and Tompkins clearly reveals how the joint venture can work to hide liabilities. The receivers at Rush and Tompkins have suggested many of its 50 joint ventures were joint in name alone with Rush and Tompkins carrying most of the risk.[25]

The regulatory response continues with the accounting profession's efforts to produce a new accounting standard to ensure the reality of risks and rewards is disclosed. But the approach is controversial. The standard has been in process since 1987 and is still at draft stage, in Exposure Draft 49 (ED49).[26] There must also be doubts as to the feasibility of effectively and sustainedly enforcing the 'spirit of the law' rather than ensuring merely formal or creative compliance.[27] Off balance sheet financing is not a UK phenomenon nor even just a European phenomenon, but a regulatory headache in the corporate sector and in banking internationally.[28]

Such creative compliance has relevance for both transparency and comparability in financial reporting. A company which can raise finance in ways which protect its balance sheet and earnings per share ratios may not only distort its own financial image but may create for itself a competitive advantage over those who offer fuller disclosure of debt and risk.

The challenges of creative compliance in a competitive market

When issues arise perceived as requiring a regulatory response, then, however powerful that regulatory response may be, it may still be rendered ineffective by the response of the regulated. Even if we could achieve harmonized rules and formidable enforcement it would not be the end of the regulatory story but the beginning of the next chapter, the regulated's response. In the context of international capital markets, variation in the stringency of different nation's laws and regulations has been pointed to as a source of competitive advantage. Indeed there are often powerful economic incentives for governments to promote a 'Delaware effect' so long as they are benefiting. But law can provide a means of competitive advantage in another way, less dependent on governments or regulators. Law must be recognized not just as a means of regulatory control but as a raw material[29] with which the competitors themselves can create rule-based advantage.

Indeed there is a paradox in using law or other forms of regulation to remove rule-based competitive advantage and create a level playing field for fair competition. The situation needs to be viewed from the perspective of the players in the competition. From this perspective the level playing field may well be something seen as an unqualified goods—*for one's competitors*. For oneself, there may be other ambitions, such as the vantage point of a little molehill of competitive advantage in the middle of that level playing field. In the competitive environment which is the goal of the SEM, there may be every incentive to use creative compliance to stay one step above levelling law.

Paradoxically, regulation, intended to remove artificial competitive advantage can also create opportunities to gain competitive advantage. A legally based level playing field opens up new sources of competitive advantage, with some more able than others to creatively escape even harmonized regulatory restrictions. The rules of the level playing field themselves become obstacles to some but not all. Regulation in effect becomes a further stimulus for innovative use of law both to defeat unwelcome regulation and to secure advantage over competitors.

This produces a dilemma for regulatory authorities, bent on a policy of free competition. How are they to encourage companies to take advantage of a competitive environment while at the same time discouraging them from gaining a competitive edge by getting round the restrictions of the rules themselves? One irony of the Single European Market is that the European Commission uses law to establish a level playing field for competitive market activity, producing, indeed, 'an immense corpus of law'.[30] But in a competitive market law may become just one more market obstacle to be overcome by the legal creativity of the regulated. The same paradox is likely to be repeated in regulation of international capital markets more generally. As one of the then Big 8 accountants we interviewed put it: 'What we are seeing is competition based on comparative creativity rather than on financial strength or traditional business links.'[31]

The significance for the international capital market is not, however, just a matter of a level playing field, perhaps always something of a holy grail. It is also a matter of risk. Global markets imply bigger deals, more volatility, and more risk. The reality of the risk that was there in the creativity of the 1980s is under the spotlight in the recession of the 1990s. Creative compliance poses a challenge not just for a competitive market but for the exposure to, and indeed creation of, risk in that competitive market. It also poses a major challenge for regulation, with no easy solution in sight. Yet unless the challenge of creative compliance can be effectively met, there can be little realistic prospect of achieving comparability in the market or of ensuring adequate disclosure of financial risk.

Notes

1. *Sunday Times*, 4 September 1988.
2. W. Landau, 'The Federal and State Roles in Regulating US Business Corporations', in B. Wachter *et al.*, *Harmonisation of Company and Securities Law* (Tilburg University Press, 1989).
3. 22 Sec Reg and Law Rep (BNA) 1111, 27 July 1990.
4. *Sunday Times*, 7 October 1990.
5. Based on analysis of law and financial techniques and interviews with leading practitioners and regulators in the UK, France, Germany, and Brussels.
6. See e.g. A. McGee and S. Weatherill, 'The Evolution of the Single Market—Harmonisation of Liberalisation', (1990) 53 *Modern Law Review* 578, 585.
7. Ibid. 591, n. 90.
8. Touche Ross, *Accounting for Europe* (Touche Ross, 1989), 18.
9. Ibid.
10. BMW annual report to December 1987.
11. *The Wirtschaftspruferkammer*, (Wirtschaftspruferkammer, Dusseldorf, 1991).
12. 90/604/EC.
13. Senior official, German Ministry of Justice.
14. D. McBarnet, 'The Construction of Compliance and the Challenge for Control: The Limits of Non-compliance Research', in J. Slemrod (ed.), *Who Pay their Taxes and Why?* (Michigan University Press, 1992).
15. Strobol, Killius, and Vorbrugg, *Business Law Guide to Germany*, 2nd edn. (CCH Editions Ltd., Bicester, 1988).
16. Directive extending the scope of the Fourth Directive on annual accounts and the Seventh Directive on companies, adopted Nov. 1990. Implementation date is 1 January 1993, but it need not apply until 1995: 90/605/EEC.
17. K. Van Hulle, *Developments in Financial Accounting and Reporting of the European Community*, 14 (KPMG, Amsterdam, 1987).
18. D. McBarnet, 'Law, Policy and Legal Avoidance', *Journal of Law and Society* (Spring, 1988); and see E. Kane on the 'regulatory dialectic' e.g. in 'Impact of Regulation on Economic Behaviour', *Journal of Finance*, 36 no. 2 (May 1981).

19. *The Times*, 27 November 1991.
20. Regulation 2137/85.
21. That is, it is directly applicable in member states.
22. For a detailed analysis of Bearer's use of a quasi-subsidiary for the acquisition of Koppers, see McBarnet and Whelan, 'Law Management and Corporate Governance', in J. McCahery, S. Picciolo, and S. Scott (eds.), *Corporate Control and Corporate Accountability* (1993).
23. *Financial Times*, 5 November 1988.
24. See McBarnet and Whelan, 'The Elusive Spirit of the Law', *Modern Law Review* (November, 1991).
25. Christopher Morris of Touche Ross, *The Times*, 30 April 1990.
26. Accounting Standards Committee, ED 49: 'Reflecting the Substance of Transactions in Assets and Liabilities' (Accounting Standards Committee, 1990).
27. See McBarnet and Whelan op. cit., n. 24.
28. For example, Bank of International Settlements, *Recent Innovations in International Banking* (BIS, 1986).
29. McBarnet, 'Law and Capital: Legal Form and Legal Actors', *International Journal of the Sociology of Law* (August, 1984).
30. P. Sutherland, 'Address by Mr Peter D. Sutherland', in Irish Centre for European Law (ed.), *The Legal Implications of 1992* (1990, 4.
31. Head of Treasury Practice Group, International Accounting firm, London.

STATE, MARKET, AND ENTERPRISE

Regulatory Reform: An Appraisal

JOHN KAY and JOHN VICKERS

I. Introduction

Britain is at the centre of an international process of regulatory reform. The frameworks of competition and regulation faced by existing and potential participants in the telecommunications, energy, transport, water, financial services, and some professional services industries are being transformed. Older, informal structures have been breaking down under the pressure of powerful economic, technological, and ideological forces, and they are being officially dismantled. This is sometimes called 'deregulation', but that is a misleading term because, as often as not, new and generally more explicit regulatory structures are simultaneously erected in place of what went before. The apparently paradoxical combination of deregulation and reregulation, which is most clearly evident in the financial services industry, is what we mean by 'regulatory reform'.

The aim of this chapter is to give an economic assessment of these new developments, drawing several lessons from recent experience. Our prime concern is with the economic performance of the industries in question—the productive, allocative, and dynamic efficiency with which they meet consumers' changing demands. This is our central criterion, and we believe that other objectives—for example, income distribution are usually better promoted by instruments other than regulation. Nevertheless distributional considerations may exert a major influence on regulatory policy in practice.

Our approach is to identify the market failures that regulation seeks to remedy, and to examine the incentive structures of alternative regulatory schemes. We compare the properties of public regulation and self-regulation, and hybrids such as 'self-regulation within a statutory framework'. Since regulatory constraint is only one of the influences that affect the decisions of economic agents, the analysis of regulation is closely bound up with questions of *ownership* and *competition*.

This is a revised and edited version of J. Kay and J. vickers, 'Regulatory reform in Britain', *Economic Policy*, October 1988.

Competition and regulation are often regarded as substitutes, and the simple maxim 'Competition where possible, regulation where necessary' indeed has merit as a first approximation for industries in which the source of market failure is the possible abuse of market power. But even in such industries, the connections between competition and regulation, and the ways of combining them, are numerous and complex. In multiproduct industries (or in industries where there are several stages in the vertical chain of production), it can be difficult to regulate one part of the business without affecting the nature of competition in other parts. One purpose of regulation may be to promote and maintain conditions for effective competition: liberalization may then alter the kind of regulation that is needed, not the need for regulation. Regulation may seek to use competitive incentives, for example, in the form of 'yardstick regulation', which seeks to encourage regional monopolists to compete with each other in cost reduction. There are some areas in which franchising ('competition for monopoly') can be used, but that still requires regulation in the form of contract administration and enforcement and franchising may be more appropriately viewed as a means of regulation than an alternative to it.

Where market failure has causes other than market power, regulation can be a prerequisite for there to be effective competition (or indeed a market at all). Without requirements of capital adequacy, the vulnerability of the banking system to bank runs would tend to have an adverse effect on competition in the market for bank deposits. Where product quality is uncertain, asymmetries of information may deter many consumers from entering the market. But, even in cases such as these regulation is not the only way of seeking to remedy market failure. Market participants themselves may be able to surmount the problem by means of reputation, brand names, warranties, and so on.

Finally, competition between the regulators themselves can have a role to play. For example, the exposure of financial fraud is likely to be carried out more energetically if 'self-regulators' within the industry compete with public regulatory bodies. Moreover, financial regulators in one jurisdiction 'compete' with regulators in other countries, in so far as investors direct their business to the most efficient financial market. Similarly, different professional bodies in the same industry (e.g. accountancy) can indirectly compete in terms of standards. These possibilities for beneficial competition between regulators in many ways mirror what happens in competition between firms in markets with asymmetric information. Indeed, the individual firm, with its mechanisms of internal regulation, is perhaps the best example of a self-regulatory organization.

In emphasizing properties of the incentives which exist under alternative regulatory regimes, we stress the distinction between the regulation of structure and the regulation of conduct. Regulators may be concerned with the way in which a market is organized (structural regulation), or with behaviour within the market (conduct regulation). Structural regulation may be preferable to conduct regulation where there is asymmetry of information between the regulator and the regulated. This arises in many contexts. Since it is impossible to determine whether a professional, faced with a conflict of interest, is acting in the best interests of his client, a sensible solution (if the possible conflict is important) may be to say that he can not act in such a case. Since we cannot judge whether a utility that controls the transmission network is offering fair terms of access to independent suppliers, a natural solution is to separate the functions of supply and transmission. Since we cannot know whether a firm is operating at maximum efficiency, the better approach is to impose a market structure (usually a competitive one) which gives incentives to maximum efficiency.

Structural regulation is often concerned with the extent to which firms operating in one regulated market are permitted to enter others. This is the issue of functional separation, often described as single capacity. Where single capacity regulation exists, there is generally pressure to dismantle it. But, at the same time, there are many cases of measures to introduce single capacity rules where dual or multiple capacity already exists. We consider why these conflicting movements exist.

These themes of regulation, ownership, competition, and information will recur throughout the chapter. Section 2 considers the rationale for regulation—the sources of market failure that it seeks to remedy—under three main headings: externalities, competition and monopoly, and information issues. Sections 3 and 4 deal, respectively, with the institutions and mechanisms of regulation. Sections 5 and 6 deal with two specific issues which appear to arise in a variety of regulatory contexts: functional separation of activities as a regulatory technique, and regulation to govern quality of service.

Our assessment of regulatory practice reveals many difficulties. In section 7 we examine mechanisms for escaping or minimizing the need for regulation, while section 8 draws some general conclusions.

2. Reasons for Regulation

The primary rationale for regulation, along with other elements of public policy towards industry, is to remedy various kinds of market failure.

Traditional analysis distinguished between *externalities* and *market power* as sources of welfare loss (see, for example, Bator's (1958) classic anatomy of market failure). More recent analysis has greatly illuminated a third major source of market failure: *asymmetric information*. Information problems feature prominently in what follows. They provide the chief rationale for much regulation—particularly in the financial system—and are essential to understanding the relationship between a regulatory agency and the firm or firms that it regulates.

The distribution of income and wealth generated by the market system is sometimes considered as another type of market failure. This is an important issue, but we do not pursue it further here. Industrial policies generally, and regulation in particular, are usually ill-suited to wider distributional ends, which are better accomplished by other instruments of public policy, particularly the tax and benefit system. Regulatory policy should be directed, in an industry-specific manner, at what it does best.

Externalities

Externalities arise when the well-being of one economic agent (consumer or firm) is directly affected by the actions of another. The textbook example is pollution: the effluent from chemical plants has an adverse effect on fishermen, which the chemical companies do not take into account.[1] The regulation of the discharge of effluent is a possible remedy; tax policy might be another. In a partial equilibrium setting, externalities are often expressed in terms of divergences between private and social costs (or benefits). At a deeper level, externalities can be viewed as an example of *missing markets*. In our illustration, if fishermen and chemical companies could trade in contracts for the water to be of given cleanliness, the externality problem could, in principle, be overcome. Of course, problems of transactions costs, contract specification, and enforcement, etc. make this a hopeless idea in practice, but it is important to understand the underlying causes of market failure. As we explain below, information asymmetries are another class of missing markets.

Externalities do feature in some of the industries that are undergoing regulatory reform. In telecommunications there are externalities arising from network effects. The benefit obtained by a subscriber depends upon who else subscribes to the same network. This externality may justify some subsidy to access charges (lines rentals, etc.) from other parts of the business, but their appropriate extent is debatable. It also gives some rationale for the requirement to provide 'universal service'. More importantly, universal service requirements are also justified by public good considerations relating to emergency services (another kind of external-ity) and social factors. Furthermore, network externalities call for regula-tion in so far as they distort competition (Katz and Shapiro 1985; Farrell and Saloner 1985).

An important kind of externality in financial services has to do with capi-tal adequacy. If a large number of depositors simultaneously attempted to withdraw their funds from a bank or building society, there is a risk that there would be insufficient funds to honour their claims. The resulting negative externality between depositors is clear, and in the limit there is zero sum game between them, in which each is scrambling for a slice of the available assets. One of the purposes of capital adequacy requirements (and related provisions such as insurance schemes) is to ensure that enough liquid funds are available to cover every reasonable eventuality. Such measures themselves give confidence to depositors and, therefore, minimize the chance that there will be a bank run in the first place. Capital adequacy requirements are also important for financial institutions dealing in contracts for future delivery, including options and insurance contracts. If there are doubts as to their ability to honour contracts if prices or cir-cumstances move against them, the market is undermined.

Monopoly and Competition

Market power is detrimental to economic efficiency in several ways, aside from its undesirability in non-economic respects. Allocative effi-ciency is undermined by the incentive for dominant firms to charge prices significantly in excess of marginal costs of supply; and the lack of competitive stimulus further blunts incentives for dynamic and produc-tive efficiency. On the other hand, despite its general advantages, compe-tition is not always for the best. In a natural monopoly, for example, economies of scale or scope imply that (actual) competition would raise costs or involve wasteful duplication. (Potential competition—the threat of entry—may have advantages even so: see Baumol 1982 on contestabil-ity theory).

In addition to the question of the desirability of competition, there is also the issue of whether it is feasible (in the absence of Government intervention). Figure 2 distinguishes these two questions.

This simple picture suggests that there are three kinds of market fail-ure to consider. First, there is the case in which competition is neither feasible nor desirable, which holds under conditions of severe natural monopoly.[2] Anti-monopoly regulation is then the only check on the firm's behaviour.

IS COMPETITION DESIRABLE?

		YES	NO
	YES	TYPICAL CASE	CREAM SKIMMING
IS COMPETITION FEASIBLE?			
	NO	DOMINANT INCUMBENT(S) PREVENTS ENTRY	SEVERE NATURAL MONOPOLY

Figure 2 Desirability and feasibility of competition

Second, there is the case in which competition is not desirable, but is feasible. It is possible to construct examples with scale economies in which single firm production is desirable (because the loss of allocative efficiency is outweighed by the gain in cost efficiency), but in which more than one firm enters the industry at equilibrium (see Mankiw and Whinston 1986; and Suzumura and Kiyono 1987 for an analysis of the relationship between the optimal and equilibrium numbers of firms).

This could not happen in a contestable market, where it is the threat of entry that disciplines incumbent firms, but the contestable markets theory has illuminated another kind of possible market failure to do with the non-existence of equilibrium: non-sustainability. A natural monopoly is said to be sustainable if prices exist that earn enough revenue to cover the monopolist's costs, but which do not attract entry by rival firms. In multi-product industries, non-sustainability is often associated with the notion of 'cream skimming', which is said to occur when entrants undercut the incumbent's profitable business segments and leave him with a loss on the rest of his activities. Such behaviour might seem a rather good antidote to cross-subsidization, in which case it should normally be welcomed, but it can occur when there is no cross-subsidization. In that event, it undermines the stability of equilibrium and has shades of 'destructive competition'.

Where competition is feasible but undesirable, the key policy question is whether there should be regulatory measures to restrict competition, e.g. by prohibiting entry into the market. In general, we would be very wary of making such a step. It may be hard even to determine whether or not natural monopoly conditions prevail. We believe that where competition would be undesirable, it will generally not come about anyway.

However, the theoretical possibility exists. But the models which display the property of undesirable competition usually do not allow for the beneficial effects of competition on incentives for internal efficiency, which are important in the overall welfare evaluation. Although the case for regulation to restrict undesirable or destructive competition cannot always be dismissed out of hand, the private interest in it is almost invariably far greater than the public interest. There is a very heavy burden of proof on those who seek to advance this case, and they should be treated with great suspicion.

Finally we come to the case in which competition is desirable but in danger of being thwarted by anti-competitive behaviour by the incumbent firm(s). The threat of predatory behaviour—by price or other means—is the clearest example of such behaviour (see Vickers 1985 for a brief account). Many regulatory measures for privatized utility companies aim to check anti-competitive behaviour by dominant firms, and we shall consider this problem further below.

To summarize, we have distinguished between three kinds of market failure involving monopoly and competition, and, correspondingly, three types of regulation, namely regulation:

1. to contain monopolistic behaviour;
2. to limit competition; and
3. to promote competition.

Information Problems

Our third category of market failure concerns information problems, which include:

1. failures in markets for information;
2. problems arising from imperfect price information; and
3. asymmetric information about product quality.

It has long been appreciated that markets for information are prone to failure. One difficulty is that the buyer of a piece of information does not know the value of what she is buying unless she knows what the information is, in which case there is no point in buying it. Trust between buyer and seller is important here, as is illustrated in many professional services, which frequently involve the supply of information by specialists. Another difficulty is the appropriability problem: once discovered, a piece of information can be sold and resold at very little cost, but incentives for discovery require that the originator of the information be rewarded at a much higher level than the marginal cost of dissemination. The appropriability problem is central to the welfare economics of innovation (see e.g. Spence 1984), and arises in markets for professional services as well.

It can also occur in financial markets. Efficient allocation of investment resources is enhanced if financial asset prices reflect information about the available economic opportunities. But if such information is rapidly reflected in prices, there is little incentive to gather it, because a superior strategy may be to sit back and deduce information from prices (see Grossman and Stiglitz 1980).

A quite distinct information problem occurs when consumers are badly informed about the prices being charged by various suppliers. Under these circumstances, price dispersion can occur even for homogeneous goods of known quality. Some consumers are likely to engage in a search to discover low prices, while others are in danger of being ripped off (see Salop and Stiglitz 1977). More generally, poor price information for consumers assists collusion between suppliers, because a price cut by any single supplier is unlikely to increase his demand greatly. An obvious solution is for suppliers to advertise their prices, since it is much cheaper for firms to inform consumers than for consumers to inform themselves. However, restrictions on advertising have been common in many of the professions. The pros and cons of such restrictions are discussed further below.

Our third information problem—asymmetric information about product quality—deserves most attention. Information asymmetries pervade markets for professional services. Indeed, demand for many professional services stems entirely from the asymmetry of information: the amateur consumer is essentially buying advice from a better informed professional. Since the consumer cannot directly judge the quality of the service that he or she is buying, indirect assurances as to quality are necessary for the effective functioning of the market. The situation is similar in respect of financial services. It is very hard for many consumers to tell directly whether their broker is offering honest advice (or whether he is 'talking his own book', e.g. by recommending clients to sell shares that his firm wishes to buy on its own account), whether their trades were executed on the best available terms, or whether a bank or insurance company with whom the customer is contemplating doing business maintains adequate margins of solvency.

The seminal article on asymmetric information about product quality is Akerlof's (1970) paper on the market for 'lemons' (American terminology for dud second-hand cars). Consumers cannot tell by inspection what is the quality of a used car, but they can draw inferences about average quality from prices. In particular, average quality will decline as price declines, because potential sellers of better cars have higher reservation prices (below which they prefer not to sell) than potential sellers of duds. Mutually advantageous trades between sellers and buyers of better quality cars are stymied, and the market may be determined altogether if there are no willing buyers at any price, given their (rational) beliefs about quality.

Insurance markets are prone to asymmetric information problems, with sellers this time being *less* well informed than buyers. If an insurance company cannot distinguish between low- and high-risk individuals, it faces an *adverse selection* problem since at any given price the high-risk people are keener to take out insurance than low-risk people. If an insurance contract was offered on terms that both types found acceptable, a competitor would find it profitable to offer a rival contract tailored to the low-risk individuals (e.g. involving less extensive cover but with a lower premium). By skimming the cream in this way, the first firm is left with the undesirable risks, and competitive equilibrium may fail to be sustained (see Rothschild and Stiglitz 1976). Insurance companies also face a *moral hazard* problem when they cannot monitor, and hence cannot condition the insurance contract upon, the risk-affecting behaviour of the insured. A contract which specifies risk-minimizing behaviour by the insured and a correspondingly low premium is then unenforceable. The worst must be assumed, and the insurance premium must be set accordingly.

In reality there are, of course, numerous ways of attempting to overcome problems of asymmetric information, many of which involve no intervention in the market by external regulatory agencies. Warranties and guarantees can act as a signal of the seller's product quality as well as giving the buyer some insurance against the risk of the product being defective (Grossman 1981). Liability rules can perform a similar function. The seller's reputation will also be of central importance.

These mechanisms are neither perfect nor costless, but in many circumstances they work tolerably well, and no external intervention (beyond general consumer protection legislation) is needed. However, under some conditions, market mechanisms are not enough. This is especially so when—as in financial and professional services—quality cannot be detected even *ex post*.[3] The forms that external regulation may take in those circumstances are discussed in the next section.

3. Regulation: institutions and problems

The Institutions of Regulation

The general economic framework for the analysis of regulation is the class of principal/agent problems. A principal/agent problem generally takes the following form. A (the principal) has objectives which can only be achieved by B (the agent), because B has immediate responsibility for the decisions, or better information, or commonly both. Given that B will typically have different incentives and superior knowledge, how does A construct a framework that ensures that the desired outcome is achieved? Attempted solutions to this problem may be characterized by differences in the degree to which the principal directs the actions of the agent.

We review the institutions of regulation in a descending hierarchy of state involvement, beginning with nationalization and ending with the internal regulation undertaken by firms themselves.

Nationalization is an extreme form of regulation and often seen as removing the need for regulation. The principal/agent problem is resolved by inviting the agent to adopt the objectives of the principal and freezing him from other constraints and obligations. But it is not apparent that nationalized boards are well equipped to determine what the public interest is, or that even if it were clear to them what it is, that they would then have incentive to pursue it; in any event such a loose definition of managerial objectives may not be conducive to efficient management and operation of the industries concerned. It follows that nationalization does not remove the principal/agent problem: it merely puts it within the context of a particular institutional structure.

In the simplest characterization of the process of regulation, A is the government and B the management of the regulated industry. This is, however, an unduly simple characterization. Commonly, there may be four interest groups involved—the voters, the government, a regulatory organization, and an industry—and a principal/agent problem involved at each link of the chain. Politicians, regulators and managers each have objectives of their own, none of which can be presumed invariably to accord with the public good, and it must be expected that these objectives will influence their behaviour.

It is difficult to assess the extent to which the evident deficiencies of the mechanisms of nationalized industry control are intrinsic to the institution of nationalization as such and to what extent they arise from failure to specify objectives and incentive mechanisms but, given that dissatisfaction with the performance of nationalization is more acute in Britain than elsewhere, we incline to the latter explanation.

The commonest form of explicit regulation is by means of the public agency. There are many such agencies. Some have specific responsibilities for particular industries. Others are defined functionally: the powers of the agency extend across most industries, but only in respect of particular areas of behaviour. In other cases public regulation is the direct responsibility of a government department.

Self-regulation is common among the professions. In some cases the self-regulatory body may receive statutory authority analogous to that which public agencies enjoy: it is usually illegal for unqualified persons to describe themselves as doctors. But anyone is free to call himself an accountant, and many people without formal qualifications do. The powers of the accountancy bodies derive in part from the legal status of the audit and partly from the prestige which attaches to the accountancy qualification itself.

An important means of regulation is internal regulation by private firms. This is of obvious significance in financial services, where reputation is central to attracting business. Since reputation is valuable, firms devote resources to maintaining it. Internal regulation is of growing importance in professional services, particularly in accountancy. Here the major international firms promise their customers higher standard (and more expensive) service than the minimum assured by professional bodies and attempt to maintain standards by common procedures and internal quality control. We discuss in greater detail in Section 6 the variety of ways in which regulatory mechanisms can influence product quality.

Regulatory Inefficiency and Regulatory Capture

The principal/agent problem results from differences in the incentives of principal and agent, and in the information available to principal and agent, and it is essentially the interaction between these issues that gives rise to difficulty. If principal and agent had identical objectives, then the fact that the agent had superior information would not be a matter of any practical significance. Equally, if the principal had access to all the information available to the agent, the objectives of the agent would not matter because monitoring his behaviour would be straightforward.

If there is a divergence of objectives between principal and agent, this divergence will remain whatever structures or mechanisms of regulation are put in place. The agent can be required to observe the regulation, but not to adopt its objectives—we can require firms to observe health and safety at work regulations, but not to reduce the incidence of accidents. The pursuit of divergent objectives within the framework of regulation may lead to inefficiency. Thus American utilities have typically been subject to price control based on a 'fair rate' of return on capital employed. If this rate of return exceeds the cost of capital to such utilities, then they can increase profits by expanding their capital base. This effect, first described by Averch and Johnson (1962) may be an explanation for the relatively high cost levels of such utilities observed by, for example, Pescatrice and Timpani (1980). Similarly, German insurance companies subject to premium regulation have, it is claimed, responded by excessive levels of marketing expenditure (Finsinger, Hammond, and Tapp 1985).

Regulatory capture occurs when a regulatory agency comes to equate the public good with the interests of the industry it regulates. The most closely documented case is that of civil aviation in the United States, where it was argued that a regulatory body established to protect consumer interests had in time come to operate a cartel on behalf of established carrier (Miller and Douglas 1974). This analysis was influential in promoting the deregulation of the industry; but it is apparent that similar tendencies exist in transport industries throughout the world. This tendency to regulatory capture is hardly surprising. The very information asymmetry which creates the need for regulation makes the agency dependent on those it regulates from the beginning, while producer lobbies are commonly better organized and better resourced than those serving consumer interests. It is a striking feature of regulatory history that industries are generally opposed both to the introduction of new regulation and to the dismantling of old regulation. Industries dislike the prospect of regulation but frequently find comfortable ways of living with it in practice.

This creates in turn several kinds of inefficiency. One reflects the costs which may result from the recasting of regulatory objectives. Quality control is, for example, a prime objective of professional services regulation: but it has been widely observed (and will be noted at several points in this paper) that such quality control has been almost entirely concentrated on pre-entry requirements with very little attention given to post-entry performance or education. This may impose high prices on consumers while giving them little substantive assurance of quality.

The possibility that regulatory structures may be turned to an industry's advantage may lead the industry to invest resources in seeking particular kinds of regulation or in influencing the behaviour of regulatory authorities. Since such rent-seeking behaviour may be very profitable, the sums which may be invested in it may correspondingly be high. Such behaviour is capable not only of leading to mistaken regulatory outcomes, but also of distorting the structure of incentives and objectives within the regulated firm.

4. Modes of regulation

There are two basic means by which a regulator can influence the behaviour of an industry with whose performances he is concerned. She can regulate the structure of the industry and she/he can regulate its behaviour. The distinction between the two categories is not always clear cut, and they are not mutually exclusive; but the general distinction is a useful one. The informational requirements needed to impose structural regulation are generally much less demanding and we will suggest that this is an important reason why it often has advantages.

These are broad categories, and a word of clarification is in order at the outset. By 'structural regulation' we mean the determination of which firms or individuals (or types thereof) are allowed to engage in which activities. By 'conduct regulation' we refer to measures concerned with how firms behave in their chosen activity or activities.

Examples of structural regulation include:

- restrictions on entry;
- statutory monopoly;
- single capacity rules;
- rules against individuals supplying professional services without recognized qualifications.

Examples of conduct regulation include:

- measures to guard against anti-competitive behaviour by dominant incumbent firms;
- price control;
- rules against advertising and other restrictions on competitive activity.

In a number of cases structural regulation and conduct are alternatives to one another. The former aims to create a situation in which the incentives or opportunities for undesirable behaviour are removed, while the latter addresses not the undesirable underlying incentives, but the behaviour that they would otherwise induce.

The recent combinations of deregulation with reregulation are less paradoxical if it is remembered that there are these two broad types of regulation. What has happened in several industries recently is a shift of emphasis between structure and conduct regulation (as in financial services), or a policy choice between the two (as with the issue of vertical separation in network industries). The choice is not so much about whether to regulate, but about which mode of regulation to adopt.

The simplest form of conduct regulation is the directive: the regulator tells the regulated what to do. Directives raise the twin problems of information and incentives in their acute form. The directive may simply instruct the regulated to adopt the regulator's objective: 'run an efficient and economical telecommunications service', in which case it is difficult or impossible for the regulator to establish whether, within the limits of what is possible, the industry has complied with the directive. The alternative is to issue more specific instructions: 'install exchange equipment of type X'. However, the regulator, less well informed than the industry about the structure of costs, the available alternatives, and the problems of day-to-day management, is in a poor position to judge whether type X is or is not the most efficient and economical means supply. The regulator is at a informational disadvantage either in composing his instruction or in monitoring compliance with it, and there is no escape from at least one of these difficulties.

Thus the weakness of conduct regulation is that to be effective it must be concerned with aspects of service provision that are readily measured; and these may be only loosely related to the issues of underlying concern. We are concerned that the monopoly enjoyed by utilities may lead to excessive profits: we therefore control the level of profits they may earn. While the level of profits is (to a degree) observable, the level of profit on particular services is difficult for an external observer to assess. In any event, profit regulation neither reassures the consumer that the costs of supplying a service are reasonable nor gives the industry an incentive to reduce them. Price regulation appears to tackle the latter problem. However, it gives the regulator no additional information about the appropriate level of costs; and if the only guide he has is the actual level of costs the practical difference between price and profit control may turn out to be slight. The general weakness of regulating outcomes is that the process generating these outcomes may prove to be inefficient. This was illustrated on pp. 429–30: the tendency of rate of return regulation to produce high costs and levels of investment which, depending on the form of regulation, may be excessive or inadequate, and the likelihood that price control will generate excessive marketing expenditures.

5. Functional separation as regulatory mechanism

An important kind of structural regulation is functional separation—in which agents are prohibited from undertaking different activities simultaneously. In utilities, the issue is whether the operator of a naturally monopolistic network should be allowed also to operate in potentially competitive business segments of its industry. In financial services there are the questions of single versus dual capacity (broking and jobbing), and of polarization (whether financial advisers may also sell their own financial services). In the professions the best example is the solicitor/barrister distinction.

It is worth stressing from the beginning that the mere fact that two functions require distinct skills does not in itself justify regulatory intervention to require functional separation. Consumers can decide for themselves which type of firm offered better value for money in relation of their own particular needs. If there are economies of scope in combining two activities, one might expect a relatively high proportion of dual capacity firms. On the other hand, if economies of scope were small or even negative, and if independent services had sufficient value added, then single-capacity firms would tend to prosper. Competition has the advantages of being flexible and economical of information. If competitive market forces are able to operate effectively, there is no need for outside regulators to prejudge what is the most efficient form or organization, and the claims of would-be self-regulators can be treated with caution. Matters may be different when investors are less sophisticated: for example, if they lack the information necessary to judge the risk of conflict of interest.

Alternative arguments for functional separation concern effects on competition. Let us begin with an example in which one activity is a natural monopoly and another is potentially competitive. The question of functional separation is whether to bar the firm which enjoys the natural monopoly from the competitive activity. An obvious instance occurs in telecommunications where local network operation is a natural monopoly but long-distance connections may be offered by competing services. Recent American policy has favoured functional separation; following the settlement of its antitrust case in 1982, AT & T was required to divest itself of its local operating companies (the 'Baby Bells'). British policy has followed the opposite course: BT was privatized intact without any restructuring. Instead, British Policy has relied on conduct regulation in the form of OFTEL's 1985 ruling on the terms of interconnection between the networks of BT and its long-distance rival Mercury. Very similar issues arise in other industries, notably the gas and electricity utilities, where network activities tend to be naturally monopolistic, but other activities (e.g. power generation) do not. The issue is whether the common carrier who provides the network should be allowed into those other businesses.

The basic problem in these cases is that a firm with a monopoly in one part of the industry has an incentive to exclude competitors from associated competitive activities by denying them access to the output from its monopoly, except perhaps on unattractive terms. By excluding them and duplicating what they were doing, it can obtain for itself the profits that competitors were making in addition to its own. Moreover, once free from constraints imposed by the presence of competitors, a firm would, in general, revise its behaviour so as to boost industry profits yet further. Exclusion therefore has the double advantage of enlarging industry profits and the share of them obtained by the monopoly.[4]

The problem for conduct regulation in these circumstances stems from the informational disadvantages facing the regulatory authorities. First, there is the difficulty of detecting anti-competitive behaviour, and of enforcing measures intended to combat it. (It is hard enough to reach an acceptable definition of 'predatory behaviour', let alone detect and deter it.) Second, even when the instrument of possible anti-competitive conduct is easily observable (as with network interconnection charges, for example), there is the question of how to regulate it. If the interconnection charge is set at too high a level, the regulator partly assists exclusion. But if it is fixed too low, there is a danger of encouraging inefficient fragmentation of the industry. In the face of asymmetries of information, conduct regulation is prone to error and evasion. On these scores, regulation of structure—by means of functional separation—has significant advantages.

6. Regulation of product quality

Much regulation is concerned with product quality. Regulation is supported, or defended, because it will raise standards. It must be recognized, however, that raising the quality of good and services provided is not, in itself, necessarily a desirable objective. This does not mean that we are not in favour of reliable electricity, safe aircraft, competent doctors, or solvent banks. Ever more stringent quality standards do, however, have a price. It is most unlikely that it makes sense to provide such a margin of excess generating capacity that the probability of power cuts is reduced to zero. Improvements in airline safety can be taken to the point at which scheduling is seriously disrupted, or costs make services uneconomic. If medical practitioners throughout the world were required to meet US standards, the result would be to deprive most of the population of the world of any access to medical treatment whatever. And if the demands imposed on financial institutions are too great, it will become impossible for new firms to enter the industry.

If consumers are themselves readily able to observe product quality, there is little case for any public intervention. Quality regulation in such a case limits consumer choice. It is likely that different consumers will make different decisions about the combination of price and quality that suits them best, and that the balance favoured by the average consumer will change over time. If telephone users wish to plug inexpensive equipment of low speech quality into the system, and are prepared to tolerate the results, and this can be done without damage to the integrity of the network, then they should be allowed to do so. Best practice is, by definition, better than the average consumer is prepared to buy.

The case for regulation arises where the consumers are poorly informed about product quality. Indeed this motivated some of the first instances of government economic regulation, when the state intervened to restrict adulteration and short measure. The problem is particularly serious when purchasers know little about product quality even after they have bought. After receiving medical treatment, I may (or may not) know whether I have recovered, but do not know how much, if anything, the treatment contributed to that recovery. The inefficiencies which may result from such a process are discussed on pp. 425–7.

Three principal mechanisms are available for relieving them. *Reputation* is the market's own device. When consumers are not themselves able to observe product quality directly, they will prefer to purchase from sellers who are known in the market place to dispense goods or services of high quality. Two public regulatory devices are *licensing* and *certification*. By licensing, the public agency seeks to impose a minimum standard on the market: commodities which do not meet the licensing requirements may not be sold. Certification occurs where the regulatory authority provides consumers with information about the levels of competence of suppliers. . . . .

7. Minimising the need for regulation

It will be apparent from the preceding discussion that no regulatory mechanism is free from problems and inefficiencies. A central objective is therefore to develop structures which minimize the need for regulation.

Privatization and Competition

The simplest cases are those where there is no evident market failure to suggest that regulation is required. The most obvious cases are peripheral areas of the public sector. The state has no advantage in running hotels, or ferries, or trucks, or laundries, and these activities suffer only disadvantages in being subject to constraints on their financing and organization structures which are appropriate or necessary where there is no commercial output or where there is political accountability for the results. It is in areas such as these that privatization has enjoyed its most conspicuously successful results.

Attention should then turn to those areas where markets do not work perfectly, but where the market failure is a relatively trivial one. A good example is the demand for universal service. There are arguments for extending the provision of basic utilities beyond the areas where that might be strictly economically justified, but there are means of ensuring this which fall a long way short of nationalization. A simple regulatory condition can deal with the problem (an alternative is contracting out the uncommercial activity—see below). Indeed it is likely that private firms will see public relations and advantages, or social obligations, in such behaviour in any event.

The more difficult areas arise where the market failure is by no means trivial. We have identified three main issues—monopoly, externalities, and information. In each of these cases, there is a trade-off between an underlying market failure and the inevitable weaknesses of any regulatory intervention designed to tackle it. The answer, whenever possible, is to find mechanisms for making markets work—to lean with market forces rather than against them.

Where monopoly is the result of statutory restriction, the obvious response is to repeal the statute. But experience has shown that this is by no means enough. The endowment which incumbent firms have built up during a period of statutory monopol—an endowment of marketing presence, and financial and technical advantages—is not easily challenged. UK experience in such varied industries as coaches and telecommunications has demonstrated that these advantages severely inhibit new competitors.

Even where monopoly is unavoidable, there are devices which harness some of the advantages of competition to reduce the need for regulation. They include franchising and yardstick competition.

Franchising

Franchising involves a competition for the market, even where competition in the market is infeasible or undesirable. Potential monopoly power in the market is held in check by the competitively determined terms of the franchise contract. Thus in theory, the problem of asymmetric information faced by the regulator can be effectively bypassed by the use of competition between informed potential franchisees: competition acts as a kind of discovery mechanism.

Our discussion of franchising can be brief, for its pros and cons have been much debated elsewhere; see, for example, Demetz (1968), Domberger *et al*. (1986), Sharpe (1982), Vickers and Yarrow (1988: section 4.6), and Williamson (1976). The simplest method of franchising is to hold an auction for the right to the monopoly, in which the winner is the bidder who offers the franchiser the largest monetary sum. Such a system helps to transfer the (capitalized) value of the monopoly to the franchiser but fails to deal with the underlying problems of market power and allocative inefficiency. Assuming that the public authorities wish to tackle those problems, we shall focus on the form of franchising sometimes known as the Chadwick–Demsetz proposal, in which the natural monopoly franchise is awarded for a period of time to the competitor offering to supply the product or service at the lowest price(s).

On the face of it, franchising appears to provide a very attractive way of combining competition and efficiency without any great burden on the regulators. This competition for monopoly seems to destroy the undesirable monopoly of information that hinders traditional regulation, and price is set by competition, not administrative decision. Franchising has also met with practical success in a number of areas, including competitive tendering in refuse collection, hospital cleaning and catering, and uncommercial bus services, not to mention its widespread use in the private sector.

But franchising is prone to a number of difficulties in some circumstances, and unfortunately the industries where regulatory problems are greatest (e.g. energy, telecommunications, and water) are especially prone to such problems. They include the following:

1. The bidding for the franchise might fail to be competitive, because there may be very few competitors, due to scarcity of requisite skills, col-

lusion between bidders, or strategic advantages possessed by the incumbent franchisee, which deter challenges to him. These could arise from experience effects or superior information over potential bidders.

2. Problems associated with asset handover in the event of an incumbent franchisee being displaced may distort incentives to invest (and indeed the nature of competition for the franchise). Valuation of sunk assets is both difficult and costly. If the incumbent expects that their value in the event of handover would be set too low (high), and if there is a chance of his/her being displaced, then his/her incentive to invest will be correspondingly too low (high). This problem is diminished if the sunk assets are under independent ownership and the franchise is simply an operating franchise, but this raises questions of how the franchiser determines the level of facilities to be provided: as usual the choice is between information or incentive problems.

3. If there is technological or market uncertainty in relation to the product or service in question, then the specification of the franchise contract will be a very complex task (especially if its duration is long, e.g. to minimize asset handover problems), and the need to monitor and administer the contract during its life is certain to arise. In the privatized utility industries, for example, it would be impossible to cater for every eventuality that might occur in the life of even a short-term contract. Thus, we are left with incompletely specified contracts, but they require continuing contract administration.

Two conclusions are implied by the considerations above. First, the attractiveness of franchising depends on the circumstances at hand. It works best where there are numerous potential competitors with the requisite skills, where sunk costs are not high, and where technological and market uncertainty is not great. Second, franchising involves an implicit regulatory arrangement for all but the simplest products and services. As Goldberg (1976) writes: 'Many of the problems associated with regulation lie in what is being regulated, not in the act of regulation itself.' Franchising should be seen not as alternative to regulation, but a form of it that seeks to use some of the desirable incentive properties of competition.

Yardstick competition

One of the main themes in this chapter has been the importance of information for effective regulation. If the regulator is relatively uninformed about industry conditions, and especially if the regulated firm has a virtual monopoly of relevant information, then the regulatory system is liable to become insensitive to cost and demand conditions. For example, if the regulator can observe actual costs but does not know the potential for cost reduction, s/he faces a dilemma. Setting prices in line with actual costs achieves allocative efficiency but provides poor incentives for cost reduction, while fixing prices for a long time ahead may create good incentives for internal efficiency but is liable to lead to serious losses in allocative efficiency as costs move out of line with prices.

Yardstick competition attempts to resolve the dilemma by bringing regulated firms in distinct markets indirectly into competition with each other in respect of cost reduction. Suppose that a national monopolist was divided into separately owned Northern and Southern units, each with a natural monopoly in its geographical region. Suppose that they face symmetric cost and demand conditions, that the regulator can observe actual unit costs, but that s/he does not know the potential for cost reduction. By making the price that North can charge depend on the unit cost level achieved by South (and vice versa), the regulator gives North incentives for internal efficiency, because North reaps the entire benefit of any cost reduction that it achieves. Given symmetry and the strong incentives to cost reduction built into the system, North's costs provide a good indication of what South may be expected to achieve, and vice versa, and since North's price is linked to South's unit cost, North's price will, in turn, be linked to North's own unit cost level. Thus, allocative efficiency becomes compatible with internal efficiency.

This illustrative argument is based on several important assumptions, which may not hold in practice. First, the firms might seek to collude to act as one, thereby undermining the indirect competition that regulation sought to promote. Second, symmetry between regions is highly improbable, but this does not affect the basic argument provided that the main differences between regions are observable and reasonably stable. Yardstick competition does not work so well, however, when they have unobservable characteristics that are uncorrelated between regions. The danger then is that North's price would be unduly affected by distinctive features of South's situation. Such 'noise' would distort allocative efficiency and would not encourage North to behave as his circumstances warranted.

Nevertheless, it is a general proposition in the theory of incentives that when a principal (in our case the regulator) has several agents (firms) under his control, it is invariably the case that the optimal incentive scheme (regulatory mechanism) involves the reward of each agent being contingent upon the performance of the other agents as well as his own. We therefore know that the best regulatory mechanisms will exploit information from comparative performance (if it is available) in some form, but the question remains of *how* to do so in any particular case. On this it would be foolish to attempt generalization, since the degree of homogeneity between regional units varies from industry to industry.

However, yardstick competition obviously relies on the existence of independent sources of information. Since the ability to make performance comparisons can greatly enhance the effectiveness of incentives, integrated industry structures that leave a firm with a monopoly of information have a major disadvantage. In short, the benefit of having a good information base for effective regulation provides a strong argument for ensuring that industry structure is such as to provide data on comparative performance. That cannot happen in the face of nationwide monopoly, but it is quite consistent with natural monopoly at the regional level. This fact has clear implications for the appropriate structure of regulated natural monopoly industries.

8. The future of regulation

General principles

We have argued that regulation is required—and only required—in the face of some market failure. It follows immediately that each regulatory regime should be targeted on the relevant failure or failures. This point seems almost too obvious to be worth making, but the reality of regulation has proved very different. The normal pattern is that market failure provides the rationale for the introduction of regulation, but the scope of regulation is then extended to a wide range of matters which are the subject of general or sectional interest, regardless of whether there is any element of market failure or not.

In devising any regulatory framework it is therefore necessary to begin by asking how markets have failed. The nature of the market will then determine the design of regulation. Of the three industries with which we have been concerned, monopoly is the principal issue in utilities and asymmetry of information in financial and professional services: externalities are a limited cause of market failure in all three activities. Where the need for regulation is the product of *monopoly*, the first requirement is to see whether structural remedies are feasible without substantial loss of economies of sale or scope. Can competition be promoted? Where it cannot be, the objective should be to 'ring-fence' the area of natural monopoly as far as possible, to ensure that unavoidable monopoly does not lead to unnecessary monopoly in other, naturally competitive markets. Within the ring-fence, regulation will be necessary to restrain prices with minimum detriment to efficiency.

Where *externalities* create the need for regulation, the objective should be to achieve solutions that lean with market forces rather than replace them. Structural remedies can again be contrasted with measures that bear directly on conduct. For example, an activity (e.g. pollution or the supply of unsafe products) that potentially generates negative externalities can be tackled either by liability rules that give aggrieved parties the right to sue for damages, or by conduct regulation. In some circumstances the former method can give good incentives to curb or modify the activity to an optimal extent, and there is no need for public intervention (and associated public information) beyond the provision of a legal framework. But where—as often with safety issues—there is limited scope for different opinions about appropriate levels of quality, and (more importantly) there are free rider problems for individuals seeking to uphold standards, then public monitoring may well be the most effective device. We would also like to see measures to bring into being the 'missing markets' which lead to over-exploitation of under-priced resources.

The most obvious remedy for market failures which result from *information asymmetry* is information disclosure, and this may often be sufficient remedy. It is perhaps, difficult for public agencies to publish information on product quality. But it is possible to subsidize the private production of such information, and it is impossible not to be impressed by the contrast between by the very small expenditure on the public good of impartial information on the qualities of goods and services available and the very large expenditures incurred by those who provide such goods and services on the private goods of advertising and public relations. Measures which seek to suppress communication of information altogether—as with the restrictions on advertising and promotional activity within the professions—seem to us particularly undesirable. Their effect, and to a degree their intention, is to inhibit the development of the market's own mechanisms for monitoring product quality—the establishment of good reputations for products and brands, relative to other products or brands. The task of policy should instead to be promote these. It is these areas that regulatory reform is most urgently required.

Notes

1. Assuming that it has the right to discharge the effluent. If, on the other hand, the fishermen possess and exercise rights to clean water, there is a sense in which they impose a cost on the chemical company, see Coase (1960).
2. In natural monopoly conditions that are not severe, competition may be desirable. Even though single firm production is the most cost-effective, rivalry can enhance allocative efficiency more than it diminishes cost-efficiency.
3. There is a well-known distinction between search goods, whose quality is apparent before purchase, and experience goods, whose quality is apparent only after consumption. Perhaps 'trust goods' could be used as a term to describe goods whose quality is not apparent even after consumption.
4. The basic argument needs modifying, and might not be valid, if competitors have a cost advantage in activity B, or if there are substantial diseconomies of scale. If there is perfect competition (and hence zero profits) in activity B, and if there is no substitutionality between the outputs of A and B, then firm F is indifferent between excluding competitors and not doing so, because it can extract all the monopoly profits either way.

References

AKERLOF, G. (1970), 'The Market for lemons: qualitative uncertainty and the market mechanism', *Quarterly Journal of Economics*.

AVERCH, H., and JOHNSON, L. (1962), 'Behaviour of the firm under regulatory constraint', *American Economic Review*.

BARON, D. P., and MYERSON, R. B. (1982), 'Regulating a monopolist with unknown costs', *Econometrica*.

BATOR, F. (1958), 'The anatomy of market failure', *Quarterly Journal of Economics*.

BAUMOL, W. J. (1982), 'Contestable markets: an uprising in the theory of industrial structure', *American Economic Review*.

COASE, R. H. (1960), 'The problem of social cost', *Journal of Law and Economics*.

DEMSETZ, H. (1968), 'Why regulate utilities?' *Journal of Law and Economics*.

Department of Trade and Industry (1988), *Review of Restrictive Trade Practices Policy*. Cm. 331, London, HMSO.

DOMBERGER, S., MEADOWCROFT, J., and THOMPSON, D. (1986), 'Competitive tendering and efficiency', *Fiscal Studies*.

FARRELL, J., and SALONER, G. (1985), 'Standardization, compatibility and innovation', *Rand Journal of Economics*.

FISINGER, J., HAMMOND, E. M., and TAPP, J. (1985), 'Insurance: competition or regulation? A comparative study of the insurance market in the United Kingdom and the Federal Republic of Germany', *IFS Report Series* 19. London, Institute for Fiscal Studies.

GOLDBERG, V. P. (1976), 'Regulation and Administered Contracts', *Bell Journal of Economics*.

GROSSMAN, S. (1981), 'The information role of warranties and private disclosure about product quality', *Journal of Laws and Economics*.

—— and STIGLITZ, J. E. (1980), 'On the impossibility of informationally efficient markets', *American Economic Review*.

KATZ, M., and SHAPIRO, C. (1985), 'Network externalities, competition and compatibility', *American Economic Review*.

KAY, J. A., MAYER, C., and THOMPSON, D. (eds.) (1986), *Privatisation and Regulation: The UK experience*, Oxford: Oxford University Press.

LAFFONT, J. J., and TIROLE, J. (1986), 'Using cost observation to regulate firms', *Journal of Political Economy*.

MANKIW, N. G., and WHINSTON, M. D. (1986), 'Free entry and social inefficiency', *Rand Journal of Economics*.

MILLER, J., and DOUGLAS, G. (1974), 'Economic regulation of domestic air transport: theory and policy', *Journal of Economic Literature*.

PESCATRICE, D. R., and TIMPANI, J. M. (1980), 'The performance and objective of public and private utilities operating in the United States', *Journal of Public Economics*.

ROTHSCHILD, M., and STIGLITZ, J. (1976), 'Equilibrium in competitive insurance markets: the economics of markets with incomplete information', *Quarterly Journal of Economics*.

SALOP, S., and STIGLITZ, J. (1977), 'Bargains and ripoffs: a model of monopolistically competitive price dispersion', *Review of Economic Studies*.

SHAKED, A., and SUTTON, J. (1981), 'The self-regulating profession', *Review of Economic Studies*.

SHAPIRO, C. (1986), 'Investment, moral hazard and occupational licensing', *Review of Economic Studies*.

SHARPE, T. (1982), 'The control of natural monopoly by franchising', mimeo, Wolfson College, Oxford.

SHLIEFER, A. (1985), 'A theory of yardstick competition', *Rand Journal of Economics*.

SPENCE, A. M. (1984), 'Cost reduction, competition and industry performance', *Econometrica*.

SUZUMURA, K., and KIYONO, K. (1987), 'Entry barriers and economic welfare', *Review of Economic Studies*.

VICKERS, J. S. (1985), 'The economics of predatory practices', *Fiscal Studies*.

—— and YARROW, G. (1988), *Privatization—An Economic Analysis*, MIT Press.

WILLIAMSON, O. E. (1976), 'Franchising bidding for natural monopolies—in general and with respect to CATIV', *Bell Journal of Economics*.

Privatization under Mrs Thatcher: A Review of the Literature

DAVID MARSH

The literature on privatization has grown at a rapid rate largely because it has become an increasingly important theme in government policy. What is more, the British privatization programme is widely acclaimed as a major economic and political success (Vickers and Yarrow 1988: 125; Veljanovski 1987: 205). In addition the scale of privatization in Britain is greater than elsewhere and the British experience is often viewed as a blueprint for other countries (Veljanovski 1987: 63).

My intention here is to review the burgeoning literature. This will also allow an interim assessment of privatization as practised in Britain. In fact, this review is divided into four sections. The first section looks at the origins and growth of privatization. The second section examines definitions, or classifications, of privatization; while the third section deals with the aims of the policy. The final substantive section, which is by far the longest, examines the extent to which the seven aims which are identified have been achieved.

Origins and growth of privatization

The government's economic goals were explicitly stated in the 1979 election manifesto:

To master inflation, proper monetary discipline is essential with publicly stated targets for the rate of growth of the money supply. At the same time a gradual reduction in the size of the Government's borrowing requirement is also vital. . . . It will do yet further harm to go on printing money to pay ourselves without first earning more. . . The state makes too much of the nation's income; its share must be steadily reduced. . . . The reduction of waste, bureaucracy and over government will yield substantial savings. We should cut income tax at all levels to reward hard work, responsibility and success (cited in Jackson 1985: 17).

David Marsh is Professor of Government at the University of Strathclyde.

The emphasis initially then was upon controlling the money supply, reducing public expenditure and cutting income tax. The manifesto did not use the term 'privatization'. Indeed, as far as most authors are concerned privatization was not a consistent, coherent policy developed in opposition and carried out in power. However, in contrast, Young argues that the policy was coherent: 'What is distinctive about the approach adopted towards [privatization] during the 1977–85 period? It has been different from what went before in the sense that it was applied as a philosophy on a sustained and continuing basis' (Young 1986: 245).

Young's argument is worth examining because he certainly presents one of the best reviews of the different forms of privatization in Britain. (For the best review of privatization in the USA see Savas 1987.) He accepts that there was an experimental element in the overall strategy but argues that the Conservatives came to power with a number of specific proposals. He is right. They did have four specific commitments in their manifesto which could be considered aspects of privatization. They pledged themselves to: sell back to private ownership the recently nationalized aerospace and shipbuilding concerns; sell shares in the National Freight Corporation (NFC); and relax licensing regulations to enable new bus services to develop. In addition, and with more electoral significance, they promised that council and new town tenants could buy their houses, at a discount increasing with the length of the tenancy. However, such commitments hardly represent a programme and they were dwarfed by the emphasis placed upon monetarism in the 1979 manifesto. At the same time, the 1979 manifesto was an inaccurate predictor of events: shipbuilding was not denationalized; the shares of the NFC were not offered to the general public and Amersham International, Associated British Ports, Britoil, and Cable and Wireless, none of which were mentioned, were sold (see Grimstone 1990: 4).

Young goes further claiming: 'The idea that there was an overall strategy is further shown by the way in which privatisation policies were pursued even when they cut across their cherished government aims' (1986: 247). He suggests that this strategy is reflected in two developments. First, privatization has been pursued even when it doesn't promote competition (pp. 247–8). Second, privatization has been promoted by the government, even when the cost of that promotion has led to increased public expenditure (p. 298). As we shall see later, few, if any of the authors under review here would dissent from either of these points. it is Young's interpretation of their meaning which is particular and poses problems. The government privatized British Telecom (BT) without breaking it up or ensuring effective competition, in large part because of the representations of the management (see below p. 453). At the same time, the government's aims in relation to privatization have changed substantially over time. As they have changed, and the political aims have become more important, so the government has offered incentives to ensure successful asset sales and broader share ownership (see below pp. 475). Far from establishing the consistency and coherence of privatization policy, as Young suggests, these developments indicate the inconsistencies and contradictions in the policy (see Mitchell 1990: 19).

Two other points about the origins and growth of privatization are important. First, the government proposals for denationalization, asset sales and contracting out were not novel. All Conservative governments since the war had been committed to some denationalization. The first asset sales in British Petroleum (BP) designed to reduce the Public Sector Borrowing Requirement (PSBR) were made by the Labour government, under pressure from the International Monetary Fund, in 1976/7 (Brittan 1984: 109; for more details see Fraser 1988: 51–2). Similarly, contracting out was common in the local authority sector in the 1950s (Asher 1987: 23). More significantly, there is little evidence of any Conservative commitment to privatization in opposition (Mitchell 1990: 17) and in its first term the government had limited horizons in this field. It was only in the second and third terms that privatization, and in particular special asset sales, became a dominant theme of economic policy.

Why did the privatization programme grow so much during its second term? Two points are clear from the literature. First, the impetus towards privatization came from the government not from the electorate (McAllister and Studlar 1989). Second, the government embraced privatization for political rather than economic reasons. As Brittan argues (1984: 110), selling public assets was politically much easier, and more popular, than cutting public expenditure. In addition, during its first term the government suffered a number of disappointments with its economic policy; unemployment rose rapidly, the recession deepened, inflation increased, manufacturing output declined and interest rates rose. Most embarrassingly, the money supply figures grew consistently faster than the government's plans, with public expenditure growth being most marked in Agriculture, Industry, Trade and Employment and Social Security. Even when inflation began to fall towards the end of the first term, this fall owed nothing to the control of the money supply, which was still rising (Whiteley 1985). It was not surprising that the government seized upon privatization as an alternative way to control the PSBR, given that the proceeds from such sales are treated as negative public expenditure and thus reduce the PSBR. In addition, as Moon *et al.* argue, the deterioration of relations between Whitehall and the nationalized industries, particularly after the election of Conservatives, also provided an incentive to privatize these industries (Moon *et al.* 1986).

Of course, in many ways privatization fitted well with the government's broader political and economic views; it was argued it would increase efficiency, reduce public expenditure and help discipline public sector unions. However, as Abromeit emphasizes:

It should not be overlooked (as most commentators seem to do when praising the Government's astonishing success in avoiding U-turns) that the privatisation policy marks a decisive U-turn in the Government's monetarist policy, of which it was originally meant to form an integral part; the sales have turned into an easy means to circumvent the fiscal constraints, following from restrictions of the money supply which ought to be the core of monetarism. Monetarism is clearly in tatters when, as *The Economist* has noted, state assets are sold because 'State treasurers want to raise money without printing it' (1988: 84).

What is privatization?

There are a number of different developments which are usually associated with privatization. (The best discussions of definitions of privatization are to be found in Wiltshire 1987: 15–29 and Savas 1987.) Young (1986) identifies seven different forms which privatization has taken in Britain: first, special asset sales, which can involve denationalization, as was the case with British Gas (BG), British Airways (BA), and British Telecom (BT), the sale of public sector companies previously bought by the government, companies such as Jaguar and Rolls Royce or the sale of government holdings in private companies such as British Petroleum (BP); second, deregulation or relaxing state monopolies which exposes individual public sector organizations to competition, as was the case in the bus industry; third, contracting out work previously done by direct labour in local government, the NHS and the civil service; fourth, the private provision of services, allowing the private sector to provide services to the public, such as private sector homes for disturbed adolescents, the mentally ill and handicapped and nursing homes for the elderly; fifth, investment projects designed to encourage the private sector to invest in projects in deprived areas and extending private sector practices into the public sector, often involving the creation of special units within public sector organizations to secure a more commercial return on assets; sixth, reducing subsidies and increasing charges, particularly in relation to the welfare services (Young 1986: 238–44). Finally, a number of authors regard the sale of council houses as an important element of privatization, given that such sales have greatly reduced public sector housing provision and therefore the scope of the public sector for housing (see Forrest 1988; for the best review of most of these developments, see Fraser (ed.) 1988; for a thinner, but entertaining, summary of asset sales see Chapman 1990).

As it reflects the existing literature, this review will concentrate on asset sales, although I shall also deal in some detail with contracting out and refer to deregulation and council house sales (for the best reviews of the privatization of welfare provision see Parry (ed.) 1989; Papadakis and Taylor-Gooby 1987; and Le Grand and Robinson (eds.) 1984).

The aims of privatization

What were the aims of the privatization policy? Some authors suggest that privatization was not a thought-out policy. Bishop and Kay 1988: 10) for example, argue that privatization was: 'a policy which was adopted almost by accident but has become politically central; a policy which has no clear-cut objectives, but has become almost an end in itself'. This is, perhaps, a trifle overstated and Abromeit (1988: 72) may be nearer the mark when he argues:

[the system of aims] was not formulated at the beginning of the policy of privatisation: we search in vain for official Government pronouncements—e.g. a White Paper—from the early years which comprehensively presents and adequately clarifies the aims and scope of the proposed measures. Only in recent times, after this policy has steadily expanded by a short of dynamic of its own, have Government members, in particular John Moore, made it their business in various speeches to equip the *de facto* policy, after the event, with a more or less consistent philosophy (see also Pitt 1990: 60 and for Moore's speeches, Kay *et al.* (eds.) 1986, chs. 2 and 4).

Even Veljanovksi, who has considerable sympathy with both the government's aims and their achievements, acknowledges that: 'the goals of privatisation evolved gradually and the emphasis given to each of these goals has been different for each privatisation' (Veljanovski, 1987: 7–8). It is clear that the privatization policy had a number of aims, which at different stages, and to different observers among both academics and Conservative politicians, received different emphases. It is perhaps not surprising that these aims were, to an extent, contradictory. In fact,

Vickers and Yarrow (1988) identify seven aims of the government's privatization programme; others produce similar, if mostly shorter, (Abromeit 1988: 71–2); Curwen 1986: 164–72; Heald and Steel 1982: 331–41; Ramanadham 1988: 12–18; Veljanovski 1987: 1–10; Mitchell 1990: 19): reducing government involvement in industry; improving efficiency in the industries privatized; reducing the PSBR; easing problems in public sector pay determination by weakening the public sector unions; widening share ownership; encouraging employee share ownership; and gaining political advantage (Vickers and Yarrow 1988: 157). How successful has the government been in achieving these aims? Overall, as we shall see, their 'success' has been limited but each aim is worthy of some consideration.

Achieving the aims of privatization

(a) Reducing government involvement in industry

The scale of privatization is immense. In fact, by early 1991: over 50 per cent of the public sector had been transferred to the private sector; 650,000 workers had changed sectors, of whom 90 per cent had become shareholders; 9 million people were shareholders, which represented 20 per cent of the population, as compared with 7 per cent in 1979; the nationalized sector accounted for less than 5 per cent of the UK output as compared with 9 per cent in 1979; about 1,250,000 council houses had been sold, most to sitting tenants under the 'right to buy' provisions; and contracting out was well established in the NHS and the local authority sector. (For the best analysis see Fraser 1988: 14 and 86–91.)

Here we are most concerned with the flotation on the Stock Market of nationalized industries and other public corporations, rather than with the direct sale of government stakes in companies or the 'hiving off' of more profitable parts of public companies (see table 1; the distinction is developed by Fraser (ed.) 1988). However, as Abromeit points out, such flotation does not inevitably, or in all ways, reduce government involvement. Indeed, privatization can be compatible with an extensive government role in the economy (see especially Graham and Prosser 1988 and 1991). In Britain, government intervention has taken a number of forms. First, in most cases the government initially retained a minority of shares in BP, British Aerospace (BAe), Cable and Wireless, Britoil, Associated British Ports and BT, although these were subsequently sold off. Second, after the majority of flotations the government retained a 'golden share' which allowed it a wide variety of powers to block types of shareholding and vary voting rights, share issues and the disposal of assets (see table 1; and Abromeit 1988; Corwen 1986: 210–11; Thompson 1990: 154). Third, the government has had to create a series of regulatory agencies which are dealt with at greater length below (pp. 469–70).

Thompson makes the point well: 'Along with the regulatory bodies and the MMC (Monopoly and Mergers Commission)—which supervises takeovers and monitors restrictive practices in the economy generally—[the goldenshare] installs very extensive powers to determine the course of these companies' development' (1990: 154). In fact, as Abromeit (1988: 80) points out the government has created hybrids which in some other European countries are called mixed-economy undertakings and would still be counted as public enterprises.

The Conservative government has generally chosen not to interfere but the powers remain and might be used differently by a government committed to greater intervention in the supply side of the economy.

(b) Increasing efficiency

Most academic economists argue that the success of privatization should be judged largely, if not exclusively, in terms of any improvements in efficiency and competition made as a result of privatization (see especially Swann 1988: 302; Vickers and Yarrow 1988: 426). Here we need to deal with three key aspects of privatization separately: liberalization/deregulation, contracting out, and asset sales. In addition, the whole question of regulation needs examining.

In its first term the government introduced legislation designed to liberalize markets and remove entry barriers in bus and coach services, telecommunications, oil, gas, and electricity supply. Subsequently, less emphasis was placed on deregulation and more on asset sales, but important steps were taken to deregulate the financial markets and the private rented housing market. These measures have not met with a great deal of success. For example, Jaffer and Thompson reviewing the deregulation of express coaches argue (1986: 64): 'The early verdicts—following in the wake of spectacular price reductions and the introduction of innovative services now look altogether too favourable'. More specifically, they suggest (p. 65): 'Incumbents, in particular National Express, have continued to dominate the deregulated market and our analysis indicates that this is a consequence of barriers to entry . . . rather than the consequence of the incumbent's relative efficiency.' Gist and Meadowcroft report a similar picture in the telecommunications industry (1986: 63):

TABLE 1 Asset Sales 1979–91

Company	Financial year of initial flotation	Golden share	Net proceeds to HMG (£ millions)	Times oversubscribed (under-subscribed)	Discount on share price (%)
British Petroleum	1979/80	No	6,149	N/A	—
British Aerospace	1980/1	Yes	390	M/A	—
Cable and Wireless	1981/2	Yes	1,024	5.6	17
Amersham International	1981/2	Yes	60	24.0	26
Britoil	1982/3	Yes	53	(0.3)	N/A
Associated British Ports	1982/3	No	97	34.0	21
Enterprise Oil (British Gas subsidiary)	1984/5	Yes	382	(0.4)	N/A
Jaguar (British Leyland subsidiary)	1984/5	Yes	—	8.3	6
British Telecom	1985/6	Yes	3,681	3.0	21
TSB	1986/7	No			
British Gas	1986/7	Yes	7,731	4.0	11
British Airways	1986/7	Yes	850	23.0	29
Rolls-Royce	1987/8	Yes	1,028	9.4	25
British Airports Authority	1987/8	Yes	1,183	8.1	12
10 Water Companies	1989/90	Yes	3,480	2.8	17
Electric Companies	1990/91	Yes	5,200	10.7	21
2 Electricity Generating Companies (Powergen and National Power)	1991/92	Yes	2,000	4.0	37

A policy of promoting competition in a newly liberalised market where the incumbent remains dominant, as BT does in communications, requires certain policy provisions if it is to be effective. In particular, the rules that govern the dominant firms' behaviour should contain a strong presumption against certain activities, such as the acquisition of industrial property rights, establishing exclusive contracts and extending existing market dominance through the acquisition of other firms. When seen in this light the regulatory regime created for the UK telecommunications industry cannot be considered a strong one. (For similar views on electricity supply see Hammond *et al.* 1986, especially pp. 30–1).

Croft (1990) and Thompson (1990: 159–62) are more positive about the effects of deregulation of financial markets while Kemp (1990) argues that liberalization of the private rented housing market may have minor positive effects. Overall, however, it is difficult not to agree with Helm and Yarrow's (1988: p. vii) assessment that the liberalizing legislation in the early 1980s had a limited effect because it lacked teeth.

The introduction of contracting out and competitive tendering has led to significant cost savings. (For a classification of the various types of contracting out see Hartley 1990: 171.) Studies report savings of 20 per cent or above for: refuse collection, whether the contract is awarded in-house or not (Domberger *et al.* 1986 and Cubbin *et al.* 1987); hospital domestic services (Domberger *et al.* 1987); a broad range of local authority and health authority services (Hartley and Huby 1985); and services in the London Borough of Wandsworth (Ascher 1987).

These studies do have major problems: different methods are used to calculate savings; often the studies assess expected savings rather than measuring actual ones; and sometimes the data are collected from interested parties, councils with an ideological commitment to privatize or even contractors who have won contracts (see Hartley 1990: 190). There is little doubt that initial bids by private contractors were loss-leaders while there is considerable debate as to whether or not the standard of services has decline as contractors cut costs (see especially Gomley and Grahl 1988).

Management buyouts have also been an important feature of the contracting out process in local government and the health service. In 1989 the privatization of public sector services accounted for over 4 per cent of all management buyouts. However, here too the main consequence of privatization has been a deterioration in the pay and conditions of workers (*Labour Research*, December 1990).

Almost all observers are agreed that asset sales have very rarely led to increased competition. Vickers and Yarrow (1988: 425–9) offer a harsh judgment on government policy:

The razzamatazz associated with stock market flotations is the most immediately visible aspect of privatisation, but in the long run the British privatisation programme will be judged in terms of its effect on economic efficiency. By failing to introduce sufficiently effective frameworks of competition and regulation before privatizing such industries as telecommunications and gas, the Government has lost a major opportunity to tackle fundamental problems experienced in the past under public ownership. By pushing the programme too far and too fast, the Government is undermining the long-run success of privatisation in Britain. (See for similar views Curwen 1986, ch. 8; Swann 1988: 295–306; Ramanadham 1988: 270–6).

It is often emphasized that asset sales have not resulted in widespread management changes (Dunsire *et al.* 1988: 382) or that there has been little change in the managerial culture in the privatized companies, precisely because competition has been severely limited (Ramanadham 1988: 276). In contrast, executive salaries in these companies have grown reasonably (see Chapman 1990: 66). More importantly, a number of authors point to the success that many privatized companies have had in fighting off the threat of competition (Curwen 1986: 258–74; Swann 1988: 3402–6; Mitchell 1990: 22; Beauchamps 1990: 57). As Abromeit (1988: 75) puts it:

Even the new and placable chairmen have proved to be a match for the Government when it came to the 'hows' of privatisation, particularly since they were rather successful in committing their sponsor departments to their own ideas, i.e. they succeeded in transferring their conflicts with Government into the Government machine. The BT managers, for instance, succeeded—quite conspicuously—in inducing the Government to drop most of its original ideas about liberalisation in the telecommunications industry (see also Curwen 1986: 258–74, and Swann 1988: 302–6).

Even Veljanovski (1987: 162) admits that: 'In British Gas's case, however, the failure to dismantle this monolith was a mistake and will place a heavy burden on the regulators'. However, he argues that it was extremely difficult for the government not to take account of the demands of the putative privatized company's management, given that it needed their co-operation (pp. 14–15).

The government also had political reasons for limiting competition. Introducing significant competition into monopoly industries would have necessitated a more complex structure for the industries which, particularly if linked to opposition from the putative managements, would have delayed privatization. Delay did not fit in with the government's political timetable (Baldwin 1990). More importantly, the government was anxious to ensure the successful sale of the privatized companies and this success was much more likely to occur if the company retained its monopoly position (Baldwin 1990: 98; see also Thompson 1990: 148). Here, there was a clear tension between the government's main economic aim—increasing competition and efficiency—and its broader political aims. In such circumstances, the political aims appear to have been paramount.

In the more recent privatizations of water and electricity, the government has introduced some elements of competition, although the fact that both these industries are natural monopolies has made this more difficult. In the case of water the ten regional water companies were privatized separately. This practice was repeated for the regional electricity companies, while the generating industry was split into two competing companies—National Power and Power Gen. There is little doubt that the government has responded to the criticism of past privatizations particularly British Telecom (see Veljanovski 1987: pp. xxi–xxiii; Pitt 1990: 72; Mitchell 1990: 20). This is also reflected in the decision in 1991 to liberalize the telecommunications market encouraging other companies to compete with BT and Mercury.

The relative lack of competition does *not* necessarily mean that there has been no improvement in the efficiency of privatized companies. Of course, there is a considerable problem with assessing efficiency because, although profitability, productivity, and output may have increased, the standard of the service may have fallen, given that many of the privatized companies retain their monopoly, or totally dominant, position in the market place. In addition, as Curwen points out, most of the early privatizations involved companies which were already relatively efficient and profitable (Curwen 1986: 166).

However, there have been a number of attempts to assess the performance of the privatized companies. Veljanovski (1990), claims that profitability increases have been impressive. Curwen (1986: 212–13, see tables 6.11 and 6.12) is more circumspect, suggesting that while the performance of newly privatized companies have been variable, most have performed well. Most other analyses are more sceptical.

Dunsire *et al.* (1991) examined patterns of productivity, profitability, and employment in a variety of companies which experienced status or ownership change including BAe, the National Freight Corporation (NFC), BT and the Royal Ordnance Factories (ROF). They found that, if they compared total factor productivity with national trends, only one of the privatized companies (NFC) showed an improved performance. If profitability was used as the measure, there was a marked improvement in only one company (ROF). There was a major labour shake-out in two companies (NFC and BAe), a limited labour shake-out in one (BT) and no employment change in the ROF.

Similar results are reported elsewhere. In particular, it is suggested that there has been little improvement in productivity as a result of privatization and a mixed pattern on profitability (Thompson 1990: 156; Bishop and Kay 1988, ch. 9).

British Telecom has received particular attention but again the picture is, at best, mixed. Pitt (1990) argues that privatization has had clear consequences. More specifically, he suggests that it now takes competition more seriously and pursues a more aggressive management style (p. 66). In addition, he points to a variety of organization changes designed to increase effective management and profitability which have occurred (pp. 68–9). In contrast, Foreman-Peck and Manning (1988: 66) examine total factor productivity in the European telecommunications industry and emphasize that the results 'do not show BT clearly performing better than its State-owned monopolistic counterparts in continental Europe'. Similarly, Foreman-Peck argues elsewhere (1990: 20):

The reorientation of British telecommunications policy in 1981 and 1984 transformed most possible influences on performance. Private ownership and competition were introduced, and the government ceased to use the system as a policy instrument on any significant scale. Yet the simulation suggests no substantial improvement in productivity and calls (the principal output) growth since liberalisation.

At the same time, even Pitt suggests that 'short-termism' has been one consequence of the increased market pressure on BT; more specifically there has been a marked reduction in BT's research and development expenditure.

There is also some discussion in the literature of the consequences to customers of privatization. Doubts have been expressed about the quality of services provided by the privatized companies (see Thompson 1990: 157), although this is clearly difficult to assess (Bishop and Kay 1988: 71 and 80). At the same time, it is suggested that a common consequence of privatization is increased prices to customers. For example, Bunn and Vlahos (1989: 144), after a detailed analysis of the likely consequences of privatization in the electricity supply industry, argue: 'looking some twenty-five years ahead . . . the effect of privatisation is a price increase above our base case, of between 40 per cent and 90 per cent depending upon the . . . required rate of return for the generating companies.' Of course, there are other economic aspects of the privatization process which might lead us to question its aims and success. The process has certainly been expensive to the taxpayer. Here, Buckland's (1987) analysis is the most thorough. He emphasizes that some of the privatization sales have been made at prices which have been significantly more heavily discounted than is normal for public sector sales (p. 245 and table 2, p. 246). Buckland's table (p. 250) indicates that the government's investment in the policy up until 1987 was between £600 millions and £1,300 millions, and he points out that the later issues 'cost' the taxpayer more when the government used them as vehicles for the creation of new shareholders.

More recent figures produced by the National Audit Office confirm Buckland's analysis (Beauchamps 1990). They calculated that by the time the electricity generating industry is privatized, the process will have cost the government £2,375 millions, more than half of which will have been spent on water and electricity. Buckland concludes, 'by every yardstick, [the] policy has been shown to be costly to the tax-payer' (p. 255; for a similar analysis see Curwen 1986: 204–8, and Abromeit 1988: 77–8). McCarthy's conclusion is even more scathing, although this, to an extent, reflects his political views; he views the government's privatization as asset-stripping (McCarthy 1988: 74–6).

The lack of competition facing the privatized companies has ensured that the question of regulation is very important. Indeed, it is one of the paradoxes of privatization that it has involved greater regulation (see Thompson 1990: 135). The government is at the centre of this regulation, despite the Conservatives' stated desire to reduce intervention (Graham and Prosser 1988: 81). In fact, the government established a series of agencies to ensure regulation, OFTEL, OFGAS, OFWAT, etc., while the Monopolies and Mergers Commission is also involved in this process.

There are clearly a series of problems involved in the process of regulation (see Helm and Yarrow 1988: p. xxix). They can lack expertise (Ramanadham 1988: 280–1) and, information from the regulated company (Vickers and Yarrow 1988: 427). The overall pattern is fairly clear. The regulatory agencies lack power, at best they have influence which they can exercise through a process of negotiation and consultation with the privatized company (see Graham and Prosser 1988: 81; Pitt 1990: 71).

It is too early to assess the affect of regulation but it is clearly, in large part, dependent on the ability of the regulating agency to maximize its powers. Even Veljanovski (1987), who is very optimistic about the future of regulation, recognizes that the relative success of OFTEL owes a great deal to the ability of its Director General, Professor Carsberg, to use his limited papers to maximum effect and, even more to the fact that: 'the tele-communications sector is perhaps unique among the utility industries because in it competition is possible. Gas, Water and the other utilities pose more serious problems and it is disturbing that OFGAS has much narrower powers and is a much smaller agency' (p. 186).

(c) Reducing the PSBR

There can be little doubt that the PSBR has been significantly improved by the sales, although there is disagreement about the importance of this as a government aim. Brittan (1984: 11–37) argues that it wasn't a significant reason for the programme, whereas most other authors suggest the opposite. As table 2 indicates, receipts from privatization sales have risen dramatically since 1979/80. In 1988/9 they topped £7 million, although this fell to £4.2 in 1989/90 and £3.7 million in the first three quarters of 1990/91.

This dramatic rise in receipts from special sales didn't result in an immediate fall in the PSBR. Even given these proceeds, the PSBR persisted at 3 per cent a year, despite the predictions in the Medium Term Financial Strategy that it would fall to 1.5 per cent (see Buckland 1987: and table 2, p. 243). Subsequently, since the financial year 1987/8 the public sector deficit has disappeared. This results in large part from the dramatic increase in privatization receipts but the public sector financial deficit has also fallen markedly, so other factors are involved (see Maynard 1988: 74–6).

At the same time, the government's policy in relation to PSBR clearly changed. Thompson (1990: 144) makes the point very well:

In a period when Government expenditure and the PSBR is seen as the main culprit responsible for the economy's ills and particularly for inflation there is a massive incentive for the Government to begin a privatisation programme independently of all the competition and efficiency arguments. This very much informed the early move towards such a programme in the United Kingdom. However, strong evidence to support the claim of a link between the PSBR and inflation (via the money supply) failed to materialise. In addition, the Government turned towards more overtly supply-side policies. In this context the proceeds from the privatisation programme could be used to offset other expenditure and finance the Government's tax-reduction aspirations—all this and the PSBR continuing to be reduced or becoming a surplus. Thus, the financial objective changed somewhat, to providing the manœuvring room for desired tax cuts in the name of their supposed supply-side incentive effects.

In essence, privatization ceased to be a means to reduce the PSBR, rather it became a way of financing tax cuts without reducing public

TABLE 2 Privatization proceeds: contribution to government expenditure financial years 1979/80–1989/90 (in billions)

	79/80	80/81	81/82	82/83	83/84	84/85	85/86	86/87	87/88	88/89	89/90	90/91[b]
Proceeds from privatization (in real terms[a])	0.475	0.520	0.577	0.425	1.4	2.5	2.9	4.7	5.1	7.5	4.5	3.90
PSBR (before privatization receipts: surplus figures in brackets)	12.6	13.1	9.1	9.4	10.9	12.3	8.5	7.8	1.7	(7.0)	(3.4)	NA
Receipts as % of PSBR	2.9	3.1	5.4	5.2	10.5	17.3	31.8	56.7	282.3	NC	NC	NA
Receipts as % of general government expenditure	0.4	0.4	0.4	0.4	0.8	1.4	1.7	2.6	3.2	4.5	NA	NA

a   Adjusted to 1987/8 price levels
b   Figures for 1990/91 are for the first three quarters only.
NA   Not Available.
NC   Not Calculated as PSBR is positive.

expenditure. This raises the broader question, which is well beyond the scope of this review, of whether the money raised was spent widely (see Thompson 1990: 148).

(d) Curbing public sector union power

There is little doubt that one of the chief initial concerns of the Conservative government was to curb union power. In part, this was because they opposed corporatist economic strategies and the resulting trade union involvement in economic policy-making but the Thatcher government also believed that the Heath government had been brought down by the trade unions, or more specifically the NUM (see Heald and Steel 1982: 344–5; both Heald 1985: 11 and Abromeit 1988: 73, pay particular attention to the Ridley report). At the same time, the trade unions in the private sector were viewed as a constraint on the operation of the market, while it was argued that trade unions in the public sector forced up wages and, thus, public expenditure and the PSBR. The government's industrial relations legislation was the main means it used to alter the balance between employers and unions (see Marsh 1992). However, as far as public sector unions were concerned, privatization was seen as a means of reducing their size, bargaining power, and influence over policy.

The unions have been particularly affected by two key aspects of privatization; contracting out and asset sales. As far as contracting out is concerned three developments are clear. First, there has been a loss of jobs, although the scale of the redundancies may be greater in the local authority sector (see Ascher 1987: 104, table 4.1), than in the NHS (Milne 1987: 154–69). Second, competitive tendering has resulted in lower wages, regardless of whether the final contract is awarded externally or in-house (Asher 1987: 107–8). Third, working conditions, notably in relation to holidays and overtime, have worsened (Asher 1987: 108–10).

The effect of asset sales on unions is more complex and there is less agreement among observers. Curwen (1986: 168–9) examined the industrial relations systems in those companies privatized before June 1984. He found that only two attempts had been made to change the bargaining systems and concluded:

The picture presented is, on the whole, quite favourable to the unions, with jobs being created as well as being lost. . . . That privatisation should bring both gains and losses is hardly unexpected, but the Government must be somewhat disappointed and the Unions pleasantly surprised, at the way in which the balance between the two has worked out in practice.

However, this conclusion may be misguided. Certainly, the TUC's publication, *Bargaining in Privatised Companies*, presents a different picture. They argue that virtually all the privatized companies have had major redundancies and that, while management salaries have risen significantly after privatization, unions have only been able to achieve an improvement in non-managerial real wages in return for important concessions on terms and conditions of employment or large-scale redundancies. In addition, the TUC specifies a number of detailed complaints against the industrial relations practices of the management of most of the privatized companies.

There seems little doubt that the situation for unions has worsened in many of these companies, but there is doubt both as to how much it has worsened and how far this change results from privatization. In fact, it appears that there is no consistent pattern (see D. Thomas 1986). Certainly the experience of BT and BG after privatization is very different. Privatization led to rapid and major changes in BT's bargaining structure but not in BG's, while unions claim a marked reduction in areas for negotiation and consultation in BT in contrast to BG. In both companies there were perceptible changes towards a more assertive management style, but this was much more noticeable in BT. In BT, privatization was followed by a major managerial initiative to change key elements in the terms and conditions of employees; indeed, in 1986–7 there was a major industrial dispute over BT's efforts to link pay increases to changes in work organization and other efficiency measures (see IRS 1989; and also Pitt 1990: 69).

If a company passes into the private sector is doesn't inevitably lead to fundamental changes in the industrial relations system. Industrial relations in many of the industries privatized, and particularly in most of the first ones sold, were good prior to the change in ownership, which may explain Curwen's results. There is little doubt that here, as elsewhere, the changes in industrial relations practice have been greatest in companies in which there was a poor history of industrial relations (see Marsh 1992).

At the same time, other factors appear to be more important than ownership in affecting industrial relations practice and bargaining. As Abromeit suggests: 'one look at the capacity-reduction policies of the British Steel Corporation [before privatisation] or [British Coal] makes the unions' contention that privatisation would increase unemployment sound slightly ridiculous.' (1988: 73). In fact, Vickers and Yarrow argue that private companies may be less able to resist union pressure because they have fewer resources while government may have more reason to stand firm or face similar demand from other public sector workers:

Both these effects were at work in the year-long coal strike in 1984–1985. The Government was content to incur massive financial losses to secure victory, and its resolve to defeat the National Union of Mineworkers was inspired in large part by the demonstration (or signaling) effect on other wage bargains in the economy—a factor that would not have entered the calculations of private sector negotiators (Vickers and Yarrow 1988: 159).

Overall, it seems fair to conclude that the change in ownership involved in privatization has had a limited effect on trade unions. It is significant that while membership of public sector unions has declined, there is no clear pattern in that decline. While the membership of unions overall fell by 21 per cent between 1979 and 1985, the membership of public sector unions like NALGO and NUPE remained relatively stable. It was in public sector industries largely unaffected by privatization (the coal industry and the railways) and in the civil service where union membership fell most dramatically. At the same time, union membership fell dramatically in many areas of the private sector; the Transport and General Workers Union membership fell from 31 per cent, the Engineers 20 per cent, and the Construction Workers 28 per cent in the same period.

(e) Wider share ownership and employee share ownership

The themes of wider share ownership generally, and increased employee share ownership specifically, became more important ones for the Conservative government as privatization progressed. The logic of this aspect of the government strategy was evident in John Moore's statement in July 1984, which only omitted the government's assessment of the electoral advantages of the changes:

As we dispose of state-owned assets, so more and more people have the opportunity to become owners . . . So these policies also increase personal independence and freedom, and by establishing a new breed of owners, have an important effect on attitudes. They tend to break down the divisions between owners and earners . . . (quoted in Abromeit 1988: 71).

Once again, the achievement is somewhat less than the aspiration. Fraser (1988: 14) reports government figures which suggest that by early 1988, 9 million people, 20.5 per cent of the adult population, owned shares compared with only 7 per cent in 1979. Of these, 13 per cent held shares in privatized companies, with 6 per cent owning only such shares, while 3 per cent of the population held shares in the companies for which they worked. In addition, he claims: 'there had been no noticeable fall in the number of shareholders in the major privatised companies, with on average roughly two-thirds of initial shareholders having retained their shares.' In fact Fraser's figures present a partial picture. Bishop and Kay (1988) report a detailed analysis of the share registers of the privatized companies (see table 19, p. 34) which was extended by *Labour Research* (June 1989). The analyses show that in some cases (Amersham and Britoil) around 90 per cent of the original shareholders had sold their shares by 1989, whilst in other cases (Enterprise Oil and British Gas) only a third of them sold. Overall, the average percentage of original share-holders who retained shares was 40 per cent, significantly less than the 66 per cent quoted by the government and Fraser. (For a similar analysis see Buckland 1987: 254.) In addition, and unsurprisingly, there is a clear class basis of share ownership (see Thompson 1990: 145–6).

The shares in the privatized companies have ended up with the finan-cial institutions which reflects the general trend in the Stock Market. As Buckland points out: 'whereas institutions owned 1.2 times the value of equities in personal sector hands during 1970, the figure has risen to 1.8 times by 1985' (1987: 255; for a similar analysis see Bishop and Kay 1988, table 18, p. 33). In some cases, 99 per cent of employees bought shares in their firms (for figures see Croft 1990). However, as Abromeit points out: 'their total share in the firm's capital nevertheless stayed ridiculously small; it fluctuated between 0.1 per cent and 4.3 per cent, the only excep-tion being the National Freight Corporation' (1988: 79). Overall, there has been a widening, but not a deepening, of share ownership (see Veljanovski 1990: 69 and Thompson 1990: 148). Initially, between 1982 and 1984 there was consistent, slightly negative, short-term return to shareholders, but after the government switched to stress the significance of wider share ownership, short-term gains escalated (see Buckland 1987, table 4, p. 253; for data on the movement in share prices since privatiza-tion see Fraser (ed.) 1988: 51).

As Buckland (1987: 253–4) emphasizes: 'Generous price margins on fixed-price offers for sale, plus directive management of application entitlement and allotment rules, have produced large returns for big institutions at one extreme and at the other for employees and shareholders.' The prices were attractive to investors and produced what Heald, very evocatively, calls a yuppy version of the football pools (Heald 1988: 44), although it must be emphasized that in this case the odds were better. However, it seems diffi-cult not to agree with Buckland's (1987: p. 255) conclusion:

The privatisation programme, therefore, is unlikely to be making much impact upon equity ownership in the UK. The deregulation of share trading and marketing in October 1986 and the expansion of decentralized information and trading systems are likely to have more far-reaching and durable effects. What the programme has undeniably done is shift the median line of the UK's public sector and redistribute large amounts of public sector wealth to share purchasers, particularly the financial institutions.

A number of economists who have examined the British privatization programme stress the political short-termism it has involved. Swann (1988: 316), for example, suggests that the programme has been 'substantially inspired by considerations of political ideology'. Vickers and Yarrow (1988: 428) are even more definite:

In our view, Mrs Thatcher's Government has been guilty of just the sort of 'short termism' that has coloured policy towards nationalized industries in the past. The desire to privatise speedily, to widen share ownership quickly, and to raise short-term revenues have stood in the way of devising adequate measures of competition and regulation for the industries concerned. . . . In the process, the Government has partly been captured by the managements of the firms being sold, since their co-operation is essential for rapid privatisation. Short-term political advantage may have been won, but longer-lasting gains in economic efficiency have been lost. (For a similar verdict, see Abromeit 1988: 83)

(f) Gaining political advantage

We have already considered what effect privatization had on economic efficiency; but are Vickers and Yarrow right when they imply that the government may have gained political advantage from the programme? Certainly the population has never favoured nationalization. What is more, support for nationalization declined significantly, particularly among Labour voters, between October 1974 and 1979, suggesting that the Conservatives' opposition to nationalization was a minor vote-winner in 1979. However, opposition to nationalization didn't increase after 1979 and indeed, Labour voters' support for it has risen during the Thatcher years (see Crewe 1988).

Of course, we don't have any opinion poll series on attitudes to privatization, which, in its present form, is a recent phenomenon. Nevertheless, the polls which have been taken about particular privatizations don't unequivocally support the view that it is a popular policy. As Crewe shows, 57 per cent of those asked thought the privatization of British Gas was a bad idea, while 56 per cent and 72 per cent expressed the same view about the privatizations of British Telecom and Electricity and

Water respectively (Crewe 1988: 42–3, these Gallup results are confirmed by an NOP Poll reported in McCarthy 1988: 823). In contrast, Veljanovski (1987: 689 and especially fig. 3.2, p. 69) suggests that support for privatization increased over time. What is not in doubt is that the sale of council houses was a popular move to reduce the size of the public sector.

There is considerable evidence however that, while privatization is not overwhelmingly popular among the general population, it has had a positive effect among those voters who have benefited from it. Veljanovski (1989: 69) reports MORI opinion poll data which suggest the overwhelming majority of first-time share buyers intended to vote Conservative; 53 per cent as compared with 14 per cent intending to vote Labour. Similarly, Crewe (1989) analyses the British Election Study data and suggests that there was a major swing to the Conservatives between 1979 and 1983 among those who bought their council houses and a smaller swing to the Conservatives between 1983 and 1987 among those who bought shares.

Of course, even if there is a clear link between privatization and Conservative voting, there is some question as to the direction of any causal relationship. Certainly, Heath *et al.* (1989: 18) argue that: 'in choosing to become shareholders and owner occupiers, these voters were more evidently affirming their existing social and political wishes rather than reorganising them.' (For data on the general social and political attitudes of earlier purchasers of council houses, see Forrest and Murie 1991.) However, McAllister and Studlar's (1989) analysis questions this conclusion. They used the British Election Study data and controlled for the effect of a range of socio-economic factors. This allowed them to isolate the independent effect of privatization by controlling for other factors, for example, class and education, which might have caused both Conservative voting and house or share purchase. They conclude:

Conservatives gained 10 per cent more of the vote among new shareholders compared with those who had never owned shares, while Labour lost 9 per cent of the vote, net of other things. Similarly, council tenants who had purchased their shares showed some 15 per cent greater levels of Conservative support, compared to stable council tenants, net of other things (McAllister and Studlar 1989: 172–3).

They also emphasize that of these two aspects of privatization the Conservatives gained more from share sell-offs, which led to a 1.6 per cent increase in their vote, than from council house sales, which led to a 0.9 per cent increase in their vote, given that almost three times as many people purchased shares as bought their own houses (see McAllister and Studlar 1989: 175–6, especially table 10, p. 175).

Conclusion

The first thing to re-emphasize is the scale of privatization. It is immense. The balance between the public sector and the private sector has been significantly changed and this appears likely to be a lasting legacy of the Thatcherite era. In essence, Britain is no longer a mixed-economy; it has moved decisively in the direction of the market.

However, privatization had a number of aims, some of which were contradictory. In particular, the aim to increase efficiency conflicted with the need to ensure quick and successful asset sales. What is more, efficiency which implied competition, was compromised because of the need to ensure management co-operation.

As such, it is hardly surprising that the government has only achieved some of its aims. As we have seen, the balance between the two sectors has altered fundamentally. At the same time, the government has gained clear political advantage from the asset sales and housing sales programmes. Elsewhere, the picture is more complex. Asset sales, and particularly contracting out, have done something to weaken public sector unions but only something; the history of industrial relations in an industry which has been privatized is still the most important factor affecting industrial relations in the new structure. Similarly, while share ownership has been widened it has not been deepened. Most significantly, however, there is considerable doubt as to whether privatization has increased efficiency. Contracting out has reduced costs but perhaps at the expense of the quality of services. The failure to improve efficiency in many privatized companies is even more noticeable. Perhaps the jury is still out, but the interim verdict must be sceptical.

As far as the literature is concerned, there are clear gaps where more research is necessary. First, we need data on the extent and success of the attempts to introduce competition, and thus greater efficiency, in the later privatization. Second, there is still relatively little work on the effect of the regulatory agencies. Third, and this take us well beyond the scope of this review, more good, comparative studies of privatization in a number of countries would help add a useful perspective on the privatization process in Britain (see Richardson (ed.) 1990; Letwin (ed.) 1988; Swann 1988; Gayle and Goodrich (eds.) 1990; McAvoy *et al.* (eds.) 1989).

References

ABROMEIT, H. (1988), 'British privatisation policy', *Parliamentary Affairs* 41, 1: 68–85.

ASHER, K. (1987), *The Politics of Privatisation: Contracting out Public Services*. Basingstoke: Macmillan.

AYLEN, P. (1989), 'Privatisation of the British Steel Corporation', *Fiscal Studies* 10, 3, 1–25.

BALDWIN, P. (1990), 'Privatisation and regulation: the case of British Airways', pp. 93–107 in J. Richardson *Privatisation and Deregulation in Canada and Britain*. Aldershot: Dartmouth.

BEAUCHAMPS, C. (1990), 'National Audit Office: its role in privatisation', *Public Money and Management* 10, 2, 55–8.

BEESLEY, M., and S. LITTLECHILD (1988), 'The regulation of privatised monopolies in the United Kingdom', *Rand Journal of Economics* 19, 454–72.

BISHOP, M., and J. KAY (1988), *Does Privatisation Work?* London: London Business School.

BRITTAN, S. (1984), 'The politics and economics of privatisation', *Political Quarterly* 55, 2: 109–127.

BUCKLAND, R. (1987), 'The costs and returns of the privatisation of nationalised industries', *Public Administration* 65, 3: 241–57.

BUNN, D., and K. VLAHOS (1989), 'Evaluation of the long-term effects of UK electricity prices following privatisation', *Fiscal Studies* 10, 4: 104–16.

CHAPMAN, C. (1990), *Selling the Family Silver: Has Privatisation Worked?* London: Hutchinson.

CREWE, I. (1988), 'Has the electorate become more Thatcherite? in R. Skidelsky (ed.), *Thatcherism*. London: Chatto and Windus.

—— (1989), 'The decline of Labour and the decline of labour', *Essex Papers in Politics and Government* No. 65.

CROFT, R. (1990), 'Deregulation and re-regulation of the financial services industry in the UK', pp. 141–51 in J. Richardson (ed.) *Privatisation and Deregulation in Canada and Britain*. Aldershot: Dartmouth.

CUBBIN, J., S. DOMBERGER, and S. MEADOWCROFT (1987), 'Competitive tendering and refuse collection': identifying the sources of efficiency gains', *Fiscal Studies* 8, 3: 49–58.

CURWEN, P. (1986), *Public Enterprise: A Modern Approach*. London: Wheatsheaf.

DOMBERGER, SIMON, S. MEADOWCROFT, and D. THOMPSON (1986), 'Competitive tendering and efficiency: the case of refuse collection', *Fiscal Studies*, 7, 4, 69–87.

—— (1987), 'The impact of competitive tendering on the costs of hospital domestic services', *Fiscal Studies* 8, 4: 39–54.

DUDLEY, G. (1989), 'Privatisation "with the grain": distinguishing features of the sale of the National Bus Company, *Strathclyde Papers on Government and Politics* No. 59.

DUNSIRE, A., K. HARTLEY, D. PARKER, and B. DIMITRIOU (1988), 'Organizational status and performances: a conceptual framework for testing public choice theories', *Public Administration* 66, 4: 363–88.

—— K. HARTLEY, and D. PARKER (1991), 'Organisational status and performance: summary of the findings', *Public Administration* 69, 1: 21–40.

FOREMAN-PECK, J., and D. MANNING (1988), 'How well is BT performing: An international comparison of telecommunications total factor productivity', *Fiscal Studies* 9, 3: 54–67.

—— (1990), 'Ownership, competition and productivity growth: the impact of liberalisation and privatisation on BT: *Warwick Economic Research Papers* No. 338.

FORREST, R. (1988), *Selling the Welfare State: The Privatisation of Public Housing*. London:Routledge.

—— and A. MURIE (1991), 'Transformation through tenure? The early purchasers of council houses 1968–1973', *Journal of Social Policy* 20, pp. 1–25.

FRASER, R. (ed.) (1988), *Privatisation: The UK Experience and International Trends*. London: Longman.

GAYLE, J., and J. GOODRICH (eds.) (1990), *Privatisation and Deregulation in Global Perspective*. Pinter: London.

GIST, P., and S. MEADOWCROFT (1986), 'Regulating for competition: the newly liberalised market for branch exchanges', *Fiscal Studies* 1, 3: 41–66.

GOMLEY, J., and J. GRAHL (1988), 'Competition and efficiency in refuse collection: a critical comment'. *Fiscal Studies* 9, 1: 80–5.

GRAHAM, C., and T. PROSSER (1988), '"Rolling back the frontiers". The privatisation of state enterprises', pp. 73–94 in C. Graham and T. Prosser, *Waiving the Rules*. Milton Keynes: Open University Press.

—— (1991), *Privatising Public Enterprises: Constitutions, the State and Regulation in Comparative Perspective*. Oxford: Clarendon.

GRIMSTONE, G. (1990), 'The British privatisation programme', pp. 3–13 in J. Richardson (ed.), *Privatisation and Deregulation in Canada and Britain*. Aldershot: Dartmouth.

GROUT, P. (1987), 'The wider share ownership programme', *Fiscal Studies* 6, 3: 59–74.

HAMMOND, E., D. HELM, and D. THOMPSON (1986), 'Competition in electricity supply: has the Energy Act failed?', *Fiscal Studies* 6, 1: 11–33.

HARTLEY, K. (1990), 'Contracting-out in Britain: achievements and problems', pp. 177–98 in J. Richardson (ed.), *Privatisation and Deregulation in Canada and Britain*. Aldershot: Dartmouth.

—— and M. HUBY (1985), 'Contracting-out in health and local authorities: prospects, progress and pitfall's, *Public Money* 5, 2: 23–26.

HEALD, D. (1985), 'Will the privatisation of public enterprise solve the problem of control?', *Public Administration* 63: 7–21.

—— (1988), 'The United Kingdom: privatisation and its political context', *Western European Politics* II, 31–48.

HEALD, D. and D. STEEL (1982), 'Privatising public enterprises: an analysis of the government's case', *Political Quarterly* 53, 3: 333–49.

—— and D. THOMAS (1980), 'Privatisation as theology', *Public Policy and Administration* 1, 2: 49–66.

HELM, D., and G. YARROW (1988), 'The assessment: the regulation of utilities', *Oxford Review of Economic Policy* 4, 2: i–xxxi.

HYMAN, H. (1989), 'Privatisation: the facts', pp. 191–219 in C. Veljanovksi, *Privatisation and Competition*. London: Institute of Economic Affairs.

Industrial Relations Services (1989), 'Industrial relations after privatisation', *Employment Trends*, pp. 12–14 No. 439, 10 May.

JACKSON, P. (1985), *Implementing Government Policy Initiatives: The Thatcher Administration 1979–83*. London: RIPA.

Jaffer, S., and D. Thompson (1986), 'Deregulating express coaches: a reassessment'. *Fiscal Studies* 7, 4: 45–68.

JOHNSON, C. (1988), *Privatisation and Ownership*. London: Pinter.

KAY, J., C. MAYER, and D. THOMPSON (eds.) (1986), *Privatisation and Regulation: The UK Experience*. Oxford: Clarendon.

KEMP, P. (1990), 'Deregulation, markets and the 1988 Housing Act', *Social Policy and Administration* 24; 145–55.

Labour Research (1989), 'Tories share out air industry', June, pp. 10–12.

—— (1989), 'Tough times for private contractors', July, pp. 19–20.

—— (1990), 'Buying out a public service', Dec., pp. 8–10.

LE GRAND, J., and R. ROBINSON (1984), *Privatisation and the Welfare State*. London: Allen and Unwin.

LETWIN, O. (1988), *Privatising the World: A Study of International Privatisation Theory and Practice*. London: Cassells.

MCALLISTER, I., and D. STUDLAR (1989), 'Popular versus elite views of privatisation: the case of Britain', *Journal of Public Policy* 9: 157–78.

MCAVOY, P., W. STANBURY, G. YARROW, and R. ZECKHAUSER (eds.) (1989), *Privatisation and State-owned Enterprises: Lessons from the United States, Great Britain and Canada*. Boston: Kluwer Academic Publishers.

MCCARTHY, LORD (1988), 'Privatisation and the employee', in V.Ramanadham (ed.), *Privatisation in the UK*. London: Routledge.

MARSH, D. (1992), *The New Politics of British Trade Unions*. Basingstoke: Macmillan.

MAYNARD, G. (1988), *The economy under Mrs. Thatcher*. Oxford: Blackwell.

MILNE, R. (1987), 'Competitive tendering in the NHS: an economic analysis of the early implementation of HC(83) 18', *Public Administration* 65, 2: 145–60.

MITCHELL, J. (1990), 'Britain: privatisation as myth?' pp. 14–34 in J. Richardson (ed.), *Privatisation and Deregulation in Canada and Britain*. Aldershot: Dartmouth.

MOON, J., J. RICHARDSON, and P. SMART (1986), 'The privatisation of British Telecom: a case study of the extended process of legislation', *European Journal of Political Research* 14: 339–55.

PAPADAKIS, E., and P. TAYLOR-GOOBY (eds.) (1987), *The Private Provision of Welfare: State, Market and Community.* Sussex: Wheatsheaf.

PARRY, R. (ed.) (1989), *Privatisation.* London: Kingsley.

PITT, D. (1990), 'An essentially contestable organisation! British Telecom and the privatisation debate', pp. 55–76 in J. Richardson (ed.), *Privatisation and Deregulation in Canada and Britain.* Aldershot: Dartmouth.

RAMANADHAM, V. (ed.) (1988), *Privatisation in the UK.* London: Routledge.

REDWOOD, J. (1990), 'Privatisation: a consultant's perspective', pp. 48–62 in D. Gayle and J. Goodrich (eds.), *Privatisation and Regulation in Global Perspective.* London: Pinter.

RICHARDSON, J. (ed.) (1990), *Privatisation and Deregulation in Canada and Britain.* Aldershot: Dartmouth.

SAVAS, E. (1987), *Privatisation: The Key to Better Government.* Chatham, New Jersey: Chatham House publishers.

SWANN, D. (1988), *The Retreat of the State: Deregulation and Privatisation in the UK and US.* London: Harvester.

THOMAS, D., J. KAY *et al.* (1986), *Privatisation and Regulation: The UK Experience.* Oxford: Clarendon.

THOMPSON, G. (1990), *The Political Economy of the New Right.* London: Pinter.

Trade Union Congress (1988), *Bargaining in Privatised Companies.* London: TUC.

VELJANOVSKI, C. (1987), *Selling the State: Privatisation in Britain.* London: Weidenfeld and Nicolson.

—— (ed.) (1989), *Privatisation and Competition: A Market Prospectus.* London: Institute of Economic Affairs.

—— (1990), 'Privatisation: progress, issues and problems', pp. 63–79 in D. Gayle and J. Goodrich, *Privatisation in Global Perspective.* London: Pinter.

VICKERS, J. and G. YARROW (1988), *Privatisation: An Economic Analysis.* London: MIT press.

—— (1990), 'Regulation of privatised firms in Britain', pp. 221–8 in J. Richardson (ed.), *Privatisation: and Deregulation in Canada and Britain.* Aldershot: Dartmouth.

WHITELEY, P. (1985), 'Evaluating the monetarist experiment in Britain'. Paper for the PSA Annual Conference.

WILTSHIRE, K. (1987), *Privatisation, the British Experience: An Australian Perspective.* Melbourne, Australia: CEDA.

YOUNG, S. (1986), 'The nature of privatisation in Britain, 1979–85', *West European Politics* 9: 235–52.

Privatization in Central and Eastern Europe

PATRICK BOLTON and GÉRARD ROLAND

This paper assesses policies of mass privatization in Germany, Czechoslovakia, Hungary and Poland. A central concern stemming from the analysis is that, in view of the fiscal crisis facing economies in transition, it is crucial for governments to try to maximize the proceeds from the sale of state assets. Because of the low initial level of private wealth, it is important, in this respect, to let potential buyers borrow from the government or issue claims on future revenues (obtained with the privatized assets) to the government in order to pay for the privatized firms. Allowing for such non-cash bids removes the government's incentive to delay privatization for fiscal reasons, reduces its ability to squander immediately the proceeds from privatization and improves the decentralization of control by allowing less wealthy but more able bidders to buy the firms they are best suited to run.

1. Introduction

The transformation process of the previously centrally planned economies of Eastern Europe has been under way for over two years. In Czechoslovakia, East Germany, Hungary, and Poland most prices have been freed and reforms aimed at achieving macroeconomic stability have been implemented. While these four countries have rapidly converged towards similar macromanagement, some of them have taken longer to design their privatization plans and all of them have devised radically different strategies. During this gestation period a voluminous literature has

We gratefully acknowledge the assistance of W. Charemza, A. De Crombrugghe, M. Dicks, G. Friebel, I. Grosfeld, M. Keese, W. Maciejewski, A. Miersman, R. Portes, I. Schmitz, W-W. Sinn, V. Stepanek, R. Stern, and J. Stymme. We have also benefited from numerous discussions with P. Aghion, R. Anderson, A. Banerjee, D. Begg, E. Berglof, J. Black, M. Dewatripont, I. Grosfeld, J. McMillan, J. Müller, M. Obstfeld, M. Pagano, A. Röell, A. Sapir, M. Schankermann, D. Scharfstein, P. Seabright, A. Simonovits, J. Tirole, S. van Wijnbergen, E-Lu. von Thadden, P. Weil, and M. Whinston. Finally, we thank our *Economic Policy* discussants M. Burda and J. Vickers, the participants at the panel and the seminar participants in Brussels, Tilburg and Toulouse for all their comments.

appeared, aiming to advise the new governments on how to proceed with the unprecedented challenge of privatizing most of the nation's wealth.

Because of the sheer size of the privatization programmes, the new governments could not rely solely on the privatization experience of the West.[1] The plans now crystalized have also adopted recommendations of this literature. Our paper addresses the issues of mass privatization policies. Although our analysis has many features in common with the more influential studies to date, our conclusions are at odds with their recommendations.

A central concern of many early studies has been to accelerate the pace of privatization and their main recommendation has been to organize mass give-away schemes of state firms as a means to transfer property most rapidly (see Lipton and Sachs 1990, and Blanchard *et al.* 1991, among others). We recommend (for both microeconomic and macroeconomic reasons) that state assets not be given away, but sold—possibly through auctions.

Auctions achieve an efficient resource allocation in situations where the seller (of a state asset) does not know which buyer has the best use for it. In addition, individual bids provide information about the underlying value of a firm to be privatized, which can be of great use to future potential private investors in those firms. Perhaps more importantly, sales of state assets provide the government with revenues at a time when it has major difficulties raising revenues through taxes. Auctions have already been used successfully in privatizing small firms. We argue that privatization through auctions ought to be expanded and even applied to large firms.

Even if the government tries to maximize the cash proceeds from the sale of state assets, there will be a serious revenue shortfall problem, since the flow of savings cannot quickly absorb the massive stock of state assets. Therefore we recommend that both cash and non-cash bids (such as debt and equity) be allowed in the auctions for state assets. When non-cash bids are allowed the constraint imposed by the small flow of savings can be removed: privatization need not be slowed in order to increase the revenues from sales. Also, if buyers can borrow from the government on the basis of the future revenues generated by the newly privatized assets, then even wealth-constrained buyers can participate in auctions. Thus, state assets will not end up entirely in the hands of the wealthy happy few; cash and non-cash bids are then more likely to reflect bidders; *willingness* rather than merely their *ability* to pay. In short, greater productive efficiency is achieved with the introduction of non-cash bids, since the bidders' willingness to pay reflects their ability to run a newly acquired firm profitably.

In the case of large firms, the winning bidder (who typically has limited wealth) is likely to obtain control over the firm without owning a very large fraction of its future cash flow. Most claims on future cash flows are likely to remain with the state for some time, since the government would excessively drive down the price if it sold too large a fraction of claims too quickly. Whether or not claims remain in state hands, there will be separation of ownership and control in those firms. In the absence of well-functioning capital markets, it may then be necessary to provide for some form of supervision of the activities of managers. We discuss the kind of supervision to which managers should be subject.

Section 2 provides an overview of the current situation in the four countries. Section 3 assesses how the existing privatization plans meet the long-term objectives of building a market economy based on private property, given the macroeconomic and microeconomic constraints of the transition period. Section 4 discusses auctions with cash and non-cash bids. Section 5 deals with important related issues such as the financial restructuring of state firms and the necessary reforms in the remaining state sector. Section 6 offers concluding remarks.

2. Background

As we are dealing with economies in transition, the picture of the economies of the four countries drawn here can only be seen as snapshots at the time of writing. Undoubtedly, many aspects may have changed by the time this paper is published. In addition, as data collection in those countries is itself in transition, some of the figures reported here should be taken with a grain of salt.

2.1. What has been achieved?

In this section, we briefly describe how far East Germany, Hungary, Czechoslovakia and Poland have gone in privatizing their economies. For a detailed account of privatization see Carlin and Mayer (1992) on Germany; and Grosfeld and Hare (1991) on Poland, Hungary and Czechoslovakia.

2.1.1. East Germany Compared to the other post-socialist countries, privatization in East Germany has been very rapid. Table 3 summarizes

TABLE 3. Privatization in East Germany

	In 1991	Total at end of February 1992
Number of privatized enterprises	5,210	6,068
Revenues (DM bn.)	19.5	21.1
Promised jobs	930,262	1,013,085
Promised investment (DM bn.)	114	120.7

Source: Treuhandanstalt.

the recent data provided by Treuhandanstalt, the East German privatization agency.

Measuring privatization by the number of privatized enterprises is an inaccurate measure of the extent of privatization, since it does not take into account the size of firms. Unfortunately, the only alternative measure available is promised employment, so far representing only 9.2 per cent of the existing labour force. In other words, less than 10 per cent of the labour force has been 'privatized' so far. This estimate of privatization is in sharp contrast to the estimate of Treuhand—based on numbers of firms privatized—according to which more than half of all Treuhand firms have been privatized.

By end-February 1992, there had been 1,041 management buyouts. Only 243 sales were made to foreign investors, representing 9.4 per cent of promised job and 8.3 per cent of promised investment.

The DM 21 bn. of revenues generated from privatization are very low, compared with initial expectations. The late Treuhand president Rohwedder declared in October 1990, that sales would generate revenues of DM 600 bn. (Sinn and Sinn 1991). On the other hand, Treuhand spending is expected to increase from DM 25 bn. to DM 30 bn. in 1992, mainly due to a reluctance to close down firms; indeed, only 700 companies have been closed so far.[2]

Treuhand opted from the beginning for selling public assets rather than giving them away, but many assets have been sold for a symbolic price. Sales are mostly the result of bilateral negotiations with an interested buyer. Auctions are rare, except for smaller enterprises. The decision to sell depends not only on the price offered (or the highest cash bid in an auction), but also on restructuring plans, and especially on promises of investment and job creation which play an important role in the selection of the acquirer. One drawback of these restructuring plans is the significant rigidities they may impose on future management. Treuhand generally favours sales for cash and is unwilling to accept deferred credit payments. It also opposes selling to buyer consortia (Sinn and Sinn 1991).

2.1.2. Hungary Table 4 gives a quick overview of what has been achieved so far. These figures should be treated with caution as they are based on asset value which are likely to be highly inaccurate given the absence of a capital market which might generate an estimate of these values.

TABLE 4. Privatization in Hungary (% shares of the book value of state assets)

	May 1990	March 1991
Commercialized firms	1.7	20
Privatized state assets	0.5	2.5
Foreign capital	1.1	5
Hungarian private assets	22.2	25

Source: Barometer of Privatization, October 91.

Commercialization, giving the enterprise a legal status like that of a joint stock company before privatizing it, has been rapid since mid-1990. The share of fully-privatized state assets, however, remains very small. But unlike the other East European countries (with the exception of Poland whose agriculture is mostly in private hands), Hungary started the post-communist era with a reasonably large and active private sector, including an embryonic private financial sector. This explains in part why foreign capital is playing an increasingly important role: Hungary received over 50 per cent of the total foreign direct investment in the whole of Eastern Europe in 1991. Admittedly though, this total inflow of capital is not very large.

The initial goal of the programme was privatization of 50–60 per cent of state assets within three to five years. Mass give-away schemes were rejected at the outset. Some free distribution has taken place, distribution of shares to the Social Security fund. In addition, 10 per cent of company shares have been made available to workers at a preferential rate. But the Hungarian authorities have been reluctant to pursue further a policy of mass distribution of shares.

A useful distinction in the Hungarian approach is between privatization from below, initiated by the enterprises themselves or by a potential acquirer, and privatization from above, called 'active privatization', initiated by the State Privatization Agency (SPA). The latter includes the SPA's 'privatization programmes' as well as 'preprivatization', the privatization of small-scale family businesses and shops. Privatization from below includes the company-initiated transformation of state-owned firms into joint stock companies, association with private partners and sales. Transformation requires prior approval of the SPA which also supervises sales, in accordance with the Law on the Protection of State property. Table 5 gives an overview of the activities of the SPA.

TABLE 5. The Hungarian State Privatization Agency (March 1991)

	Number of enterprises	Value of assets (bn. for.)	% of book value of existing state assets	SPA participation (%)	Foreign participation (%)
Approved transformations	45	68.7	3.6	64.5	19
Approved associations with foreign participation	40	37.9	2	—	45.3
Approved associations with domestic partners	35	34.7	1.8	—	—
Sales under property protection	54	6	0.3		
First privatization programme	20	90.4	4.7	36	42
Reprivatization	95	0.8			

Source: State Property Agency, *Annual Report*, August 1991.

Privatization from below has until now primarily involved small and medium-sized companies in processing industries. It usually occurs when a strategic foreign investor appears. By end-September 1991, 104 transformations had already been approved, concerning assets valued at 267 bn. forint. There has thus been a noticeable acceleration between March and September.[3] At the time of writing, 616 cases of transformation were still in progress. Direct sales are rarer than association with a foreign or a domestic partner. Up to September 1991, 43 per cent of the sales contracts approved by SPA involved contributions in kind, the rest being sales contracts.

'Preprivatization' of small businesses takes place through auctions, and bidders may receive a 'livelihood loan' for the purchase of assets. This programme has, however, not been well prepared and its implementation has been constantly delayed: it is not clear how many shops are to be included in the auctions, no credit structure has been set up, and initially only leasing rights were to be auctioned off. By 15 June 1991 only 203 shops had been sold for 80 mn. forints (less than 11 mn. dollars).

As for privatization from above, the first programme initiated by the SPA included 20 enterprises. Additional programmes are under way. However, in September 1991—a year after the announcement of the first programme—not one of the 20 enterprises of SPA's first privatization package had been fully sold off. SPA revenues from sales and rental fees amounted to 9.4 bn. forint in September 1991, sharply below the 40 or 50 bn. initially projected. This method of privatization thus does not appear to have been as successful as initially anticipated.

2.1.3. Poland
After months of parliamentary debate the first Privatization Bill was passed by Parliament in July 1990. Workers organized in Solidarity—whose power in enterprises strongly increased with the end of the communist regime—have resisted attempts to reassert state ownership of enterprises through their transformation into joint stock companies. The law of 1990 represented a compromise. It simply provides a legal framework for privatization, without favouring any particular method. The transformation of state enterprises into joint stock companies is not a necessary step towards privatization. The Polish authorities have also undertaken so called privatizations through liquidation, which by-pass the commercialization stage.

Only a small fraction of SOEs have been transformed into state treasury companies so far. In contrast, privatization through liquidation seems to work fairly well, mostly for smaller enterprises. Of the 950 privatization cases accepted through liquidation, 466 involved cases of asset sales, 20 inclusion in joint stock companies, and 340 cases of leasing; the remaining 124 have adopted a mix of the three procedures. Most of the sales (339) concerned enterprises with less than 200 employees. Most of the leasing contracts have been signed with worker collectives. (See Table 6).

Individual sales have so far generated 2,086 bn. zloty revenues for the government, much lower than expected. In August 1991, the Bielecki government had a deficit of 20 tn. zloty, partly due to the shortfall of 14 tn. zloty expected from the sale of state assets (Slay 1991).

TABLE 6. Privatization in Poland (end-1991)

	Changed into state treasury companies	Privatization through liquidation	Individual sales
Number of enterprises:	308	950	24
less than 200 workers	25	561	
between 200 and 500 workers	68	243	
more than 500 workers	215	146	
Total (as a % of the number of state enterprises)	3.7	11.5	0.3

Source: Prwatizacja przedsiebiorstw panstwowych, March 1992.

Prepared for June 1991, the mass privatization programme of Minister of Ownership Lewandowski involves 400 enterprises (25 per cent of industrial output and 12 per cent of the labour force). The plan provides for five to 20 'national wealth management funds', which would receive 60 per cent of the enterprises' shares, with 33 per cent of the shares in any given firm going to a single fund; this fund would then have a controlling interest in the firm. In addition, 10 per cent of the shares would go to the workers and 30 per cent to the state treasury. The directors of the funds are appointed by the President, and the funds will be managed by Western managers. Many of the important details of the plan have not yet been finalized, in particular the important question of how the controlling blocks of shares in the firms ought to be allocated to the various funds.

The mass privatization plan, however, has met important difficulties. When proposed in parliament in August 1991, the plan was halted. Many criticisms were formulated, the most important being concerns about budgetary revenues, the dangers of concentrating economic power and its administrative complexity (Slay 1991).

Small privatizations have taken place mostly through auctions at the municipal level. In some cases, employees received pre-emptive rights and preferential rates for leasing. This part of the privatization package has been successful. More than 75 per cent of shops have been privatized this way, amounting to about 100,000 small and medium retail and wholesale shops (Grosfeld 1991).

In contrast to the slow pace of privatization expected, the growth of the private sector through the creation of new private enterprises has been very impressive. Private activity accounted for roughly 40 per cent of GDP in 1991, and 45 per cent of employment.[4] One should recall that in Poland, about 85 per cent of agricultural production was kept private. But even outside the agriculture sector, private employment in 1991 had risen to an estimated 2 mn. people. Data from March 1991 show that private activity accounted for 22.1 per cent of industrial output, 43.9 per cent of construction and 16.3 per cent of transport. At the same time, joint ventures grew rapidly, from 1,645 at the end of 1990 to 3,512 in September 1991. Foreign investment is around 700 mn. dollars.

2.1.4. Czechoslovakia   Privatization in Czechoslovakia has taken place along two tracks: 'small' privatization, according to a law passed in October 1990 and 'large' privatization, according to a law of March 1991. Small privatization is run by local committees through auctions. Foreigners are excluded from the first round. Roughly 10 per cent of all small firms have been sold through this method in 1991, generating revenues of about Kcs 10 bn. in Czech lands and Kcs 5 bn. in Slovakia. These funds are transferred to the National Property Fund, the agency responsible for privatization.[5]

the Law of April 1991 on large privatizations specifies two methods: direct sales and the voucher system. The latter system has attracted most attention so far. These two schemes are roughly organized as follows: in a first stage, 1,700 Czech and 700 Slovak firms had to prepare privatization plans, submitted to their ministry. In the next stage, the assets of these enterprises are transferred to the Czech and Slovak National Property Funds. Direct sales are allowed if there is an offer for purchase of equity. Foreign investors are not excluded. All equity not sold is to be included to offer about 60 per cent of their equity to the voucher programme. For a flat fee of Kcs 1,000, any citizen over 18 can purchase a booklet of vouchers worth 1,000 points, with which to bid for shares. At the time of writing, 8.5 mn. people have purchased booklets. The book value of the counterpart of a booklet of vouchers has been evaluated at more than Kcs 30,000. The Czech scheme is thus essentially one of free distribution. Before bidding starts, all voucher holders are given basic information about the firms to be privatized. Individuals can then bid either directly—through one of the many computer terminals to be set up across the country—or indirectly through a financial intermediary. The actual bidding game is rather elaborate; up to six rounds of bidding are planned and complicated price updating rules are specified. It is not clear that these pricing rules cannot be manipulated through strategic bidding. Perhaps as a result of these complications as well as a total lack of information about the values of these firms, many individual buyers will let financial intermediaries bid for them.

Indeed, most vouchers will probably be concentrated in the hands of a few investment funds like *Provni Investicni* or *Harvard Capital Consulting* (which had accumulated over 500,000 voucher-booklets by the end of March 1992). More generally, over 60% of all booklets have already been put in the hands of the financial intermediaries, of which Caseka Sporitelna (the Czech savings bank) alone has gathered over 10 per cent. These investment funds could play an important role monitoring the recently privatized firms. There are 450 investment funds to date, but the bulk of vouchers is concentrated in the 10 biggest investment funds (*Financial Times*, 25 May 1992). Thus, on of the main differences between the Czechoslovak mass privatization plan and the Polish plan is likely to disappear. The Polish plan has been designed specifically to meet the problem of the separation of ownership and control. One of the main purposes of the Polish holding companies is to monitor the activities of the newly privatized firms (the other important function of these companies is to act as interim privatization companies by gradually divesting most of the firms in their portfolios). It is ironic that an important unresolved issue in the Polish plan—how to allocate firms to holding companies (see Frydman and Rapaczynski 1990)—has found an unexpected solution in Czechoslovakia.

Finally, it is worth noting that the government is opposed to debt write-offs for public enterprises, but banks will be allowed to exchange bad debts for equity in the privatized enterprises.

2.2 What remains to be done?

Except for East Germany, privatization in Eastern Europe has been much slower than expected. In contrast to the success in the privatization of shops and small businesses, privatization of bigger enterprises is still in an initial phase, more than two years after the demise of communism. Early expectations were that 50 per cent of public assets would be sold within three years.

However, if one takes into account the rapid growth of the growth of the private sector, the task of mass privatization in Eastern Europe appears less formidable. Reducing public ownership from say 90 per cent to say 25 per cent does not require the privatization of 65 per cent of public assets: we must also take account of the parallel creation of new private firms and the closure of inefficient public firms. Accordingly, Kornai (1990), Murrell (1990), and others have emphasized the important role of 'organic' spontaneous growth of the private sector in completing the massive reallocation of labour and investment to the private sector.

Some simple back-of-the-envelope calculations may give a rough idea of the fraction of state assets to be privatized once one takes into account the parallel growth of the private sector. Privatization may involve only about half as many state assets as was initially estimated, when the independent growth of the private sector was not taken into account.

Centrally planned economies have been characterized, among other things, by two important biases: first, a bias in favour of heavy industry, and second a bias in favour of large firms. As a consequence, the service sector has been seriously underdeveloped and there hardly exists a network of small and medium enterprises. The introduction of the market and the opening up to the world economy is thus likely to lead to an important economic restructuring that correct these biases. To take this into account, we made the following simple calculation. We looked at the actual distribution of labour, across sectors, and across firms of different sizes in industry, and compared this with the distribution of labour in comparable Western economies. In the absence of meaningful prices for capital and for marginal productivity, and because of the uncertainties surrounding value-added statistics, labour is a meaningful indicator of economic activity. The added advantage of focusing on labour is that we get a picture of the extent of labour redeployment in the economy. Assuming that economic restructuring will lead to the adoption of a Western *sectoral* and *size* distribution, and assuming full employment, one calculates the part of the labour force that will leave industry for the service sector and the part which will move towards smaller firms. In our scenario we make the extreme assumption that most of the labour redeployment from manufacturing to services and from large firms to small firms will take place through the spontaneous emergence of a private sector with smaller firms, mostly in the service sector but also in manufacturing. This part of the labour force will therefore not be affected directly by privatization.

The basis of comparison chosen for the size effect in industry is the Federal Republic of Germany, which is more concentrated than France or Italy. This would tend to underestimate the redeployment towards small firms. We assume that only the structurally 'excessive' part of bigger enterprises will be closed down; this also tends to slightly exaggerate the extent of required privatization The basis of comparison chosen for the sectoral effect is the average of the eight poorer OECD countries, where the secondary sector and the service sector represent respectively

29.5 and 52.6 per cent of the labour force, with 27.5 per cent of industrial labour in public industries and 45.6 per cent of service labour in public services. We have left out agriculture because cross-country variations in its share are too large, and concentrated on the labour force in industry and services that is potentially concerned with privatization of their enterprise. The results are shown in Table 7.

TABLE 7. The potential extent of privatization in industry and services

% of labour force potentially concerned by privatization decomposed as:	GDR	CSFR	Hungary	Poland
% of industrial labour	31.1	23.9	45	44
(as a share of total labour)	(13.7)	(11.2)	(16.3)	(15.9)
% of labour in service sector	47.7	42.3	48.3	34.2
(as a share of total labour)	(21.9)	(17.6)	(22.4)	(12.5)
% of total labour, excluding agriculture	35.7	28.8	38.7	28.4
(excluding the size effect)	(43.3)	(39)	(43.7)	(33.8)

This simple calculation reduces the importance of privatization in industry and services to slightly more than 32 per cent of the labour force. This means that all the rest of the growth of the private sector happens through direct redeployment of labour from state-owned firms to newly founded private firms. Table 7 also suggests that privatization in the service sector is likely to be more important than in industry, except in Poland. Of course, our calculations reflect our assumption that labour redeployment will mostly take the form of closure of old firms and creation of new firms. We believe that this is a plausible assumption.

If the extent of privatization is to be smaller than initially thought, because of the closure of many state firms, then concern about the slow speed of privatization appears somewhat misplaced. An equally important concern is the creation of well-functioning labour and capital markets that facilitate the movement of labour from the state sector to the private sector. Roughly half of the working population is likely to change jobs during the transition period.

3. What privatization process?

The previous section reveals that each country is adopting a different privatization programme. Two countries have opted for a strategy of piecemeal sale of state assets (Germany and Hungary) while the two other countries favour mass privatization programmes with give-away schemes. This is only one among many distinctions one can draw between the four programmes. Naturally this diversity raises the question of which programme is likely to perform best, and more generally whether there exist more suitable programmes than the four described above. To some extent the answer to this question depends on country-specific factors; the important differences between the German experience and the experiences of the other three countries are obvious. It is, however, less clear that the economies of Poland, Czechoslovakia and Hungary differ enough from each other to call for such radically different privatization programmes.

In Bolton and Roland (1992), we develop a simple general equilibrium model in which the main trade-offs can be analysed and the costs and benefits of the various privatization plans can be assessed. In this section, we briefly report the main policy conclusions of that analysis.

Speed is the main advantage that has been claimed for the Polish and Czech mass privatization plans favouring give-away schemes. But it is not clear how much time such schemes can save. Even if the valuation stage can be by-passed, it is still necessary to take inventory of what is given away, otherwise property rights are not well defined. Taking inventory, producing opening balance sheets, transforming enterprises into joint stock companies and other decisions which should be taken before privatization, such as allocating environmental liabilities or restructuring financial debts, are time consuming and make plans of overnight privatization impossible. Moreover, the option to give away state assets increases the potential rents various interest groups can obtain through lobbying, thereby reinforcing the political fight for those rents, possibly leading to stalemate and delay in decision-making. Evidence to date does not indicate that privatization in countries that have opted for give-away schemes is taking place at a faster pace.

Free distribution schemes also have the important advantage of creating a large constituency in favour of privatization and market reforms. If every voter receives an equal share of the spoils of the communist state, everyone is concerned with the problem of improving the efficiency of the system. This general concern may be a useful counter-thrusting force against vested interests opposed to the privatization process, such as trade unions and management lobbies (see Roland and Verdier 1991, for a detailed discussion).

The main drawback of give-away schemes is their budgetary impact.

All economies in transition are in the process of restructuring their tax base, introducing new tax systems and setting up tax administrations. This process takes time. In the meantime the existing tax base of these economies is eroding (see Bolton and Roland 1992). Tax revenues in 1991 in Poland for example were 20 per cent lower than expected, with an accelerating budget deficit in the last months of the year, despite temporary success of the 1990 stabilization measures emphasizing cuts in expenditures. Macroeconomic stability is a key condition for the success of reforms and a revival of growth. This objective would clearly be jeopardized by giving away state assets, at a time when revenues from state firms are the only substantial source of revenue for the state.

Another drawback of give-away schemes is that incumbent management is left in place at the moment of privatization and no satisfactory procedure is set up to remove inefficient management or to replace existing managers—whose skills are mostly those of coping in a command economy—by new managers—who are better acquainted with Western commercial, accounting and financial practice. Better marching of managers with firms is achieved by policies of auctioning state firms, since the sales price serves as a screening device, sorting out unsuitable potential acquirors and to attracting efficient ones.

A policy of sales of state assets as in Eastern Germany and Hungary, however, is not likely to meet the fiscal constraint since the revenues generated by a massive sale of state assets would be low. The main reason is what we refer to as the *stock-flow* constraint. Briefly, in a closed economy without preexisting private wealth or capital markets, the most the government can get from selling the *stock* of state assets is a *flow* of savings.

Note that this stock-flow constraint may also apply to financial intermediaries in Czechoslovakia, when they must honour their hasty promises to pay individual voucher-booklet holders ten times the initial purchase price of a booklet after one year. In order to meet those promises, they may have to sell part of the shares acquired with the vouchers. But sales on the massive scale required to meet the bulk of the promised payments are bound to result in a substantial fall in stock prices, so much so that some of these intermediaries may not be able to meet their promises. Clearly, a chain of such failures may discredit the entire scheme and the functioning of the future stock market.

An important consequence of privatization is that the government gives up the right to the residual returns generated by the privatized asset. As the price at which the asset is sold to private owners is likely to be substantially below the Net Present Value of the asset (unless this value is close to zero) privatization implies a *net* intertemporal revenue shortfall for the government on all assets which have a strictly positive value. Indeed, even if the government can cut subsidies to the newly privatized firm, the Net Present Value of the firm—and therefore the price at which the firm is sold—will be lowered commensurately with the cut in subsidies to that firm.[6] Moreover, the assets most likely to find a buyer are those that generate a net return to the government before privatization. Despite reduced revenues, the government is likely to be unable substantially to reduce total subsidies to the remaining state-owned sector and to cut its other expenditures on public goods.

The stock-flow constraint can be relaxed by letting foreigners purchase state assets. However, foreigners are often less well informed and more importantly in the case of Eastern Europe they face exchange rate risk which is difficult to hedge: it is not surprising that so far foreign capital has been only trickling into Eastern Europe. Finally, the stock-flow constraint creates an incentive for governments artificially to delay privatization to increase the revenues generated from sales.

4. Breaking the stock-flow constraint

In principle it is straightforward to eliminate the stock-flow constraint. It suffices to introduce securities which allow the government to sell state assets in exchange for claims on future cash-flows generated by the asset. Suppose that every year the total stock of government land produces 100 mn. bushels of wheat and that the discount rate in the economy is 10 per cent, so that the net present value of the aggregate stock of land in terms of what is 1,000 mn. bushels. If the government sells the entire stock of land within one year in return for wheat, the most it can get is 100 mn. bushels and, taking into account minimum consumption and investment constraints, probably much less than that. But if the government can sell the stock of land in exchange for a claim on future yearly production of, say 50 per cent, then it can get a return from the sale of the entire stock of land of 500 mn. bushels in net present value. An important added benefit of this privatization method is that the government can in principle accelerate the pace of privatization without substantially reducing the total proceeds from the sale of state assets. This solution was identified by the Chilean authorities when they faced a similar mass privatization problem. To quote Hernan Buchi, the Chilean minister of finance from 1985 to 1989:

Especially, from our experience, it was very clear that if you want to privatize, you have to realize that all the assets are currently in the hands of the government. If you want some of those assets, or a large proportion of those assets, to be in the private sector, you have to realize that you have to transfer those assets. If you sell those assets, then you are not transferring net property, you are transferring an asset, normally, plus a debt. The private sector has to incur debts in order to pay for assets, because the wealth is not in the private sector, the wealth is in the public sector. You have to be conscious that to do something like this, you have to make a transfer to assets, and you can do it in a stock way, or in a flow way, and probably you have to do it in both ways. What we did was both ways—stocks, plus designing our macroeconomic policies in such a way that there was a permanent flow in the way we changed our taxes and in the way we changed our pension schemes, that allowed year by year, an increase in the capital base of the private sector. (Buchi 1991: 11).

Besides debt, another standard type of security that could be used for this purpose is equity. Several analysts of the Eastern European privatization process have also emphasized variants of this basic method. Most notably, Sinn and Sinn (1991) have suggested that Treuhand ought to sell only a fraction of a firm to be privatized commensurate with the size of the pledged investments by the new acquirer, instead of selling the entire unit in exchange for cash. The remaining fraction of equity would then provide the Treuhand or government with future revenues. They also suggest that the recent deal between Volkswagen and Skoda—where the German acquirer receives a larger and larger fraction of equity in the Czechoslovak firm as it commits higher and higher investments—could be seen as a model for other privatizations. Similarly, Blanchard *et al.* (1991), Bauer (1991), Borensztein and Jumar (1991) and Bös (1991) have suggested that in order to guarantee a minimum source of income to the government in the future, some fraction of equity (in the form of preferred or common stock) ought to be retained by the state.

In this section we go further and propose that the government or privatization agency ought to organize auctions where (potential) buyers could submit both cash and non-cash bids. Such auctions would not only resolve the revenue shortfall problem but also achieve better matching between firms and managerial teams. This scheme differs significantly from the above proposals that privatization should be in stages (that is, the government distributes only a small fraction of the shares in state-owned firms at a time. First, the latter scheme does not allow for the creation of a market for managers: only cash-flow claims are privatized, not control (under the staged privatization scheme, incumbent managers remain in place). Second, the staged privatization process does not allow for a system whereby the share of the claims in state hands varies from firm to firm, the state maintaining a bigger share in the more efficient firms. This has adverse effects both on the government budget and on the government's ability to insure potential acquirers against the uncertainty about the underlying value of the firm. It is useful to distinguish between two phases in the privatization of state firms: the phase of transfer of control (which can be achieved by auctioning state assets in exchange for non-cash bids) and the phase of transfer of claims (which can take place in stages). This section deals mostly with the first phase.

We focus here on the microeconomic issues raised by the organization of auctions with non-cash bids. We would draw attention to one macroeconomic property of this scheme. The use of non-cash bids implies that the government transfers productive assets to the private sector in exchange for, say, nominal debt or equity claims. This introduces an anti-inflation bias into the economy, since inflationary policies would erode the real value of the claims on the private sector held by the government (see Lucas and Stokey 1983; Persson, Persson, and Svensson 1987 and Obstfeld 1990). In addition, if the government receives rights to future revenues rather than cash it will not be able to dissipate immediately the proceeds from privatization.

An important aspect in the evaluation of the bids concerns the effects on the new acquirers' incentives of pledging a fraction of future revenues to the government. Basically, by allowing buyers to submit non-cash bids one allows then to design their post-privatization capital structure. Therefore one has to address the question of how the capital structure affects the (new) managers' incentives.

4.1. Sales with non-cash bids

To simplify matters we only consider three types of non-cash bids: standard debt, voting shares (or common stock) and non-voting shares (or preferred stock). Other related types of non-cash bids that have been suggested are leasing contracts and management buy-outs (see Sinn and Sinn 1991). While it is easy to see how the introduction of debt or equity can increase the government's revenues from the sale of state assets, it is less obvious how these non-cash bids affect the future owners' incentives and how these bids allow the privatization agency to screen buyers who can make efficient use of the asset from other (potential) buyers. Accordingly, this section discusses mostly the incentives and informational issues related to privatization.

One important advantage of non-cash bids is that many (potential) buyers with little current wealth can bid for state assets by committing either to sharing future revenues with the state or to fixed future debt repayments to the state. In this way, a team of managers or workers with little initial wealth but with the expertise to run a given firm efficiently may be able to outbid a wealthier but less efficient bidder. To put it differently, privatization based on sales only for cash may produce bids that mostly reveal the *ability to pay* of the bidder. This is likely to be the case when the expected price of the asset is substantially below the net present value of the asset in its most efficient use. In that case, even an inefficient but wealthy management team can make a profit from the acquisition. In contrast, when non-cash bids are allowed, the winning bid reveals the willingness to pay of the bidder; that is to say, the bidder's ability to run the business efficiently. Thus, with non-cash bids better matching can be achieved. In addition, incompetent but wealthy *nomenklatura* members will be in a less favourable position to outbid other less wealthy buyers. An additional advantage of non-cash bids is that better insurance can be provided, as well as better screening between inefficient and efficient acquirers (see McAfee and McMillan 1987).

One risk of allowing non-cash bids, however, is encouraging frivolous bids: some bidders may offer very high future payments to the state which they will not be able to meet but, before they are called to honour their commitments, they will be able to enjoy the private benefits of running the firm. To the extent that frivolous bids are made, the introduction of non-cash bids could potentially induce worse matching than if they were not allowed. To discourage such bids, the government has to impose either minimum cash payments or severe penal sanctions on the new managers if they fail to make the promised payments. Failing that, the privatization authorities may have to carefully monitor the seriousness of each bid. This will introduce additional delays in the process.

Besides minimum cash payments, the question remains of what kind of non-cash bids should be favoured? Given that one aim is to decentralize control, bids of common stock such that the government retains a majority (or the biggest block) of shares should be discouraged; if possible, the government should only retain non-voting shares. However, the government—like any investor—must have some minimum protection against the firm's new owners never making the promised dividend payments. One of the weakest protections is to retain cumulative preferred stock, which does not prevent the firm from missing dividend payments, but requires it to pay the cumulated dividend payments that have been missed in the past before it can pay dividends on voting shares. Thus, if the firm tries to expropriate the state by repeatedly missing dividend payments on non-voting shares it will have greater and greater difficulties in raising new equity.

However, the firm will not necessarily have greater difficulty in raising new debt, since in case of financial distress debt has priority over equity (provided the new bankruptcy laws incorporate this feature common to all bankruptcy laws in industrialized nations). Therefore, to give the state minimum protection it may be necessary to let some fraction of the non-cash bids be in the form of debt. Debt gives the government some leeway to extract payments from the firm by threatening to close the firm in case of default (see Bolton and Scharfstein 1990, and Hart and Moore 1991). Another advantage of letting the government hold debt is that it may induce the new managerial team to runt the firm as efficiently as possible in order to reduce the risk of financial distress (see Grossman and Hart 1982). All in all, it may be a good compromise to have a combination of debt and (non-voting) equity in the non-cash bids. Of course, the exact proportion cannot be determined at this level of generality. In fact the right mix between debt and equity has to be determined firm by firm.[7] Moreover, the current state of corporate finance does not enable us to make firm recommendations about the right mix between debt and equity.

A difficult question which needs to be resolved is how the government or privatization agency determines the winning bid when several bidders make non-cash bids—some pledging higher debt repayments, others higher cash payments and yet others a higher fraction of shares? There is no general fool-proof rule that can be determined to rank the various bids and it may be necessary to delegate the choice of the winner to a committee of independent experts. Note, however, that such difficulties are commonly encountered by Western administrations dealing with procurement auctions for, say, public works or defence contracts. Despite these ranking problems and other potential inefficiencies, such auctions are perceived to be the best method of determining the best deal the public authorities can get from private contractors.

Yet another potential difficulty with non-cash bids is how to evaluate extreme bids such as a bid offering 100 per cent (non-voting) equity to the government. Even if the new acquirer seems serious, the government may legitimately wonder what incentives the new owner will have to manage the company efficiently, when he gets none of the residual returns. In fact, because of the effect on incentives, the government may end up obtaining higher expected proceeds from the sale if it sells the firm to a bidder offering only 80 per cent of equity to the government. Here again the determining of the winning bid may have to be left to a committee of experts—despite the obvious drawbacks of such a solution—or else the privatization agency may have to set ceilings above which (potential) buyers are not allowed to bid, such as, say, a rule that a maximum of 90 per cent can stay in state hands. Then if several applicants make the same maximum bid the privatization agency can select the most suitable buyer.

For the sake of concreteness, consider the following sketch of auctions with non-cash bids on a vast scale. In the initial stages it is easiest to follow in the steps of the Treuhandanstalt. Firms should first be commercialized; in a second stage a set of firms to be auctioned off should be advertised. A deadline should be specified for the submission of sealed bids to the privatization agency in charge of the auction. The rules of the auction should be clearly spelled out and basic information about what exactly is being privatized should be made available to the bidders. Bids should comprise a minimum cash bid (to discourage frivolous bidders) together with non-cash bids. The minimum cash bid may be determined on a case-by-case basis by the privatization agency.

The main difficulty in setting up an auction mechanism with non-cash bids is establishing a ranking of bids. To this end, each bidder must submit a business plan with an estimate of future cash flows. Then part of these cash flows can be pledged to the privatization agency in the form of non-voting shares or in the form of nominal debt repayments. To preserve the incentives of the winner, a ceiling of say 80–5 per cent (depending on the size of the firm) of non-voting shares that can be pledged may be imposed. Similarly, a maximum debt–equity ratio may be specified so as to reduce the risk of default.

The ranking of the bids would be made on the basis of the estimates of future cash flows derived from the business plan. If the selection committee disagrees with the estimates provided by the bidders, they may modify these estimates, but their decision must be backed by numbers. At this stage, the committee could request additional information from bidders; one can also envisage some direct negotiations between the winner of the auction and the committee. If one is concerned with the committee favouring some candidates on grounds other than the maximization of the proceeds from the sale, then bidders should be given the right to appeal the committee's decision. The appeals court could then be composed of independent financial analysts, possibly from the West.

This sketch indicates that the committee's job is basically that of an investment bank. It has to evaluate the future stream of cash flows to determine both the value of the non-voting shares pledges to the privatization agency and the credit rating of the debt incurred with the agency. Moreover, once the auction is over, the agency may have to monitor the firms in order to preserve the value of its portfolio of securities. Given the nature of their task, it is then conceivable to eventually transform the privatization agencies into fully-fledged financial intermediaries. The proposal described very briefly here obviously must be given more body, especially concerning the operational aspects. The above sketch should be seen more as an indication that such a programme is feasible than as the skeleton of a precise auction scheme.

The difficulties with the implementation of a privatization plan based on sales of assets in exchange for both cash and non-cash bids are not insurmountable. In fact such schemes have been used in the past in Chile (Buchi 1991). Another noteworthy example is the case of auctions for television rights at the Seoul 1988 Olympics, where NBC won the broadcasting rights in exchange for a bid comprising a cash payment of $300 mn. and a non-cash bid specifying a revenue sharing provision of two-thirds of any revenues in excess of $600 mn. to the Games' organizers (McMillan 1991).

Perhaps such auctions are slightly easier to organize for small or medium-sized firms, where it makes sense to have manager-owners and otherwise a reasonably concentrated ownership structure. Although in principle there is no major added difficulty in organizing such auctions for even the largest firms, greater attention must obviously be paid to these firms as the stakes are so much higher. Thus, the identity and intentions of the (new) management teams as well as their ability to run their firms efficiently must be carefully checked. As Carlin and Mayer (1992) point out, this monitoring activity is in fact an important part of Treuhand's sales strategy. For very large firms it is likely that the managers will hold only a small fraction of the equity, so that these auctions, so that these auctions will resemble more auctions for managerial positions than auctions of ownership titles of the firm. As mentioned above, the privatization of large firms can be divided into two separate auctions. First, managerial positions are auctioned off, bringing about an efficient matching of managers and assets; then shares of the enterprises are auctioned off to the public. In that case, sales of the (non-voting) shares owned by the state can be made gradually since this would have little effect on productive efficiency once control has already been handed over to a new managerial team.[8] Interestingly, China has introduced reforms allowing for auctions for managerial positions in state-owned firms, but not for auctions of shares (McMillan and Naughton 1991).

4.2. Auctions versus bilateral negotiations

So far auctions have only been used to privatize small businesses and shops. For industrial firms the preferred method has been to sell these on a firm-by-firm basis while negotiating with a single buyer at a time. Naturally, if firms are sold for cash there are likely to be few buyers wealthy enough to put up the cash for the larger firms, so the privatization agency is likely to deal with only one potential buyer (or consortium of buyers) per firm. But if non-cash bids are allowed there is likely to be more competition. One may wonder whether the auction method should not then be extended to industrial firms irrespective of their size. Maskin (1991) has shown that the absence of wealth constraints, sales through auctions (with cash bids only) are efficient not only in terms of revenue maximization but also in terms of achieving the best possible matching between owner-managers and productive assets. He also suggests that even in the presence of wealth constraints they are likely to perform well in terms of matching. Moreover, auctions reveal useful information about the underlying common value of firms through the bids of all the participants (Milgrom and Weber 1982); this information is particularly useful in facilitating the emergence of new capital markets as it informs future private investors about the value of the newly privatized firms.

When bidders are wealth-constrained but can make non-cash bids, auctions have to advantages over bilateral negotiations with a single buyer. First, by forcing buyers to compete for the public asset higher bids can be generated. In bilateral negotiations, if the buyer knows that the state is eager to privatize quickly, he will act as if the asset is not worth much to him. As a result, the privatization agency may be forced to sell the asset at a much lower price than the buyer is likely to be willing to pay. This is an additional reason why Treuhand sold firms at such low prices. If, however, the buyer is uncertain whether he faces competition from another buyer, he will make higher bids even if it is known that the privatization agency wants to privatize quickly. The second advantage of auctions is that, to the extent that higher bids come from more efficient management teams, better matching is achieved than if firms are sold on a first-come-first-served basis.

Auctions may also save time on the valuation of the assets to be privatized; if buyers compete for the acquisition of an asset, the privatization company can learn more about the asset's intrinsic value from the winner's bid than from an *ex ante* valuation. True enough, *ex ante* valuations may help generate higher expected bids by reducing the uncertainty bidders face, but the time saved may well justify the loss in expected revenue. In contrast, when the government is involved in bilateral negotiations with an acquirer, the only way for the government to get the buyer to pay more may be to provide hard information about the value of the asset to be sold, so that it is costlier to by-pass the valuation stage.

Finally, from the point of view of *ex post* incentives, auctions with non-cash bids do not distort incentives beyond what non-cash bids determined through bilateral negotiations would: Laffont and Tirole (1992) show that the only effect of auctions is to reduce the informational rent of the winner. Otherwise, *ex post* incentives are as in any efficient bilateral contract.

4.3. Corporation taxes and non-cash bids

Both non-cash and future corporation taxes are ways for the government to obtain future revenues from firms. Why should the government go through all the trouble of selling state assets in exchange of debt or non-voting equity when it can simply tax the future revenues of the privatized firms? A general answer is that taxing corporate profits *ex post* is not the same as having firms committed *ex ante* to pay the government a fraction of future profits. For one thing, the government need not be concerned about the effects non-cash bids committed to the government by privatized firms may have on the future investment incentives of other firms. In addition, when the government sets a corporation tax affecting all firms across the board, it must worry about the effects of an announced increase in the tax on investment incentives. More practically, enforcing the payment of pledged debt repayments or dividend payments is not the same as enforcing tax payments. A government with a debt claim is in a much stronger position to force the newly privatized firm to pay out than a government trying to enforce payment of corporation taxes. If the firm does not meet its debt obligations the government can force the firm into bankruptcy, whereas if the firm does not pay any corporation taxes the government must first establish whether the firm indeed had positive net revenues and only then can it impose penalties for non-payment of taxes. Moreover, these penalties are likely to be softer than the threat of bankruptcy. Similarly, enforcing payment of dividends may be easier since presumably the newly privatized firms will be eager to establish a reputation for paying dividends in order to be able to make new equity issues if these are necessary.

We close this section by raising an important issue. If most state assets are sold in exchange for debt, there is a risk that the government may quickly end up again controlling a substantial fraction of firms which were not able to meet their debt obligations. As in Chile in 1982, the government may be forced to renationalize *de facto* a fraction of the newly privatized firms. More generally, if the government holds substantial fractions of debt in most of the privatized firms it may be able to exercise indirect control over these firms, as the German and Japanese banks exercise control over firms to which they lend. If this is the case there would not have been a complete privatization of the state-owned sector. In order to avoid excessive concentration of power, the government could first limit its debt holdings in the privatized firms and, second, attempt to achieve as widely-dispersed ownership as possible. This may involve in particular the creation of financial intermediaries who would manage part of the state's portfolio of assets together with other private securities.

5. Related issues

All the issues raised by mass privatization cannot be addressed here. Some issues, like demonopolization, have been dealt with extensively elsewhere (see in particular Carlin and Mayer 1992, Mayhew and Seabright 1992, Newbery 1991a, b, and Tirole 1991). We briefly discuss only two additional related issues in this section: financial restructuring and the management of the state sector.

5.1. Financial restructuring

Several analysts have suggested that existing debts in state firms should be written off entirely (*inter alia*, Begg 1991, and Begg and Portes 1992, Frydman and Rapaczynski 1990, Newbery 1991a). The basic rationale is that the allocation of credit to firms in the past has not been based on any sound financial principles so that many firms with a positive net continuation value have ended up with excessive liabilities. Instead of distorting these firms' incentives by leaving them with an excessively leveraged capital structure, the suggestion is to let newly privatized firms start their new life with a clean slate. While debtors would clearly benefit from such a move, creditors are going to be hurt by it. The latter are state banks, who have used individual deposits as well as government subsidies to make loans to firms. If these loans are written off, the state banks will go bankrupt and the government, as well as individual depositors, will be hurt. The individual deposits will have to be compensated so that the ultimate loser is the government. Thus, the real cost of writing off debts is an increase in government expenditures at a time when public finances are already severely strained. As Carlin and Mayer (1992) explain, the Treuhandanstalt has opted for massive write-offs (up to 75 per cent of the debts) despite the dramatic public finance consequences. Of course, in Germany this bill can be picked up by West German taxpayers, but in the other three countries one may wonder how the government will finance this increased expenditure.

Now, if firms are auctioned off in exchange for cash and non-cash bids, as described in Section 4, then debt write-offs will have no adverse consequences on the state budget. Any reduction in existing debt will be immediately reflected in the net present value of the firm and therefore in the bids made for the firm. The combination of debt write-offs with auctions will amount to a swap of securities, with existing debt being exchanged for either cash or shares and debts in the newly privatized firm. This process will allow the new owners of the firms to optimally redesign their capital structure, thus implementing the desired result. Debt write-offs thus go hand in hand with auctions.[9]

5.2. Improving the efficiency of the state sector

Even with a strong commitment towards rapid privatization, several years will be necessary to complete the privatization of the bulk of state assets. Therefore some attention has to be directed towards improving the efficiency of the state sector awaiting privatization. In this respect, several useful lessons can be drawn from the recent Chinese experience.

There is no necessary sharp discontinuity between private ownership and public ownership; it suffices to look at the examples of the British or French economy to see this. This Chinese reform process was a largely successful attempt to move state-owned firms towards what privately-owned firms look like, without going all the way towards full-blown privatization. At the same time, conditions were set up for the emergence of a private sector which would eventually compete with the state sector. State-owned firms are gradually transformed into semi-private firms by giving them greater autonomy over production decisions and by allowing them to retain a greater fraction of the profits they generated. The Chinese government also introduced auctions for top managerial jobs where potential candidates would submit bids promising minimum performance targets for the future (McMillan and Naughton 1991). These auctions could play a similar role to auctions for private ownership in terms of achieving better matching. The combination of all of these reforms has had a tremendous impact on productivity (Hussein and Stern 1991, and Groves *et al.* 1991). This shows that sensible partial reforms can substantially increase the efficiency of the state sector. Note, however, that in the case of Hungary, Poland and the Soviet Union, previous partial reforms allowing greater autonomy in decision-making and giving higher retained profits were not as successful, most often yielding little gain and unleaching inflationary pressures. But Chinese reforms were much more radical to the extent that they involved the creation and development from below of a significant private sector.

Another important difference between Eastern Europe and China should be noted. When the state firms were reformed in China there was no expectation that they might be privatized in the near future. The mere expectation of privatization may create incentive problems that are difficult to control. An extreme form of perverse incentives created by the expectation of privatization is the plundering of assets by incumbent managers that has been witnessed in Poland and Hungary. There are many less visible manifestations of this type of behaviour, and in order to counteract these perverse incentives it is important to provide incumbent managers in the state-owned firms with a stake in the privatization of their firm. This could be achieved, for example, by letting incumbent managers do a leveraged buy-out when no alternative serious buyer appears. Alternatively, incumbent managers ought to be allowed to participate in the auction for their firm, or they should receive compensation for losing their jobs after privatization if they can show that their management effort prior to privatization has enhanced the efficiency of the firm.[10]

An important aspect of the management of the public sector in the transition period is centralized control over expenditures and access to credit. In East Germany, the Treuhandanstalt monitors the management of its enterprises by controlling their access to liquidity and investment credits (Carlin and Mayer 1992). Hardening the budget constraint in the public sector essentially means limiting the expenditures of public enterprises and using the threat of bankruptcy to obtain higher effort. These instruments are, however, imperfect. Indeed, squeezing access to public-sector funds can induce enterprises to reduce their costs, but can also reduce the quality and quantity of their services. As for the threat of bankruptcy, its credibility will remain low as long as capital markets are not developed enough, and as long as the rate of entry of new firms is not great enough to compensate for exiting firms. If bailing out privatized firms may prove difficult to resist in the near future, this will *a fortiori* be true for state-owned enterprises.

Finally, one should also mention the importance for the efficiency of both the state and private sectors of the introduction of well-functioning labour and housing markets. These dimensions, as well as those concerning the underlying legal structure, are of paramount importance, but a full treatment of these issues is unfortunately beyond the scope of this paper.

6. Conclusions

Four central policy conclusions emerge from the above analysis. First, privatization through give-away schemes is likely to create a budgetary crisis, unleashing inflation and destabilizing the young and fragile democracies in Eastern Europe. In our opinion, the most important issue concerning privatization in Czechoslovakia, Hungary, and Poland is the dramatic effect on the government budget of the loss of cash-flows from the previously state-owned firms. There is mounting evidence that even in the remaining state sector the tax authorities are having increasing difficulties in collecting tax revenues. These difficulties will be even greater once these firms are privatized. Therefore, the main priority of the privatization plans in these countries should be the maximization of the proceeds from the sale of state assets. The pursuit of this objective may go against accelerating the place of privatization. We believe that this is a small cost to pay for the guarantee of a smooth transition process. The recent experience of China in reforming its planned economy indicates that, following the decentralization of decisions in state firms, the government quickly lost control over the revenues generated by those state firms and, despite a sharp increase in productivity, government revenues declined: the government deficit increased sharply despite the fact that the economy was booming. This increase in the deficit in turn led to an increase in inflation, which was so sharp that the government was forced to interrupt the reform process and to trigger a severe recession at the end of the 1980s. A similar scenario awaits Czechoslovakia, Hungary, and Poland, if they do not control the erosion in state revenues following the privatization of the bulk of state assets.

Second, privatization through mass give-away schemes creates an environment which is too favourable to incumbent management. In

Czechoslovakia, the voucher scheme will lead to the privatization of cash-flow claims but it will not lead to the privatization of control; incumbent managers will remain in place and, without well-functioning capital markets, inefficient managers will not easily be removed through take-overs. Neither is product market competition going to impose discipline on these inefficient managers, since there has been no attempt at breaking up the monopolistic structure of the old state sector. In Poland, a mechanism for controlling incumbent management has been proposed—mainly the creation of financial intermediaries playing a supervisory role—but it is unclear how effective these holding companies will be or how they in turn will be monitored effectively by the regulatory authorities.

Third, privatization through sales has been dismissed too soon because of the difficulties arising from the level of private wealth, the resulting stock-flow constraint and valuation problems in the absence of capital markets. These problems can and must be solved, even though the solutions cannot be perfect. We have suggested a policy of auctioning off state assets in exchange for cash and non-cash bids, involving the transfer of control into private hands in exchange for debt claims or other securities, thus transforming the government into a net nominal creditor. Such a policy reconciles several desirable policy objectives: speed of privatization, higher efficiency, introduction of capital markets and balanced budgets. It also allows the government to write off the existing enterprise debts without substantial revenue loss, since the debt write-offs will be reflected in higher bids for the state firms. The important added advantage of writing-off debts before privatization is that the government will not be faced with the prospect of having to write off some of these debts in the future in those firms that have inherited an unusually high stock of debt, thus introducing doubts in the minds of managers about the government's commitment to enforcing debt repayments.

Fourth, however, one should not underestimate the difficulties ahead, in particular the enormous administrative and management efforts associated with mass privatization. A generalized policy of sales in exchange for cash and non-cash bids may require similar monitoring efforts, in identifying serious buyers, to those undertaken by the Treuhandanstalt. This will then inevitably slow down the pace of privatization. In addition, the larger firms to be privatized are likely to see a separation of ownership and control, as the winning bidders will only own a small fraction of the cash flow claims. These firms' management teams may need to be supervised by the newly privatized banks. Alternatively, they may be monitored effectively by supervisory boards similar to those existing in Germany.

Discussion

John Vickers
Oxford University

This paper addresses two-and-a-half of three fundamental questions about privatization in Eastern Europe:

  (i) How fast should it be done?
 (ii) Should assets be sold or distributed free, and how?
(iii) Should restructuring (demonopolization, etc.) happen before or after privatization?

Eminent economists such as Blanchard *et al.* (1991) have given a clear answer—speed is of the essence and therefore privatization in Eastern Europe must proceed by free distribution and before restructuring. Bolton and Roland say the opposite—assets should be sold, in particular by auctions involving non-cash as well as cash bids, and at a moderate pace so as not to jeopardize the government's fiscal position. Both sides of the argument invoke considerations of microeconomic incentives, macroeconomic stability, public finance, fairness and political acceptability. Who is right?

A follower of the privatization experience of a market economy such as Britain's might incline to the Bolton–Roland view—but for a somewhat different reason from theirs. The best recipe in that case appears to be to restructure first in order to create competitive market structures where possible and then to sell the assets in a way that maximizes revenue. But of course the economic, political, and legal circumstances in Czechoslovakia, Hungary, and Poland are altogether different from those in the West and the lessons from there cannot be applied straightforwardly.

Bolton and Roland build an impressive case for their view and they construct an ingenious way of easing the tradeoff between efficiency and revenue considerations. They show that considerations of fairness and politics do not unambiguously favour rapid privatization by give-away, and they highlight the legal and administrative need to define ownership titles whatever happens (but is privatization perhaps an essential part of this?). They present detailed analyses of the matching and incentive benefits of methods of asset sale. However, they do not convince me in every respect.

First, even for small firms, the idea of privatizing in a way that leaves the private sector with substantial debt obligations to the government seems dangerous, especially when there is massive uncertainty about relative prices, wages, and the general level of macroeconomic activity. In particular it carries the risk of large-scale endogenous reversals of privatization via bankruptcy, as in Chile in 1982–3, depending on the government's toughness. In any event, the microeconomic efficiency benefits of bankruptcy threats are not clear cut, especially when there is a lot of exogenous noise, and there are obvious disadvantages of debt in the presence of risk-aversion.

An alternative is partial equity sales, in which the state retains a substantial fraction of shares. Philippe Aghion and I, in a similar spirit to Bolton and Roland, have analysed the trade-off between the incentive disadvantage of low-powered incentive schemes and the 'sorting' advantage of the government retaining a larger stake. The sorting advantage is that the probability of ability rather than wealth endowment determining the winning bidder is greater when the fraction being privatized is smaller. Much turns on the correlation between ability and wealth endowment.

Given the emphasis that Bolton and Roland place upon the stock-flow constraint, an important alternative may be to lease some capital assets owned by the state, at least for a time. This is not a perfect solution in any industry, and it would be totally unsuitable for some, but the combination of private operation with deferred capital asset transfer appears to have some attractions, particularly in the early stages.

Second, the authors' proposals seem better suited to small enterprises than to large firms, though the latter have accounted for an unusually high proportion of economic activity in Eastern Europe. It is true that financial intermediaries such as holding companies and mutual funds are not a panacea and that they multiply rather than solve the 'who monitors the monitors?' question, but their risk-spreading function in current circumstances is surely of first-order importance. Pension funds in particular would seem to be a useful way of ameliorating the stock-flow problem that is central to the paper.

Third, while this paper says a great deal about ownership reform, it says relatively little about competitive markets (other than potential auction markets for privatized assets.) As for sequencing (question (iii) above), references are made to other literature, trade liberalization is mentioned as a source of competition, and it is pointed out that demonopolization may lose the state revenue, but more emphasis should be given to markets and competitive restructuring. The matching, sorting and informational benefits of competition are not confined to asset auc-tion markets, and, as is noted, product market competition allows man-agerial incentives to be improved. Industrial structure in Eastern European economies, with its high degree of horizontal and vertical inte-gration, is the legacy of centralized planning. Unless immediate privatiza-tion is imperative for political reasons, or because it is the only way to stem anarchic rent-grabbing, the benefits of pro-competitive restructur-ing would appear to be large and indeed an essential part of the proper development of market-based economies. Since divestiture is best done before sale, the consequence is that some privatizations will be delayed.

These industrial organization considerations are complementary to the public finance reasons in the paper for moderating the pace of privatiza-tion. They are more important, I think, than the paper suggests. The case for pro-competitive restructuring is strong. Perhaps the privatization experience of market economies, despite the vast differences, is of some relevance after all.

Michael Burda
INSEAD

Although the detail of this thorough analysis of the economics of privati-zation risks becoming outdated, its main message is robust: regardless of how quickly Eastern Europe wants a private sector, it will have to trade this desire against budgetary and macroeconomic stability. My discussion will focus on practical issues. It seems evident that in countries where the central government is only beginning to regain credibility (and, more crucially, control), simple solutions should be preferred. Auctions are complicated affairs and require considerable information to yield maxi-mum income to the auctioneer (the state). In Central and Eastern Europe, information is a scarce resource which confers significant eco-nomic rents to the owner (the current managers); the commercialization process will require considerable time to collect and disseminate the data to achieve the matching benefits claimed for the auction mechanism.The state must organize thousands of these auctions. A competent auction bureaucracy will be required, that is capable of comparing apples and oranges. Which is superior: a bid of Kzs 100 mn. cash plus Kzs 300 mn. of 10-year debt or Kzs 250 mn. of cash plus Kzs 100 mn. of five-year debt? The authors' proposal presumes the existence of a financial infrastructure with experts able to value and rate the debt. Does the debt have the same seniority as that already on the firm's books? Does one consider the qual-ity of the management team as well? These issues pose difficulties for sophisticated Western investment bankers. How can we expect the Eastern Europeans to crack this nut? How many consultants and investment bankers will the authors' proposal require? To add to all this, to obtain credible bids, there must be a threat of bankruptcy in case of default on the tendered debt. This presumes a functioning, credible body of bankruptcy law. A hallmark of the ex-communist economies (even East Germany) is their reluctance to implement or apply even existing bankruptcy law to moribund firms.

Several simpler alternatives exist to auction-style, mixed-bid privatization, despite its considerable theoretical appeal. The authors' ultimate aim is to preserve a residual stake for the state in the privatized enterprises, a sort of sleeping partner. The simplest procedure would be to withhold some fraction of the business's equity from privatization, and to privatize the rest by whatever means it chooses. As with the authors' proposal there is no deadweight loss associated with the corporate tax and probably fewer collection problems. A still simpler but theoretically similar alternative is leasing, or lease-buy-back arrangements (such as the small privatization in CSFR).

Another approach to rapid privatization is to use the state's property to recapitalize banks, insurance companies and pension funds, by simply transferring ownership to these often seriously undercapitalized financial intermediaries. This approach has been adopted most recently by Czechoslovakia (see Hrnzír 1992, or Janázek 1992). It would also have the advantage of cancelling a non-arbitrary fashion the non-bank business sector's debt to commercial banks. With sufficient technical assistance from the West, Eastern European banks could learn to become large stakeholders and exercise appropriate continental European-style control. Western techniques and self-discipline would be applied to new loans at the margin.

Still another stop-gap (and cheap) idea is simply to invest lots of resources in appointing and training competent supervisory boards for state enterprises. Workable supervisory boards can prevent state capital from being taken either by managers (by asset-stripping or spontaneous privatization) or by workers (via excessive wage claims).

Finally, the authors' case against asset giveaways seems incomplete. Their claim that inefficiency in matching has been responsible for poor enterprise performance is not sufficiently substantiated. Are we sure there are new managers to be found? Existing enterprise managers possess considerable human capital and skills. Arguably, they are the same people who would have made it to the top in a capitalist world. They just need to be retooled if possible—and, more importantly, monitored. Why can't institutions—Kozuny's Harvard fund in Czechoslovakia or the banks and pension and insurance companies in Hungary—perform this role? With sufficient technical help, large stakeholders maximizing their own interests will induce proper managerial behaviour, just as in developed capitalist economies.

More generally, I think the underlying stress on matching assets with managerial talent may be excessive. Enterprise restructuring (including killing off the dinosaurs, which trap labour and management resources, as well as having considerable political influence) is more important than transferring ownership. And the redeployment, remotivation and retraining of workers may be at least as urgent as that of managers.

Although they have complications, the case for mixed-bid auctions should still be taken seriously, and the alternatives I sketch rest on the authors' solid analysis. I believe that this paper will serve as a standard for future work in the area.

General discussion

Some of the panel discussion focused on the authors' diagnosis of the problem with existing schemes, and some on the details of their proposed remedy. Beginning with the diagnosis, Maurice Obstfeld thought the stock-flow constraint was less severe than it looked: it could be alleviated by allowing firms to issue debt abroad. Rafael Repullo pointed out that the stock-flow constraint was really a liquidity constraint, due to the inability of borrowers credibly to pledge future income as security; borrowing abroad might not help. David Begg argued that the governments too were liquidity-constrained, and the crisis in public finances would happen too soon for the authors' proposed solution to make much difference.

Others doubted the significance of the matching problem. Jacques Drèze thought the need for training was much more important; private markets could not be relied upon to do the job. Bidders for firms should be assessed, he argued, partly by their ability and willingness to train workers and managers. The state, for its part, could establish intermediaries specializing in training, who could retain substantial shareholdings in firms. It could also promote training via its residual influence on supervisory boards where these existed. John Flemming disagreed, thinking that other incentives were needed to solve the training problem than continued government involvement in the management decisions of firms.

Coming to the merits of the authors' solution, there was much discussion of the particular form in which firms could pledge to make future payments to the state, Maurice Obstfeld was unconvinced that the government would be able to enforce debt obligations credibly, especially for large firms. Guido Tabellini argued that it was desirable in principle to tax existing capital heavily while taxing marginal capital investment as little as possible. He was concerned that the authors' proposal caused distortions by being effectively a tax on profits, a concern that was echoed by Martin Hellwig who thought nothing should be done to dampen the signalling role of profits for new investment. Richard Portes thought profits taxes too easily evaded to be a significant source of revenue. However, John Flemming and Hans-Werner Sinn both proposed that cash-flow-based taxation could overcome these problems.

Alan Manning said that the advantages of auctions with non-cash bids over existing proposals depended entirely on the criteria that would be used to evaluate non-cash bids. He wished the authors had been more explicit about these criteria. Replying, the authors acknowledged there was work still to do on their proposal, but argued that their main purpose had been to shift discussion away from questions of speed onto the important implications of privatization for public finances. In addition, non-cash bids allowed for the decentralization of the important decisions that would have to be taken about firm restructuring, including closure of the firms with the worst prospects. It was important to find ways to take these decisions quickly without taking them arbitrarily. Even if it turned out that mismatching of managers to firms was not an important problem, this could not be decided *a priori* but should be left to markets to evaluate.

References

BAUER, T. (1991), 'Building Capitalism in Hungary' presented in June at the conference in Kiel on 'The transformation of socialist economies'.

BEGG, D. (1991), 'Economic Reform in Czechoslovakia: Should we Believe in Santa Klaus?', *Economic Policy*.

—— and R. PORTES (1992), 'Enterprise Debt and Economic Transformation: Financial Restructuring of the State Sector in Central and Eastern Europe', CEPR Discussion Paper No. 695.

BLANCHARD, O., R. DORNBUSCH, P. KRUGMAN, R. LAYARD, and L. SUMMERS (1991), *Reform in Eastern Europe*, MIT Press, Cambridge, Mass.

BOLTON, P., and G. ROLAND (1992), 'The Economics of Mass Privatization: Czechoslovakia, East Germany, Hungary, Poland', Cahiers du Laboratoire d'Econométrie de l'Ecole Polytechnique, No. 375, Paris.

BOLTON, P., G. ROLAND and D. SCHARFSTEIN (1990), 'A Theory of Predation based on Agency Problems in Financial Contracting', *American Economic Review*.

BORENSZTEIN, R., and M. KUMAR (1991), 'Proposals for Privatization in Eastern Europe', *IMF Staff Papers*.

BÖS, D. (1991), "Privatization in East Germany: A Survey of Current Issues', mimeo, IMF.

BUCHI, H. (1991), 'Practical Aspects of Privatization: The Case of Chile', lecture given at CERGE in Charles University, Prague, Sept. 28.

CARLIN, W., and C. MAYER (1992), 'Restructuring Enterprises in Eastern Europe', *Economic Policy*.

FRYDMAN, R. and A. RAPACZYNSKI (1990), 'Markets and Institutions in Large Scale Privatizations', in V. Corbo and F. Coricelli (eds.), *Adjustments and Growth: Lessons for Eastern Europe*, World Bank.

GROSFELD, I. (1991), 'A Note on Privatization in Poland', mimeo, Delta.

—— and P. HARE (1991), 'Privatization in Hungary, Poland and Czechoslovakia', *European Economy*.

GROSSMAN, S., and O. HART (1982), 'Corporate Financial Structure and Managerial Incentives', in J. McCall (ed.), *The Economics of Information and Uncertainty*, University of Chicago Press, Chicago.

GROVES, T., Y. HONG, J. McMILLAN, and B. NAUGHTON (1991), 'Autonomy and Incentives in Chinese State Enterprises', mimeo, UC San Diego.

HART, O., and J. MOORE (1991), 'Default and Renegotiation: A Dynamic Model of Debt', mimeo, MIT.

HRNZIR, MIROSLAV (1992), 'Die Währungs- und Fiskalsphäre bei der Transformation der tschechoslovakischen Ökonomie', presented at a conference on 'Macroeconomic Problems of Transformation' held at Wissenschaftszentrum Berlin, June.

HUSSAIN, A., and N. STERN (1991), 'Effective Demand, Enterprise Reforms and Public Finance in China', *Economic Policy*.

JANAZEK, KAMIL (1992), 'Transformation of Czechoslovakia's Economy: Results, Prospects, Open Issues', mimeo, Bank of Finland, April.

KORNAI, J. (1990), *The Road to a Free Economy*, Norton Press, New York.

LAFFONT, J. J., and J. TIROLE (1992), *A Theory of Incentives in Regulation and Procurement* (forthcoming).

LIPTON, D., and J. SACHS (1990), 'Privatization in Eastern Europe: The Case of Poland', *Brookings Papers on Economic Activity*.

LUCAS, R., and N. STOKEY (1983), 'Optimal Fiscal and Monetary Policy in an Economy without Capital', *Journal of Monetary Economics*.

MASKIN, E. (1991), 'Auctions and Privatization', mimeo, Harvard University.

MAYHEW, K., and P. SEABRIGHT (1991), 'Incentives and the Management of Enterprises in Economic Transition: Capital Markets are not Enough', CEPR Discussion Paper No. 640.

McAfee, P., and J. McMillan (1987), 'Auctions and Bidding', *Journal of Economic Literature*.

McMillan, J. (1991), 'Bidding for Olympic Broadcast Rights: The Competition before the Competition', *Negotiation Journal*.

—— and B. Naughton (1991), 'How to Reform a Planned Economy: Lessons from China', mimeo, UC San Diego.

Milgrom, P., and R. Weber (1982), 'A Theory of Auctions and Competitive Bidding' *Econometrica*.

Murrell, P. (1990), 'Big Bang Versus Evolution: Eastern European Reforms in the light of Recent Economic History', *PlanEcon Report*, June 29.

Newbery, D. (1991a), 'Reform in Hungary; Sequencing and Privatisation', *European Economic Review*.

—— (1991b), 'Sequencing the Transition', CEPR Discussion Paper No. 575.

Obstfeld, M. (1990), 'Dynamic Seignoriage Theory: An Exploration', National Bureau for Economic Research.

Persson, M., T. Persson, and L. Svensson (1987), 'Time Consistency of Monetary and Fiscal Policy', *Econometrica*.

Roland, G., and K. Sekkat (1992), 'Market Socialism and the Managerial Labor Market', in P. Bardhan and J. Roemer (eds.), *Market Socialism: From the Classics to the Modern* (forthcoming).

—— and T. Verdier (1991), 'Privatization in Eastern Europe: Irreversibility and Critical Mass Effects', CEPR Discussion Paper No. 612.

Sinn, G., and H.-W. Sinn (1991), *Kaltstart, Volkswirtschaftliche Aspekte der deuschen Vereinigung*, J. C. B. Mohr (Pal Siebec), Tübingen.

Slay, B. (1991), 'The "Mass Privatization" Program Unravels', Radio Free Europe Report, November.

Tirole, J. (1991), 'Privatization in Eastern Europe: Incentives and the Economics of Transition', mimeo, MIT.

Vickers, J., and G. Yarrow (1988), *Privatization. An Economic Analysis*, MIT Press, Cambridge, Mass.

Notes

1. See Vickers and Yarrow (1988) for an excellent overview of the issues raised by privatization in the West.
2. *Financial Times*, 7 Nov. 1991.
3. *SPA Newsletter*, October 91.
4. Sources for figures in this paragraph: Grosfeld (1991) and *Die Zeit* no. 45, November 1991.
5. *Financial Times*, 8-11-91.
6. There may be exceptional circumstances where the sale of state assets may actually increase the government's net revenues of the sharp increase in profitability resulting from privatization.

7. Some of the government's debt must be secured, otherwise the threat of bankruptcy may be ineffective.
8. In order to avoid creating a situation where most of the voting shares are in the hands of the managers and the bulk of remaining shares (owned by the state initially) are non-voting, one can specify provisions giving a voting right to the shares once they end up in private hands.
9. An additional benefit of this procedure is related to the credibility of bankruptcy as an incentive scheme. Privatization is like a change of regime and being soft on debtors during the regime change does not necessarily signal that the government will be soft with debtors in the future. On the other hand, if the government fails to write off debts before privatization and allows such write-offs to take place after privatization when firms are in financial distress, then the government may find it difficult to enforce a hard budget constraint on the newly privatized firms. We thank Paul Seabright for this remark.
10. One natural countervailing force inducing managers to run a state-owned firm efficiently even if the firm is likely to be privatized soon is the reputation managers are likely to acquire. This reputation may help then to find a job in the emerging private sector just as a reputation for efficient administration in, say, the French civil service can allow a civil servant to get a high managerial position in the private sector (see Roland and Sekkat 1992).